HIGH PERFORMANCE

ORACLE8
Object-Oriented Design

David A. Anstey

High Performance Oracle8 Object-Oriented Design
Copyright © 1998 by The Coriolis Group, Inc.

All rights reserved. This book may not be duplicated in any way without the express written consent of the publisher, except in the form of brief excerpts or quotations for the purposes of review. The information contained herein is for the personal use of the reader and may not be incorporated in any commercial programs, other books, databases, or any kind of software without written consent of the publisher. Making copies of this book or any portion for any purpose other than your own is a violation of United States copyright laws.

Limits of Liability and Disclaimer of Warranty
The author and publisher of this book have used their best efforts in preparing the book and the programs contained in it. These efforts include the development, research, and testing of the theories and programs to determine their effectiveness. The author and publisher make no warranty of any kind, expressed or implied, with regard to these programs or the documentation contained in this book.

The author and publisher shall not be liable in the event of incidental or consequential damages in connection with, or arising out of, the furnishing, performance, or use of the programs, associated instructions, and/or claims of productivity gains.

Trademarks
Trademarked names appear throughout this book. Rather than list the names and entities that own the trademarks or insert a trademark symbol with each mention of the trademarked name, the publisher states that it is using the names for editorial purposes only and to the benefit of the trademark owner, with no intention of infringing upon that trademark.

The Coriolis Group, Inc.
An International Thomson Publishing Company
14455 N. Hayden Road, Suite 220
Scottsdale, Arizona 85260

602.483.0192
FAX 602.483.0193
http://www.coriolis.com

Library of Congress Cataloging-In-Publication Data
Anstey, David A.
    High performance Oracle8 object-oriented design / by David A. Anstey.
      p.   cm.
    Includes index.
    ISBN 1-57610-186-X
    1. Oracle (Computer file) 2. Database design. 3. Object-oriented methods (Computer science) I. Title
QA76.9.D26A57   1997
005.75'75—dc21   97-51992
                                                                                         CIP

Printed in the United States of America
10 9 8 7 6 5 4 3 2 1

CORIOLIS GROUP BOOKS
an International Thomson Publishing company I(T)P®

Albany, NY • Belmont, CA • Bonn • Boston • Cincinnati • Detroit
Johannesburg • London • Madrid • Melbourne • Mexico City
New York • Paris • Singapore • Tokyo • Toronto • Washington

Publisher
Keith Weiskamp

Acquisitions
Stephanie Wall
Jeff Duntemann

Project Editor
Ann Waggoner Aken

Production Coordinator
Michael Peel

Cover Design
Anthony Stock

Layout Design
April Nielsen

CD-ROM Development
Robert Clarfield

Acknowledgments

When a person acknowledges his success, he recognizes those that have contributed to it. I have been extremely fortunate to have worked with some extraordinary people on some pretty extraordinary projects over the years.

To Tom and Karen, one of the best development teams I have ever worked with, even in terribly nasty weather.

To Stan, who took a chance on me those many years ago. You and I, we have gone a long way.

To Steve (Mr. La), my friend of friends and brother in faith.

To Pete, who got me into this.

To the fantastic folks at the I.T. department in Galderma Labs: Ken, Mark, Henry, Steve, Nancy, Houng, Cathy, Liz, and Ruben. The best tech group anywhere.

To the great folks at Coriolis: Ann, Mary, Michael, Robert, Josh, and Tony.

To Aspen and Spruce, my two dogs who stayed with me for this entire project and had enough sense to pull me away from the PC when it was too late to be up.

And last, but certainly not least, my two sons David and Zachary who fill me with pride every day, and my beloved wife Cindy, who has always believed when I doubted. I love you.

A Note From Don Burleson

Today's Oracle professionals are standing at the turning point. As Oracle technology moves into the twenty-first century we are seeing the complexity of database systems becoming almost unfathomable. Today's Oracle professional must be an expert in database performance and tuning, database administration, data warehousing, using Oracle with the Web, using OLAP and spatial data, and many other areas. These robust new features of Oracle present unique challenges to anyone who must use Oracle technology to deliver solutions to complex data-oriented challenges.

Oracle, the world's leading database management system, provides a mind-boggling wealth of features and options—far more than one Oracle professional can easily digest. The Oracle market is filled with new possibilities as Oracle introduces the management of objects, data warehouses, and Web-enabled applications; Oracle professionals everywhere are struggling to understand how to exploit these new features.

It is no longer acceptable for Oracle professionals to be generalists—they must become intimately familiar with all facets of Oracle technology and understand how these technologies interoperate. Rather than simply breadth of knowledge, the Oracle professional must have enough depth to effectively apply the technology. To get this knowledge we must rely on experts to guide us through the labyrinth of complicated tools and techniques, and we do not have the luxury of wading through mundane technical manuals.

What we need is clear, concise advice from seasoned Oracle professionals. That is the purpose of The Coriolis Group's High Performance Oracle series. As you are challenged to keep pace with this exciting new technology, we are challenged to provide on-point books to help guide you through the myriad of Oracle features and ensure your success.

—*Don Burleson*

Contents

Foreword   xvii

Introduction   xxi

Chapter 1   An Introduction To Oracle8   1

Evolution Of Database Systems   3
Legacy Systems   4
Relational Model   6
Referential Integrity   8
Oracle8 And Object Orientation   9

The Next Wave: Object-Relational Databases   11

Modeling For Oracle8   13
When To Implement Object-Oriented Design   14

Object-Oriented Concepts   16
Classes   17
Methods And Messages   18
Polymorphism   18
Inheritance   19
Abstraction   20
Encapsulation   21

Object-Oriented Features Of Oracle8   23
Oracle8 Semantics   24
Abstract Data Types (ADT)   24
Methods   26
Pointers   27

Support Of Unstructured Data 28
Support For Complex Objects 28
Support Of Client-Side Objects 29
Object Views 29
Upcoming Features: Inheritance And Extensibility 29

Summary   30

Chapter 2 The New Systems Development Life Cycle With Oracle8   31

The Importance Of System Analysis   33
The Oracle System Modeling Conventions   35
Strategy Phase 36
Analysis Phase 38
Design Phase 39
Build Phase 41
User Documentation Phase 43
Transition Phase 44
Production Phase 46

Oracle8 And Database Design   46
Designer/2000 And Oracle8 46
How Oracle8 Affects The CASE Method Life Cycle 48

Functional Decomposition And The Impact On Design   50
A Functional Decomposition Example 51

Analyzing Process Flow   54
Basic Entity Relationship Modeling   56
Entity Relationship Modeling And Object Extensions 58
One-To-One Relationships 59
One-To-Many Relationships 60
Many-To-Many Relationships 60
Recursive Relationships 62

Exclusive Relationships 64
Redundancy And Other Thoughts 65

Modeling The Real World — 66
Common Design Issues And Problems 68

Summary — 70

Chapter 3 The New Frontier Of Database Design — 71

An Overview Of Database Modeling And Designing With Objects — 73
Creating A Database Object Model 75
The Relational Meta-Model 79
The Object Meta-Model 83
Reconciling The Relational And Object Paradigms 88
Benefits And Design Considerations Of The Database Object Model 94

Aggregate Objects — 96
Variable Arrays (VARRAYs) 97
Nesting Tables 98
Basic Rules For The Use Of VARRAYs And Nested Tables 101

Modeling Non-First Normal Form Data Structures — 102

Summary — 104

Chapter 4 Modeling For Oracle Supported Data Types — 105

Oracle Supported Data Types — 108
Built-in Data Types 108
User-Defined Data Types (ADTs) 120

Planning A Hierarchy Of Data Types — 136

Summary — 139

Chapter 5 Oracle Reference Pointers And Database Design — 141

Recalling Data Structures 101 — 144
What Are Pointers? 145
Pointers In Oracle8 148

The Oracle8 Pointer Constructs — 149
Object Identifiers (OIDs) 150
The REF Construct 151
The DEREF Construct 153
Dangling REFs 155
The VALUE Construct 156
The OIDINDEX 156

Relationships With Oracle8 Pointers — 157
Recursion 157
Circular Referencing 159
Nested Dereferencing 161
Re-Sequencing Of Pointers 164
A Complex Object View Example 167

Summary — 172

Chapter 6 Method Design And Oracle8 — 173

What Are Methods? — 175
PL/SQL Constructs 177
Reasons For Using Methods In Oracle8 185

Using Methods In Oracle8 — 186
Comparison Methods 187
External Procedures 190
Building Methods In PL/SQL 194

Planning A Method Topology — 204
Creating Method Prototypes 213

Summary — 217

Chapter 7 The Tools Of The Trade 219

Oracle's Object Database Designer 222
An Overview Of Object Database Designer's Components 223

Logic Works' OR-Compass 236
An Overview Of The Major Components In OR-Compass 237
A Look At The Design Environment In OR-Compass 239
Building Model Elements With The Diagram Window And The
   Property Dialogs 240
Relations In OR-Compass 243
Internal And External Routines In OR-Compass 246
Forward And Reverse Engineering In OR-Compass 248

Summary 251

Chapter 8 Putting It All Together: A Comprehensive Object Relational Design 253

The Acme Telephone Company 256
Identifying The Requirements 258
Understanding The Constituent Parts 258

Undertaking The Modeling Effort 261
Analyzing The Components 261
Defining The Relationships 266
Putting System Behavior Into The Design 276
A Review Of The Completed Data Model 280

Expanding The Basic Design: Tracking Objects By Order 284

Summary 289

Chapter 9 An Oracle8 Modeling And Design Methodology 291

A New Approach To Model Diagrams 293
Basic Modeling Diagram Conventions Of The UML 294
Relationships In The UML Modeling Diagrams 298
The Modeling Diagrams Of The UML 303
The Object Relational Model And The UML 317

Implementing New Diagrams In The Object Relational Design 321
Using Use Case And Activity Diagrams In Method Design 322
Implementing The Static Structure Diagram 327

Summary 329

Chapter 10 Oracle8 Design For The Data Warehouse 331

An Overview Of Data Warehousing 334
Data Marts 337
Online Analytical Processing And Multidimensional Databases 339

Oracle8's Data Warehousing Features 342
Bitmapped Indexes 342
Index-Organized Tables 344
The Partitioning Option 346

Oracle8 And Data Warehousing 351
Planning The Data Warehouse In Oracle8 352

Summary 361

Chapter 11 Oracle8 And Distributed Systems — 363

An Overview Of Distributed Systems — 365
Types Of Distributed Databases — 370
Horizontal Distribution   370
Vertical Distribution   371
Architectural Distribution   372

Features And Properties Of Oracle8 Distributed Database Systems — 373
Heterogeneity And Transparency   374
Data Replication   376
Database Applications In A Distributed Environment   380

Understanding Distributed Transactions — 384
The Prepare Phase   385
The Commit Phase   386
A Two-Phase Commit Example   386

Designing A Distributed Architecture With Oracle8 — 389
Snapshot Design Considerations   392
Performance Enhancements With Oracle8   393

Summary — 394

Chapter 12 Object Extensions To SQL And The Emerging SQL3 Standard — 395

The Emerging SQL3 Standard — 398
The SQL3 Development Effort   399
Additional SQL3 Enhancements   408
SQL3 And Java   409
Issues Affecting The New Standard   409

An Overview Of The New Features In PL/SQL — 411
Object Type Support 412
Database Extensibility 422

Summary — 423

Chapter 13 Planning For Class Hierarchies And Inheritance In Oracle8 — 425

An Object-Oriented View Of Classes And Inheritance — 428
Classes Revisited 429
Inheritance 431
Multiple Inheritance 436

Oracle8 And Type Classes — 438
Oracle Implementation Of Classes 439
Dealing With Multiple Inheritance Issues 446
Designing Class Hierarchies 449
Mapping Methods To Oracle8 Classes 450

Summary — 452

Chapter 14 Current Trends And Future Directions — 453

The Current Technological Trends In Oracle8 — 456
Oracle8 And Java 456
Oracle Cartridges 458

Future Initiatives With Oracle8 — 460
Server-Side Advancements With Oracle8 460
Application Development Tools And PL/SQL 461

Summary — 465

Appendix A Naming Convention Standards   **467**

Glossary   **477**

Index   **485**

Foreword

I've been working with computers for more years than I care to admit, having received my B.S. in Information and Computer Science in 1973 from the University of California, Irvine (UCI).

In my two years at UCI, I received an incredible education in all aspects of software engineering, from life-cycle methodology to twiddling hardware. Not only did we have a leading-edge faculty, with the likes of John Seely Brown, Rusty Bobrow, and Peter Freeman, I also had an incredible mentor in a fellow student, Daryle Lewis, who had been working as a computer programmer for many years.

UCI was a hotbed of research in artificial intelligence, and I was heavily involved with the ongoing research, particularly in the areas of programming languages and object-oriented (OO) techniques. I graduated with OO techniques firmly and permanently implanted in my approach to software development.

It was also my great fortune to attend a seminar by Dr. Codd on his research on relational database techniques. With a great deal of embarrassment, I confess that I was extremely skeptical about the potential performance and doubted it would ever catch on.

Through the years, I've been witness to new techniques of all types: new modeling techniques, new programming language, and new methodologies. Fanatical adherence by true believers amused many of us. Who can forget (or remember) the ferocity of the debates between the "data siders" and "process siders" of the late 70s and early 80s? Whatever happened to the artificial intelligence revolution of the 80s? Who remembers "HIPO" diagrams?

A number of these techniques proved useful and became standard practice in many organizations. The work of Yourdon, Demarco, Palmer, and Chen all had a strong influence on today's development practices.

Despite the hubris of my youth, relational database techniques have come to dominate the market for persistent data storage, with Oracle of course being the most popular product. Even though object-oriented programming dates back to 1967 (Simula '67), OO is in many ways a relative newcomer. The introduction of object-modeling techniques and language into the mainstream is relatively new, having truly gained widespread use with C++.

Although I personally used what I considered the best aspects of all of these approaches, I never expected to see a book about a commercial product that would be a true synthesis of the past 30 years in software development. But this is precisely what David Anstey has written!

Oracle8 is a marriage of the relational world and the object-oriented world. Successful use of the new features in Oracle8 requires a combination of techniques that will be unfamiliar to many developers.

This book provides a comprehensive explanation of the new data features in Oracle8. David doesn't just provide technical details. He clearly describes how to use the new features and how to decide whether to use them. He describes drawbacks as well as benefits.

The sections on modeling bring together a unique approach to using multiple techniques not seen elsewhere. Object-oriented design eliminates the false dichotomy between "data" and "process." David emphasizes the importance of both. He provides excellent coverage of entity relationship modeling and OO class modeling. His approach to the use of dataflow diagrams, a technique that has fallen into disuse over the past few years, is superb and should cause many designers to revisit this valuable discipline.

But this is a book about Oracle8, not a theoretical treatise on the object/relation paradigm (ORP). Oracle8 is the first large-scale ORP product. In the relational world, we were limited to tables, columns, and scalar datatypes. Normalized vs unnormalized design was our primary consideration. We weren't subject to both the blessing and curse of the many data design features that ORP provides. Unfortunately, we do not yet possess the depth of experience needed to confidently prescribe when to use which feature. Features that intuitively appear to be the "correct" solution may have drawbacks that would adversely affect both implementation and performance. David clearly and concisely presents both the positive and (potentially) negative aspects of each of the new capabilities.

Foreword

David also presents the type of concrete examples and advice that is so critical to understanding and using Oracle8. ORP presents new challenges and issues for designers and developers. No longer is data design sufficient. Server-based executable code becomes an important issue for everyone, including DBAs. David's examples are clear, understandable, and complete.

As we approach the 21st century, the options and complexities for software development are increasing at a staggering rate. For the past several years, I have served as president of the Oracle Development Tools User Group (ODTUG), which started as the Oracle CASE Special Interest Group (http://www.odtug.com). ODTUG membership includes many of the leading practitioners of Oracle development from organizations in over 40 countries. In the past four years, I have been privileged to watch and listen as the range of interests and topics covered by the group exploded. *High Performance Oracle8 Object-Oriented Design* will lead the way into the next generation of issues to be faced by ODTUG members.

As we race into the enormous complexities of developing applications in the object relational world, David's work will be considered a milestone, uniquely combining theory and practicality in what is essentially the first book of its kind.

—*Jeffery Jacobs, President, Oracle Development Tools User Group*

Introduction

An exciting chapter in the saga of database development is unfolding before our eyes. The marriage of object-oriented functionality into the relational paradigm brings about a sense of excitement and reservation all at once. There is no doubt that the treatment of objects will require a fresh new perspective on planning, designing, and building new object relational applications. At the same time, a clear understanding of the object extensions in Oracle8 will be needed to successfully execute any new ORDBMS endeavor.

Object-oriented methodology lies on the opposite spectrum from relational methodology. Interestingly enough, what was a liability to one was a strength to the other. It was certainly only a matter of time before we witnessed a convergence of the two in order to solve problems that neither dealt with adequately.

One thing of certainty in a profession that offers few, is that designing and developing database applications for Oracle8 will not be business as usual. There is no way that it can be, nor, for that matter, should it be. The object extensions will expand the capability of the database developer like never before. Before jumping ahead into an object relational database project, the prudent developer will carefully assess the tools and methods at his or her disposal. That is where this book comes in.

High Performance Oracle8 Object-Oriented Design is aimed at analysts and developers facing a system application effort with Oracle8. The book strives to accomplish two basic goals. The first is to provide a detailed familiarization with the new object extensions found in Oracle8. Beyond a basic explanation of what each feature is, there is material here that explains how to use it.

The second goal of this book is to guide the reader from a purely relational methodology to the new object relational paradigm. Conventional means of planning and analysis are no longer adequate. The entity relationship diagram that we have all grown comfortable with will not adequately depict all of the new constructs at our disposal in Oracle8.

INTRODUCTION

There will be a number of books on the store shelves that give a basic itemized introduction to the new features found in Oracle8. The one thing that makes the book that you now hold unique is that it delves further into how objects should be used, when they can and should be used, and, most importantly, how to design your next database application system with objects in mind.

The chapters of this book are arranged in a logical progression to give the reader the proper perspective of how object extensions fit into the grand scheme of things. The first chapters of this book will give you valuable insight into the object extensions themselves. An entire chapter is dedicated to most of the new features like methods, reference pointers and OIDs, and user-defined data types. The initial portion of the book also deals with the object relational paradigm and how new design concepts like the Unified Modeling Language will change the way that database systems are conceived.

The next section of the book introduces new modeling tools that complement the object relational environment. The first generation of products have already emerged and will prove to be indispensable to object relational database design.

A sample case study is also presented that brings together the major concepts discussed in the book. A real-world example is used to demonstrate database design and implementation techniques. From a broader perspective, the use of Oracle8 in data warehousing and distributed environments is discussed. In the first release of Oracle8, there are many limitations to the use of objects and that valuable information can be found here.

The last portion of the book anticipates upcoming features and functionalities to Oracle8 that the database developer will have to be concerned about. The emerging SQL3 standard, type classes, inheritance, and more can be found in this single volume.

The incredible popularity of the World Wide Web, the demand for richer, more complex data types beyond characters and numbers, and the fact that software applications today are more sophisticated, means that the database supporting such applications must be just as rich and robust. As analysts and developers, we must also meet the technological challenge ahead. For users of Oracle8, this book is the first step.

An Introduction To Oracle8

HIGH PERFORMANCE

CHAPTER 1

Order and simplification are the first steps toward the mastery of a subject—the actual enemy is the unknown.
—Thomas Mann

HIGH PERFORMANCE

An Introduction To Oracle8

The overwhelming success of relational databases in general, and Oracle in particular, is due in large part to the fact that relational databases provide unprecedented access to data needed for making decisions. In addition, relational databases ushered in a new era of data management. With relational databases, data integrity could be governed by relational operations, and the data itself could be structured to a simple model based on mathematical set theory. Of greater importance to database developers was the innate flexibility of the relational schema. Relational databases offered unprecedented ease in modifying table structure. For example, adding data columns to existing tables or introducing entire tables remains an extremely simple operation. In terms of design methodology, not a lot has changed, although numerous extensions to SQL and the database have stretched database capabilities markedly since Dr. Codd first introduced the relational model, nearly three decades ago. Since then, the relational model has been endlessly studied, debated, and put into practice. The advent of the relational database signaled the end of mainframe-based supremacy (whose limited access to valuable data conjures up the image of an often-circulated office cartoon stating: *You want it when?*). In the sections that follow, we will discuss current relational methodology and introduce the object-relational paradigm. A brief overview of the object extensions to Oracle8 is presented to familiarize the reader with the key points to be found in the book. A discussion of the object-oriented concepts that are so vital to the understanding and implementation of Oracle8's exciting new features is given to prepare the reader for the material in succeeding chapters.

Evolution Of Database Systems

From an evolutionary perspective, the science of data storage and retrieval has made significant advances. Today, the hierarchical database architecture is considered to be a legacy system, even though hierarchical databases have established a reputation for speed in the arena of online transaction processing (OLTP). When we consider that only a few short decades ago, companies used file cabinets as a primary means for data storage, the technological transition has been mind-boggling. Not even man's venture into flight can eclipse the dramatic progress of data automation. Data management has witnessed a number of evolutionary changes since the introduction of disk-based storage. In just a few short decades, data management has moved from its auspicious beginnings on magnetic tape to flat files, hierarchical architecture, networked, relational, and now object-relational. Each of these represented a dramatic leap from its previous technology.

Legacy Systems

Early on, commercial implementations of a "database" consisted of magnetic tape storage. This was due, in large part, to the prohibitive expense of physical drum storage. At this point, retrieval of data was quite cumbersome and difficult to execute. Complete reliance on the good graces of the system administrator was unavoidable. He alone controlled the daily collection of data archived on tape. Data stored on tape served as input to statistical programs that aggregated the data and produced meaningful summaries.

Magnetic tape-based systems gradually gave way to early disk-based systems utilizing a flat file approach. Flat files supported sequential storage and a technique known as indexed sequential access method (ISAM). One popular access method developed during this time, BDAM (Basic Direct Access Method) used what is known as a hashing algorithm to take the symbolic key and convert it to a location address on the physical medium. Despite the gross inefficiency of this technique (BDAM file structures consume vast amounts of storage space), it is very fast and is quite popular today in data warehousing implementations.

Hierarchical systems emerged after the problems with the early flat-file systems became clear. Hierarchical databases used pointers to establish relationships between data elements. IBM fielded the first commercial database known as the Information Management System (IMS). IMS lent itself well to applications of a hierarchical nature, but it stumbled on more complex efforts requiring many-to-many or nested relationships.

In the 1970s, the Committee on Development of Applied Symbolic Languages (CODASYL) formulated what would become a network model for databases. Network databases like IDMS and MDBS2 gained wide acceptance and dominated in the 1980s. Their ability to handle complex data relationships coupled with good performance traits made them a natural selection for mission-critical systems. Unfortunately, data structures were difficult to work with, forcing programmers to navigate between data elements to extract needed information. Programmers would have to determine exact access paths to the data to return requested aggregates.

Hierarchical systems are the legacy systems of today. Hierarchical and flat-file systems use pointers to establish relationships among data. While this structure is extremely effective when modeling systems with a hierarchical nature, more complex systems are difficult to implement. For example, if you consider the pricing mechanism used in Oracle's Order Entry application module, you will find a complex schema where many products can have many price lists. It is this kind of data relationship that poses significant data design problems for legacy systems.

In addition, legacy systems are also overly complex. The tasks of programming and administration are difficult and require a significant amount of training and experience. You don't need to look any farther than the current craze over the year 2000 dilemma to realize how complex it is to administer changes.

So, what is it that makes legacy systems so complex? Flat-file systems are unable to establish data relationships as database administrators have become accustomed to in the relational world. This results in a denormalization of the data and therefore, widespread redundancy throughout the system. Maintenance of these systems can be extremely difficult because structure changes in a file cannot be easily traced to a calling program. It is of little comfort to think that finding discrepancies can be located by running all of your programs and watching to see which ones bomb out.

Case In Point: Legacy Vs. Client/Server

I recently worked on a contract for a client who was making the gradual transition from a legacy system to a client/server system. The project was to proceed in stages in which one business unit at a time would migrate to the Oracle database. The project had a very tight timeline, and we were forced to economize our efforts wherever possible. The most difficult part of our job turned out to be the migration of the data itself from the mainframe to the new relational database. We met with the system administrator to devise a plan of action. After our discussion, it was clear that it would require months for his staff to produce the flat

> files that we requested. We ultimately compromised on a file structure and assumed the lion's share of the responsibility for massaging the data by creating numerous PL/SQL scripts. Our task was tedious, but it paled in comparison to what the legacy system people would have faced.

The introduction of each new database approach presented the database designer with different advantages and disadvantages. Each step improved access mechanisms to the data but did not always provide an adequate methodology for designing the database entities. The challenge of dealing with these problems would change with the introduction of the relational model.

Relational Model

The introduction of the relational model offered a method to the madness of structuring data. The concept of data normalization had been discussed for years, but at last a serious implementation was delivered in the form of the relational model. I can recall my first encounter with the relational modeling concept, many years ago. It all seemed to make perfect sense to me, in fact, I couldn't help but wonder why it wasn't universally implemented at that time. The relational database did away with pointers and allowed navigation through data in a declarative fashion. This is accomplished through the English-like structured query language, or *SQL* as it has come to be known. Using the relational model, data retrieval can span a number of tables linked together with shared columns. The framework of the relational model makes it easy for developers and users alike to understand the ways in which the data is structured and organized. See Figure 1.1 for an illustrative example of the relational concept.

The elegance of relational design is succinctly stated in the rules of normalization, set forth by Dr. Codd:

- *The Precursor*—Ensure each occurrence of an entity is uniquely identifiable by a combination of attributes and/or relationships.

- *First Normal Form*—Remove repeated attributes or groups of attributes to their own entity.

- *Second Normal Form*—Remove attributes dependent on only part of the unique identifier.

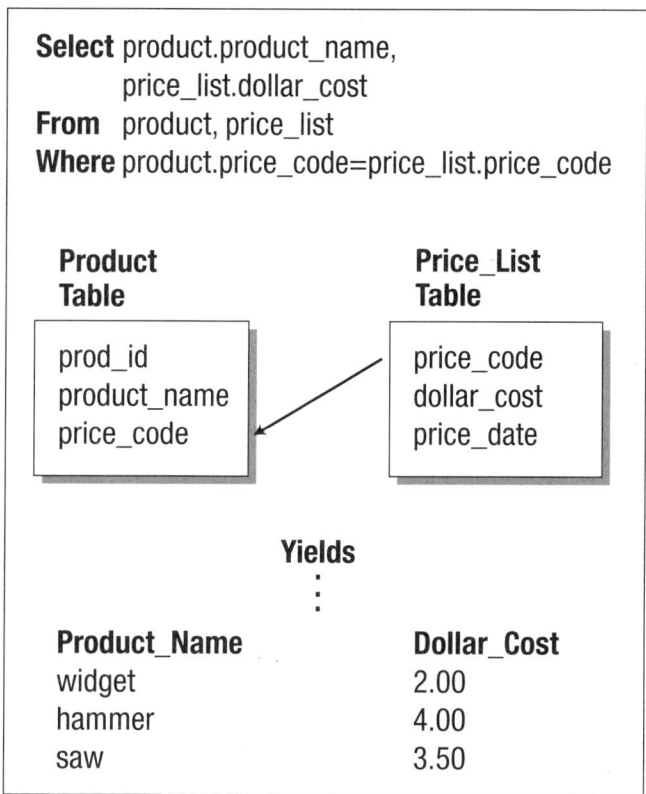

Figure 1.1
An example of a relationship between tables.

- *Third Normal Form*—Remove attributes dependent on attributes that are not part of the unique identifier (primary key).

When I first learned the rules of normalization, the popular catch phrase for second normal form was: *The key, just the key, and nothing but the key.* The application of third normal form requires you to eliminate *transitive dependencies* that depend on whole primary keys and other non-key attributes. For example, if we were to create a **PERSON** entity with an attribute called eye color, third normal form would have us move the eye-color attribute out to its own table. Interestingly enough, for all of their simplicity, you will almost never find a production system normalized to third normal form. This is because intentional redundancy improves performance and eliminates unnecessary complexity from the data model. There are data constructs in the Oracle8 object extensions that actually violate second and third normal form intentionally. In Chapter 5 we will discuss the use of Object Identifiers (OIDs) and how their implementation bypasses the need for referential integrity between data elements that use them. VARRAYs and nested tables, as well as non-first normal form, are introduced in Chapter 3. Before we explore these exciting new features, let's concern ourselves with another important aspect of relational models, namely, referential integrity.

Referential Integrity

From a database design perspective, the introduction of referential integrity (RI) played an important role, because referential integrity enables business rules to be controlled through the use of constraints. Constraints are executed during the execution of data manipulation language (DML) statements. The role of constraints is to prevent the violation of data integrity and, thereby, its normalization. For an illustration of referential integrity enforcement, look at Listing 1.1. The code is typical of syntax used to create RI. Listing 1.1 displays a table created with embedded referential integrity clauses.

Listing 1.1 A table-creation script with embedded referential integrity clauses.

```
DROP TABLE REF_EXAMPLE;

CREATE TABLE REF_EXAMPLE
   (EMPNO NUMBER(6) PRIMARY KEY CONSTRAINT PK_EMP_REF_EXAMPLE,
    DEPTNO NUMBER(6) CHECK (DEPTNO BETWEEN 100000 AND 600000),
    DEPTNAME VARCHAR2(15) CHECK (DEPTNAME IN ('ACCOUNTING',
        'MANAGEMENT', 'SALES', 'MARKETING', 'SUPPORT') )
    FOREIGN KEY (DEPTNO)
    REFERENCES REF_EXAMPLE2
ON DELETE CASCADE;
```

Listing 1.1 might not be what you envision as the ideal table, but it serves as an adequate example of how referential integrity is enabled. In this listing, there is a constraint to establish the column **EMPNO** as the primary key while **DEPTNO** and **DEPTNAME** have **CHECK** constraints to enforce a reduced set of entries. Finally, there is a table constraint that causes the deletion of all child records in the related table **REF_EXAMPLE2** should the parent record be deleted. Users of the

Designer/2000 product are accustomed to having scripts like this generated for them once the business rules have been applied to the tool.

Following the implementation of referential integrity, Oracle8 ushered in a new era of database functionality. Oracle8 has stepped back from the rigid enforcement of referential integrity by introducing objects that reflect the behavior of the hierarchical database's use of pointers. In fact, implementation of OIDs is the reintroduction of the pointer concept. The astute reader will note that in the absence of referential integrity, there is no mechanism for preventing a pointer to a deleted object. We will discuss what is known as a "dangling" pointer in Chapter 5, but suffice it to say, Oracle has anticipated such occurrences and has developed an **IS DANGLING** clause for use in PL/SQL. You'll see in the next section, the underlying force behind Oracle8's new functionality really has evolved over many years.

Oracle8 And Object Orientation

The advent of client/server technology enables more robust systems to be designed and built. The lead into client/server was somewhat akin to the change in American culture when television made the transition from black-and-white to color. What everyone soon discovered was that, despite the dramatic improvement in what users could accomplish, moving work from the server to the client introduced a plethora of new problems, including: network bottlenecks, hardware conflicts, high maintenance costs, and complex system designs. All along the way, Oracle supported the demands for data storage, but much of the work shifted to client stations.

It wasn't long before there was a realization that the cost of client/server deployment was very high. Add to this the recent explosive popularity of the World Wide Web and the Internet, not to mention the coming of age of Java and C++ as truly legitimate commercial development tools. The Internet has changed the way the world does business. It is quickly becoming business suicide to ignore this avenue of trade and commerce. Figure 1.2 serves to illustrate the evolutionary progress of database design.

If the Internet is a glimpse into the future, then database technology must advance to accommodate the demands of an object-oriented world. This has lead to what is now Oracle8. Oracle8 has been fundamentally redesigned with the perspective that the next step in the evolutionary ladder of computer technology will be the thin client or Network Computing Architecture (NCA).

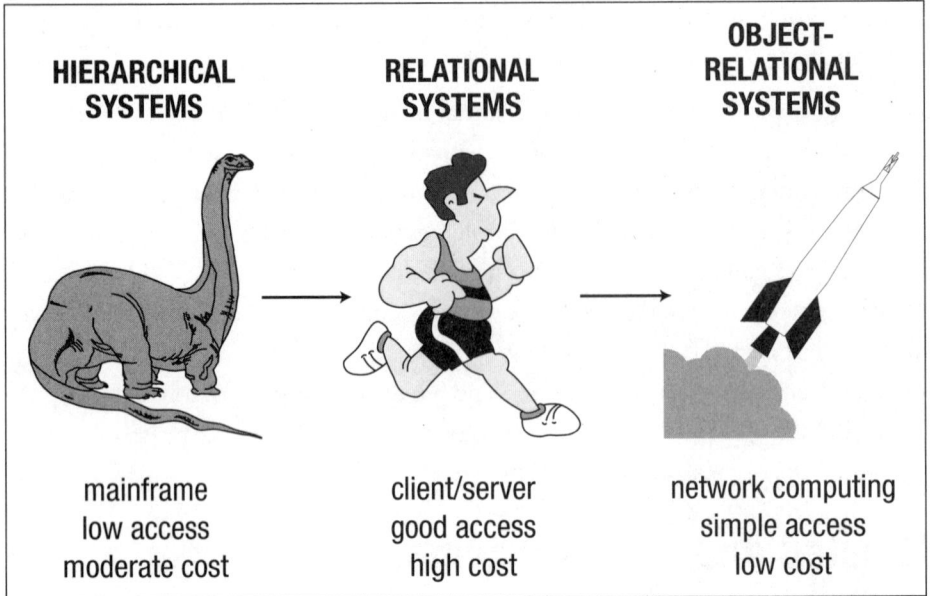

Figure 1.2
The evolution of database design.

The Web has demonstrated that rickety terminal screens have given way to multimedia systems sporting spectacular graphics and sound. Once you've taken the user to Paris, he isn't going back to the farm. Suddenly, the demands on the database to support modern technology began to strain the limits of what relational databases could support.

Despite arguments for the adoption of object-oriented functionality, many relational database designers have been reticent to adopt the new extensions. Part of it could be rooted in an unfamiliarity with object-oriented design. Part of it could be the concern over how such new functionality would affect normalization and the inner workings of SQL. Regardless of developers' reticence, fear has certainly given way to necessity because it is readily accepted that current relational databases do not model the real world adequately. Even if designers dismiss the immense popularity of the Web, designers are still left with the fact that there are real-world systems that remain problematic to design because of their complex business rules.

Add to this the fact that the logical model doesn't necessarily lead to a good viable physical model. Theory and practice are rarely synonymous, and it has been the challenge of producing an efficient physical model that often frustrates database developers and designers.

The redesign of Oracle's database does not mean that the migration from version 7 to version 8 will be difficult. On the contrary, Oracle8 fully supports existing relational systems. So, why migrate? Improved performance, scalability, and maintenance (need I say more?). But what about the object-oriented extensions? Is that sufficient reason? The answer to that question depends on your system. Chances are, you will find that one or more of Oracle8's object-oriented extensions will prove to be extremely useful. It's a safe bet that systems targeted for NCA and the Web will most certainly demand this new functionality. New functionalities demand a new way to model the system. For this reason, database modeling enters the next evolutionary stage: object-relational.

The Next Wave: Object-Relational Databases

For those of you well-versed in relational methodology, object-oriented design presents a significant paradigm shift. Most likely, there are instances that you can recall where the power of object-oriented design would have proven to be indispensable. Unfortunately, you were tethered to the limited set of object types, a restrictive relational methodology (normalization, tables, and columns) and the limits of SQL. Even when data was only words and numbers, some implementations proved hard to design and develop effectively.

Later in Chapter 8, we'll look at a case study illustrating a perfect example of a situation where the complexity of the objects being modeled, coupled with the fact that behaviors were to be included, made for a challenging design task. In fact, since the original design was restricted to a relational database implementation, the final product is fraught with compromises. The outcome is quite different utilizing the object-oriented extensions in Oracle8.

Attempting to force object-oriented concepts into a relational database model always results in compromise. Leaning a compromise in favor of relational methodology results in lost functionality, such as polymorphism and inheritance. Leaning the other way means sacrificing some degree of normalization and introducing some

Chapter 1

level of entity abstraction in order to simulate object-oriented behavior. Pure object-oriented designs suffer from a lack of flexibility, since data relationships are established with pointers versus the declarative relationships used in the relational model. In Oracle8 we are able to take advantage of object-oriented behavior with the exception of encapsulation. Since SQL allows objects access outside of their methods, pure encapsulation is violated. Encapsulation and methods are discussed later in this chapter and in Chapter 6. Support for inheritance and polymorphism are currently planned for the version 8.1 release of Oracle8.

For the first time since the introduction of the relational database, an entirely new level of design flexibility is being introduced through the advent of the object-oriented extensions in Oracle8. But, as with any new technology, the introduction of this marvelous new technology is not without its ramifications. As you shall see, Chapter 2 shows how Oracle8's new object-oriented extensions will affect the way developers design databases in the future.

What then is to become of the design methodologies that developers have grown accustomed to? The methodologies will have to adapt. The object-relational database is serving as the catalyst for a new unified data model. Two initiatives of major significance are currently underway. The first is the development of the SQL3 standard. The second is the formulation of the Unified Modeling Language (UML).

The American National Standards Institute (ANSI) is currently in the process of developing an object-extensible version of SQL to be called SQL3. Even at this early stage, many consider the new definition to be incomplete. Database vendors are not waiting around to see what happens next. Most are taking the initiative to develop their own implementations. Relational database companies are working in the direction of SQL3 while the object-oriented database proponents favor the Object Data Management Groups (ODMG) vision: ODMG/OQL. OQL permits the selection of objects via SELECT statements. Both systems build on the SQL-92 standard, and the two committees (ANSI and ODMG) are making efforts to merge the direction of the two standards. It is uncertain at this point how the separate efforts of the various vendors will impact on the SQL3 initiative or on standardization of an SQL language in general. Numerous vendors are in support of this standard, which will allow access to traditionally non-relational object types.

The Rational Software Corporation is spearheading an effort with the support of many large vendors to define a standard to the Object Management Group (OMG) for the UML. The UML will encompass the best techniques of designing software systems to include business modeling. The UML combines the concepts originally set forth by Booch, Object Modeling Technique (OMT), and the Object-Oriented Software Technique (OOSE). The resulting product is a unified modeling language standard. The UML incorporates new semantics, notation and process specific extensions with the goal that it will become the industry standard. The UML is intended to be treated as a process, even though the focus is on a standard modeling language. Oracle's new product, Object Database Designer, implements type modeling from this new emerging open standard.

While all of this satisfies the question of what direction database modeling is taking, it is appropriate to consider the rationale for pursuing this direction in the first place.

Modeling For Oracle8

The increasing complexity of today's business environment requires corporations to find new ways to stay ahead. Doing so has meant that business rules have grown more complex. Incorporating these business rules into a workable model has posed a tremendous challenge to developers required to maintain system speed and agility while increasing functionality. Object-oriented extensions to the relational database is the natural evolution to solving part of this problem. The new improvements in Oracle8 provide more than sufficient rationale for migration. New advances in query optimization, support for large databases, and so forth will enhance performance and reduce the complexities of maintenance. All these things can be used to great advantage, but in the end they do nothing to change the methodology under which the database is designed.

So, why model for Oracle8? Primarily, a shift in design philosophy will be required if you intend to capitalize on the object-oriented extensions. Use of these extensions is almost unavoidable if the system you are designing is targeted for the Web or if you are faced with a real-world application like the one found in the case study used later in this book.

The introduction of methods (described in detail later in this chapter) poses significant design implications on the designer and DBA. With the ability to move code into the database, the developer will be responsible for greater emphasis on analysis and design. The DBA will inherit the added responsibility of maintaining these new extensions.

Oracle8 supports more data types. Not only is it possible to utilize text, but now spatial (e.g., 3D mapping), images, and video can be stored as objects in a database. Furthermore, support for user defined data types is now included. The design methodology changes to handle these new data types. In order to access images, video, and other large files, the use of **REFs** and OIDs are utilized. The detailed discussion on these two items is found in Chapter 5. **REFs** give a developer the ability to directly reference one object from another. In other words, relationships can be established without the use of SQL **JOINs**. In addition, OIDs will facilitate the aggregation of data objects without the necessity to build **JOINs**. This will have far reaching effects on how normalization and database design are treated.

The introduction of abstract data types (ADTs as they were commonly known, Oracle refers to them as user-defined data types) will have far reaching effects on design methodology. Through the use of ADTs, it is possible for a column in a table to contain an array of values or even an entire table. Aggregation of data in this manner will have a dramatic effect on how database objects are defined starting at the analysis phase.

Oracle8 allows the creation of business objects, which can be anything a user defines, such as a purchase order or a hotel reservation. Essentially, a business object captures the semantics of a process and places it in the data server rather than disperses it as application logic in various locations. Developers will realize a reduction in design time because less effort will be required to sift through the minute details of data aggregation to adequately capture business rules. While this concept may seem somewhat vague right now, a greater understanding will be gained in Chapter 8 from the case study.

When To Implement Object-Oriented Design

Too many times when a new technology is introduced, there is a compulsive drive to rework perfectly functioning systems to squeeze out some small performance or cost benefit. If you are faced with the question of whether or not object-oriented design is appropriate, you should consider the arguments presented in this section.

If the system in question is an existing application in production and its performance is not in question, then object-oriented design is probably not appropriate. Consider also whether or not this system is targeted for NCA. The answer is still

"No," because the existing architecture most likely migrates well to a thin client so long as the application has not been designed with significant processing logic on the client side. Take for example, an order-entry system currently in place. Chances are, the users have no need for additional sophistication in this application. Such a system that has no need for functional improvement is better left alone or simply migrated under its current configuration.

The corporate environment under which object-oriented design is being considered is perhaps the most significant factor of all. The following three crucial factors must be in place before a technological shift as significant as object-oriented design should be undertaken:

- *Assets*—The organization must have the fiscal strength to undertake what amounts to a reengineering effort of their deployed production systems. Client/server technology taught an important lesson in fiscal reality. Cost savings from such an implementation are not realized in the short term. The corporate culture must understand that the benefits to be reaped are long term. Often the benefit realized is not in real dollars but in improved productivity, which is an indirect financial gain. The bottom line is that new technologies have a real price associated with them and an organization considering such a venture must be able to absorb the necessary costs.

- *Resources*—This refers to the hardware and software infrastructure required to implement the new technology. If a company is unable or unwilling to replace the dumb terminals with PCs or network computers or if a host of various other tangibles (such as application servers or networking components) are not possible, then designing for the new object-oriented extensions might not be appropriate. There are many reasons why organizations will not commit to new resources, but the two most common are usually cost (the asset factor) or corporate culture. If the rationale is corporate culture and you are consulting for such an organization, it might not be possible to glean this fact when you first start the project. A few interviews with the staff are always a prudent investment of time, in order to gather the information you will need.

- *Expertise*—In the long run, an organization must have its own internal talent to assume ownership of an application system when the consultants are gone. If a company is fortunate enough to have its own group of talented people to assume the task of developing with a new technology, then this is better still. In either case, designing and developing with the new object-oriented extensions (or any new technology for that matter!) should not be taken lightly. Projects that lack the necessary expertise to carry them through to completion are doomed to failure and are better off not attempted in the first place. During my tenure as a consultant, I was party to only one project where the permanent personnel had absolutely no expertise in the new technology and yet were able to pull off a successful project. On Friday afternoon, they left work running their applications in COBOL on an IBM mainframe. On Monday morning, the users came to work and ran their new Oracle applications from a VAX platform. Such is the exception rather than the rule. Granted, they had brought in a number of consultants to help execute the changeover, but I recall a statistic on client/server implementations that indicated that only 10 percent of such "cold turkey" attempts are ever successful. In this particular case, I attribute the personnel's motivation as a factor of success as much as anything else.

In my earlier consulting days, I was often struck by the percentage of companies that I visited that were still banging away on character-based applications in SQL*Forms3.0 when the rest of the world (as it seemed to me) was hotly pursuing the holy grail of graphical user interfaces and client/server deployment. Over time, I came to realize that one or more of the three factors just mentioned could not be attained. The lesson to be gained from this is that both corporate and technological factors determine whether object-oriented design is appropriate in a particular scenario. Regardless of the current trend, the individual needs of the client site ultimately dictate what methodology is best.

Object-Oriented Concepts

In order to gain a better appreciation for the object-oriented extensions in Oracle8, it is important to understand some of the concepts of object-oriented design. The definitions provided here are intended to give some insight into how object-oriented methodology is utilized in a pure programming environment—like that of C++. These are the origins from which the Oracle8 extensions have evolved, yet their implementation differs from C++. Languages like C++ and Smalltalk draw their beginnings from structured programming languages. The benefit of object-oriented languages is that the same structure remains but with the added ability to organize and structure in a different way. Many of the concepts are taken for granted in everyday life where they occur on a continual basis. During your waking hours, you are unconsciously grouping and categorizing things that are a part of your world. You react to events that you recognize but are oblivious to the details of how they occur. These things and more draw a parallel between the real world and the concepts described here. Concepts we'll discuss include the following:

- Classes
- Methods
- Messages
- Polymorphism
- Inheritance
- Abstraction
- Encapsulation

Classes

A *class* is a data type that consists of data members and their functions. This is perhaps one of the most important concepts in C++ and is fundamental to its use. Classes define object types in C++. Functions and variables that are part of the class declaration of a class definition are considered to be **public** members of that class. Likewise, functions and variables declared inside of the class are said to be **private** members. PL/SQL packages display this same behavior where public and private program units and variables can be declared. This is where the similarity ends, however, because packages do not define data classes. In a future release of Oracle8, currently anticipated to be 8.1, class hierarchies for data structures will be supported allowing not only a cascading of object properties but also support for polymorphism.

It is important to note that classes are a logical abstraction defining new data types and what properties they will have. An object declaration is the actual physical manifestation of the object. The principle of polymorphism will be carried out by associating one or more methods within two or more distinct object tables in a class hierarchy. Polymorphism is achieved when the single method can achieve a different outcome for each of the two object tables. See the example in the polymorphism section.

Methods And Messages

It is difficult to discuss one of these concepts without the other. A *method* in object-oriented programming is a function of a particular class. Objects receive messages from programs by calling methods. A *message* is essentially an executed function belonging to a class member. The message will include the function call and its associated arguments. To think of this in another way, if the message is the set of instructions being delivered to an object, then the method is the vehicle that gets it there. Figure 1.3 illustrates the relationship between methods and messaging.

Polymorphism

The first time you hear the word *polymorphism*, it conjures up an image of some exotic tropical skin disease. In reality, it is defined as the ability for different objects in a class hierarchy to have different behaviors in response to the same message. Polymorphism derives its meaning "many forms" from the Greek language. A single behavior can generate entirely different responses from objects in the same group.

As an illustrative example, take an event called *paycheck distribution*. Also, assume that there is a general class called *employee*. As part of the **employee** class, there are **managers** and **programmers**. The **paycheck distribution** event can generate the behavior

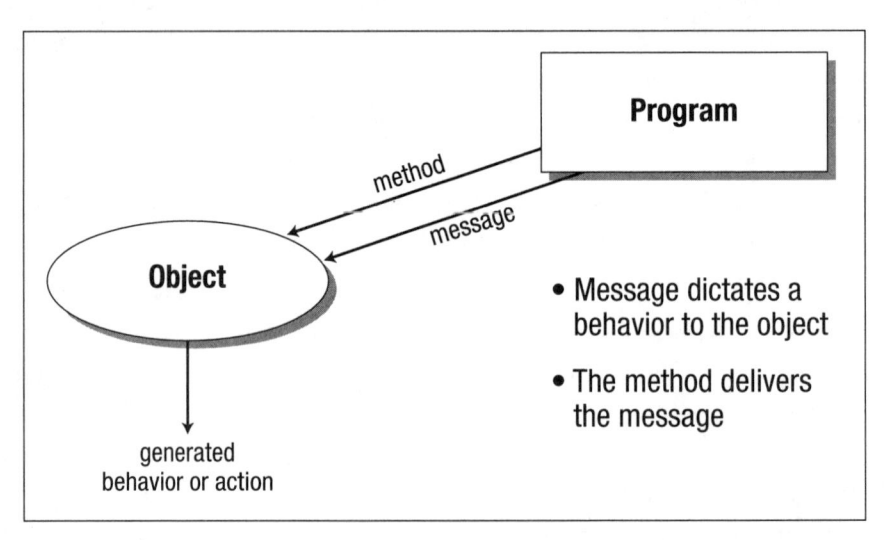

Figure 1.3
An example of methods and messaging.

of laughter from the type **management** while the same event produces the behavior of tears from the type **programmer**. Although this example is simplistic, you can see that polymorphism allows you to specify a general type of action. Within the framework of the program, the internal mechanism determines what specific action should take place. In C++ programming, the use of the same function name for different purposes is known as function overloading. To experienced PL/SQL programmers, this is not an alien concept. It is accepted as good practice to develop overloaded PL/SQL packages whenever possible. Overloaded PL/SQL packages are flexible and require little revision when thought out carefully. For those inexperienced with overloaded packages, Listing 1.2 illustrates the script for an overloaded PL/SQL package.

Listing 1.2 A sample overloaded PL/SQL package.

```
CREATE OR REPLACE PACKAGE  OVERLOAD_SAMPLE
IS
PROCEDURE POLY_1 (PAY_EMP IN VARCHAR2, DEF_CODE IN VARCHAR2);
PROCEDURE POLY_1 (PAY_EMP IN VARCHAR2, DEF_CODE IN NUMBER);
END OVERLOAD_SAMPLE;
```

The procedure **POLY_1** is defined with two distinct input types for the second parameter. The user can pass either a character or number valued parameter and get the same or different results, depending on the code for each iteration of the procedure. This is just one example. Executing polymorphism through class hierarchies will not be available in Oracle8 until perhaps version 8.1.

The most important thing to remember about polymorphism is that a greater degree of complexity can be handled through a standard interface such as a commonly named function. Figure 1.4 illustrates the concept of polymorphism using the paycheck_distribution example just described.

Inheritance

Inheritance is the ability for one class to inherit the properties of its ancestor. This concept is also known as *subclassing*. Inheritance allows an object to inherit a certain set of attributes from another object while allowing the addition of specific features. The concept of inheritance is familiar to anyone who has used Developer/2000. Within the Forms tool, it is possible to create property classes that are comprised of a selected set of attributes that will be passed to any object assigned to the property

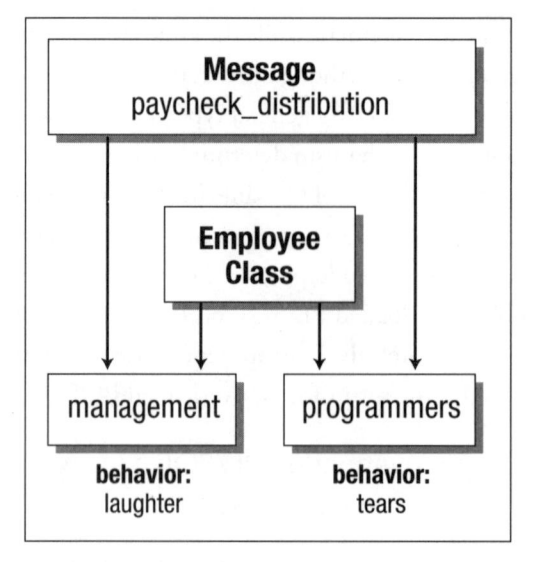

Figure 1.4
An example of polymorphism.

class. In other words, the objects inherit those attributes that make up the property class. Property classes in the Forms tool should not be confused with data classes, which are also defined in the Forms tool. Figure 1.5 displays a property class sheet showing inheritable properties.

Abstraction

Abstraction is performed when a data class is designed containing only the essential elements of that class. In object-oriented design, this customarily means that a "class" is created but it has no objects itself. This abstract class represents a hierarchy from which lower-level detail objects share a commonality. For example, if you create an object class called *automobile*, then you could assume that this class would be a subclass to an abstract class called *vehicles*. The relationship between the new abstract class **vehicles** and the subclass would be known as a supertype to subtype relationship, if you were designing these objects for the logical model in a relational database. As mentioned before, because the class **vehicles** is an abstract class, it has no actual instances of objects in it. It exists to describe general features that pertain to all vehicles, not just automobiles. Abstraction will be discussed in detail in the case

PC_CANVAS_MAIN	
Name	PC_CANVAS_MAIN
Class	
Type	
Canvas-view Type	Stacked
Display	
Displayed	True
Width	600
Height	410
Bevel	Lowered
Font Name	Arial
Font Size	10
Font Style	Plain
Font Width	Normal
Font Weight	Medium
Foreground Color	black
Background Color	gray16
Fill Pattern	transparent
Charmode Logical Attribute	
White on Black	False
Functional	
Window	WINDOW0
Raise on Entry	False
X Position on Canvas	0
Y Position on Canvas	0
Direction	Default
Stacked View	
View Width	600
View Height	410
Display X Position	0
Display Y Position	0
View Horiz. Scroll Bar	False
View Vert. Scroll Bar	False

Figure 1.5
A property class sheet from Forms4.5 showing properties to be inherited.

study in Chapter 8 later in the book. Figure 1.6 depicts the concept of abstraction using the vehicle example cited above.

Encapsulation

Encapsulation is defining a class with data members and functions into a definition. In other words, it is the mechanism that binds code and data together while protecting or hiding it from outside of the class. The actual implementation is hidden from the user who only sees the interface.

CHAPTER 1

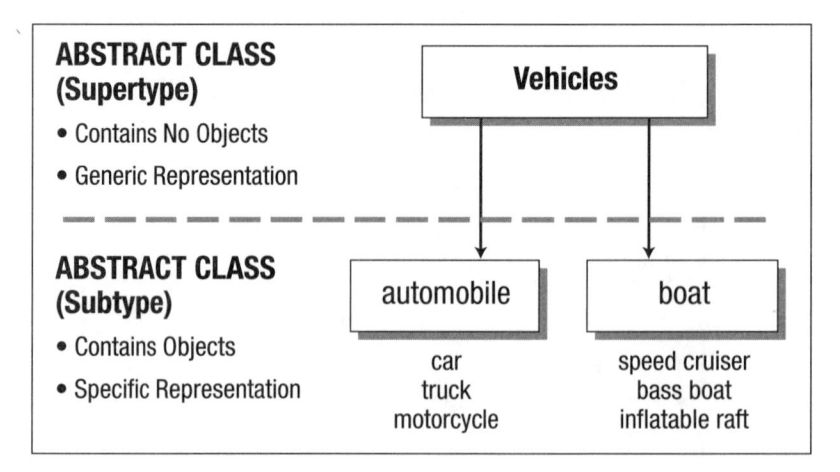

Figure 1.6
An example of the concept of abstraction.

As an illustrative example, think of a car engine. You can open the hood and see that it is there, and you can get in the car and start the ignition. The engine causes the car to move. Although you can see the motor, the inner workings are hidden from your view. You can appreciate the function that it performs for you without ever knowing all of the details of what occurs inside or even how. Another example that draws from experience more familiar to Oracle developers is that of privately declared program units in a PL/SQL package. For example, look at Listing 1.3.

Listing 1.3 A private program unit in a PL/SQL package.

```
CREATE OR REPLACE PACKAGE   ENCAPSULATION_SAMPLE
IS
PROCEDURE ENCAP_1 (PAY_EMP IN VARCHAR2, PAY_AMT IN OUT NUMBER);
END ENCAPSULATION _SAMPLE;

CREATE OR REPLACE PACKAGE BODY ENCAPSULATION_SAMPLE
IS
FUNCTION ENCAP_2 (EMP IN NUMBER) RETURN DATE
IS
H_DATE    DATE;
BEGIN
   SELECT HIREDATE
   INTO    H_DATE
   FROM    EMP_HISTORY
   WHERE EMP_NO - EMP;
RETURN H_DATE;
```

```
END ENCAP_2 ;

PROCEDURE ENCAP_1 (PAY_EMP IN VARCHAR2, PAY_AMT IN OUT NUMBER)
IS
BEGIN
   SELECT SALARY
   INTO PAY_AMT
   FROM PAY_TABLE
   WHERE EMPLOYEE = PAY_EMP
   AND HIREDATE > ENCAP_2(PAY_EMP);

EXCEPTION WHEN NO_DATA_FOUND THEN
   NULL;
END ENCAP_1;
```

If you look closely at Listing 1.3, you can see the function **ENCAP_2** in the package body. The function is a private program unit and cannot be addressed from outside of the package itself. The function performs a role in determining the value fetched when the procedure **ENCAP_1** is executed, but this functionality is hidden from the user. Note that under encapsulation, objects may only be accessed by their own methods. In Oracle8 we violate this principle because SQL provides the means to circumvent this innate security.

Now that we have taken a moment to explain the basic principles that describe the object-oriented methodology, it is appropriate that some attention is directed to the object extensions in Oracle8.

Object-Oriented Features Of Oracle8

There are over 20 volumes that comprise the entire Oracle8 documentation set. Fortunately, our focus is on the object-oriented extensions offered in this new version. In the chapters that follow, we will discuss those extensions and detail the steps in which to incorporate an object-oriented design methodology into your work. The reason that we are discussing the Oracle8 extensions apart from the object-oriented concepts described earlier is because Oracle's implementation of these concepts differs somewhat with the pure definitions. Oracle has maintained the correspondence of its object constructs very closely to those of its relational constructs to build on the familiarity that the current developer generation has with the Oracle relational methodology. The features explained below embody these object concepts in a way that can be exercised through the mechanism of the database. Our discussion of Oracle8's new object extensions will touch upon several subject areas: semantics, user-defined data types (also referred to as ADTs), methods, pointers, support for unstructured data, support of client-side objects, and object views.

Oracle8 Semantics

It is of some interest to note that, despite the new functionality, Oracle8 maintains the same transactional semantics that it always had with the relational data. What this means is that it is not necessary to discard all that you have learned about SQL and working with data. However, you will have to change how you define your data and design it into your system.

Oracle8 has the ability to aggregate objects via pointer constructs, thus eliminating the need to create views to assemble composites at runtime as SQL must do. Objects in Oracle8 assume an independent character, even if they are composed entirely of small atomic pieces from various tables. Not only does this impact on how SQL is used, but it carries design ramifications with regard to normalization.

Abstract Data Types (ADT)

ADTs (sometimes called *object types* or *user-defined data types*) extend the relational data type system beyond the conventional text, numbers, and dates. ADTs are essentially data types composed of subtypes. At its simplest, an ADT is merely a collection of smaller, basic data types that can then be used as a single data object. Oracle implements ADTs through the use of a **CREATE TYPE** definition statement. This definition can define domains of all subtypes that will exist within the new data type.

Abstract data typing utilizes the concept of encapsulation, as described earlier. Previous attempts to utilize encapsulation in the relational database environment failed because of the declarative nature of relational design and SQL. The use of ADTs offers the following valuable characteristics:

- ADTs support the creation of aggregate data types. Aggregate data types are those that contain other data types. For example, an aggregate data type called *ship_to* might contain the data fields necessary for a freight delivery such as **point_of_contact**, **ship_location**, and **delivery_date**.

- ADTs allow the nesting of ADTs within other data types. Data structures can now be created that can be easily reused in Oracle tables and by PL/SQL. Drawing from the previous example of the data type **ship_to**, the data field **ship_location** can itself be an ADT with data types **street_address**, **city**, and **zip_code**. Figure 1.7 shows a representation of abstract data types nested into columns of a data table.

Through the use of ADTs, data fields can now be a set range of values or they can contain an entire table. Value domains can be defined in this way. Referring again to Figure 1.7, if you assume that only valid values can reside in the **ship_location** table, then you have utilized domain integrity.

ADTs come in two varieties: persistent and non-persistent. *Persistent* ADTs are those that are derived from physical database objects, such as tables. Persistent ADTs are assigned Object Identifiers (OIDs). **OIDs** are discussed in greater detail under the section describing pointers. *Non-persistent* ADTs are memory-resident objects, such as PL/SQL tables, and, because they are temporary, will have no **OID**.

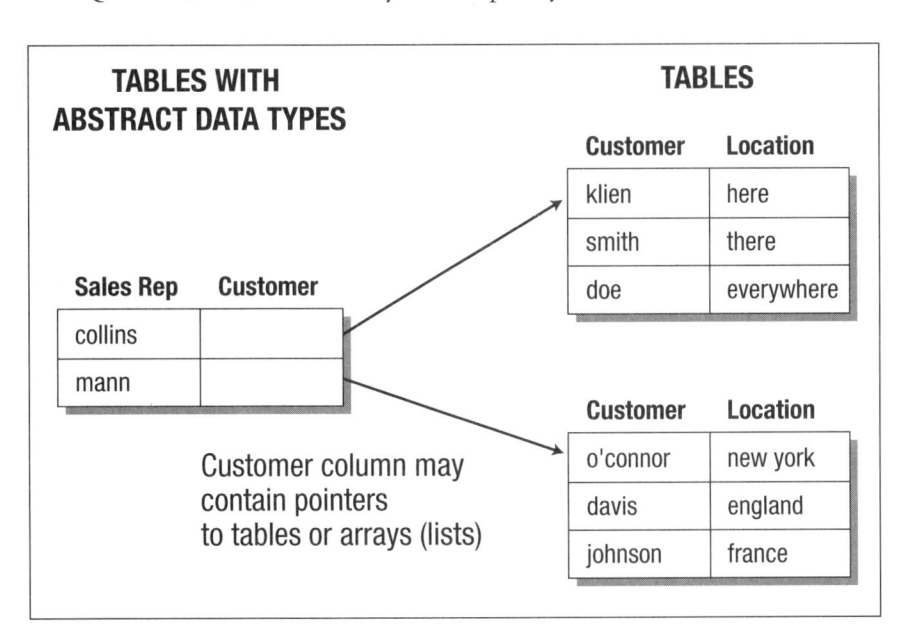

Figure 1.7
An example of Abstract Data Types (ADTs).

Other ADT concepts introduced in Oracle8 include:

- *Object Tables*—These are tables that contain instances of complex data types, such as those described earlier in this section.
- *VARRAY*—This is a multivalue column. **VARRAY**s are intended for use when there is a small, finite set of multiple values to be linked to a data column.
- *Nested Tables*—These are tables stored within other tables. In other words, a single column in one table can contain another table. Tables that have been nested can contain nested tables themselves. This offers new possibilities for modeling complex aggregate objects. One restriction to this feature is that each column must contain a pointer to a table with the same column definition.
- *REFs*—These are pointer values that directly reference one object from another. Functionally, they behave much like foreign keys do in SQL.

Methods

Methods in Oracle8 are essentially relational database packages and procedures. Oracle7 was the first version of the database to support the procedural option. In the case of Oracle8, the packages and procedures can be associated directly to a database table. This is not the same as a database trigger, however. In a database trigger, the referential integrity is maintained for the table. In a method, the behavior of a data object in a table is manipulated. In this particular case, methods are the coupling of the data with its behavior.

Developers familiar with creating and implementing PL/SQL packages will adapt quickly to the use of methods. As with standard PL/SQL packages and procedures, developers can create **public** and **private** methods. Methods need not be written in PL/SQL, however. Oracle8 also supports methods written in C and Java. In Oracle8, this action is conducted through an object name and associated method specification. Methods encourage code reusability and encapsulation. Reusability is achieved because a properly constructed method will become a module to be used in the same manner regardless of the object it is executed against. In other words, you create it once and use it many times. Oracle programmers are not required to hunt through existing code or rewrite it, so long as they know the name of the data object class. The list of methods are easily displayed from this information alone. Encapsulation is also achieved because the inner workings of the method become transparent to the person using it.

Methods for use with data objects are searched based on the class under which the data object resides. When a method is invoked, the database will first look within that data class for the method. If it is not found, then it will search up the data class hierarchy until it is found.

Pointers

Although it may seem like déjà vu, pointers have been introduced as an Oracle8 extension. A pointer is a data type and happens to be an **OID**. **OID**s are 128 bytes in length and are not repeated, even after they have been deleted. Oracle guarantees that this uniqueness will extend for perpetuity. Much like a traditional pointer from earlier programming languages, such as PL1, an Oracle pointer provides the ability to reference another row somewhere in the database. There are significant ramifications to the use of pointers in Oracle8. Relationships among tables can now be effected without the declarative mechanism of SQL. What this means is that data among tables can be linked directly without having to perform a table join operation. Pointers in Oracle8 possess the following capabilities:

- *Related rows in other tables can be referenced as sets*—First normal form can now be violated, and cells in a table can contain a pointer to repeating table values. This feature is known as *nested tables*. Aggregate objects can be pre-built so that all of the specific rows in an aggregate table can be pre-assembled.

- *Pointers can reference non-database objects in a flat file*—A table cell can contain a pointer to a flat file referencing a non-database object such as a picture or sound clip.

- *Use of pointers allows the establishment of data relationships without a JOIN operation*—Through the use of pointers, table columns can contain references to another table's rows, thus eliminating the need to perform an SQL **JOIN** to retrieve the desired data.

Besides this functionality, Oracle also provides the following extensions to the basic pointer:

- A single pointer to other rows.
- Lists of pointers to other rows. This extension is called the *VARRAY*.
- Lists of pointers to pointers that point to other rows. This is known as a *Multi-dimensional VARRAY*.

- A pointer to another table. This is also known as *nested tables*.
- Lists of pointers to other entire tables. These are known as *Multidimensional arrays of OIDs*.

Support Of Unstructured Data

Oracle8 now supports the ability to store large objects, such as video clips and graphic images, in the database. The Large Object (LOB) data type can be supported in one of two ways: hosted in the database, either inline or in a separate tablespace; or as an operating system file. Support for LOB data types represents a vast improvement over the LONG and LONG RAW data types in Oracle7. LOBs offer the means to store larger objects in more ways than Oracle7 was able to support. Through the use of Oracle's OCI and DBMS_LOB utilities, the methods in which large objects can be manipulated have improved. This includes the ability to update and insert new objects. Multiple LOB columns can now be supported in the same table, and the data types of the columns can vary. Oracle8 supports random access to this data, reducing the LOB into chunks that can be retrieved in a single round trip to the client. The LOB data type utilizes a stored value called a *locator*. The locator indicates the location of the LOB, whether it is stored out-of-line or by an external file in the operating system. Oracle8 now provides the programmatic interface and PL/SQL support to perform operations on LOBs.

Multimedia support is also provided through the use of *cartridges*. Cartridges allow users to store and access each of the specific data types supported (text, image, video, spatial data, and time series data).

Support For Complex Objects

Oracle8 provides the means to model complex objects by utilizing a combination of the constructs described here. Useful aggregations of data can be devised through the nesting of user defined data types within other user defined data types. For example, a VARRAY can be constructed and linked to a column that, when combined with other columns, describes a new user defined data type. This data type could then be used in an object table thus representing several layers of data aggregation.

Just as important as the ability to specially aggregate data types, is the ability to couple behaviors (methods) with the user defined data types resulting in a robust and rich data construct effectively emulating the most important features of object-oriented design. The true benefit of the object extensions for Oracle8 will be in the creative design of these complex objects to solve real-world modeling problems.

Support Of Client-Side Objects

Oracle8 supports the use of client-side objects outside of the database. This is an important point to note from a design perspective because this means that calls to external programs can be made from within the database. External programs written in C, C++, and Java can be utilized. External procedures are also allowed to interface with other external procedures or even specialized devices.

In addition, objects in a client application can be traversed by means of an application cache. A complex hierarchy of objects can be retrieved into an object cache without an overabundance of network retrievals. This provides a fast and efficient way to use objects in a client application that more closely emulates native object-oriented code.

Object Views

Object views combine objects from one application with those from another. They allow the synthesis of business objects that exists in relational tables or object types. Object views function much like object tables. They can incorporate methods, point to other object views, be part of collections, and can be accessed from SQL or pointer traversal. Because Oracle extended the view mechanism in Oracle8, object views are fully updateable through the use of special trigger types, known as **INSTEAD OF** triggers. Figure 1.8 displays the versatile nature of object views and their ability to span relational and object tables.

Upcoming Features: Inheritance And Extensibility

Inheritance is not a feature available in the current release of Oracle8, but it is slated for an upcoming version. As the name implies, inheritance will provide for subclass objects to inherit or assimilate the data structures and behaviors of the class above it in the hierarchy (also known as a *superclass*). As with the object-oriented definition, an abstract class can exist for the purposes of passing inheritable data and behaviors or methods.

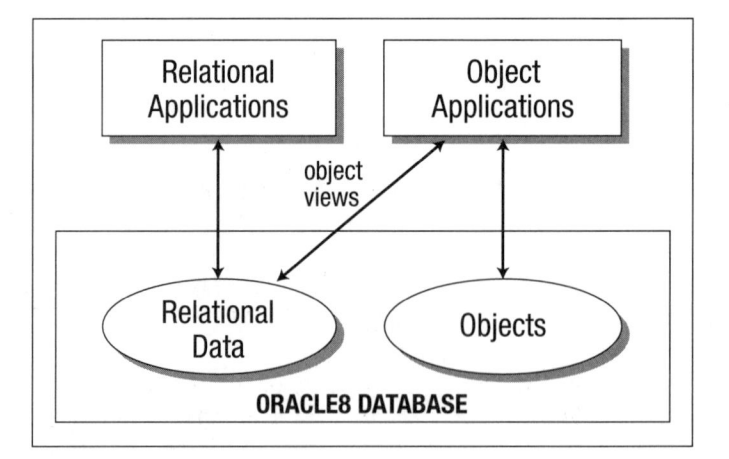

Figure 1.8
Oracle8 object views.

Extensibility will allow users to create software cartridges consisting of objects, methods operators, and aggregates defined by the user. The server will subsequently treat these cartridges as native data types.

Summary

In this chapter, we have briefly reviewed the evolution of database systems from the days of hierarchical storage to the new object-relational structure of Oracle8. We have discussed the emerging standards of the object-oriented extensions in Oracle8 and provided a comparison to the object-oriented programming standards found in languages like C++. Now that a basic understanding of the tools is in place, we're ready for the next chapter, which covers the systems development life cycle and how real-world problems impact design.

HIGH PERFORMANCE

The New Systems Development Life Cycle With Oracle8

CHAPTER 2

The 90-90 Rule of Project Schedules: The first ninety percent of a project takes ninety percent of the allotted time; the last ten percent takes the other ninety percent.
—From the 18 Unnatural Laws Of Science

The New Systems Development Life Cycle With Oracle8

Part of doing a job is devising a plan. Database design is certainly no exception to this rule. Over the years, there has been much published on the subject of development life cycles and analysis. While the methodologies have varied from one study to another, they have shared one thing in common: a framework for synthesizing a problem and a structured organization for solving it. Before moving into the detailed aspects of Oracle8's object-oriented extensions in the chapters that follow, we must first focus on the techniques used to analyze the system and touch upon common design issues and problem areas related to current analysis techniques.

The Importance Of Systems Analysis

The concept of a systems development life cycle was not a frivolous idea on the part of a handful of computer systems gurus intent on selling a few books. A guideline for good analysis came about because, like other disciplines, computer scientists need a detailed blueprint or plan delimiting how to perform their work so their products will perform as intended. Without a doubt, the computer science industry has exercised its share of "on the fly" development. Unfortunately, such an approach rarely leads to a successful outcome. The computer science industry is a relatively new practice when compared with other industries in the engineering disciplines. This probably accounts for the growing pains associated with formulating a structured approach. Systems analysis, however, is no less complicated than its brethren in the engineering world and therefore relies on an effective and detailed methodology to solve problems.

Let's consider the massive effort of constructing a major freeway. To those of us who must navigate through the detours for months or years on end, it might seem like there is no plan. (I have been convinced of this many times.) As the freeway network begins to take shape, however, it becomes apparent that a great deal of thought has gone into things like determining the height of each overpass, at what point exits should be started, and at what angle the exit ramps should slope to meet the other sections of the road. All of this is evidence that an excruciating amount of detailed planning took place in order to make the freeway come together. The construction company didn't start out by bulldozing everything flat and then wondering how the freeway should be built. It only seems that way to us—the motorists—during the initial stages of construction. The art of database design should be treated just as seriously. After all, what we are attempting to do is construct the virtual freeways (and parking lots) that a company will use to do business. If the roads are poorly planned and constructed, you will hear about the traffic jams from your virtual motorists!

I had a high school teacher whose mantra was, "Plan your work, and work your plan." His intent was to get us to focus on the effort of writing research papers, which was an accomplishment in itself because most of us were barely organized enough to get to class, much less write coherent research papers. But, there is much truth in those words when applied to almost anything you do. This mantra should belong to today's system analysts and database designers. And, it becomes even more apropos with the advent of object-relational databases. As you will see in upcoming chapters, access to new functionality adds complexity to analysis and design.

The introduction of new data constructs will change the way normalization is treated in the analysis and design phases. Introducing the concept of pointers in relational tables certainly circumvents the reliance we have developed for SQL, not to mention the rules of normalization that we have come to embrace. Through the course of discussion in this chapter, you will find that the problems have only grown more complex. The tools we have at our disposal to navigate through these new systems must adapt if we are to be successful at developing the systems of the future.

The role of the systems analyst is crucial to the execution and ultimate success of any project. While the majority of discussion in this book focuses on dealing with the data model, the systems analyst must cross the boundaries of other areas to include business functions, process development, customer liaison, and project lead. Analysts must be able to manage both staff members' and the customers' expectations, while maintaining control of the project scope to prevent "feature creep." The successful systems analyst understands how to balance requirements within budget and time constraints, and can negotiate suitable compromises with the customer when needed.

The first step in our journey to successful system modeling is a review of the tried and true conventions that are an inseparable part of building Oracle applications. In the next section, we will discuss essential topics for designing and deploying successful relational Oracle-based systems. In subsequent sections, we will discuss how certain conventions are affected by the introduction of object extensions.

The Oracle System Modeling Conventions

Many programming languages have established methods for constructing applications, and Oracle is no exception to this. A life cycle is so termed because all aspects of application development are strictly guided and planned from initial concept through deployment. The chart in Figure 2.1 illustrates the essential steps in an Oracle life cycle.

Many organizations that have deployed Oracle-based systems have done so through the aid of Oracle's CASE product or its current incarnation, Designer/2000. Designer/2000 is ideally suited for such efforts because it is specifically designed to handle the complete life cycle of Oracle databases and tools (e.g., forms, reports, and so forth) through its design and generation process.

Most life cycle methodologies adopt a top-down approach, and Oracle's methodology is no exception. This means that the coarse generalities of a company's business objectives are identified first and placed into the framework of the system to be built. Once the scope of the project has been defined, the detail begins to take shape in the subsequent stages until a working system is in production.

The life cycle phases we are most concerned with in this chapter are the first three: strategy, analysis, and design. However, we will review the others, as well, in order to gain a complete perspective.

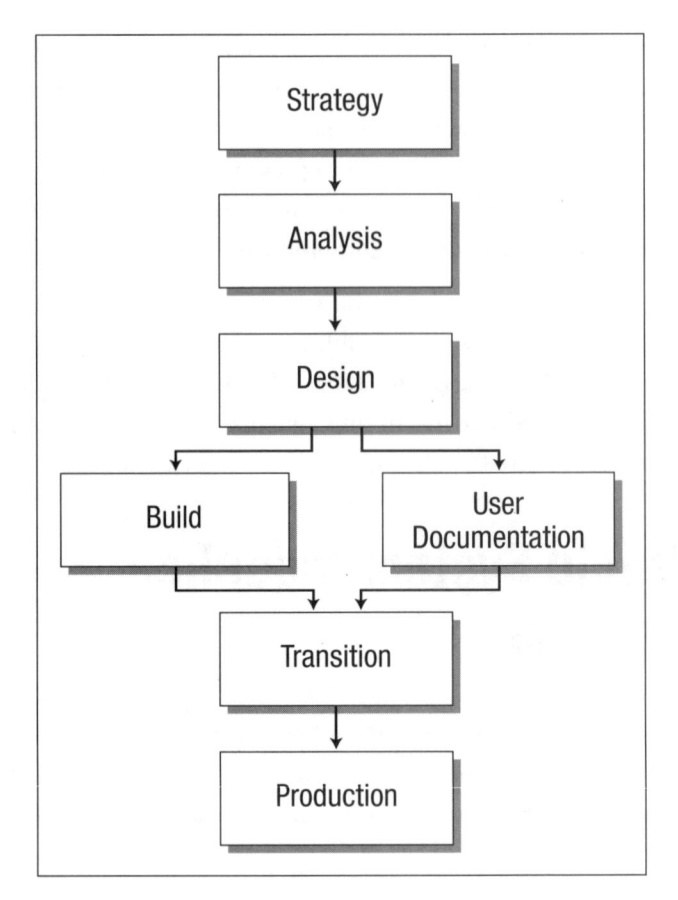

Figure 2.1
The Oracle Computer-Aided Software Engineering (CASE) method life cycle development process.

Strategy Phase

The strategy phase is where the system to be built is first introduced. At this stage, the scope is general in nature with the intent of formulating a business model for the system under consideration. Participation with key members of the company through the interview process, as well as developmental partnering, is important. This way, you can gain an understanding of the scope of the application to be built. The sense of ownership that is so important to the success of any project starts here. Members of the company must feel a proactive sense so that the "we" concept takes hold. The final outcome will only be as successful as the interest and level of participation. The consultants must be the catalyst for creating this synergy.

Never take the interview process lightly. If you are a consultant, there is a reasonable chance that you are unfamiliar with the corporate culture and the business of the client. In all likelihood, you might not know everything about the pharmaceutical industry, to name an example. The time made available to you for interviewing by the corporate staff is very precious, and you must absorb a great deal of information in a short period of time. Asking the vice president of manufacturing where he likes to play golf might be a fine ice breaker, but once the meeting starts, you must glean every relevant fact from those present while you can.

Interviews are conducted to identify the key business objectives to be addressed in the application. Constant communication is maintained through sample models and feedback. Junior developers should be included in this effort because they benefit in two ways: It sharpens their communication skills, and it gives them an appreciation for the big picture. Understanding the motivations behind business objectives provides a clearer understanding of the interrelationship of the functions and processes they will be expected to address in the design and build phases.

The chart in Figure 2.2 shows the tasks that should be accomplished during the strategy phase.

The scope of the project should be defined during this phase. Conducting the strategy phase will give you a sense of how big the "bread box" is and what business units comprise it. An initial function hierarchy is produced that will inevitably spawn detailed requirements and aid in the documentation effort later on.

An initial data flow diagram and entity relationship diagram are also generated during this stage. At this point, specific attributes are not yet introduced. The context of both diagrams must be easy to understand so that management can evaluate the accuracy of the work to date.

In short, your work during this phase should identify the following:

- Clearly understood statement of work (requirements and scope)
- Business objectives
- Business functions with dependencies
- Preliminary data flow diagram
- Initial entity relationship diagram
- Agreement of time and budget limitations

Strategy Phase

- interviews
- functional hierarchy
- entity relationship diagram (preliminary)
- data flow diagram

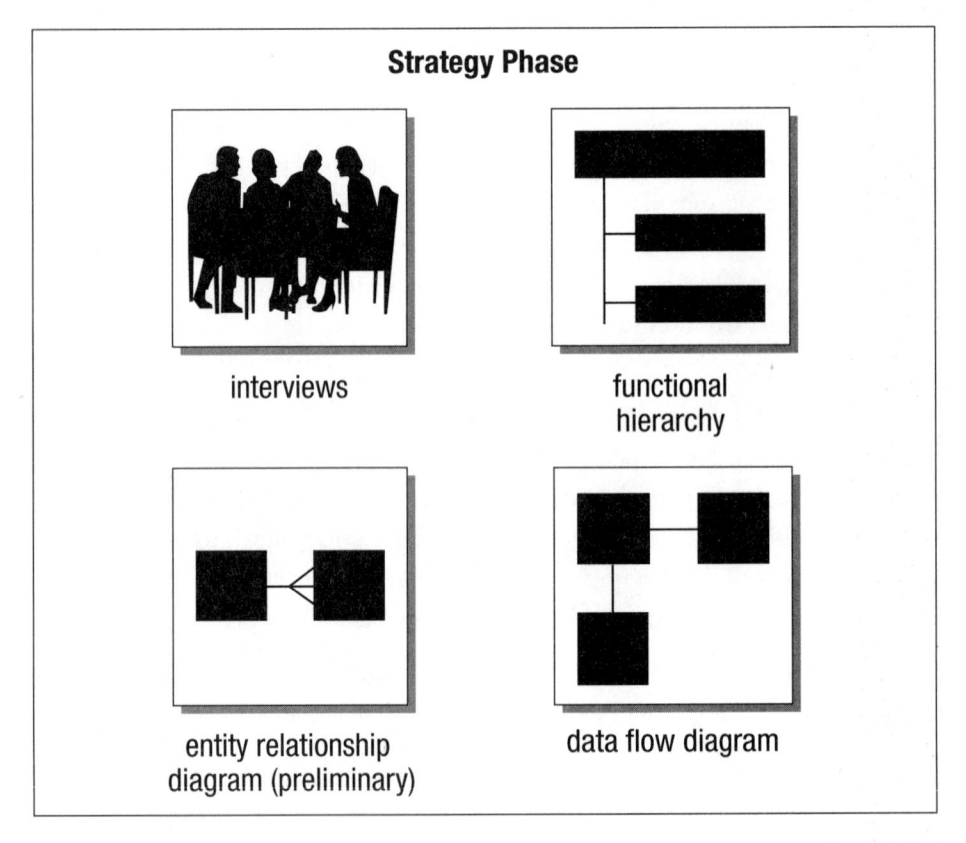

Figure 2.2
Task objectives of the strategy phase.

Analysis Phase

The analysis phase decomposes the business objectives and identifies functions defined in the strategy phase. All the business units are clearly defined, and the business functions are completely represented in a function hierarchy. Note that the function hierarchy is a representation of business functions and not algorithms or specific pieces of code. Functional decomposition is discussed in greater detail in a section to follow, but suffice it to say that this activity forms the cornerstone of how the design will progress, whether good or bad.

At this stage, all efforts are focused on the logical aspects of the system. Actual process constructs are introduced later, during the design phase. During the analysis phase, there is no preoccupation with programming languages or database products.

The client might prefer index cards to computers, but that will be resolved in design. Serious attention must be paid to the logical organization of the function hierarchy to make sense of how the business operates, as well as to avoid confusion and redundancy. Think of the function hierarchy as a great library. Libraries have a very precise way of organizing and placing books. The available space is sectioned in order to group subjects or categories together. Within the categorical groupings, the volumes are placed in such a way as to indicate a precise order. Duplicate books are found easily because they reside together. Imagine if you were to go to the library one day to do research only to discover that the library staff had abandoned their cataloging efforts and had begun placing books wherever they fit. Finding a specific title would become a tedious process, and one might never know if duplicate volumes existed.

A detailed entity relationship diagram is also produced during this phase. An association between the items in the function hierarchy and the entity relationship diagram is established. This will define those functions that have a direct data processing role and those that do not. Figure 2.3 illustrates the essential steps of the analysis phase.

This is the last phase in which any requirements should surface. Never enter the design phase and add requirements after the fact if at all possible. (*Hint:* Don't make it possible!) If your objective is to create a never-ending project with lots of workarounds and spaghetti code that is difficult to maintain, then, by all means, continue adding requirements later in the life cycle process. No system is without change, but altering the face of any project is one sure way to encourage failure. Ad hoc requirements are how functions end up getting drawn on paper napkins.

Design Phase

The design phase introduces the preliminary, and ultimately final, database design. Armed with the knowledge gained from the detailed function-to-entity matrix, the analyst can focus on those functions that have a direct bearing on the data. Besides the database itself, other key ingredients of the system begin to take shape. The implementation of functions to modules is determined. The formulation of the processes that will allow business functions to take place is performed in this phase. (Later in this chapter, we'll differentiate between functions and processes.) The interface applications begin to take shape as functions are mated to screens, reports, and behind-the-scenes code. Suitable mechanisms to accomplish processing and data storage are examined and selected. It is at this point that either C++, Basic, Java, or

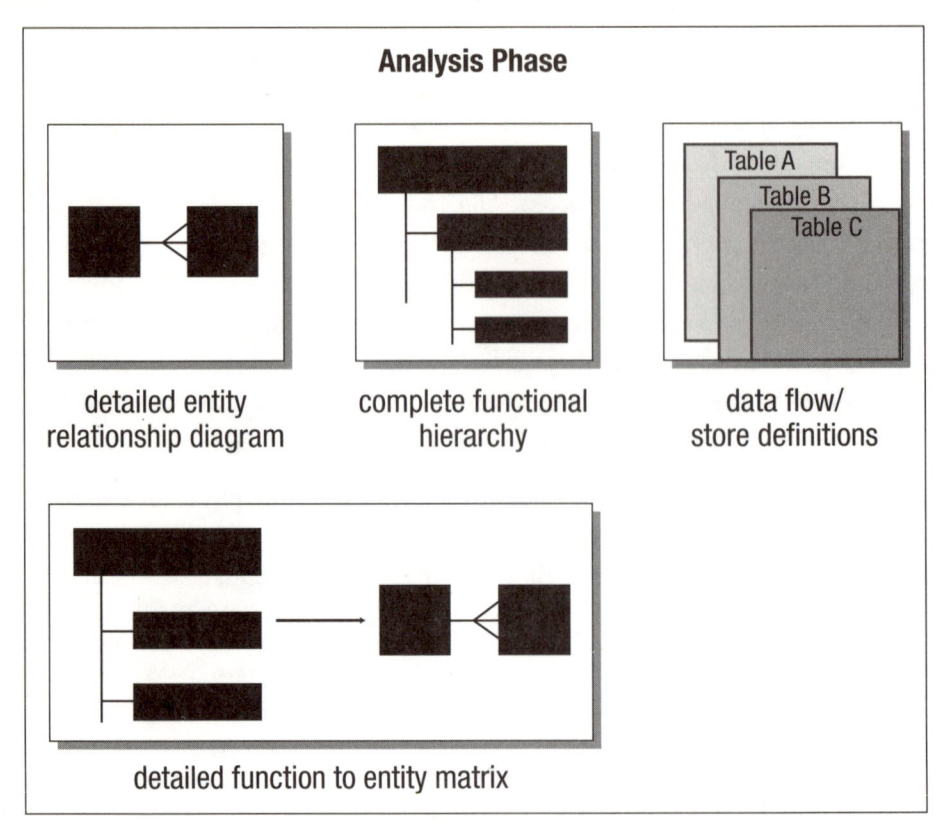

Figure 2.3
Task objectives of the analysis phase.

Oracle Forms should be identified as the best tool for addressing a specific process. The interrelationships between processes is evaluated to ensure that there are no technological hindrances or conflicts. Compatibility and performance are also considerations in this evaluation.

At this point, data estimation and table size requirements are calculated. It is worth the trouble to be as thorough as possible because it is easier to create the database with properly sized objects the first time than it is to alter tables, indexes, tablespaces, and so on when they turn out to be too small. A seasoned DBA should perform the necessary estimations and evaluate the database design for maintainability, performance, possible data conversion, and capacity planning. I have worked with several DBAs who have developed useful routines to perform such estimations, and their time is worth the rates they charge.

The DBA can also perform a review of data tables to identify the proper use of indexes to improve performance. It is good practice to evaluate not only the structure of the table, but also the content. Knowing whether or not a single value repeats 90 percent of the time is useful in determining what kind of index to use or even if one is not appropriate at all. DBAs and developers alike should be conversant with the use of the **ANALYZE** command to determine the selectivity and distribution of column values. This exercise aids in the proper assignment of indexes, as well as subsequent SQL structure, later when PL/SQL blocks must be written.

During the design phase, you should pay particular attention to performance-critical functions. Look for bottlenecks in the design that could contribute to slow response times. An inordinate number of retrievals back and forth from the database add to the overall processing time for an event or request for data. Look for such functions, and place as much processing as possible on the server side to reduce I/O requests. Processes and functions that fire recursively should be evaluated with an eye toward streamlining event flow. An example of such an instance might be a forms application with complex item-level validation logic. Modules that require "in the moment" validation of text items before a commit is ever executed are prime targets for redesign because validation fires every time the item changes. The essential steps of the design phase are illustrated in Figure 2.4.

Build Phase

The build stage represents the point where programs are generated and the database is created. This is also the stage that generally causes the most friction between the interface developers and the database designers. In an environment using Designer/2000, an effort is made to completely generate forms and reports as completely as possible. This is known as 100 percent generation. If a complete Oracle solution is being implemented, the forms and reports are spawned from the information gathered in the Designer repository. The completeness of the generated modules is in direct proportion to the thoroughness of the analysis and design phases. If details were overlooked, then the modules will fall short of their intended result. Complete generation is rarely achieved and often hands-on modifications are required to obtain desired results. In an environment where Designer/2000 is not used, or where Oracle tools are not used on the front end, all of the interfacing modules must be created manually. A complex database design does not necessarily lend itself to straightforward

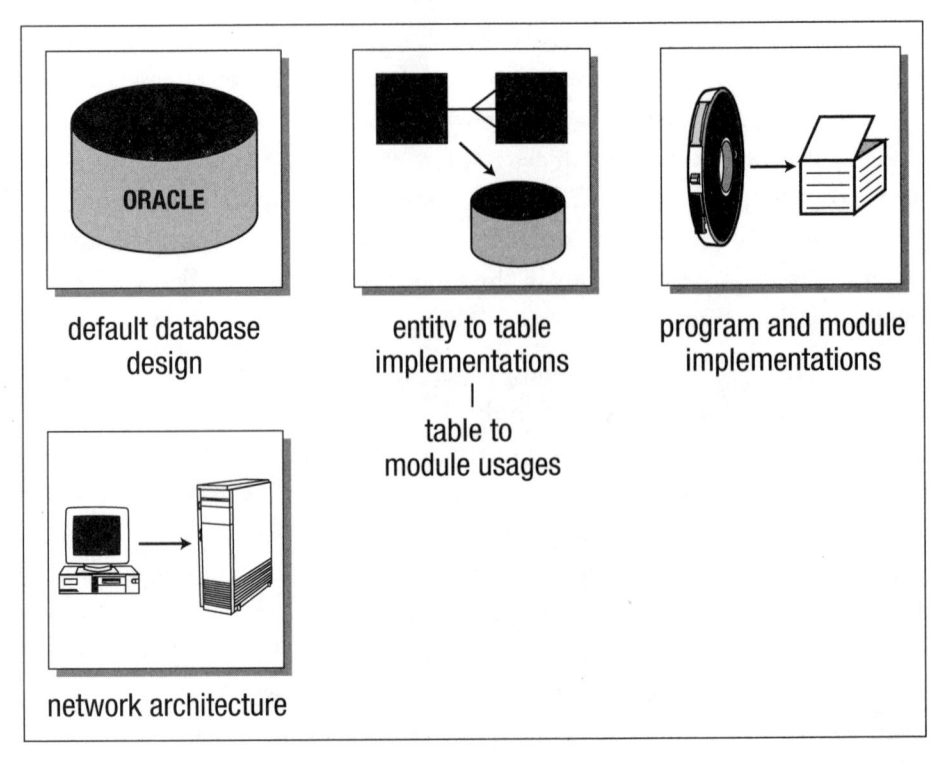

[default database design | entity to table implementations | table to module usages | program and module implementations | network architecture]

Figure 2.4
Task objectives of the design phase.

screens. The database designer strives for the elegance of a perfectly normalized database schema while the application developer looks for ways to simplify the modules to be built. Complex data retrieval and data manipulation language (DML) commands affect performance and functionality. To relieve these burdens, the application developer will try to persuade the database designer to "relax" certain rules of normalization or create additional views. A classic example of this would be the monthly summary report that is to produce aggregated sums with numerous subtotals and categorical groupings. The objectives just described for the build phase are shown in Figure 2.5.

The complexities of resolving any process incompatibilities not identified in the design phase must be addressed to a satisfactory conclusion. Ideally, the theoretical questions of process-to-process integration will have been answered during design. It is not unusual for problems to arise in complex systems at this late stage. Careful planning in design eliminates the lion's share of possible late-breaking process conflicts.

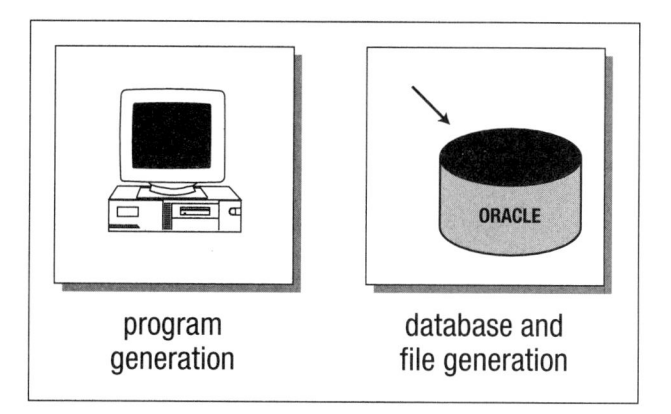

Figure 2.5
Task objectives of the build phase.

User Documentation Phase

At this stage, all system documentation is produced. The documentation should relate closely to the requirements specified during the strategy and analysis phases. In fact, there should be a one-to-one correspondence between topics in the documentation and the business objectives/functions defined. This also applies to the test documentation, which should thoroughly address every aspect of the system design. It is usually the case that the one function left out of the test procedures or the documentation will be the one that fails in production or cannot be found when the system is modified later on.

Those individuals familiar with DOD Standard 2167A have witnessed documentation rigidity at its most extreme. While DOD Std 2167A usually generates more documentation than code, it is unquestionably thorough in its treatment of matching requirements to design, and perpetuating the one to one correspondence between each step all the way to the test phase. As a matter of fact, subparagraph numbering between the phases must correspond one-to-one! It is not acceptable under this standard to detail a subrequirement and not readdress it in each and every phase that follows. Omissions under this methodology are easy to detect merely by comparing paragraph numbers.

User guides should be written to "the lowest common factor," meaning that even the least experienced user should be able to understand and use a system based solely on the user guide. Such a task can be particularly trying when the system to be deployed represents a significant paradigm shift for the user. For example, users that have always used character-based terminals will have a difficult time adjusting to a GUI application on Windows-based PCs. I witnessed this on a recent project which proved to be my greatest user-education challenge. The challenge did not come from the application we built; instead it stemmed from having to explain what a program group was and how to use the mouse. Figure 2.6 shows the essential elements of the documentation phase.

Transition Phase

The transition phase is where pre-production testing of the new system takes place before deployment. The test material produced in the prior phase is now exercised to determine if any shortcomings exist. User testing is also conducted to apply the "acid test" to what has been produced. Two statistics should be determined from testing: whether an application works correctly and whether it can be broken. The latter seems to be the more difficult of the two to accomplish. Applications that respond incorrectly or unpredictably when illegal keystrokes are performed are not acceptable. Testing for every possible combination is extremely difficult, however. I found that ordinary users are best at this sort of testing because they will do almost anything out of sheer curiosity—"I wonder what happens if I do this?"

Early in my career as a software engineer, I was involved in a project to develop an application for radar testing. During the testing phase, the users beat up on the application mercilessly, finding one minor glitch after another. My partner and I retreated at the end of the day to our office to develop a way of finding the problems

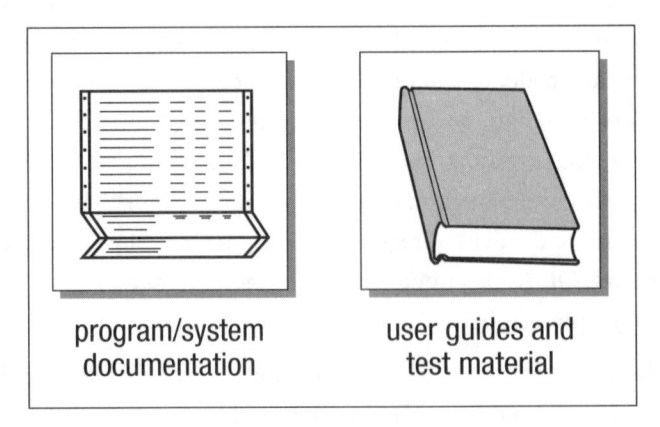

Figure 2.6
Task objectives of the user documentation phase.

before the customer did. Due to the late hour, we were alone in the office except for the cleaning lady. After a contemplative moment, my partner remarked that perhaps we should have the janitorial staff test our software. It never actually happened, but we did devise a testing method that we named, "The non-English speaking cleaning lady test." The test consisted of an entirely new approach to how we would treat the new applications. Although we never really employed the assistance of the janitorial staff, we tested each module with the mindset that we had never seen a computer before. We tried to do things that "non-programmers" would do. Our efforts paid off, and we successfully deployed the system. The moral of the story is that testing should be conducted with a novice's attitude, not with a programmer's mindset.

The transition phase is also where some effort is spent in performing a reverse engineering study. The objectives of the transition phase can be seen in Figure 2.7. Such

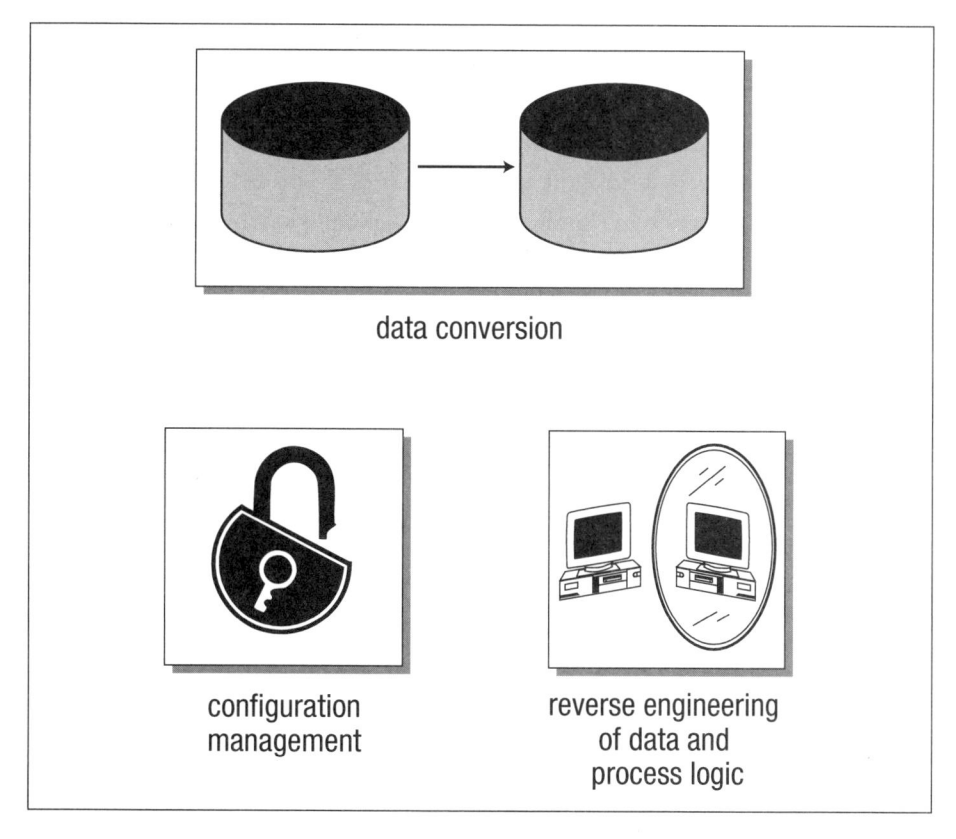

Figure 2.7
Task objectives of the transition phase.

an activity is useful for gaining insights into how the new system will integrate with other existing systems. Reverse engineering will identify data flow patterns and dependencies with functions and processes. This effort serves to validate the accuracy of what has been produced. If it makes sense in both directions, then the design is probably sound.

Production Phase

The production phase ushers the new system into general use by the organization. Corrections are made in the user guides and other documentation, and versioning of the software is conducted for proper configuration management. It is not uncommon for the new and old systems (if a predecessor exists) to be run in parallel for a short period of time until all users and resources can be transitioned over. By this time, the client will assume full ownership of the system, and they will have been properly trained in how to use and maintain it. Figure 2.8 shows the tasks involved in executing the production phase.

Now that we have discussed the phases of the life cycle as they apply to a purely relational database system, let us now consider some of the issues regarding Oracle8's influence. The introduction of the object-relational paradigm requires us to consider new data constructs and to incorporate behaviors in the modeling effort—only two of the many extensions and features that will drive the way we do business in the future.

Oracle8 And Database Design

When the development life cycle that we have just discussed was first formulated, the mainstream focus of database designers was on the relational paradigm. While the phases just described offer sound principles for routine database application systems development, there is no escaping the fact that the shift to an object-relational paradigm will require some changes in how the life cycle is performed. In the next sections we will consider some of the factors that impact on the life cycle.

Designer/2000 And Oracle8

In the late 1980s and early 1990s, Oracle set out to develop a product suite that would make them a complete solution vendor. To support the challenges faced by

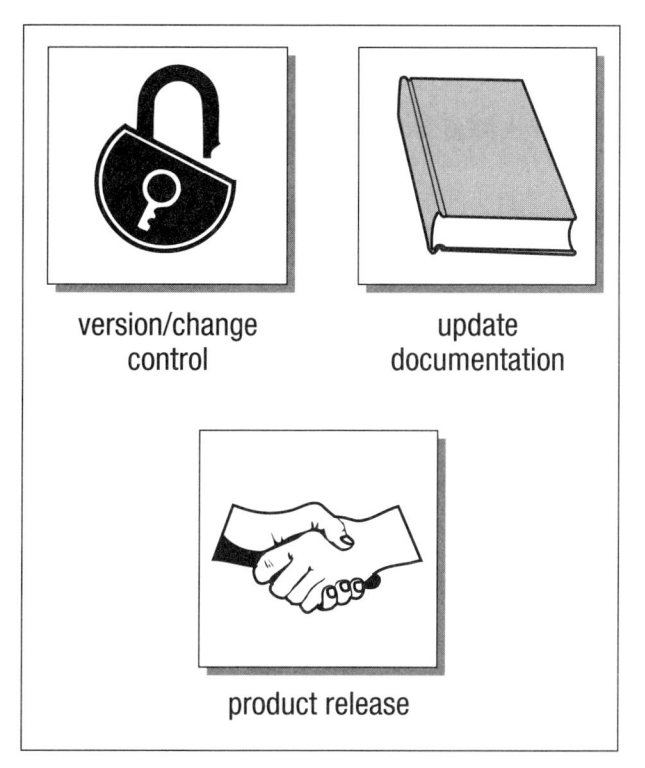

Figure 2.8
Task objectives of the production phase.

developers, Oracle produced a Computer-Aided Software Engineering (CASE) product, now known as *Designer/2000*, as well as a supporting methodology, called the *CASE method*. The Designer/2000 product supports the life cycle phases described in the previous section. The greatest strength of the product, however, lies in its ability to support the first three phases (strategy, analysis, and design). At the time of this writing, the current version of Designer/2000 is not equipped to handle the new object-oriented extensions found in Oracle8. Despite this fact, the methodology offers a good foundation in database design practice. The introduction of Oracle8 poses a significant challenge to the existing versions of this product. Its sister product, Developer/2000 is also lacking in support for Oracle8 extensions. It is anticipated that a future release of both products addressing the extended functionality is on its way. In the meantime, creative database developers and designers are devising workarounds until full product compliance is attained, once again.

In the short term, Oracle is introducing a product called Object Database Designer. This new tool has been designed to work specifically with the new Oracle8 database. The underlying methodology is based upon the Unified Modeling Language. The tool will facilitate the modeling of object-relational data types and objects. It is anticipated that the tool will be integrated into the Designer/2000 product in later releases.

Third party products are also emerging to fill the design gap created by the emergence of object-relational databases. Companies like Logic Works also have products that adequately model object-relational databases. A detailed discussion of two of these new tools is found in Chapter 7.

How Oracle8 Affects The CASE Method Life Cycle

With the introduction of user-defined data types, methods, and pointers, Oracle8 adds a new dimension to the life cycle approach. In the days of Oracle7, the process of database and code generation could be visualized in three steps. Figure 2.9 illustrates the conventional means by which the build phase was executed.

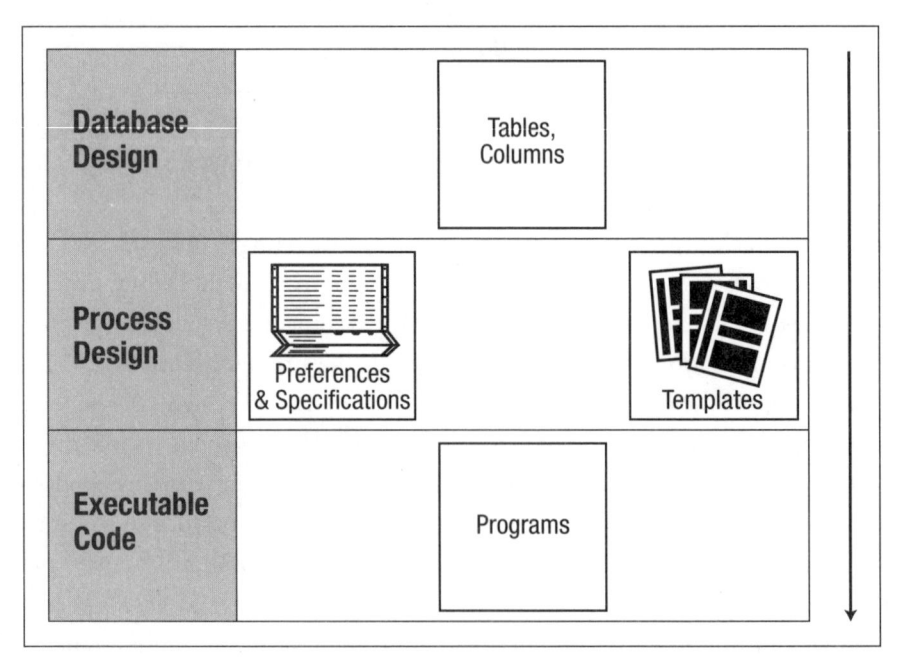

Figure 2.9
The steps of database and code generation.

Because of the introduction of the object-oriented extensions in Oracle8, the distinction between the database design and process design stages is beginning to blur. This is because the dichotomy between data and process has been diminished. Methods represent executable functions stored in the database. The database is no longer just for data. Incorporating object behavior extends the notion of characters, numbers, and dates as the exclusive set of database content, as does the idea of user-defined data typing. Such concepts permeate through all aspects of the database from data structure to index definition.

Oracle8 will have a dramatic effect on most phases of the life cycle. The strategy phase remains as it always has because of its broad nature of defining a system and because the mechanisms for addressing business objectives are not specified. Subsequent phases, however, will be affected. The idiosyncrasies of each new extension will be covered in subsequent chapters, but a brief list of impacts includes the following:

- The process of defining the entity relationship diagram in the analysis phase changes as a result of the introduction of **REFs**, pointers, nested tables, and methods. A suitable compromise in design must be attained to determine appropriate use of normalization versus denormalization through the use of table-to-table linkages without enforced constraints between them. A total abandonment of normalization represents chaos. Guidelines for when to use relationships versus pointers and nested objects will be established.

- The task of developing a function-to-entity matrix will change with the addition of methods. Methods represent a construct tied to the data as opposed to a separate object outside of the data table. Functions will have to be categorized by their suitability to be translated into conventional stored procedures and packages or behaviors attached to the data. Methods will be ideally suited to processes that perform actions on the data.

- The very schema of the database itself will be affected by how normalization and referential integrity are adjusted to implement data types like **VARRAY**s and nested tables. **VARRAY**s are well-suited to replace small reference tables. Nested tables do not require foreign key associations with their host table. Nested tables can also contain user-defined objects, adding further complexity to the database design.

- In the current environment, developing interface applications for Oracle8 will be more difficult. Developer/2000 is not currently suited to the new database structure. Data access and manipulation via current forms technology must be facilitated with server-based logic.

Now that we have reviewed some of the factors impacting the system development life cycle, let's look at one of the most important activities in any system design, functional decomposition.

Functional Decomposition And The Impact On Design

Functional decomposition is the activity of defining and organizing the substructure of the business objectives identified within a system. Business functions relate back to the business and define a specific activity, but they do not define the way in which the activity is performed. Processes define the mechanism used to execute a function. The collection of business functions within a system describes how the business objectives will be achieved. Functions and processes are not distinct players in the concept of system design. On the contrary, the two are somewhat similar and are inseparable when analyzing and designing a system.

Performing functional decomposition provides a guideline for the development of a new system. Functional models are free of any description about process dependency or any other technological specificity. An objective evaluation of the system can then be made without bias to one technological solution or another. Implementation plans are developed in the design phase to identify the best course of action in how the supporting process will be implemented.

Traditionally, functions are grouped or categorized into a hierarchy. Each function is clearly and succinctly described in a single statement starting with a verb to denote action. On many occasions, the analyst will identify interdependent functions. Interdependent functions utilize a concept known as *events*. Events are triggers for functions. Events come in three varieties: external, realtime, and system.

- External events are associated with input entering the organization from outside. For example, payment entering the system for a processed order. Receipt of such an event usually generates events for other business functions. In this particular example, check receipts generate the function of payment posting and payment status reconciliation.

- Realtime events are those that pertain to specific time requirements or constraints. For example, the last day of the calendar month might spawn the production of an end-of-month sales report.

- System events involve activity within the system itself. For example, an event might be triggered when the requirements for one or more business functions have been satisfied. More complex functions require an exacting detailed list of steps to accomplish a particular business function. The outcome of some events could require alternative events to take place. The detailed logic of a function should be clearly defined so that the effort of creating the processes can be translated cleanly to the appropriate programming vehicle (i.e., 3GL and 4GL languages).

The highest-level business functions do not associate directly to data entities. Business functions regard the system in its entirety, and it is, therefore, incumbent on the system analyst to interpret which functions will have a direct impact on the data. Business functions can also be implemented to determine the success or failure of a particular business objective. Business objectives are defined during the strategy phase and provide quantifiable goals for the business to attain, generally within a specified time frame. For example, a company might articulate a business objective stating that loss due to damaged goods is to be reduced by five percent before the end of the calendar year. A business function defined to calculate overall loss to damage would then be created. Figure 2.10 illustrates the functional support of the business objective described in this example.

There has been a temptation to disregard functions unrelated to data processing. This is discouraged in the business life cycle that we have discussed. Particular attention should be given to all classes of business functions because of the possibility of interdependence. Functions that fall into this category might not execute until some set of initial conditions has been met, usually some other function. A complete treatment of the functional hierarchy exposes these interdependencies.

To illustrate the importance of functional decomposition in the analysis effort, let's take a look at a brief example of how business objectives are broken down.

A Functional Decomposition Example

Suppose for a moment that you have been contracted to build an inventory system for Fred's Freight And Storage. Fred's Freight accepts goods for short- and long-term storage in a large warehouse. On any given day, numerous trucks arrive, dropping off

Chapter 2

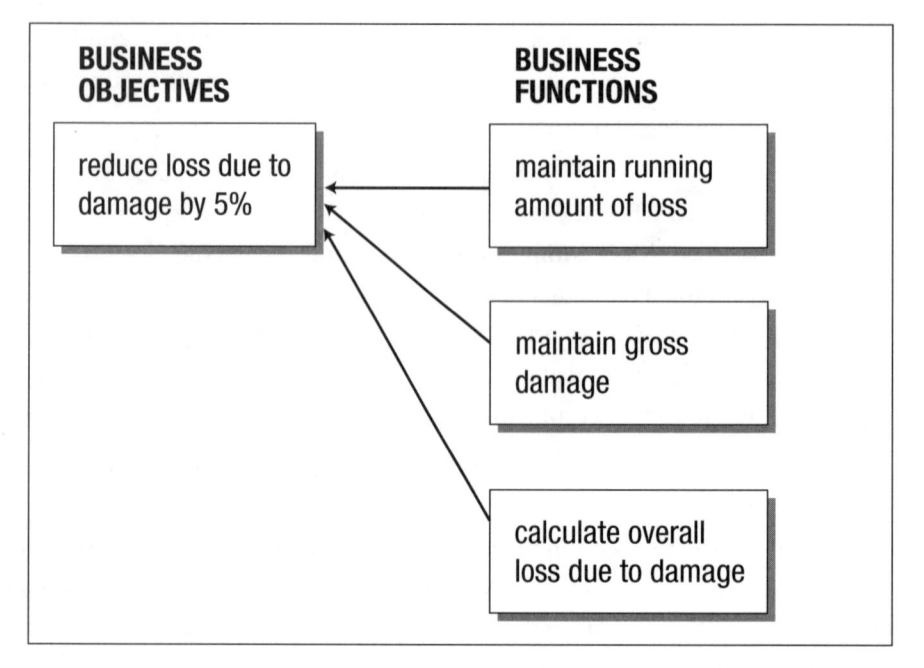

```
BUSINESS                    BUSINESS
OBJECTIVES                  FUNCTIONS

┌─────────────────┐         ┌─────────────────┐
│ reduce loss due │◄────────│ maintain running│
│ to damage by 5% │         │ amount of loss  │
└─────────────────┘         └─────────────────┘

                            ┌─────────────────┐
                            │ maintain gross  │
                            │ damage          │
                            └─────────────────┘

                            ┌─────────────────┐
                            │ calculate overall│
                            │ loss due to damage│
                            └─────────────────┘
```

Figure 2.10
Business function support of a business objective.

cargo. Upon prior arrangement, trucks come to pick up stored freight and deliver it to its owners. Fred needs an automated system to track and inventory goods from the time it arrives until the time it is picked up.

Analyzing Fred's operation, you can identify the following business functions:

- Receive delivery of freight
- Reconcile inventory to manifest
- Catalog freight
- Store freight
- Receive pick-up order
- Retrieve freight from warehouse
- Produce shipping manifest
- Load truck

Each of these business functions can be decomposed into smaller functions. Decomposition for database implementations should continue until individual steps equate to a single query where data events occur. An equivalent level of decomposition should likewise be performed against non-database functions to facilitate the derivation of the requisite processes.

If you evaluate the business function to Reconcile Inventory To Manifest, you can see that it decomposes further into the subfunctions shown in Figure 2.11.

When the functional decomposition is complete, you can proceed in identifying the processes necessary to accomplish each function. In this case, the subfunction Scan Incoming Items is processed via hand scanner.

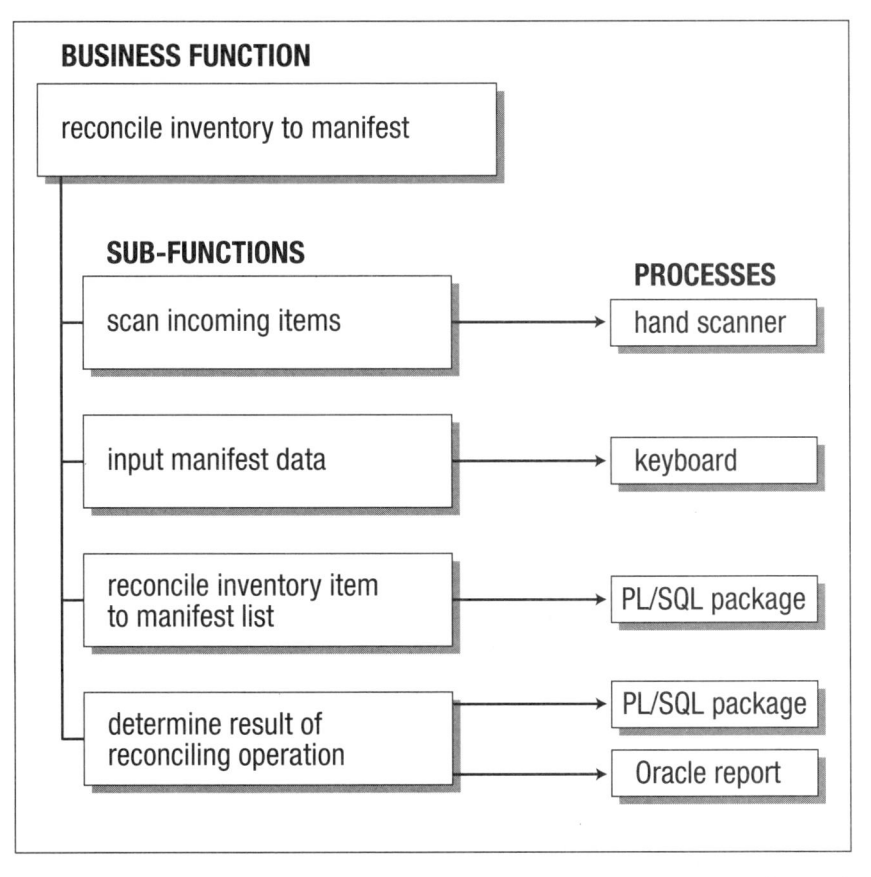

Figure 2.11
Functional decomposition with supporting processes.

Although this is a simplistic example, it serves to illustrate business functions, how they are decomposed, and the resulting processes developed to support each function.

As noted earlier, there is a distinction between functions and processes. Let's now turn our attention toward analyzing processes and understanding their role in the development of the new application system.

Analyzing Process Flow

A process is somewhat similar to a function, but a distinction lies in the fact that a process defines "how" and functions describe "what." Processes define the physical or mechanical means of how one or more business functions will be executed. Processes do not model business behaviors but rather system behaviors. When implemented, processes ultimately manifest themselves as interfaces, reports, procedures, or other actions performed by humans or machines. For example, the list could include C programs, Web cartridges, scanners, automated manufacturing equipment, or even an employee. Processes can also be grouped into collections of activities. When defining a system, it is possible to say that it is a representative collection of processes or mechanisms that, in turn, fulfill business functions and data manipulation.

Unlike business functions, processes include the methodology to be used in executing particular events. For example, a grocery store scanner represents a mechanical device representative of a process. It reads the bar codes on the groceries, deciphers a numerical code for the product, and retrieves the price from the database. The electronic cash register maintains a running balance of the purchase amount and the products scanned.

Analyzing the process flow should not be done in isolation from the activity of the business function analysis because processes will define the methodology under which business functions will be executed. It is entirely possible that multiple processes must be executed to complete one business function, as illustrated in the grocery store example. A cross check of the two activities should be conducted in order to ensure completeness of business function utilization and to guarantee that each process has its place in the system. It is entirely possible that one or more processes will be required to properly execute a business function. A direct correlation between the two is necessary to avoid process redundancy and prevent procedural gaps under a business function. The reader is directed to Figure 2.12, which illustrates a business function to process relationship.

BUSINESS FUNCTION

scan grocery item

PROCESSES

decipher bar code

retrieve price list

add to running balance

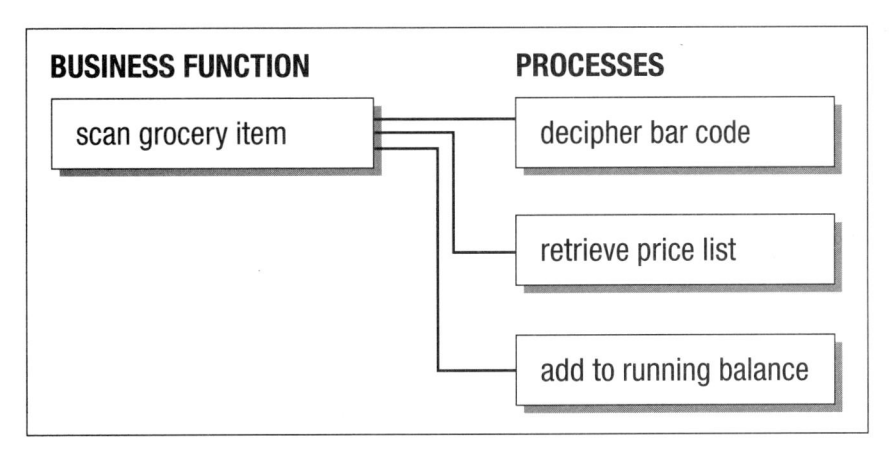

Figure 2.12
A business function to process relationship.

Processes should be evaluated for commonality to determine where redundant behavior exists. Redundancies can then be eliminated, and a single process can be utilized by more than one business function. Processes should also be screened for possible dependencies to other processes. Particular dependencies can be introduced by technological issues. For example, a barcode reader could have specific software interfacing requirements with the database. It is not unusual for this process interdependency to require execution of a process subset before others are allowed to continue. Serial execution of processes indicates that one or more prerequisites must be achieved before additional processes can be executed. For example, adding a product to inventory must be performed before it is placed on the shelf by the automated forklift. Such an interdependency must be documented so that the logical model is accurate. Nested processes, such as those just described, are generally subordinate to one business function, but this rule is not absolute. Process logic is added once the structure of the process flow has been determined. The iterative effort of deriving the process logic also helps to identify shortcomings in the design. Based on the technology used to create the process logic, it might be determined that the design does not support the intended process logic to be executed. This will, in turn, point out areas in the design that require reevaluation.

Now that we have discussed the principles of performing a methodical system design, we will turn our attention to a subject familiar to the database designer: entity relationship modeling. For relationally based designs, this tool has proven to be indispensable to defining a solid, workable database. In this chapter and others that follow, we will see that the graphical interpretation of the database system is no less important when dealing with Oracle8.

Basic Entity Relationship Modeling

The original entity relationship, or ER, model was conceived by Peter Chen in 1976. The intent was to formulate an effective way to conceptualize networks and relational views of database constructs. The entity relationship diagram has gained universal acceptance as a valuable modeling tool for the relational paradigm. The strength of this concept is that it is easily understood yet offers sufficient flexibility to represent very complex relationships. Entity relationship modeling assumes that the world can be considered entirely of entities and the relationships between them. In the purest sense, an *entity* represents a clearly definable thing, while a *relationship* is the association between two entities. An example of the entity-to-relation concept can be seen in Figure 2.13.

Entities are given further depth with the addition of *attributes*. Attributes are individual characteristics that give an entity detailed definition. For example, if you create an entity called *Animal*, then you might define attributes such as type, height, and weight. A set of attributes for a given entity are sometimes referred to as an *entity type*. When entities have been migrated to physical tables, attributes manifest themselves as columns.

Attributes can fall under the umbrella of a *domain*. A domain is a set of properties or rules that applies to a specific group of attributes. Domains are commonly used to validate ranges or subsets of values applicable to the attribute set. For example, an attribute "height," describing how tall an individual is, could be restricted to values

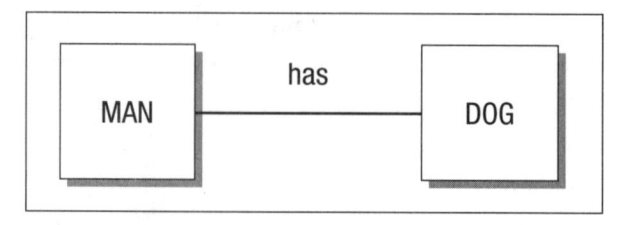

Figure 2.13
The concept of entity to relation.

that fall between three and eight feet. This would describe the qualified range for attribute height. Domains can also consist of value sets. For example, the attribute "sex" could have a domain consisting of the values **M** and **F**, for male and female. Any other value would be considered invalid for this attribute. Once domains have been defined, they can be applied to any attribute that you wish to impose that restriction upon, regardless of which entity the attribute belongs to. The domain created for height in the animal entity would also be applicable to the height attribute for another entity, such as structure.

In dealing with relationships, it is important to understand the meaning of *cardinality*. Cardinality for a relationship expresses the combination of minimum and maximum occurrences for each entity on each side of the relationship. Cardinality has everything to do with how primary and foreign keys are defined, and whether keys are mandatory or optional. Relationships are categorized by degrees of cardinality. A one-to-many relationship indicates each individual parent will have one or more child records in the detail table. Cardinality can also be defined to an exacting level. For example, *more* could be defined to mean exactly three. By defining more to mean, zero, one, or more, the mandatory or optional condition of the relationship is determined to mean optional or, in other words, not mandatory. Figure 2.14 contains examples of cardinality.

All of this, of course, begs the question: Can entity relationship modeling incorporate the concepts of object-oriented design? The answer, in a theoretical sense, is "Yes," because behaviors can be represented as attributes to an entity. In a realistic sense, doing so has proven to be cumbersome at best, at least with the current tools available on the market. The current choices for entity relationship modeling tools have limited data types for use in attribute definition. This, of course, makes it extremely difficult to create a "method" attribute while being forced to categorize it as a character, number, or date. Restrictive data typing, as seen here, is not a part of the conceptual model proposed by Chen. It is the commercialized adaptations of his model, intent on serving a relational database paradigm, that institutes limited data type functionality.

Now that we have described the component parts of entity relationship modeling, it is a good idea to review the valid relationship constructs.

Chapter 2

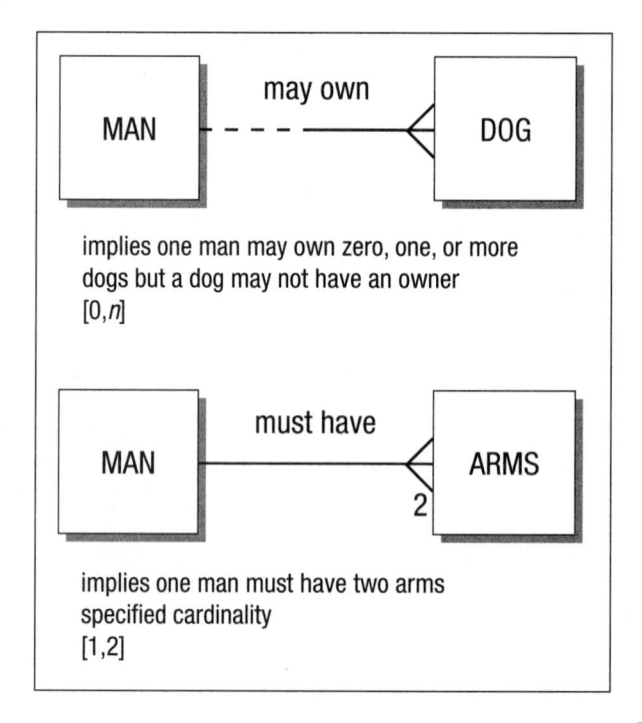

Figure 2.14
Examples of cardinality.

Entity Relationship Modeling And Object Extensions

The introduction of object extensions presents certain modeling problems to the conventional entity relationship diagram that we describe here. In the object-relational paradigm, it is important to divert from third normal form and utilize aggregate objects like nested tables, **VARRAY**s, and object views. We also will find it necessary to incorporate behaviors as methods and even allow for the creation of user-defined data types, which may themselves be an assortment of other user-defined data types. We will reserve the detailed discussion of how these problems are to be solved for Chapter 8 and focus our current attentions to the long standing rules that we must not forget, even in the light of these exciting new object-oriented functionalities. In the long run, it will be demonstrated that the old rules still apply, subject to enhancement by the new object features at our disposal.

One-To-One Relationships

One-to-one relationships are uncommon and generally manifest themselves only when an entity contains overlapping subtypes with categorical differences. Each subtype would have its own rules for mutual exclusivity within the supertype. For example, a person either is or is not a member of a group. At the same time, the same person will either be alive or dead.

Mandatory one-to-one relationships indicate that the entity attribute definitions need to be reevaluated as this represents an invalid relation construct. Figure 2.15 shows common variations of the one-to-one relationship.

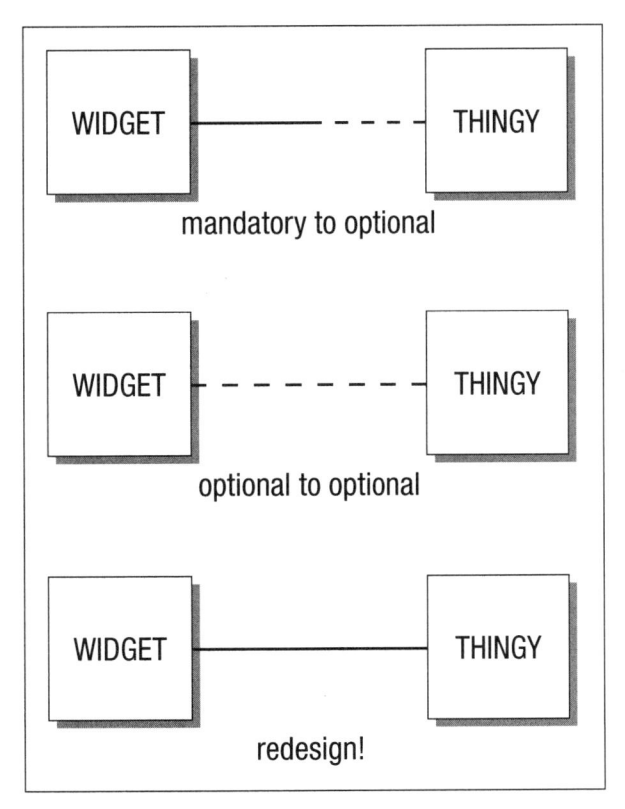

Figure 2.15
One-to-one relationships.

One-To-Many Relationships

Many-to-one or one-to-many relations are the most common. Many-to-one relations can occur in three varieties, depending on the cardinality specified: mandatory-to-optional, optional-to-optional, and mandatory-to-mandatory.

- A mandatory-to-optional relation infers that one or more detail records can exist only if there is one master record. On the other hand, a master record can exist without any detail records.

- An optional-to-optional relation infers that the master or detail records can exist without the presence of the other. This relation does not occur as frequently as mandatory-to-optional relations.

- The mandatory-to-mandatory relation infers a master detail relationship where one or more detail records must be created for each master record. Performing any kind of DML statement under this construct is far more restrictive because of the close association between the master and its detail records. Behavior under record deletion is limited to cascading functionality because master cannot exist without detail and vice versa. The examples in Figure 2.16 illustrate the three varieties discussed here.

One-to-many relationships can also be handled in Oracle8 through the use of repeating groups. The execution of repeating groups is done through a construct such as a **VARRAY**. For example, rather than establish two distinct entities to represent **STUDENT** and **TEST SCORES**, where each student may have many test scores, we can create a **VARRAY** and embed the data object into the **STUDENT** entity. We discuss **VARRAY**s and other collection types in greater detail in Chapters 3 and 4.

Many-To-Many Relationships

This type of relation always raises warning flags to the database designer. And, it should, because such relations indicate an unresolved state between the two entities in question. During early analysis, it is not unusual to find an optional-to-optional variety of this relation. This merely indicates that further analysis is required to resolve the interaction between the two entities.

While a mandatory-to-optional variety can occur, its sibling, the mandatory-to-mandatory, is not possible, and both should be resolved further. Bridging many-to-many

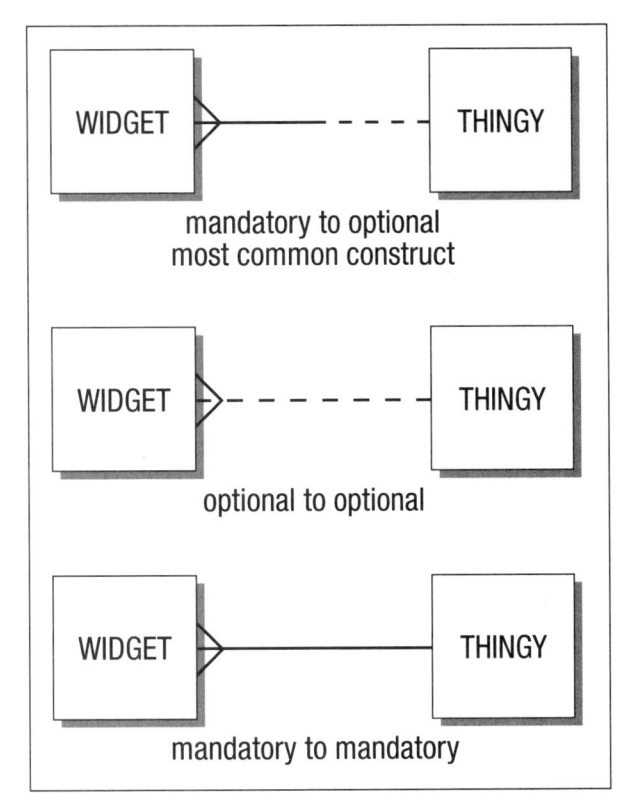

Figure 2.16
One-to-many relationships.

relations is commonly done by creating an intersection or associative entity. The intersection entity resolves the many-to-many relation into two many-to-one relations between the two original entities and the new intersection entity. Intersection entities exist only in the context that the two original entities become reference entities to it. Figure 2.17 shows the implementation of an intersection entity to resolve the many-to-many relationship.

Oracle8 has provided an alternative means for the resolution of many-to-many relationships by introducing aggregate objects like the nested table. The nested table and its implementation is introduced in Chapter 3. Unfortunately, the nested table does not lend itself to modeling in the conventional entity relationship diagram. We discuss this topic starting in Chapter 8.

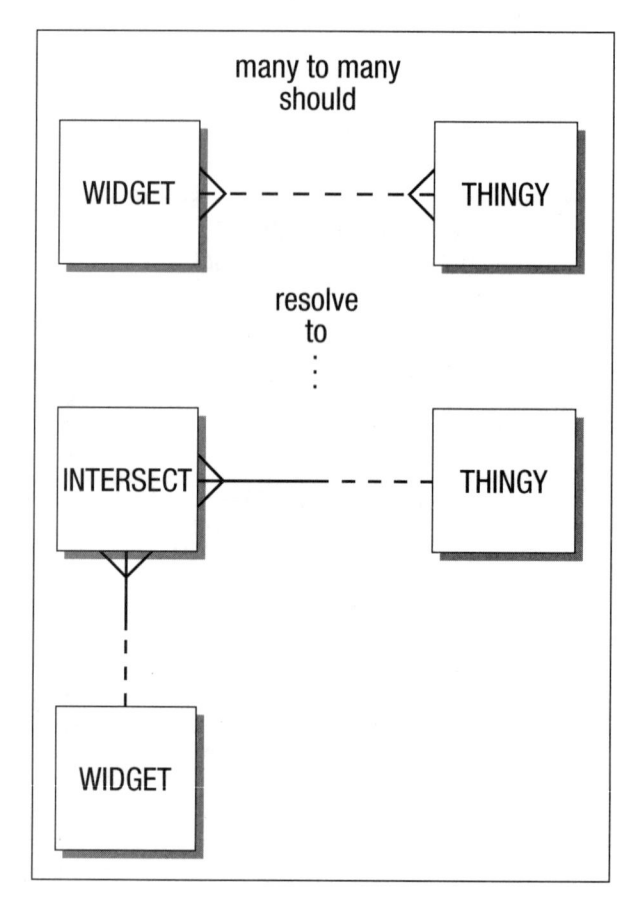

[Figure 2.17 diagram: WIDGET many-to-many THINGY ("should"), resolve to INTERSECT—THINGY, with WIDGET below]

Figure 2.17
Many-to-many relationships.

Recursive Relationships

Recursive relations, also called *pig's ears* or *pig tails*, indicate that an entity has a relationship with itself. Recursive relations are useful in mapping entities grouped into hierarchies or classifications. They can also be used to describe alternative records within the same entity. While there are numerous invalid combinations of this relation, there are, in fact, only two valid instances. Coincidentally, both are optional-to-optional in nature. This is because a mandatory cardinality on either side introduces impossibilities, like infinite loops, into the design.

The optional-to-optional many-to-one is the first valid construct. It is used to create hierarchy within the entity. The second is the optional-to-optional one-to-one. This second iteration is used to show relationship alternatives within the entity. Figure 2.18 shows two valid examples of the recursive relationship.

Recursive relationships are all too common in real world applications and present confusing constructs that impact adversely on system performance. Recursive many-to-many relationships are often called *Bill-of-Materials relationships* because of their appearance in order entry type applications. For example, let's assume that a company has created a continuing training program for their employees. Each training class might have one or more prerequisites (in the form of other classes) that must be taken before the training class. At the same time, the training class itself may be a prerequisite for another training class. It can be seen from this simple example that extracting data relative to the training class and its prerequisites requires many sub-passes through the same table to obtain the final output.

Understanding a relationship like this one is difficult and requires the aid of effective graphical representation. The entity relationship diagram does not always provide the necessary visual explanation needed to convey what is really occurring. On some occasions it may make sense to "split out" the relationship in question and conceptualize the activity taking place in order to understand it properly. This can be accomplished with a simple flow diagram to show the exchange of activity between the

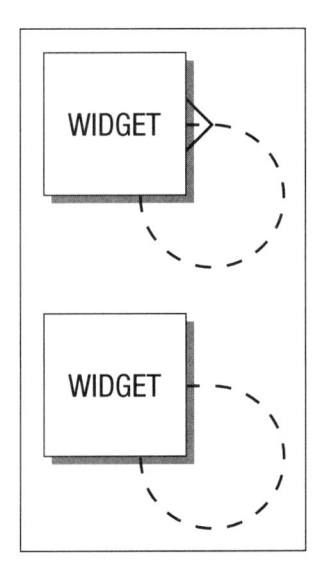

Figure 2.18
Recursive relationships.

different data elements. Going back to the data flow and functional hierarchy diagrams is a useful exercise to resolve misunderstandings of how the data may be interacting.

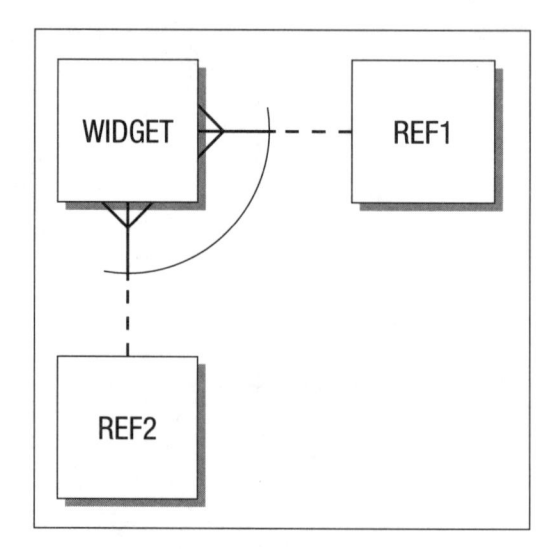

Exclusive Relationships

Exclusive relations are useful when it is necessary to define alternating choices between one entity and two or more others. In others words, the multiple relationships from a single entity will be mutually exclusive. Most commonly, the "many" side of a relation will be with the entity with the exclusive relationship. A common example appears in Figure 2.19.

It should be noted that an entity with an exclusive relation must exhibit the same cardinality to the other entities with which it shares this exclusive relationship. Note in Figure 2.19 that the Widget entity has a mandatory many-to-one relationship to entities Ref1 and Ref2. The relations must both be mandatory or optional but not a combination of the two. Likewise, if one of the relationship ends is part of a unique key, then the same end on the other relation(s) must be also. Keep in mind that a relationship cannot be a member to more than one exclusive combination. Subtypes within a supertype must be treated separately, as shown in Figure 2.20.

Figure 2.19
Exclusive relationships.

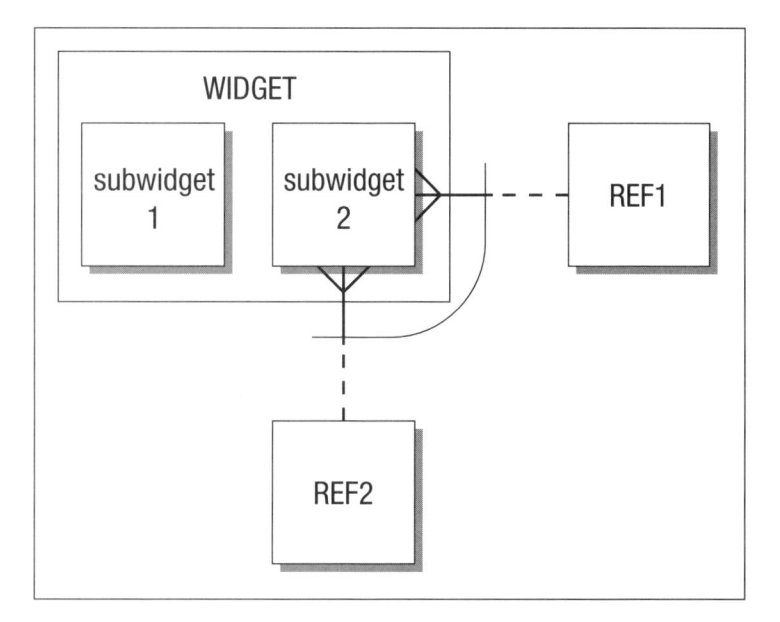

The New Systems Development Life Cycle With Oracle8

Figure 2.20
Exclusive relationships with subtypes.

Redundancy And Other Thoughts

When constructing relationships between entities, it is often possible to establish relationships that create redundancies. On occasion, these redundancies prove useful for performance improvement. This is because a circuitous path between entities is replaced with a direct relationship or shortcut. The resulting SQL is much simpler and requires the user to access fewer tables. Rather than joining three or four tables, it is possible to directly join only the two needed to satisfy the conditions of the query. True redundancy is in effect when the association between the first two entities can always be circumvented by the new relationships to the other entities. This is generally not good practice unless there is some mitigating performance issue at stake. Figure 2.21 shows how relational redundancies are manifested between a group of entities.

While the examples cited above provide good textbook situations of how entities are to be modeled, they fail to consider all of the real-world situations that will have an impact on a database system you may be developing. The next section explores some of the issues you might be faced with when the time comes to put theory into practice.

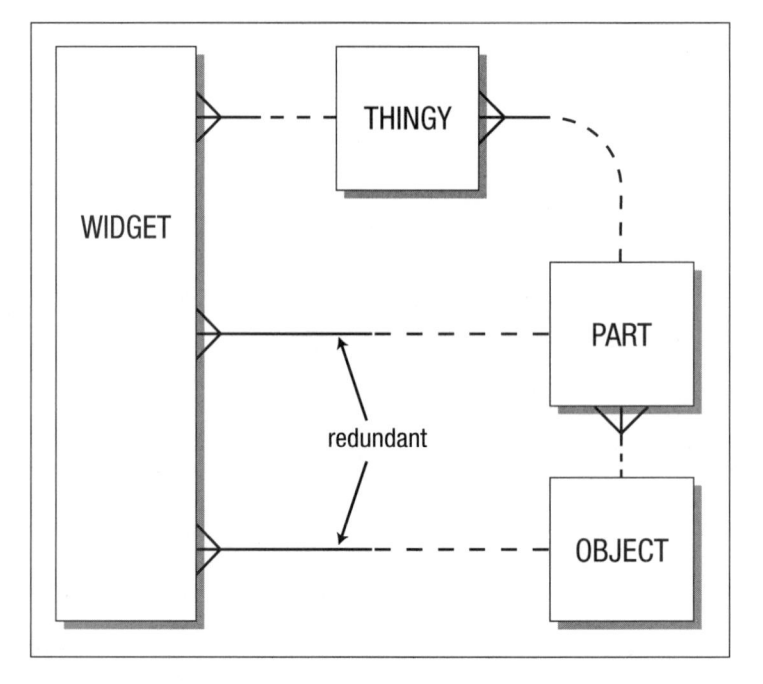

Figure 2.21
Redundancy between relationships.

Modeling The Real World

Most academic studies of the relational concept, and now object-relational concept, offer examples of implementation that demonstrate the proper execution of the respective methodology. What is left to the common designer and developer is an implementation in which system requirements and functions don't fit the mold as easily as before. The business world that we work in grows more complex and yet more intangible each day. Problems in the real world boil down to "gray areas." Business functions become so complex that they almost defy categorization.

I can recall taking Calculus in college, many years ago. I would watch attentively as the instructor worked through an entire problem, explaining each step as he went along. "How straightforward," I thought to myself, confident in the feeling that I would easily work the assigned problems that evening. More times than not, I found myself completely wrong in my assumption as I struggled for hours to solve what I was certain was a similar problem to the one demonstrated earlier that day. It usually turned out that the homework problems involved a bit more complexity than the ones demonstrated in class (at least, I hope that was the case!).

Resolving system design issues is a formidable task when you are new to it. The sense of confidence comes over time as your experience increases and your proficiency with the tools of the trade improves. Up until the present, resolving some database design issues was like trying to do automotive work with a screwdriver and a ball-peen hammer. The new extensions to Oracle8 will improve the design task because the tools at your disposal have improved. New technologies introduce new problems, and the problems we face with the new object-oriented extensions involve analysis and design.

The real world complexities which will arise, and for which Oracle8 is better suited, are not necessarily "new" problems; rather, they have been relegated to other mechanisms (e.g., third-generation programming languages) when the relational paradigm was unable to resolve them effectively.

The first of these is the introduction of aggregation to the entity relationship model. From our previous discussion, we know that aggregation represents a violation of the rules of normalization. But what about the real world? Aggregation is a highly effective means to an end for data warehousing applications and overall simplification of database design. This is pointed out further in several of the chapters to follow.

The second, and arguably one of the most important issues to be resolved, is the coupling of behavior with data. True object-oriented systems encapsulate behavior with data. These behaviors are known as methods. Behavior and data are inseparable in the real world, and the ability to model them together offers the database designer terrific opportunities to solve process-to-data modeling problems. A detailed discussion of methods is handled in Chapter 6.

Finally, objects in the real world are classified into groups. We all do it unconsciously everyday, but it is extremely important to do so when designing an application system. In the relational modeling world, the closest approximation to classes was the super-type-sub-type concept. This is a poor substitution for classes, as discussed in Chapter 1 when we described the object-oriented nature of C++ language. Although the ability to model class hierarchies is not available in the current version of Oracle8, it is scheduled for version 8.1.

Aside from the conceptual, let us illustrate some common design issues and problems that can be expected.

Chapter 2

Common Design Issues And Problems

On occasion, a customer will present a requirement that presents a true modeling challenge. Let's assume that Bob's Fertilizer Corporation produces a special compound formulated for tropical plants in California. In order to produce their special formula, certain chemicals must be mixed in a deliberate sequence. The Research And Development branch wishes to utilize the chemical data stored in the database to produce a graphical rendering of the manufacturing process. The company wishes to maintain this "recipe" in the database along with the procedural steps needed to produce it. On occasion, "custom blends" are produced in order to satisfy specific customer requirements. These derivations must also be captured in the database so that future batches can be produced. Custom orders must be graphically charted, as well.

At first glance, you can see that the manufacturing process itself can be decomposed into specific functions that produce the desired effect. The problem arises when we must retrieve the formula from the database in a specified order to produce the graphical recipe. In this scenario, we must have the ability to group data and order it. Because the compound can be customized to suit customer needs, the recipe has a dynamic behavior unsuitable for static storage techniques like **LONG RAW**. Figure 2.22 illustrates the process of formulating the fertilizer recipe.

The task of grouping or collecting the ingredients is not the challenge in this scenario. The real challenge lies in developing design logic that ensures the correct ingredients are mixed in the right order. The scenario indicates that a certain intelligence in the data is required to successfully produce the recipe. On first impressions only, it seems that some sort of recursive relationship could be in order. Two things confound this approach: One chemical must have another to combine with (insinuating a mandatory relationship and, as you might recall from the discussion on recursive relationships, this is taboo), and the order in which they are combined is crucial. I'm not going to give away the end of this story because we'll address this very dilemma in a case study found later in this book.

Such a design challenge is indicative of the increasing problems systems designers face. One alternative would be to introduce a C or C++ layer to handle this complicated task. Under a purely relational paradigm, this option would soon gain some appeal.

There are modeling situations in which a supertype spawns numerous subtypes. In order to capture the true nature of the entities being modeled into the relational

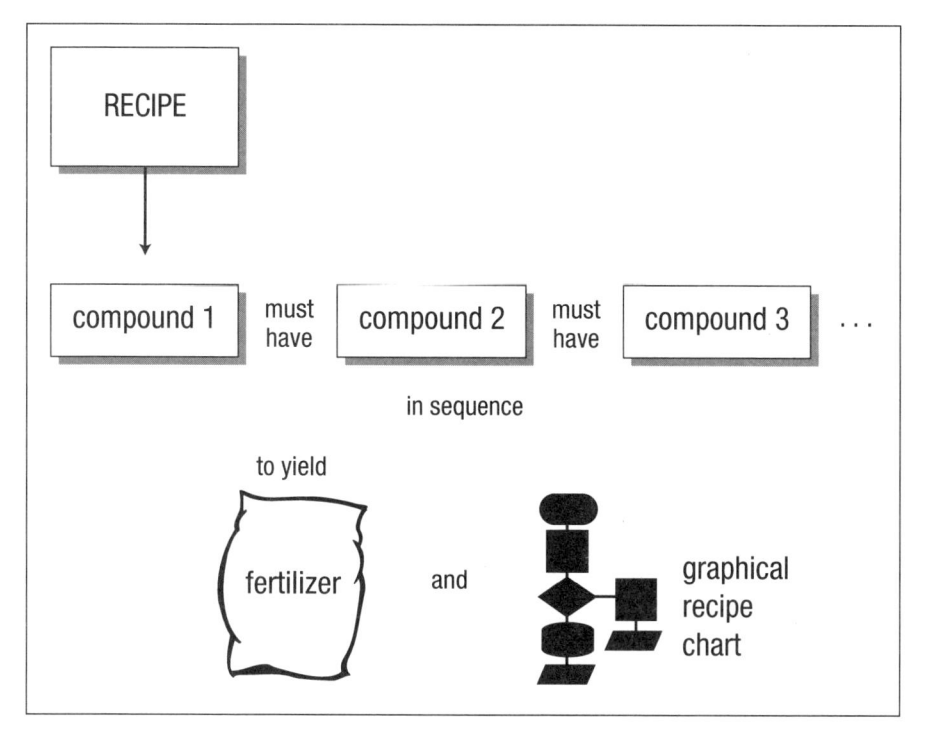

Figure 2.22
Producing the fertilizer recipe (determining record order).

paradigm, one or more abstract supertypes are required to resolve the design problem. It is a classic object-oriented example of defining abstract classes. Abstraction in a relational database has limitations that, once crossed, have a derogatory effect on performance and on the database design itself. Problems such as this are not at all uncommon. They manifest themselves in businesses that must maintain an ever-changing inventory of "similar-but-not-quite-the-same" objects, particularly when these objects satisfy the same business function or supporting process.

A future release of Oracle8 is slated to support the creation of class hierarchies. Class hierarchies will allow the inheritance of behaviors from the superclass to the subclasses. At the time of this writing, this installment of Oracle8's extensions is slated for version 8.1.

In light of the problems you will encounter in the real world, keep in mind the following basic principles to guide your design efforts:

- Normalize your database for functionality, not theoretical perfection.
- Don't lose sight of the business objectives you're asked to address.
- Simplicity speaks volumes. Take pride in usefulness, not complexity.
- Maintain good client-analyst communications. You might not be designing what the customer asked for.
- Never hesitate to get a second opinion.

Summary

In this chapter, we discussed the importance of the system development life cycle in designing systems. We focused on the role of the systems analyst and detailed the steps taken in a normal development process. A brief review of important design concepts, such as functional decomposition and entity relationship modeling, reinforces topics that will fall under considerable scrutiny in upcoming chapters. Chapter 3 initiates detailed discussion of database design with the new object-oriented extensions. We will explore the implications of the new extensions on database normalization and begin the formulation of a new modeling paradigm.

HIGH PERFORMANCE

The New Frontier Of Database Design

CHAPTER 3

HIGH PERFORMANCE

These are times in which a genius would wish to live. It is not in the still calm of life, or the repose of a pacific station, that great characters are formed...Great necessities call out great virtues.
—Abigail Adams

The New Frontier Of Database Design

In Chapter 2, we established that object-oriented functionality will have a dramatic impact on several phases of the systems development life cycle. In this chapter, we begin the discussion of what steps need to be taken to transform the database design effort from a purely relational perspective to one that embraces the object-oriented paradigm. The way in which data is perceived and the processes that change it will undergo a metamorphosis of sorts. Oracle8's object-relational model does not abandon the concepts or functionalities developed over the years. The model incorporates many of the best features of object design while preserving much of the declarative nature of the purely relational method. What will be demonstrated is the effective utilization of complex data typing, behaviors, and aggregation so prevalent in object-oriented design. By the end of the chapter, we will propose a new object database model for use in the design phase of future database system development.

An Overview Of Database Modeling And Designing With Objects

The concepts of object-oriented design have witnessed numerous variations since their inception in the mid-1970s. Although the concepts gained gradual acceptance over a number of years, the dramatic rise in popularity took place between 1989 and 1994. It was recognized early on that none of the methods developed offered a complete solution to the problem of modeling. In 1994, Grady Booch, Jim Rumbaugh, and Ivar Jacobson collaborated to develop a unified method which was later to become the Unified Modeling Language (UML). The intent of this effort was to bring about a standardization of notation and semantics to the object modeling community. The UML became the response to the Object Management Group's (OMG) request for a proposal of a definition of a standardized modeling solution. Although the UML incorporates all aspects of system design, the treatment of data and data manipulation is addressed in a way that proves viable to the modeling of Oracle8 extensions.

The UML does not espouse one particular implementation technique over another. This is to say that the methodology proposed by the UML should apply itself capably under many languages and software products. The future of database design with regard to Oracle is evolving in the direction of the UML. This is evidenced by Oracle's Object Database Designer, which adopts the methodology and notation of the UML's new open standard. In Chapter 7, we will present an overview of the Object Database Designer and the OR-Compass tool by Logic Works and demonstrate the ease in which the tools move the database modeling effort into the object-relational spectrum. With the advent of object-oriented type elements and behaviors introduced to the database arena, a standardized approach to design is needed. Particularly, because more contemporary system solutions demand the integration of a greater variety of hardware and software products. For example, newer applications integrating C++ or Java with Oracle8 require seamless access to data. Use of a C++ generator to create persistent classes for these objects simplifies application development by reducing the work needed to develop database-access mechanisms later. The modeling tools described in Chapter 7 incorporate this functionality.

The methodology prescribed by the UML serves as the basis for object-oriented discussion in this book for two reasons:

- Oracle has adopted this standard, and the standard will become more pervasive as newer releases of Oracle tools roll out.

- The UML is anticipated to become an industry standard modeling solution, and many influential organizations and vendors have already embraced it.

Key partners in the development of the UML include:

- Digital Equipment
- Hewlett-Packard
- i-Logix
- ICON Computing

- MCI Systemhouse
- Microsoft
- Oracle
- Rational Software
- Texas Instruments
- Unisys

Not unlike the effort to standardize ANSI SQL, the UML is intended to bridge the gap of inconsistent practice across system modeling in the software industry. With a new industry standard to guide us, let us next compare the relational and object-oriented paradigms in order to formulate a working database object model for Oracle8.

Creating A Database Object Model

As you might recall from Chapter 2, the analysis phase of the development life cycle is affected by the introduction of object-oriented functionality to the database design. In this section, we'll focus on synthesizing a modeling paradigm that suits the new character of Oracle8. The pure relational model is inadequate while the purely object-oriented model is not entirely appropriate for database use. What you will discover is that a combination of the two is possible and that the compromise of features is dramatically reduced with the introduction of Oracle8 object extensions.

One of the dissimilarities between the two paradigms is the handling of abstraction and encapsulation. This dissimilarity of abstraction and encapsulation handling first manifests itself while performing detailed analysis of the data flow diagram. Because of the unique qualities of abstraction and encapsulation that object-oriented structures bring to the database, the data flow/store definitions must reflect the aggregate character of complex data types. Data flow diagrams help in defining the function-to-entity and function-to-attribute associations. At their most general level, a clear determination of data structure within the data flow diagram is not made, but, as substantive detail is added, a decision is required as to the mechanism that will be used (e.g., reference entity versus **VARRAY**). Because we are able to incorporate complex data types in Oracle8, the effort of translating the function-to-attribute association becomes more complex. Nested tables and aggregate objects represent a violation of basic normalization. In a section to follow, we will consider non-first

Chapter 3

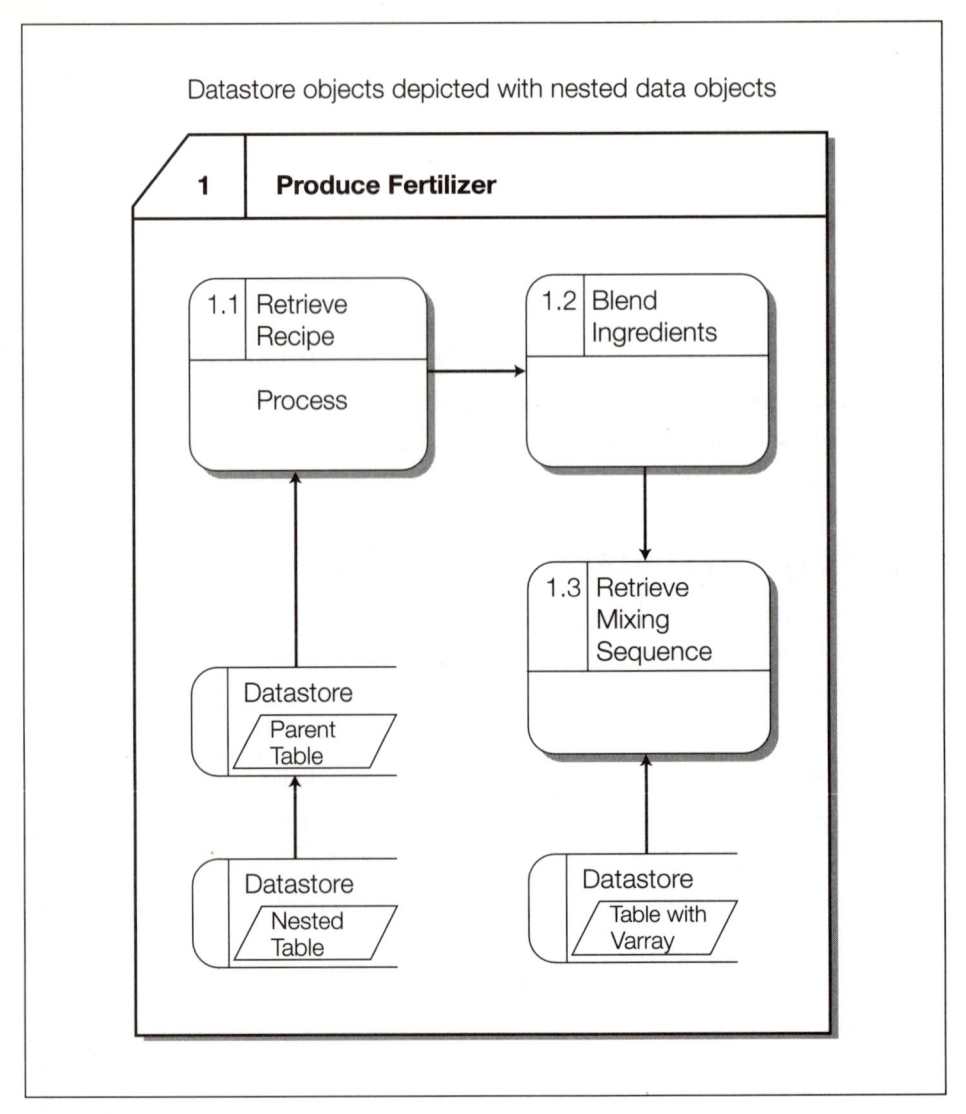

Figure 3.1
Data flow diagram with alternate constructs.

Datastore objects depicted with nested data objects

1. Produce Fertilizer
- 1.1 Retrieve Recipe — Process
- 1.2 Blend Ingredients
- 1.3 Retrieve Mixing Sequence
- Datastore: Parent Table
- Datastore: Nested Table
- Datastore: Table with Varray

normal form and its implications on overall database design. Figure 3.1 illustrates the use of collection types like nested tables in the data flow diagram.

One of the most important dissimilarities between the two paradigms is that of inheritance. Inheritance is a natural characteristic of object-oriented design because of its treatment of object types and classes. Classes can be defined that describe the general or detailed characteristics of an object type. The set of properties or characteristics is inherited by object types subordinate to the defining class. Recall that a class does not identify an instance of an object but only its properties. This ability to categorize types is extremely useful in modeling because a hierarchical progression of properties can be defined, thus emulating objects in the real world. The relational paradigm is incapable of employing true inheritance as we have just described. In Chapter 13 we discuss the planning of class hierarchies, a feature planned for version 8.1 of Oracle8.

Under the structured environment of Designer/2000, data flow diagrams can be bypassed in the development of a database system. This is because the other modeling tools and diagrammers will absorb the necessary information and generate the required database objects and modules. In all development environments, however, data flow diagrams offer insight into four key areas:

- *Functions/processes*—Data transforming mechanisms.
- *Data flows*—Descriptions of the movement of data between processes.
- *Data stores*—Representations of data in a system.
- *External objects*—Objects that send or receive data from outside of a system's scope.

Data flow diagrams are useful, primarily for documenting and communicating the iterative flow of data to your clients. In the development of the database object model for Oracle8, data flow diagrams are significantly more important because they help in determining where abstract data types and denormalized constructs might be required. Although data flow diagramming represents a generalization of the interaction between data and processes, the initial evaluation of their implementation to actual entity mapping begins here. Before an accurate transition to the detailed entity relationship diagram can be made, a concept of the new database object model must be formulated.

The obvious question at this point becomes, "How can you discern the rationale for using a conventional database construct or an abstract data type?" Although we will present further detail in following chapters that suggests one method over another, here are a few general questions to consider when faced with the question of conventional database construct versus abstract data type:

- *Simplicity*—Does the selected database object, whether conventional or complex, simplify the database schema?

- *Modularity*—Does the database object support a modular approach? Is it a good candidate for reuse?

- *Performance*—Does the database object hinder or improve database performance?

- *Maintainability*—Does the database object increase the amount of overhead needed to maintain it later in production?

- *External Impact*—What, if any, are the ramifications on processes required to access or manipulate the database object?

Chances are, you will have to balance the results of your question and make a calculated estimate. It might be that the preferred database construct improves performance but degrades maintainability. The construct might increase database simplicity but pose extreme difficulties in process interfacing. Rank the answers to the five questions based on the objectives and requirements of the system you intend to build. Remember what you are attempting to accomplish and make decisions toward that end.

Performance, for example, can be a particularly sensitive subject. The type of system being developed might have special performance needs. Consider, for a moment, the design implications of a data warehouse. A data warehouse implementation, by its very nature, requires a degree of denormalization and high levels of aggregation to improve retrieval of data. In such a case, performance would be the overriding factor in selecting the database object type used. User-defined objects might be the likely choice. The use of data types incorporating pointers will be faster than their relational cousins because collections and aggregates can be directly addressed, thus eliminating the need for table scans to locate pertinent data. See Chapter 10 for restrictions on using object extensions for data warehousing.

The database object model must incorporate aspects of the object meta-model. By utilizing the semantics defined in the UML, we will enhance the relational meta-model to formulate a database object model that captures the functionality of the new Oracle8 extensions. More importantly, a marriage of object-to-relational is created that successfully integrates the two paradigms. The first step in developing the database object model is to reconcile the differences between the object meta-model and the relational meta-model.

A meta-model is merely a model of how a model is defined or expressed, or in simpler terms, a model of a model. At first glance, this concept might seem rather obtuse. It should not be alien to anyone in the relational design business because meta-models are widely used to describe system models as well as the modeling mechanism itself. Designer/2000 makes use of the meta-model, providing a valuable set of elements that describe the data held in a Designer/2000 repository. For example, element types such as entities, attributes, relationships, tables, columns, and so forth have a relationship with one another, and the meta-model describes those relationships. Meta-models can also be portrayed in entity-relationship diagram fashion. The technique is widely used in relational design methodologies and serves to cross-check the validity of the intended database design. Before creating the new database object model, we will examine the characteristics of each meta-model that defines the distinction between relational and object-oriented meta-models. Figure 3.2 illustrates a simplified graphical representation of a meta-model for the relational model.

So, what exactly will we gain from a meta-model comparison? Specifically, the comparison will reconcile the *capabilities* of the relational meta-model with the *functionalities* of the object meta-model. The derived database object model will become the new standard for Oracle8 development. But first, let's take a look at the relational and object meta-models.

The Relational Meta-Model

The relational meta-model can be succinctly described by three components: data structure, data manipulation, and data integrity. The major characteristic of this meta-model is simplicity. There are very few distinct objects in the meta-model and each has a simple, straightforward purpose with an easily described function. We

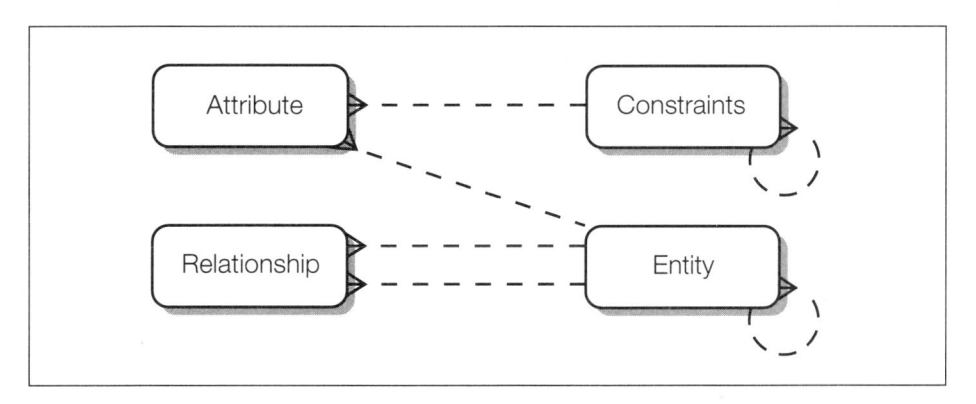

Figure 3.2
An example of a meta-model.

will dispense with a lengthy discussion of these objects and proceed to the facts that are germane to this chapter because this material should be quite familiar to you. We will summarize the key points and proceed with a more in-depth discussion of the object meta-model whose characteristics are more alien.

The relational meta-model has a proven versatility due to its combination of intuitiveness, simplicity, and theoretical foundation. A valid comparison between it and the game of chess could be made. In chess, there are only six types of playing pieces: pawn, rook (castle), knight, bishop, queen, and king. Each playing piece has a specific domain of valid moves that it can execute. The rules are simple—navigate the playing pieces in such a way that your opponent's king cannot escape capture. Those of us that have played chess can attest to the fact that these humble guidelines often spawn an extremely complex game of strategy. In the relational meta-model, think of entities, attributes, tables, and so on as the playing pieces. Relationships determine the set of allowable "moves" that the pieces can make, while functions define the processes and constraints that define the rules. Figure 3.3 illustrates this comparison of the relational meta-model with the game of chess.

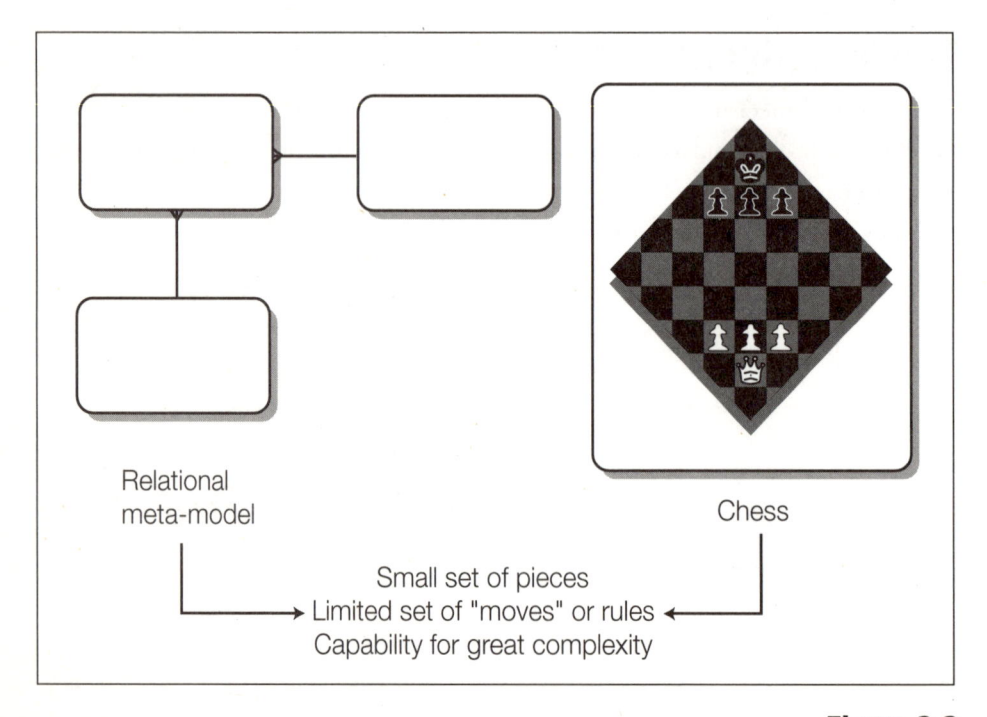

Figure 3.3
The correlation between the relational meta-model and chess.

Now that we have provided a brief description of the simple construction of the relational meta-model, let's move on to describing the characteristics of the constituent parts.

Basic Characteristics

There are three constituent parts of the relational meta-model: entity, attribute, and relationship. From our discussion in Chapter 2, entities represent objects for which specific information is maintained, such as customer, vehicle, and employee. Attributes specify the detailed properties of an entity, such as name, age, and height. Relationships describe the significance or association that one object has with another. It is common practice to assign meaningful names to constituent parts, which identify their role in the database system.

There are six properties that comprise the characteristic of data structure. The key players governed by this characteristic are entities and attributes. The essential rules for data structure are:

- Column entries contain a single value.
- Column entries are of the same kind.
- Each row in a table is unique.
- Column sequence is insignificant.
- Row sequence is insignificant.
- Columns have unique names within a table.

Data manipulation describes the types of operations that can be performed on the data. There are two varieties of manipulation available. The first variety of manipulation is assignment (DML statements), and this includes the operators **INSERT**, **UPDATE**, and **DELETE**. Assignment manipulation covers operations that alter the data itself. The other variety of data manipulation involves the use of relational operators such as **SELECT**, **UNION**, **INTERSECT**, and so forth. Relational operators group and gather data into various aggregations but do not alter it. Data manipulation manifests itself most commonly in business functions and processes. For example, assume there is a function called *PLACE_ORDER*. The supporting process would execute an **INSERT** statement to the **ORDERS** table to fill the customer's request. A corresponding process might print the resulting invoice using a **SELECT** to retrieve the necessary data from the **ORDERS** table.

Data integrity refers to the rules of normalization that we have already discussed and how the rules serve to constrain permissible values in the data tables. Data integrity is the enforcement of the business rules identified in the system to be built and are executed through the use of constraints and enforced relationships. Referential integrity constraints come in five varieties: **NOT NULL, UNIQUE, PRIMARY KEY, FOREIGN KEY**, and **CHECK**. Figure 3.4 shows how each constraint is used in the relational meta-model. Data integrity can also be enforced through the use of domains. Recalling our earlier discussion in Chapter 2, domains comprise business validation rules that apply to one or more attributes.

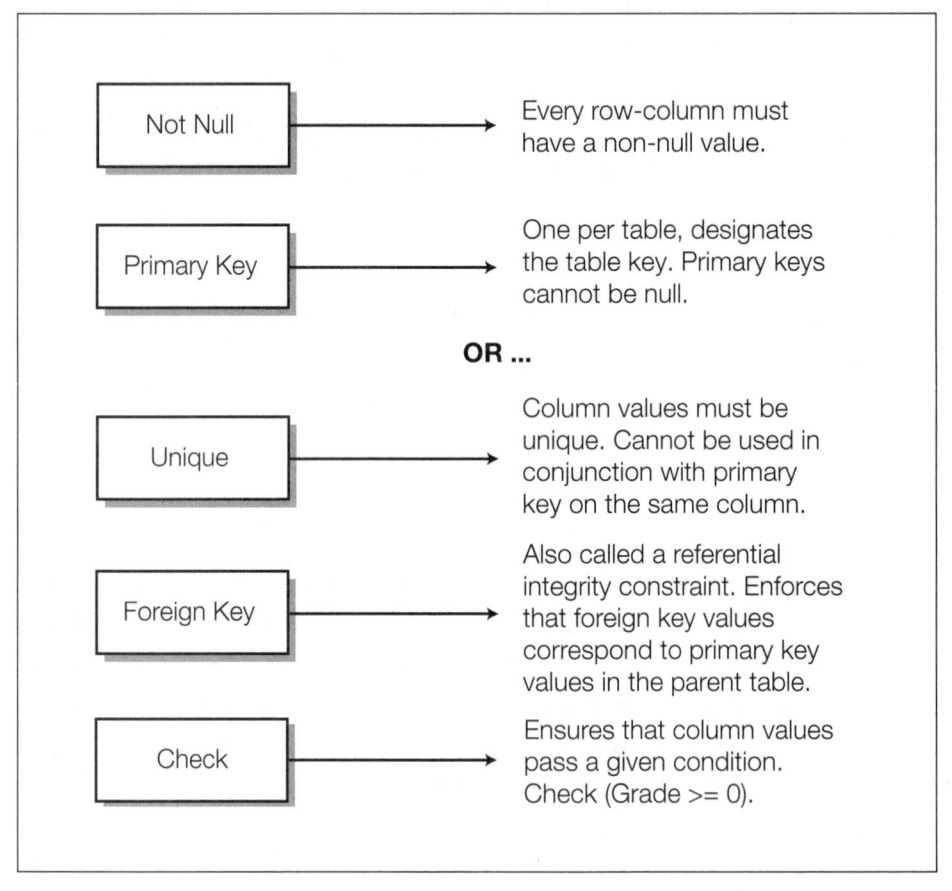

Not Null → Every row-column must have a non-null value.

Primary Key → One per table, designates the table key. Primary keys cannot be null.

OR ...

Unique → Column values must be unique. Cannot be used in conjunction with primary key on the same column.

Foreign Key → Also called a referential integrity constraint. Enforces that foreign key values correspond to primary key values in the parent table.

Check → Ensures that column values pass a given condition. Check (Grade >= 0).

Figure 3.4
Referential integrity constraints in the relational meta-model.

The Object Meta-Model

The object meta-model of the UML is a robust, feature-rich language that integrates the best practices of several methodologies. While a detailed discussion of the semantics is appropriate, we will forego much of this until Chapter 9 and focus our immediate attention on the key aspects that define the meta-model. Needless to say, most of the objects described in this section are constructed of other constituent objects. Many of the objects in the UML will have a similarity to those in the relational meta-model. The method in which the UML is constructed allows for the nesting of objects within other objects of the same type. This concept becomes more clear in the paragraphs that follow. A graphical representation of these components appears in Figure 3.5. The basic core elements that define the meta-model include the following:

- *Element*—The most basic object in the set is referred to as an *element*, and elements comprise the base class for most objects in the UML. Elements are one of the basic building blocks and can describe the most atomic level of a system.

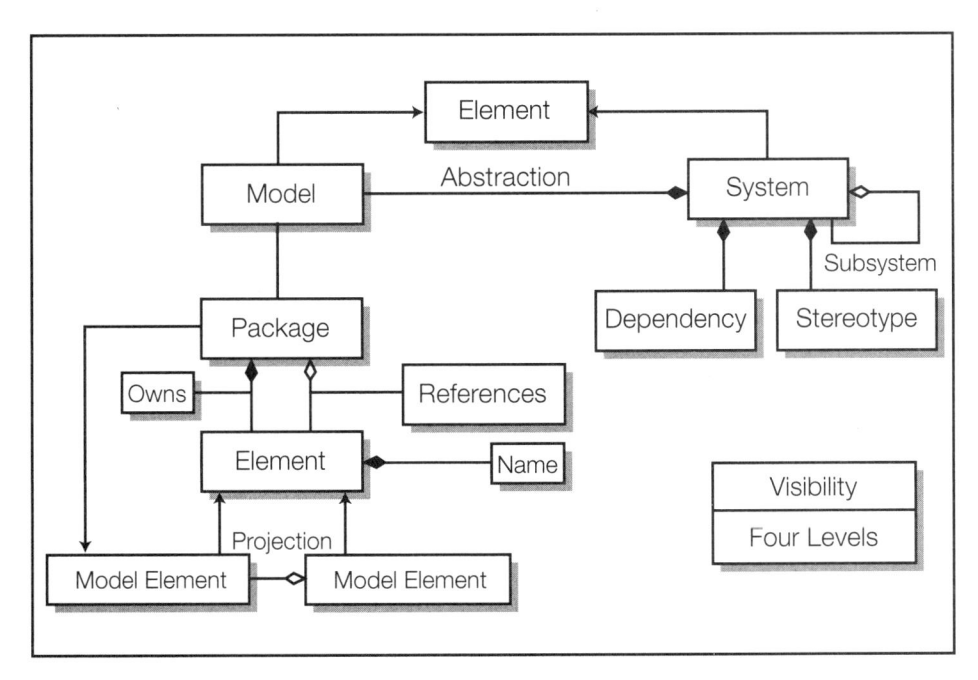

Figure 3.5
A depiction of the core components of the object (UML) meta-model.

Elements can also take on more abstract levels because they can describe models, packages, and other sub-elements described here. It should be noted that element carries with it a somewhat generic nature because it is capable of describing so many levels of objects within a system. Elements in this context can be synonymous with relational entities, or they can represent a larger abstraction, like a business function. Elements can also contain attributes composed of various data types, including complex or abstract varieties. Within a model instance, elements are related by reference, but outside of this scope, they are related by name.

- *Model*—This is considered to be a subtype of element defining an abstraction of the system or a subsystem being modeled. Models represent a collection of related element objects that can stand independently of other subsystems. In comparison to the relational model, think of models as business functions. Each model can be evaluated independently while maintaining relationships to other functions.

- *ModelElement*—This component is one of only two immediate subtypes to element. A model element describes an abstraction drawn from the modeled system. There is a close association to this component type and ViewElements (described shortly). Think of a ModelElement as a subset of an element that describes certain properties associated with the element being modeled. ModelElements are subtyped and specify information such as element relationships, data domains, and notes.

- *Dependency*—This is nearly synonymous with the relational concept of relationships. Dependencies differ from their relational siblings in that they are unidirectional. In this case, a source object has a dependency on a target object. They, too, can specify particular constraints, and it is interesting to note that, in a mechanical sense, they represent a many-to-many relationship among types. Dependencies are one of the five relationships identified in this list (see *Relationships* in this list).

- *Name*—This component performs exactly as its name implies. It is the label given to an element, and it is one of the five relationships identified in this list. Like the relational model, elements must be named. It is customary to select unique names within a system, but, under this meta-model, it is not a requirement. Duplication of names within a model is permitted because elements are related by reference rather than by name. This means that changing an element name does not alter the reference mechanisms associated with it.

- *Owns*—Serves to define what elements are aggregated or owned by a specific package. Owns is also one of the relationship types. Every element can be owned by no more than one package. With the exception of the top-most system element, all elements must be owned by a package. Interestingly, a package can't have elements, but this is usually the case only early in the design phase. Owns also determines how an element is "seen" by other elements outside of its owning package. This is performed via the visibility component described shortly. If no visibility specification is made, then the element is considered to have public access.

- *Package*—This component provides a generalized grouping mechanism for elements. When a group of elements are gathered under one package, they are referred to as the *package contents*. Packages represent a logical grouping in the design and do not manifest themselves as real objects in the database when it is created. Just as functions in the relational model synthesize into tangible processes, packages dissolve into the concrete elements which they serve to group and categorize. Elements in a package can also include other packages. This assumes a nesting behavior of these objects, and it means that the nested packages are implicitly imported or a part of the larger package.

- *References*—Serves to provide a means by which a referenced element can be addressed or seen by other elements not within the same package. Referencing also resolves conflicts due to naming duplication by specifying a new name for one or another of the elements. This is known as *aliasing*. Referencing elements also implies that an element is visible to the element that has imported the package that owns the element in question. For example, an element (element A) can reference a package (package B) containing one or more elements. A reference established from element A to an element in package B is visible (see the definition for Visibility) and can be aliased if the calling element (element A) owns, or is part of, a package with an element of the same name. Even though references are destroyed if a package is deleted, referenced elements and packages will remain intact. References are one of the relationship types. The illustration in Figure 3.6 gives a graphic description of the definition of referencing.

- *Stereotype*—Stereotypes are the classification instrument for elements. This component is a subtype of ModelElement. In simple terms, stereotypes are a means to classify an object or define object classes. Recall the discussion in Chapter 1 where the concept of class definition was offered. Stereotypes can be assigned to

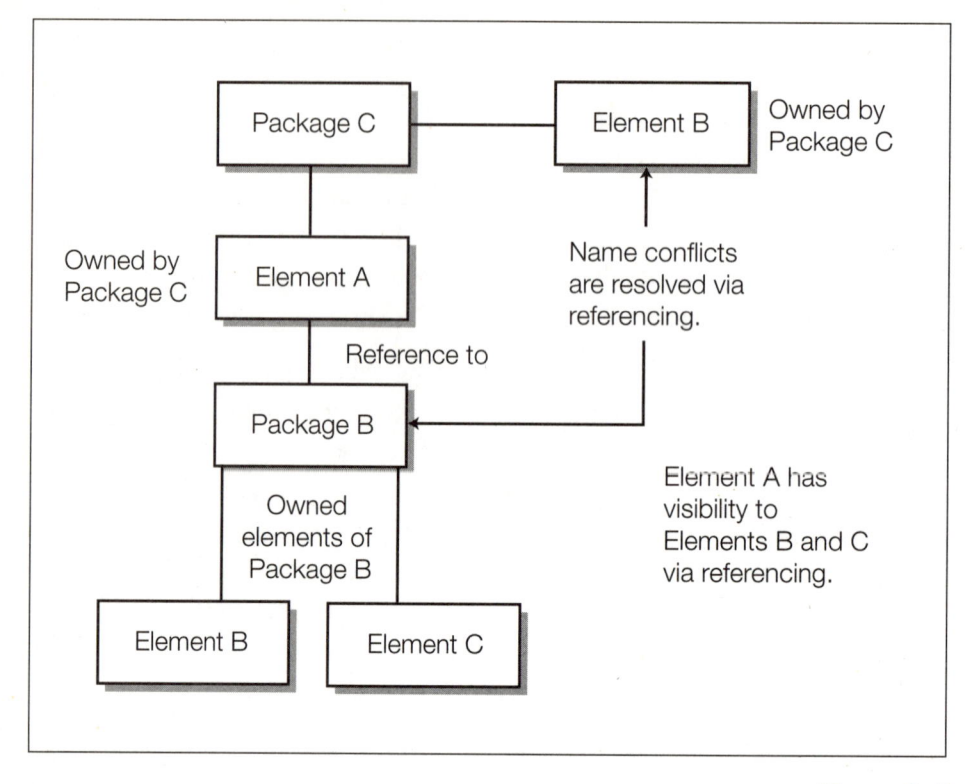

Figure 3.6
An example of referencing.

elements, but it is not required for an element to have a stereotype. The UML has 35 predefined stereotypes that apply to various objects in the meta-model, but the meta-model affords the ability for the user to create others, if necessary.

- *System*—This is also a subtype of element and represents a collection of objects gathered to perform a specific purpose. Systems can be described by one or more models and identify a real world activity or domain. Systems can be compared to subsystems in the relational life cycle model described in Chapter 2. Systems contain all the elements, dependencies between models, and stereotypes that apply to the higher-level element that describes the database or application under construction. It should be noted that even though model and package are also subtypes of element, a package can never own a model or system. This infers that model and system reside on a higher level than package.

- *ViewElement*—This component is a textual and graphical depiction of a collection of model elements. This component is the second of only two immediate subtypes to element. ModelElements can be projected into ViewElements. In this context, projection means that the ViewElement represents a human readable format for the ModelElements that it contains. ViewElements can manifest themselves as charts, diagrams, or other documentation-related media. ViewElements can depict the same information about a ModelElement in different ways, much like an entity relationship diagram and data flow diagram represent the same data stores in different ways.

- *Visibility*—Visibility establishes the degrees to which an element can be seen from outside of its enclosure, whether the enclosure is a package or a model. This component relates to encapsulation in that the inner mechanisms of an object can be hidden from another object or process even though that process can have the ability to access or execute it. The UML defines four degrees of visibility going from least to most restrictive. The four degrees are: public, protected, private, and implementation. Public visibility is the default, and this indicates that the object is open to all other objects, including those outside of its package. Protected and private visibility indicates that the element is not visible outside of the package that owns or references it. There are caveats to the execution of these two that require a detailed discussion of dependencies. That discussion is saved for Chapter 9. Finally, implementation visibility means that the element is not visible outside of a package that owns or references it under any conditions.

- *Relationships*—These are used to create a semantic connection between two instances of element. Relationships are a subset of ModelElements described earlier, and there are five fundamental types:

  - *Dependency*—A common mechanism that applies to all elements. Dependency is unidirectional from a source to a target element.

  - *Association*—A bi-directional connection between two objects.

  - *Generalization*—A unidirectional inheritance relationship used in supertype/subtype hierarchies.

  - *Transition*—A behavioral relationship that specifies the state change of an object.

- *Link*—A relationship type that specifies the instances of processes and elements that describe an interaction.

As mentioned, further discussion of these relationship types takes place in Chapter 9.

Reconciling The Relational And Object Paradigms

As you can see, the two meta-models present a divergent philosophy in their treatment of data and functions. Traditional relational types demand decomposition of constituent objects to the most primitive level. This is due, in large part, to the declarative structure of SQL. The relational design model requires data objects to exist in a rudimentary state—numbers, characters, and dates. The introduction of SQL offered tremendous benefits to data access because cumbersome navigation of data structures (e.g., tables) was eliminated. The use of pointers, so commonly found in hierarchical and network databases, was not needed to establish relationships between data tables. Data access is accomplished through the use of primary and foreign keys. The most outstanding benefit of the declarative structure is that the actual navigation path is hidden from the user. The work is performed by the SQL optimizer which determines the navigation path. However, it can be seen that the declarative approach is inadequate when working with complex data types, such as nested tables, because such objects cannot be referenced by key. This is the reason for the reintroduction of pointers in Oracle8. Figure 3.7 shows the declarative approach of SQL and the difficulty of dealing with complex data types like collections.

The object design model allows for complex data that does not fall into one of the three categories listed earlier in the relational meta-model section. Complex data object implementation calls for a technique known as *persistent storage*. Persistent storage is the concept that an object will have a physical location on the storage media even when the object is not in use. For example, an object called **EMPLOYEE_BACKGROUND** might be created to store attributes such as skill level, specialty, and department. In the object meta-model, such a construct would become an abstract type physically residing in storage. As you might recall from the first rule under data structure in the relational meta-model section, a column must contain a single value. Complex data typing of the variety proposed by persistent storage is not possible under the relational model. In the relational meta-model, the individual attributes might exist in different tables and would be retrieved via query

THE NEW FRONTIER OF DATABASE DESIGN

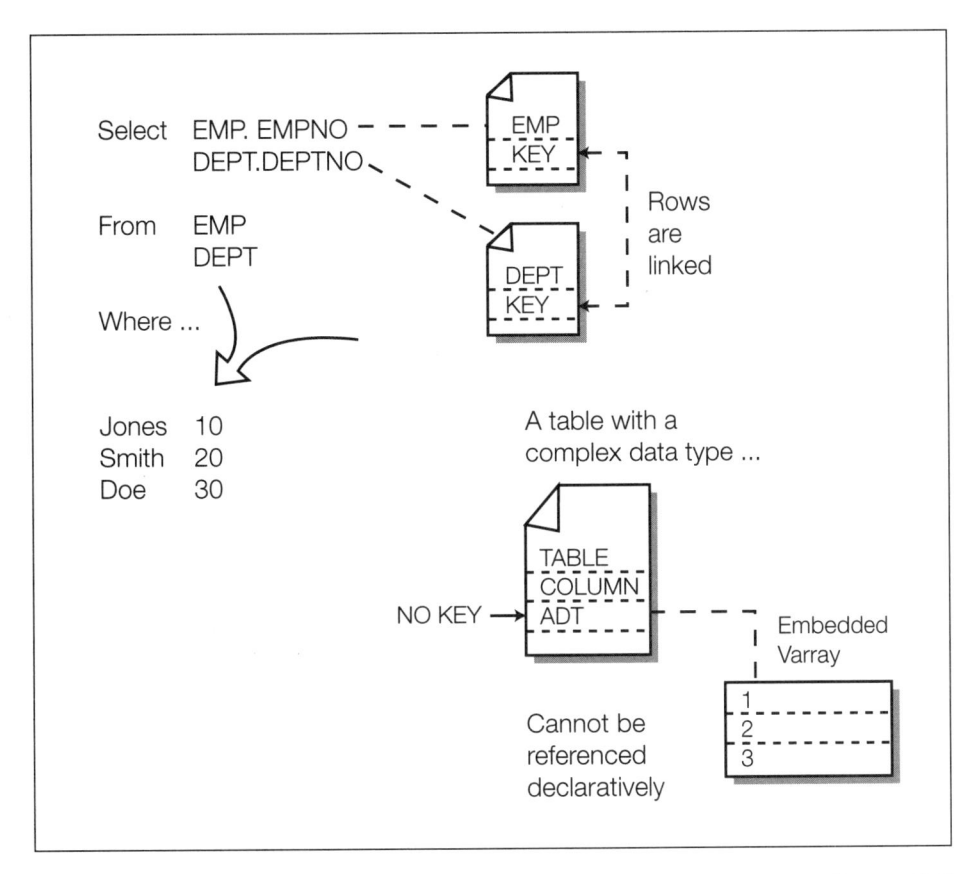

Figure 3.7
The declarative structure of SQL.

to assemble the aggregate data. No physical storage of the aggregate would take place except for the atomic elements spread about in various tables. Figure 3.8 illustrates the concept of persistent storage.

For relational databases to approximate the same behavior, it is necessary to dynamically retrieve the necessary data through the use of **JOINs** in a **SELECT** statement. The result set of such an operation does not exist in the database in the retrieved format; rather, the constituent parts are scattered throughout the database and brought together when needed. The inability of relational models to exercise the concept of persistent storage is often referred to as the *impedance mismatch*.

Further complicating this issue is the ability of object-oriented methodologies to encapsulate information preventing external activities from changing or sometimes

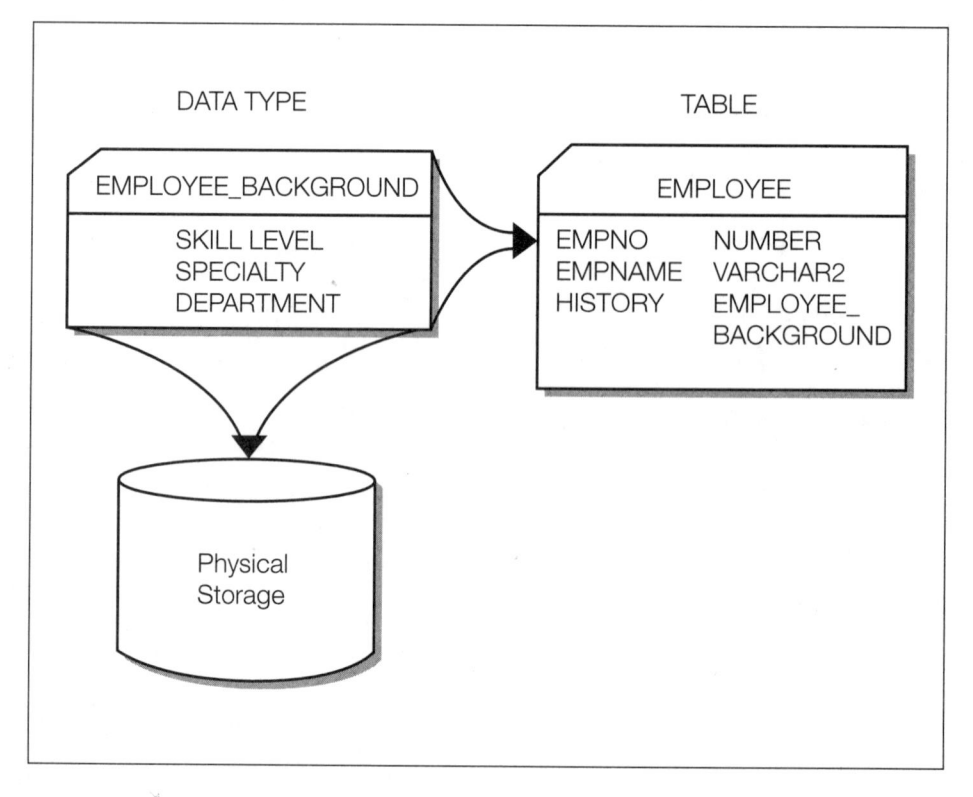

Figure 3.8
An example of persistent storage.

gaining access to the internal properties or data. Because of the declarative nature of SQL, external access is permitted in the relational model. Enforcing data encapsulation proves to be difficult, if not impossible.

For example, in the relational functional hierarchy, let's say you have defined a function called *POST_PAYMENT* which credits a customer's account upon receipt of payment. The proper billed items must be credited in order to maintain an accurate log of what has and has not been paid for. Perhaps there are items that have not been paid for, in which case, an "account overdue" flag might be generated. With the power of the SQL language, it is possible to manually update the customer's account external to the function and therefore violate its logic. This represents a violation of encapsulation because this action would not be possible in a pure object-oriented environment. As we can see, ad hoc SQL proves to be counter to the concept of encapsulation because the inherent protection afforded an object can be violated through the use of a DML statement. Figure 3.9 illustrates the concept how the relational model violates encapsulation.

In the relational meta-model, such problems are handled by creating constraints on the tables. Constraints vary from encapsulation for two reasons: constraints are not restricted to maintaining the behavior of a single object, and they are external to the property set for the aggregated data type.

The object meta-model defines more types of relationships than the relational meta-model. Object relationships are primarily unidirectional in nature. This means that

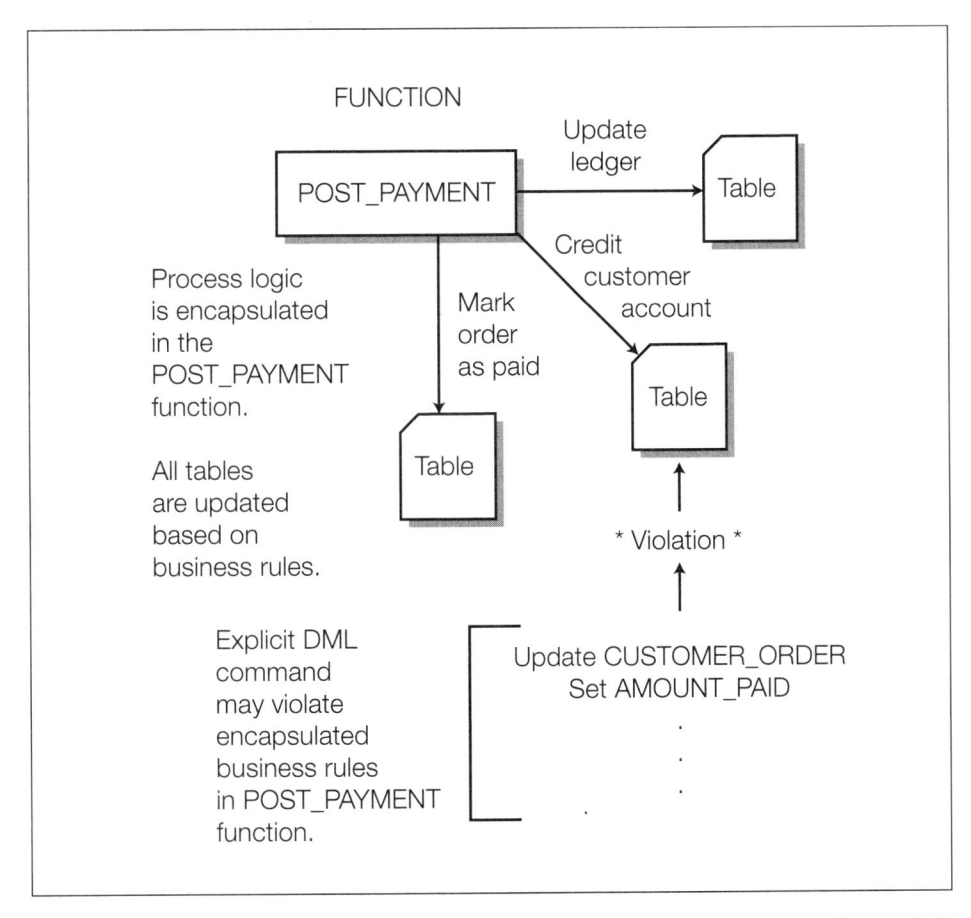

Figure 3.9
An example of the relational model violating the concept of encapsulation.

the database object model must address this disjointed correlation by mapping the object relation behavior to that of a conventional relationship. The object meta-model provides the following information:

- Relationship name
- Relationship type
- Multiplicity (or cardinality) of the object-to-object relationship

The database object model incorporates this information while also ascertaining the following:

- Implemented direction of the relationship
- Intended implementation for stored object type (single values use standard relational data types; aggregates and complex data will use **VARRAY**s, nested tables, and so forth)
- Appropriate data object selection (**VARRAY**s and nested tables), if a relationship indicates a multiplicity (aggregation)

This incorporation is required to properly map the logical expressions from the database design to the physical implementation in the database. Business object relationships from the database object model can specify an implementation in only one or both directions. For example, consider **EMPLOYEE** and **DEPARTMENT** tables. You'll find that an employee can implement a department as an attribute. Conversely, a department incorporates multiple employees. You can see that in each case, the individual relationships do not infer nor negate the possibility of the other. Figure 3.10 shows the nature of implied direction in the use of relationships.

For Oracle8 to decipher the implementation of object types to relationships, a series of steps are performed in order to establish the proper object type needed to support the relationship(s). The following criteria are used to make the necessary assertions.

1. What is the direction of implementation for the relationship?
2. What is the multiplicity (cardinality) of the relationship?
3. Is the cardinality *many*?
4. What is the data or collection type based on the response from the question in Step 3?

The New Frontier Of Database Design

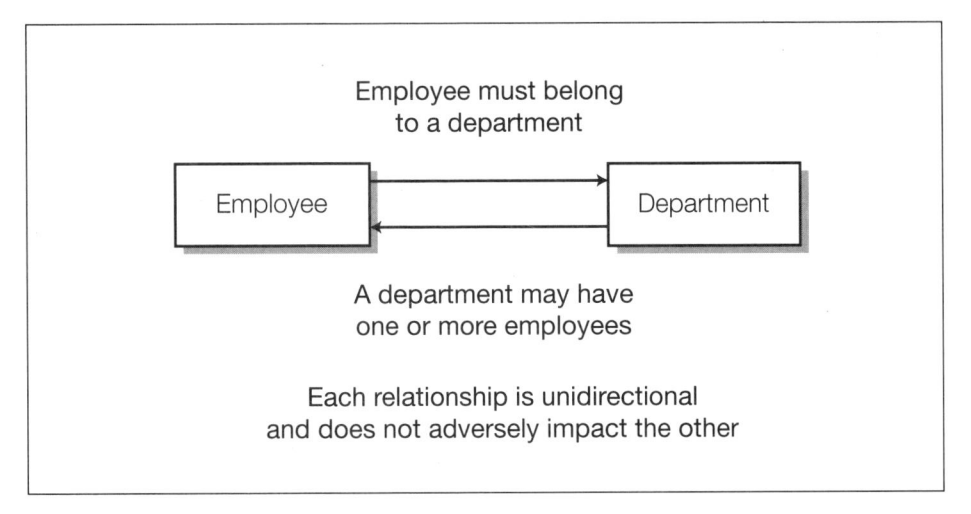

Figure 3.10
Implementing the direction of relationships.

> Employee must belong to a department
>
> Employee ⇄ Department
>
> A department may have one or more employees
>
> Each relationship is unidirectional and does not adversely impact the other

5. What is the cardinality of the relationship in the other direction (if applicable)?

6. Is embedding or referencing used to satisfy the relationship?

When the answer to the question in Step 1 is *unidirectional*, then the relationship is implemented via conventional DDL and the answer to the question in Step 6 is *none*. At this point, it is useful to define what exactly is meant by *referencing* and *embedding*. Referencing is used when an instance of an object can be used by one or more objects at the same time. For example, a company could be a client, supplier, and distributor. The company holds three responsibilities but, the fact remains, that all three responsibilities are executed by one company.

Embedded relationships are relationships where the object is not visible to the rest of the system or where the object has no relative significance outside of its relationship. For example, a shipping manifest can contain numerous line items. Outside of the context of the shipping manifest, the line items lose meaning.

If the answer to the question in Step 1 is *bi-directional*, then the cardinality of the relationship type must be determined in Step 2. If multiplicity is indicated (a many relationship), then the questions in Steps 3 and 4 determine that an aggregation (**VARRAY**, nested table) is needed, and a specification as to which will be used is also made. Step 5 evaluates the bi-directional nature of the relationship. If the relationship is unidirectional, then there is no impact on whether or not embedding or

93

referencing is used. Now that we have reconciled the main differences of the relational and object paradigms, let's move on to the next logical step that is the product of our efforts, the database object model.

The Database Object Model

There are two conclusions that we can draw from our comparison of the two meta-models. From a design perspective, it is possible to embody much of what the object meta-model has to offer. The basic components described from the UML enable a designer to effectively execute encapsulation, class typing, abstraction, aggregation, and other techniques necessary for the deployment of complex systems designs. The UML offers a sound framework from which to launch a design effort. The second conclusion we can draw is that the implementation of the resulting design effort must coexist within the current framework of SQL. Despite the extensibility offered by the new features in Oracle8, SQL remains as the primary vehicle for data manipulation. The natural evolution from design to implementation must address the inconsistencies between the nimble mechanisms of the object design and the declarative workings of SQL. Oracle8 introduces a number of new extensions to SQL for the purpose of handling the new object-oriented features. These extensions will be discussed in detail in Chapter 12. Table 3.1 illustrates the comparison between the relational, object-oriented, and resulting database object models.

Now that we have reviewed the nature of the two meta-models, it is appropriate to summarize the character of the new database object model we will use.

Benefits And Design Considerations Of The Database Object Model

What we have determined is that the database object model is an extension of the conventional relational model. The previous mechanisms remain intact, but overall functionality is greatly enhanced through the incorporation of the object meta-model components. The new SQL extensions (addressed later in this book) provide the necessary vehicle for dealing with the complex relationship structure introduced by the object model. Decomposition of database objects will no longer proceed to the most atomic level now that support for collections, groups, and abstractions is present. A direct benefit of reduced decomposition is that there will be a reduction in the quantity of entities and derived tables in the database.

Table 3.1 A meta-model comparison.

Feature	Relational Meta-Model	Object Meta-Model	Database Object Model
Object Types	Primitive	Complex	Complex
Relationships	Bi-directional	Unidirectional	Bi-directional
Constraints	Yes	Yes	Yes
Normalization	Yes	No	Yes
Persistent Storage	No	Yes	Yes
Abstraction	No	Yes	Yes
Aggregation	No(limited)*	Yes	Yes
Class Typing	No	Yes	Yes**
Encapsulation	No	Yes	Yes
Methods	No	Yes	Yes
Pointers	No	Yes	Yes
Data Navigation	Declarative	Pointers	Declarative, Pointers

* Aggregation in the relational model is generally achieved by the creation of views. While this often achieves the desired result, this method lacks the robustness and persistent storage of the object model.

** Class typing and the construction of class hierarchies is a feature that will be supported in a future release of Oracle8. Currently, it is anticipated for version 8.1.

From the standpoint of design and implementation, the effort required to properly synthesize the design to physical components in the database has grown more complex. The importance of decomposing the data flow diagram and mapping the necessary function-to-attribute relationships could dictate the success or failure of a system to be deployed.

The following list depicts what is gained from the conceptualization of the new database object model:

- Retained functionality of the declarative structure of SQL and the addition of new extensions.
- An expanded scope of entity definition.
- Additional functionality for incorporation of C++ structures.
- Extended definition of relationships and relation types.

Chapter 3

- Incorporation of user-defined data types.
- The ability to incorporate structures or objects outside of the database.
- A method for resolving the impedance mismatch of SQL with object-oriented technology by incorporating persistent storage.
- A richer classification of relationships and their functionality.

Now that we have gained a better understanding of the new database object model, let's examine one of the most important aspects of database design under the new approach in Oracle8, namely, aggregate objects.

Aggregate Objects

The idea of aggregate objects has been bantered about in this chapter, but, in this section, we will examine what aggregate objects are and how they are implemented. An aggregate object is essentially a data type definition that can be composed of many subtypes coupled with behavior. Referring to the example in Chapter 2 for Bob's Fertilizer, let's say you wish to create a user-defined data type called *RECIPE*, as depicted in Listing 3.1.

Listing 3.1 Data type **RECIPE**.

```
CREATE OR REPLACE TYPE
   Recipe (
        chemical            VARCHAR2(20),
        purity_level        VARCHAR2(20),
        quantity            VARCHAR2(15));
```

From this example, you can see that each of the constituent items of the new data type **RECIPE** is essentially an attribute from several tables. By creating the data type **RECIPE**, you can now embed the data type into another table as an individual attribute, as shown in Listing 3.2.

Listing 3.2 Use of data type **RECIPE**.

```
CREATE OR REPLACE TABLE
   Fertilizer (
      name          VARCHAR2(20),
      fert_mix      RECIPE));
```

In the **FERTILIZER** table, you can see that the **fert_mix** field now contains an entire range of values. This is an example of complex or unstructured data typing. Domain integrity can be enforced through this construct because you can ensure that only valid entries are entered into the **RECIPE** data type.

Up until this point, you have created a user-defined or abstract data type (ADT). If you take this one step further, you can create a predefined behavior or method to embed new recipes called *NEW_FERTILIZER*. For example:

```
Fertilizer.new_fertilizer('SuperGrassGrow', 'SuperGrassRecipe');
```

The important concept to be gained from this basic example is how grouped data can be nested in the single field of another table. In Chapter 4, we will pursue user-defined data types in detail, and, in subsequent chapters, we will discuss pointers, methods, and other object-oriented extensions. Let's take a moment to introduce two new constructs in the new object extensions for Oracle8. Both **VARRAY**s and nested tables fall under the category of collection types. An additional detailed discussion of collection types appears in Chapter 4, but the following discussion will help in the explanation of other topics that will appear in the sections and chapters to follow.

Variable Arrays (VARRAYs)

Variable arrays or **VARRAY**s can be thought of much like PL/SQL version 1 tables. **VARRAY**s are suitable when the subset of information is static and the subset is small. Developers familiar with Developer/2000 are reminded of *poplists*. Poplists are basic forms constructs that allow only a small set of valid entries in a field. Poplists function much like domains in that only values in the list are considered valid entries. A suitable implementation of a **VARRAY** might be in the same context where a reference entity might be used. The contents of reference entities remain relatively static and serve to validate entries in the referencing table. For example, a reference entity called *MARKETS* might be created to store the valid set of areas where a company does business. In the same way, a **VARRAY** might be substituted to perform the same reference and validation.

VARRAY constructs are stored inline. This means that the **VARRAY** structure and data are stored in the same data block as the rest of the row as a **RAW** data type. Although they bear some similarity to PL/SQL tables, **VARRAY**s are a fixed size.

Altering a **VARRAY** requires a DDL statement. Accessing individual elements of a **VARRAY** is limited. This task can be done only via the index within the PL/SQL code. Individual **VARRAY** elements cannot be queried. The following code excerpt illustrates the syntax used for the creation and subsequent population of a **VARRAY**.

```
CREATE OR REPLACE TYPE
   Markets AS varray(4) of VARCHAR2(20);

CREATE OR REPLACE TABLE
   Market_Area (
      id                 NUMBER    primary key,
      market_name        Markets);

INSERT into Market_Area values (
     1, Markets ('Domestic', 'Mexico', 'Canada', 'Brazil'));
```

In this example, note that the **MARKETS VARRAY** is comprised of four values. If it becomes necessary to add a fifth item later, then the **VARRAY** would have to be altered to hold the additional value. Unfortunately, the **MARKET_AREA** table structure would also change, and the data would have to be moved. The **VARRAY** is the first member of the collection type family. Now that we have a basic understanding of this new data construct, let's introduce the nested table.

Nesting Tables

A *nested table* is essentially a table embedded within another table and linked to a specific column. Nested tables are suitable in situations where a table of one or more columns are to be used as parameters, variables, or ADTs. They are also ideal when the number of items is indeterminate and the storage must be directly managed. Nested tables are stored out-of-line and have a more robust access than **VARRAY**s. Keep in mind, too, that the nested table is a somewhat clumsy structure when compared to a conventional table with attributes. This is because the nested table becomes an attribute for another table. The most recognizable benefit of these structures is that they are fast because of their use of pointers instead of relational keys. They also provide a cleaner design alternative to many-to-many relationships than the use of associative entities.

A nested table is stored in a store table which must be specified in the **CREATE TABLE** command for each nested table used. In order to implement a nested table, a pointer is defined in the column which references it. If a column is so designated to reference the nested table, then all column entries for that column must contain a pointer to a nested table of the exact same definition.

Outward appearances suggest that the pointer in the column "points" to a whole table. In actuality, the internal mechanism of the object-relational database subordinates the contents of the nested table to the controlling table.

Let's examine a real world example where the utilization of a nested table would be feasible. Suppose that in a given database there are two entities: **EMPLOYEE** and **TASKS**. Assume, for a moment, that you have a many-to-many relationship between these two entities because many employees can have many tasks. In a conventional situation, you would resolve the many-to-many relationship with an associative or intersection entity. The new entity would contain the primary keys from **EMPLOYEE** and **TASKS**, as shown in Figure 3.11.

A nested table implementation in this scenario would eliminate the need for the additional entity as well as the three-way join to retrieve the necessary data.. A proper implementation of this scenario using nested tables would look something like this:

```
CREATE OR REPLACE TYPE Tasks_t (
    task_name           VARCHAR2(20),
    manpower_lvl        NUMBER,
    duration            NUMBER);

CREATE OR REPLACE TYPE Emp_List_t (
    Emp_id              Number,
    Last_Name           VARCHAR2(20),
    First_Name          VARCHAR2(15),
    Task_List           Tasks_t);

CREATE OR REPLACE TABLE Employee_List  of Emp_list_t
    nested table Tasks_t store as
        Task_List_tbl;

ALTER TABLE Employee_List ADD
    CONSTRAINT PK_Employee_List
        PRIMARY KEY (Emp_id);
```

From this example, you can see that a type was first created of the necessary task data. A basic employee type was also created with an attribute called *task_list* of type

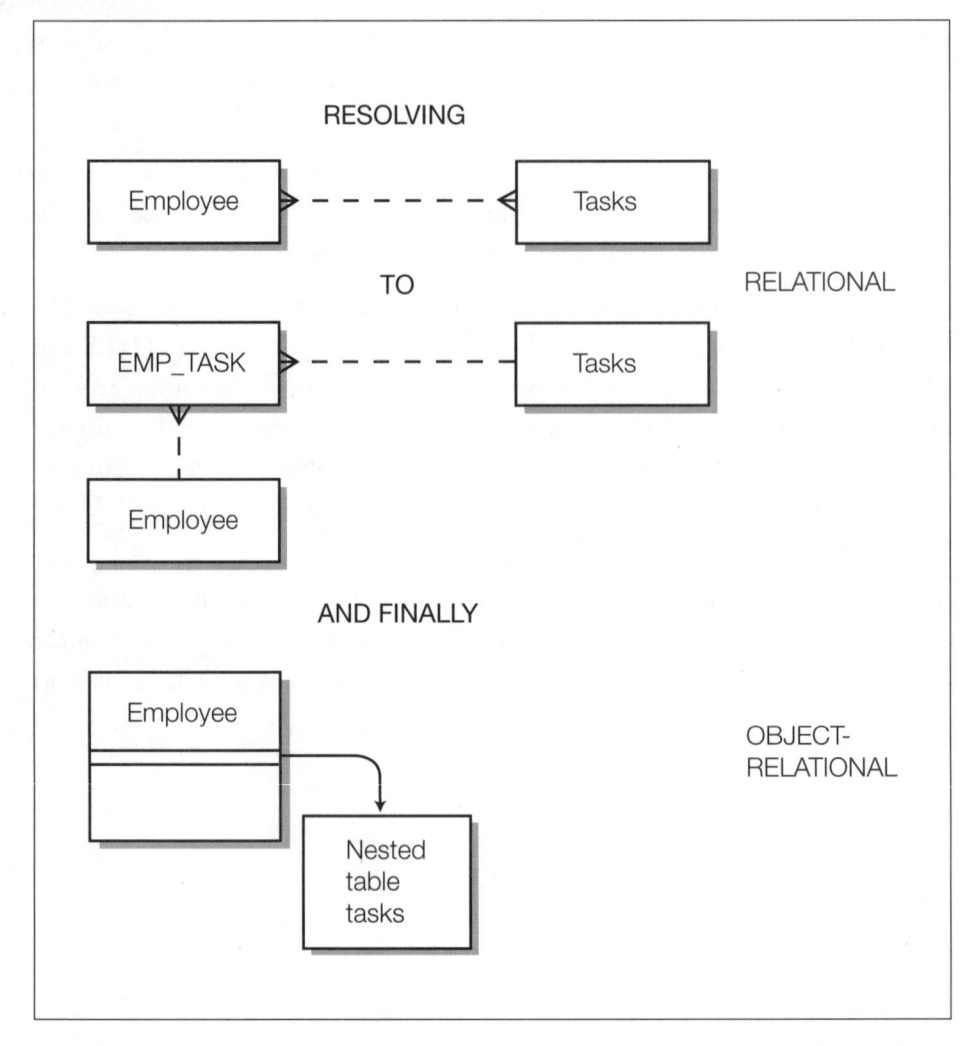

Figure 3.11
A sample many-to-many relationship.

tasks_t. This attribute becomes the pointer to the nested table. You could then create the table **EMPLOYEE_LIST** with the necessary syntax. Note that the primary key is added in an **ALTER** statement and not included in the initial creation. This is because constraints cannot be issued against nested tables during creation.

The implementation of nested tables lends itself well to the modeling of hierarchical structures. Nested tables offer a simpler database design by reducing the number of actual tables created or traversed during data manipulation. It has not been substantiated absolutely whether there are distinct performance advantages to utilizing them versus the conventional method described before; however, the use of pointer structures is expected to generate performance gains over the use of relational keys. In the final analysis, other mitigating design factors individual to each system design effort will have to be examined. Much like the current use of the TRACE and EXPLAIN PLAN utilities to find problems in performance, so too these same utilities will be run to ensure the best performance possible in Oracle8 applications.

While the temptation might be great to jump up and litter your new application with **VARRAY**s and nested tables, a few rules and restrictions must be taken into consideration during the design phase to determine whether these constructs are suitable.

Basic Rules For The Use Of VARRAYs And Nested Tables

The following rules must be considered before implementing **VARRAY**s and nested tables.

- A **VARRAY** or nested table cannot contain another **VARRAY** or nested table as an attribute.
- A store table must be specified to store the records of a nested table.
- Store tables inherit the physical attributes of the parent table.
- Default values cannot be specified for **VARRAY**s.
- Constraints of any kind cannot be used in type definitions. Rather, they must be specified using the **ALTER TABLE** command.
- A table column specified as a **VARRAY** cannot be indexed.
- A table using **VARRAY**s or nested tables cannot be partitioned.
- **VARRAY**s cannot be directly accessed via SQL.
- Incomplete types are allowed. However, only complete types can be used in a **CREATE TABLE** command. (Incomplete types are used for circular reference situations. A typical situation might be where a type referenced a second type, which, in turn, referenced the first type. For example, the hierarchical relationship of supervisor to employee where the supervisor becomes his superior's employee.)

- The scalar parts of a type can be indexed directly in the parent table.
- **VARRAY** and nested table sub-attributes cannot be indexed directly on a parent table.
- Store table attributes for nested tables can be indexed.

With the introduction to collection types complete, we are ready to embark on a concept that is practically an anathema to most relational database designers, but one that will play an important role in the development of object-relational database implementations.

Modeling Non-First Normal Form Data Structures

To most database designers, the thought of repeating data in data tables is somewhat distasteful. A great deal of effort goes into developing an elegant design that follows the essential tenets of normalization. If you handed most DBAs an entity relationship diagram and told them you intended to introduce repeating data items, they would spontaneously combust. As unnatural as this act may seem, earlier database engines such as IDMS allowed for repeating groups. Later, the "set" concept was proposed by C. J. Date that allowed for such constructs in the relational world. As part of the transition to object-relational methodology, we need to recognize the importance of this concept.

If we are to accept the idea that it is allowable to violate first normal form, then the following set of guidelines is needed, to establish cases when first normal form violations are acceptable:

- Repeating data items should be small in size.
- Repeating data items should be static and rarely, if ever, changed.
- Repeating data must not be queried as a set or collection.

A real world example of this case might be a scoring system for a gymnastics meet. Each competitor is granted three attempts at a specific event, say, vaulting. One method to model this would be to create a single table as follows:

```
CREATE OR REPLACE TABLE Comp_Score (
    Athlete_id        NUMBER,
```

```
Athlete_Name         VARCHAR2(20),
Score_1              NUMBER,
Score_2              NUMBER,
Score_3              NUMBER);
```

This option requires only one table but it is relationally messy. Another consideration would be to displace the scores to another table and normalize the schema. This alternative is most frequently implemented in a pure relational environment. With the addition of new data types and constructs in Oracle8, it makes more sense to utilize a **VARRAY** in this particular case, as follows:

```
CREATE OR REPLACE TYPE
   Scores AS varray(3) of NUMBER(3);

CREATE OR REPLACE TABLE Comp_Score (
   Athlete_id        NUMBER,
   Athlete_Name      VARCHAR2(20),
   Ath_Score         Scores);
```

As you can see, use of database extensions is a means to streamline design and functionality and not an overt attempt to wreck the clean structure of a properly normalized database. At this point, it would be appropriate to consider some advantages and disadvantages of this approach.

The primary advantage of implementing repeating groups is a gain in performance. Data from repeating groups is available when the table row is fetched without the use of a table join as is done in previous versions of the database. Because additional tables are not created, there is a realized reduction in the use of disk space. One of the disadvantages of the repeating groups (particularly **VARRAY**s) is that the entire set of data cannot be retrieved as is possible in a conventional table. Another disadvantage of repeating groups is that it is not possible to tell which data cells can be null until they have been checked individually.

Consider also that aggregate entities comprised wholly of pointers to nested tables and VARRAYs might also be implemented to resolve many-to-many relationships. For example, consider the relationship between a student, his many classes, and the corresponding grades earned in each of those classes. Each student attends several classes in a term. Some students enroll in more and some enroll in less. For each class, a set of grades is given out during the term that must be tracked in order to determine the student's performance. Traditionally, we resolve such many-to-many relationships with an associative entity. In Chapter 5 we will present a more detailed discussion on pointers and the data constructs that use them.

In the final analysis, use of non-first normal form becomes an effective means of modeling repeating data groups. Use of this functionality must be weighed against the particular disadvantages, namely, the lack of accessibility to set data outside of the controlling table or construct. Because **VARRAY**s and nested tables obviate the need for foreign keys, the overall impact on the database design should be considered carefully.

Summary

In this chapter, we compared the relational and object-oriented meta-models. The result of this comparison was the formulation of a viable database object model that incorporates the best features of both methodologies while sacrificing none of the features of the relational paradigm. We examined the derived benefits of the new approach to database modeling, and we discussed the first of the new object-oriented extensions, namely **VARRAY**s and nested tables. Finally, we explored the idea of non-first normal form and how it impacts everyday implementations. In Chapter 4, we will begin a detailed discussion of user-defined data types. We will also discuss other data types, such as large objects (**LOB**s), and we will address how to plan a hierarchy of data types.

HIGH PERFORMANCE

Modeling For Oracle Supported Data Types

CHAPTER 4

HIGH PERFORMANCE

Beauty is no quality in things themselves. It exists merely in the mind which contemplates them.
—David Hume

Modeling For Oracle Supported Data Types

Oracle8 has catapulted database design and development to the next level of the evolutionary database chain with the introduction of the object-relational paradigm. The change that accompanies any shift in thought or approach has not escaped the discipline of database design. As you saw in Chapter 3, new features require new ways to incorporate them into the whole. A pure relational modeling approach is no longer adequate, and so, the concept of the database object model was born.

The new Oracle8 extensions give database designers a whole new freedom to create data types that are limited only by the resourcefulness of the designer. This is not to say that structure has given way to creativity. From outward appearances, it seems that concepts like *rapid application development* should move to the forefront of database design now that database development resembles the behavior of object-oriented languages. On the contrary, the demand for a structured method is now greater because there are now many ways to do the same thing (and every way will not be the ideal way). Database designers must maintain their discipline to adhere to a structured methodology and not drift into ad hoc development.

Maintenance and performance of a database can be affected in a variety of ways based on the selection of data type constructs. As you will see later in this chapter, two or more data constructs can be used to solve the same problem but one might be more advantageous than the other due to access requirements or performance considerations. There will be a temptation to utilize the object extensions at every opportunity because, let's face it, they're new. The database designer must prudently consider the appropriateness of each construct and exercise some restraint. The responsibility of discernment now rests with the database designer who must correctly decide the best implementation for the circumstances at hand.

In this chapter, we will take a closer look at the data type mechanisms now available in Oracle8. The types from previous releases are still here, some with extended functionality. The data types of greatest interest, however, are the user-defined variety. Although Large Objects are not user-defined data types, a detailed discussion of their makeup is presented due to their importance in future development efforts. A great deal of the design talk, covered up until now, centers on how these new constructs are dealt with. In the sections that follow, we will focus on what user-defined data types are and how they are used.

Oracle Supported Data Types

Categorically, the Oracle8 database provides support for two distinct types of data: built-in and user defined. Previous releases of Oracle only included the first type. The introduction of user-defined data types opens the way for design constructs that were previously impossible. Taking advantage of user-defined data types allows database designers to develop a data type hierarchy, which is described later in this chapter. Object types are supported through the use of several constructs very similar to the standard relational types. For example, object tables and object views are very nearly the same as relational tables and views with the exception that they support user-defined data types. Object tables and views are held to the same semantic standards for DML, DDL, and storage as their relational cousins. (See Figure 4.1.) To begin our discussion of Oracle supported data types, let's focus first on built-in data types.

Built-In Data Types

In any chapter describing data types, it is appropriate to discuss the standard data typing conventions. Oracle8 supports seven distinct built-in data types for use in column definitions. The built-in data types represent a superset of what was available in previous releases. If you are interested in pursuing greater detail on the mechanics of the Oracle built-ins, you should refer to the Oracle Documentation set. The seven built-in data type categories are as follows:

- Character
- Number

Modeling For Oracle Supported Data Types

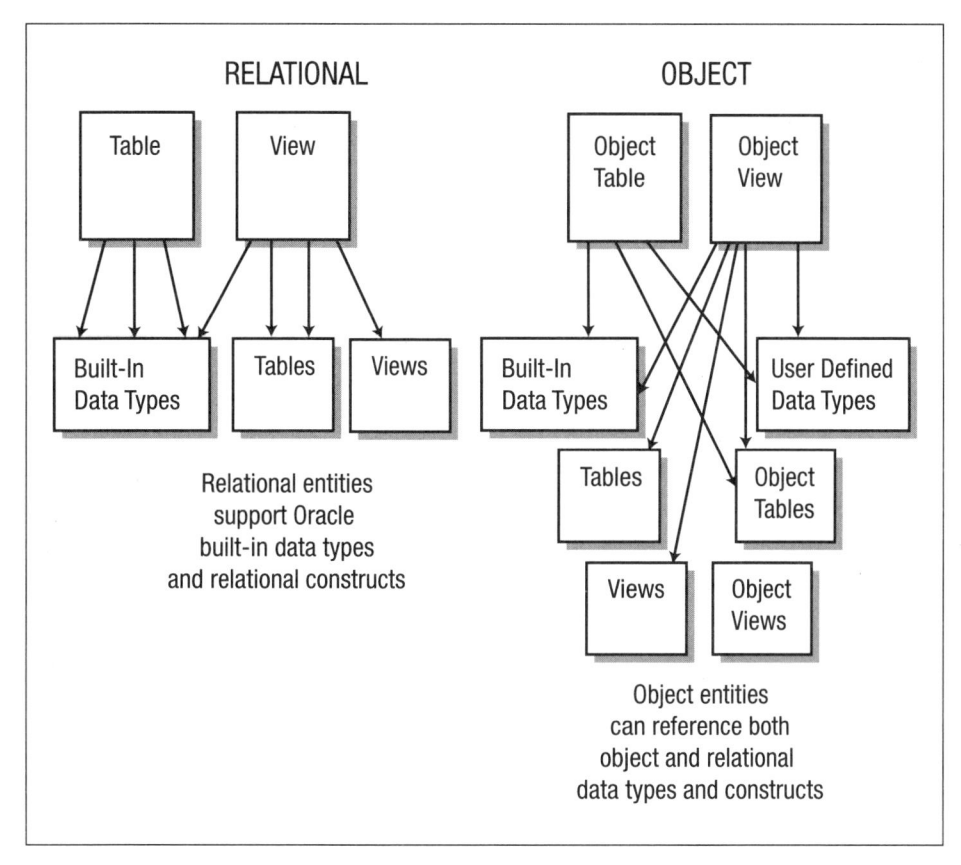

Figure 4.1
A comparison of object and relational tables and views.

- Date
- **RAW** and **LONG RAW**
- **ROWID**
- **MLSLABEL**
- Large Objects (**LOB**)

The character type is further broken into five subtypes, and the **LOB** category is broken into three subtypes. The upcoming sections present a discussion of each data type, starting with the character data type.

Character Data Types

Character data types are used for the storage of alphanumeric strings. This is the most commonly used data type and requires very little introduction. The five subtypes that comprise the data type character are:

- **CHAR**—This data type is used for fixed-length strings. Once a string length is specified at creation time, then the column will retain that length. Note that data added to a **CHAR** type column is padded with blanks if it is not the same as the specified length. For example, if you declare a column **NAME** to be **CHAR(20)** and you insert the name **Smith**, then 15 blanks will be appended to the end of the name string. The **CHAR** data type can be up to 2,000 bytes in length.

- **VARCHAR2**—This data type stores variable length character strings. It differs from the **CHAR** data type in that entries in a column are not blank padded. Therefore, if you add **Smith** to a **NAME** column declared as **VARCHAR2(20)**, you store only **Smith**. This is an important distinction to make. I have witnessed data retrieval problems at more than one client site that has combined the use of these two subtypes, not realizing that there is a semantic comparison difference. **VARCHAR2** data types are capable of storing up to 4,000 bytes of data.

- **VARCHAR**—Oracle has created this data type for use in future releases of the database. The current functionality is that of **VARCHAR2**, but developers are warned against using it in this way because its definition is subject to change.

- **NCHAR** and **NVARCHAR2**—These data types support Oracle's National Language Support (NLS) feature. NLS enables the conversion between different character sets of other languages. **NCHAR** and **NVARCHAR2** correspond to their **CHAR** and **VARCHAR2** counterparts. Storage limitations for **NCHAR** and **NVARCHAR2** are 2,000 and 4,000 bytes, respectively.

- **LONG**—This data type is variable in length and supports lengths of up to 2GB in Oracle8 databases. The **LONG** data type is intended for backward compatibility with older applications. New development efforts should utilize Large Objects (**LOBs**), which are described later.

Number Data Types

The number data type allows for the storage of both fixed and floating point numbers. Oracle supports up to 38 digits of precision. Columns can be defined as **NUMBER** types without specifying the scale or precision, for example:

```
AGE            NUMBER;
```

Precision refers to the number of significant digits, while the scale indicates the number of digits to the right of the decimal point. Let's look at the following two useful examples:

```
AMOUNT_PAID      NUMBER(9,2);
AVERAGE_TONS     NUMBER(10,-2);
```

In the first example, a typical input value might be stored as 4512836.11. In the second example, a negative scale causes the value to be rounded to the nearest hundred, so an input value of 4382247 would become 4382200.

Date Data Types

Date data types are for the storage of dates and times as the name suggests. Oracle is capable of storing date and time ranges from January 1, 4712 BC all the way through December 31, 4712 AD (Also referred to as CE, or Common Era. This is the default if nothing is specified in the format mask.). Typically, when date type data is input or output, the default format is **01-JAN-98**.

For every date entry, the year (and century), month, day, hour, minute, and second is stored in an internal format that can be accessed through the use of an appropriate format mask. As we approach the year 2000, it will make more sense to alter the format to reflect a four-digit year in order to resolve the discrepancy between the two centuries. The default date format can be changed for a database instance through the setting of the **NLS_DATE_FORMAT** parameter. Alternately, the format can be set for individual sessions with the **ALTER SESSION** command.

Oracle also supports the use of a Julian date calendar. Julian dates are a way of continuously tracking time by numbering the days in a sequential fashion from a given starting point. Oracle Julian dates start on January 1, 4712 BC. Other non-Oracle systems do not necessarily adopt the same starting point, so exercise caution if you are comparing Julian dates from multiple database sources.

With the approach of the year 2000, the date-format issues regarding time-based data cannot be disregarded. One need look no further than the major technical journals to recognize the impact that two digit year dates (e.g., YY) will have on data processing in the very near future. Although Oracle has anticipated this issue by devising a means to seamlessly transition the internal mechanism to go from 1999 to

2000 with two digit year groups, the transition will not be as simple for the users of your applications.

Consider for a moment a data entry system where date columns are a vital part of what is entered by your users. Let's assume that the two digit year format has remained. Oracle will recognize the difference in time but what if the user must enter a date for 1999? Will the user be confident that they have entered 1999 or fear that their entry will become 2099? The wise thing to do is implement a four-digit year format. Oracle accommodates this through the setting of the **nls_date_format** parameter. The **nls_date_format** will accept one of three settings:

- DD-MON-YYYY—This indicates that four-digit years are required for data entry and querying.
- DD-MON-YY—This indicates that two-digit years are used for query and data storage where the current century is prefixed to the year digits.
- DD-MON-RR—This indicates that two-year digits are used, but the century 19 is prefixed for year digits ending in 50 through 99, while the century 20 is prefixed to those ending in 00 through 49.

RAW And LONG RAW Data Types

Much like the **LONG** character data type described earlier, **RAW** and **LONG RAW** data types are provided for backward compatibility with existing systems. These too, should be replaced with Large Objects. **RAW** and **LONG RAW** are intended for use with binary and byte string data, such as graphics, sound clips, video, and other data of that nature. **RAW** is variable in length, similar to the **VARCHAR2** data type. **LONG RAW** data cannot be indexed, but **RAW** data can.

ROWID Data Type

ROWID data types are used for the unique identification of each row of data in a non-clustered table. In a clustered table environment, it is possible for rows in different tables residing in the same data block to have the same **ROWID**. **ROWID**s are not actual columns in a database, but are considered *pseudocolumns*.

Oracle8 provides for the use of two **ROWID** constructs. The standard convention is the use of the extended **ROWID**, which internally records the data object number, the data file, data block, and row. Restricted **ROWID**s are a binary representation of the data row's physical address and contain the following information: data block, row, and data file. Restricted **ROWID**s are intended for backward compatibility to prior versions of Oracle. **ROWID**s are used by Oracle to build indexes where each key is associated with a **ROWID** pointing to the row's address. Figure 4.2 illustrates the two types of **ROWID** constructs.

Of particular interest to database designers and developers is the behavior of **ROWID**s. **ROWID**s do not change unless a row is exported and imported, or if a row is deleted. If a row is deleted, the **ROWID** is recovered and available for use again on another row. It is not possible to change the value of the **ROWID** through the use of DML statements (**INSERT** and **UPDATE**) nor can you delete the value of a **ROWID**. It is possible to create tables with columns defined as data type **ROWID**. **ROWID**s

Restricted Row IDs used for backward compatibility

Row ID

00000AB4	0005	0002
Data Block	Row	Data File

In hexadecimal notation

Extended Row IDs for use in Oracle 8

Row ID

AABA8A	AAE	BAABAA	AAC
Data Object Number	Data File	Data Block	Row

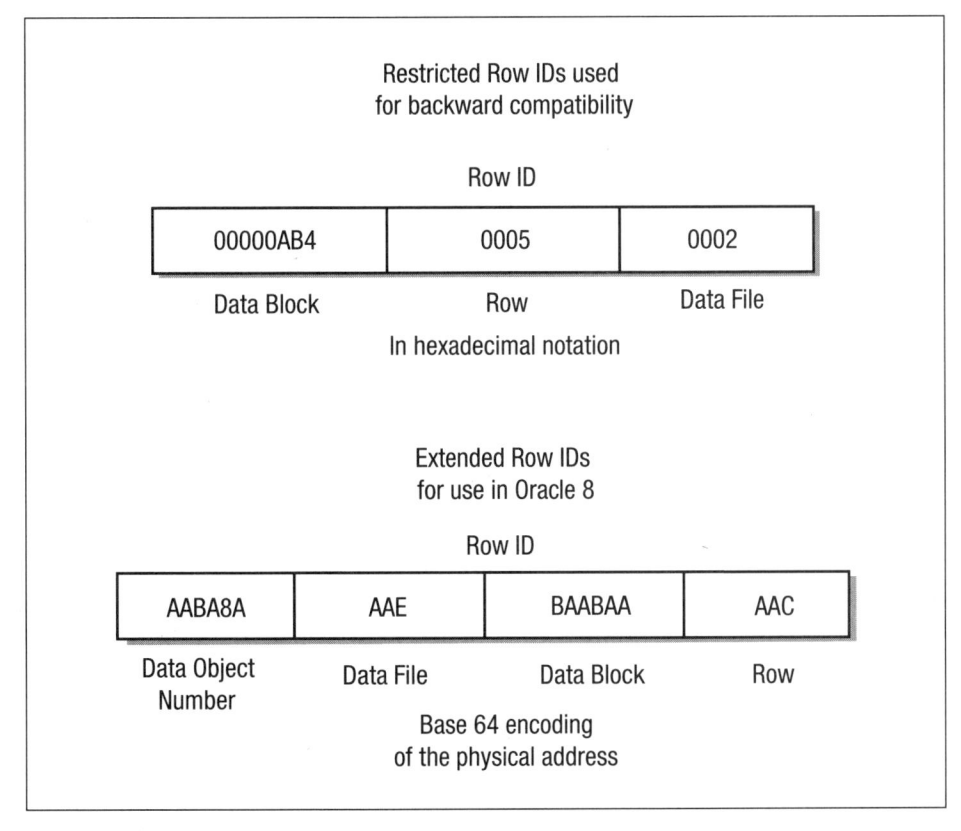

Base 64 encoding of the physical address

Figure 4.2
A comparison of restricted and extended **ROWID** constructs.

can be useful because they provide fast access, show table organization, and represent a unique identifier for rows in a specific table. Developers can utilize **ROWID**s in their SQL statements, but care should be exercised to ensure that values will not change. Any attempt to access an invalid **ROWID** results in an error. If you execute DML statements using **ROWID**s, the intended rows should be locked so other actions performed on the same table do not circumvent the process in question.

MLSLABEL Data Type

MLSLABEL is used with Trusted Oracle and represents iterations of labels in multi-level secure operating systems. Labels are used to control database access, much like Access Control Lists (ACLs) in OpenVMS and privilege classes in IBM systems. (ACLs and privilege classes are used to compartmentalize individual user access to directories and files.) Every row in a table created in Trusted Oracle receives an appended column called *ROWLABEL*, which is of type **MLSLABEL**. **MLSLABEL** data type columns can be created in Oracle8 for compatibility with Trusted Oracle, but the only valid value accepted in the Oracle8 schema is **NULL**.

Large Objects (LOBs)

We will give the topic of Large Objects greater attention than the other built-in data types for two reasons. First, as technology and its implementation moves toward greater use of multimedia, the demand for accessing and storing video, sound, and other objects will increase. The second reason for giving **LOBs** special attention is because, as a category, developers have less experience and understanding of this data construct than any other. It is important to note that **LOBs** replace the older **LONG**, **RAW**, and **LONG RAW** data type constructs. For this reason, we will discuss the specifics of what **LOBs** are, how they are used, and how to integrate them into a database application.

LOBs can be categorized into two types: internal and external. Internal **LOBs** are objects that are physically stored in a database. **LOBs** stored in the database are subject to the same conditions as other object types. For example, a **LOB** data type can be updated, selected, and so forth, much as a **VARCHAR2** or **NUMBER** data type. Internal **LOBs** come in the following three varieties:

- **BLOB**—This **LOB** subtype contains values composed of raw or unstructured binary data.

Modeling For Oracle Supported Data Types

- **CLOB**—This **LOB** subtype contains values composed of single-byte fixed-width character data corresponding to the character set used in the database.
- **NCLOB**—This **LOB** subtype contains values having fixed-width multibyte character data that corresponds to the NLS character set defined in the Oracle8 database. Figure 4.3 shows the implementation of internal and external **LOB**s.

Note that none of the aforementioned subtypes support varying width character data. It is possible to store varying width characters in a **BLOB**, but this requires the

INTERNAL LOBs
- BLOB
- CLOB
- NCLOB

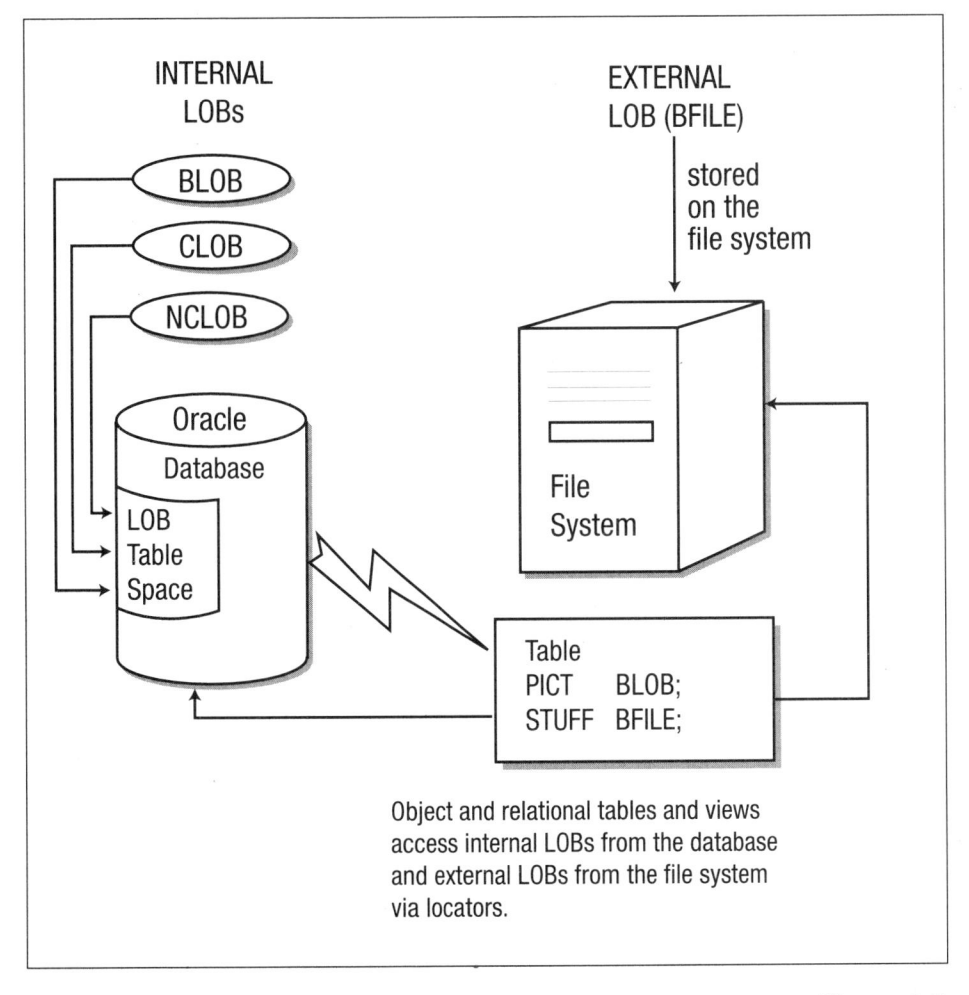

Oracle Database
LOB Table Space

EXTERNAL LOB (BFILE)
stored on the file system

File System

Table
PICT   BLOB;
STUFF   BFILE;

Object and relational tables and views access internal LOBs from the database and external LOBs from the file system via locators.

Figure 4.3
Internal and external **LOB**s.

user to perform the character set conversion manually. This technique is not recommended by Oracle because the offset and amount parameters are measured in bytes rather than characters. In such a situation, it is possible to retrieve the text from a **BLOB** and inadvertently cut a varying character width in half, thus getting an erroneous return. **BFILEs** (described in detail later in this chapter) can also be used to store text data, but the same conversion problems apply here as well.

Should it become necessary to convert **LONG** data to a **LOB** data type, the following steps are suggested:

1. Create a table with at least one column defined as a **LOB** data type.
2. Write the **LONG** data to a file on the server.
3. Use the **CREATE DIRECTORY** command to specify the location of the **LONG** data file.
4. Use one of the following two commands to populate the new LOB with the data file:
   - **OCILobLoadFromFile()**
   - **DBMS_LOB.LOADFROMFILE()**

Keep in mind that there is no loader support for **LOBs**; therefore, these two built-ins are the only mechanisms available to perform such an operation.

Oracle provides two methods for the manipulation of both internal and external **LOBs**: Oracle Call Interface (OCI) and PL/SQL built-ins DBMS_LOB. A detailed discussion of either method is too lengthy to present here. If you wish to seek a greater understanding of these utilities, you should consult Oracle's documentation.

Internal **LOBs** must be stored in tables. That is, a table must be created with at least one column data type defined as a **LOB**. Table columns originally defined as **LONG** cannot be redefined as **LOBs**. Internal **LOBs** should be stored in a tablespace apart from the data. If the system being built contains relatively active **LOBs** (both internal and external), then frequently accessed **LOBs** should be divided into different tablespaces to reduce device contention.

An **LOB** index is an Oracle internal structure closely associated with the storage of **LOBs**. Users are highly encouraged to fully specify storage parameters when defining **LOBs**, because the system might default to settings which are neither advantageous

Modeling For Oracle Supported Data Types

nor desirable. For example, the following list illustrates how the system performs allocation in the absence of direct instruction:

- If a tablespace is not specified for the **LOB** data or index, then the tablespace of the **LOB**'s host table will be used for both.
- If a tablespace is designated for the **LOB** data but not the index, then both will be placed in the tablespace set aside for the **LOB** data.
- If a tablespace is designated for the **LOB** index but not the **LOB** data, then the index will be placed as directed, but the **LOB** data will be located in the tablespace of the **LOB**'s host table.

Internal **LOB**s are initialized prior to use by creating the table host and setting the **LOB** column to be empty. Empty **LOB**s have zero length and are not to be confused with having a **NULL** value. External **LOB**s are created as attributes in an object type and can be initialized with a **NULL** value. In either case, accessing the host table yields a locator, which, in turn, can be used to populate the **LOB** with data by utilizing the OCI or DBMS_LOB programs. A sample initialization appears as follows:

```
CREATE TABLE Candidate_bio (
    Candidate_id       NUMBER,
    Resume             BLOB,
    Photo              BFILE);

INSERT INTO Candidate_bio VALUES (
    1000, EMPTY_BLOB(), NULL);
```

When a **SELECT** command is issued to retrieve a **LOB**, Oracle responds by returning a locator for the **LOB** rather than the actual value. The locator is generally passed into a PL/SQL variable that can then be used with the OCI or DBMS_LOB routines to perform various functions on the **LOB**. For example, consider the following code segment where a **BLOB** is read using the DBMS_LOB utility:

```
PROCEDURE read_blob IS
    blob_loc           BLOB;
    buffer             RAW;
    amount             BINARY_INTEGER := 32767;
    offset             INTEGER := 2147483647;

BEGIN
    SELECT Resume INTO blob_loc
```

```
   FROM      Candidate_bio
   WHERE     Candidate_id = 12;

   LOOP
      DBMS_LOB.READ ( blob_loc, amount, offset, buffer );
      offset := offset + amount;
   END LOOP;

   EXCEPTION
      WHEN NO_DATA_FOUND THEN
         DBMS_OUTPUT.PUT_LINE (' That's all there is.');
END;
```

In this example, you can see that the **LOB** (in this case a **BLOB**) is retrieved into the variable **blob_loc** by iteratively retrieving portions of the object via the **DBMS_LOB.READ** routine. The **buffer**, **amount**, and **offset** variables represent the size of the buffer, the amount to be fetched at each iteration, and the offset position for each retrieval, respectively.

Other operations are also possible, such as determining the length of the **LOB**, appending two **LOB**s together, copying one **LOB** to another, erasing, loading, trimming, and more.

> **Note:** *If an internal **LOB** value has been modified through the locator via the use of OCI, DBMS_LOB, or DML commands, then the locator moves from being a read-consistent locator to one that is updated. These activities automatically start transactions that lock the row. At this point, the locator can no longer be used outside the current transaction. The moral of the story is that **LOB** locators cannot span transactions.*

Only one external **LOB** type is currently defined: **BFILE**. **BFILE**s are composed of binary or raw data stored in a server-side operating system file. External **LOB**s do not manifest themselves as columns in a table but, rather, as attributes of an object type that must be referenced. Unlike internal **LOB**s, the file system hosting the external **LOB** must enforce integrity and durability. Single external **LOB**s cannot extend from one device to another. In other words, the entire **BFILE** must remain contiguous in one location on the file server. **BFILE**s are read-only and are, therefore, not updateable through conventional SQL and PL/SQL commands.

Referring to the earlier example on **LOB** initialization, the following statements are needed to set up the external **LOB**:

```
CREATE DIRECTORY cand_image AS '/usr/home/candidates/photos'

CREATE TABLE Candidate_bio (
   Candidate_id        NUMBER,
   Resume              BLOB,
   Photo               BFILE);

INSERT INTO Candidate_bio VALUES (
   1000, EMPTY_BLOB(),
   BFILENAME ('cand_image', 'Jones.jpg'));
```

Note in this example that the **CREATE DIRECTORY** command is implemented first. In order to link an operating system file with the attribute of type **BFILE**, it is necessary to first create a **DIRECTORY** object. The **DIRECTORY** object administers the access of **BFILE** data types in Oracle8. **DIRECTORY** serves as an alias for the physical directory on the host server where the binary file is located and names the file to be used. Use of the **DIRECTORY** object obviates the need for any hard coding of directory paths. Conveniently, file location references can be changed from this object without affecting application logic used in the retrieval of the **BFILE**. It is important to note that the directory object name defaults to uppercase, unless the name is enclosed in quotes (in which case, it will retain its case sensitivity). Because **DIRECTORY** is a system-owned object, users intending to use it must have two new system-level privileges:

- CREATE ANY DIRECTORY
- DROP ANY DIRECTORY

> **Note:** Because of the reference-based nature of **BFILE** assignment, it is possible for more than one **BFILE** column to reference the same file. This is the case even when the columns reside in the same record.

Two important points need to be emphasized in the use of the **DIRECTORY** object. First, never map a **DIRECTORY** object to the same location as Oracle data files, control files, log files, or other system files. Inadvertent damage to any of these files could lead to database or operating system corruption. Second, never drop

DIRECTORY objects while the database is in operation because any OCI and DBMS_LOB routines from any active sessions will fail. If this should happen, system resources from these files will not be released until the sessions in question are shut down.

Now that we have reviewed the built-in data types supported by Oracle8, let's move on to the newest and perhaps most interesting of all, the user-defined data types.

User-Defined Data Types (ADTs)

User-defined data types, or ADTs, are provided with the Objects Option for Oracle8. They are not included as part of the baseline product but are considered an add-on functionality in the current version. ADTs allow for the definition of objects that model structure and behavior beyond the conventional Oracle built-in data types. *Methods*, which represent the behavior aspect of ADTs, represent a new dimension in data type functionality and are covered in Chapter 6.

User defined data types can store structured business data without decomposing it to the most atomic level. This ability represents a value-added feature because database objects will now share a similar modularity as constructs used in 4GL languages, like C++. The important concept here is that abstraction can be actively used in the design of data constructs. By incorporating data abstraction into the design of database elements, the atomic-level complexities of a database's organization and behavior can remain hidden. The design and coding effort will become more refined as new data objects incorporate other user-defined data types into their structures. For example, if you create a data type of **CHEMICAL_PROCESS** used to store various pieces of data pertaining to the manufacture of fertilizer, it, in turn, can be constructed of additional data types such as **VARRAY**s that control the manufacture sequence. (See Figure 4.4.)

User-defined data types can be divided into two categories—object types and collection types—both of which are described in this section. User-defined data types are schema objects, much like their brethren built-ins except that their structure and behavior (via the use of methods) can be defined by the developer. User-defined data types support the development of complex data models because the business functions can be constructed intact while retaining the declarative behavior of the relational database. For example, assume that a company has adopted a complex pricing structure for its products. Because of the way sales are negotiated, it is possible for a

Modeling For Oracle Supported Data Types

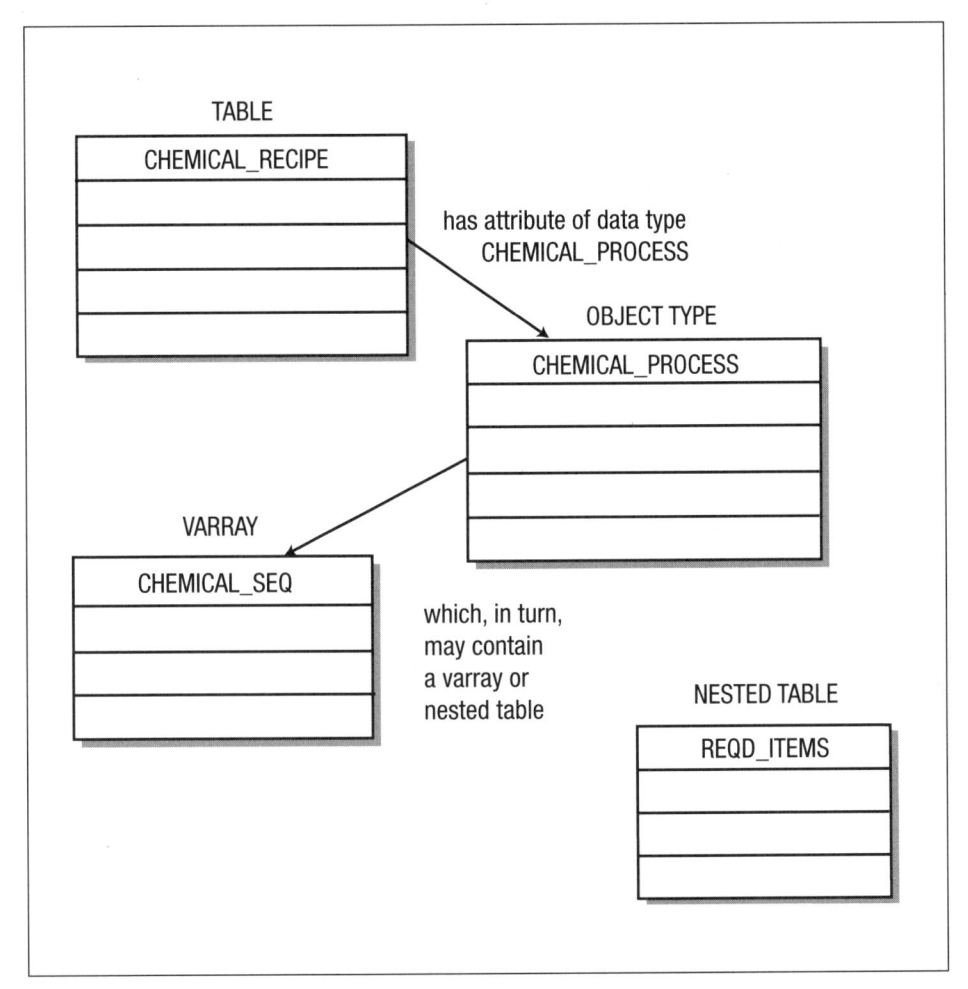

Figure 4.4
The concept of data type abstraction in a table.

single sale to have more than one discounting structure applied. By incorporating the pricing structure in an object table, the data and its behavior (in this case, the business rules governing the application of discounts) is stored in one convenient database object. Furthermore, by exercising this kind of abstraction in the data object, the server is able to support the client request in a single retrieval, thus reducing transmission traffic and improving performance.

The complex structure of user-defined data types is hidden from users by Oracle's internal mechanisms. Data from user-defined data types is stored in tables, and the database system automatically maps these constructs into the simpler relational table constructs familiar to users.

Object types are structured similarly to a tree. The lowest level nodes, known as *leaf-level attributes*, are the most atomic level (where no further decomposition takes place). The next branch up consists of user-defined data types and collections comprised of leaf-level attributes. Finally, object tables are constructed of built-in and user-defined data types. For each data type, down to and including the leaf-level attribute, Oracle creates a table column. Figure 4.5 depicts a representation of this architecture.

When a leaf-level attribute exists outside of a collection, it is considered a *leaf-level scalar attribute*. The actual data from leaf-level scalar attributes and **REF** objects (**REF**s will be covered in Chapter 5) are stored in a column in the object table. This rule is also true for **VARRAY**s of less than 4,000 bytes in size. Now that we have provided a brief introduction to the user-defined data type, we will move the discussion on to object types.

Object Types

Object types created in Oracle8 represent abstractions of real world entities. Object types are considered templates for objects that internalize their structure. An object

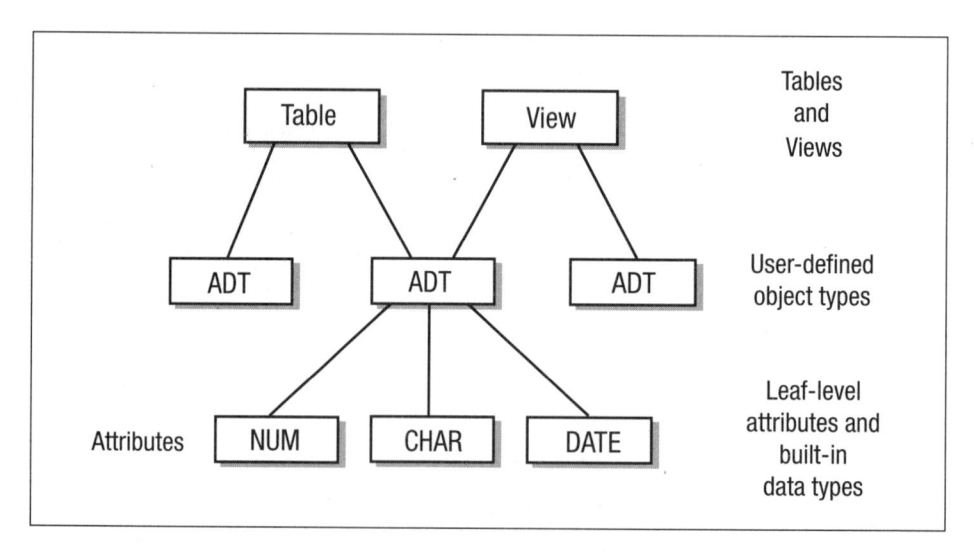

Figure 4.5
A graphical depiction of the tree-like structure for data storage.

type can be defined and created once and utilized by many objects. All object types are composed of three distinct components:

- *Name*—Uniquely identifies an object.
- *Attribute*—Defines the nature of the entity being modeled. Attributes are comprised of Oracle built-in data types and/or user-defined data types.
- *Method*—Dictates the behavior of an object. Methods can be composed of PL/SQL program units stored in the database or C programs stored externally in the file system.

Creation of a typical data type might start out like this:

```
CREATE TYPE Chemical_t;
CREATE TYPE Buyer_address_t;
```

At this point, no further definition is provided. Oracle considers these declarations incomplete object types. Incomplete declarations are allowed and indicate to the database that complete definitions will follow. Such an approach is useful when details about a data type have not been finalized but other constructs depend on the incomplete declarations in order to compile correctly. In the next code snippet, the data type definition is completed:

```
CREATE TYPE Buyer_address_t AS OBJECT (
    Address_id      NUMBER,
    Buyer_name      VARCHAR2(30),
    Address_ship    Address_t
    );
```

Note from the preceding example that the attribute **Address_ship** is declared as a user-defined data type. The data type **Address_t** could be declared as follows:

```
CREATE TYPE Address_t AS OBJECT (
    Address1        VARCHAR2(30),
    Address2        VARCHAR2(30),
    Address3        VARCHAR2(30),
    City            VARCHAR2(20),
    State           VARCHAR2(2),
    Zip             NUMBER(5)
    );
```

As you will see, one distinction between object types and collection constructs (**VARRAY**s and nested tables) is that collection constructs are limited by the object types that they can contain, whereas basic object types are not. In the next section, we will discuss a data type that was briefly introduced in the previous chapter—collection types.

Collection Types

Collection types are introduced briefly in Chapter 3 as **VARRAY**s and nested tables. You might recall from that discussion that both describe a data unit made up of an indefinite number of elements, each of the same data type. Collection types are similar to arrays except that collections can have only one dimension. Third-generation languages, such as Pascal, allow for multiple dimensions indexed by various enumeration types, while collections must index by integer. Collections can be passed as parameters, so they can act as the vehicle for moving data between the database and client-side programs.

VARRAYs are single dimension arrays of fixed length. Let's assume for a moment that you wish to store a data type called *RECIPE_STEPS* as a **VARRAY**. The statement to create such an object might appear like this:

```
CREATE TYPE Recipe_steps_t AS VARRAY (10) OF VARCHAR2(50);
```

This declaration produces a data type element capable of storing 10 recipe steps.

On occasion, you might determine that a nested table would make a better choice of construct than a **VARRAY**. Here are some instances when this determination would make sense:

- When querying the contents of a line item that requires casting a **VARRAY** to a nested table in order to retrieve its entire contents. **VARRAY** cells are normally addressed directly by cell to obtain a specific piece of data.

- If indexing is required on a column containing the **VARRAY** data.

- If the user wishes to order the data based on the column value and not the order of the **VARRAY** cells.

- If the collection of data does not have a specified upper boundary (a defined set of elements) and the data requirements remain indeterminate.

Note also the minor distinction between the creation of an object table and a nested table. In an earlier example, we showed that a typical **CREATE** statement for an object table might appear like this:

```
CREATE  TABLE address OF Address_t;
```

The same **CREATE** statement for a nested table, however, would appear as follows:

```
CREATE  TYPE address_list_t AS TABLE OF Address_t;
```

Each row of the nested table would contain one instance of **Address_t**. Compare this to the object table that also has one row containing an instance of **Address_t**. The difference is that the nested table is linked to a column in another table whereas the object table is a standalone entity.

Nested tables are placed in store tables that must be specified in the **CREATE TABLE** command for each nested table type used. The syntax for this appears as follows:

```
CREATE OR REPLACE TABLE Recipe_List  of Recipe_list_t
   nested table Ingredients_t store as
    Ingredients_List_tbl;
```

Table 4.1 shows a comparison of **VARRAY**s and nested tables.

Now that we have discussed collection types, we will move on to the next type of construct—the object table.

Object Tables

Object tables are special tables that hold objects while providing a relational view of those objects' attributes. Attributes in an object table are composed of top-level

Table 4.1 The differences between **VARRAY**s and nested tables.

Property	VARRAY	Nested Table
Maximum size	Yes	No
Delete individual elements	No	Yes
Data storage	In-line	Out-of-line
Retain ordering and subscripts	Yes	No

attributes of a particular type. For example, an object table might have attributes defined as object types like **Address_t** (created in the previous example)

```
CREATE TABLE address OF Address_t;
```

by introducing

```
CREATE TABLE address OF Address_t
   (Address_id   PRIMARY KEY);
```

to the object table declaration. Here, a constraint is implied on the table and not on the objects of **Address_t**.

> **Note:** *Constraints apply only to tables and not to data type definitions.*

In this case, an object table 'address' is created, holding address objects of type **Address_t**. Every row in the object table will contain an instance of **Address_t**, and each instance is given a unique object identifier (OID). OIDs are discussed in greater detail in Chapter 5. Figure 4.6 illustrates this interesting correspondence between the object table and its contents.

Object tables comprise one of two basic constructs that enable the object-relational approach to resolving the association between relational entities and user-defined data types. We began this section by introducing the object type.

It is important to note that certain dependencies exist between object tables and the object types that they reference. In PL/SQL programming, if a package with a dependency to an outside program unit loses its relationship to an external program by means of alteration or deletion, then the package will not run. Similarly, a parallel behavior exists between object tables and the object types that they reference. Here are a few points to keep in mind regarding this dependency:

- If a type definition used by an object table is changed, then the data in the table becomes inaccessible. Actions that cause this behavior include the loss of privileges required by the data type or a dropped data type that the data type in question relies on.

- An invalidated table resulting from missing privileges will automatically regain its validity if the required privileges are reinstated.

MODELING FOR ORACLE SUPPORTED DATA TYPES

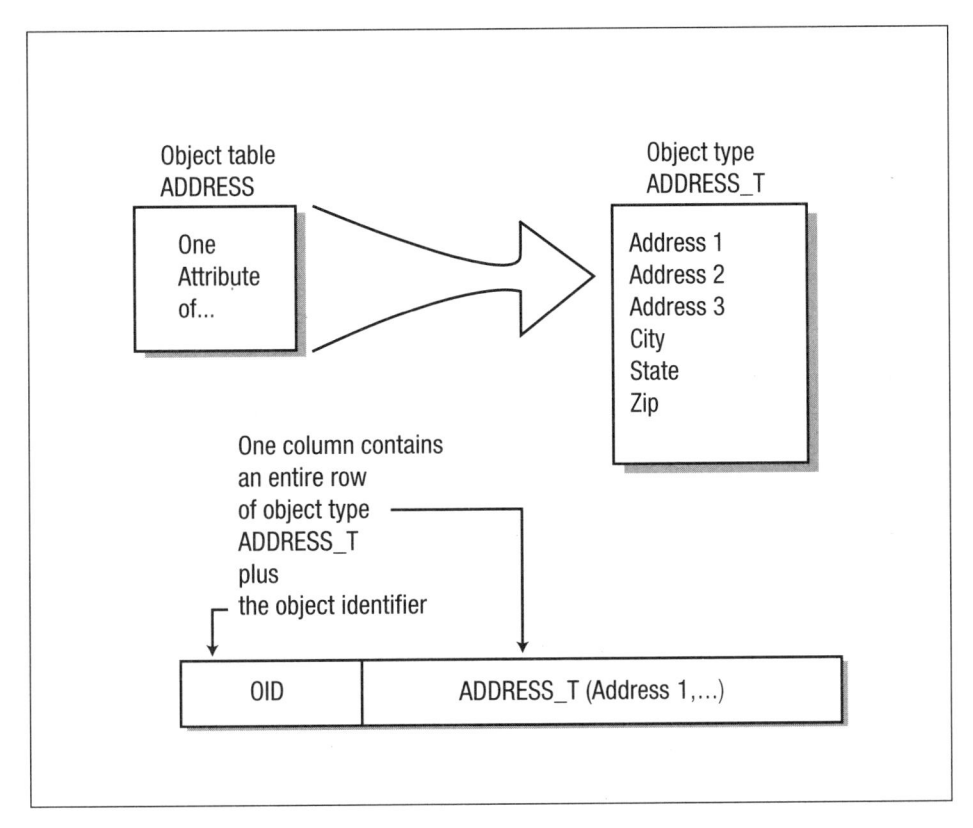

Figure 4.6
An object table and its contents.

- A table that is invalid because of its dependency to a type that has been dropped cannot be accessed again. The table must be dropped and recreated.

- If a user attempts to execute **REVOKE** or **DROP TYPE** against a data type that other objects depend on, then the command will return an error and terminate. Using the **FORCE** option on either command will override the error, but the affected object types will no longer be valid.

These points can become painfully apparent during the build phase when a change to a data construct inadvertently invalidates a series of dependent objects in the database. This shows the importance of good configuration management and structured design technique. Now that we have introduced the object table, we will next discuss the object view, which has many similarities to the object table.

Object Views

Object views can be thought of much like conventional views. Just as relational views are a virtual representation of one or more tables, object views are a virtual representation of one or more object tables. As an extension of the view functionality, object views become a virtual object table of built-in and user-defined data types from relational and object tables in the database. For example, an object view might contain attributes of type **NUMBER**, **VARCHAR2**, and an assortment of user-defined data types gathered from one or more relational and object tables. Object views can even be created from other object views. Object views are extremely useful in situations where a data conversion effort is planned from pure relational to object-relational, and the team wishes to employ a gradual migration strategy. They are also effective in the employment of legacy relational data with newer object-oriented applications. In this situation, an object view will allow the development team to experiment with various object-oriented programming efforts without actually converting any of the existing data. Figure 4.7 illustrates the versatile nature of the object view.

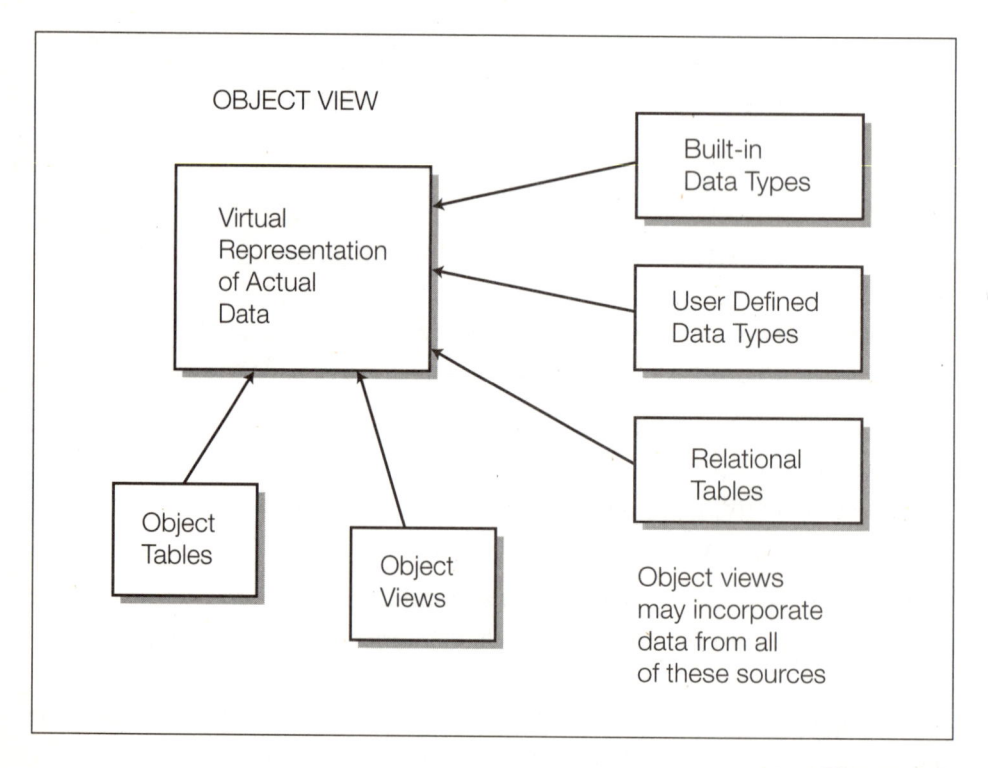

Figure 4.7
An object view.

MODELING FOR ORACLE SUPPORTED DATA TYPES

As noted earlier in this chapter, data for an object view can originate from multiple sources. Object views provide the ability to restrict access to data that is not appropriate to all users of the system by screening out particular columns. Deletions are not possible from the view without the creation of an **INSTEAD OF** trigger, so data is protected from accidental or intentional misuse. The coding steps for creating an object view are demonstrated in the following code:

```
CREATE OR REPLACE TABLE Customer_address (
    Address_id      NUMBER;
    Address1        VARCHAR2(30),
    Address2        VARCHAR2(30),
    Address3        VARCHAR2(30),
    City            VARCHAR2(20),
    State           VARCHAR2(2),
    Zip             NUMBER(5)
    );

CREATE TYPE Address_t AS OBJECT (
    Address_id      NUMBER;
    Address1        VARCHAR2(30),
    Address2        VARCHAR2(30),
    Address3        VARCHAR2(30),
    City            VARCHAR2(20),
    State           VARCHAR2(2),
    Zip             NUMBER(5)
    );

CREATE VIEW Cust_addr_view OF Address_t
    WITH OBJECT OID (Address_id) AS
    SELECT   c.Address_id, c.Address1,
                c.Address2, c.Address3, c.City,
                c.State, c.Zip
    FROM     Customer_address c
    WHERE    c.zip <= 40000;
```

Notice in the last **CREATE** statement that the **WITH OBJECT OID** option is exercised. This specification indicates to Oracle that the object identifier corresponds to the primary key of the **CUSTOMER_ADDRESS** table. Keep in mind that the specification of an object identifier in an object view must reference a unique data item, such as a unique or primary key. In addition, any column addressed in the **WITH OBJECT OID** clause must also be an attribute of the referenced object type—in this example—data type **Address_t**. If the object view involves a join of two or more tables, then it is incumbent on the user to specify the key to be used as the unique identifier for the view.

Join views are not updateable, nor are single table views updateable if they have set operators or group functions. To get around this problem, Oracle has introduced the **INSTEAD OF** trigger. The **INSTEAD OF** trigger replaces the standard functionality of a DML statement. When an **INSERT**, **UPDATE**, or **DELETE** is executed against the object view, the trigger replaces the DML statement behind the scenes. For example, look at the following code:

```
CREATE OR REPLACE TRIGGER
   Cust_addr_view_insert_tr INSTEAD OF INSERT ON Cust_addr_view

BEGIN
   INSERT INTO Customer_address VALUES (
      :NEW.Address_id,
      :NEW.Address1,
      :NEW.Address2,
      :NEW.Address3,
      :NEW.City,
      :NEW.State,
      :NEW.Zip );
END;
```

This example is somewhat simple in nature, but it adequately illustrates the use of the **INSTEAD OF** trigger. Specific triggers are also required for **UPDATE** and **DELETE** operations. Keep in mind that the trigger code can be taken to fairly sophisticated levels when the object view is a representation of complex user-defined data types and collections. For example, if one of the attributes happens to be of type **VARRAY**, then a loop must be constructed to update the appropriate entry as follows:

```
CREATE OR REPLACE TRIGGER
   Recipe_view_insert_tr INSTEAD OF INSERT ON Recipe_view
DECLARE
   Recipe_list    recipe_list_t;
   tIngredient1 Recipe_steps.Ingredient1%TYPE := NULL;
   tIngredient2 Recipe_steps.Ingredient2%TYPE := NULL;
   tIngredient3 Recipe_steps.Ingredient3%TYPE := NULL;
BEGIN
   IF Recipe_list.COUNT = 1 THEN
      tIngredient1 := Recipe_list(1);
END IF;
```

```
IF Recipe_list.COUNT = 2 THEN
     tIngredient2 := Recipe_list(2);
END IF;

IF Recipe_list.COUNT = 3 THEN
     tIngredient3 := Recipe_list(3);
END IF;

INSERT INTO Recipe_steps VALUES (
   :NEW.Recipe_id, :NEW.Recipe_name,
   tIngredient1, tIngredient2, tIngredient3);
END;
```

In this case, the appropriate ingredient of the fertilizer recipe is evaluated to ensure that the proper value in the **VARRAY** is updated or entered. Now that we have discussed the various user-defined data types, let's move on to an example to illustrate how some of them might be used.

The Consult-Rite Example

To illustrate some of the material we have just covered dealing with various data types, this section examines a hypothetical recruitment database for the Consult-Rite Corporation. Recruiters are a concept that most Oracle developers can relate to, in one way or another.

Consult-Rite wishes to create a database of all its candidates such that any recruiter can query an individual's personal information, a copy of their resume, and a photo. The personal information will be entered manually at the time a candidate is recruited. The resume will be scanned and stored on the system, making it accessible whenever a candidate's biography screen is displayed. Finally, a photo of each candidate will appear on the screen to help familiarize the recruiter with each candidate. Figure 4.8 illustrates the Consult-Rite database application.

The first step is to determine the data structures that will be used. Let's assume that a proper analysis of the problem has been conducted, and the process is moving into design. The basic biographical data is easily captured in the following tables:

```
CREATE TYPE Address_list_t AS OBJECT (
   Address_id       NUMBER;
   Address1         VARCHAR2(30),
   Address2         VARCHAR2(30),
```

```
    Address3        VARCHAR2(30),
    City            VARCHAR2(20),
    State           VARCHAR2(2),
    Zip             NUMBER(5)
    );

CREATE TYPE cand_name_t AS OBJECT (
    First_name      VARCHAR2(20),
    Last_name       VARCHAR2(30),
    Middle          VARCHAR2(15)
    );

CREATE OR REPLACE TABLE Candidate (
    Candidate_id    NUMBER,
    Photo_id        NUMBER,
    Resume_id       NUMBER,
    Candidate_name  cand_name_t,
    Cand_address    address_list_t
);
```

As you can see, two user-defined data types support the **CANDIDATE** table. The first data type is an aggregation of the candidate's name, and the second data type is a grouping of the address information. Note how the table attributes **Candidate_name** and **Cand_address** are declared on the user-defined data types. If you want to add telephone information, you have several options. Assuming that each candidate will have a work and home phone number, you could include the information as attributes in the **CANDIDATE** table, add the information as attributes to the **address_list_t** data type, or, you could create a **VARRAY** of two elements and embed it in the **address_list_t** data type. The code to do the latter would appear like this:

```
CREATE TYPE Phone_list_t AS VARRAY (2) OF NUMBER(10);

CREATE TYPE Address_list_t AS OBJECT (
    Address_id      NUMBER;
    Address1        VARCHAR2(30),
    Address2        VARCHAR2(30),
    Address3        VARCHAR2(30),
    Phone           Phone_list_t;
    City            VARCHAR2(20),
    State           VARCHAR2(2),
    Zip             NUMBER(5)
    );
```

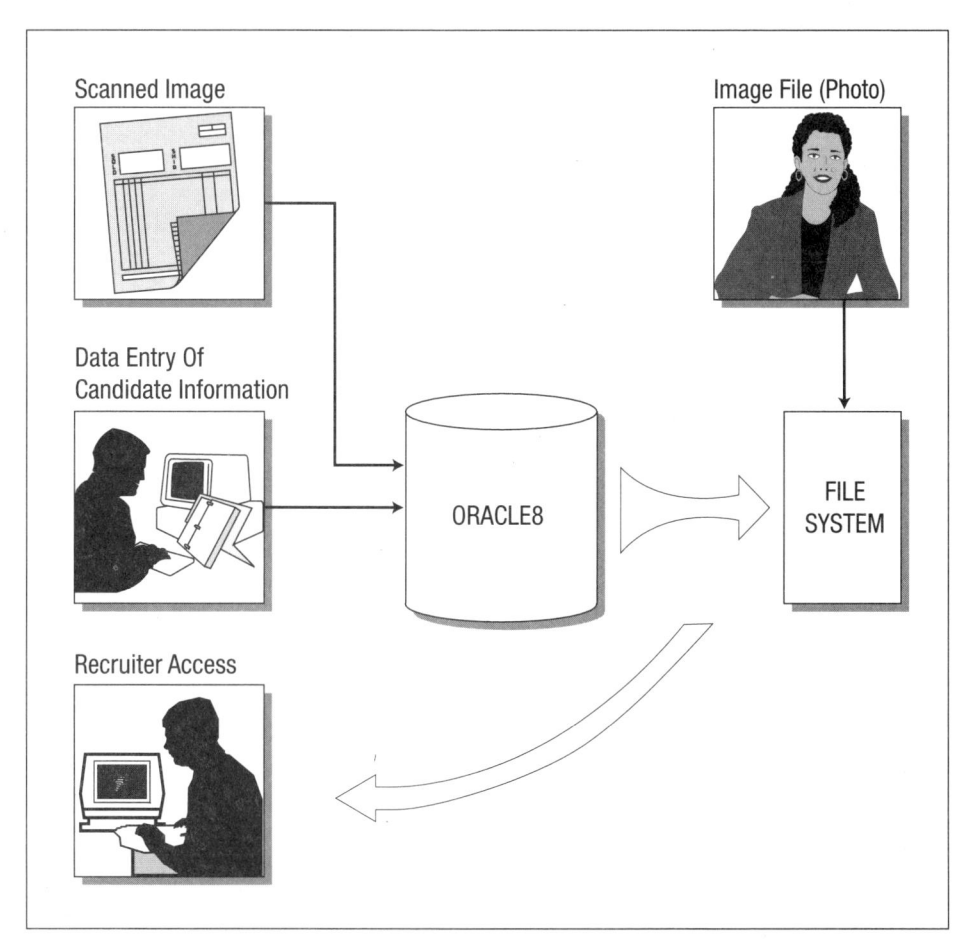

Figure 4.8
The Consult-Rite database application.

Consult-Rite also needs an object table to store the pertinent resume and photo for each candidate. The code for this activity appears next:

```
CREATE DIRECTORY cand_image AS '/usr/home/recruiters/candidates/photos'

CREATE TABLE Candidate_resume (
   Resume_id        NUMBER,
   Resume           BLOB);

CREATE TABLE Candidate_photo (
   Photo_id         NUMBER,
   Photo            BFILE);
```

```
INSERT INTO Candidate_resume VALUES (
   1000, EMPTY_BLOB());

INSERT INTO Candidate_photo VALUES (
   1000, BFILENAME ('cand_image', 'Jones.jpg');
```

Note that there is a key relationship between the **CANDIDATE** table and the **CANDIDATE_RESUME** and **CANDIDATE_PHOTO** tables. Both of the latter tables have been initialized, and the **RESUME** table is ready for population.

If you wish to restrict DML activity from the general user while gaining the advantage of a single-data retrieval for each candidate's data, you might consider consolidating some or all of the data from the three tables into an object view. For example, the following code creates an object view of selected data elements:

```
CREATE VIEW Candidate_view OF Candidate
   WITH OBJECT OID (Candidate_id) AS
   SELECT   a.Candidate_id, a.Candidate_name,
               a.Candidate_address, b.Photo
   FROM     Customer_address a, Candidate_photo b
   WHERE    b.Photo_id = a.Photo_id;
```

As you can see, great flexibility and robustness are keenly apparent in the new user-defined data types. Note how leaf-level attributes are combined into more functional data types that could then be incorporated into simpler table and view constructs.

As an additional illustrative example of how user-defined data types are altering the playing field of data object design, let's return to Bob's Fertilizer corporation.

A Study In Collections: Bob's Fertilizer Revisited

Because your last assignment was completed so successfully, Bob has asked you back to consider the following design problem. Bob's special blend of fertilizer has become so popular that, in addition to private buyers, the company has expanded sales to larger chains. The existing billing system has become inadequate to handle the task of multiple clients with many shipping destinations. Presented here is one approach to the entities used in the billing scheme. Figure 4.9 illustrates the added complexity of many shipping destinations.

Assume that there are many direct sales clients whose billing address and delivery address are either the same or such that the ratio is one-to-one. Under such conditions, the data types could be adequately modeled with the following constructs:

Modeling For Oracle Supported Data Types

```
CREATE TYPE Address_t AS OBJECT (
   Address_id      NUMBER;
   Address1        VARCHAR2(30),
   Address2        VARCHAR2(30),
   Address3        VARCHAR2(30),
   Phone           Phone_list_t;
   City            VARCHAR2(20),
   State           VARCHAR2(2),
   Zip             NUMBER(5)
   );

CREATE TYPE Address_list_t AS VARRAY (2) OF Address_t;

CREATE TABLE Customer (
   Customer_id     NUMBER,
   Customer_name   VARCHAR2(30)
   Address         Address_list_t
   );
```

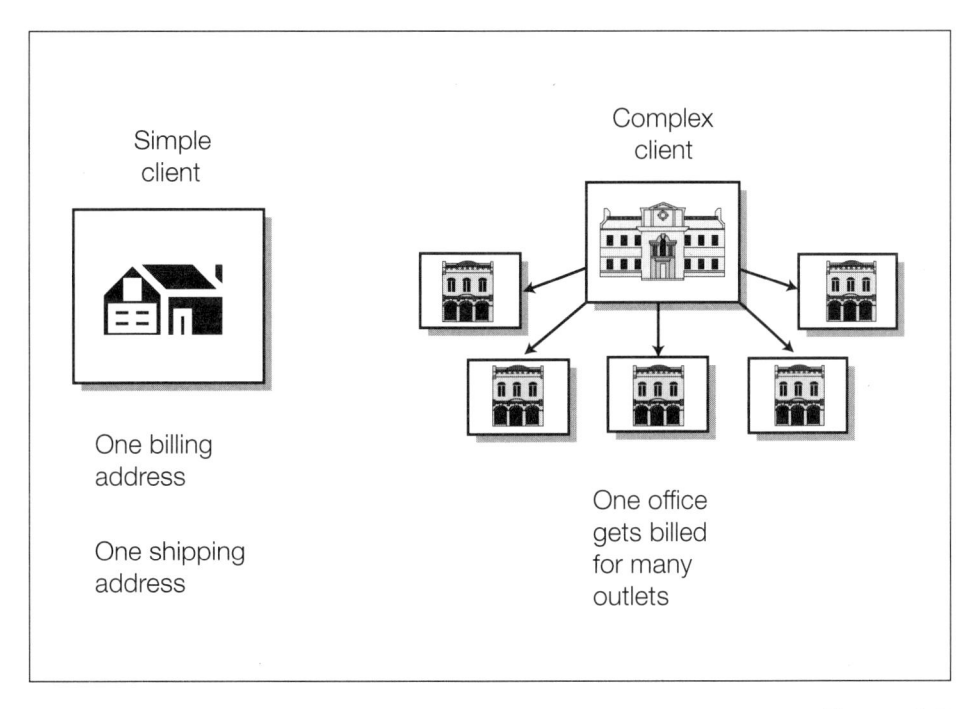

Figure 4.9
Billing and shipping destinations for Bob's Fertilizer.

By utilizing the **VARRAY**, you can use one cell for billing information and the other for shipping. The problem in Bob's case is that he must now deal with store chains with many outlets, so the **VARRAY** is no longer adequate. The company must now contend with an indeterminate number of shipping addresses for each billing address, so the most likely approach would be to utilize a nested table as follows:

```
CREATE TYPE Address_t AS OBJECT (
   Address_id      NUMBER;
   Address1        VARCHAR2(30),
   Address2        VARCHAR2(30),
   Address3        VARCHAR2(30),
   Phone           Phone_list_t;
   City            VARCHAR2(20),
   State           VARCHAR2(2),
   Zip             NUMBER(5)
);

CREATE  OR REPLACE TABLE Customer (
   Customer_id     NUMBER,
   Customer_name   VARCHAR2(30),
   Address         Address_t)
    nested table Address_t store as
        Address_List_tbl;
```

This case study illustrates how many indeterminate shipping addresses can be associated to a single customer through the implementation of a simple nested table. Now that we have established a basic understanding of the user-defined data types, we will move into the subject of organizing those data types into a hierarchy.

Planning A Hierarchy Of Data Types

If you are experienced in the creation of PL/SQL packages, then you can appreciate the importance of building reusable modules to reduce the amount of generated code. Oracle provides a set of PL/SQL built-ins that can be incorporated into customized program units. For example, **TO_DATE** is a function that performs a data conversion for the user. When this functionality is needed, you don't need to rewrite the same code over again. Instead, you use the existing built-in. Consider also that behind a very simple procedure call, lies many lines of executable code. The picture becomes clear why building a data hierarchy is important. The same outward simplicity, combined with the encapsulated nature of what goes on behind the scenes, benefits data constructs as much as it benefits executable code. The applications that you build can be simplified by exercising the same concept in the construction of data types and objects.

The idea behind developing a data type hierarchy is that basic core components are developed with the intent that they will form simple, easy-to-use representations of objects that would normally be complex or tedious to use. Figure 4.10 illustrates the concept of the data type hierarchy.

The hierarchy concept means that you should build from the atomic data level and gradually move up the chain to larger data constructs, such as tables and views. The

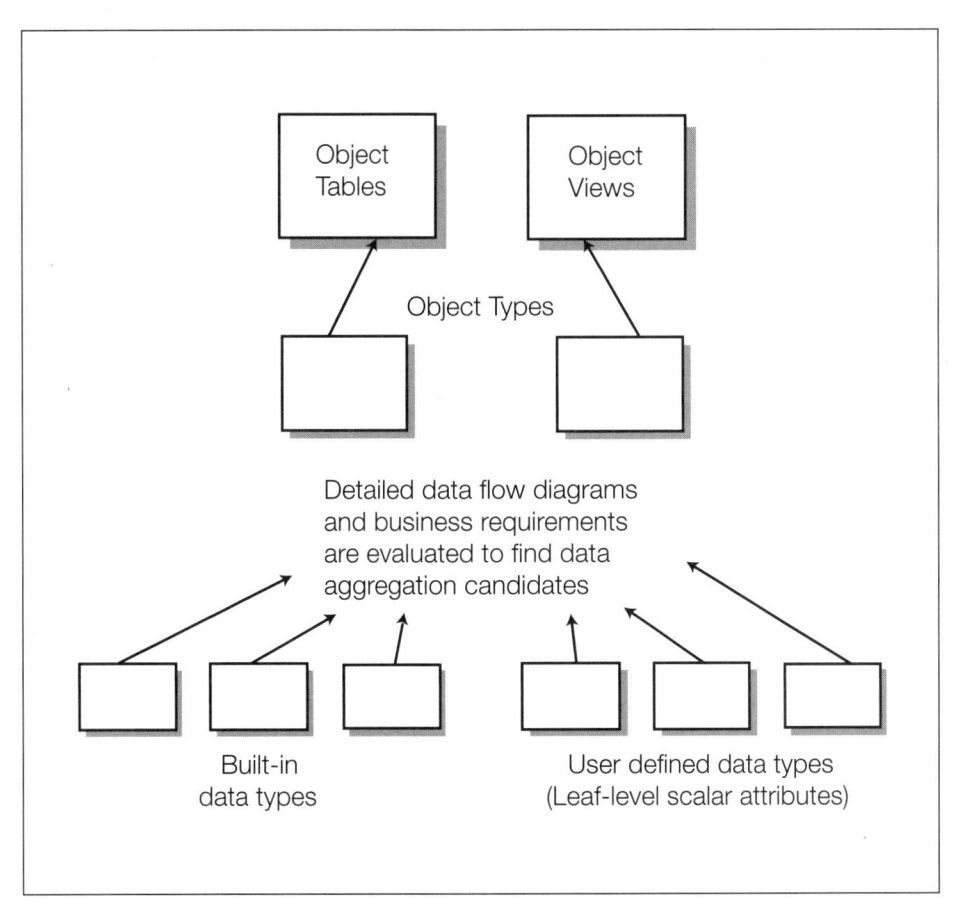

Figure 4.10
The data type hierarchy concept.

intent is to reduce as much of the leaf-level attribute referencing as possible and incorporate attributes into self-contained data types suitable for reuse in many parts of an application. A well-documented library of user-defined data types reduces the complexity of business objects. Simple, easy-to-access data objects, tables, and views replace circuitous SQL statements needed to ferret out the appropriate aggregations.

The first questions that generally arise are: Where to start? and, What strategy should be used to accomplish the goal? Therefore, the first step is to evaluate the system requirements and business rules. Once this effort has begun, you should address the following:

- Does the targeted aggregation resolve a complex business rule that is difficult to solve with standard relational structures and atomic-level attributes?
- Will the proposed object be reused in more than one place in the application?
- Will the object under consideration improve performance through reduced I/O or simplified retrieval?
- What are the maintenance ramifications of the new object?
- Does the proposed object perform a vital role as an attribute to another object, such as object table, object view, and so on?
- Does the planned object cleanly resolve a many-to-many relationship?
- Will the proposed data object simplify interaction with the user interface?

An effective opportunity to initially target data hierarchy prospects is during the detailed phase of creating the data flow diagram. It is at this point when natural data aggregations, complex data constructs, and unusual business criteria manifest themselves on the data stores and intended entities. You should select aggregations carefully so that they are flexible. Adding too many "special interest" attributes reduces the probability that the composed data type will have utility in other parts of the application. In addition, select attributes and group them logically, much as you would relational tables, in order to achieve the highest level of normalization possible. Data redundancy is acceptable, but why introduce it if it isn't necessary?

A good example of data constructs that will lend themselves well to the concept of the data type hierarchy are those that make use of what is known as the IS-A relationship. The IS-A relationship naturally grows into a hierarchy of object classes because each constituent member or object is a part of the next object class. For example, an automobile engine is comprised of parts—the engine is a part of the automobile. IS-A relationships imply a successive level of attributes or properties that gradually define a class hierarchy. This subject will be discussed in greater detail in Chapter 13. In short, devise a plan for the logical consolidation of leaf-level attributes for the purpose of simplifying data access and program design.

Summary

In this chapter, we discussed the basic data types supported by Oracle8. We covered built-in data types in an effort to address the enhancements added to existing constructs since the introduction of Oracle8. We examined **LOB**s in added detail to highlight their importance to emerging development efforts and to raise your overall understanding of these unconventional data types. In addition, we examined user-defined data types with an eye toward future discussion to include an in-depth case study in an upcoming chapter. Finally, we looked at two straightforward examples of data type implementation, and we held a discussion on data type hierarchies. In the next chapter, we'll look at Oracle's reference pointers and discuss how the concepts of data access and normalization are impacted by what many consider to be an art from the past.

HIGH PERFORMANCE

Oracle Reference Pointers And Database Design

CHAPTER 5

HIGH PERFORMANCE

Science moves, but slowly, slowly, creeping on from point to point.
—*Lord Alfred Tennyson*

Oracle Reference Pointers And Database Design

The greatest impact on normalization in object-relational databases is the use of pointers. This concept is so important to the modeling of database systems in Oracle8 that this entire chapter is devoted to the discussion of how pointers and their supporting constructs are implemented. The reintroduction of pointers into the database design methodology harkens back to the days of hierarchical structure with tools like IMS. Does this mean that database design is regressing? Absolutely not. The addition of reference pointers adds a new dimension to how aggregate objects can be modeled. The use of pointers brings the database designer closer to accurately modeling the real world.

The object-relational paradigm incorporates the best of both the relational, CODASYL Network and hierarchical worlds. This new paradigm produces a robust and flexible design capable of accommodating complex data structures previously impossible to model. Pointers represent the only way complex data objects can be effectively linked. Declarative statements in SQL have proven inadequate to the task. An infusion of navigational techniques is needed to complete the picture of how data in the object-relational database can be associated. In the sections to follow, we'll review the basics of pointer usage, introduce the pointer constructs in Oracle8, and finish up with some pertinent examples of real-world implementation techniques you might face.

Recalling Data Structures 101

At some point in your past, you were probably subjected to a computer science course on data structure. As I recall, the course material did not always hold my undivided attention as it probably should have. This could have been due to the fact that I took it in the spring semester after lunch. Or, maybe it had something to do with the fact that my instructor spoke to the chalkboard. In any case, I never dreamed that one concept would hold such staggering consequences to the way I would perform my work so many years later.

The science behind data structures came about as a way to logically order data elements to improve access and retain system performance. Modularity of programming languages ushered in a natural application to data stores, as well. Organizing data in physical storage requires a means to access it. Early constructs, like sequential allocation, provided a neat and organized way to deal with data. Sequential allocation, as you probably know, is a technique of storing equivalently sized data elements in sequential order on a physical device or in memory. Figure 5.1 shows how a typical construct of this type is physically placed. Notice in Figure 5.1 that the address of the next data element is easily determined, because the data elements are the same size, and they are stored end to end.

Although sequential allocation is very efficient, two glaring drawbacks present themselves immediately. The first drawback concerns the complexities involved when inserting an element between two others. What becomes of the sequential list then? To maintain the integrity of the allocation structure, the elements that trail the new one must be "moved over" to make room in physical storage for the new element. This approach is highly inefficient and demands a significant amount of system resources.

The second drawback is rooted in the fact that not all data stores are created equal. This is to say that different data stores can require different lengths. Again, this complicates the use of sequential storage because the addresses for individual data stores can no longer be determined with ease.

These shortcomings led to the next logical step in database development—the linked list. The introduction of linked lists involved adding an address column to data stores that allowed elements to "point" to items, regardless of physical ordering on the storage media. Updates and changes could be easily executed, without an inordinate amount of effort on the part of system resources or programming constructs.

ORACLE REFERENCE POINTERS AND DATABASE DESIGN

Address	Data	Pointer
1		10
10		20
20		30
30		40
40		50
50		60
60		70
70		80

Address values are easily determined because of consistent data element sizing

Equivalently Sized Data Elements

Storage Medium

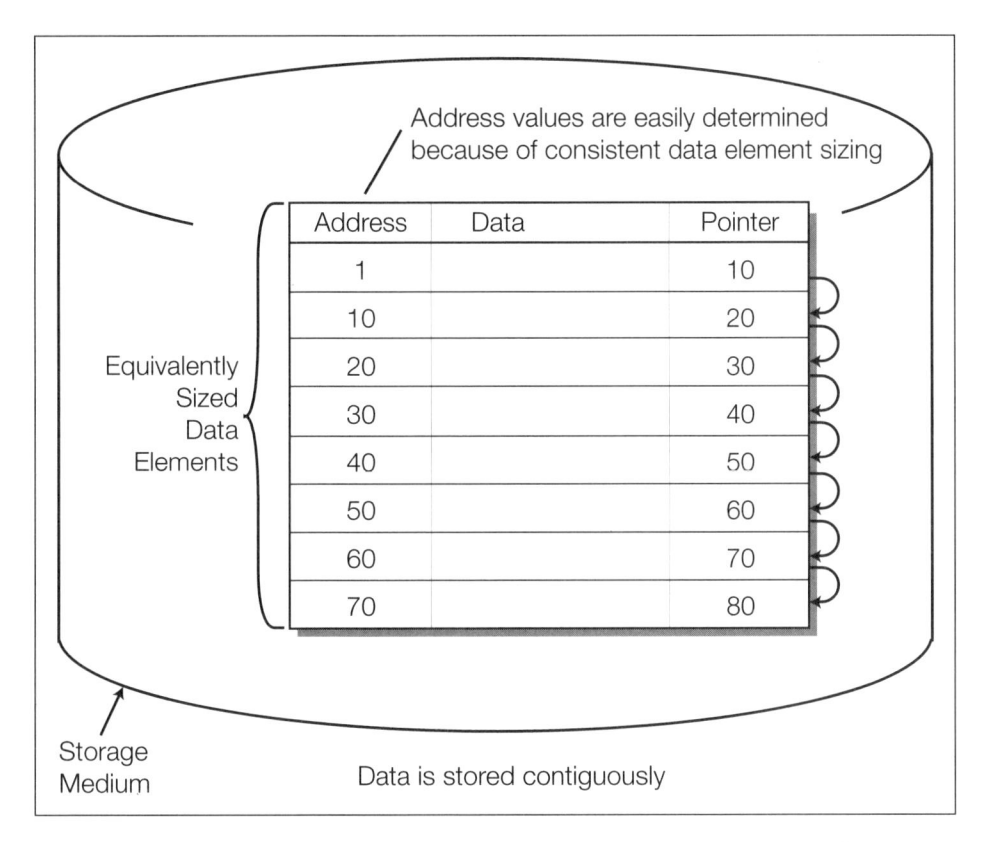

Data is stored contiguously

Figure 5.1
Data elements utilizing sequential allocation.

This hierarchical approach to associating data stores demonstrated great power reflected in terms of performance and efficiency. Figure 5.2 depicts the use of linked lists as a means to associate data elements.

The key ingredient to linking data elements was the pointer. Pointers freed programmers from calculating the location of the next required element and introduced flexibility regarding the physical storage of data. Let's take a moment to discuss pointers in greater detail.

What Are Pointers?

Pointers, in the most basic sense, are merely addresses. Pointers come in two varieties: address and symbolic. Address pointers make use of the physical address of a targeted data element. Symbolic pointers are functionally the same as address pointers

CHAPTER 5

Address column

| 100 | → | 108 | → | 116 | → | 124 | → | 132 |

Pointers from starting data element to the next data element

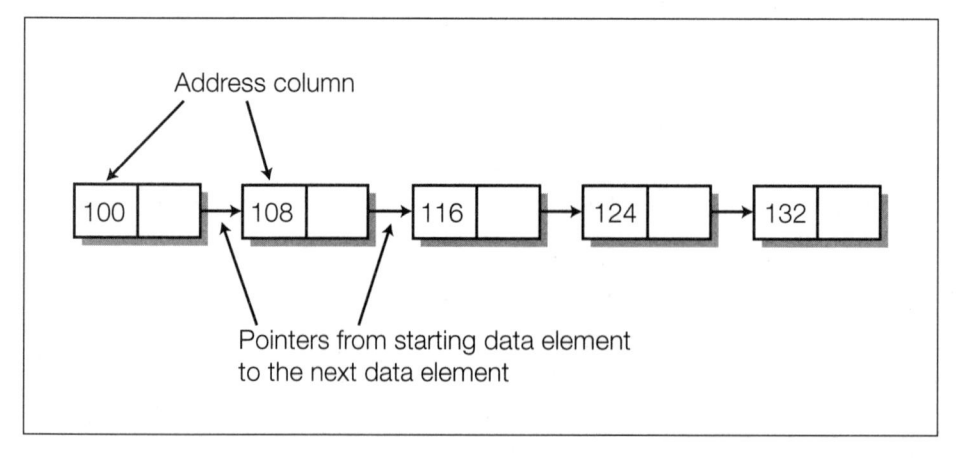

Figure 5.2
A linked list construct.

except that a symbolic pointer is composed of a unique name or identifier, instead of a physical location address. In other words, a symbolic pointer makes use of a symbolic destination.

The address construct is the actual physical address of the data element where it can be found in storage. The hosting data element maintains an extra column to host the pointer so that future references to the target are easily retrieved. To an outside viewer, the perception is given that the entirety of the target element is contained in the pointer column. To illustrate this point, we can refer to our earlier discussion of nested tables in Chapter 4. A nested table can be composed of one or more attributes. By nesting a table in the column of another table, you give users the perception that the entire nested table resides in the column of the host table. In reality, a pointer resides in the host column and references the nested table. Figure 5.3 illustrates the concept of creating a nested table by using a pointer.

A symbolic pointer would fulfill the same role as that of the address pointer. If we were to make a side-by-side comparison of the two, we might find something like the following example

```
Employee(237123)
```

versus

```
Employee(new)
```

146

ORACLE REFERENCE POINTERS AND DATABASE DESIGN

THE USER'S PERCEPTION

Employee Table

EMP_NO	NAME	ADDRESS 1	CITY	STATE	ZIP

THE ACTUAL NESTED CONSTRUCT

Employee Table

EMP_NO	NAME	ADDRESS_T (REF)

pointer to

Nested Table ADDRESS_T

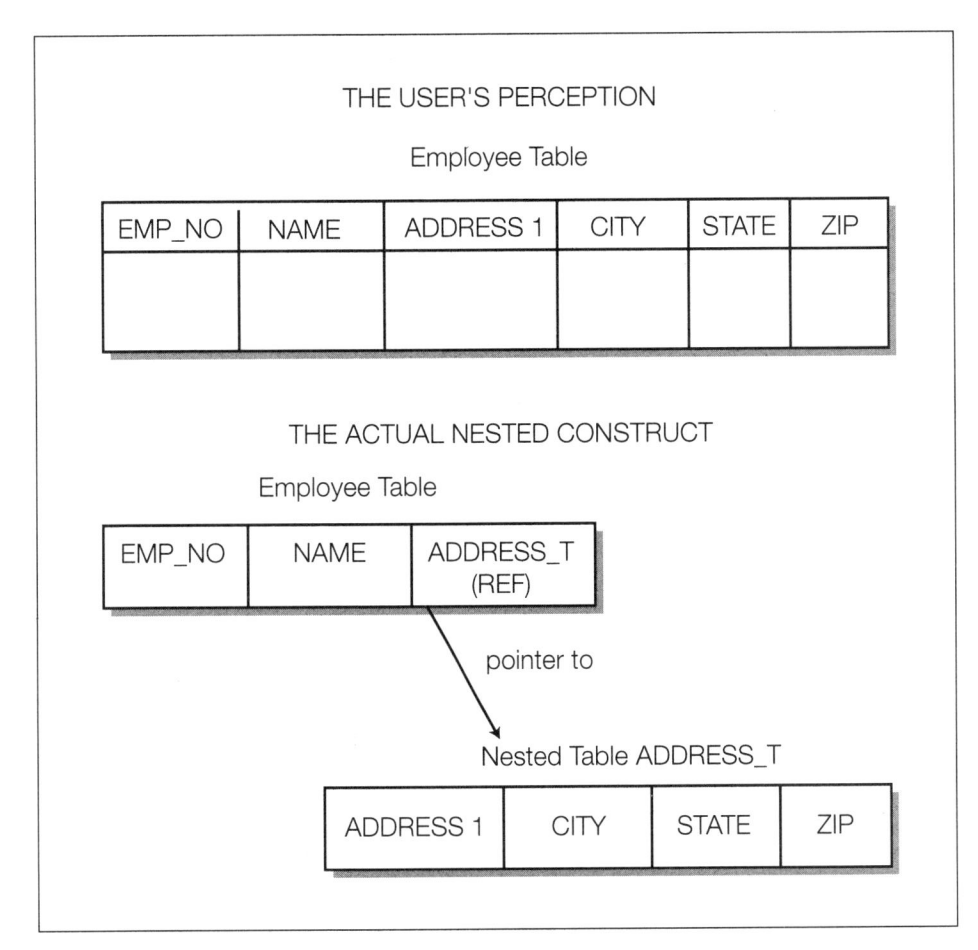

ADDRESS 1	CITY	STATE	ZIP

Figure 5.3
An example of pointer usage by means of a nested table.

In both cases, the pointers might refer to the same individual record, but in the case of the symbolic pointer, the location of the employee record is represented by the parameter or symbol "new."

A pointer does not point to more than one data element or object at a time. It is possible for the targeted object to be composed of multiple attributes, as in the case with nested tables, but the nested table is still one entity.

At the same time, using a number of pointers plays a key role from a hierarchical perspective in establishing an order or sequence. From a hierarchical perspective, it is important to have the ability to link multiple objects or data elements in a sequential fashion in order to establish an order or hierarchy. Early on, such constructs were known as *linked lists*. The difference between linked lists and the use of pointers explained earlier in the chapter is that linked lists tie data objects in a sequential order. Figure 5.4 shows a series of elements tied together in a hierarchy where the top-level element accesses the second element, which in turn accesses the third, and so on.

The concept of linked lists is important to our discussion of Oracle8's use of pointers later on. In the sections that follow, we will examine complex modeling concepts using circular referencing, nested dereferences, and more. Oracle8 provides the functionality to model real-world constructs like arrays of pointers. These arrays constitute another technique for dealing with aggregate objects as each pointer may reference a collection type or other user-defined data object that groups several atomic level attributes.

Pointers In Oracle8

Pointers in Oracle8 resurfaced as a means to link the complex data types introduced with object-oriented extensions. Although pointers utilize a navigational approach to data access, the two concepts (relations via SQL and pointers) do not operate independently in the Oracle database engine. Pointer mechanisms are, in fact, accessed

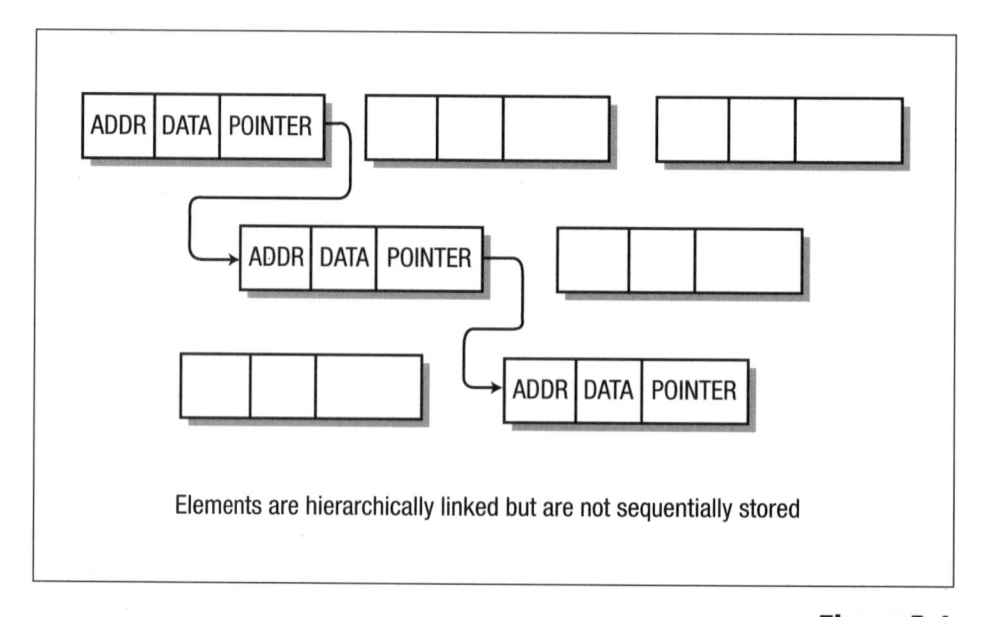

Elements are hierarchically linked but are not sequentially stored

Figure 5.4
An illustrative example of a linked list.

via SQL through the use of new, extended functionality. This behavior is a step toward the highly anticipated SQL3 standard.

Many pre-relational databases incorporated pointer constructs and linked-list data type structures. The pointers were useful in defining one-to-many and many-to-many relationships between data entities. But, despite their elegance and efficiency, both network and hierarchical databases were difficult to navigate, primarily because the burden of identifying each location, name, and pointer type was incumbent on the programmer.

A more significant problem was that structural changes to data entities were extremely difficult. Data relationships were hard coded, making the addition of new pointers difficult to integrate. In Oracle8, there is no need to concern ourselves with complex programming efforts to realign pointers or add new pointer columns to existing tables. Such efforts are facilitated with the **ALTER TABLE** command. In the upcoming sections, we will examine the new Oracle8 constructs that make the use of pointers possible.

The Oracle8 Pointer Constructs

The implementation of pointers in Oracle8 has spawned the creation of several new constructs and SQL extensions. The traditional Oracle database concept is taken one step further by facilitating the access of data constructs that were difficult or impossible to maintain with ordinary tables and attributes. Oracle8's expansion into this new territory gives us the following advantages:

- *Set referencing*—First normal form can be violated, and a tabular column cell can contain a pointer to repeating values. The true benefit of this approach is that pre-built aggregations can be created, simplifying database design in the long run.

- *Accessing non-database objects in a flat file*—We discussed the importance of multimedia objects in new application systems in Chapter 4. **LOB** data types can be stored in the database or on the file server. Pointers supply the means to effectively access these constructs.

- *Data relationships without referential foreign keys*—Utilization of pointers obviates the need for conventional SQL **JOIN** operations because each column instance references the object table containing the necessary aggregate data. The steps and syntax required to perform such operations are described in a later section.

To obtain these benefits, Oracle has created object identifiers and several new extensions to SQL for use in manipulating the data constructs, as well as the data.

Object Identifiers (OIDs)

As defined earlier in this chapter, pointers are a basic physical storage address for a targeted data object. Oracle8's object identifiers (OIDs) are essentially the reincarnation of the pointer construct. OIDs are intended for use with objects such as nested tables and not for conventional built-in data types like **VARCHAR2** and **NUMBER**. When an object table is created, a corresponding OID is added for every row that can be used in **REF**, **DEREF**, and **VALUE** commands. These new SQL commands are described in detail later in this chapter. OIDs should not be confused with the **ROWID** construct. **ROWID**s are used by conventional tables and can change during the life span of that table. OIDs are used only by object tables, and they do not change or repeat.

An OID is a 128-byte base-64 number generated internally by the Oracle engine. OIDs are never reused once they are discarded, and Oracle guarantees OIDs are globally unique, even across a distributed system. The value range for OIDs has been set to a maximum of 2^{128}. This represents a number which I doubt any organization will exhaust for the time being. Oracle defines the OID construct as an opaque structure. This means that the internal workings are not accessible to developers, and Oracle warns against manipulation because the OID construct is subject to change at their discretion.

OIDs are created implicitly whenever an object table is created. For example, in the following **CREATE** command, an OID is generated for the object table:

```
CREATE TABLE fertilizer OF fertilizer_t;
```

In this case, an object table called *FERTILIZER* is created of object type **fertilizer_t**. When the **FERTILIZER** table is created, an OID is created for it by the Oracle database engine.

While the OID is the tool that describes the new pointer scheme, the mechanisms that utilize the tool are the new clauses added to SQL. A description of each clause follows in the next sections.

The REF Construct

In order to make use of the OID in object tables, it is necessary to execute an Oracle supplied routine called *REF*. The **REF** command returns the OID of an object instance. In itself, this information is rather meaningless because the returned value is a 42- through 46-byte number. The OID contains no actual data but merely "points" to the object table in question. The **REF** construct allows a row object to be "referred" to from other objects or tables. **REFs** encapsulate reference activity between host and target objects.

A table can consist of top-level **REF** columns or **REF** attributes that have been embedded inside an object type column. Tables can have a combination of **REF** columns and **REF** attributes, each referencing a different object table. For example, the following **CREATE** command shows embedded **REF** columns in the definition:

```
CREATE OR REPLACE TABLE Candidate (
    Candidate_id        NUMBER,
    Cust_bio            REF cust_info_t ,
    Photo_id            NUMBER,
    Resume_id           NUMBER,
    Candidate_name      cand_name_t,
    Cand_address        address_list_t
);
```

This **CREATE TABLE** command shows an object table comprised of conventional data types (**NUMBER**), two user-defined object types (**cand_name_t** and **address_list_t**), and one reference to another object type (**cust_info_t**).

The previous example of conventional referencing is one of two methods possible. The second method is called a *scoped reference*. Scoped referencing implies strong typing because the referential focus is limited or specified to a definite source. A scoped reference is used when the intention is to limit the reference to a particular table. If the **SCOPE** option is selected when a table is created, then all further instances of data in the table must reference the scoped table. For example, let's say you were to change the preceding statement to read as follows:

```
CREATE OR REPLACE TABLE Candidate (
    Candidate_id        NUMBER,
    Cust_bio            REF cust_info_t  SCOPE IS cust_info,
    Photo_id            NUMBER,
    Resume_id           NUMBER,
    Candidate_name      cand_name_t,
```

```
    Cand_address         address_list_t
);
```

The change in the **CREATE TABLE** command now indicates that values must be obtained from the object table **CUST_INFO**, which is described as a type of **cust_info_t**. Utilizing the **SCOPE** clause reduces space requirements and speeds access because the target table is isolated. In all likelihood, the majority of applications will utilize the scoped reference. There will be fewer instances where you will want to access multiple object tables from the same **REF** column.

While we are speaking of improving access speed, you might wonder if other means of performance improvements exist. The answer to this question is yes. For example, you could rewrite the previous script to include a **ROWID** reference, like this:

```
CREATE OR REPLACE TABLE Candidate (
    (Candidate_id_r      WITH ROWID
        SCOPE IS Candidates),
    Cust_bio             REF cust_info_t  SCOPE IS cust_info,
    Photo_id             NUMBER,
    Resume_id            NUMBER,
    Candidate_name       cand_name_t,
    Cand_address         address_list_t
);
```

In this case, the **CREATE TABLE** command stores the **ROWID** and the **REF** value together in the specified column. This action improves the performance of dereferencing operations, which are explained later in this chapter. The disadvantage of using the **WITH ROWID** clause is that additional space is needed to store the column. If the **WITH ROWID** clause is not specified in the **CREATE TABLE** command, then the default is to not impose it. From a database design perspective, consider the option carefully to determine if the use of additional storage is worth the performance gain.

The **SCOPE** clause can be used in two slightly different ways. The two methods of implementation are described here:

- **SCOPE IS**—This restricts a column's **REF** values to a specific object table. In other words, the values for the **REF** column must come from the specified object table. Only one scoped table can be specified in any **REF** column. If there are additional **REF** columns in the same table they, of course, can specify other object tables. The object table specified in the scope clause must be of the object type defined in the first part of the statement.

- **SCOPE FOR**—This restricts a column's **REF** values to a referenced column name from a referenced object table. The referenced column name is either the name of a **REF** column in an object table or an embedded **REF** attribute from an object column in a relational table. The value in the **REF** column points to an object in the table identified in the **SCOPE** clause.

Remember that **REFs** can only refer to a single entry in a referenced object table, so the relationship between these two entities must go from the dependent table to the controlling table. In other words, **REFs** imply a many-to-one relationship.

In addition, keep in mind that a **REF** clause can not be used on a **REF** column in a nested table during the **CREATE TABLE** command. To accomplish this, the **ALTER TABLE** command must be used after the table has been created. For example, the following **ALTER TABLE** command adds the **REF** clause after initial table creation:

```
ALTER TABLE cust_info
    ADD ( SCOPE FOR (emp_bio_t) IS emp_bio );
```

This **ALTER TABLE** command points out two items from our discussion. First, the **emp_bio_t REF** column for the nested table is now declared. Second, the use of the **SCOPE FOR** clause is demonstrated, where **emp_bio_t** must be in the **emp_bio** object table.

If the **SCOPE** clause is not implemented during the initial table creation and becomes desired at a later point, it can only be added if the target table is empty.

Now that we have described how OIDs and **REFs** work together, let's examine implementations using some of the other new SQL extensions. The other extensions work with **REF** to provide the user with the functional ability to manipulate data stored in user-defined data types.

The DEREF Construct

The OID is a piece of data devoid of any intelligence, meaning that it is only a pointer value from 42 through 46 bytes. If you execute the following statement in SQL*Plus, the resulting output might be somewhat underwhelming:

```
SELECT REF(cust_info_t)
FROM   Candidate;
```

You could expect the output to appear something like this:

```
0000280A656BEEEF112B811D1AD5B00609CFBAD567CDA1
```

Despite the fact that what you have just retrieved is the actual OID, keep in mind that the contents can be referenced. As I mentioned before, the output is not very impressive. So, what are you to do when an actual value needs to be retrieved? The answer is to utilize the **DEREF** routine. The **DEREF** routine is used to retrieve the value or values pointed to by a **REF** statement. SQL **SELECT** statements do not support the implicit dereferencing of **REF**s within PL/SQL programs but do so in SQL*Plus. The use of **DEREF** is required to obtain the value(s) contained in the target table within a PL/SQL block. A simple illustration of this concept appears in the following code:

```
DECLARE
    info            cust_info;
    cust_info_t     REF cust_info;
    name            VARCHAR2(20);
BEGIN
    SELECT DEREF (cust_info_t)
    INTO     info
    FROM     DUAL;

    name := info.customer_name;
END;
```

This PL/SQL block begins by dereferencing the **cust_info_t** object. The reason that the **SELECT** statement is against the **DUAL** table and not the specific object table is because Oracle utilizes the unique OID assigned to the object table as part of the **REF**. The attribute **customer_name** is found in the object type for **cust_info**, so the actual value is assigned to the placeholder, **name**. The value in this placeholder can then be passed outside of the PL/SQL block via one or more mechanisms, such as the Oracle built-in DBMS_OUTPUT.

Thus far, you are probably pleased with the way database constructs have evolved. But one point is missing in our discussion of referenced tables—what happens if a **REF**ed value is deleted without removing the **REF** value in the dependent table?

Dangling REFs

When a **REF**ed value is deleted without removing the **REF** value in the dependent table, it is known as a *DANGLING REF*. **DANGLING REF**s occur when an application has not been properly coded. It is also possible for this situation to occur if privileges to one or more of the tables has somehow been revoked from the intended user. Indeed, such actions should not be permitted in your applications, and the appropriate coding measures should be taken to maintain **REF** integrity. If such an episode occurs, then any DML-type commands will fail because the navigational linkage cannot be established. Such a disintegration of the pointer to target object presents certain problems, not the least of which can be violations in referential integrity. The use and manipulation of pointers introduces a new level of complexity in maintaining data integrity in the database. Where pointers are employed, we cannot count on constraints and referential integrity enforced with keys to prevent dangling **REF**s. The appropriate course of action to prevent this type of situation is to use the **DANGLING** clause. An example UPDATE statement using this clause is shown here:

```
UPDATE cust_info_t
   SET cust_info = NULL
   WHERE cust_info
   IS DANGLING;
```

In this example, the **UPDATE** command is used to ensure that no dangling **REF**s exist in the **CUST_INFO_T** table. The clause can also be used with **IS** and **IS NOT** modifiers. An example of the latter usage is illustrated in the following **SELECT** statement:

```
SELECT  cust_id, cust_name, DEREF (cust_info)
FROM    cust_info_t
WHERE   cust_info IS NOT DANGLING;
```

Here, you can see that a check is first made against the **REF** column **cust_info** to ensure that the **SELECT** statement is not executed against a **REF**ed column that has been left dangling. It is very important that you do not access a dangling **REF** column. Session termination can occur if someone attempts to improperly access a dangling **REF**.

The VALUE Construct

VALUE is the next of the new operators and, as its names implies, it returns the value of an object. In order to use **VALUE**, a correlation variable must be passed as an argument. The correlation can take the form of a row variable or even a table alias associated with a row from an object table. For example, the following code segment will fetch a set of **cust_info_t** objects and insert them into the **CANDIDATE** table:

```
BEGIN
   INSERT INTO candidate
      SELECT   VALUE (c)
      FROM     cust_info_t c
      WHERE    c.last_name LIKE '%Anstey';
END;
```

The **VALUE** operator can also be used to access and update object values. In the next example, the contents of one of the columns is changed:

```
DECLARE
   name1           cust_info;
   name2           cust_info;
BEGIN
   SELECT VALUE (c)
   INTO    name1
   FROM    cust_info_t c
   WHERE   c.last_name LIKE '%Anstey';

   name2 := name1;

   name1.cust_name := name1.cust_name||' Jr.';
...
END;
```

In this case, the **cust_info** object held by **name1** has the new value **Anstey Jr.**. This is only a local reassignment. If the developer chooses, the new value can be used for further DML operations.

The OIDINDEX

As with other normal data constructs in the Oracle repertoire, indexes can be built from columns containing OIDs. Indexes created on OIDs are termed as *OIDINDEX*.

Oracle Reference Pointers And Database Design

The benefit of having an **OIDINDEX** is that the performance of **REF**-type queries can be improved. An **OIDINDEX** can be added to the **CREATE TABLE** script, but it cannot be added later as an **ALTER TABLE** or **CREATE INDEX** command. The use of this construct should be given careful consideration because it is not possible to add it later without recreating the entire table. This becomes problematic if there are other tables with dependencies to the table that has to be dropped. The following section of code illustrates this implementation:

```
CREATE OR REPLACE TABLE Candidate (
    Candidate_id        NUMBER,
    Cust_bio            REF cust_info_t  SCOPE IS cust_info,
    Photo_id            NUMBER,
    Resume_id           NUMBER,
    Candidate_name      cand_name_t,
    Cand_address        address_list_t
) OIDINDEX odx1 (TABLESPACE prod_idx_1);
```

Now that the basic pointer constructs have been introduced, we will discuss some real-world modeling problems and how they can be dealt with using Oracle's new tools.

Relationships With Oracle8 Pointers

The topics presented in this section describe complex activities that developers are certain to encounter in real-world design efforts. These activities are described here to point out the power and, oftentimes, the difficulty of putting pointer constructs to work in various circumstances. We will examine a number of interesting design patterns, including recursion, circular referencing, nested dereferencing, and more.

Recursion

You might recall from an earlier discussion that recursion is the condition where an entity has a relationship to itself. The question in this case is how recursion (also referred to as *self-association*) is dealt with when the table in question is an object table with one or more **REF** columns. Figure 5.5 illustrates the recursive relationship where the link to the object table is the **REF** column.

There are four possible self-association relationships that can be created from an object table when the recursion is based on a referenced column. Remember that

```
                    Object Table
                    FERT_RECIPE

                    ┌──────────────────┐
                    │    RECIPE_ID     │ ⇐┐
                    ├──────────────────┤  │
Object Type         │   RECIPE_PARTS   │  │
┌─────────┐         ├──────────────────┤  │
│ VARRAY  │         │ GEN_RECIPE (REF) │ ─┘
│   1.    │         ├──────────────────┤
│    .    │         │       MIX        │      The object table
│    .    │         └──────────────────┘      contains a self-
└─────────┘                                   association via a
                                              REF back to the
Object Type                                   object table itself
┌─────────┐
│ Formula │
└─────────┘
```

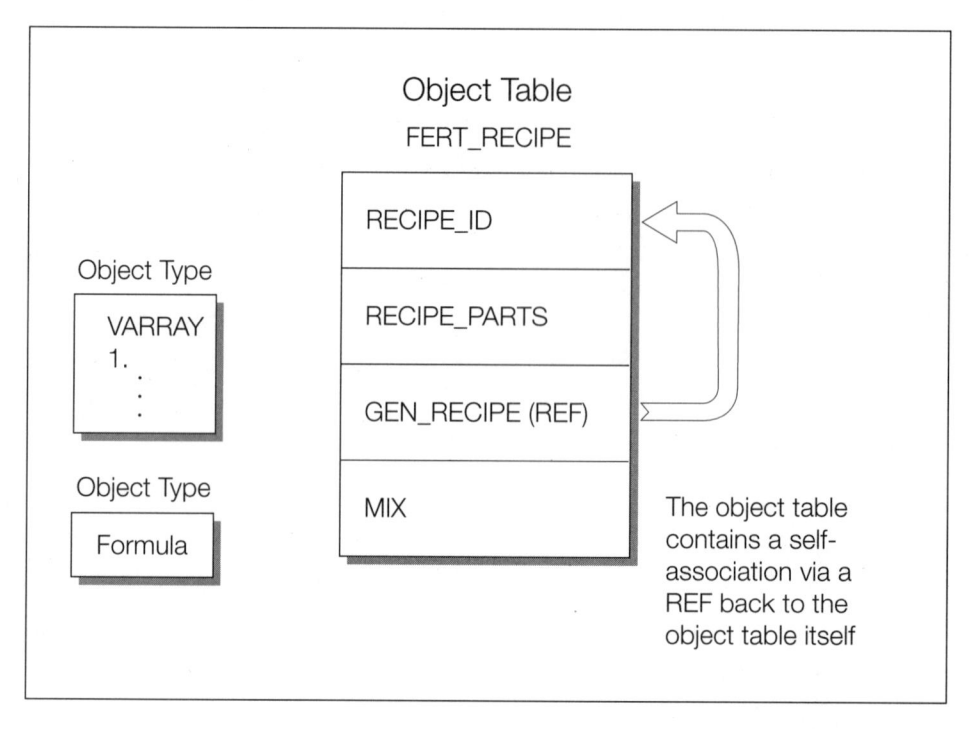

Figure 5.5
An illustration of recursion with an object table.

REFs only describe a relationship in one direction. The column or attribute must exercise one of the following:

- One or single reference
- Zero reference (none)
- **VARRAY** reference
- Nested table reference

Keep in mind that the design acquired from the data flow diagram might require a bi-directional relationship. For example, if we use Bob's Fertilizer company, a recursive roll-up of the recipe table could have a relationship to a 'general recipe' (higher level), while the recipe in question could also have a collection of sub-recipes used to produce the final mix. For this implementation, you might create a **REF** back to the 'general recipe' while the collection of sub-recipes might be implemented using a collection object such as a **VARRAY** or nested table. To demonstrate this scenario, the following code segment can be used to create the constructs:

```
CREATE TYPE recipe_t OF recipe;

CREATE TYPE parts_t AS VARRAY(10) OF VARCHAR2(30);

CREATE TABLE fert_recipe
   ( recipe_id      NUMBER,
     recipe_parts   parts_t,
     gen_recipe     REF fert_recipe,
     mix            formula
);

ALTER TABLE fert_recipe
   ADD ( SCOPE FOR (gen_recipe) IS fert_recipe);
```

Note that the referenced object table is the **FERT_RECIPE** table itself. Recursion has been introduced using the **REF** construct. The sub-elements of each recipe are contained in the **VARRAY parts_t**.

Now that you've seen a rather esoteric example of how recursion might be modeled with object tables, let's take a look at a more common example of table dependency—circular referencing.

Circular Referencing

The concept of circular referencing is similar to recursion except that the circular dependency involves two or more tables. Figure 5.6 illustrates a typical set of tables in a schema that requires circular referencing.

Circular references are created when two or more objects require information about each other. This is not the same as a relationship dictated by foreign keys. Circular relationships reflect a bi-directional implementation of one-to-one, zero-to-one, or one-to-zero. In each case, a **REF** is used. Figure 5.6 shows a suitable example for circular referencing, in which a department in a company is made up of a group of employees. Assume that the company has many departments. Finally, an employee (upper management) has responsibility for one or more subsidiaries of the company. Drawing from this example, you can see that departments require employees, companies (subsidiaries) require departments, and employees (certain management varieties) require companies.

CHAPTER 5

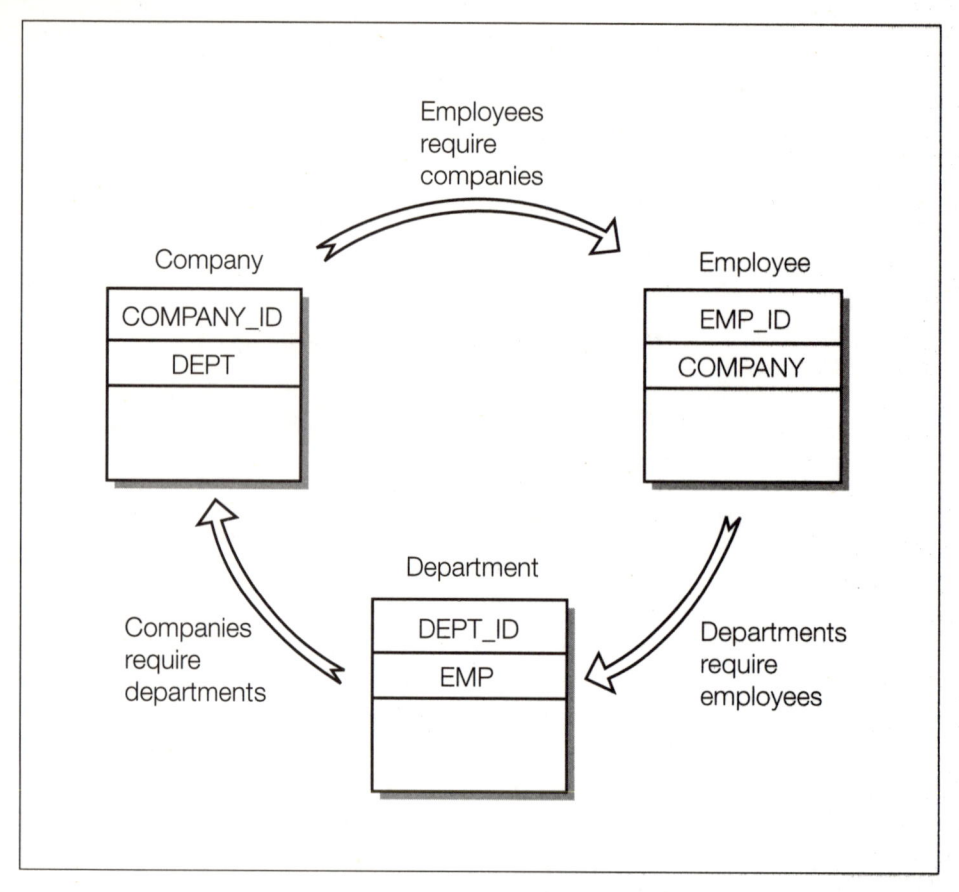

Figure 5.6
A set of tables linked together in circular referencing.

Situations such as this are relatively common in data modeling problems. The key to solving this using the object functionality of Oracle8 is to create the individual object types and tables in the correct order. The necessary steps appear as follows:

```
CREATE TYPE employee;

CREATE OR REPLACE TABLE department
    ( dept_id       NUMBER,
      emp           REF employee,
      location      VARCHAR2(20)
    );

CREATE OR REPLACE TABLE company
    ( company_id    NUMBER,
```

Oracle Reference Pointers And Database Design

```
      comp_dept     REF dept_id SCOPE IS department,
      function      VARCHAR2(20)
   );

CREATE TYPE employee AS OBJECT
   ( emp_id        NUMBER,
     emp_name      name_t,
     division      REF company,
     position      VARCHAR2(20)
   );
```

The first action taken in this code creates an incomplete type definition for employee. The code does not fully specify employee at this time because one of the intended attributes is a **REF** column back to company, which is not yet possible because company has not been defined at this point.

The second step taken in this code fully declares the **DEPARTMENT** table using the incomplete employee type by reference. The **COMPANY** table is also fully declared, in this case referencing the **DEPARTMENT** table. Finally, the full specification for employee can be created and the **REF** back to company can be included. This then, assembles the circular reference.

While the concept of circular referencing is not uncommon, certainly the next scenario occurs even more frequently. The implementation of a many-to-many relationship is described under nested dereferencing.

Nested Dereferencing

Common database design practice in the relational model has shown that the most prudent action to take when dealing with many-to-many relationships is to resolve them to a simpler form. This is generally accomplished using an intersection or associative table to break down the relationship to two one-to-many relationships. In the past, designers did this to preserve the state of normalization.

Recall that a **REF** can reference only one object. Remember also that a nested table is a collection (many) contained or referenced from a column or attribute (one). Faced again with a many-to-many relationship between two entities, is there an alternate solution available using the object tools available in Oracle8? Consider for a moment the marriage of **REF**s and nested tables to provide a viable solution to the many-to-many problem. Figure 5.7 illustrates a viable strategy.

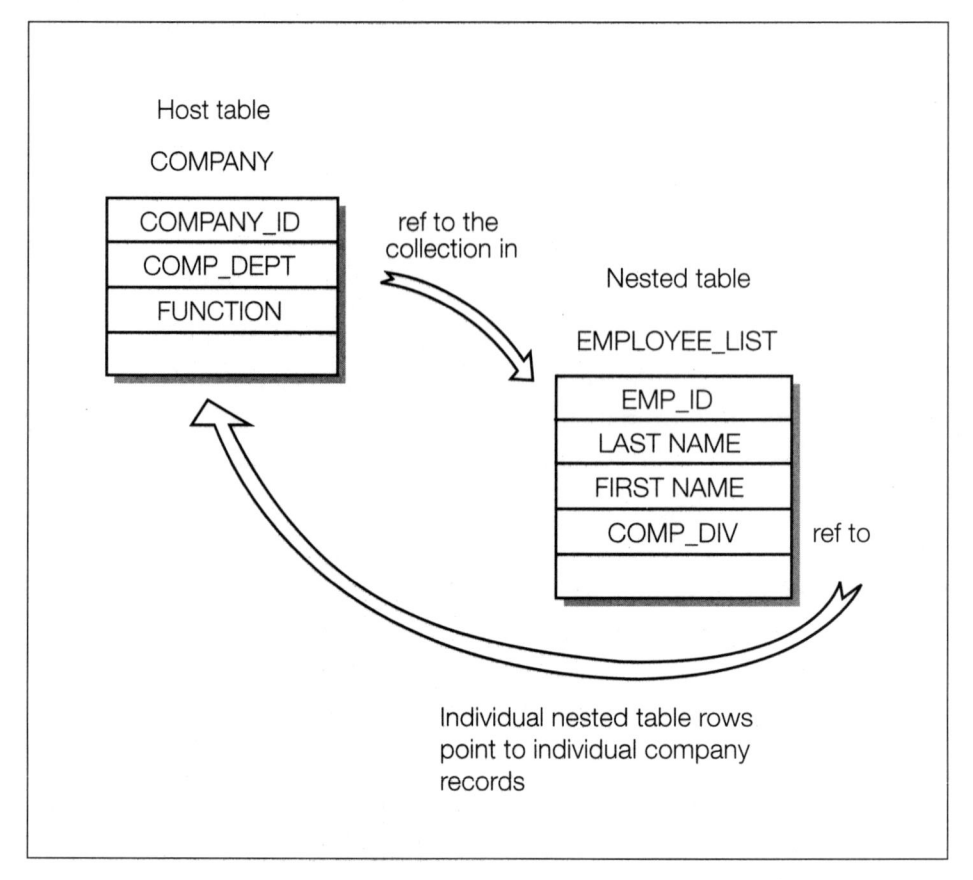

```
                    Host table

                    COMPANY
                    ┌──────────────┐      ref to the
                    │ COMPANY_ID   │      collection in         Nested table
                    │ COMP_DEPT    │
                    │ FUNCTION     │                            EMPLOYEE_LIST
                    │              │                            ┌──────────────┐
                    └──────────────┘                            │ EMP_ID       │
                                                                │ LAST NAME    │
                                                                │ FIRST NAME   │
                                                                │ COMP_DIV     │   ref to
                                                                │              │
                                                                └──────────────┘


                              Individual nested table rows
                              point to individual company
                              records
```

Figure 5.7
An approach to many-to-many resolution with nested dereferencing.

The devised implementation goes something like this. A table is created with a **REF** column that references a nested table. The nested table is composed of **REF** columns. To establish the bi-directional nature of the many-to-many, **REF** columns from the nested table refer back to the host table. The following code segment shows how this can be created:

```
CREATE OR REPLACE TYPE Tasks_t (
   task_name          VARCHAR2(20),
   manpower_lvl       NUMBER,
   duration           NUMBER);

CREATE OR REPLACE TYPE Emp_List_t (
   Emp_id             Number,
```

Oracle Reference Pointers And Database Design

```
    Last_Name         VARCHAR2(20),
    First_Name        VARCHAR2(15),
    comp_div          REF company_id SCOPE IS company,
    Task_List         Tasks_t);

CREATE OR REPLACE TABLE Employee_List  of Emp_list_t
   nested table Tasks_t store as
        Task_List_tbl;

CREATE OR REPLACE TABLE company
   ( company_id       NUMBER,
     comp_dept        REF emp_id SCOPE IS Employee_List,
     function         VARCHAR2(20)
   ) nested table Employee_List store as
     Employee_List _tbl;

ALTER TABLE Employee_List ADD
   CONSTRAINT PK_Employee_List
        PRIMARY KEY (Emp_id);

 ALTER TABLE company ADD
   CONSTRAINT PK_ company
        PRIMARY KEY (company_id);
```

Note from the sample code that bi-directional referencing has been placed where **EMPLOYEE_LIST** is a nested table to **COMPANY** while **EMPLOYEE_LIST** retains a **REF** back to **COMPANY**. A PL/SQL block is the most effective means of extracting the requested data under these circumstances. Dereferencing this data composition can occur like this:

```
DECLARE
    emp             Emp_list_t;
    comp_dept       REF Employee_List;
    comp_div        REF company;
    div             company _t;
    div1            VARCHAR2(30);
    emp1            VARCHAR2(30);
BEGIN
  SELECT DEREF (comp_dept) ,
    INTO      emp
    FROM      DUAL;

SELECT DEREF (comp_div) ,
    INTO      div
    FROM      DUAL;
```

```
    div1 :=    div.function;
    emp1 :=    emp.Last_name;
END;
```

Keep in mind that **REF**s point to a single value. Retrieving both **REF**s simultaneously results in a one-for-one combination of the linked data. The final output from a simultaneous retrieval does not produce a master detail styled output but, rather, one parent for each child. The many-to-many relationship has been artificially reintroduced by establishing a **REF** from the nested table to the parent table.

In the next section, we'll review a scenario representing a sequential, or hierarchical, data scheme that emulates the linked list behavior. The question pondered is what to do when the sequence needs to be realigned.

Re-Sequencing Of Pointers

The idea of re-sequencing pointers is as old as pointer technology itself. Pointer re-sequencing is also known as *twizzling*. Consider the abstraction of linked data types in Figure 5.8. A series of data objects are linked through the use of pointers in a sequential pattern.

This abstraction could represent the hierarchy of a personnel management scheme, or it could represent a series of customer orders where subsequent entries are back orders of the original. In either case, the collection of data objects can be relatively small or significantly large. Up until this point, we have not addressed the possibility of defining order or access direction in one-to-many relationships. In languages such as C++, pointers to objects can be easily manipulated using pointer arithmetic.

Before we delve into the possible methods of re-sequencing linked list type compositions, let us first consider the ways in which sequential specificity can manifest itself in Oracle8. The first and most obvious way is through the creation of a **VARRAY**. The individual cells are addressed by number, and so, a rank ordering, of sorts, can be instituted by this means. The two disadvantages to the use of **VARRAY**s in this context are that the collection set must be small and the number of elements must remain static. This is an unsuitable criteria for use with the back order example mentioned earlier because the number of back orders remains indeterminate.

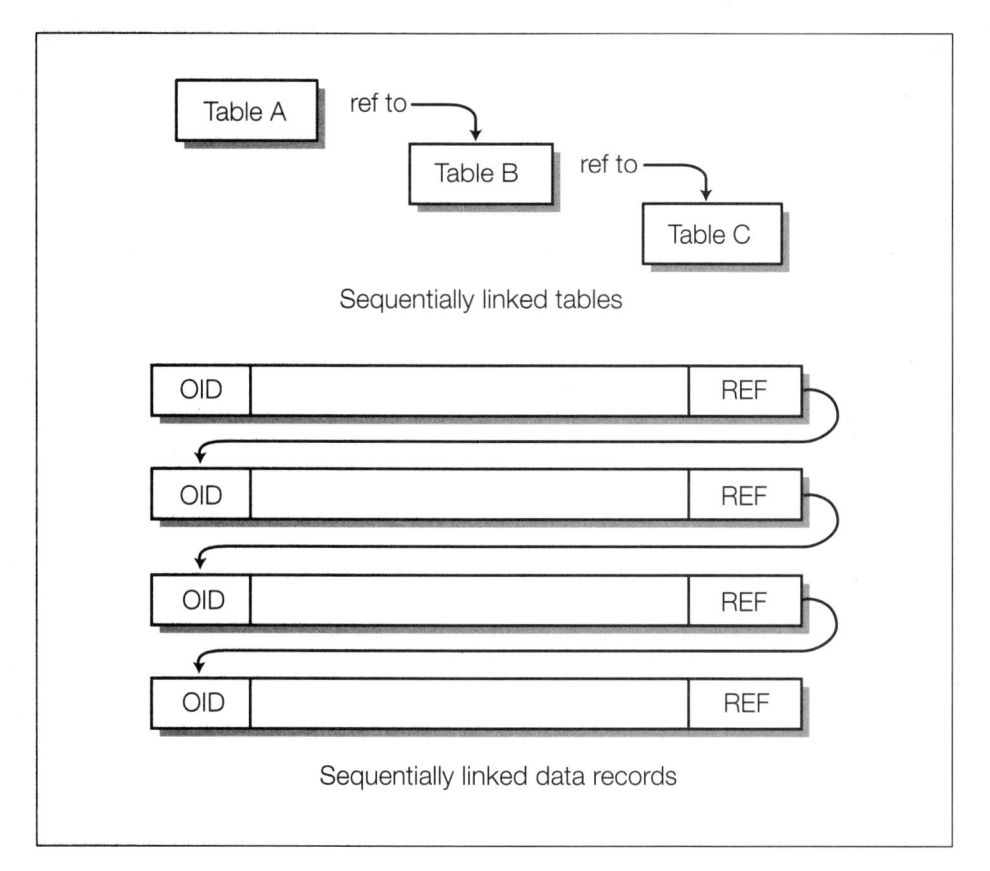

Figure 5.8
A series of sequentially linked data objects.

The second method of introducing linked list behavior is through the use of a nested table. The nested table is not limited to a predefined number of elements, but it is awkward to specify order without introducing a mechanism like a sequence column.

The final application of this concept is through the linkage of separate data entities. This is a replication of a hierarchical data dependency, such as departments in a company. Undoubtedly, there are limits to this style of implementation.

Although the three options cited have various differences in execution and semantics, the principle behind re-sequencing is essentially the same. A sort mechanism is needed to realign the constituent members into the desired order.

The simplest of the three methods to alter, or re-sequence, is the linked data entities method. The individual **REF**s can be redirected to point to a new respective target table. This is possible so long as the **SCOPE** operator was not declared when the objects were created and each of the objects selected to switch places are of the same object type. If indeed the **SCOPE** option was utilized, then the objects must be recreated. This highlights a possible advantage to not using the **SCOPE** operator.

The **VARRAY** implementation is the next simplest method for re-specifying order. A simple sort routine using a placeholder can be written to swap data between cells. This is essentially a twist on the bubble sort routine taught in school in basic computer science. The current row is copied to the placeholder and the next adjacent cell is retrieved for comparison purposes. The two compared rows can be swapped around depending on the sort criteria. Keep in mind that sort routines must make several passes through the collection to ensure a thorough re-sequencing has taken place.

The nested table option is the most difficult to work with because dictating row order in a PL/SQL cursor is very cumbersome. Recall that the **ORDER BY** clause cannot be used in the **SELECT** statement of the cursor. This means that some qualifiable column other than the **ROWID** is necessary for use in a looping mechanism in order to reset the sequence column. For example, you could use an order number column, starting the loop with the smallest order number and incrementing it with each pass of the loop. Each pass of the cursor could fetch the row that matches the order number value on the order number counter. When a row is fetched, the sequence column could be updated, and the process could continue until the data is exhausted. A simple illustration of this concept appears in the following code:

```
DECLARE
counter      NUMBER := 0;
new_seq      NUMBER := 0;

CURSOR EMP IS
   SELECT    seq_num
   FROM      fert_order_t
   WHERE     fert_order_num = counter;

R_EMP    EMP%rowtype;

BEGIN
   SELECT    min(fert_order_num)
   INTO      counter
   FROM      fert_order_t;
```

```
OPEN EMP;
FETCH EMP INTO R_EMP;
WHILE EMP FOUND LOOP
counter := counter + 1;

SELECT  var_seq_ord.nextval
INTO    new_seq
FROM    dual;

UPDATE  fert_order_t
SET     seq_num = new_seq
WHERE   fert_order_num = counter;

FETCH EMP INTO R_EMP;
END LOOP;
CLOSE EMP;
COMMIT;
END;
```

Sequencing data objects is not the most common situation presented in this section. But, it is an interesting topic that bears some thought because it presents certain challenges to developers and designers under specific conditions.

A more likely scenario is described next. Developers will be faced with ample opportunities to utilize the new object view, which presents an excellent means of making the complex much simpler.

A Complex Object View Example

From a design perspective, there are two reasons why the creation of a complex object view might become necessary. The first reason is that complex data structures can be aggregated to a simpler form for access by users of the system. The second, and perhaps more important, reason is that many current application tools (Developer/2000 being one of them) are not suited to handle the new object types in Oracle8. This means that the task of simplifying entities for use by application software is the responsibility of the database designer. For discussion purposes, consider the data constructs found in Figure 5.9.

Let's return to Bob's Fertilizer company again, where you have modeled certain aspects of the fertilizer sales module. The aim in this discussion is to construct an object view that effectively consolidates the data shown in Figure 5.9. The final object view should show each of Bob's customers with their detailed fertilizer order

CHAPTER 5

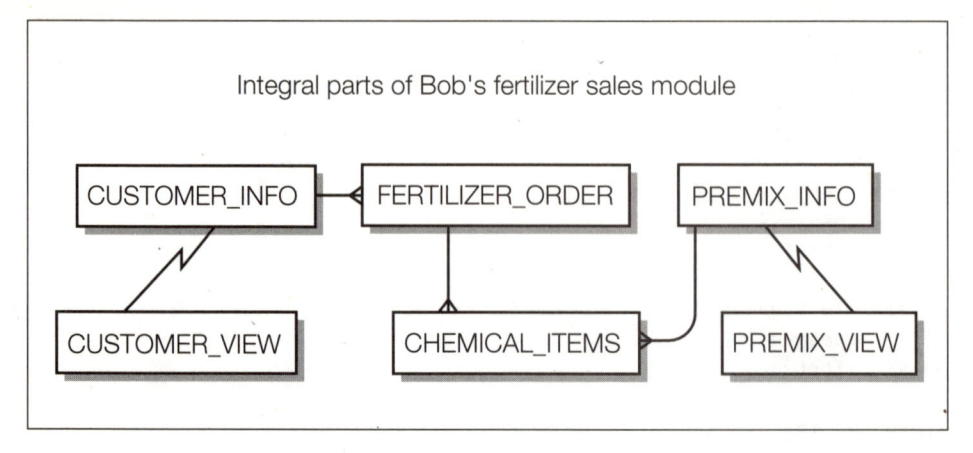

Figure 5.9
The data constructs comprising the complex object view.

data. Representative data structures for the following entities have been created: chemical items, fertilizer order, and customer info tables; fertilizer order, customer info, and premix object types; and two supporting views—customer and premix. The essential code for this example is shown followed by the final consolidated object view called *fertilizer view*.

```
CREATE OR REPLACE TABLE chemical_items (
    chemitemno      NUMBER,
    fertno          NUMBER REFERENCES fertilizer_order,
    premixno        NUMBER REFERENCES premix_info,
    quantity        NUMBER,
    PRIMARY KEY (fertno, chemitemno )
);

CREATE OR REPLACE TABLE fertilizer_order (
    fertno          NUMBER,
    custno          NUMBER REFERENCES customer_info,
    orderdate       DATE,
    s_date          DATE,
    s_street        VARCHAR2(40),
    s_city          VARCHAR2(40),
    s_state         VARCHAR2(2),
    s_zip           VARCHAR2(20),
    PRIMARY KEY (fertno)
);
```

Oracle Reference Pointers And Database Design

```sql
CREATE TYPE fertilizer_order_t AS OBJECT (
   fertno               NUMBER,
   custref              REF customer_info_t,
   orderdate            DATE,
   shipdate             DATE,
   chemical_item_list   chemical_item_list_t,
   s_addr               address_t
);

CREATE TYPE customer_info_t AS OBJECT (
   custno      NUMBER,
   custname    VARCHAR2(40),
   address     address_t,
   phone_list  phone_list_t
);

CREATE TYPE premix_t AS OBJECT (
    premixno   NUMBER,
   cost        NUMBER
);

CREATE OR REPLACE VIEW
customer_view OF customer_info_t WITH OBJECT OID (custno) AS
   SELECT   C.custno, C.custname,
            address_t (C.street, C.city, C.state, C.zip),
            phone_list_t (C.phone1, C.phone2, C.fax)
   FROM     customer_info C;

CREATE OR REPLACE VIEW
premix_view OF premix_t WITH OBJECT OID (premixno) AS
   SELECT *
   FROM   premix_info;

CREATE OR REPLACE VIEW
fertilizer_view of fertilizer_order_t WITH OBJECT OID (fertno) AS
   SELECT F. fertno.
      MAKE_REF (customer_view, F.custno),
      F.orderdate, F.s_date,
      CAST (
         MULTISET (
            SELECT chemical_item_t (
               C. chemitemno,
               MAKE_REF (premix_view, C. premixno),
               C.quantity,
               )
```

```
              FROM  chemical_items C
              WHERE C. fertno = F. fertno
              )
           AS chemical_item_list_t
        ),
        address_t (F.s_street, F.s_city,
              F.s_state, F.s_zip)
     FROM fertilizer_order F;
```

The final view is based primarily on the **CHEMICAL_ITEMS** and **FERTILIZER_ORDER** tables with additional data drawn from the two supporting views **customer_view** and **premix_view**. The graphical depiction of this final object view can be found in Figure 5.10.

Notice the use of several new clauses in the creation of the final view. The **MAKE_REF** clause indicates to create **REF** for the row object of the view named. For example, the line

```
MAKE_REF (customer_view, F.custno)
```

indicates that a **REF** should be created for the row object in the **customer_view** object as identified by **custno**. This **REF** becomes the **custref** column defined in the **fertilizer_order_t** object type.

The next new construct is **CAST**. The **CAST** operator converts the specification enclosed in the parentheses into a nested table of type **chemical_item_list_t**, in this particular case. The use of the **MULTISET** operator is the signal to tell the Oracle engine that the addressed object type specification should be treated as a multiset (collection). The result is that the nested table becomes the **chemical_item_list** column in the object view.

Object views are also extremely effective in the implementation of multidimensional pointer schemes. To illustrate this concept, assume we have a natural hierarchy of descending one-to-many relationships like that found in the student-course-grades example. Each entity would contain pointers to the next detailed level. The object view can be constructed to consolidate this natural hierarchy into a meaningful and easy to access aggregate object.

The Fertilizer View

1) FERTNO — from TABLE FERTILIZER_ORDER

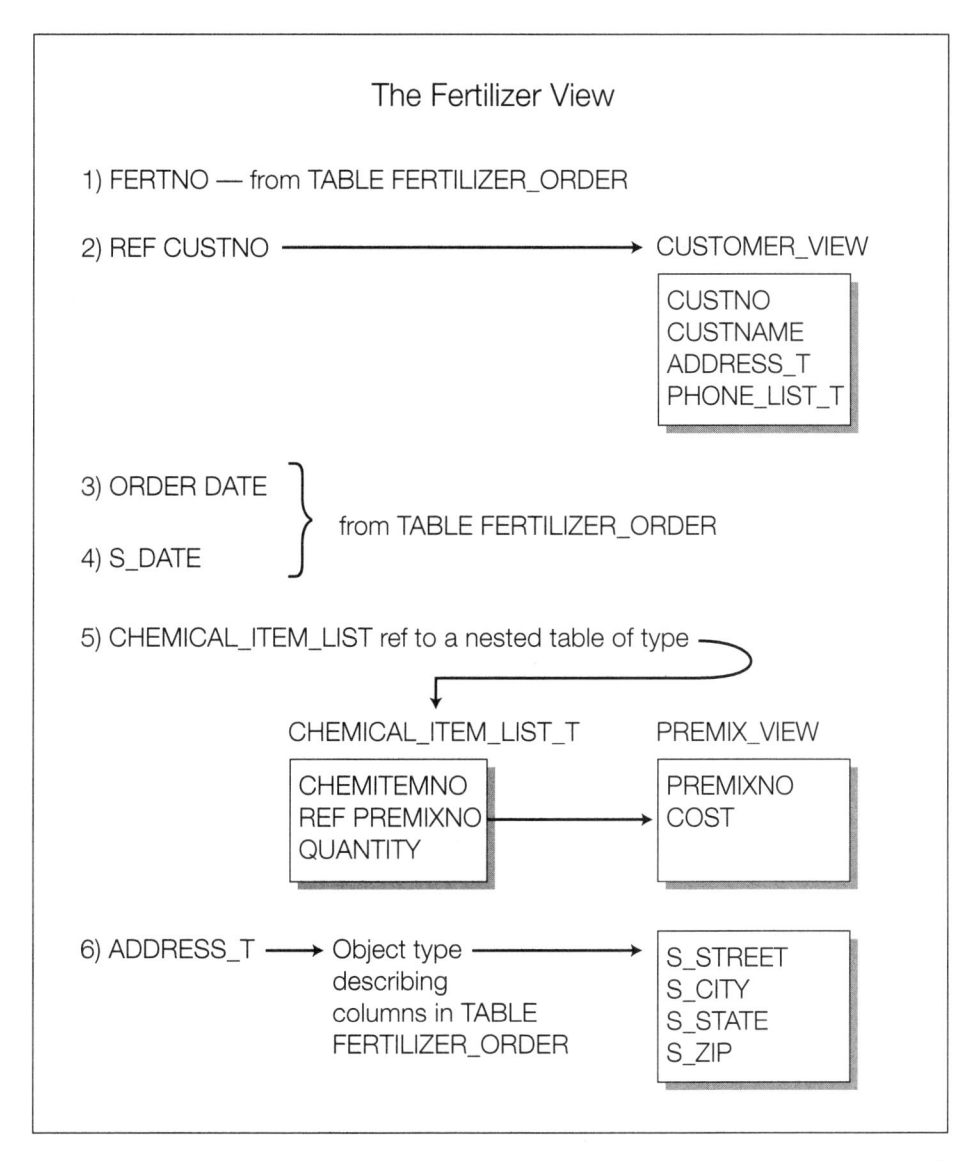

2) REF CUSTNO ⟶ CUSTOMER_VIEW
   - CUSTNO
   - CUSTNAME
   - ADDRESS_T
   - PHONE_LIST_T

3) ORDER DATE ⎫
4) S_DATE ⎭ from TABLE FERTILIZER_ORDER

5) CHEMICAL_ITEM_LIST ref to a nested table of type

   CHEMICAL_ITEM_LIST_T
   - CHEMITEMNO
   - REF PREMIXNO ⟶ PREMIX_VIEW
   - QUANTITY

   PREMIX_VIEW
   - PREMIXNO
   - COST

6) ADDRESS_T ⟶ Object type describing columns in TABLE FERTILIZER_ORDER ⟶
   - S_STREET
   - S_CITY
   - S_STATE
   - S_ZIP

Figure 5.10
A graphical depiction of the fertilizer view.

Summary

In this chapter, we discussed one of the most powerful new features in the object-oriented extensions for Oracle8—pointers. By utilizing these new constructs, it is now possible to design new aggregated objects linked together not by relational keys but through the direct navigational ability of pointer structures. The face of database design is changing with the advent of allowable violation of first normal form. We covered the new operators **REF**, **DEREF**, **VALUE**, and the supporting clauses that enable this exciting new functionality. Finally, we discussed the use of the new pointer constructs under some fascinating real-world situations. The next chapter discusses an equally important topic in regard to the new object-oriented functionality, namely, methods. Methods represent an important step toward fulfilling a greater object-oriented behavior in the database paradigm.

HIGH PERFORMANCE

Method Design And Oracle8

CHAPTER 6

HIGH PERFORMANCE

Though this be madness, yet there is method in it.
—William Shakespeare, Hamlet, *Act 2*

Method Design And Oracle8

In the past, the one aspect of modeling database applications in the real world that confounded developers was the ability to adequately combine the behavior (business rule) of an element with the data itself. Dealing with the processes that evolved from the decomposition of the detailed data flow diagram meant creating application code (usually PL/SQL) in the form of detached triggers and procedures. Often, this detached approach yielded client-side code (e.g., DML in Oracle Forms), which was prevalent in two-tier client/server applications. Fundamentally, it was recognized that the encapsulation of data with its associated behavior, as is commonly done in the object-oriented paradigm, was key to the effective modeling and implementation of complex systems. Part of the tremendous appeal of the object-oriented paradigm was this ability to encapsulate the two together. The exciting new object extensions in Oracle8 bring this sorely needed functionality to the object-relational paradigm. In this chapter, we will explore the implementation of methods in detail. We'll start with an explanation of what methods are, how Oracle8 treats them, and how to use them in your applications.

What Are Methods?

Recalling the discussion from Chapter 1, a *method*, in the purely object-oriented paradigm, is the incorporation of a specific behavior assigned to an object or element. A method is a function of a particular class. Objects receive messages from programs by calling methods. A *message* is essentially an executed function belonging to a class member. Recall that class members manifest themselves as user-defined data type objects in the context of Oracle8. The message will include the function call and its associated arguments. For languages like C++, the method is an integral part of an object construct. The method is the means by which objects communicate with one another. The coupling of data with behaviors also creates a condition where database objects "know" their behaviors.

The implementation of methods in Oracle8 blurs the distinction between methods and messages. Oracle8 uses PL/SQL to define a method. The resulting event generated from the PL/SQL program unit can be considered the message. PL/SQL is the essential element for creating methods in Oracle8. Although routines written in C and Java are supported for use with methods, they cannot be declared directly from the method definition. Instead, they are incorporated as external procedures, which are covered in greater detail in a subsequent section.

As a developer, you'll find PL/SQL programming to be a familiar venue for data manipulation. This is natural because PL/SQL has been the de facto tool for use with relationally stored data in Oracle. Precompilers have also been used to handle programming tasks where PL/SQL has been unsuitable. A perfect example of this is the use of Pro*C in the Oracle Financials modules to perform particularly complex tasks, such as pricing schemes in the Order Entry module. In all these cases, the code is detached from the actual data, making encapsulation impossible. In fairness, however, object-orientation was not intended in the purely relational paradigm. Now that technology has advanced to the point in which the marriage of object and relational models is feasible, it only makes sense to redirect our design efforts to capitalize on the extended functionality.

In the pure relational model, the interaction between data and behavior is disjoint. Figure 6.1 illustrates how data and processes interact.

Note how programs are outside the database and manipulate data from separately collected modules comprised of PL/SQL and often a variety of third-generation languages. The advantage of this technique is that the events or processes can be maintained in a centralized location, such as a set of libraries on the client or application server. Unfortunately, there is no way to encapsulate this code with the data elements they are designed to affect.

Now, let's consider the object-relational model and how you can associate data with its related methods. Figure 6.2 illustrates how this association takes place.

The implementation of processes as methods to data objects does not prevent you from maintaining code modules outside your database. If anything, you now have a more robust environment for data and processes.

Because of the importance of PL/SQL programming in the development of methods, we will take a moment to discuss PL/SQL constructs and cover topics pertinent to the subsequent discussion on developing methods.

METHOD DESIGN AND ORACLE8

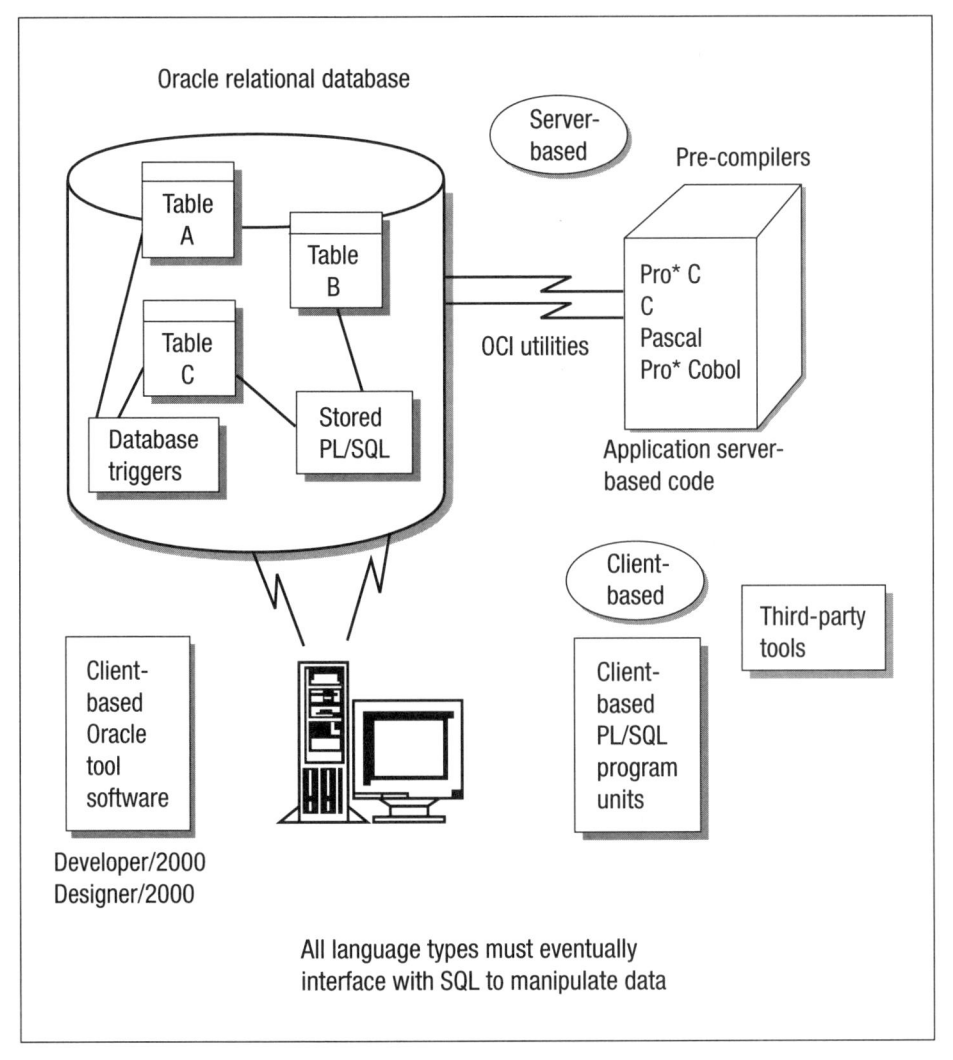

Figure 6.1
Conventional means of incorporating behavior into the relational model.

PL/SQL Constructs

PL/SQL program units will be the primary vehicle for creating methods, so let's take a moment to briefly review their structure and implementation. PL/SQL program units can manifest themselves in the following several ways:

- Anonymous PL/SQL blocks
- Triggers

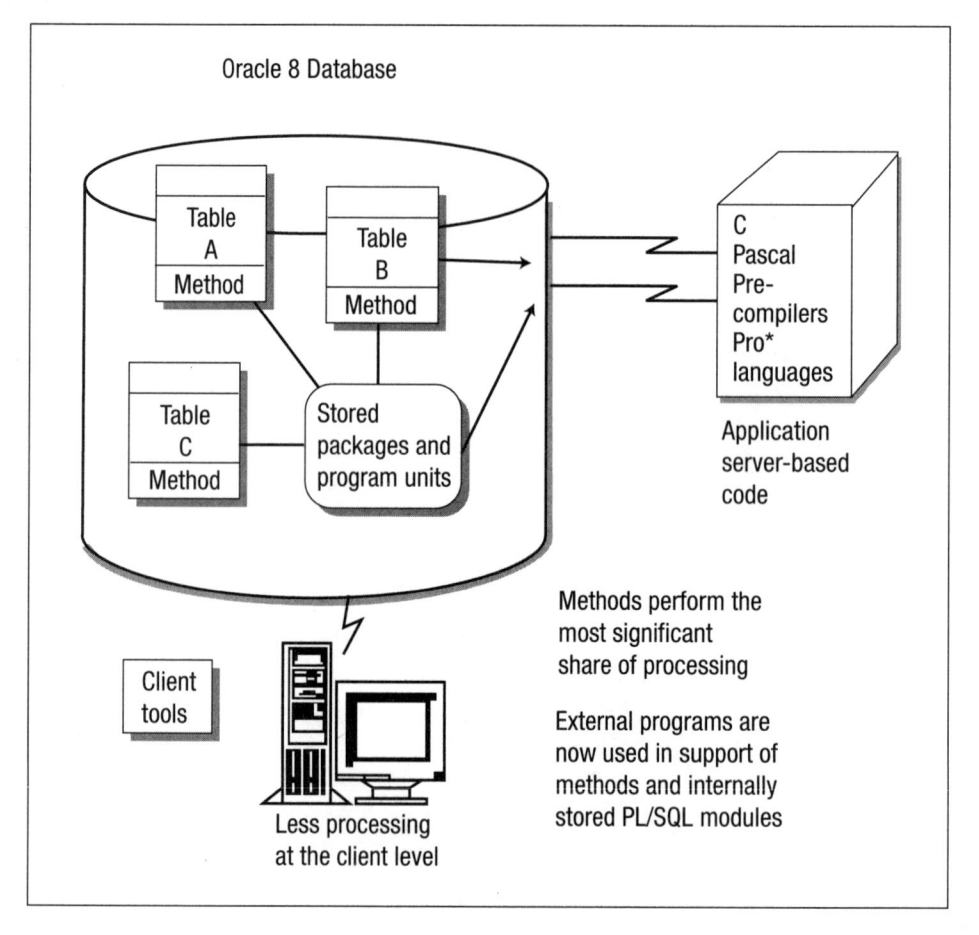

Figure 6.2
Incorporating behavior in the object-relational model.

- Standalone procedures and functions
- Procedures and functions incorporated into packages

The most common and simplest form of PL/SQL that developers are accustomed to using is probably the anonymous block. Basically, the anonymous block consists of an optional declaration, followed by an executable body, and finished off with optional exception handlers. A simple example of an anonymous block appears in Listing 6.1.

Listing 6.1   A sample anonymous block.

```
BEGIN
   IF error_code = 10206 THEN
      show_msg_mod('0-10206', v_button);
   ELSIF error_code = 10239 THEN
      show_msg_mod('0-10239', v_button);
   ELSIF error_code = 40010 THEN
      show_msg_mod('0-40010', v_button);
   ELSE
      message(to_char(error_code)||'-'||
         error_text,ACKNOWLEDGE);
      raise form_trigger_failure;
   END IF;
EXCEPTION
   WHEN OTHERS THEN
      NULL;
END;
```

The code example in Listing 6.1 is typical of what might be found in an Oracle Forms trigger. Good coding practice would dictate to move as much of the code as possible into libraries or procedures, but this example adequately illustrates common usage.

The anonymous block is important because it sets the groundwork for the creation of methods to be discussed soon. The declarative portion is optional when there are no variables or cursors used in the block. The exception handlers are also optional but highly recommended. Without the aid of exception handlers, conditions that cause failure will prevent complete execution of the program unit itself, not to mention any called procedures or routines. With respect to system design, it is never a good idea to leave programming "holes" or potential points of failure that cause applications to abort with an error condition. This concept becomes especially critical when the program unit in question becomes nested in other PL/SQL constructs, thereby multiplying the potential point of failure. Developers must carefully evaluate every program unit for possible outcomes, no matter how unlikely. Later, I'll introduce the use of both standard and user-defined exception handlers under the section entitled "Building Methods In PL/SQL."

The second type of PL/SQL program unit is the database trigger. Database triggers are merely specialized anonymous blocks stored in the database and defined to fire before or after certain DML statements. A good example of a database trigger is shown in the code example found in Listing 6.2.

Listing 6.2 A sample database trigger.

```
CREATE OR REPLACE TRIGGER EMP_UPDATE
   AFTER INSERT
      OR UPDATE OF
         emp_no, emp_name
      ON employee
   FOR EACH ROW
DECLARE
   v_emp_no            NUMBER;
BEGIN
IF UPDATING THEN
      v_emp_no := :old.emp_no;
END IF;

IF INSERTING THEN
   INSERT INTO employee_archive
   values ( :new.emp_no, :new.emp_name,
            :new.emp_address);
END IF;

IF UPDATING THEN
      UPDATE  employee_archive
      SET emp_no := :new.emp_no,
          emp_name := :new.emp_name,
          emp_address := :new.emp_address
      WHERE emp_no = v_emp_no;
END IF;
END;
```

The database trigger in Listing 6.2 writes data to an archive table whenever the primary table has new records inserted. The **INSTEAD OF** trigger, for use with views described in Chapter 4, is also an example of a database trigger. Database triggers are a useful construct for maintaining referential integrity; however, they have no bearing on our discussion of methods, so we will dispense with any lengthy explanation of their use.

The third type of program unit is the standalone stored procedure or function. Stored procedures and functions have names and can accept parameters and return values. The stored function can only return one value. Because this type of program unit is stored in the database, it must have a legal PL/SQL identifier as a name. Typical examples of both constructs are shown in Listing 6.3.

Listing 6.3 Stored procedures and functions.

```
PROCEDURE print_analysis_list is
BEGIN
  DECLARE
     pl_id ParamList;
     pl_name varchar2(10) := 'reportlist';
  BEGIN
    pl_id := get_parameter_list(pl_name);
    IF not id_null(pl_id)
       THEN destroy_parameter_list(pl_name);
    END IF;
    pl_id := create_parameter_list(pl_name);
    add_parameter(pl_id, 'analysis_list',data_parameter,
       'NEW_ANALYSIS_GROUP');
    run_product(REPORTS,'analysis_list',synchronous,
        runtime,filesystem,pl_id,null);
    message('ANALYSIS PRINT READY! Handing off to default
       Windows Printer.');
  END;
END;

FUNCTION fget_alpha (valpha1     VARCHAR2)
    RETURN    VARCHAR2
    IS
    valpha2    VARCHAR2(1);
    c_dummy_1  NUMBER;
    BEGIN
      IF ascii(valpha1) >= 65 and ascii(valpha1) <= 89 THEN
         BEGIN
            select ascii(valpha1)
            into   c_dummy_1
            from   dual;

            c_dummy_1 := c_dummy_1 + 1;

            select chr(c_dummy_1)
            into   valpha2
            from   dual;
         EXCEPTION
            when no_data_found then
                null;
         END;
      END IF;
      RETURN  valpha2;
    END fget_alpha;
```

The stored procedure code is an example of a useful routine that creates a parameter list and passes an Oracle Forms record group to an Oracle Reports module. The stored function code illustrates a routine that evaluates an alpha character input and returns the next alphabetic letter. Such a function is useful when item codes are used and the next sequential value requires the next letter in alphabetic sequence. In both cases, note that each has a unique name that conforms to PL/SQL naming standards. Keep in mind that stored procedures and functions are subject to the same access restrictions as other objects stored in the database. For example, if other users are to execute the program units created by a particular user, then the appropriate grants must be run. This is done in the same way that grants to tables, sequences, and so forth are granted to users with a requirement to use particular database objects.

Stored procedures and functions are capable of accepting parameters. Parameters can be declared as **IN** for parameter values going into the program unit, **OUT** (procedures) for values to be returned, and **IN OUT** for parameters that traverse in both directions. The default is **IN**. Functions deal with return values in a slightly different way. The **RETURN** clause is used to indicate what is to be passed back. Note from the previous example that a variable **valpha2** is defined, populated, and returned. Functions are intended for the return of single values only. If more than one value is required from a program unit, then a procedure should be used. Note that in the parameter declaration, a data type is specified. The data type selected should be consistent with the item to be populated on the receiving end of the function or procedure. We will discuss a useful concept known as *overloading* in the section entitled "Building Methods In PL/SQL" that demonstrates an effective strategy for polymorphism. Stored procedures and functions are important to our discussion of nesting methods found later in this chapter.

The last type of program unit is the package. The effective implementation of a method network or hierarchy (described later) will make tremendous use of the PL/SQL package. The package is an extremely effective way to modularize code and insulate users and applications from frequent algorithmic changes. A package is composed of two parts: specification and body. The specification declares what program units will appear in the body, as well as define what parameters are required for each. Source code for each program unit does not appear in the specification.

The package body contains all source code and, occasionally, program units or localized variables that have not been included in the specification. Program units and variables that appear in the body and not in the specification are localized to that package only and cannot be directly addressed by the user. Such localization is useful when you do not want users to have the ability to directly manipulate values or behaviors.

The values of localized variables can be guarded from direct manipulation, thereby maintaining the integrity of the variable. For example, let's say you declared a localized variable and fixed the value to the ending date of your company's fiscal year. The variable might be used for comparison purposes during which budget figures are calculated. If the variable is declared in the specification, a user with access to the owning package could manually alter the value. If the variable is localized, then no such manipulation can occur. Localized units can only be called from program units within a package, while those declared in the specification can be called from other packages or routines.

Localized declarations also serve to hide code that users have no need to see. This behavior represents a form of encapsulation for the package because the internal details are hidden from the user. The code segment shown in Listing 6.4 demonstrates a typical package script with a complete specification and body:

Listing 6.4 A sample package script.

```
CREATE OR REPLACE PACKAGE invoices
/*
||  Program: invoices
||   Author: David Anstey
*/

IS

FUNCTION  fgen_invoice_nbr (vinv_type IN VARCHAR2)
          RETURN VARCHAR2;

FUNCTION  fget_price_list_name (vprice_id IN NUMBER)
          RETURN VARCHAR2;

END invoices;
/

CREATE OR REPLACE PACKAGE BODY invoices
IS
```

```
      FUNCTION fgen_invoice_nbr (vinv_type VARCHAR2)
         RETURN   VARCHAR2
      IS
      vinv_nbr1      NUMBER;
      vinv_nbr       VARCHAR2(20);
      c_inv_source   VARCHAR2(32);
      BEGIN
         BEGIN
            select invoice_nbr_sequence
            into   c_inv_source
            from   sales_invoice_types
            where  invoice_type_name = vinv_type;

            vinv_nbr1 := sequences.fget_next_seqnum(c_inv_source);
            vinv_nbr := to_char(vinv_nbr1);

         EXCEPTION
            when no_data_found then
               null;
         END;
         RETURN vinv_nbr;
      END fgen_invoice_nbr;

   FUNCTION fget_price_list_name (vprice_id NUMBER)
      RETURN     VARCHAR2
      IS
      vprice_name  VARCHAR2(40);
      BEGIN
         BEGIN
            select price_list_name
            into   vprice_name
            from   sales_price_lists
            where  price_list_id = vprice_id;
         EXCEPTION
            when no_data_found then
               null;
         END;
         RETURN vprice_name;
      END fget_price_list_name;

END invoices;
```

Keep in mind that if a function or procedure is declared in the specification, then the source code must appear in the body in order for it to generate without errors. A package specification can be created without a body much like a user-defined object type can be declared as incomplete.

Now that we have reviewed some of the essential elements that go into the construction of methods, let's examine some of the reasons for using methods in Oracle8.

Reasons For Using Methods In Oracle8

At this point, it is clear that moving procedures out of the application programs and into the database engine is a significant benefit of Oracle8's object-relational methodology. Not only does this provide a more secure repository for the code, but it encourages the concept of code reuse. If you combine these aspects with the ability to represent aggregate objects, then you have an extremely robust framework for dealing with complex real-world application designs.

With the ability to move process code into the database, the role of the database administrator changes. This new responsibility means that DBAs must be even more adept at maintaining objects stored in databases. A DBA's role must expand to include a greater understanding of the code and also how to administer it. For example, methods make use of roles and permissions much as data objects do. A DBA must ensure that users have access to methods that manipulate the data. More importantly, if methods include nested calls to other procedures, then the DBA must be cognizant of these relationships, as well as ensure that all components work together. Developing applications in Oracle8 heightens the importance of DBA involvement throughout the development and design process.

The role of the programmer will change just as much as that of the DBA. With greater control of the code that enters the system, programmers will no longer have the ability to run renegade, creating ad hoc code in isolation. Adherence to strict design and coding standards will be necessary. Coded modules will become a part of an integrated design approach and must pass muster with the DBA and project leader before inclusion into the database. The focus will now shift to smaller, generic, reusable components. More on how the design effort incorporates this philosophy is found in the upcoming section on designing a method network.

What are the reasons, then, for introducing methods in Oracle8? From a pragmatic point of view, the following reasons are given:

- *Code Reusability*—Process code only needs to be written once. Cleanly debugged and generated program units can be used in other modules and applications.

- *Configuration Management*—Storing code in a central location in a common format, namely, the database, supports rapid code retrieval and simplifies the maintenance task. The database can also be used for tasks like code searches and code backup.

- *Proactive Tuning*—Because the SQL is stored in the database, DBAs and developers can extract and test the methods used in applications. Information garnered from these tests can be used to pinpoint areas where indexes are needed, identify tables that can benefit from caching in the buffer pool, and other performance tuning techniques.

- *Application Portability*—Because code is resident in the database, the code is immune to platform changes like operating system changes or multiplatform execution. Portability from platform to platform is simplified because the executable code will not require recompilation.

- *Process Cross-Referencing*—Documentation of a method's use in an application is simplified through the use of a data dictionary. Method calls can be examined to identify data and program dependencies. Maintenance is also simplified because all applications that reference a particular entity can be identified easily.

Now that we have provided sufficient background into the introduction of methods, let's examine the ways in which they are used in Oracle8.

Using Methods In Oracle8

Methods will be unavoidable if you intend to make use of the object extensions in Oracle8. In this section, we will begin with some of the elementary uses of methods in Oracle8. Believe it or not, every time a user-defined data type is created, a method is generated. Take the following code segment in Listing 6.5, which defines an object type, as an example:

Listing 6.5 Sample code for creating a user-defined data type.

```
CREATE TYPE Address_t AS OBJECT (
   Address1    VARCHAR2(30),
   Address2    VARCHAR2(30),
   Address3    VARCHAR2(30),
   City        VARCHAR2(20),
   State       VARCHAR2(2),
```

```
    Zip      NUMBER(5)
    );
```

While no explicit declaration is made in Listing 6.5, Oracle creates a system-defined *constructor method*. A constructor method is a function that creates the new object based on the definition stated in the object type's specification. Oracle names the new constructor method the same name as the new object type. The parameters are the same as the attributes named in the object type definition. From the standpoint of method execution, think of the use of the object type name as the invocation of the constructor method. For example, let's say you used the previously defined object type as an attribute in another DML statement like the one in Listing 6.6.

Listing 6.6 A DDL statement that invokes a constructor method.

```
INSERT INTO employee ( emp_no,
                       emp_name,
                       Address
                      )
VALUES(1000675,
 'Jones, Davy',
 Address  ( '123 Maple Street', 'Albuquerque', 'NM', '87505')
 );
```

In this case, your use of the **Address** data attribute in the **VALUES** clause of the **INSERT** statement invokes the constructor method. The constructor method returns an object that becomes the **Address** data attribute. Users and developers could consider this a "built-in" method because the explicit coding and execution is eliminated. In the section that follows, you'll be introduced to the first of the explicitly declared method types and shown how Oracle manages comparison of user-defined data objects.

Comparison Methods

In Oracle8, methods can be used in comparative functions when used with user-defined object types. In the traditional relational model, scalar values of type **VARCHAR2** and **NUMBER** were easy to compare and contrast. This simplicity diminishes when the data types are more complex, such as those we have seen so far. The answer to dealing with these complex types in a comparative element is to implement one of the two comparison methods now available with the object extensions.

Map methods provide a way to compare two objects to determine a quantitative outcome. For example, let's say you defined an object type of **VEHICLE**, you might specify an attribute that describes the maximum speed. Map methods could perform a comparison to determine the vehicle with the fastest or slowest maximum speed. The syntax associated with the map method would appear like the code in Listing 6.7.

Listing 6.7 Code demonstrating a **MAP** method.

```
CREATE OR REPLACE TYPE vehicle (
   veh_id            NUMBER,
   speed             NUMBER)
MAP MEMBER FUNCTION  find_max_speed
   RETURN INTEGER IS
      BEGIN
         RETURN  speed;
      END;
);
```

Because map methods allow recursive behavior, you can ascertain that they are well-suited for aggregate operations such as **GROUP BY** and **ORDER BY**, based on the object type. What if the attributes under consideration do not offer a straightforward comparison such as this? If that is the case, then the next comparison method type might be more appropriate.

Order methods offer a different perspective. Order methods use internal logic to compare two objects. Order methods are well-suited for making comparisons of small groups of instances against a single value. An order method returned value is not quantitative but, rather, qualitative. In other words, a return value would state that object A is less than object B (return value of -1), objects A and B are the same/equal (return value of 0), or object A is greater than object B (return value of 1). The following code segment in Listing 6.8 shows a simple example of the syntax used for an order method.

Listing 6.8 Sample code for an **ORDER** method.

```
CREATE OR REPLACE TYPE vehicle (
   veh_id            NUMBER,
   speed             NUMBER
ORDER MEMBER FUNCTION  find_max_speed (speed   INTEGER)
   RETURN INTEGER IS
      BEGIN
         IF speed < SELF.speed
```

```
            THEN
                RETURN  -1;
            ELSIF site > SELF.site
            THEN
                RETURN 1;
            ELSE
                RETURN 0;
            END IF;
        END;
    );
```

Note how the order method is used on a one-time basis where the input value is compared to the current instance value, while the map method maps all instance values into scalars. Figure 6.3 illustrates the difference between the two comparison methods.

If comparison methods are used with an object type, only one or the other can be used, but not both. Comparison processes can still take place in the absence of an

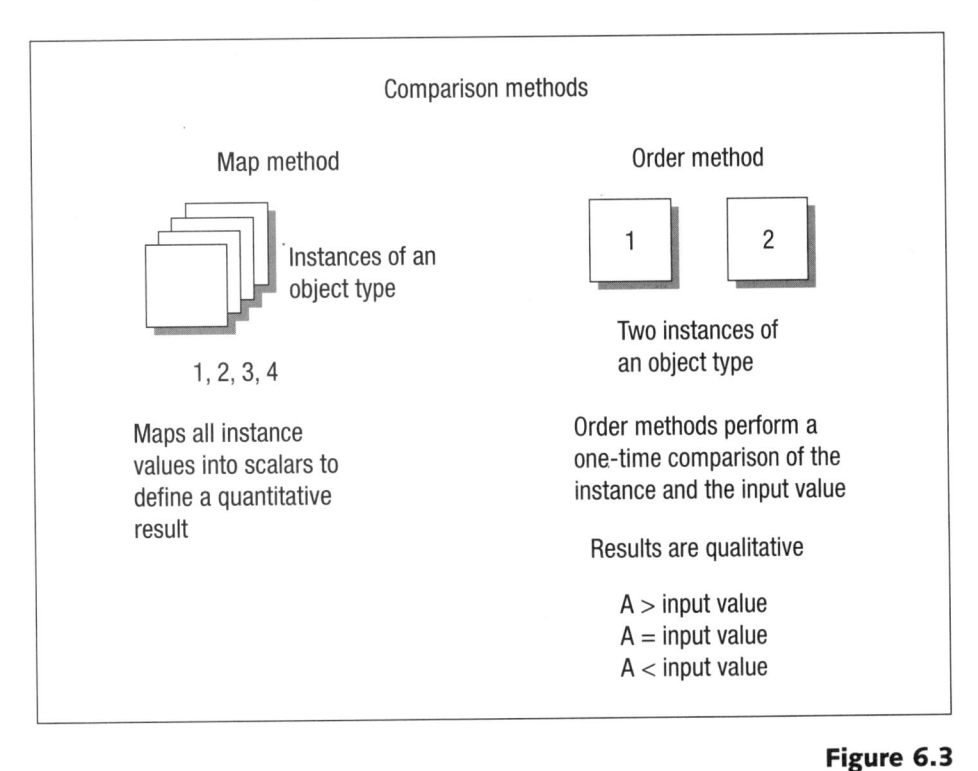

Comparison methods

Map method

Instances of an object type

1, 2, 3, 4

Maps all instance values into scalars to define a quantitative result

Order method

Two instances of an object type

Order methods perform a one-time comparison of the instance and the input value

Results are qualitative

A > input value
A = input value
A < input value

Figure 6.3
The difference between map and order comparison methods.

explicitly declared comparison method, but the scope of what can be determined is diminished. Oracle can still evaluate the corresponding attributes to determine if they are equal. **NULL** values play a role in the effectiveness of the evaluation. If the common attributes are not **NULL**, then the values can be scrutinized, and an equal or not equal determination can be made. If any of the attributes contain **NULL** values, then the result of the comparison is said to be not available or **NULL**. This is similar to the behavior found when an arithmetic operation is performed in SQL with two or more attributes and one happens to be **NULL**. The entire result of the arithmetic operation will yield a **NULL** value. This is an important fact to consider when developing user-defined object types and associated methods. Rarely is a **NULL** value from a called function of much use, even when no error condition is raised.

So far, all of the discussion has focused on basic method implementation via PL/SQL. The next section sheds some light on how third-generation languages can extend process functionality.

External Procedures

For all the power and flexibility found in PL/SQL, there will be occasions when a lower-level language is better suited for a particular function or operation. Previously, I mentioned that routines not written in PL/SQL could not be directly declared in the method definition. In order to support the use of third-generation languages, Oracle provides for the use of *external procedures*. External procedures are routines stored in a dynamic link library and registered with PL/SQL. In the current release of Oracle8, any routine that can be called from C code is supported for use in an external procedure. Commonly, the use of external procedures shows their greatest value when there is a need to interface with an event or function outside of the Oracle database. Frequent examples include processing scientific and engineering problems, data analysis, and integration with physical devices and processes. An appropriate example is the grocery store price scanner, which is a manifestation of a physical device that reads a bar code placed on merchandise. External procedures would represent the code that handles the communication between the scanner and the ultimate changes in the data tables that propagate as a result of the sales transaction. Figure 6.4 illustrates the relationship of external procedures to the process flow in the database application system.

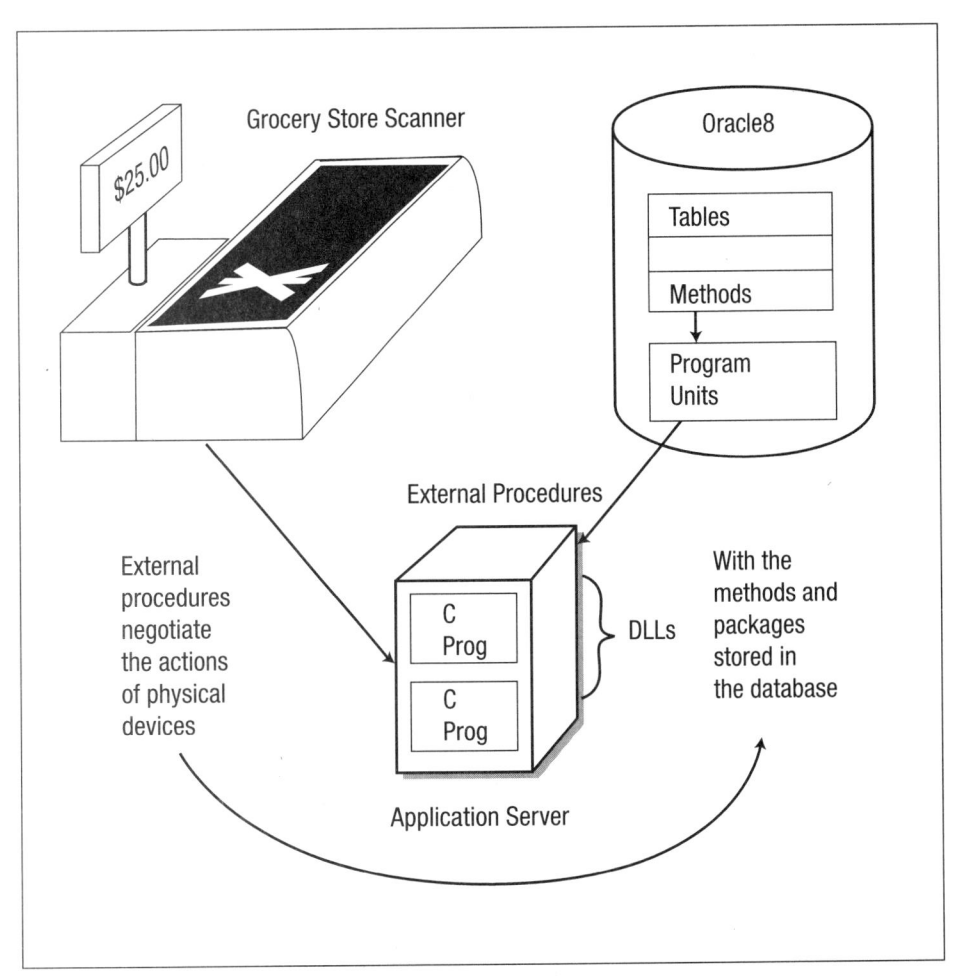

Figure 6.4
The relationship of external procedures to the database process flow.

Note: While the propensity of focus in external procedures is placed on the use of dynamic link libraries in the Windows development environment, any platform that supports dynamically loaded and shared libraries (Solaris, to name one) can make use of this feature.

Control of the operating system file-based library is handled by a DBA. As with many of the other constructs in Oracle, a schema object, called an *alias library*, representing the DLLs must be created. This is performed with the use of the **CREATE LIBRARY** command. Users authorized to implement the DLLs must be granted **EXECUTE** privileges on the alias library. The following code segment illustrates these last two concepts:

```
CREATE LIBRARY  grocery_progs AS '/home/dlls/scanner.dll';

GRANT EXECUTE ON grocery_progs TO anstey;
```

The PL/SQL program unit used to call the external procedure must have knowledge of the whereabouts of the library. To accomplish this, the library must be *registered*. Registering is performed by creating a standalone PL/SQL package to act as the proxy for the external procedure. The syntax for registering an external procedure is shown in Listing 6.9.

Listing 6.9   Code for registering an external procedure.

```
CREATE   FUNCTION grocery (
    sc1             BINARY_INTEGER;
    sc2             BINARY_INTEGER;

RETURN   BINARY_INTEGER AS EXTERNAL
    LIBRARY         grocery_progs
    NAME            "groc_scan"
    LANGUAGE   C
    CALLING STANDARD   C;
```

In the code example found in Listing 6.9, a PL/SQL proxy is created for the external procedure. The function has the same name as the external procedure, and, whenever the external procedure must be invoked, it is done by calling the proxy PL/SQL program unit. This is the only way third-generation language routines can be called as methods in Oracle8. In the previous code's syntax, the **EXTERNAL** clause indicates to Oracle that an external procedure is being used. The **LIBRARY** clause is the only required modifier in this definition. It defines what library the external procedure is located in. Recall that the library is already defined in the **CREATE LIBRARY** command, which must proceed all other external procedure statements. The **NAME** clause identifies the specific procedure to be addressed. Note that the use of quotation marks around the name preserves the case sensitivity. The **LANGUAGE** clause indicates the language that the procedure is written in. If this clause is not included, Oracle assumes the C language. The **CALLING STANDARD** clause indicates the

METHOD DESIGN AND ORACLE8

Windows NT calling standard used to compile the external procedure. The choices for this option are C and Pascal.

There are two other clauses not shown in Listing 6.9. The **WITH CONTEXT** and **PARAMETERS** clauses are used together and serve to indicate information about context pointers and passed parameters. For example, let's say you include the following lines of code:

```
WITH CONTEXT
   PARAMETERS (
      CONTEXT,
      sc1 BY REF,
      RETURN INDICATOR);
```

The **WITH CONTEXT** clause provides the external procedure with information on parameters (shown), exceptions, and other useful information. The **PARAMETERS** clause allows a user to specify certain conditions that are not covered in the formal declaration section (this is the area **sc1** and **sc2** variables are defined). The **PARAMETER** clause allows us to specify whether a parameter should be passed by value or reference, where the parameters are in the list (position), **NULL** and **NOT NULL** indicators, lengths of parameters, and non-default external data types. The **INDICATOR** property is shown in this example to highlight an interesting point. Even though the handling of **NULL**s is a default functionality in Oracle, it might be necessary to notify third-generation language procedures that a working value is **NULL**. **INDICATOR** can be used with parameters and function results.

> **Note:** It is good practice to associate an indicator with all formal parameters because PL/SQL's default behavior is to assume that a parameter cannot return a **NULL** value.

This is, by no means, an exhaustive study of external procedures. If you are interested in pursuing how to work with external procedures and write C code, refer to the *Oracle8 PL/SQL Users Guide And Reference* and to suitable texts describing the C language.

At this point, we've covered some of the fundamental concepts of PL/SQL, and methods have been introduced. Now, we will discuss further aspects of constructing methods, including some sound approaches to designing your program units.

Building Methods In PL/SQL

Methods in Oracle8 are useful for far more than value and data object comparisons. All the power and utility that developers have grown accustomed to, and more, can be integrated into methods. If you intend to create sophisticated methods in your applications, then it is highly recommended that a complete knowledge of PL/SQL programming be attained. Much like any other programming language, it is possible to write good and bad PL/SQL programs. Over the years, I have witnessed the best and worst of what can be done with this tool. In general, the bad code is not as much a function of low-level expertise as it is a function of haste and poor planning. The construction of methods can single-handedly bring down a development effort through poor documentation, unclear guidelines, and a lack of testing and quality assurance. As we enter a new era where less and less of the mechanics are visible, both to users and developers alike, it stands to reason that what developers write must be written cleaner and designed better. The methods of today will become the legacy from which future applications will spring. It is up to analysts and developers to make sure the foundation is rock solid.

The Basics Of Building Methods

When you enter into the process of designing and building methods, there are several key points that should retain your focus and assist in the development plan. The first point is to strive for encapsulation of object type behaviors. This might sound rather trite and certainly repetitive, but it really cannot be overemphasized. Encapsulation is not an old concept for those deeply entrenched in the relational paradigm. Let's consider, for a moment, an important manifestation of object type and method design. Figure 6.5 shows an object type with two subtypes. The supertype has a defined method as part of its definition.

When methods are defined for a supertype, they are inherited by all subtypes under the supertype. This points out two important aspects of object type and method design: Created behaviors are shared under an object type class, and each subtype receives the exact same behavior (method). The first of these aspects represents an economy of effort because behaviors and processes will cascade down a class hierarchy. The obvious disadvantage is pointed out in the second aspect because it is probably not desirable for all subtypes to be processed or treated in the same way. Otherwise, subtypes might not have been created in the first place.

Method Design And Oracle8

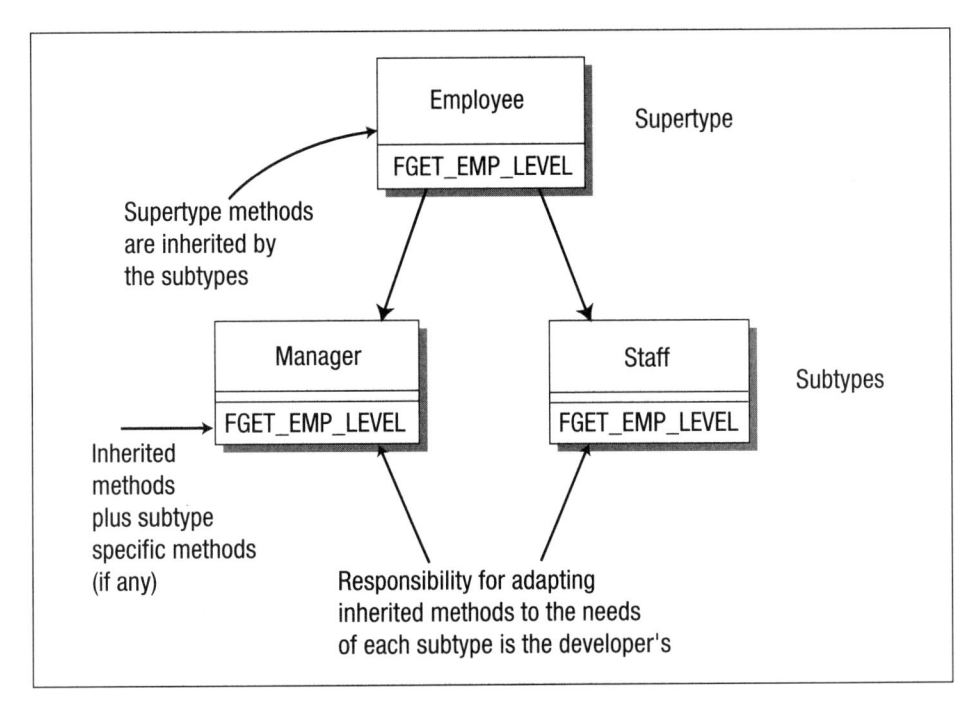

Figure 6.5
Object type and method design in a supertype/subtype configuration.

The dilemma in the last case brings us to the next key point—the incorporation of polymorphism into the method design. Recall our discussion of polymorphism in Chapter 1. Multiple behaviors can be derived from the same process. In order to accomplish this in method design, the developer must explicitly address the multiple behaviors to be performed. As with almost everything else in Oracle, there is more than one way to accomplish this, and each way has one or more design considerations behind it.

The first approach to addressing this problem is to use *overloaded* program units. Overloading is PL/SQL's answer to polymorphism. Basically, overloading is the creation of more than one program unit with the same name but each program unit differs in function and parameters. The difference in functionality is attained based on what you send to the program unit rather than which program unit you call. In simple terms, it works something like this: You create multiple program units of the same name, but one or more of the input parameters varies. For example, the first parameter accepts the employee ID and a number, the second parameter accepts the employee ID and a character string, and the last parameter accepts the employee ID and a date. The code example that follows in Listing 6.10 shows the package specification for an overloaded program unit scheme:

Listing 6.10 A sample package specification using overloaded program units.

```
CREATE OR REPLACE PACKAGE emp_promote
/*
||   Program: emp_promote
||   Author: David Anstey
*/

IS

FUNCTION  fget_emp_level (vemp_no IN NUMBER,
            vemp_grade IN VARCHAR2)
   RETURN VARCHAR2;

FUNCTION  fget_emp_level (vemp_no IN NUMBER,
            vemp_grade IN NUMBER)
   RETURN VARCHAR2;

END emp_promote;
/
```

This overloaded function example illustrates how a promotion-level process can be constructed when there are two employee types: managers and staff. Note how the overloaded functions are integrated into a single package. While this is not a functional requirement, it demonstrates good programming technique and (you guessed it) encapsulation. This form of polymorphism shown in Listing 6.10 has been available since version 7.0 of Oracle7. True polymorphism as it is defined in object-oriented programming will be available in a future release of Oracle8.

Packages offer significant benefits in PL/SQL programming. Spending the time and energy to develop packages properly results in simpler applications development in the long run, with less effort expended to create programs. Besides enforcing a modular coding structure, packages help stabilize an application's environment. The two-part structure of a package insulates your applications from coding changes. If a package specification is changed, then all modules (to include other packages and program units) that call it must be recompiled. On the other hand, if a code change occurs that affects only the body of the package, then only the body itself requires recompilation. This means that the core portions of your application code can be placed in package bodies. Changes can be contained to one specific piece of code as opposed to being scattered all over the application system. Keep in mind that if a change requires the number of parameters to adjust or if the data types of any parameters should switch, then this constitutes a change to the specification and all calling modules must be recompiled.

Returning to the previous code example, the Oracle engine is intelligent enough to ascertain the data types being passed when a program unit is called. Based on the data types being passed, Oracle selects the right version of the program unit by matching the known data types against the parameter list for each. Figure 6.6 illustrates the process that Oracle goes through to execute overloaded program units.

Overloaded program units do not have to match in number of parameters. It is acceptable to have a different set of parameters for each overloaded unit. There are a couple of reasons why this might be a desired design approach:

- You might not want to pass a variety of numbers and characters to achieve a desired result. The addition of another parameter provides a way to differentiate various program units.

- An additional parameter is necessary to drive an entirely different behavior, and the additional information is necessary to perform a desired event.

The second way in which you can achieve polymorphism is by nesting program unit calls into a primary method. For example, let's say a procedure is declared for the supertype method. The necessary logic is placed within the body of the supertype procedure to determine which of several other procedures should be executed to achieve the desired results. Figure 6.7 shows an illustration of this approach.

In this particular case, the supporting program units might not be resident in the same package as the primary method, if such a package has even been created. This way of designing methods is not as elegant and certainly not as organized as overloading. This is not to say that there are not appropriate times to structure methods with nested program units. As you will see in the section "Planning A Method Network," this approach is very powerful.

The next key point we must address is method dependency. Dependencies arise in situations like the one just described where one or more program units are nested inside one another. As mentioned earlier in this chapter, if a nested program loses its

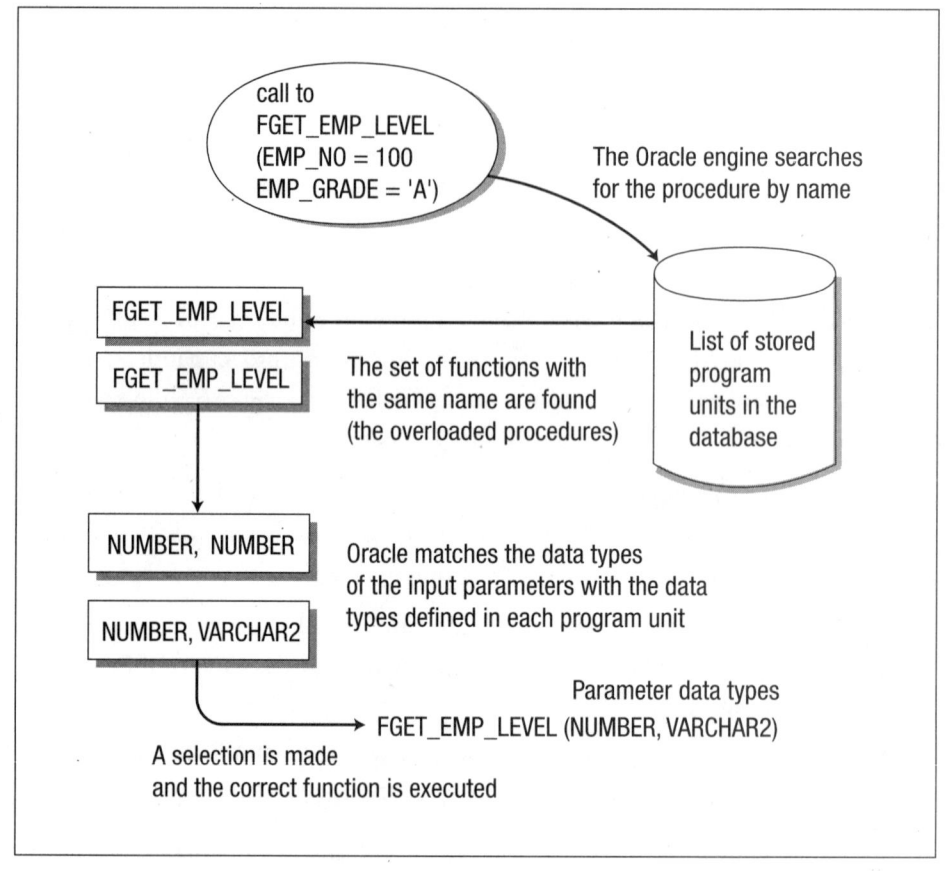

```
                    ┌─────────────────────┐
                    │   call to           │
                    │   FGET_EMP_LEVEL    │
                    │   (EMP_NO = 100     │──────▶ The Oracle engine searches
                    │   EMP_GRADE = 'A')  │         for the procedure by name
                    └─────────────────────┘
```

Figure 6.6
The Oracle process of executing overloaded program units.

generated state, for whatever reason (accidental deletion, changes in privileges, and so on), then the host program unit will fail to execute properly. What happens, in all cases, is that Oracle raises an error condition, usually indicating that the object (subprogram unit) does not exist. Oftentimes, this error is masked by a far more generic and less meaningful error, which makes debugging of the problem very difficult. The learning point here is that designing and developing with methods requires far greater diligence on the part of the entire team, making it necessary to focus on the design and to document, document, document.

To summarize our key points of method design and development, strive to adhere to the following principles:

- Work to encapsulate object behaviors.
- Plan ahead, and design for situations where polymorphism is called for.
- Analyze the design carefully to identify method dependencies.

In the upcoming section entitled "Planning A Method Network," we will integrate some of these concepts further. Before we move on to the next section, however, there are a few other items involving method use and design that need to be addressed.

Earlier, I mentioned the importance of good exception handling in program units. The appropriate attitude to take when formulating exception handlers is that almost anything can go wrong. Under most situations, it is not desirous for an active process

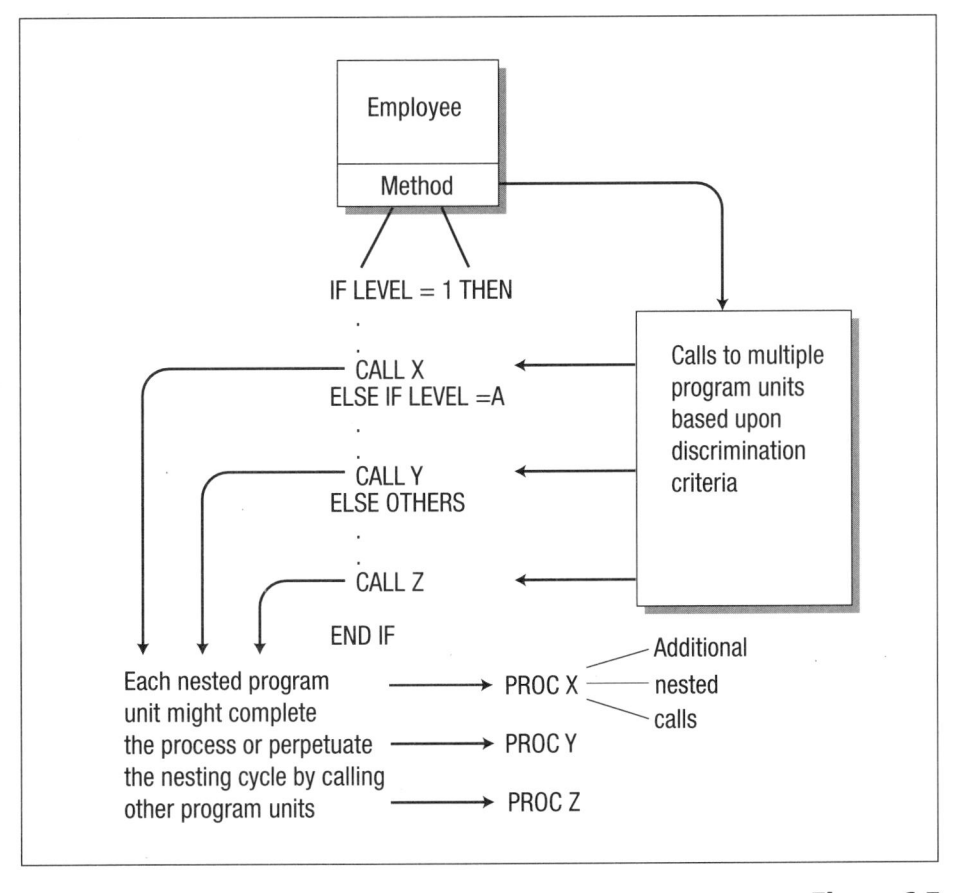

Figure 6.7
The use of nested procedures to achieve polymorphism.

to halt and prevent further activity due to an unhandled situation in your code. Halts in processing mean calls from users telling you the application is broken. Halts also mean that there are holes in the design; otherwise, the particular contingency would have been addressed.

Start with addressing the incoming parameters. Is it possible for parameters to enter the program unit **NULL**? Could the wrong data type be passed in? If this is the case, then exception handlers should be created for each situation. Examine the SQL code next. Could there be a possibility that no rows are found? Despite the best of intentions in regard to referential integrity, is it possible that duplicate rows might be retrieved? These possibilities, and more, are fertile ground for identifying possible exception handlers.

Earlier in the example of the anonymous block, a basic exception handler was shown. A standard failure condition was identified, and a basic response to that condition was provided, as follows:

```
EXCEPTION
      when no_data_found then
      null;
   END;
```

It is useful to know that almost anything can be included as the functional response to a raised exception. For example, in the previous code, you could choose to reset a variable value as follows:

```
EXCEPTION
      when no_data_found then
      sc1 := 1;
   END;
```

It is also entirely appropriate to insert a call to another program unit, as depicted in the next code segment:

```
EXCEPTION
      when no_data_found then
      grocery_proc;
   END;
```

This is very useful, but what if you want to define your own exception handlers? That too is possible, as the following code segment in Listing 6.11 demonstrates.

Listing 6.11 A code segment utilizing a user-defined exception handler.

```
DECLARE
   vinv_nbr1         NUMBER;
   vinv_nbr          VARCHAR2(20);
   c_inv_source      VARCHAR2(32);
   too_high          EXCEPTION;
BEGIN

   select  invoice_nbr_sequence
   into    c_inv_source
   from    sales_invoice_types
   where   invoice_type_name = vinv_type;

   IF c_inv_source > 1000000 THEN
      RAISE  too_high;
   ELSE
      vinv_nbr1 := sequences.fget_next_seqnum(c_inv_source);
      vinv_nbr  := to_char(vinv_nbr1);
   END IF;

   EXCEPTION
      when no_data_found then
         null;
      when too_high THEN
         DBMS_OUTPUT.PUT_LINE('The maximum invoice
            number has been exceeded.');
   END;
```

In this case, a new spin is put on an example program unit used earlier. As you can see, a user-defined exception is first introduced in the program unit declaration. In the body, an evaluation of a retrieved value is performed to see if it has exceeded a predetermined maximum value. If the condition evaluates to be **True**, then the user-defined exception is raised, and the specific actions are iterated in the exception portion of the program unit. User-defined exceptions are useful for controlling the manipulation of data within a program unit. Use of these constructs should not be overlooked during method design.

One last feature of exception handling that should not be left out of this discussion is the use of **RESTRICT_REFERENCES PRAGMA**. When functions are created as standalone entities, Oracle can automatically determine the impact (from a DML perspective) that the function will have on data. Interestingly enough, if the same function is placed in a package body or created as an object type method, Oracle is unable to determine what effect the function will have on the data it works with. This is also termed *side effects*, and they can prevent the parallelization of a query, yield indeterminate results, or even require that a package state be maintained across user sessions, which is not allowed. To work around this problem, Oracle has provided what is known as the **RESTRICT_REFERENCES PRAGMA**. Basically, this command allows a developer to explicitly state what effect (also referred to as the *purity level*) a function will have. The syntax for the use of this **PRAGMA** is shown in the following code snippet:

```
PRAGMA   RESTRICT_REFERENCES
   (fget_alpha, WNDS, WNPS, RNDS, RNPS);
```

The **PRAGMA** immediately follows the function declaration in the package specification. The four modifiers shown in the example represent the various purity levels that can be asserted. Only the **WNDS** level is mandatory. The meaning of each level is as follows:

- **NDS**—Writes no database state. The function will not modify any database tables.
- **WNPS**—Writes no package state. The function will not modify any package variables.
- **RNDS**—Reads no database state. The function will not read any database tables.
- **RNPS**—Reads no package state. The function does not read any package variables.

Failure to declare the **RESTRICT_REFERENCES PRAGMA** can cause Oracle to reject the function when it is executed if a violation of **WNDS** is detected or suspected. You might find that a package does not compile because you have asserted too high of a purity level. If this happens, eliminate one assertion at a time until you strike a balance. Keep in mind that **WNDS** is mandatory and, therefore, cannot be omitted from the declaration.

The use of this **PRAGMA** seems to cause a significant amount of consternation with developers, if the volume of email on the Oracle listservers are any indication. I have found that there are often other mitigating factors preventing the proper execution of a function that have nothing to do with purity levels. At the risk of sounding simplistic, rudimentary troubleshooting should be considered first. For example, does the user have the necessary grants to execute the function? Have the necessary synonyms been created? You might be surprised how often something as simple as this manifests itself as a possible purity problem. Purity-level problems are not merely in the domain of user-generated packages. There are certain Oracle built-ins (**DBMS_OUTPUT**, to name one) that do not incorporate **PRAGMA**, as late as version 7. This is a documented issue slated to be addressed in an unspecified upcoming release.

Now that we have discussed the important concepts of method construction, let's place some focus on how methods are called.

Calling Methods

There are two types of methods that you might find necessary to call in your application development. The first method type is the constructor type, which I described earlier. The second method is the conventional method.

Constructor methods assume the name of the object type for which they are created. Calls to a constructor method are allowed wherever standard function calls can be used. Consider the following code segment:

```
DECLARE
    addr        Address_t := Address_t ('123 Maple Street', 'Albuquerque',
                                        'NM', '87505');

FUNCTION locator ( vaddr  Address_t) RETURN Address_t IS

BEGIN
...
```

Note that the function call includes the constructor as part of the data type expression and return data value. Likewise, if you want to call a standard method in a program unit, you would do so as illustrated in the next code segment:

```
DECLARE
    addr        Address_t;

BEGIN
    addr := Address_t ('123 Maple Street', 'Albuquerque', 'NM', '87505');

    addr.find_me;
...
```

The example illustrates the desire to execute the packaged subprogram **find_me**. Methods adhere to the use of dot notation, much as any other packaged subprogram, hence, the syntax **addr.find_me**.

From a design and execution standpoint, it is important to know that methods can be *chained*. Chaining method calls means that each method will be executed in a series and in the order in which they appear in the chain. For example, let's say you wrote the following line of code:

```
addr.find_me.business_loc;
```

This code indicates that the **find_me** and **business_loc** methods will be executed one after the other, starting with the leftmost method. The ability to chain methods represents a boon to developers because a sequence of behaviors can be tied together and associated as a single process. Think of the derived benefit from combining small iterative processes to create a larger core process.

There are a couple of rules to keep in mind if you intend to chain methods. First, parameterless methods must include empty brackets throughout the chain except for the last called method. Second, it is not possible to chain any further methods to the right of a procedure. This restriction does not apply to functions, however. When multiple function methods are called, the first function must return an object that can be passed to the second function.

We have covered the essential aspects of method design, construction, and use. It is now time to address a crucial design planning strategy for use in the deployment of methods in an application system.

Planning A Method Topology

The concept of developing a method network or hierarchy can be compared to the discussion on planning a hierarchy of data types in Chapter 4. The principle is essentially the same, except that the focus of the hierarchy is on the various levels of process functionality rather than data types. However, remember that while methods may be mapped as a hierarchy, in reality they have a many-to-many relationship to other methods, and a method may have many sub-methods, while at the same time participating as a method in many super-methods. There are three types of

Method Design And Oracle8

processes to consider during the design phase that will impact the method hierarchy. The three types are:

- Processes independent of database objects.
- Processes attached to base-level database objects.
- Processes attached to aggregate database objects.

Remember, you now have the ability to nest methods one inside the other. At first glance, it would seem that methods proliferate throughout the application system. This daunting aspect is exactly what must be brought under control, and, to do so, there must be a detailed plan of action. Remember, just as data can have sub-elements and at the same time be a part of a larger data element, behaviors can be composed of sub-behaviors, while at the same time being a sub-behavior in a larger method. Figure 6.8 illustrates the recursive many-to-many nature of nested methods.

In Figure 6.8, we see that the **check_credit**() method is composed of the sub-processes **check_payment_history**() and **check_credit_references**() methods. At the same time, **check_credit**() participates in the **place_order**() and the **hire_employee**() methods.

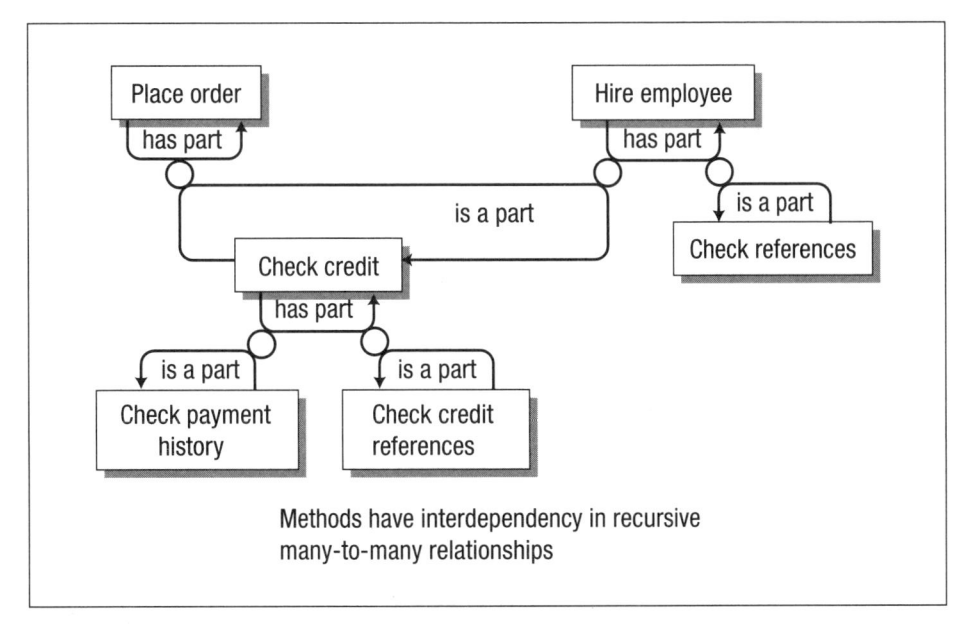

Figure 6.8
The recursive many-to-many nature of nested methods.

Chapter 6

Considering the number of options, where do we begin developing the methods? An organized approach is always best, perhaps by developing a set of rules by which to work. A good rule of thumb is to develop a series of steps to accomplish this effort of mapping data to methods. The following steps provide a good starting point for doing so.

1. Create and refine the following essential analysis and design documents:
   - A complete set of fully decomposed data flow diagrams. This becomes the starting point for all the methods that will be generated. The data flow diagrams assist in determining method names, input and output values, and a preliminary plan for nested methods.
   - A detailed object-relational element diagram (an entity relationship diagram in the relational paradigm) used for identifying the base classes in the application system.
   - A diagram showing the aggregate objects that will be used to associate the higher-level processes with the appropriate methods.
2. Create a prototype for each process identified in the data flow diagram in order to define input and output requirements as well as to track method dependencies.
3. Identify any standalone program units in the system, and trace their relationships to other program units and data objects.
4. Perform an initial mapping of method prototypes to data elements.

There are two ways to proceed once the listed steps have been performed. A top-down or a bottom-up strategy can be implemented. The disadvantage of the latter is that it is difficult to ascertain early in the effort which atomic-level program units are needed to fulfill the project requirements. The top-down approach is effective because only those processes required to meet the business objectives will be targeted.

To illustrate the importance of method prototype mapping in the steps for creating the method hierarchy, we will present a simple mapping example based upon the sub-processes contained in the **fill_order** process for the Order Entry module of a small company.

The effort begins with either a traditional data flow diagram or a functional model. We will start with a short review of object analysis. A functional specification for any system describes the complete logical model and consists of three documents:

- The data flow diagram, which is a pictorial description of all of the processes in the system.
- The data dictionary, used to define all of the data flows and data stores in the system.
- The process logic specifications that are used to describe each process, showing how the data flow is modified within each process.

The DFD diagrams the processes, data flows, and data stores as we decompose the system. While these documents may be known by different names depending upon the analysis methodology that is chosen, they should contain a complete description of all of the entities in our system. In Figure 6.9, we will take a level-one data flow diagram and show the breakdown of the **fill_order** processes.

The overall specification for the **fill_order** process is displayed, and all of the incoming and outgoing data items are easily identified. In this case, **cust_info** is shown coming in as the input to the **fill_order** process. Of course, **cust_info** does not reveal

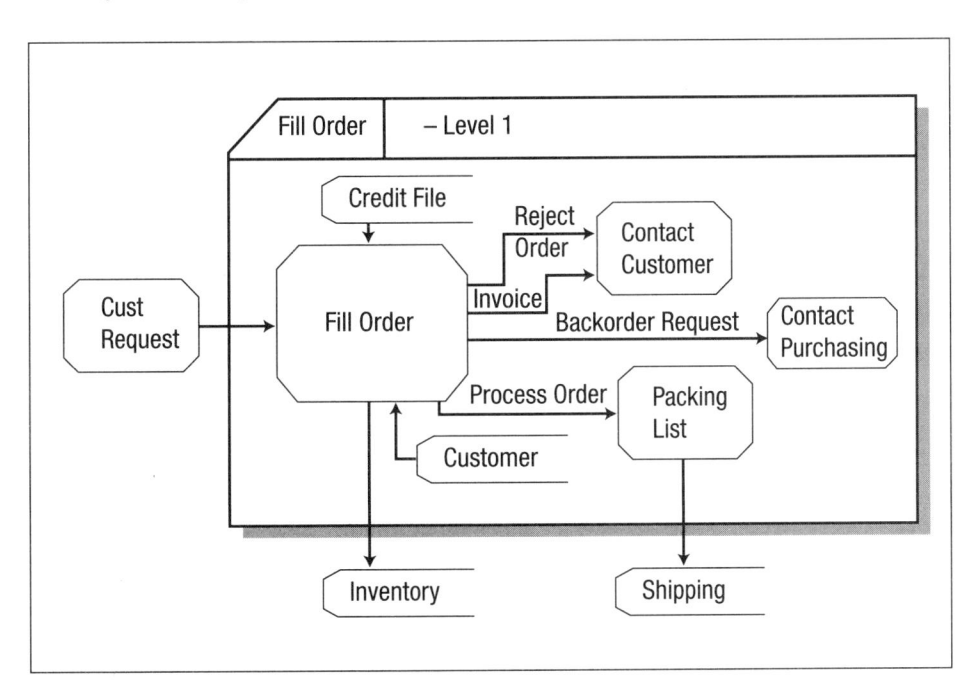

Figure 6.9
The fill_order data flow diagram (first level).

the details of this data flow, so the data dictionary is consulted to identify the contents of **cust_info**:

```
cust_info =

cust_full_name +
      cust_last_name
      cust_first_name
      cust_middle_initial

cust_full_address +
      cust_street_address
      cust_city_name
      cust_state
      cust_zip_code

cust_phone_nbr +

1
{ item_ID + item_quantity }
n
```

The data dictionary definitions are used to retrieve data items that are of interest to each process in the data flow diagram. Remember, the purpose of designing methods is to map the incoming and outgoing data flows to clean, well-defined procedures that can be coupled with the database entities.

Next, we examine the **fill_order** process further by decomposing it into lower level DFDs. Looking at the next lowest level DFD, we see that **fill_order** is broken down into three sub-processes: **check_customer_credit**, **check_inventory**, and **prepare_invoice**. The DFD in Figure 6.10 shows all of the input and output data flows for these processes.

In the second level data flow diagram, we see another level of detail for the **fill_order** process. This process is broken down into three sub-processes, each with its own data flows and processes. As the reader has probably ascertained, the departitioning of the processes will correspond to the departitioning of the methods for the object-relational database.

We can complete the foundation for our methods by showing the next level DFD for some of the lower-level processes. For illustrative purposes, we will use the **prepare_invoice** process (see Figure 6.11). We can assume that this is a functional

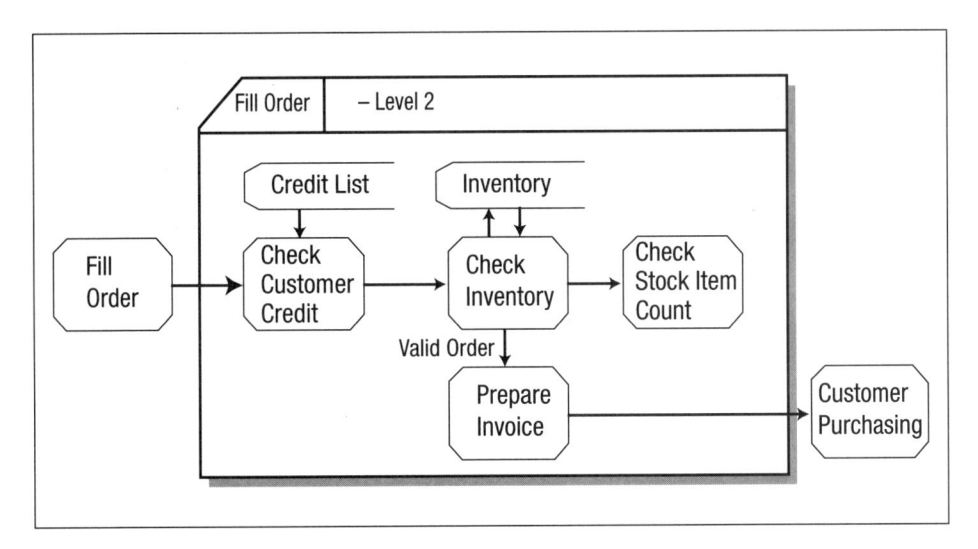

Figure 6.10
The second level data flow diagram for **fill_order**.

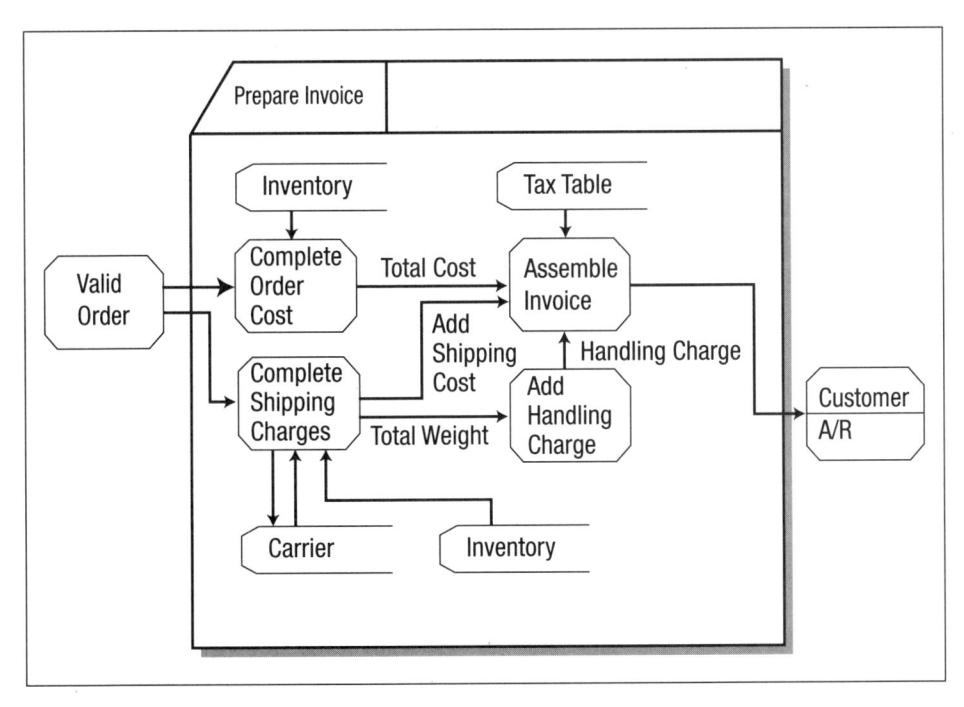

Figure 6.11
The data flow diagram for the **prepare_invoice** process.

primitive or atomic level process, and it will serve as the lowest level method in the example.

It is important for the mapping of methods to database objects to understand when a process has been departitioned to a level that corresponds with the functions of a database entity. We could continue to departition this DFD, making each process smaller and smaller, but the sub-processes would not easily map to the database objects. Hence, when a process on the DFD deals with a single function on a single database entity, we know that we have reached the functional primitive level, and the analysis is complete.

The process of developing the method network is somewhat akin to playing the shell game. As more facts surrounding the relationship between the methods are uncovered, more of the submethods will be moved to different parts of the network. As we stated earlier, the effort starts with the data flow diagram or functional model. The data dictionary is used in conjunction with the data flow diagram to associate the atomic-level attributes participating in the data process flow. At this stage, processes have a much broader scope, and it is fully understood that further decomposition will yield further sub-processes.

As you progress from one level of detail to the next, you should find the sub-processes required to perform the overall tasks for which they are assigned. At each level of analysis, you should perform an evaluation to identify duplicate process behaviors under different higher-level processes. The visualization of this procedure is shown in Figure 6.12.

At this stage of analysis, duplicated processes are not eliminated or consolidated because further analysis at greater granularity might reveal subtle differences in the processes after all. What is done is that the two (or more) processes are labeled to identify their system duplicity and the analysis proceeds. Ultimately, you'll want to proceed until decomposition is no longer possible. At that point, the effort turns to organizing the defined processes. In which case, you start by grouping the processes into the three categories named earlier: independent, base level, and aggregate.

The next step is to revisit the duplicated processes and consolidate them. This is not to say that you will create one big package and put redundant sub-processes together. Instead, the effort is focused on organization. Later, redundant processes will be grouped categorically by function. These steps have proven to be a most effective means of code organization in terms of maintenance and deployment.

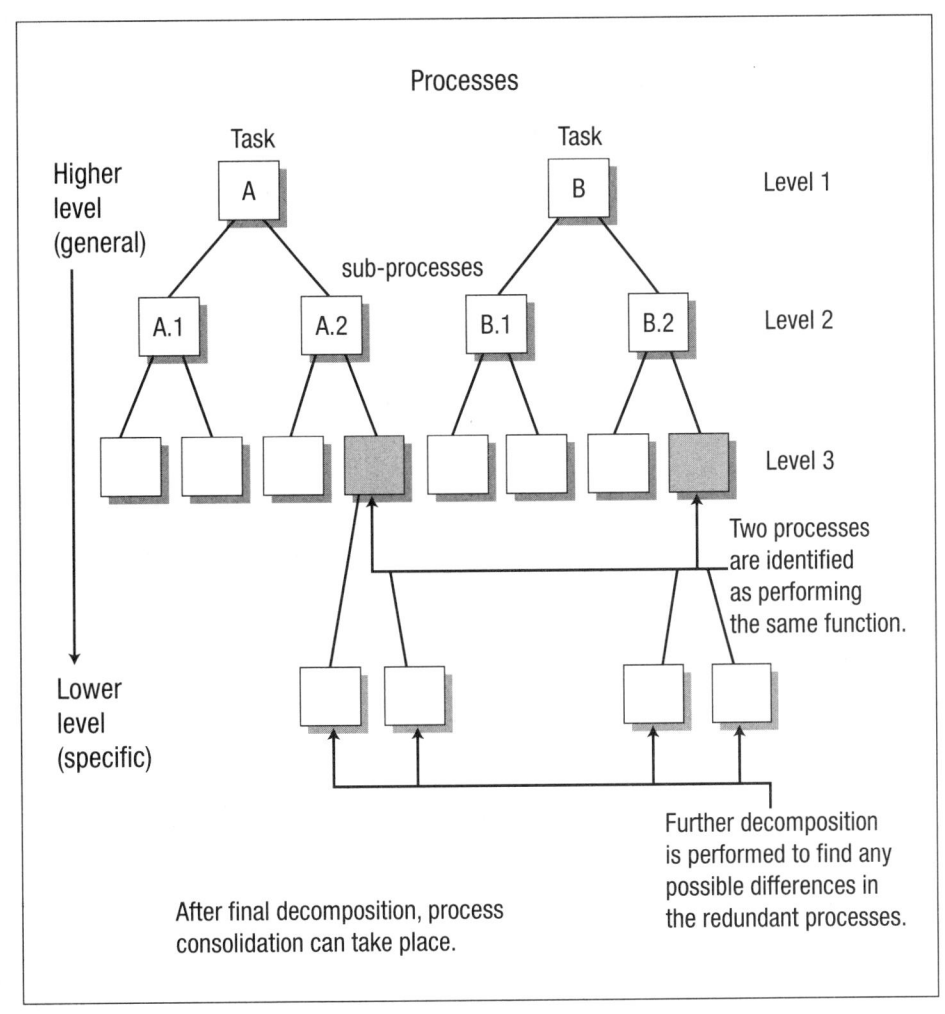

Figure 6.12
Identifying duplicate behaviors under different tasks.

Once categorization is complete, the groundwork for the method hierarchy will be in place. Figure 6.13 illustrates the concept behind the method network.

The benefits of developing a method network are threefold.

- It serves to provide much-needed information regarding method interdependency and, toward that end, provides the stepping stone to effective documentation of the system being built.

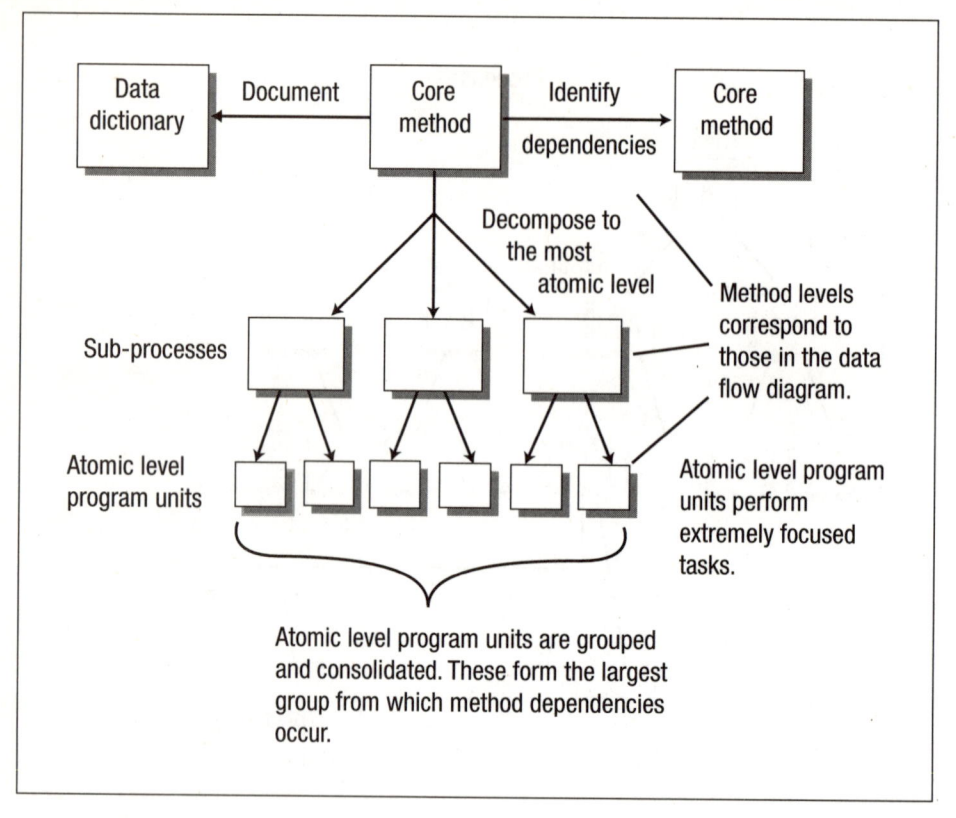

Figure 6.13
The concept of the method hierarchy or network.

- It provides the mechanism for decomposing processes so that more generic and useful atomic level sub-processes can be created, thus reducing the brunt of coding activity in the long run because reuse is encouraged.

- The process of creating a method network serves to reduce the confusion level that is sure to ensue when there is a propensity of code embedded in the database in the form of coupled behavior with data elements.

Now that the preliminary aspects of method topology have been discussed, let's take the concept of mapping methods a bit further and discuss a means to prototype them in our applications.

Creating Method Prototypes

Now that several aspects of constructing the method hierarchy have been explained, we will discuss the process of prototyping methods. In order to illustrate the concept of method prototyping, the data type definitions from the data dictionary and the functional decomposition will be used to complete our understanding of the hierarchical mapping of methods. If the analysis has been performed properly, it will be possible to reference the set of data flow diagrams, beginning at level one (describing the **fill_order** process from the earlier example) and proceeding downward to include all of the lower-level data flow diagrams.

We begin by listing each process, showing its constituent sub-methods:

```
1 - fill_order

        1.1 - check_customer_credit

        1.2 - check_inventory
                1.2.1 - check_stock_level
                1.2.2 - generate_backorder_notice
                1.2.3 - decrement_inventory
                1.2.4 - prepare_packing_slip

        1.3 - prepare_invoice
                1.3.1 - compute_order_cost
                1.3.2 - compute_shipping_charges
                1.3.3 - add_handling_charge
                1.3.4 - assemble_invoice
```

It should now be possible to identify all nested methods subordinate to other methods. Once this natural hierarchy has been developed, we are ready to define the mapping of these processes to the database classes.

The lowest level data flow diagrams represent "functional primitives," or atomic level processes that cannot be decomposed any further. Although, the functional primitive processes will become methods, it does not mean that they will never have sub-components. If the analyst has performed his or her job properly, there will be no sub-methods in these processes with the exception of standalone methods, such as a **compute_shipping_charge** method.

Starting with the atomic level processes, we design a method that accepts the same values as noted on the DFD and returns the same values to the program that invokes the method. For example, in Figure 6.11 we see that the **complete_shipping_charges** process accepts a **valid_in_stock_order** as input. Inside this process, it gathers the weight and cost of the items, computes the charges, and returns the shipping charge and total weight.

Essentially, a prototype is a formal definition of a method that describes all of the input and output data flows. The accepted form for a prototype is:

```
return_data_type Method_name
     (input_data_name_1  input_data_type_1,
      input_data_name_2  input_data_type_2,
      . . .);
```

In object-oriented terminology, we design the "prototype" for each process on our DFDs. For example, we will begin by examining how to design the prototype for the **compute_shipping_charge()** method.

From the DFD, we see that **compute_shipping_charges** accepts a **valid_in_stock_order**, and outputs the **shipping_charge** for the order. Therefore, we could create a prototype that shows **compute_shipping** charges as returning an integer (the shipping charge) and accepting a pointer to an order object.

```
int compute_shipping_charge(valid_in_stock_order *order);
```

Returning to the data dictionary it can be established that **valid_in_stock_order** contains four values that are required to compute the shipping charges:

1. The objects weight in pounds.
2. The desired class of shipping.
3. The origination zip code.
4. The destination zip code.

How is it possible to obtain these items, when only a pointer to an order is given? The method will de-reference the pointer to the order object and gather the required information. This means that the method will grab the OID and issue the appropriate SQL to accept all of the data items from the object. The following code segment shows how the SQL within the **compute_shipping_charges** method might appear:

METHOD DESIGN AND ORACLE8

```
SELECT
    item_weight,
    shipping_class,
    origination_zip_code,
    destination_zip_code
FROM
    ORDER
WHERE
    ORDER.OID = :valid_in_stock_order;
```

This function returns the shipping charge, expressed as an integer number. If a pointer to the order object were not passed to this method, the prototype for **compute_shipping** charges becomes far more complicated. The code samples that follow show the method prototypes in pseudocode and are not intended to be syntactically correct to PL/SQL.

```
int compute_shipping_charge
      (weight int, class char(1),
       origination_zip_code number(9),
       destination_zip_code number(9));
```

Note that the first token **int** refers to the data type of the value that is returned by the method. For methods that do not return a value, the first token in the prototype is **void**. For example, a method called **give_raise** would not return a value and could be prototyped as:

```
void give_raise(emp_ID number(9), percentage int);
```

Now that the basics of prototyping have been explained, let's prototype every method from our example data flow diagrams.

```
*order        fill_order(cust_info *customer);

int           check_customer_credit(cust_info *customer);

int           check_inventory(item_number int);

*invoice      prepare_invoice(valid_in_stock_order *order_form);

int           check_stock_level(item_number int);

*backorder    generate_backorder_request(item_number  int);
```

```
void                decrement_inventory(item_number int);

*packing_slip prepare_packing_slip(valid_in_stock_order *order_form);

int                 compute_order_cost(valid_in_stock_order
*order_form);

int                 compute_shipping_charges(valid_in_stock_order
*order_form);

int                 add_handling_charge(total_weight int);

*invoice            assemble_invoice(item_total_cost   int,
                                     shipping_charge int,
                                     handling_charge int);
```

Let's now describe these prototypes, in order to achieve a level of comfort with the definitions. In these prototypes, some methods return an integer number, some return on values, and others return pointers to objects. In object-oriented databases, it is not uncommon to combine assignment statements with method calls. For example, the following process code will do two things: it will compute the shipping charges for the order, and it will assign the result to a variable called **my_shipping_charges**:

```
my_shipping_charges = compute_shipping_charges(:my_order_form_OID);
```

At the same time, we can also return an OID in a method call, so we can embed the OID into another object. In the following code, assume that we have defined the data type for order OID as a pointer to order. We can now do two things in a single statement. Below we are invoking the **fill_order** method and at the same time returning the OID of the new order object into our **order_OID** variable:

```
order_OID = fill_order(:cust_info);
```

A complete specification for each method has now been created, stating the name and data type of every input and output variable. Each of these methods will be independently tested, and the internal variable may not be known to the calling method. This is known as information hiding and is used when "private" variables are declared and used within the method. This is also a key characteristic of encapsulation. Keep in mind that the objective is to make each method into a reusable black box that can always be counted on to function properly. This is the very foundation of object method reusability.

Summary

In this chapter, we discussed one of the most important new features to come about as a result of the object extensions to Oracle8, namely, methods. We defined what methods are and covered important information regarding their use and implementation. We have looked at the steps required to build them, and we discussed some important facts about their interaction. We finished the chapter with a review of good system development using methods by building a method network.

In the next chapter, I present a brief tour of two of the emerging tools that will aid developers and designers in their struggle to create systems in Oracle8's object-relational environment: Oracle's Object Database Designer and Logic Works' OR-Compass.

HIGH PERFORMANCE

The Tools Of The Trade

CHAPTER 7

Man is a tool-using animal...Without tools, he is nothing; with tools, he is all.
—Sartor Resartus, Thomas Carlyle

The Tools Of The Trade

Designing database application systems is a science of logic and organization. In Chapter 2, I described the methodical life cycle approach to synthesizing business objectives and requirements into working database systems. In Chapter 3, we discussed how the shift in database design philosophy is forcing systems analysts and developers to rethink their approach to designing database systems in the object-relational paradigm.

Throughout the discussion in this book thus far, we have not addressed specific examples of how automated tools help analysts and designers. There are two reasons for this. First, and foremost, a thorough understanding of the new object extensions and their ramifications needs to be demonstrated without masking the mechanical details. To illustrate this point, let's compare the activity of database design with learning math in school. Before the teacher allows students to use calculators to work various equations, students must demonstrate they've gained an understanding of the concepts and fundamentals used in solving the assigned equations. Accordingly, the concepts and fundamentals of the new object extensions must be presented, so analysts and developers can have a clear understanding of the object extensions before they use automated tools to generate them.

The second reason for avoiding tool-specific examples thus far is because object-relational modeling tools are still in their infancy. Many analysts and developers are unfamiliar with the specifics of the new generation of tools. Therefore, using the tools in the illustrative examples presented so far would have complicated the important discussion of the new object extensions in Oracle8.

The field of object-relational modeling tools is still rather small but continues to grow every day. Two likely candidates for modeling your object-relational database systems are presented here. Both of these products are available at the current time, and both have been designed to work with Oracle8. The first product described in this chapter is Oracle's new modeling tool called *Object Database Designer*. The second tool is the new modeling tool from Logic Works called *OR-Compass*. The following discussion is not a product review that seeks to contrast the various strengths and weaknesses of each product against the other. Rather, the intent is to highlight the use and functionality of each so that you can gain a better understanding as to which tool might serve your specific needs. Also, this chapter serves to highlight the kind of capabilities offered in this first generation of object-relational modeling tools. Features and functionalities will most likely be added as the functionality of the object-relational database approaches maturity.

Oracle's Object Database Designer

The Object Database Designer is a new tool from Oracle Corporation intended for use with Oracle8 and its object extensions. Unfortunately, at the time of this writing, the product was unavailable for direct evaluation. I will, however, present a somewhat comprehensive description of the product and outline its many features. Before you can use Object Database Designer, you must have version 8.0.3 of the database, at a minimum.

In order to use Object Database Designer effectively, you should have a basic knowledge of relational and object-relational database modeling concepts. If you want to use the C++ components, you must master the language first. The tool is designed so that much of the tedious, manual hands-on coding of C++ and SQL are eliminated, thereby freeing up the developer to concentrate on other parts of the system-development effort. It is Oracle's claim that a developer does not need to know a great deal of SQL in order to produce a successful database design with this tool. A great deal of the tool's emphasis has been placed on the creation of C++ runtime libraries for use in a client-side object cache. This would indicate that a greater focus is being placed on application languages centered around C++.

To provide a migration path for Oracle7-based database systems, the tool provides a reverse-engineering utility to retrieve design information from existing database schema. The developer can then make enhancements and modifications in the Type Modeler (described in the next section) and regenerate the schema into Oracle8, thus allowing the use of the object extensions. From this brief overview, let us now move on to a description of the major components that comprise the Object Database Designer.

An Overview Of Object Database Designer's Components

Object Database Designer is a full-featured modeling tool that supports all aspects of the object-relational database management system (ORDBMS) design and creation. The underlying methodology is based heavily upon the Unified Modeling Language described in Chapter 3. There are six components of the Designer included in the tool (see Figure 7.1):

- *Type Modeler*—The Type Modeler is used to design the application diagram and present a graphical representation of it much like the entity relation diagram is used in relational modeling. The Type Modeler allows users to define types representing schema objects and identify the relationships between them. It also allows the creation of operations (methods) and attributes for defined types. Interestingly, object types can be created that are not a part of the schema.

- *Navigator*—The Navigator provides a structured hierarchical tree-like view of the objects in the schema being created. Developers familiar with other Oracle tools, like Designer/2000, will find an immediate familiarity with the Navigator as it resembles and operates like the Navigator in Designer/2000. The Navigator allows the developer to browse through the repository objects. More on the repository will be discussed later. Objects in the Navigator can be selected and dragged into the type modeler for viewing or for editing with a property screen.

- *C++ Generator*—The C++ Generator component of the Object Database Designer creates C++ class definitions from the object types that have been defined in the Type Modeler or Navigator. The resulting C++ object layer becomes the interface between the database and any supporting applications developed in C++. The generated classes represent the objects from the application that are stored in the database. The classes contain transparent persistency to the database, but they can be treated as regular C++ objects. Creation of these classes removes the need for the programmer to manually code the underlying mechanisms required to communicate with the database.

- *C++ Runtime Library*—The C++ Runtime Library consists of classes that maintain important functionality between the database. Classes for maintaining database connections, executing SQL transactions, pointers, and so on are managed from the runtime library. The generated classes created from the C++ generator are also maintained here.

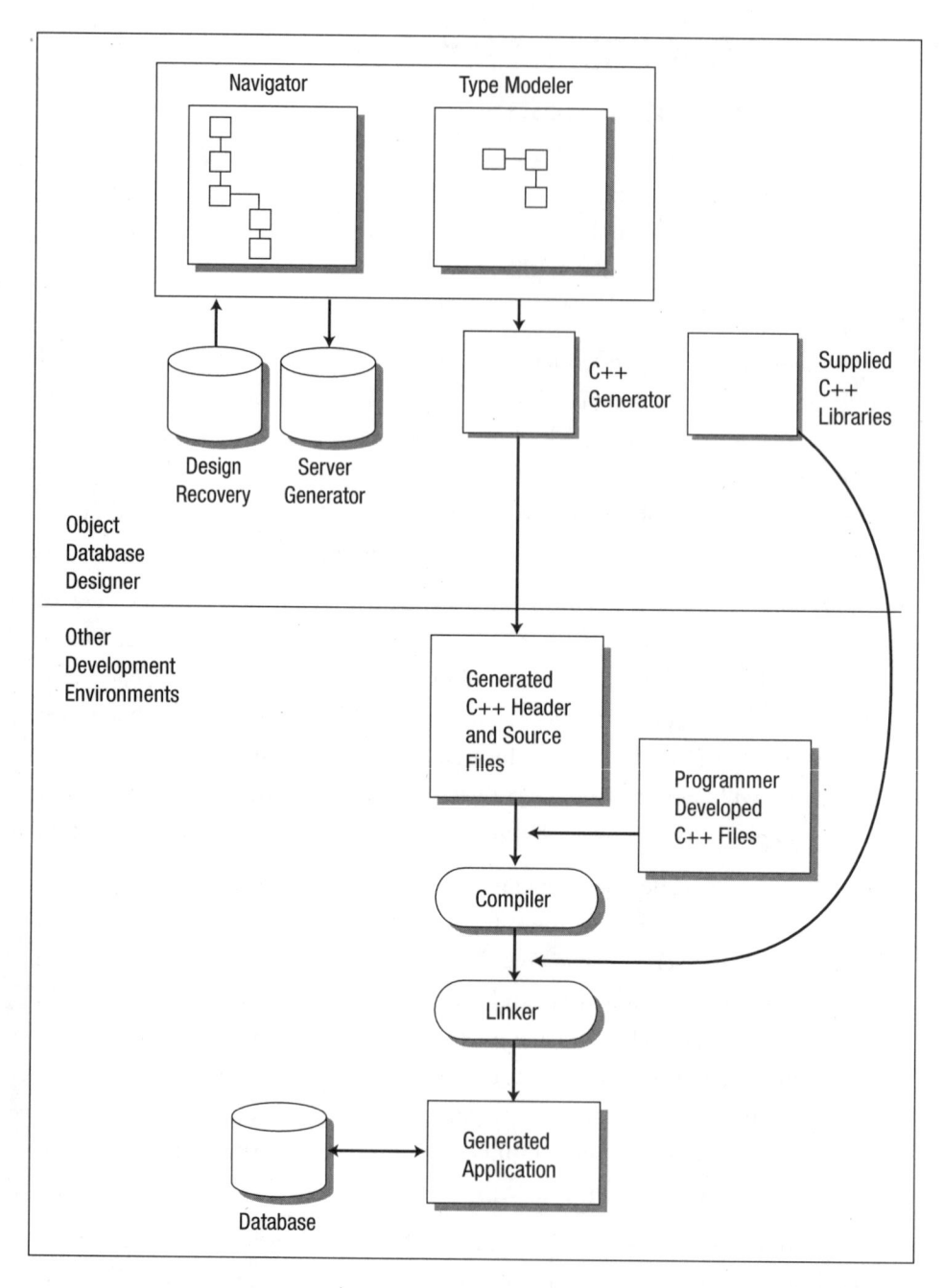

Figure 7.1
The six components of the Object Database Designer.

- *Server Generator*—The server generator takes the design information and generates the necessary SQL DDL statements to create the database schema. This component is similar to the Server Generator used in Designer/2000.

- *Design Recovery*—The Design Recovery component allows a developer to upgrade existing Oracle7 database applications by reverse engineering the relational schema into the Object Database Designer. Once the relational schema is loaded into the tool, it can be graphically depicted in the Type Modeler and redesigned to incorporate the object-relational functionalities in Oracle8. From this redesign effort, a user can generate the necessary SQL DDL and C++ class definitions.

Although not mentioned as one of the six components, the Object Database Designer requires a repository on the database, much like the Designer/2000 tool. Although specific information is not available at the time of this writing, the repository stores the information about the database application being created. The repository is comprised of a set of tables and views created during the installation of the Object Database Designer. Use of the tool is incumbent upon the successful installation of the repository. For further information, you should refer to the Oracle installation guide for the Object Database Designer.

The structure and functionality of Object Database Designer is designed to provide utility to several different members of a design team. Database administrators will find the Type Modeler useful to understand the object types represented in the database schema. Systems designers will find the product useful in understanding how design information is stored in the repository. Designers will also find the Navigator particularly helpful in managing the objects in the repository. Finally, programmers will find the Type Modeler and C++ Generator of great benefit in representing class diagrams, generating classes, and integrating their own code with the object-layer code. Now that we've introduced the six basic components of the Object Database Designer and described its basic makeup, let's look at the Object Database Designer working environment. After that, we'll examine each component in greater detail.

Design Environment Basics Of The Object Database Designer

For designers and developers familiar with other Oracle tools, the working environment of the Object Database Designer presents an easy learning curve due to its consistent Oracle-like look and feel. The starting point of any session is with the shell. The shell contains separate windows for the Type Modeler and the Navigator, as well as a toolbar that offers shortcuts to various options in the menu. The data contained in the Type Modeler and Navigator is the same; only the Type Modeler provides a graphical depiction of application objects, while the Navigator shows the same objects organized in a hierarchical tree. A Messages window can also be displayed, which shows the progress of any quality checks and object generation. The following generators and services will automatically invoke the Messages window:

- C++ Generator
- Server Generator
- Design Recovery
- Quality Check Utility

The Quality Check Utility is not a separate component of the Object Database Designer, but rather, a tool provided for monitoring completeness of generated code and retrofitted schema under the Design Recovery function. The Quality Check Utility will be discussed further in an upcoming section.

As mentioned, the toolbar provides shortcuts to many of the options available from the main menu. The toolbar includes the following buttons:

- *New*—This button is used to create a new application diagram.
- *Open*—This button opens an existing application diagram.
- *Save Diagram*—This allows a developer to save the current active diagram.
- *Revert Uncommitted Data*—This button reverses unsaved changes made in the Property Palette for a given object.
- *Requery Selection*—This button compares highlighted elements in the active Type Modeler or Navigator window with its repository definition. If differences between the repository and the element(s) in the active window exist, then the data in the window is made consistent with the values in the repository.
- *Zoom In*—This button allows a developer to magnify the selected working area in the active window.
- *Zoom Out*—This button functions in the opposite manner as the Zoom In button. Magnification is decreased while maintaining the selected view centered in the active window.

THE TOOLS OF THE TRADE

- *Fit To Selection*—If one or more items have been selected, this button magnifies the active window to the maximum size that will accommodate the viewing of the selected items.

- *Fit To Area*—This option allows a developer to increase the magnification of a selected area so that it fits within the active window.

- *Fit To Diagram*—This button adjusts the viewing area in the active window so that a complete diagram can be viewed at once.

- *Use Property Palette*—This button allows a developer to use a Property Palette to edit object properties rather than a Property dialog.

- *Use Property Dialogs*—This button reverses the condition performed in the Use Property Palette button.

- *Context Sensitive Help*—This button enables the context-sensitive help.

Two of the listed button choices refer to Property Palettes and Property dialogs. Both Property Palettes and Property dialogs provide for the entry of detailed information about an object type. Specific information about attributes and operations (behaviors or methods) is indicated using one of these two tools. The Property dialog organizes the data entry effort into tabbed screens or canvases. Developers can choose from the various tabbed categories (Object Type, Attributes, Operations, Database, and C++) and define those properties for each object created in the application diagram. Likewise, the same information can be entered into a Property Palette. The Property Palette is laid out in tabular form on a single page or sheet. Properties are listed sequentially in the Palette and grouped much like the categories in the Property dialog. The additional benefit of using the Property Palette is that the developer can elect to have it display as a spread table. This allows for the entry of properties of more than one object at a time.

Now that we have reviewed the basic working environment of the Object Database Designer, let's review each component.

The Type Modeler And Property Screens

The Type Modeler window is where graphical representations of the application diagram appear. The Type Modeler uses the convention specified by the UML for object representation. Recall the discussion of the UML in Chapter 3. In Chapter 9,

227

we'll conduct a detailed discussion on the symbols and notation used in the object-relational design methodology based on the concepts prescribed in the UML. In this section, we'll address the core components where most of the database design work is performed.

Much of the design work can take place in the Type Modeler. The Type Modeler is composed of a drawing surface and a toolbar. This is not the same toolbar described earlier, but one that has functions specific to the Type Modeler. The toolbar consists of buttons for a selection arrow (cursor), element types (object type, interface, value type, attribute, and operation), relation types (generalization, association, composition, and aggregation), and general drawing preferences (fill color, font, line color, and line width). Objects in the Type Modeler are created by selecting the appropriate item from the toolbar and clicking on the open canvas of the Type Modeler. When an object type is created, a highlighted area above the object rectangle appears. The object name is entered in this space. The object type is created once the Enter key is pressed. Further definition of the object type continues by double-clicking the object type's rectangle. The Property Palette (or Property dialog) appears, and the individual attributes, operations, and so on can be defined. Once the Property box has been dismissed, the information is automatically saved to the repository.

The Object Database Designer defines an *interface* to be a collection of operations that one or more object types can implement. To create an interface, follow the steps for creating an object type, select the interface button from the toolbar, click on the Type Modeler canvas, and draw the rectangle. Double-clicking an interface will invoke an Interface Object Type dialog box where similar information to the Property box can be entered.

Relation types are created using the Generalization, Association, Composition, and Aggregation buttons from the Type Modeler toolbar. The Generalization button is used to specify the association between a subtype and its supertype. A generalization can adopt one of two settings: generalization and specialization. If the association (the new term for relationship in the object-relational paradigm) between two object types denotes a subtype, then the setting is a generalization. Likewise, if the association described is a supertype, then it is considered a specialization. To illustrate, assume you created the object type **PERSON**. It is further assigned the attributes of **NAME** and **ADDRESS**. If you next create an object type of **EMPLOYEE** with attributes of **HIRE_DATE** and **DEPARTMENT**, then the association from **EMPLOYEE** to

The Tools Of The Trade

PERSON becomes a specialization. In other words, the **EMPLOYEE** object is a specialization of **PERSON**. In addition, the **EMPLOYEE** object will inherit the **NAME** and **ADDRESS** attributes from **PERSON**. Figure 7.2 illustrates this example.

The following steps show how simple it is to create a generalization in the Type Modeler:

1. Click the Generalization button.
2. Click the object type that is to be the specialization (the subtype).
3. Drag the cursor to the supertype object.
4. Release the mouse button.

The resulting graphical representation of the generalization will show an arrow pointing toward the supertype and away from the subtype.

Note: *The Object Database Designer allows for the representation of multiple inheritance in the application diagram, but this functionality is not supported by the C++ and Server Generators.*

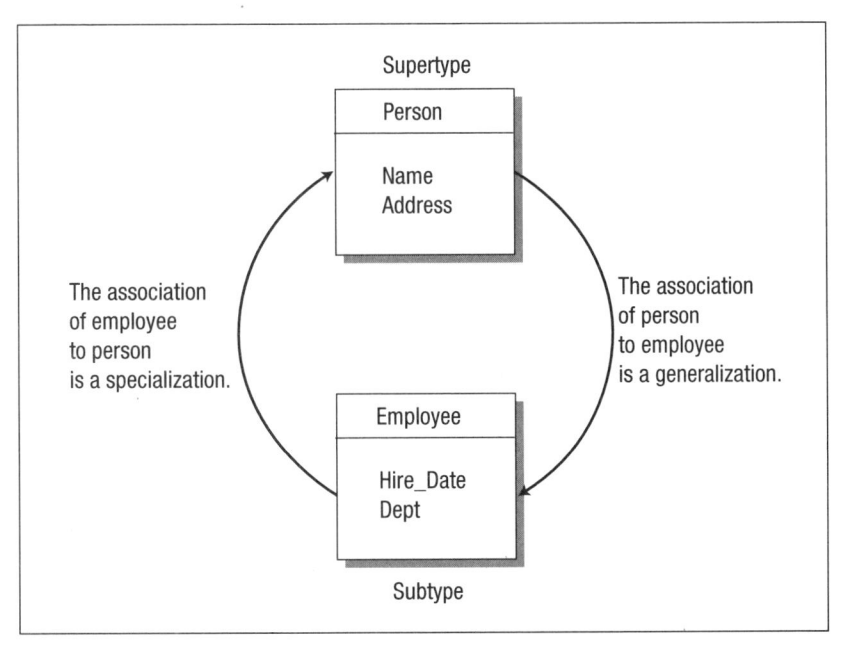

Figure 7.2
The use of generalization and specialization.

CHAPTER 7

Creating an association between two object types is accomplished in the same manner performed for generalizations. Because associations in the UML are unidirectional, each side of an association in the Type Modeler creates what is known as a *role*. A role describes only one side of the association and describes what that object type's relationship is with the connecting object type. Associations can be created using the Association, Aggregation, or Composition buttons. To specify the characteristics of an association just created, an Association dialog box can be invoked by double-clicking the Association line in the Type Modeler. The following information can be defined in the Association dialog box:

- Basic association information, such as the statement verb and the direction in which the association is to be read.

- The name of the association role and the identification of the two object types being linked.

- Role type information, such as multiplicity, visibility, scope, and so on. See Chapter 3 for a discussion on associations and relationships.

- Class member information, persistency of the association, and other information specific to the C++ and Server Generators.

Attributes for individual object types are created using the Attribute button or by double-clicking on the object type and selecting the Attributes tab from the Property dialog box. As with associations, various types of information can be entered for attributes, such as:

- Basic attribute information, such as name, visibility, scope, and so on. See Chapter 3 for definitions of these terms.

- Basic characteristics of an attribute, such as length, datatype, and whether the attribute inherits the properties of a created value type. Value types are described in the next paragraph.

- Whether an attribute is an array of value and, if so, the size of the array.

- Class member information, whether the attribute should contain **NULL** values and other information specific to the C++ and Server Generators.

Value types are considered to be a specialization of a predefined scalar datatype. Object Database Designer supports predefined and user-defined value types. There are seven predefined value types: **String, Integer, Real, Date, DateTime, Boolean,**

LargeString, LargeBinary, and **Binary**. The predefined value types cannot be deleted or altered. User-defined value types consist of a specialization of one of the predefined value types. For example, let's assume that you have created the following value type:

- **CURRENCY**—Used to represent dollars.

The **CURRENCY** value type would be a specialization of **Real** and would inherit its properties, but **CURRENCY** might also have additional properties associated with it, such as a specific length or number of decimal places. User-defined value types can only specify one other value type, as this example illustrates. Multiple inheritance of value type is not supported. Value types can have only one allowable value or a range of values.

Operations or behaviors for object types can be defined through one of the two Property boxes (palette or dialog). Operations are the methods that will be generated as part of the object types. Object Database Designer allows for the following information to be specified when defining operations:

- The operation name, return type, scope, and whether it changes the state of its parent object.
- Class member information, whether the operation is persistent, whether it can be overridden by another specialized type, and other information specific to the C++ and Server Generators.

By this point, you have probably ascertained that little or no actual coding takes place. This is not to say that customized modules cannot be integrated into an application built with the Object Database Designer; however, the tool has been designed to generate as much code as possible to reduce the burden of the programming activity.

The Property dialogs (or palettes) used in conjunction with the Type Modeler are an important combination in the development of an application. Basically, these two tools cover the four fundamentals of developing the applications diagram. The fundamental steps are:

1. Identifying and creating object types.
2. Defining the properties (attributes) of each object type.
3. Defining the behavior (operations) of each object type.
4. Establishing associations (relationships).

Now that we have discussed the basic operation of the Type Modeler and Property dialogs, let's move on to look at the Navigator screen.

The Navigator Screen

The Navigator screen maintains the same look and feel as other navigator screens found in other Oracle tools. The conventions used for navigator screens in general are becoming more and more standardized throughout the industry, as more software manufacturers adopt the hierarchical tree notation to display code and objects in the application environment. The notation is structured and easy to understand, and it subjugates objects to their logical object parents in such a way as to make the relationship of one item to another easy to see.

Almost all of the editing functionality found in the Type Modeler can be performed in the Navigator. Oracle suggests that the Navigator be used primarily for browsing, checking, and fine-tuning objects while the bulk of development is performed in the Type Modeler. This, of course, is a matter of personal preference, but the pictorial representation found in the Type Modeler might be easier to use.

Elements in the Navigator are organized in the order in which they might be addressed while developing a new application (object types appear first, followed by value types, and so forth). Each element in the application tree can be comprised of one or more sub-elements. When this is the case, a small + (plus) sign appears on the branch in front of the element containing sub-elements. The view on the tree can be expanded or exploded to view all sub-elements simultaneously. Editing of an element can be performed by double-clicking an element. This action invokes the appropriate Property dialog box.

The Navigator supports the use of drag-and-drop functionality. That is to say that an element from one part of a tree can be selected and dragged to another area on the tree. There are logical restrictions to this behavior, as you might imagine. You cannot drag and drop an element onto an area that does not support the item type being dragged.

One of the features included in the Navigator that serves to simplify a developer's job is the use of an element filter. The element filter allows only a subset of the elements to be displayed. The filtering option is invoked through the use of the right mouse button. A branch of the tree is selected first, then a right-click invokes a small menu that displays the following three filtering options:

- *Filter*—This option lets a developer filter out instances of a particular element type. Only instances of elements meeting the filter conditions will be displayed.

- *Order By*—This allows a developer to specify the order in which instances of a particular element will be displayed.

- *Displayed Properties*—This allows a developer to specify which properties will be displayed.

Removing filters is easily accomplished by selecting the branch in question, right-clicking, and selecting Clear Selected Filters from the option list.

We have successfully reviewed the integral parts of the Object Database Designer that deal with the application design activities. Now, let's take a closer look at the generators that will produce the code for database applications.

Using The C++ And Server Generators

There are two generators in the Object Database Designer: C++ Generator and Server Generator. The purpose of the C++ Generator is to help developers create C++ applications that can seamlessly manipulate object data found in the database. This is done through the creation of C++ class definitions and implementations drawn from the application diagram.

Although not every organization will choose to develop interfacing applications in C++, the C++ Generator greatly simplifies the work required to do so. C++ does not support database concepts like query sets and relationships. By the same token, there is no correspondence between an object stored in the database and one held in memory. Writing C++ code to access objects in the database is a long, tedious process. The C++ Generator solves this process by automatically creating the code necessary to negotiate the bridge between application and database. The C++ Generator also helps to insulate application code from changes in the database model. Changes to a database can be accommodated by rerunning the C++ Generator—removing the need to manually modify or customize the code.

The C++ Generator produces or generates a class for each object type in an application diagram. Generated classes fall into one of two categories: mapped and support. A *mapped class* is one that maps directly to an object type. A *support class* is one that provides mechanisms through which objects are accessed. The C++ Generator also produces a set of standard member functions to enable various DML and DDL events, like **CREATE**, **QUERY**, **UPDATE**, **DELETE**, and so on. The C++ Generator produces four types of code:

- Implementation code for the mapped classes.
- Implementation code for the support classes.
- Definition or header code for the mapped classes.
- Definition or header code for the support classes.

Developers can write application code to use the generated classes, and, upon completion, the source code files containing both the application code and the generated code will be compiled. A library is included with the generator to link the generated code with the application.

Before the C++ Generator can be invoked, at least one class set must be defined. A class set can be thought of as a C++ project or *makefile*. The class set must include the object types that will be used by the application. Small projects can only require one class set, while larger projects might find it advantageous to group object types into multiple class sets. Regardless of the number of class sets to be created, the C++ Generator only generates them one at a time. As part of the preparation for generating your class sets, it is advisable to perform a series of quality checks on the definitions. Quality checking is described in the utilities section later.

The Server Generator is the mechanism that creates the scripts to generate the database from the application diagram created in the Object Database Designer. The resulting DDL code is generated from the information stored in the repository and written to a command file that can be run on the Oracle8 database. Developers can merely create command files, or they can create and run command files.

In order for objects to be included in the generate function, they must be marked as **PERSISTENT** and **COMPLETE**. Objects that do not meet this criteria will be omitted from the generation command file. Also, keep in mind that, if an object to be created already exists on the database, you must delete it before running the generated DDL script. The progress of the generation script can be monitored in the Messages window, and any objects that fail to create can be addressed individually.

In a nutshell, this is a basic overview of the generator components in the Object Database Designer. Let's move to the topic of dealing with existing database applications and the use of the Design Recovery component.

Using The Design Recovery Component

The Design Recovery component allows developers to extract type definitions from an existing database schema. Developers are then free to redesign or enhance an existing database application and migrate it to Oracle8. Definitions can be recovered from an existing Oracle database, a DDL script file with the table definitions, or a non-Oracle database via ODBC connection.

The Design Recovery component supports Oracle's concept of *round-trip engineering*. Round-trip engineering takes the approach that software development is a controlled, iterative process that understands the changing nature of user requirements. In this process, an application can go through the development life cycle several times. When an application is determined to be "complete," the planning stage begins again, and new requirements and enhancements are added. The Design Recovery component supports this process because the database definition is stored in the repository. Incremental changes can be incorporated by regenerating the database schema and the C++ class sets, if necessary.

Now that we have discussed the components of the Object Database Designer, let's briefly describe the Quality Check Utility.

The Quality Check Utility In The Object Database Designer

Earlier in this chapter, I mentioned the Quality Check Utility. The Quality Check Utility is invoked prior to running either of the generators. The checks performed by this utility ensure that all information required to create C++ or DDL code is consistent and complete. Quality checks can be performed on selected objects or on an entire application system. Oracle recommends running this utility against each object type individually before marking it **COMPLETE** for generation purposes. The Quality Check Utility has its own dialog box and is called from the menu by selecting Utilities|Quality Check. The utility can perform the following three checks:

- *Check General Quality*—This option performs a general quality check, specific to neither generator.

- *Check Quality For C++ Generation*—This option performs the necessary quality checks for the generation of C++ code. Note that this option also performs a DDL quality check.

- *Check Quality For DDL Generation*—This option performs a check only for DDL generation.

Results of the Quality Check, as well as actions performed by the Design Recovery components and both generators, will appear in the Progress Message window. The Progress Message window is automatically invoked whenever one of the Quality Check operations is executed. A toolbar at the top of the window allows for scrolling through the messages or copying selected portions to the clipboard.

As you can see from this basic introduction of the Object Database Designer, the development of Oracle8 applications using an object-relational modeling tool will progress much more smoothly using such software tools. In the next section, I will introduce another modeling tool from Logic Works, a major software vendor with a history of producing quality modeling software.

Logic Works' OR-Compass

As mentioned at the beginning of this chapter, the new tool for modeling object-relational databases from Logic Works is called *OR-Compass*, and this tool is hotlinked from the book's accompanying CD-ROM. Logic Works has a long-standing history of producing quality data modeling software to the software community. Previous versions of their modeling product were based on the IDEF1X methodology, which was originally a government standard developed by Texas Instruments. The new entry, OR-Compass, offers several major features in functionality. The highlights of these features are listed here:

- The ability to completely forward engineer a schema design directly to the database or into a script file.

- Complete reverse engineering of a schema from the database or a script file.

- A compare feature allowing incremental updates to and from the database.

- Change management to preserve data during database updates.

- An add-in architecture that allows third-party modules to extend the modeling capability of the OR-Compass tool.

- Full undo and redo capability, limited only by the available disk space on the target system.

- Complete accessibility of user-defined datatypes and behaviors showing the contents of functions and packages.

- Support for user-defined datatypes with an element known as *ModelBlades*.
- Wizards to simplify the migration task.
- Direct migration of modeling information from ERwin/ERX.

OR-Compass provides a rich modeling environment in which to create object-relational database schema for Oracle8. OR-Compass places less reliance on constructs like C++ class sets and more emphasis on robust object-relational object types supported by the database. The depth of supported objects in the tool shows this commitment to complete modeling in the object-relational environment. Users will find the product easy to learn and use. As with Oracle's product, Object Database Designer, a complete understanding of relational and object-relational modeling concepts should be acquired before using this tool. In the next section, we'll examine the major components of OR-Compass.

An Overview Of The Major Components In OR-Compass

The OR-Compass modeling tool is composed of six basic components: Package Explorer, Model Explorer, Routine Explorer, docked and floating toolbars, a Diagram window, and property sheets. Figure 7.3 illustrates a typical screen with the major components displayed. Following is a brief description of each component:

- *Package Explorer*—The Package Explorer displays objects available from imported Data Cartridges that can be used in modeling an application using the Cartridge's predefined objects. It includes the details of all imported cartridges including extended data types, alternative indexing methods, and so on. Data Cartridges are currently available for spatial data and many multimedia data types. The ability to extend the modeling environment to support extended functionality of object relational databases is important to understanding the use of the new object relational features.

- *Model Explorer*—This component lists all objects in the model, including those that are not visible on the diagram. The Model Explorer is organized in a hierarchical tree fashion, where each element is displayed as a sub-element of another object that "owns" it. As mentioned earlier, hierarchical object navigators are becoming a standard convention for displaying the many elements in an application

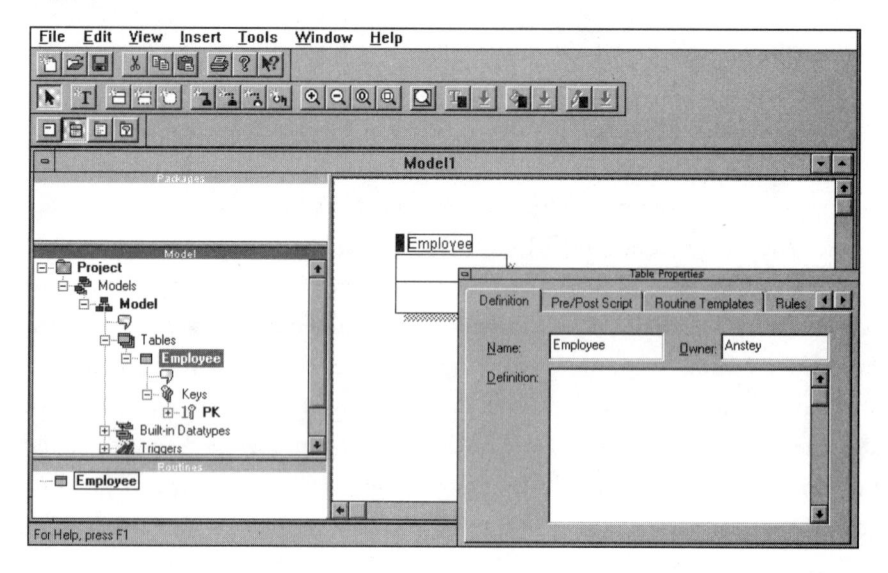

Figure 7.3
A view of the basic working environment in OR-Compass.

environment. Each element in the Model Explorer shows the name and description of the item. In-place editing of the name and description is allowed.

- *Routine Explorer*—This component lists the methods associated with a specific object type selected. It categorizes each program unit by the association it has with the object type. The Routine Explorer only displays information for the currently selected object. That is, it is sensitive to the object selected in the diagram, Model Explorer, and Package Explorer.

- *Docked and floating toolbars*—OR-Compass offers easy access to the most frequently accessed functions in the tool. The tool allows developers to dock toolbars on any side of the OR-Compass window or float them anywhere on the desktop. Toolbars also have context-sensitive help to indicate their function.

- *Diagram window*—The Diagram window is used to show a graphical depiction of the model. Not all elements are displayed, but it is possible to gain an intuitive visualization of the object types and their relationships. Tables, views, text blocks, and so on can be created directly on the diagram using the tools from the toolbar.

- *Property sheets*—The property sheets in OR-Compass are context sensitive. That is, they display information for the currently selected item or element. Property sheets appear as boxes with tabbed pages for easy access to categorical groups of properties.

Now that we have touched on the major components of OR-Compass, let's proceed to a discussion of the design environment.

A Look At The Design Environment In OR-Compass

The physical design of OR-Compass is structured to facilitate the use of the components simultaneously. The starting point for any new application design effort is the creation of objects in the diagram screen. All relevant information is kept synchronized from one window to the next whenever objects are edited or created. The OR-Compass toolbar provides all the functions necessary for the creation of objects in the diagram. The initial position of all toolbars is at the top of the working window, but each toolbar can be moved away to "float" on another part of the screen to avoid obscuring the view of one or more of the component windows. The available functions from the OR-Compass toolbar are as follows:

- *Selection Arrow*—This button returns the cursor to its normal state as a pointer.
- *Text Block*—This button allows a developer to create a text block on the diagram canvas.
- *Table*—This button allows developers to create table objects.
- *Typed Table*—This button allows for the creation of user-defined object types.
- *View*—This button provides the functionality to create a view in the diagram screen.
- *Identifying Relation*—This button allows the creation of a relationship where the existence of the child entity is dependent on the parent entity.
- *Non-Identifying Relation*—This button allows the creation of a relationship where the existence of the child entity is independent of the parent entity.
- *Derivation*—This button creates a derivation-type relationship showing the link between a table or view and another view.
- *Inheritance*—This button creates a relation between two typed tables in which a subtype participates in an inheritance hierarchy with a supertype.

Chapter 7

- *Zoom In*—This button allows a developer to magnify the selected working area in the active window.

- *Zoom Out*—This button functions in the opposite manner as the Zoom In button. Magnification is decreased while maintaining the selected view centered in the active window.

- *Zoom Normal*—This button returns the view to its default setting.

- *Zoom Fit Diagram*—This button adjusts the viewing area in the active window so that a complete diagram can be viewed at once.

- *Zoom To Rectangle*—This option allows the developer to increase the magnification of a selected area so that it fits within the active window.

- *Various text and line color settings*—There are six buttons that allow for the selection of text color, setting the text color, selecting a background color, setting the background color, selecting a line color, and applying a line color.

The three Explorer components are stacked on the left-hand side of the development shell. Changes and additions are kept up-to-date with any activity that takes place in the Diagram window. When a new item is created or an existing item is edited, the focus in the Model Explorer shifts to that item in the tree.

You should now have a good feel for the working environment of OR-Compass. Let's move on and examine its features by walking through the creation process of some basic object types. The upcoming, brief sample session points out the key capabilities of this tool.

Building Model Elements With The Diagram Window And The Property Dialogs

To illustrate the broad functionality of OR-Compass, we will create some basic objects and point out the tool's abilities along the way. A categorical examination of each and every feature found in OR-Compass is too lengthy to present here. Instead, some features are described, while others are only listed.

A good starting point to demonstrate the use of OR-Compass is to create an object type such as a table. A table is created by selecting the table button from the OR-Compass toolbar and clicking on the Diagram window. Columns and properties for the created table can be defined. To add columns to a table, select the table using the right mouse click context menu and INSERT|COLUMN or INSERT|PRIMARY KEY COLUMN from the menu. Once selected, a new column immediately appears in the table box of the diagram and in the Model Explorer. To define properties for a new column, you need to invoke the property screen for the column by double-clicking the column icon in Model Explorer or the PROPERTIES selection can be made from the context menu. Note that the property dialog is modeless and changes based on the object type selected (i.e., column properties when columns are selected and table properties when tables are selected). The column property sheet includes five tabbed pages of properties. The five tabbed page groups are Definition, Datatype, Rules, Physical properties, and User-defined properties. Figure 7.4 shows a typical column property sheet.

OR-Compass supports a lengthy list of predefined datatypes—26 in all. Included in this list is support for Large Objects (LOBs). The location on the physical device can be specified for the files populating a LOB in the physical properties page of the property sheet.

OR-Compass supports two table types: conventional and type table. The *type table* is a representation of an object type, as introduced in Chapter 4. Recall that an object type called **ADDRESS_T** might be comprised of several address columns, a city column, a state column, and, lastly, a zip code column. A type table in OR-Compass is a representation of such an object type. Use of type tables requires the creation of *row types*, which are the equivalent of user-defined datatypes. OR-Compass supports two row types: named and unnamed. *Named row types* are strongly typed. That is, their definition is complete, or they are completely defined object types. *Unnamed row types* equate to incomplete object types. Unnamed row types cannot be used for the creation of type tables.

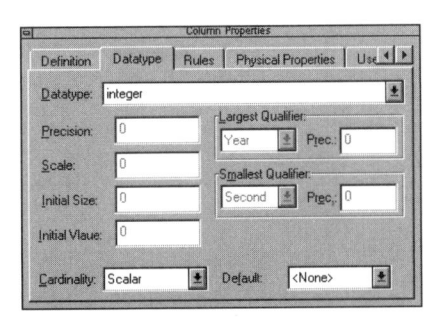

Figure 7.4
An example of a column property sheet.

Named row types are extremely useful in OR-Compass because of their support for type tables and because they facilitate the creation of *inheritance hierarchies*. An inheritance hierarchy is a structure in which row subtypes automatically inherit fields from a selected row supertype. The row subtypes in the inheritance hierarchy also support the defined behaviors of the row supertype.

For illustrative purposes, let's assume that a row type **ADDRESS** was created for an **EMPLOYEE** table. The row type **ADDRESS** was assigned a datatype of **DAVE** which was created via the menu option INSERT|DATATYPE|ROW TYPE. A type table **ADDRESS_T** was then created to represent the user-defined datatype of the column **ADDRESS** found in the **EMPLOYEE** table. Figure 7.5 illustrates the result of this activity.

OR-Compass also supports the use of other object-relational constructs described in Chapter 4 of this book. Besides built-in datatypes, OR-Compass allows developers to build the following:

- *Distinct Datatypes*—A distinct datatype is a user-defined datatype based on a built-in, collection, or row type datatype. These datatypes are strongly typed and cannot be directly compared with other datatypes.

- *Opaque Datatypes*—These datatypes are a completely encapsulated complex datatype not derived from a built-in datatype. Opaque datatypes require additional handling by a developer who must write all functions to enable access, comparison, or manipulation of these datatypes.

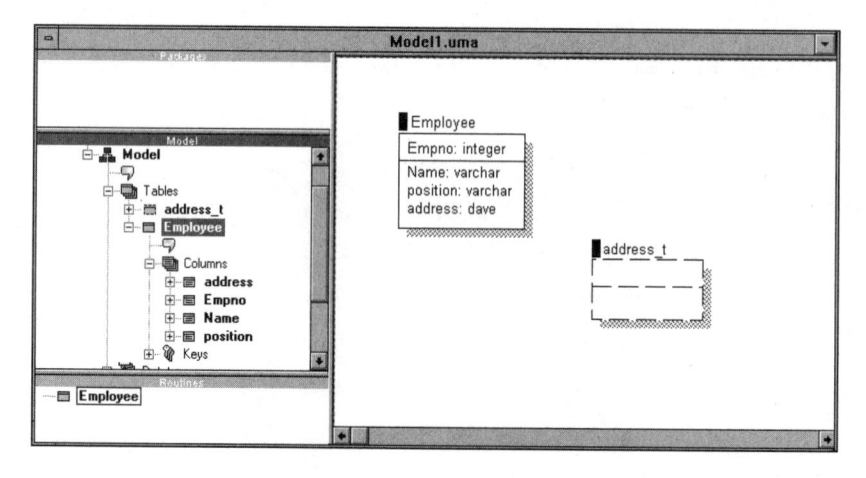

Figure 7.5
A view of the working screen after creation of a row type and type table.

- *Collection Datatypes*—Collections are a user-defined, complex datatype that can be used to store multiple pieces of data that have the same datatype. In OR-Compass, a collection can be a set, multiset, or list.

- *Row Types*—Row types are a user-defined, complex datatype capable of storing multiple pieces of data of different datatypes within a single column. Row types are illustrated in the previous paragraph.

Now that you have been introduced briefly to the basic elements of tables, columns, and datatypes, it's time to look at the major aspects of working with relations in OR-Compass.

Relations In OR-Compass

The relation types used in OR-Compass borrow part of their methodology from the IDEF1X modeling notation. There are four relation types supported in OR-Compass:

- *Identifying*—An identifying relationship is one where an instance in a child table is identified through its association with an instance in the parent table. In such a relationship, the child table is dependent on the existence of the parent table.

- *Non-Identifying*—This type of relationship indicates that a child table is independent of any instances in the parent table. Non-identifying relationships can be optional (indicating that nulls are allowed) or mandatory (null values are not allowed).

- *Derivation*—A derivation is a contributing relationship that shows tables or views from which a view derives its columns. This relation type is used with views only.

- *Inheritance*—This relation is used between two typed tables and is used to denote a hierarchy between the typed tables. The concept of the inheritance hierarchy is used in OR-Compass to create situations where subtables inherit the properties of the supertable. Inheritable properties include referential integrity, triggers, physical storage, locking options, indexes, and constraints.

Figure 7.6 illustrates the notation used by each relation type.

Creation of a relation between two tables is performed by selecting either the Identifying or Non-Identifying relationship button on the toolbar. The relationship is attached by selecting the parent table first, followed by the child table. The relationship drawn on the diagram will depict a large dot on the child table end. Figure 7.7 shows an identifying relationship between two tables.

Relation Types In OR-Compass

- Identifying Relationship
- Mandatory And Optional Non-Identifying Relationship
- Derivation (For Use With Views Only)
- Inheritance (For Use With Typed Tables)

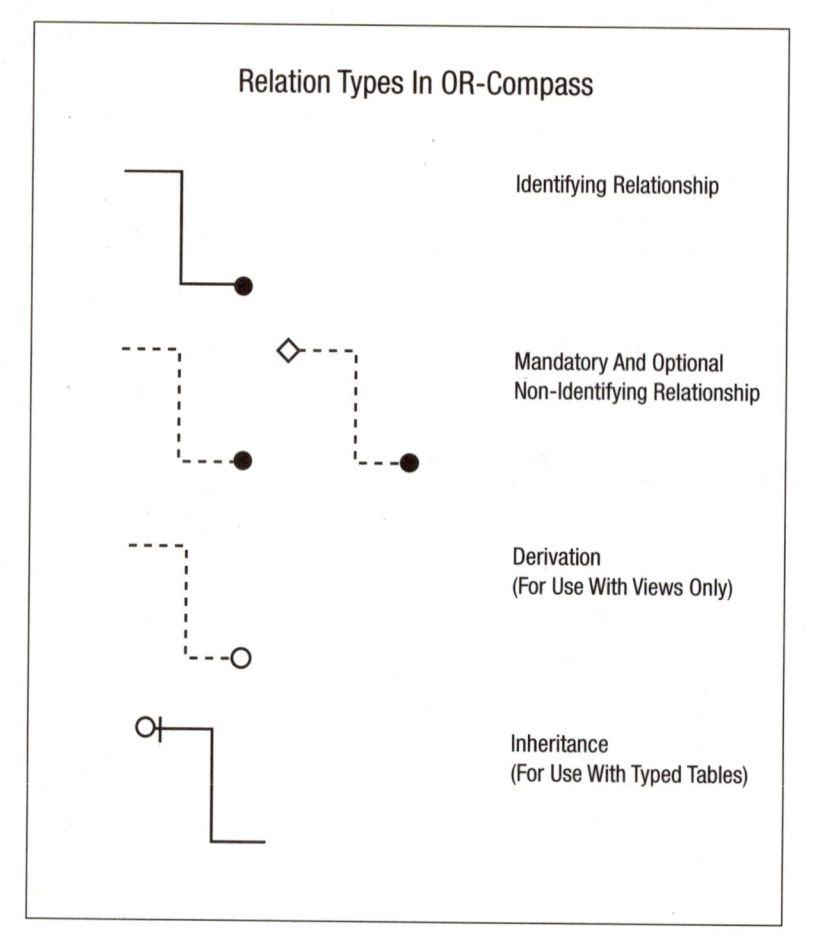

Figure 7.6
The four supported relation types.

Note in Figure 7.7 how the shape of the rectangles depicting the tables are different. The **DEPT** table has sharp square corners, because it is an independent entity, meaning it is not dependent on another table for its identity. The **EMPLOYEE** table, however, has rounded corners. This indicates that it is a dependent entity and relies on the foreign key from **DEPT** to establish its identity. The nature of these two entities is automatically set by OR-Compass when the relationship is defined. Likewise, when the identifying relationship was created, the foreign key to **EMPLOYEE** was automatically created.

THE TOOLS OF THE TRADE

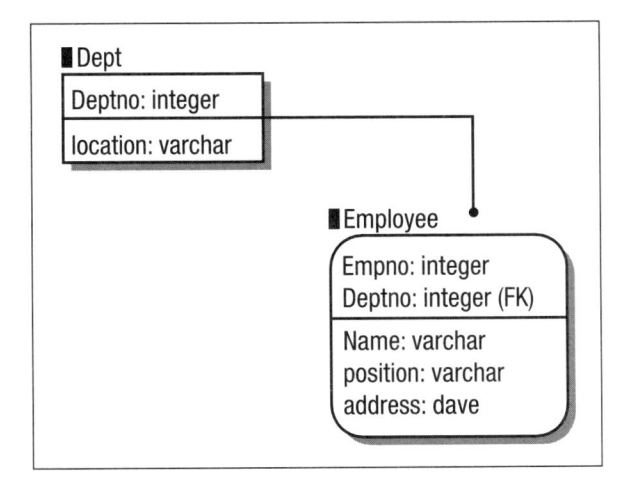

```
Dept
Deptno: integer
location: varchar

Employee
Empno: integer
Deptno: integer (FK)
Name: varchar
position: varchar
address: dave
```

Figure 7.7
An identifying relationship between two tables.

The property sheet for relationships allows a developer to specify the relation name, definition, cardinality, type, null option, and referential trigger options. In keeping with the modeling standards of the UML, each side of the relationship can have a specified verb phrase. The phrases tab in the relation property sheet provides areas to specify both.

A particularly useful feature included in the relation properties is the ability to specify exact cardinality. Figure 7.8 shows the relation property sheet open to the type tab.

The cardinality represents the fact that each parent table instance has a specific number of associated child instances related to it. The four options supported in OR-Compass are as follows:

- *Zero, one, or more*—This indicates that for each instance in the parent table there are zero, one, or more child records.

- *One or more*—This indicates that each instance in the parent table has one or more associated child records.

- *Zero or one*—This option indicates that for each parent record, there is only zero or one child record.

- *Exactly*—This option implies that there is an exact number of child records for each parent record.

245

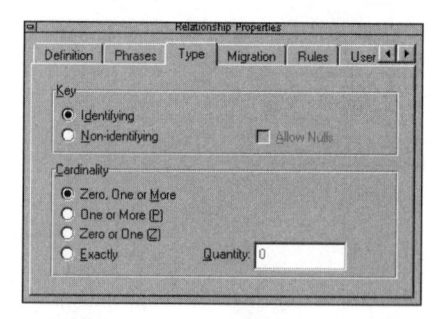

Figure 7.8
Specifying type properties for a relation.

Complicated relationships can be created in OR-Compass. For example, a hierarchical recursive relationship can be created whereby the parent table and child table are the same table. Figure 7.9 illustrates this with a supervisor-to-employee example.

This concludes our discussion of the implementation of relations in OR-Compass. The next section presents a brief description on how internal and external routines are supported.

Internal And External Routines In OR-Compass

OR-Compass supports the creation and reverse engineering of internal and external routines. An internal routine is a named set of precompiled SQL statements stored

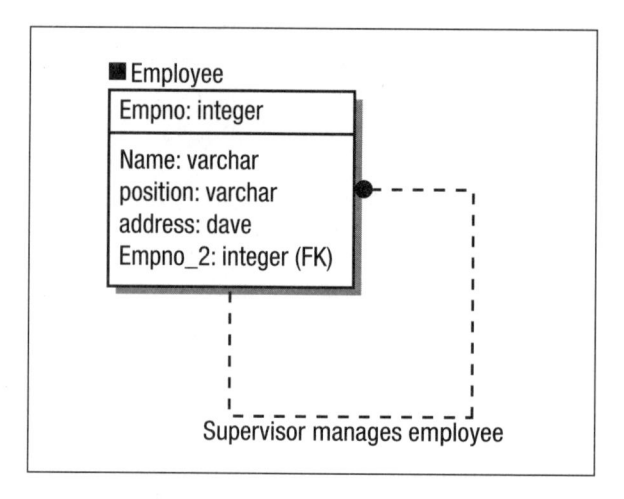

Figure 7.9
An example of a hierarchical recursive relationship.

on the server but are invoked from the client side by a remote procedural call. Internal routines can consist of PL/SQL packages, procedures, and functions. OR-Compass can be used to reverse engineer the code for an internal routine. During the reverse engineering process, OR-Compass retrieves the information in the database or script file and automatically creates a diagram based upon this information.

To create an internal routine, follow these simple steps:

1. Selecting INSERT|ROUTINE|INTERNAL ROUTINE from the menu. This invokes the Internal Routine property sheet.
2. On the Definition card, enter a new name and definition for the routine.
3. On the Arguments card, enter the appropriate input and output parameters.
4. Select the Code tab, and enter the source code for the program unit.
5. Finish the process by selecting the Options tab and defining the new routine as *internal*.

An external routine is stored externally from the database and is written in C, C++, or Java. The function and purpose for external routines is much the same as it is for internal routines. External routines provide the opportunity for developers to create C++ object layers forming the interface between the database and any supporting applications developed in C++. Developers can create classes for maintaining database connections, executing SQL transactions, pointers, and more.

The process for creating an external routine is essentially the same as it is for creating internal routines. The only difference is that there are a few additional options available to specify in the External Routine property sheet.

Routines can also be associated with several types of modeling objects. For example the internal routine we just created above can be associated with an entity in object-oriented fashion. Select the table you would like to associate the internal routine with using the context menu; then, right mouse click and pick PROPERTIES. The properties dialog contains a tab called routines. From the routines tab, you can associate the internal routine just created with the table. Note that the functions associated with a table are displayed at the bottom of the entity below a double line.

Now that support for internal and external routines has been discussed, let's examine the forward and reverse engineering capabilities in OR-Compass.

Forward And Reverse Engineering In OR-Compass

The process of generating a data model in OR-Compass from a physical database or script file is known as *reverse engineering*. Likewise, the process of generating a physical database from a model in OR-Compass is known as *forward engineering*. Both of these activities are fully supported in OR-Compass. OR-Compass can also be used to perform model updates and synchronize changes to a database. This process is known as *Complete-Compare*. OR-Compass adopts the concept of a full life cycle approach, as depicted in Figure 7.10.

Performing a forward-engineering process in OR-Compass is a three-step activity. The steps involved are as follows:

1. *Set options for forward engineering*—The settings in the Forward Engineering dialog box are quite detailed and allow you to specify a number of preferences for the inclusion or omission of certain database objects.

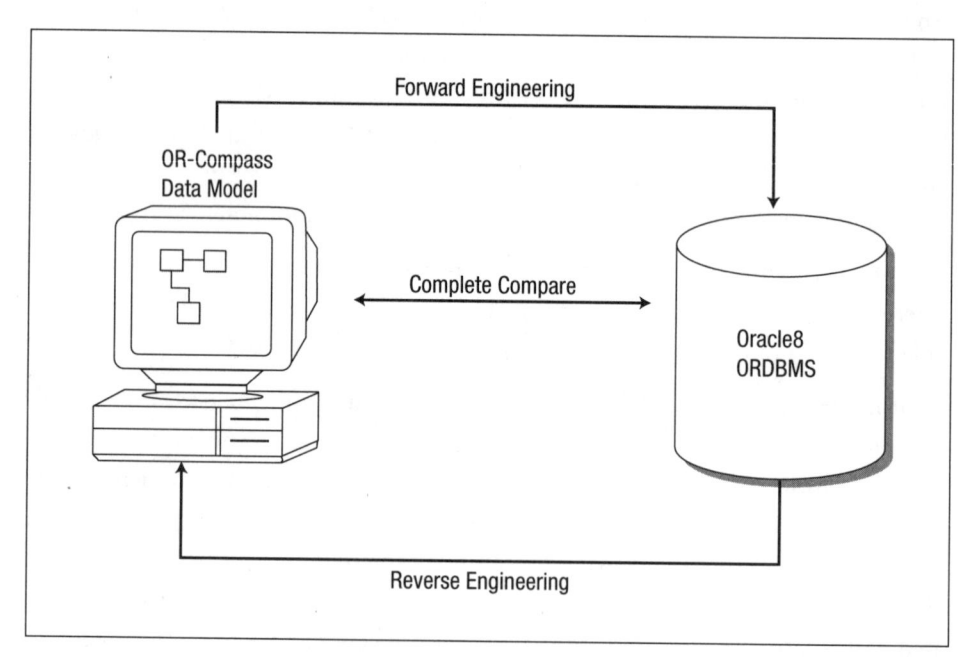

Figure 7.10
The full development life cycle approach with OR-Compass.

2. *Preview the schema DDL script*—Prior to execution, you should scrutinize the script to be used for the database generation.

3. *Generate the database schema*—In this step, OR-Compass is connected to the target server, and the new schema is generated. The script used to perform generation can be saved for future use. If you choose to save the script to a file, then the file must be run against the server as an extra step. The saved script is produced in a format easily read in Windows Notepad.

To illustrate some of the functionality offered in the forward-engineering utility, Figure 7.11 shows the Schema tab of the Forward Engineering Options dialog.

The reverse-engineering process in OR-Compass captures the information in the database or script file including tables, columns, relations, triggers, stored procedures, constraints, user-defined datatypes, and so on. A model is created in OR-Compass based upon the information gathered. A model resulting from reverse-engineering activity can be edited and modified or redefined, if necessary.

OR-Compass also provides the option to selectively choose what portions or items of a database schema are to be reverse engineered back into the tool. In this way, incremental portions of a database can be evaluated for changes and modifications. Figure 7.12 shows the Reverse Engineering Options screen.

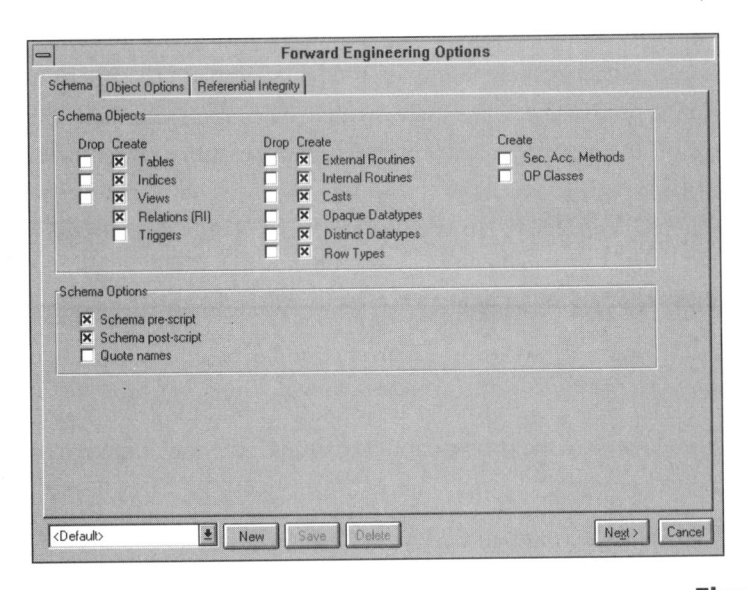

Figure 7.11
The schema page for the Forward Engineering Options dialog.

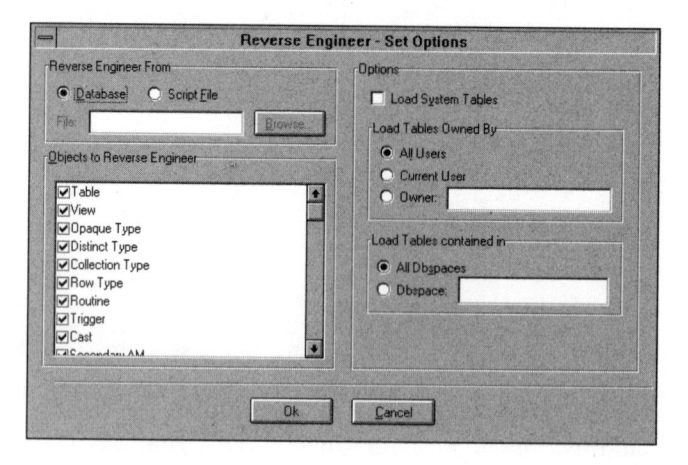

Figure 7.12
The Reverse Engineering Options screen.

The final utility to be discussed is Complete-Compare. Recognizing that today's database environment is dynamic, managing change is an important aspect to maintaining a good working production environment. OR-Compass allows developers to keep the model and database synchronized through the forward- and reverse-engineering utilities. To identify differences between the model and the database before any generation takes place, OR-Compass provides the Complete-Compare feature. Complete-Compare can be run against a target database, the DDL script for an existing database, or even against a different OR-Compass model. Complete-Compare finds differences between a model and a database so that developers can take the necessary actions to reconcile discrepancies. Complete-Compare allows the following actions in response to a list of differences:

- Allows developers to selectively undo changes in the data model.

- Documents changes by printing a report that lists the differences.

- Allows developers to update the current model based on the changes in the database.

- Allows developers to update the database through the use of the synchronization feature.

Figure 7.13 shows the Complete-Compare Options screen.

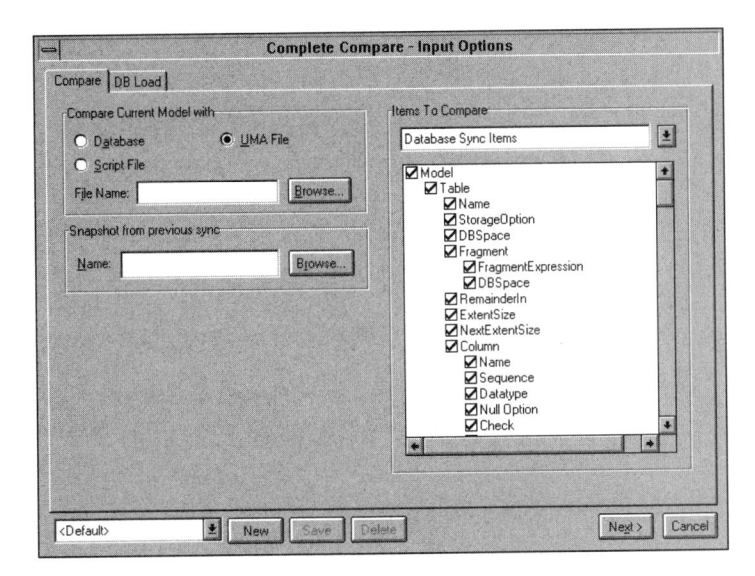

Figure 7.13
The Complete-Compare Options screen.

Summary

There is a small but ever-growing choice of modeling tools at database designers' disposal. In this chapter, we reviewed two viable options for use by developers who require a tool supporting the object-relational paradigm. We first examined Oracle's Object Database Designer, which adopts the conventions prescribed by the UML and offers users a familiar Oracle look and feel. The second tool discussed was Logic Work's OR-Compass, which includes an impressive level of support for user-defined objects and complex datatypes. Both products offer great flexibility and functionality.

In the next chapter, we'll move away from our discussion of modeling tools and enter into a real-world case study that combines the object-relational concepts we have discussed thus far.

Putting It All Together: A Comprehensive Object Relational Design

HIGH PERFORMANCE

CHAPTER 8

HIGH PERFORMANCE

Well building hath three conditions. Commodity, firmness, and delight.
—*Sir Henry Wotton*

Putting It All Together: A Comprehensive Object Relational Design

In the previous chapters of this book, we discussed the features and functionalities of the new object extensions in Oracle8. In a step-by-step approach, we discussed how the paradigm shift to object relational modeling will change the way systems analysts and database designers will perform their tasks. The next logical progression is to look at some real-world examples that make use of the object relational design methodology.

Increasingly, applications systems in today's workplace are becoming more complex. With greater frequency, the relational model proves inadequate for describing real-world systems accurately. The inability to successfully deliver application systems that meet customer needs and expectations was a key factor in the eventual introduction of object methodology into the relational model. The business community demands tools with the ability to represent complex business objects while encapsulating data with behaviors and creating new data types. This inherently object-oriented focus should not come at the cost of data access and performance—two features that have become the hallmark of the relational database. Database systems must rise to the challenge and offer the best of both worlds. And so, with this thought in mind, let's begin a study of what might be considered a typical problem by today's technological standards.

CHAPTER 8

The Acme Telephone Company

In order to illustrate the power of object relational modeling and incorporate as many of the object features in Oracle8 as possible, a suitably complex example must be chosen. The real benefit of using objects is in producing applications that don't map well in a traditionally relational environment. In a general sense, those systems that possess a networked architecture have proven to be difficult, if not impossible, to model in the relational paradigm. Network architecture type problems are not uncommon in the business world. As a matter of fact, the general concept of this type of modeling problem has been around for quite some time. Consider trying to develop a system model for the power and utility company in your hometown. At face value, this might seem somewhat straightforward, but have you ever stopped to think of what's involved in designing the electric company's network? (Perhaps you have been on such a project, in which case, this challenge is all too familiar.) Consider that a single plant must generate and distribute adequate energy to thousands (or millions) of destinations. Keep in mind that consumption levels of each node must be monitored. This information must, in turn, be fed back to the plant for constant update of power flow and, of course, billing purposes. Figure 8.1 illustrates the network architecture of the electric company.

Successful relational modeling solutions to network-type architectures have one major drawback: They require the introduction of new entities and/or attributes if new objects are introduced or if existing ones are modified. This presents an interesting design challenge for a system analyst responsible for devising a database schema that will support such an architecture when the client wishes to avoid changes in the schema.

Another example of a real-world system with networked architecture is the phone company. Although the example we'll use has been fictionalized, the basis for this case study is drawn from an actual project conducted for a large telecommunications firm. The problem that it describes is very real and certainly not uncommon in today's workplace. In fact, telephone companies constitute a large segment of users of the "pure" object-oriented database because of the limitations found in the relational database model.

For this case study, you have been assigned to act as the chief database designer for the Acme Telephone Company. Acme has undertaken the effort of installing a fiber-optic system throughout the country. The fiber-optic network is composed of

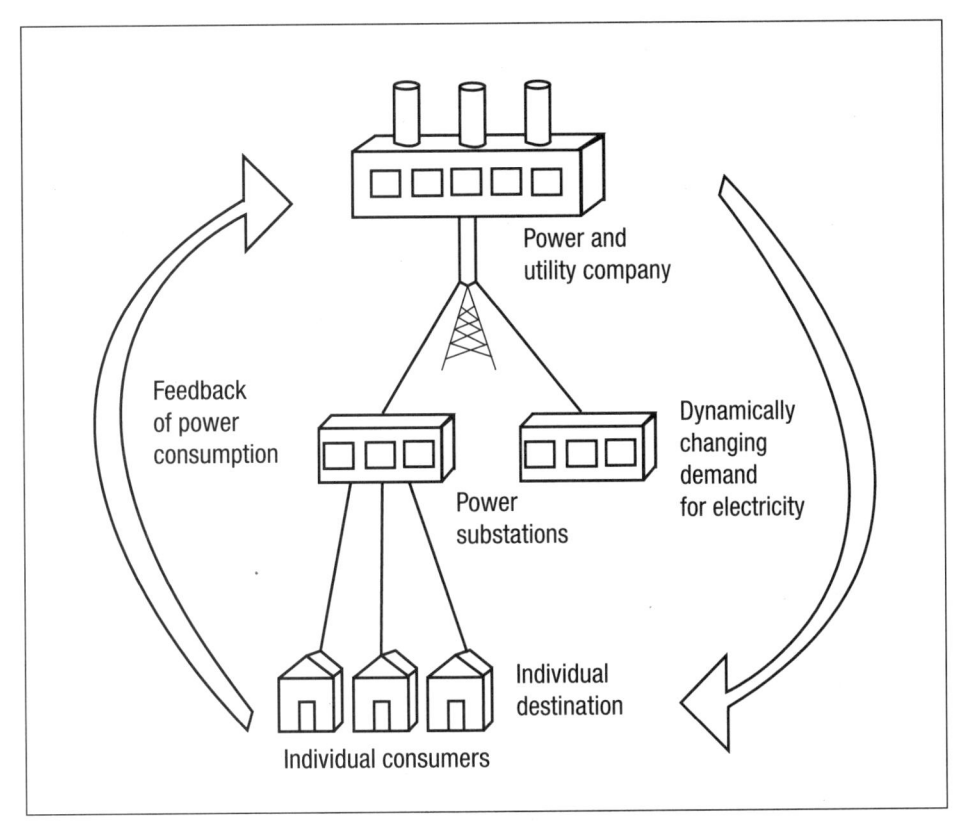

PUTTING IT ALL TOGETHER: A COMPREHENSIVE OBJECT RELATIONAL DESIGN

Figure 8.1
The network architecture of an electric company.

numerous telecommunication devices that relay a signal from one point to another via fiber-optic line. Fiber-optic networks communicate information by transmitting a light wave of one or more specific wavelengths along the fiber in a digital format. The purpose of the database system is to provide an automated capability to record and store data for transmission equipment on the fiber-optic network. Within the scope of this case study, we'll define the entities, attributes, and methods that adequately model the physical devices used and their associated behaviors.

Despite the fact that the scope of this case study is kept at a basic level, it should become apparent to you, early on, that design concerns can elevate in complexity rather quickly. Now that I have introduced the system to be modeled, let's review the requirements of the system to be built.

Identifying The Requirements

The overall purpose of the Acme Telephone Company database system will be to provide a capability to the engineering staff to review, plan, and design network changes of transmission equipment for the fiber-optic network. The database will also act as the repository for all equipment deployed to the field. Beyond this general business statement, there are several business objectives that must be met by the system before it can be implemented. The general requirements for the system are as follows:

- The database must accurately track all objects and their properties.
- The database must accurately detail all instances of objects at any given location.
- The database design must be robust enough to allow the introduction of new equipment types and their properties (attributes), without requiring the modification of the database schema.
- The database must accurately model the relationships between objects in the database (i.e., each connection between two pieces of equipment must be maintained).
- The "rules" for connections between devices must be maintained in the database in order to perform validation.
- Site maps must be stored for use by the field engineers to help in locating out-of-the-way or difficult-to-find equipment sites.

It should come as no surprise that in an industry driven by technology, such as telecommunications, that new equipment frequently emerges on the scene. The dynamics of such an environment add to the challenge of designing a database schema that does not require regular modification. The addition of new devices can mean the introduction of new capabilities on the part of these devices. These new capabilities must, in turn, take their place in the database.

Now that we have covered the basic requirements for the system design, let's take a moment to describe the elementary objects that comprise a fiber-optic network.

Understanding The Constituent Parts

Before attempting any kind of design effort for this problem, it is important to understand what the constituent elements are, what they do, and how they work. By way of general introduction, we'll identify the basic physical objects that exist in the fiber-optic system and define their purpose:

Putting It All Together: A Comprehensive Object Relational Design

- *Fiber*—The actual fiber-optic thread used to carry a communication packet via light wave. Fibers are no thicker than a human hair. They are manufactured to exacting tolerances because they must carry a signal without aberration or obscuration. Fibers are designed to carry one or more specific wavelengths of light simultaneously. Fibers are generally paired so that each fiber supports a specific direction of communication.

- *Cable*—A bundle of fibers, always packed in even numbers, most commonly 44. Cables can host as few as 22 fibers and as many as 144. The fiber count is determined by the model and manufacturer.

- *Connector*—A device used to connect two fibers together. Connectors come in three varieties: optical send, optical receive, and optical send/receive. One connector must be placed on the end of each fiber to be connected. For example, one fiber end will have an optical send connector. Another fiber end joined to it must have an optical receive connector. Optical send/receive connectors must be paired with connectors of their own type.

- *Lightwave Terminating Equipment (LTE)*—A final destination, or "terminating" point, for a transmission. An LTE can be thought of as the junction box that either receives an incoming system (see the definition for system later in this list) or is the starting point for a system. LTEs come in various configurations, but all have one incoming fiber and one outgoing fiber.

- *Lightwave Regenerating Equipment (LRE)*—A device that regenerates a transmission and forwards it to a further destination. The normal configuration for an LRE is two incoming fibers and two outgoing fibers. Newer versions of this device are capable of supporting multiple pairs of fibers.

- *Amplifier*—A device that amplifies or strengthens the power of the transmission running on the fiber. The light signal on a fiber begins to diminish or weaken after a certain distance. The amplifier serves to boost the signal so that it can proceed to the next location. Amplifiers come in the following three varieties:

    Post-amplifier—Post-amplifiers have one fiber running in and one fiber running out. Post-amplifiers are placed after a transmitter on the sending line of an LTE or LRE.

Line-amplifier—Line-amplifiers have one fiber running in and one fiber running out. Line-amplifiers can be placed anywhere on a line and do not have to be paired with other devices like LTEs or LREs.

Preamplifier—Preamplifiers have one fiber running in and one fiber running out. Preamplifiers are placed on the receiving line of an LTE or LRE.

- *Site*—The physical location at which one or more pieces of equipment is positioned. A site is a location wherever fibers must be amplified or regenerated, or where a junction exists which consists of two or more systems requiring LTEs, LREs, and so on. Because the signal on a fiber has to be regenerated after a certain distance (we'll assume a maximum distance of 10 miles), sites must be placed within the maximum limit. For this reason, it is not uncommon for sites to be situated in very remote locations.

- *System*—A completely configured and operational two-way transmission line normally consisting of two fibers and the devices and equipment necessary to make the system function. Systems have a specific starting point and run through many sites before reaching a final destination. For example, a system that runs from Phoenix to San Diego includes the Phoenix and San Diego points as well as every site in between.

Figure 8.2 illustrates how the components presented in the preceding list are used together. It shows a typical segment of a system between two sites.

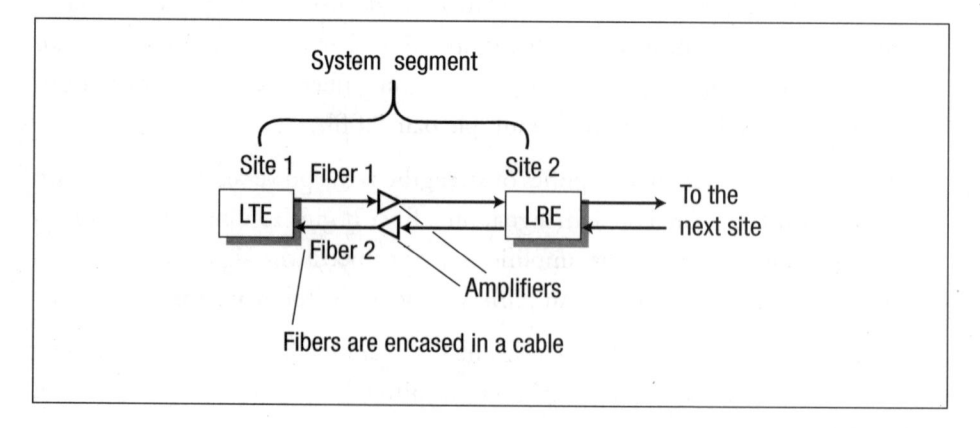

Figure 8.2
A typical system segment for a fiber-optic network.

Putting It All Together: A Comprehensive Object Relational Design

Now that I have described the physical devices used in a fiber-optic network and listed the requirements for the system design, let's proceed with the effort of designing the elements that will comprise the database schema.

Undertaking The Modeling Effort

By now, it should be apparent from the description of the various objects comprising a fiber-optic network that there are numerous complex relationships between both data entities and behaviors. There are also countless details in the real world that have been omitted from this case study in order to permit a detailed discussion of the principle aspects of this database design. The issue most germane to this chapter is a demonstration of the modeling techniques used in a real-world system with respect to the object extensions discussed in previous chapters. We'll disregard much of the detail of telecommunications because it would only complicate our discussion. Instead, we'll focus on the aspects of our modeling problem that make it so interesting yet commonplace in today's technology-driven business environment.

In order to give you an appreciation for the system that we are about to model, the discussion will focus first on the individual objects and their properties. The second step will be to determine the relationships between the defined entities. The third step will be to identify the behaviors or methods needed to reflect events and processes. Finally, we'll conclude by reviewing the finished model.

Analyzing The Components

Building a working fiber-optic system is much like assembling the tracks on a toy train set. All of the tracks must be connected to form a loop if the electrical connection is to take place. Understanding how the devices in a fiber-optic system work together to "complete" a system will give you insight into how the various entities must be modeled. If you evaluate the nature of each component or device carefully, you will notice that there are many similar shared properties.

A fiber-optic system segment in its most basic state requires the following: one LTE, one LRE (alternatively two LREs), two fibers, an "owning" cable, and two amplifiers. Where there are fiber-splice points, there will be two connectors at each fiber junction. This basic set of objects gives us the starting point for a number of business rules. The following list identifies the rules that we can glean from the basic description of a system segment:

Chapter 8

- An LTE must connect to two fibers.
- Fibers must be bundled in a cable.
- Fibers and cables must terminate at a site.
- Sites may or may not be the terminating point for fibers and cables.
- Each site must have one or more pieces of equipment (devices).
- An LRE must regenerate one or more pairs of fibers.
- A connector must be placed on each fiber end.
- An amplifier can be connected to only one fiber.

To help illustrate the analysis effort to this point, Figure 8.3 shows a preliminary data flow diagram of the Acme Telephone Company's fiber-optic network.

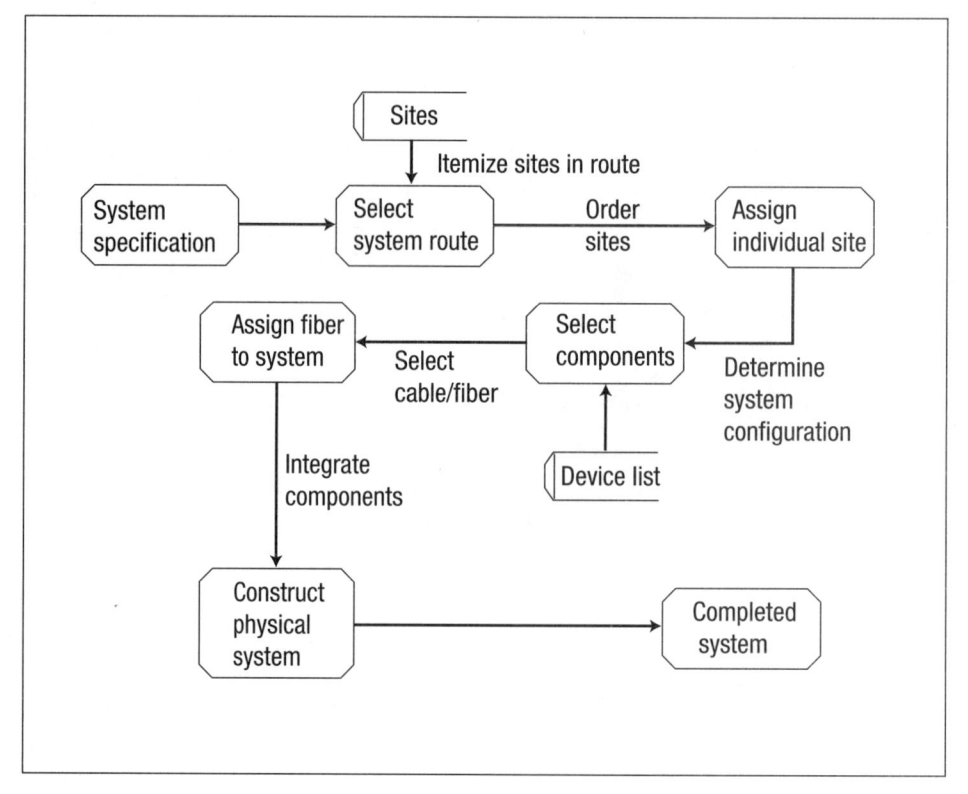

Figure 8.3
The preliminary data flow diagram of the fiber-optic network.

Putting It All Together: A Comprehensive Object Relational Design

A proper analysis of the devices reveals that several properties are held in common by all. For example, the following list shows the attributes that all devices have in common:

- *Manufacturer*—This attribute lists the company responsible for the manufacture of the device for which the attribute is attached.

- *Device class*—This indicates when you are dealing with an LTE, LRE, amplifier, connector, and so forth.

- *Device type*—All devices come in various models or versions. For example, fibers are produced in three varieties: dispersion unshifted (DU), dispersion shifted (DS), and multimode (MM).

- *Location or site*—The notable exceptions to this rule are cables and fibers, except that the ends of these devices must reside at a site. A detailed discussion dealing with the disjoint nature of cables and fibers is continued shortly.

LTEs and LREs share the most common properties. The major difference between the two is that LTEs start or end a system, while LREs continue the transmission of a system. Each device also has a number of specific properties associated with them. As previously stated in the general requirements sections, new device types will be introduced, and these devices could possess additional properties not currently defined. Figure 8.4 shows the preliminary list of known properties for the existing set of devices.

By now, you have probably surmised that the nature of the physical devices makes them good candidates for type classes. This is because a general set of attributes or properties can describe the majority of the devices used. In essence, we could define a general class that defines one or more classes of the fiber-optic devices. Sub-types to this abstract class would provide detailed properties applicable to individual device types. Recall the discussion on classes and abstraction from Chapter 1. The object relational methodology is naturally suited to the design effort of this project for several reasons. First, it will be necessary to encapsulate data and behaviors in order to properly model this system. Second, there are numerous many-to-many relationships that lend themselves to the use of aggregate objects and collections. Third, a degree of abstraction will be useful to reduce the number of actual tables created. We will accomplish this with user-defined data types.

The object relational paradigm allows us to create type classes and class hierarchies to model the complex equipment types. The current release of Oracle8 does not yet

```
LTE
    Device type (model)
    Fiber pairs supported
    Manufacturer
    Bit rate
    Signal type

LRE
    Device type
    Fiber pairs supported
    Manufacturer
    Bit rate
    Signal type

Amplifiers
    Amplifier type
    Supported wavelengths
    # of systems supported
    Manufacturer
    BI-DIRECTIONAL_YN

Connectors
    Connector type
    Connection type
        (splice, optical patch)
    Manufacturer

Cables
    Cable number
    Manufacturer
    Length
    Fiber count

Fibers
    Fiber number
    Manufacturer
    Supported wavelengths
    Fiber type
    BI-DIRECTIONAL_YN
    Owning cable
    OPERATIONAL_YN
    Signal dispersion
```

Figure 8.4
Known device types and their associated properties.

support object classes and inheritance. In this chapter, we'll present a solution to this system design that is supported by the current version of Oracle8. In Chapter 13, we'll revisit portions of this case study to introduce class hierarchies and inheritance for future releases of Oracle8.

Despite the fact that the devices have been analyzed and the business rules (those that have been communicated by the client or distilled through the analysis process) have been listed, there can be a sense that the design effort lacks focus. For a project to be successful, there must be a singular goal or an individual element that is the reason for the system's existence. I call this the *center of the universe* rule. The inability to locate a single focus for a system seems to occur more frequently in projects that involve a great deal of technological complexity, such as the modeling problem with the Acme Telephone Company. Many complex physical devices with intricate relationships and behaviors tend to divert the analyst's attention away from the strategic goal. In other modeling efforts, the central focus is far more obvious. For example, in a human resources database that maintains important data for company employees, the main element is the employee entity. Everything is designed around the support of the central focus (in this case, the employee entity) in order to achieve the primary business objective. Figure 8.5 illustrates the center-of-the-universe concept.

This is a much overlooked aspect of system analysis and design. A fair number of projects have failed because the design didn't address the central problem. Textbook examples used in the discussion of database modeling generally direct their attention on situations that are easily defined. Unfortunately, the real world rarely offers such simple and direct interpretation. Take into consideration what we know of the physical

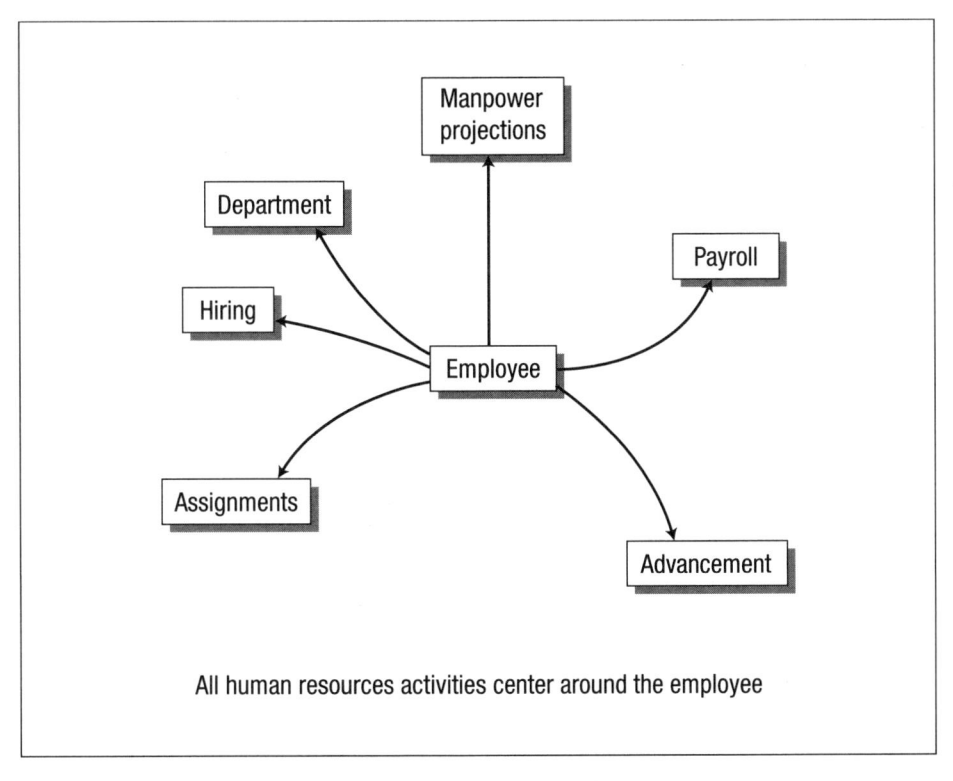

All human resources activities center around the employee

Figure 8.5
Discerning the central focus of a system design.

components of the fiber-optic system and revisit the general business objective for the system design. Is the main element easily discernible? In the real-world system from which this case study is based, the answer eluded the first design and development team and was not "discovered" until a second group was recruited to revise the design created by the first group. In the course of performing the client interviews during the strategy phase, it is quite common for each department visited to claim ownership of the central focus. It is the responsibility of the system analyst to sort the input from the information at hand and accurately map the general business objective to the main element. Before I provide an answer to the question that I just posed, let's evaluate the relationships that exist between the entities in the fiber-optic network.

Defining The Relationships

The analysis of the components revealed opportunities for a number of relation types. In addition, it demonstrated the various natures that the objects will take when mapped to database entities. In the object relational model, we treat the concept of relationships somewhat differently than we do in the purely relational model. Recall from Chapter 3 that object relational relationships are unidirectional in most cases. The semantic connection between two elements is completed when the relationship from each element to the next has been addressed. In the case of the fiber-optic network, most of the relationships will consist of dependencies, associations, and generalizations. To review the context of each of these relation types, consult Chapter 3. The next step is to evaluate the relationships between the various components in the fiber-optic network. We will begin our discussion with many-to-many relationships.

Also, since we are designing both data entities and methods, we must look at relationships from three aspects: what the data relationships are, what the behavior relationships are, and how the data is coupled with the behaviors. Unlike a traditional relational data model where we could only model the world at its lowest level, we now have the ability to model aggregates, and we must also plan for aggregation of both data entities and of methods.

Listing The Many-To-Many Relationships

As stated earlier, there is ample opportunity to incorporate collection types (aggregation). In a purely relational sense, numerous many-to-many relationships have been

Putting It All Together: A Comprehensive Object Relational Design

identified from the study of the data flow diagram and the analysis of the system components. The many-to-many relationships resulting from our analysis are as follows:

- Systems and fibers
- Systems and devices
- Sites and systems
- Sites and cables
- Sites and fibers
- Systems and cables
- Fibers and devices (this is to mean LTEs, LREs, amplifiers, and so on)

The first many-to-many relationship is between systems and fibers. A completed system can be comprised of two or more fibers. At the same time, one or more systems can run on a single fiber. There is a dependency that runs from a system to each supporting fiber. That is, systems rely on the fibers that carry it. Fibers, however, are not dependent on a specific system as they are capable of supporting more than one system simultaneously. Figure 8.6 illustrates the implementation of systems and fibers in the field.

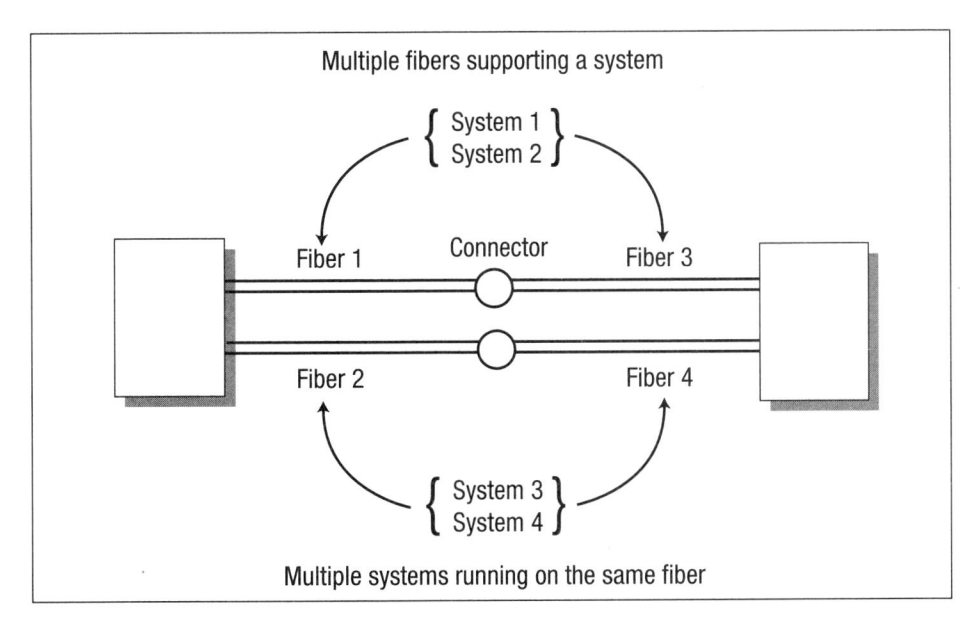

Figure 8.6
The many-to-many relationship between systems and fibers.

In order for a complete system to be constructed, a variety of devices must be installed and connected between the start and end points. Likewise, individual devices must host more than one system. When system configurations are being constructed, a check of the existing equipment at a site should be performed to see if any capacity vacancies exist. For example, a particular model of LRE might support four systems simultaneously. If only one slot has been filled, then the next vacant position is assigned to the next system to be built. Figure 8.7 illustrates this last example of the many-to-many relationship between systems and devices.

The relationship between sites and systems indicates that one or more systems will traverse a site. This is largely due to the way fibers and cables are deployed. As stated earlier, fibers are bundled in multitudes within each cable. Fibers cannot be removed from their parent cable, and therefore, many systems are supported within each cable. At the same time, a single system must traverse at least two sites, but, as a rule, this number is much greater due to the distance that a system must run. Sites and systems share an association because there is a bi-directional relationship between them. Figure 8.8 shows the relationship between systems and sites.

The relationship between sites and cables is very nearly the same as the relationship between sites and fibers. The multiplicity of cables to sites is obtained when multiple cables are run through a site. An interesting hierarchical relationship exists between these three devices. A site can have several cables, and each cable can contain dozens

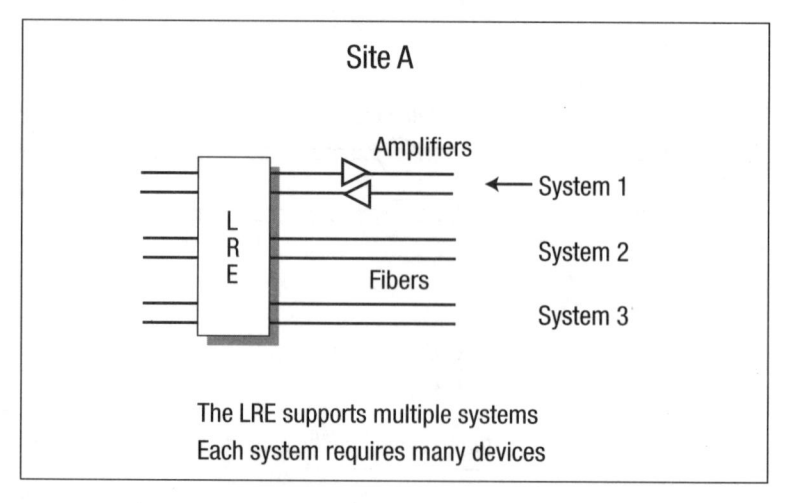

Figure 8.7
The many-to-many relationship between systems and devices.

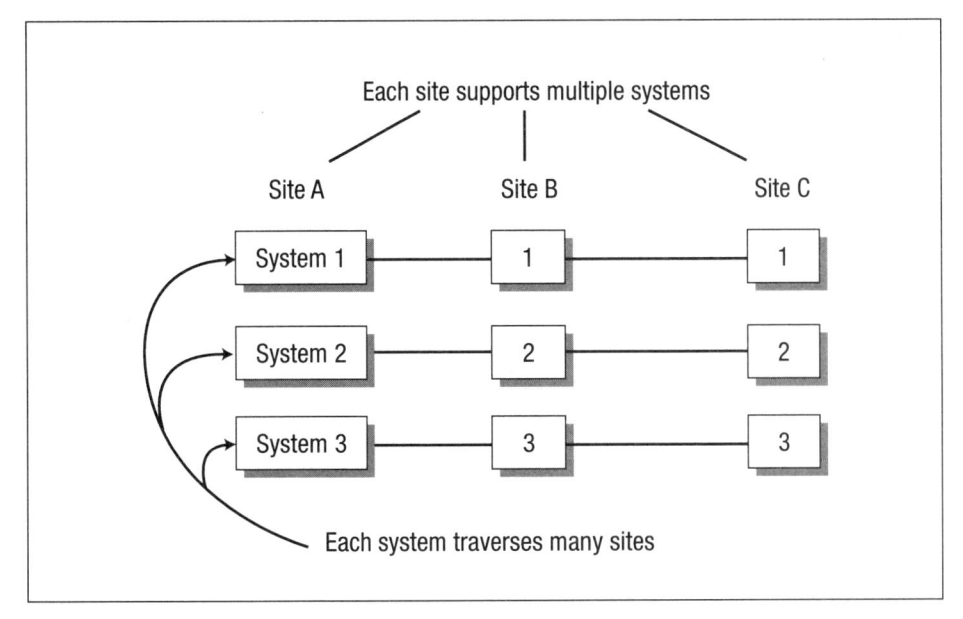

Putting It All Together: A Comprehensive Object Relational Design

Figure 8.8
The relationship between systems and sites.

of fibers. In turn, each cable and fiber traverses at least two or more sites. Recall the discussion on circular referencing found in Chapter 5. Although circular references are created when two or more objects require information about each other, they also reflect a bi-directional implementation of one-to-one, zero-to-one, or one-to-zero. This is not the case with the sites, cables, and fibers. The many-to-many nature of their relationship prohibits them from forming a true circular reference. Their nature indicates a relationship more closely affiliated with a network. There is a mutual dependency between sites to cables and sites to fibers. These devices share an association due to their bi-directional connection. Refer to Figure 8.9 to review the relationships between sites, cables, and fibers.

At first glance, it would seem that a system should only reside in one cable because the fibers that carry it must be housed in one cable. The reason that this is not a one-to-many relationship is that a system will continue beyond a fiber-to-fiber splice point. Whenever two fibers are connected, the fiber and cable designation changes. For this reason, it is possible for a system to negotiate many cables before reaching its final destination. Figure 8.10 illustrates both a fiber splice point and the many-to-many relationship between systems and cables.

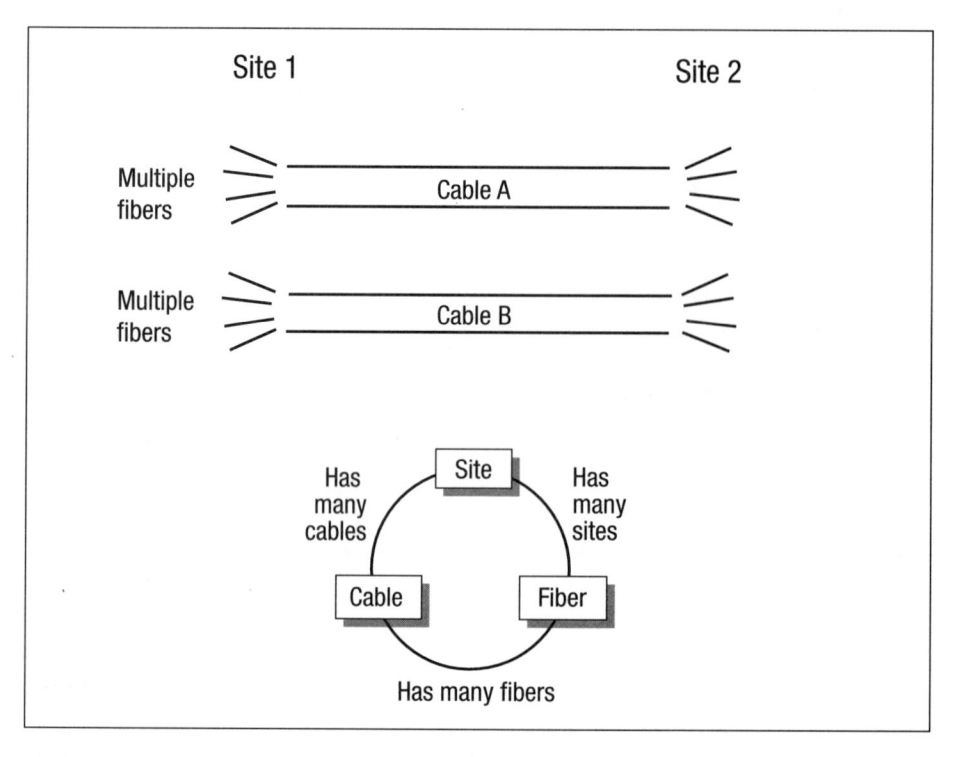

Figure 8.9
The many-to-many relationships between sites, cables, and fibers.

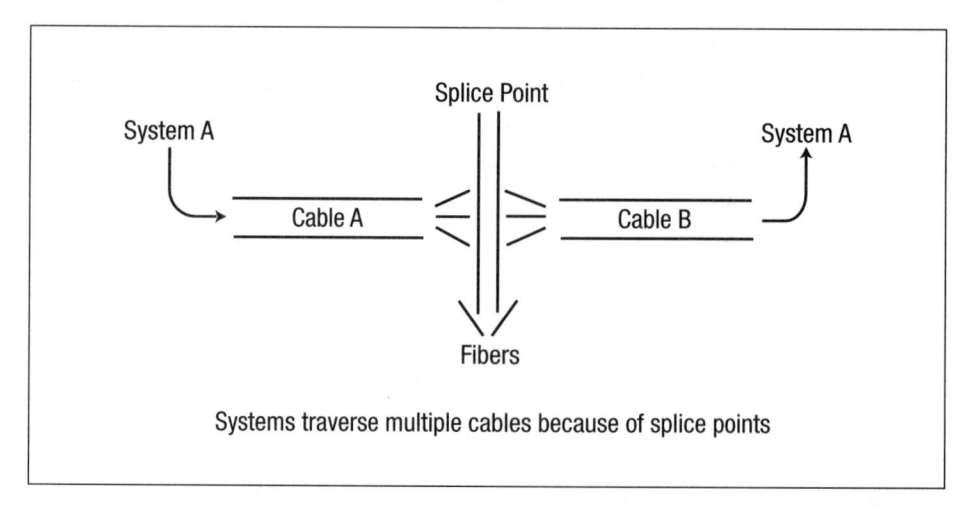

Figure 8.10
The many-to-many relationship between systems and cables as a result of a fiber splice point.

Putting It All Together: A Comprehensive Object Relational Design

Fibers and devices share a many-to-many relationship because each fiber will traverse many devices (amplifiers, LREs, and so on). Most but not all devices will support multiple fibers. The notable exception to this rule is amplifiers. Amplifiers support one and only one fiber. In this particular case (referring to amplifiers), there exists a one-to-many relationship. Figure 8.11 differentiates the relationships among various device types and fibers.

Now that we have examined the many-to-many relationships, let's move on to the one-to-many relationships found in the fiber-optic network.

Listing The One-To-Many Relationships

While there seemed to be a propensity of many-to-many type relationships, one-to-many relationships exist between the following components in the fiber-optic network:

- Sites and devices (includes all the devices described earlier with the exception of cables and fibers)
- Cables and fibers
- Fibers and special case devices (amplifiers and connectors)

An individual site can contain many devices from one or more systems, but a device can only be at one site. The glaring exception to this rule is the relationship between sites and cables/fibers. We will discuss the special circumstances for cables and fibers

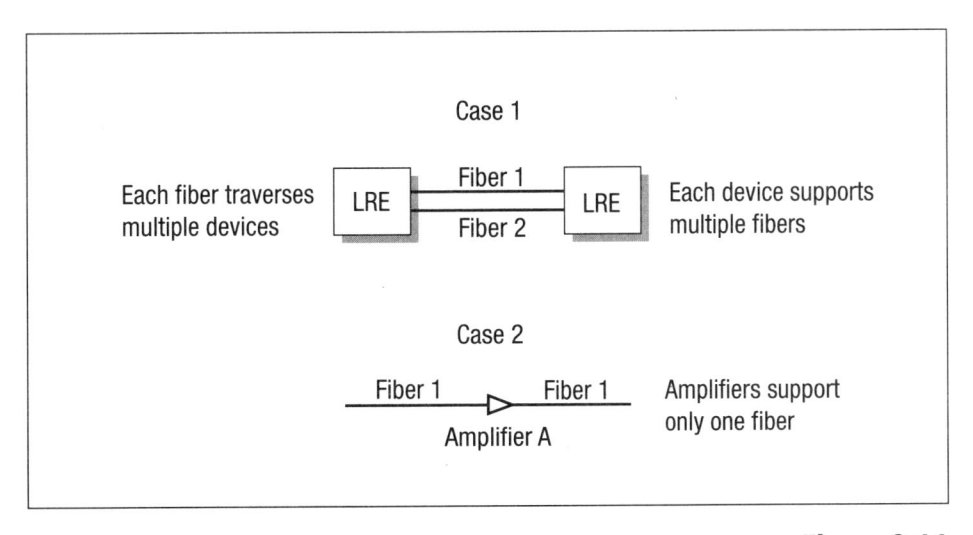

Figure 8.11
Device relationships to fibers.

shortly. Devices are dependent on sites for spatial identity. The only way to locate an instance of a device is through its relationship with a site. Figure 8.12 shows the one-to-many relationship between sites and devices.

Cables and fibers possess one of the most basic relationships in the entire fiber-optic network model. The relationship is a strongly defined association between one cable and many fibers. Fibers are not allowed outside the context of an owning cable. Cable and fiber start and end points are always the same. Fibers can inherit certain properties from cables because of their physical limitations. For example, location (start and end points), length, and system association are all shared properties. In a broad interpretation, cables can be thought of as "super-fibers" and, as such, can act as the supertype to the fiber's subtype. This interpretation gives the two devices a generalized relationship, reflecting an inherited hierarchy. Figure 8.13 illustrates the generalized relationship between cables and fibers.

Earlier, I mentioned the special relationship between fibers and amplifiers. These devices are special-purpose components and do not share many of the same attributes with the other devices. The relationship between fibers and amplifiers is one-to-one, because one amplifier goes with one fiber. Amplifiers must be treated separately from the standpoint of their relationship to fibers. If you model amplifiers as you do the remaining devices with respect to entity creation, then it would be possible to control the fiber-to-amplifier relationship through the use of a constraint or method.

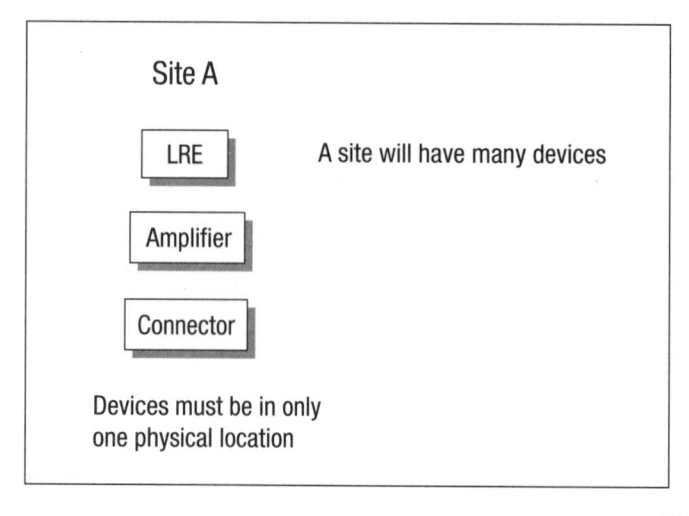

Figure 8.12
The relationship between sites and devices.

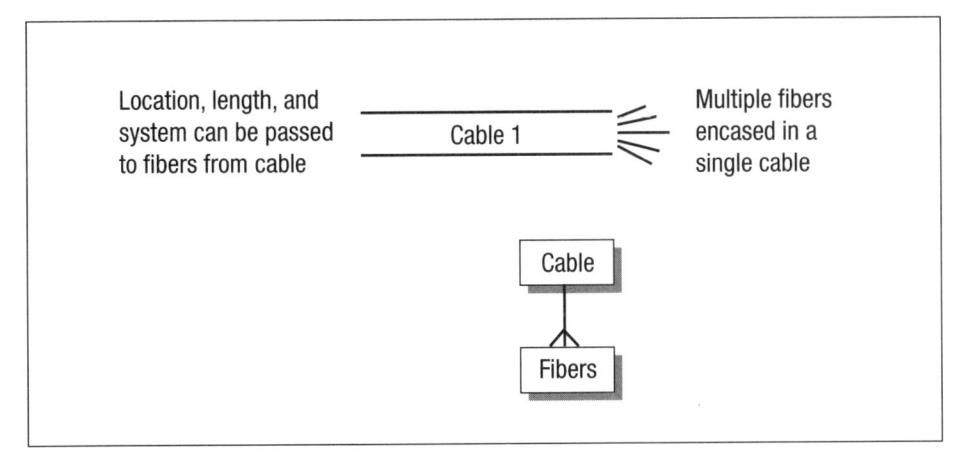

PUTTING IT ALL TOGETHER: A COMPREHENSIVE OBJECT RELATIONAL DESIGN

Figure 8.13
The generalized relationship between cables and fibers.

Now that we have categorized the relationships between the components in the fiber-optic network, it is appropriate to step back and evaluate the ramifications that these relationships have on the nature of the model.

Interpreting The Evolving Nature Of The Fiber-Optic Network Through Its Relationships

After reviewing the various relationships in the fiber-optic system, it would be easy to conclude that almost everything has a many-to-many relationship with everything else. It would be easy to categorize this case study as a *Bill-Of-Materials* problem. The one crucial factor that prevents it from being so is that none of the devices maintain a recursive relationship, where a data entity has a many-to-many relationship with entities of the same type. Rather, this is really a classic example of a network modeling problem. This is not an inference to the fact that we are modeling a fiber-optic network but, rather, network models in the data modeling sense. A network structure is one that supports many hierarchies simultaneously. The fact that so many elements of this project are involved in a many-to-many relationship indicates that almost any sub-element can be derived by following the path of relationships between the main element and those it is connected to. Figure 8.14 illustrates this concept using conventional entity relationship notation, while illustrating a few of the devices from the fiber-optic model.

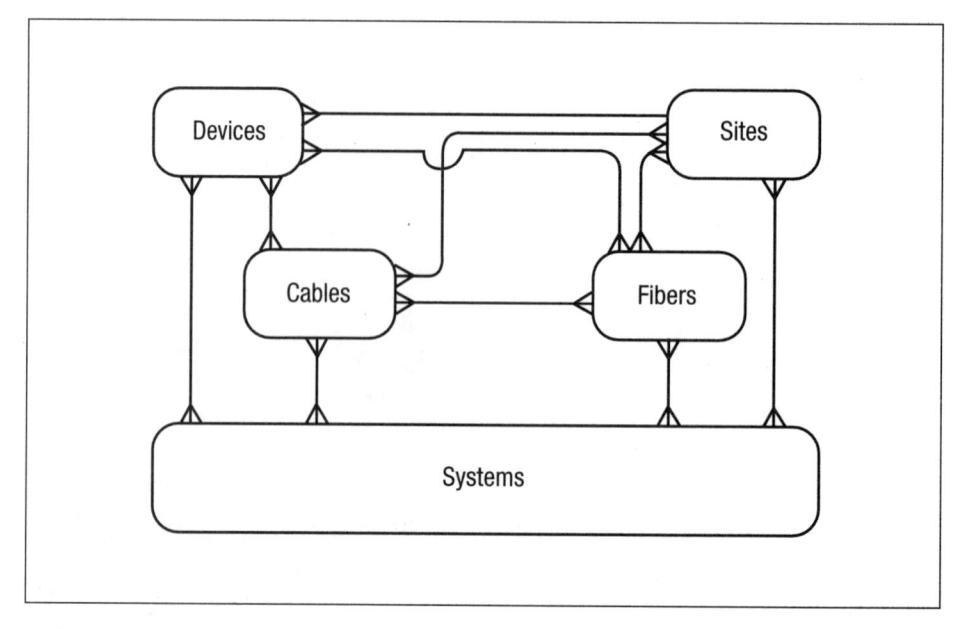

Figure 8.14
The concept of a network structure model.

One of the most annoying problems to surface in the analysis of the various devices is that cables and fibers cannot be distinctly "located" or placed at only one site. Cables and fibers link one site to the next and, therefore, cannot be identified as being at any one specific place. Cables and fibers require the association of two sites to pinpoint their location. The treatment of cables and fibers is unique to the other devices in this respect. All other instances of equipment can and are associated with a single site. To identify the true path of a cable or fiber it is necessary to list the start and end sites as well as all of the sites in between. It is entirely possible for the path of a cable (and its fibers) to divert from what appears to be a straight path. For example, it is possible to have a junction-like site that contains crisscrossing systems. Figure 8.15 illustrates two of the possible scenarios that can occur at a junction site.

This behavior on the part of cables and fibers with respect to sites explains why the many-to-many relationship exists. The problem that arises from this relationship is that it deviates from our ability to group or categorize instances of objects by location. The difficulties that arise from this problem manifest themselves to a greater extent on the application side of the development effort. User reports and screens that represent device groupings by location are difficult to write and can be misleading

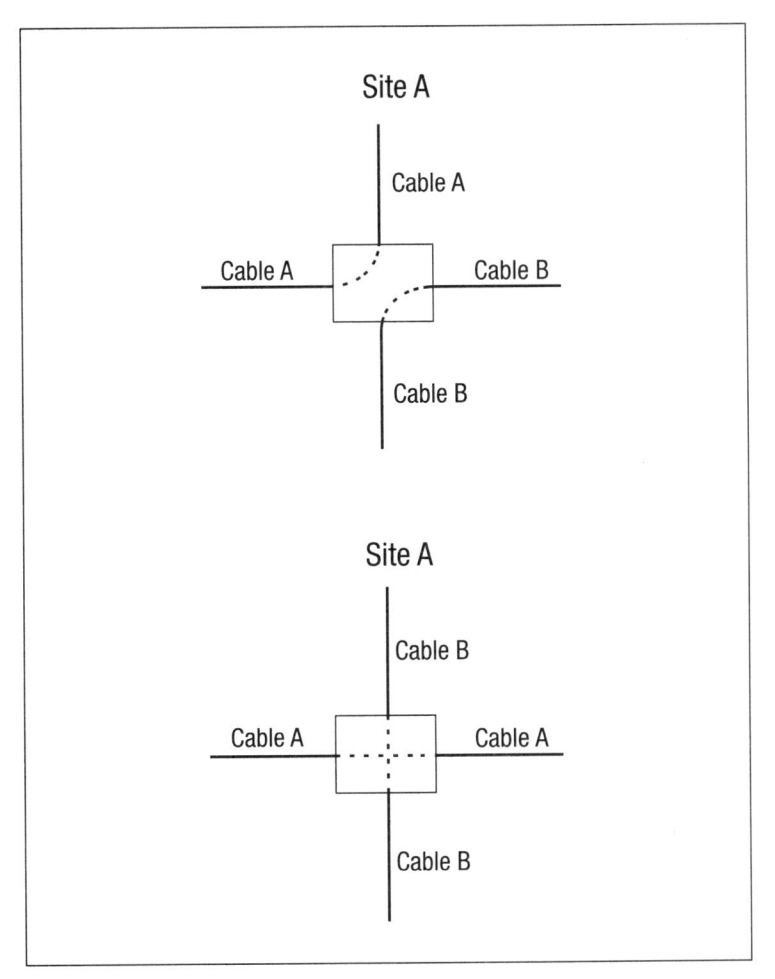

PUTTING IT ALL TOGETHER: A COMPREHENSIVE OBJECT RELATIONAL DESIGN

Figure 8.15
Possible cable routing scenarios at a single site.

to a user. It is possible for a cable/fiber combination to merely pass through a site. It is also possible that the fibers are spliced at that location, indicating that the continuity of the fiber-optic system must recognize the change in cables/fibers at that location before the system is passed on. A complete fiber-optic system might traverse several cables and fibers before reaching its final destination. After all, a roll of cable can only be so long.

In the earlier section entitled "Analyzing The Components," I posed a question regarding the importance of finding an application's central goal or center of the universe. Having gained a better appreciation for the components and relationships that make up the fiber-optic network, what do you surmise is the central goal for our example? Based on the existing capabilities of the object extensions in the current version of Oracle8, a good answer would be "systems."

Why did I present the existing capabilities caveat to the answer? Because the additional functionality of class hierarchies and inheritance offered in Oracle8 version 8.1 will change how we can model this application. With the additional object-oriented robustness at our disposal, we might have the ability to place the design focus on another aspect of the system model. The additional freedom to model applications in a manner that more closely resembles the real world will also give us the latitude to acknowledge and model objects (and build them) in a way that is not possible with today's tools. In the original project, it was determined after much research and analysis that the organization's most important factor about the fiber-optic network was the interworking relationship between devices. In the end, the goal was never a tangible object that you could put your hands on. Unfortunately, this fact was missed in the real-world version of this project, which is what lead to the second design group effort. In the sections that follow, we will pursue the remainder of the design effort with the central focus on systems. In Chapter 13, we'll revisit a portion of this case study to discuss how class hierarchies and inheritance change the way this model might be structured.

Now that we have gained a better understanding of the relationships between the physical devices in the fiber-optic network, let's formulate the methods that will be used by the data tables before pressing on to the effort of creating the objects in the database.

Putting System Behavior Into The Design

We have ascertained that the intricate relationships between the various devices call for specialized behaviors. These behaviors can be manifested in the form of methods assigned to the various data tables. The encapsulation of data with its associated behavior, as is commonly done in the object-oriented paradigm, is key to the effective modeling and implementation of complex systems. The coupling of data with behaviors also creates a condition where database objects "know" what their indigenous actions or events are. Refer to the discussion in Chapter 6 for further information. In this case study, we'll use methods to perform the following:

Putting It All Together: A Comprehensive Object Relational Design

- Help enforce data integrity between user-defined data types.
- Control the proliferation of collection types represented as embedded user-defined data types in object tables.
- Execute processes derived from a functional decomposition.

Recall from Chapter 6 that the purpose of designing methods is to map incoming and outgoing data flows to database entities. Data integrity can be enforced through the use of methods. Methods can provide a mechanism to ensure that any reliance components have on other objects is satisfied. For example, an LRE must have at least one pair of fibers entering and one pair exiting. A method can be written to ensure that fiber pairs have been assigned to the LRE so that the system can proceed. This is accomplished by attaching the following method to the **TRANS_DEVICES** entity:

```
CHECK_FIBER_CONNECTION
```

Another example is a method that checks to see that a piece of equipment has been assigned and placed at a designated site. For example:

```
DEVICE_SITE_PLACEMENT
```

The control and proliferation of collection types is an extremely important aspect of method utilization in this application. Cables "own" a collection of fibers, which can be represented as a **VARRAY** or nested table. Either collection type will suffice because the number of fibers is finite and there is no requirement to retrieve the entire set simultaneously. In this particular case, the controlling method will manage the association of the individual fibers with its designated devices and systems.

Methods are the Oracle8 constructs that will be used to implement some of the processes identified in the data flow and functional decomposition diagrams. For example, the construction of a system requires that the route between the start and end points is determined. This means that the affected sites must be identified sequentially. A method can be used to identify the system route. In the listing that follows, some of the methods used in this application by the various components are listed by type or class of object:

```
SITES:
  LIST_EQUIPMENT
```

Chapter 8

```
SYSTEMS
   GET_DISPERSION
   GET_SYSTEM_ROUTE
      FIND_SITES
      ASSIGN_SITE
      SELECT_COMPONENTS
      ASSIGN_FIBER

TRANS_DEVICES (OTHER THAN CABLES AND FIBERS)
   GET_DEVICE_TYPE
      GET_PROPERTY_LIST
   CHECK_FIBER_CONNECTION
   GET_SITE
      DEVICE_SITE_PLACEMENT

CABLES
   GET_FIBER_COUNT
      GET_MANUFACTURER
   GET_TERMINAL_SITE
   GET_SITE_TO_SITE

FIBERS
   FIBER_TERMINATE
   GET_TERMINAL_SITE
   GET_AMP
   GET_WAVELENGTH
   GET_LOSS_READING
```

Needless to say, many of the events and processes just described would not be performed with a single program unit. What has been created is an aggregation of behaviors or methods. The work necessary to accomplish each process requires the implementation of a method hierarchy. Recall from the discussion in Chapter 6 that a method hierarchy is created by decomposing an event or process into atomic-level (yet modular) functions and procedures. Note that indented methods in the preceding code are subordinate to the previous method in the hierarchy. If we use the **SELECT_COMPONENTS** process from the data flow diagram and decompose it to its constituent elements, it becomes apparent that further detail and sub-methods support this individual method. The method hierarchy for **SELECT_COMPONENTS** can be derived as shown here:

Putting It All Together: A Comprehensive Object Relational Design

```
SELECT_COMPONENTS
    FIND_OPEN_FIBER
        FIBER_END_YN
            ADD_CONNECTOR
            ADD_AMPLIFIER
    FIND_OPEN_LRE
        ADD_MODIFY_LRE
    SYSTEM_TERMINATE_YN
        ADD_MODIFY_LTE
```

The sub-elements below **SELECT_COMPONENTS** represent packages and the subprograms needed to perform the component-selection task.

We don't have the benefit of creating actual object classes in this version of the database, so we'll simulate this action by creating the necessary methods to give the outward appearance that object classes exist. The first question that arises is, "How can this be done?" The answer is that we will employ nested program units in the **MAP** and **ORDER** methods that employ our method-hierarchy approach to guide the appropriate behavior in controlling attribute population and device selection. In addition, we will employ external procedure calls, if necessary, to handle some of the sophisticated behavior surrounding system construction. For example, overloaded packages embedded in our method hierarchy can ascertain the device type to be modified based on the parameters passed to the packages. Look closely at the illustration in Figure 8.16. The first-level functional decomposition for device types like LTEs, LREs, and so on is depicted.

Conceptualize a supertype entity that incorporates LTEs, LREs, amplifiers, and connectors. There are two subsets of attributes that each device type possesses—attributes common to all and specialized attributes specific to each device type. Besides incorporating a sense of polymorphism, overloaded packages differentiate device types by focusing on the specialized attributes. Figure 8.17 illustrates the use of overloaded packages embedded in methods to achieve the result just described.

Now that the requirements, analysis, relationships, and behaviors have been adequately addressed, let's proceed to the completed data model and review the actual scripts necessary to create the database objects.

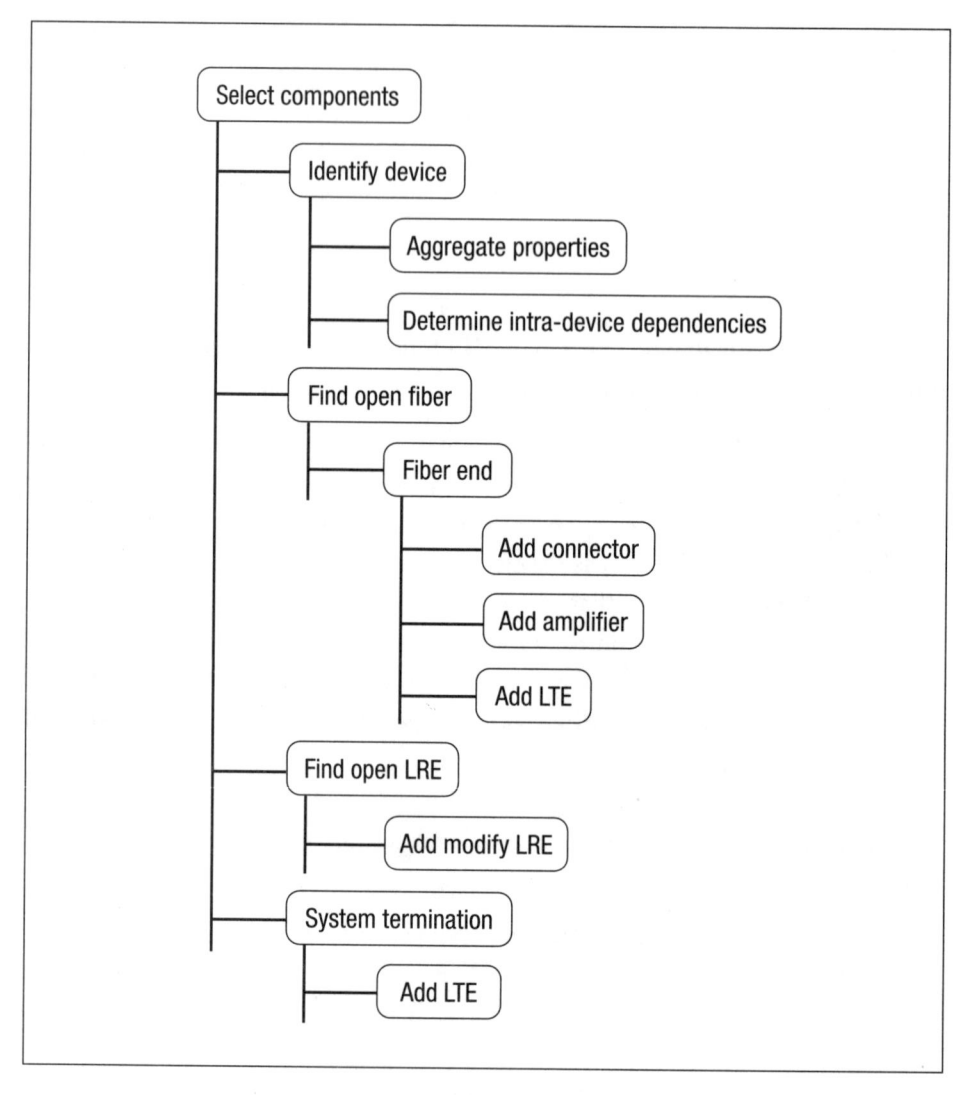

Figure 8.16
The functional decomposition for assorted device types.

A Review Of The Completed Data Model

The next step in the process of producing our database system design is the generation of the database schema. In an iterative fashion, we will present portions of the DML statements and discuss them, and then we'll proceed to the next portion. For the sake of brevity, the detailed source code for the methods used in this application will not be displayed.

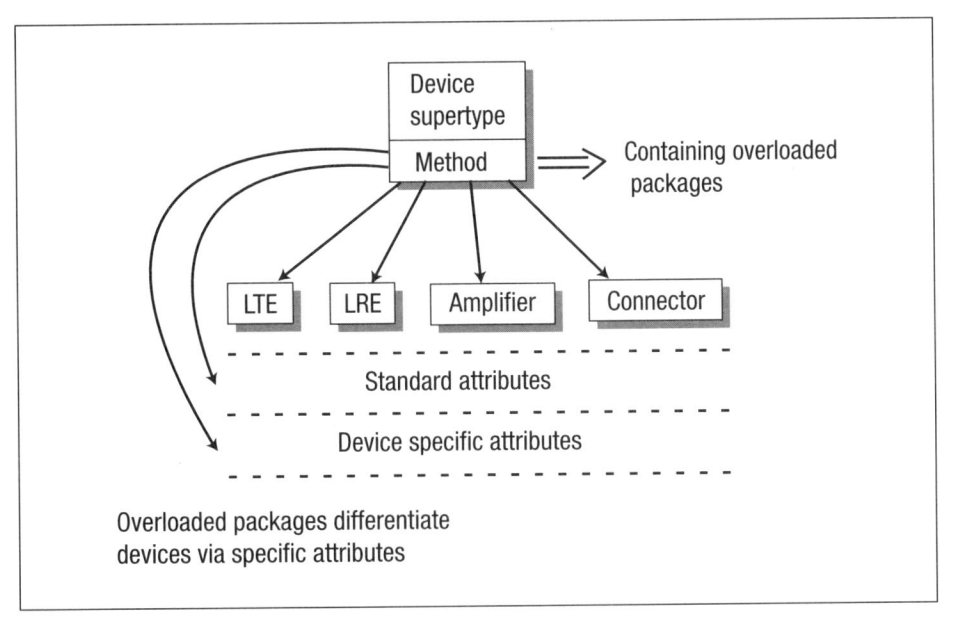

Putting It All Together: A Comprehensive Object Relational Design

Figure 8.17
The use of overloaded packages in methods to maintain device types.

```
CREATE DIRECTORY site_image AS '/usr/home/sites/maps'

CREATE TYPE trans_device_t;

CREATE TYPE manufacturer_t;

CREATE TYPE site_t;

CREATE TYPE cable_t;

CREATE TYPE fiber_t;
```

The first lines of code show that we must establish some baseline definitions for object types used in the next series of DML statements. Recall that an incomplete type can be declared so that other objects will compile. The specific declarations for each of these types takes place later in the DML code script. Note that the **CREATE DIRECTORY** command is used. One of the requirements for the fiber-optic network is to provide maps for all sites in the field. This will be accomplished by storing map images on the file server and referencing them with a **BFILE** data type in the **SITES** table. From this point, we proceed with several detailed object type and table declarations, as follows:

```
CREATE TYPE property_t AS OBJECT (
    property_id     NUMBER,
    description     VARCHAR2(30),
    value           VARCHAR2(15));

CREATE TYPE address_t AS OBJECT (
    address_id      NUMBER,
    address_1       VARCHAR2(30),
    address_2       VARCHAR2(30),
    address_3       VARCHAR2(30),
    city            VARCHAR2(20),
    state           VARCHAR2(2),
    zip_code        NUMBER);

CREATE TABLE Sites (
    Site_id         VARCHAR2(10),
    Location        VARCHAR2(30),
    Map_coord       VARCHAR2(15),
    Site_map        BFILE,
    Equip           trans_device_t)
    nested table trans_device_t store as
    device_list_tbl
    MAP MEMBER FUNCTION list_equipment;
```

The first two DML statements that appear in the preceding code are unremarkable in that they merely create user-defined data types for use in succeeding tables and objects. It is worth pointing out that the **BFILE** attribute mentioned in the last paragraph now appears in the **SITES** table. Also, note that the **EQUIP** attribute is a nested table of devices from **TRANS_DEVICE_T**. This provides our representation of many devices being hosted at a single site. In the next few lines of code, the **SYSTEM** table is created:

```
CREATE TABLE System (
    System_id       NUMBER,
    Sites           REF site_t SCOPE IS Sites,
    Equipment       REF trans_device_t SCOPE IS trans_device
    Cable           REF cable_t SCOPE IS cables)
    MAP MEMBER FUNCTION get_dispersion,
    ORDER MEMBER FUNCTION get_system_route;
```

Note that the **SYSTEM** table contains several **REF** attributes to other database entities. In this case, the **SITES**, **TRANS_DEVICE**, and **CABLE** tables. Two of the methods described in the previous section are also declared.

Putting It All Together: A Comprehensive Object Relational Design

```
CREATE TABLE manufacturer (
   Comp_id           NUMBER,
   Company_name      VARCHAR2(30),
   address           address_t);

CREATE TABLE trans_device_t OF trans_device;

CREATE TABLE manufacturer_t OF manufacturer;
```

The manufacturer table is used to identify the contractors that produce the components and devices used in constructing the fiber-optic network. Two more object types are created for use in the next set of object tables, as shown here:

```
CREATE TYPE trans_device AS OBJECT (
   Device_id         NUMBER,
   Device_type       VARCHAR2(15),
   Device_model      VARCHAR2(15),
   Property          property_t)
   nested table property_t store as
   property_list_tbl
   MAP MEMBER FUNCTION get_device_type,
   MAP MEMBER FUNCTION check_fiber_connection,
   MAP MEMBER FUNCTION get_site;

CREATE TYPE fiber_t AS OBJECT (
   Fiber_id          NUMBER,
   Length            NUMBER,
    Sites            REF site_t SCOPE IS Sites)
   MAP MEMBER FUNCTION fiber_terminate,
    MAP MEMBER FUNCTION get_terminal_site,
    MAP MEMBER FUNCTION get_amp,
    MAP MEMBER FUNCTION get_wavelength,
    MAP MEMBER FUNCTION get_loss_reading,

CREATE TYPE fiber_list_t AS VARRAY(144) of fiber_t;

CREATE TABLE cables (
   Cable_id          NUMBER,
   Company           REF manufacturer_t SCOPE IS manufacturer,
   Sites             REF site_t SCOPE IS Sites,
   fiber             fiber_list_t,
   Property          property_t)
   nested table property_t store as
   property_list_tbl
```

```
    MAP MEMBER FUNCTION get_fiber_count,
    MAP MEMBER FUNCTION get_terminal_site,
    ORDER MEMBER FUNCTION get_site_to_site;
```

Finally, the core device elements are created. The first core device element is the **TRANS_DEVICE** table, which represents all devices except cables and fibers. The **TRANS_DEVICE** table contains a nested table of properties for each device listed. Each device class can have its own set of properties that it maintains in the nested table. As stated earlier, methods are used to control the properties assigned, based on device type. This helps fulfill the requirement that further database modifications are to be avoided because new device types can be easily integrated into this entity.

An object type is also created that is subsequently used in the creation of a **VARRAY** to store the individual fibers in the cable. The **CABLES** element maintains the **VARRAY** for the fibers. The **CABLES** element maintains **REFs** to the sites and manufacturer. With the exception of the primary key, all other attributes are user-defined data types.

Now that we have worked through the basic design of the fiber-optic network, let's present an amendment to the original requirements in order to highlight an interesting modeling concept—namely, the specification of object order.

Expanding The Basic Design: Tracking Objects By Order

Now that we are satisfied that a functional database design has been created, let's introduce an additional business rule that will allow us to demonstrate an interesting modeling problem. Let's assume that our client has requested that the database provides the ability to determine the physical order of devices connected to each other at each location or site.

Defining this sequential relationship is by far the most interesting yet abstract of the modules discussed in this case study. The requirements leading to the development of this portion of the database lies outside the scope of this case study. We will assume, however, that it is now necessary for a software module written in C to have the ability to extract data from the database and construct a graphical representation of the fiber-optic network. Detailed information pertaining to the object relationships, or "connections," are needed for correct performance of the graphical application.

Putting It All Together: A Comprehensive Object Relational Design

In formulating this module, two distinct parts or sections are involved. The first is that of object groups commonly known as *fiber rings*. Fiber rings are transmission systems that span a certain geographical region. For example, a continuous system running along the Florida peninsula and returning to the point of origin might be considered a fiber ring. As such, all sites along this ring are "members" of the ring. Figure 8.18 illustrates the fiber-ring concept.

The second part of this module describes the object-to-object connectivity that is established when transmission systems are constructed. For example, a relationship exists between an amplifier and the fiber to which it is connected.

The concept of object groups affords the ability to trace object memberships. The decomposition of a group identifies all constituent members (objects). Fiber rings are one type of group named earlier but other types exist, as well. It is possible to catalog all objects at a specific site as a site group. If the user wishes to describe all of the equipment at a particular site that continues a transmission to another site, then that becomes an example of a location-centric group. Objects comprising a single transmission system and spanning multiple sites (commonly known as *modsects*) are

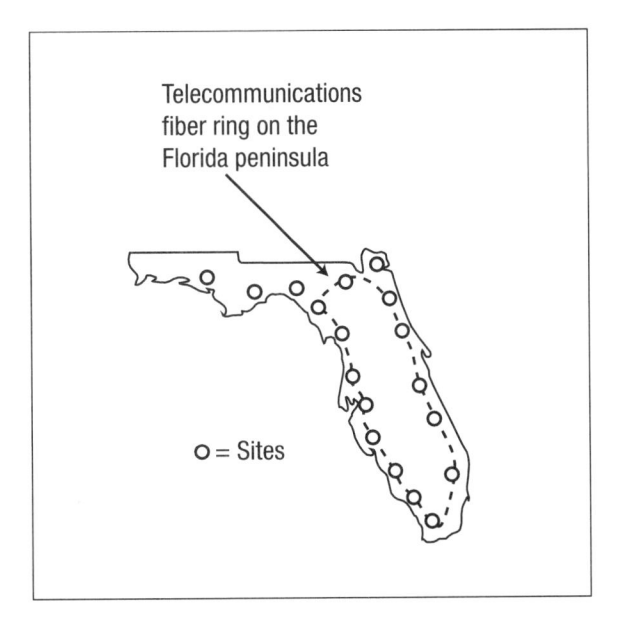

Figure 8.18
An example of a fiber ring.

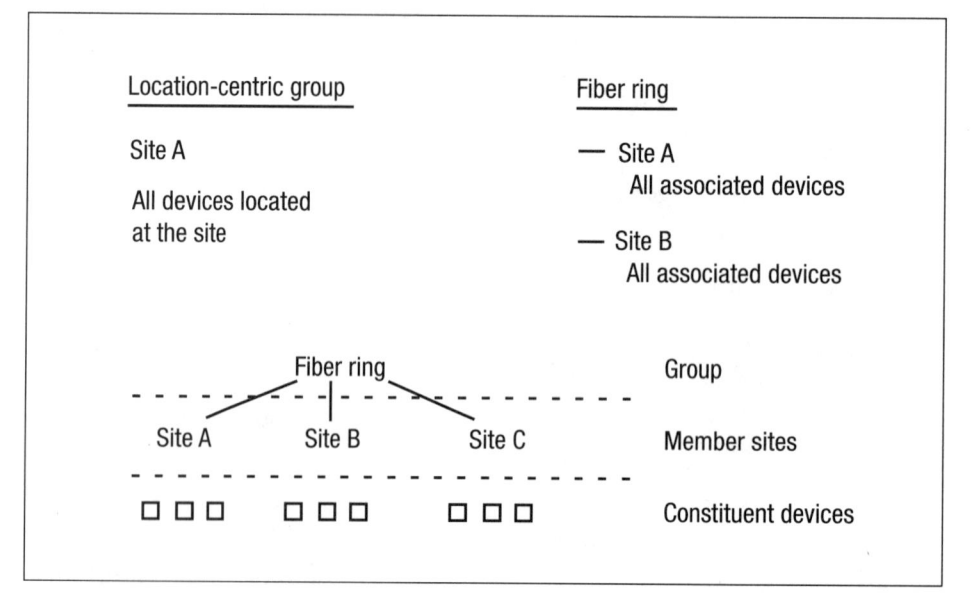

Figure 8.19
The concept of object membership.

classified as a non-location-specific group. Figure 8.19 illustrates the concept of membership that objects can have in the fiber-optic network.

The object-group concept does not require device order specificity. It is perfectly adequate to simply include a device in a group. Under this concept, it is possible for an instance of an object to be a member in more than one group. For example, a site might be a member in a modsect and a fiber ring. Therefore, the object-group concept does not allow for exclusive membership.

The treatment of groups offers relief in querying disjointed sets of objects where location is a part of the selection criteria. The classic example of this problem is apparent when objects such as connectors, LTEs, LREs, and amplifiers exist at a specific location. Cables and fibers lie between two sites and, therefore, cannot be uniquely associated with a specific location. In creating object groups, it becomes easier to make disjointed associations.

In order to track object groups, it is necessary to create another entity to represent groups. Groups should have the ability to be uniquely identified, identify each constituent member, and indicate the group type (modsect, fiber ring, and so forth).

Putting It All Together: A Comprehensive Object Relational Design

```
OBJECT_GROUP
┌─────────────────┐
│    GROUP_ID     │
│   GROUP_TYPE    │    Nested table
│    MEMBERS   ══════▶ of constituent
│  DESCRIPTION    │    objects in the group—
└─────────────────┘    each uniquely identifiable
```

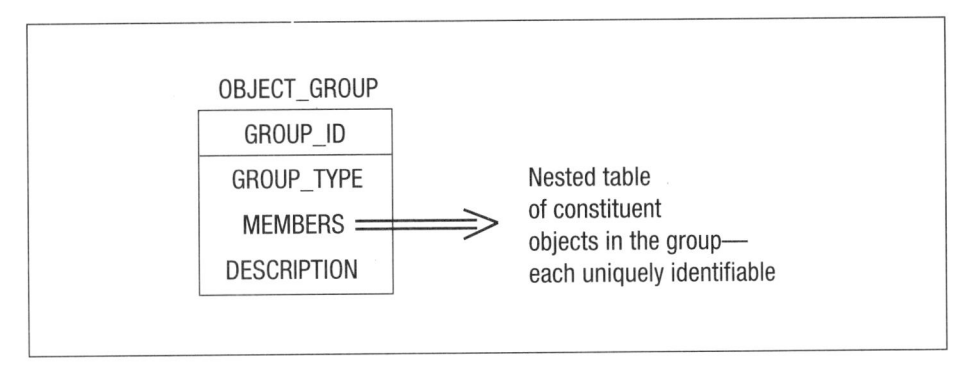

Figure 8.20
The object group entity.

Figure 8.20 shows the new entity constructed to support the accountability of object groups. The DML to create this entity is straightforward and is left as an exercise for you to pursue.

Dealing with the concept of object-to-object connectivity is more complex because what is being requested is a way to maintain a strict sequential order for the entire network. In addition, distinct order must be maintained in an environment that does not natively support this function. For example, the relational database (and now the object relational database) does not store data records in a data-driven order. Retrieval of data relies on the declarative nature of SQL. If we institute a system of object order, then it must be accomplished through our own design.

To begin the construction of this part of the model, we must acknowledge that each instance of a device will interact with many others. In order to inject a sense of organization into this concept, each ordered relationship must be uniquely identified. The links or connections that an object has with another object are termed *object relations*. Figure 8.21 illustrates the object relations that a single object can have at different levels.

An object relation has only one relationship, and it is assigned a unique relation ID. Object relations should be thought of as the interaction one object or device has with another. Just as a Lego block has the ability to snap into an assortment of other types of Lego blocks, an object or device must connect or associate itself with another device or object. The properties of that relationship can be described with two attributes. The two attributes are identified as the following: relation-type codes and

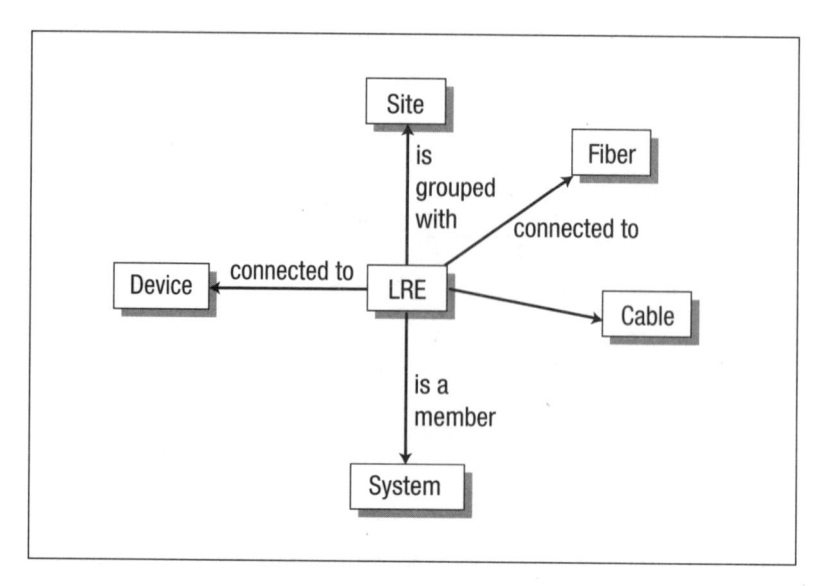

Figure 8.21
The concept of object relations.

scopes. A relation scope defines what kind of object-to-object association is being made. Examples of scopes are cable-to-site, fiber-to-cable, or equipment-to-equipment. In other words, an instance of a cable is associated with a specific instance of a site, or a specific instance of a fiber is associated with a specific instance of a cable, just to name two. Relation scopes identify the specific types of devices or objects as the previous example just illustrated. It should be noted that some scope descriptions are generic simply because a greater level of detail is not required. The relation scope "equipment-to-equipment" is an example of a generic description. The use of the term scope used in this context is not the same as that defined in the description of object relational semantics found in Chapter 3. In order to complete the definition of the object-to-object concept, we must have an additional attribute that defines order or logical placement. This is accomplished with the relation-type code.

Relation-type codes, by definition, can have one of three values: is connected to, is grouped with, and is a member of. These three codes determine whether a relationship is commutative. Relationships in this table can be commutative or non-commutative. If the relationship is commutative, the object order does not matter. If the relationship is non-commutative, then object order becomes significant. The code *is connected to* indicates a specific order (at least by the definition of this database design)

Putting It All Together: A Comprehensive Object Relational Design

Object-to-Object Entity

- RELATION_ID
- OBJECT_PAIR → VARRAY of two objects listed in order
- RELATION TYPE ← Identifies one of the commutative or non-commutative relation types
- SCOPE ← The type of object-to-object association

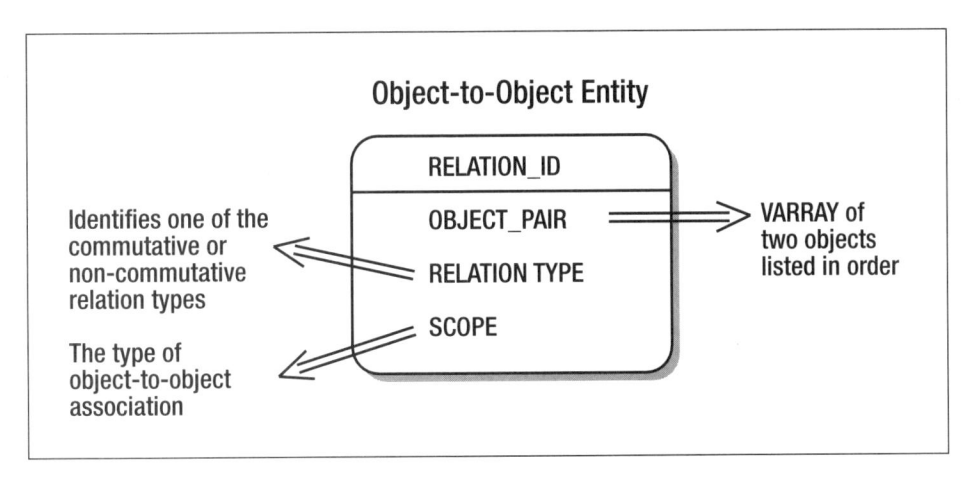

Figure 8.22
The entity representing the object-to-object concept.

and is therefore non-commutative. The same is true of the code *is grouped with*. The only commutative code created for this database is *is a member of*. In Figure 8.22, the object-to-object entity is illustrated. Note that the unique identifiers for each object instance are stored in a **VARRAY** collection type, and the relation type and scope become attributes of the object-to-object entity.

The two attributes, scope and relation type code, provide a data driven means of logically constructing the fiber optic system as it physically exists in the real world. This is the intent of the object-to-object concept: to store the physical nature of the fiber optic network as textual data in the database.

The logical means of populating the object-to-object table is through the use of method calls. As each system is being built, the necessary object pairings should be assembled and stored in the **OBJECT_RELATIONS** table, and the method call should be added to the method hierarchy for the **SYSTEMS** table.

Summary

In this chapter, we analyzed a real-world modeling problem drawn from the technology-driven environment of today's business world. The Acme Telephone Company's fiber-optic network demonstrates the level of complexity that systems analysts and database designers should come to expect. The object relational model supports the

Chapter 8

design of complex applications in a way that the relational model can't. The ability to deal with aggregates, create user-defined data types, and incorporate behaviors (methods) into the database schema allows today's analysts and designers to more accurately model real-world applications. In Chapter 9, we'll expand on the discussion started in Chapter 3 by introducing a modeling and design methodology based on the concepts found in the Unified Modeling Language.

An Oracle8 Modeling And Design Methodology

HIGH PERFORMANCE

CHAPTER 9

HIGH PERFORMANCE

Logical consequences are the scarecrows of fools and the beacons of wise men.
—T.H. Huxley

An Oracle8 Modeling And Design Methodology

An essential component of developing a working application system is producing its graphical representation. When using the relational methodology, we produced data flow and entity relationship diagrams. These tools, particularly the entity relationship diagram, were adequate in the relational model because entity types were simple and the set of relation types correlated to the mapping of normalized data structures. With the advent of the object-relational database, the standard diagrams of the relational model are no longer adequate for accurately describing the more complex nature of object tables, collection types, and new relation types. Keep in mind also that the entity relationship diagram required developers to follow the rules of normalization, which do not allow for constructs like pointers. In addition, the concept of non-first normal form, as proposed in Chapter 3 of this book, cannot be implemented in an entity relationship diagram. Complex systems are also often difficult or impossible to accurately model using the entity relationship diagram. The introduction of object-oriented functionality in Oracle8 requires an equally robust method of graphically describing the new database systems. With this presumption in mind, we will focus our attentions on a new family of modeling diagrams.

A New Approach To Model Diagrams

The basis for our discussion of modeling diagrams comes from the Unified Modeling Language (UML). Recall that the UML became the response to the Object Management Group's (OMG) request for a definition of a standardized modeling solution. Besides the fact that the UML is becoming the industry standard for system design, many of the tools that database designers will use to build Oracle8 applications are based on the UML. A specific example of this is Oracle's Object Database Designer. The new database object model proposed in Chapter 3 is also based heavily on the concepts introduced in the UML, and, therefore, it follows that a new approach to modeling diagrams should share a common basis. Recall from the introduction of the UML in Chapter 3 that the UML is not a methodology but a language. The architects of the UML intentionally designed it as a process-independent mechanism in order to create as great a range of applicability as possible throughout the software community. The environments under which software development takes place varies greatly with organization, culture, and application. Certain aspects of the UML will have greater relevance to the design of object relational databases than others. It is incumbent upon the system analyst and database designer to find the proper implementation of features that the UML has to offer in the design of Oracle8 applications. Fortunately, the material presented in this chapter takes all of the experimentation and guesswork out of this effort. The first step in achieving this understanding is through a basic introduction of the modeling diagrams that the UML supports.

Basic Modeling Diagram Conventions Of The UML

The UML offers a set of diagrams for graphically depicting various aspects of a system. While all of the diagram types are not needed to produce a working Oracle8 application, each serves the purpose of graphically rendering difficult-to-understand concepts about a system under construction. In a later section, we will discuss the design considerations that influence a design team's selection of diagrams. Many notational elements used in the UML model diagrams can be found in more than one diagram. Most diagrams used in the UML are composed of nodes connected by paths. All of the diagrams are two-dimensional in nature and make use of four basic constructs:

- Icons
- Two-dimensional symbols
- Paths
- Strings

Icons are graphical symbols with a fixed size and shape that do not adjust to accommodate various contents. Icons can appear within other elements, on the ends of paths, or as standalone symbols with or without connections to other symbols.

Two-dimensional symbols have variable dimensions enabling them to contain text and other objects. Most two-dimensional symbols are partitioned into compartments in order to differentiate among an element's properties or functions.

Paths are merely line segments whose endpoints are attached to icons, two-dimensional symbols, and so on. The elements attached to the ends of a path give the path meaning. Just as a relationship line in an entity relationship diagram is meaningless without the entities it links together, so it is with paths.

Strings are used to display information about a specific element in a model. Examples of string usage would be the syntax for element attributes, operations, and even transitions. The use of strings in UML diagrams is subject to extension by the tools being used in the application development process. For example, string syntax used in the development of an Oracle8 system could reflect the specific syntactical constraints and specifications used in PL/SQL. Strings can also be used as labels on elements and symbols, paths, and standalone elements in a diagram.

Constraints are defined in UML diagrams using paths, icons, and two-dimensional symbols. The UML does not specify any particular language that a constraint should be written in, rather, this capacity is the responsibility of the tool or language being used for the application development. As mentioned in Chapter 3, the UML allows for user-defined constraints as well as those specified in the UML itself. The syntax contained in a user-defined constraint is the responsibility of the tool being used in the development process. For example, Oracle's Object Database Designer might specify PL/SQL and C++ syntax in any user-defined constraint syntax. Figure 9.1 illustrates the use of graphical symbols to identify constraints.

Notice in Figure 9.1 that constraints between two graphical symbols are depicted as a dashed arrow labeled by a string contained in brackets. The two-element example shows how a single cable can be a subset of many that traverse a single site. When three or more graphical elements are connected by a constraint, the string for the constraint is placed in a note symbol. Note symbols are boxes with the corner folded over and the text string displayed as its contents. This appears as the second example in Figure 9.1.

As a general convention, the UML groups model elements into *packages*. Refer to the discussion of elements and packages found in Chapter 3. Packages can contain subordinate packages or regular model elements. In the UML methodology, an entire

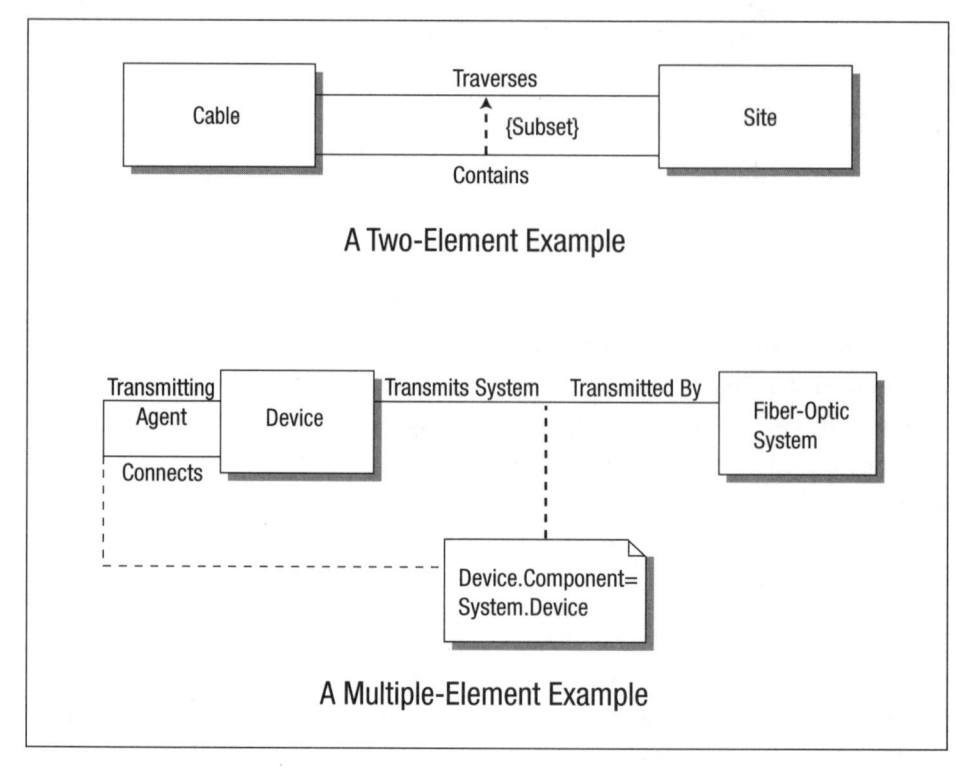

Figure 9.1
The graphical symbology for constraints.

application system can be thought of as a high-level package. Packages are denoted as a rectangle with a small tab usually attached to the upper-left corner. The appearance is somewhat akin to a tabbed manila folder. Figure 9.2 shows a basic example of the package graphic with subordinate packages enclosed.

Note that packages have an inherent hierarchical, or nesting, property. This makes packages suitable for the modeling of applications with multiple levels or layers. The way in which developers can model varying degrees of detail with packages is similar to the decomposition of a data flow diagram or a functional decomposition chart. This comparison is made to aid you in associating functionalities found in the UML with the more familiar system design features of relational modeling described in Chapter 2.

The modeling diagrams in the UML make use of a concept known as *type-instance dichotomy*. Type-instance dichotomy is the preparation of generic descriptions that define multiple specific items. Most of the modeling concepts found in the UML

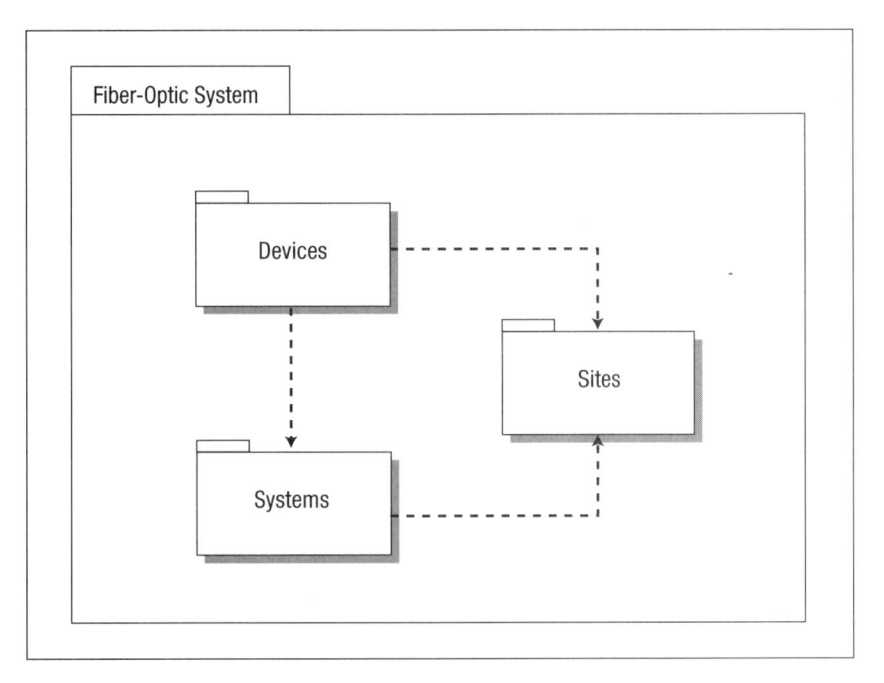

Figure 9.2
The graphic notation for a package.

exercise this behavior, and the dichotomy is manifested by two paired elements. The first is the generic descriptor for the element, and the second specifies detail of the individual item. For example, the specification of type class paired with object instance or parameter type paired with parameter value.

Model diagrams in the UML also make use of *stereotypes*. Stereotypes are basically a new class of element that is introduced at modeling time. Stereotypes allow developers to extend classes in the UML in a controlled fashion. For example, if an element instance called *A* were to be classified with the stereotype *S*, then it is equivalent to a metamodel class *S* belonging to a supertype called *A*. Stereotypes support high levels of abstraction because the stereotype can define a very generalized class of element. One of the restrictions on their use is that they must be based on an existing class supported by the UML metamodel. Stereotypes possess a complex classification hierarchy, and manipulation of these classifications are best left to developers with substantial expertise in using the UML. Stereotypes are indicated in a model diagram by placing the name within *guillemets*. Guillemets look like angled parentheses, << >>. Figure 9.3 illustrates the use of stereotype notation in model diagrams.

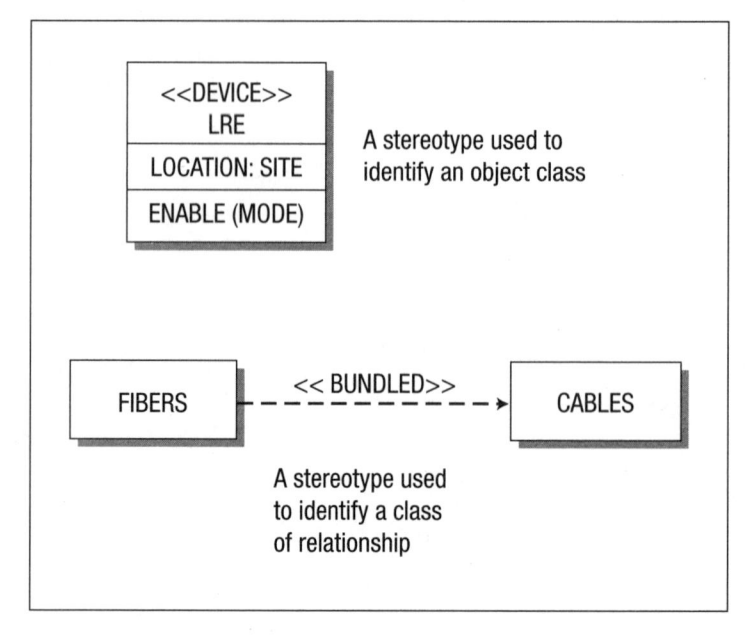

Figure 9.3
Examples of stereotype usage in model diagrams.

Now that some of the basic notational conventions for UML model diagrams have been presented, let's move next to a brief discussion on the complex nature of relationships and their importance in the UML.

Relationships In The UML Modeling Diagrams

The first introduction to the interesting characteristics of relationships in the UML appears in Chapter 3. Recall that the relational paradigm offered users an extremely limited set of relationship constructs from which to work. The benefit of this approach was that the rules could be learned quickly and applied by developers with some sense of assurance that the relationships would be properly utilized. The UML presents a double-edged sword to the modern developer, because the object paradigm expands the capability of accurately representing the complex nature of real-world systems via a robust set of relationships. At the same time, the number and nature of the new relationship types and their behaviors present developers with the daunting task of learning far more relationship types and their rules. The properties associated with the relationship set found in the UML are not all that intuitive, especially to first-time object relational converts. The purpose of this section is not to reiterate material covered in Chapter 3 but to expand on two areas that bear further examination: relationship types (dependency, association, generalization, transition, and link) and the concept of visibility.

The Five Relationship Types

An understanding of the five relationship types is important because of their universal applicability throughout the UML. The relationship types are introduced in Chapter 3 and are discussed or mentioned to some degree in ensuing chapters. Relationships bind elements and objects together. Understanding exactly what significance is being communicated when a relationship type is assigned means the difference between understanding a graphical representation and misinterpreting it. The ramifications of misinterpretation should be quite clear, as this results in miscommunication among development team members and, worse, an inaccurate database schema. A continuing dialog about relationships is found in the remaining sections of this chapter, so it is important for you to gain a solid appreciation of what each type represents. Here again, but in greater detail, are the five relationship types:

- *Dependency*—This is a common mechanism that applies to all elements. Dependency is unidirectional from a source to a target element. A lengthy discussion is omitted here because dependencies are extensively discussed in the section entitled "The Concept Of Visibility."

- *Association*—This is a bidirectional connection between two objects. When using associations, it is important to understand *association roles*. Association roles are composite aggregations of an association relationship to its roles. Roles are defined to be a shared aggregation of an object instance to a collection of type instances. This means that roles represent the part (in the UML, this is also termed *face*) that an object is playing at a specific moment in time. Keep in mind that a role is a subset of all roles (functions) that an object can perform. Association roles can have an attribute that specifies multiplicity, which indicates the number of instances of a type participating in the association. Four other attributes set the character of an association role. These are isNavigable, isAggregate, isChangeable, and isOrdered. The isNavigable attribute indicates that one or more of the type instances is reachable by the association relationship. The isAggregate attribute indicates whether the type instance is a whole or part association. For types that are given the whole designation, it signals that all other types are parts. This serves to differentiate individual versus aggregate behavior.

The isChangeable attribute indicates that the association relationship remains intact even though the participating type instance is replaced or merely changed. Finally, the isOrdered attribute shows whether the participating object instances are ordered. Although much of this might seem complex, what is transpiring with the complex nature of association relationships is a sophisticated method of describing and maintaining a many-to-many relationship.

- *Generalization*—Generalizations specify a unidirectional inheritance relationship used in supertype/subtype hierarchies where an instance of the subtype is substitutable for an instance of the supertype. A *GeneralizableElement* is an abstract class that identifies an instance of an element that can participate in a generalization relationship. Under this relationship type, an instance of GeneralizableElement can have zero, one, or more supertypes or be a supertype for zero, one, or more subtypes. Elements cannot be supertypes or subtypes for themselves. Keep in mind that class hierarchies will not be supported in Oracle8 until version 8.1.

- *Transition*—This is a behavioral relationship that specifies the state change of an object. A transition is the first of the behavioral elements in the relationship types. Transitions represent a composite aggregation of a state machine to a collection of transitions. Transitions basically mark the passage of an object's state from one transitional point to the next. For example, the state of object A moves from **OFF** to **ON**. The modeling of state diagrams in general, and state machines in particular, can become a very complex task.

- *Link*—This relationship type specifies all the instances of processes and elements that describe an interaction. This behavioral element is also used to describe the object participating in interaction-type diagrams. Both links and transitions are used in state diagrams. The use of both, where appropriate, serves to complement the meaning or significance of the state diagram. Links describe the relationships between processes and elements, and transitions describe the relationships between elements and their associated state changes.

The five relationship types just described are categorized in the following way: association, dependency, and generalization are structural elements, while transition and link are considered behavioral elements. The structural elements are geared toward model diagrams that represent the more physical aspects of the system being designed, while the behavioral elements focus on operational aspects. In the next section, we'll integrate the concept of visibility, a property that impacts relationships.

The Concept Of Visibility

Recall that visibility establishes the degree to which an element can be seen from outside of its enclosure, whether that be a package or a model. The UML defines four degrees of visibility going from least to most restrictive. The four degrees are:

- *Public*—Indicates that the object is open to all other objects, including those outside of its package. This is also the default level of visibility.

- *Protected*—Indicates that the element is not visible outside of the package that owns or references it.

- *Private*—Indicates that the element is not visible outside of the package that owns or references it. Although this seems a restatement of the protected visibility, there are additional caveats that set the private visibility apart. These caveats are discussed in the paragraph following this list.

- *Implementation*—Indicates that the element is not visible outside of a package that owns or references it under any conditions.

Taken individually, each of the four degrees are simple enough to comprehend. Any developer who has worked on Digital's VMS operating system and has used Access Control Lists (ACLs) will quickly master the concept behind each of the four degrees of visibility. The caveats that differentiate the characteristics of the four levels of visibility are affected by *dependency*. Dependency is a metamodel class in the UML and one of the five relationship types described in the previous section. In basic terms, a dependency is a unidirectional relationship running from one or more source objects to one or more target objects. A source has a dependency on a target. Dependencies are considered a many-to-many relationship among types. Dependencies are assigned various stereotypes that impact the behavior of the relationship between connected objects. If a target object is destroyed or altered, then the source object will be affected to the degree that the stereotype for the dependency specifies. Of the 35 defined stereotypes in the UML, there are 15 standard stereotypes that apply to the dependency metamodel class. They are listed here:

- *Becomes*—This stereotype infers that the source and target instances are the same object. It is possible that different values, states, and roles are at play. For example, instance A becomes instance A'. This stereotype infers transition.

- *Bind*—This is a stereotyped dependency whose source object is an instantiated type and the target object is a template type. This stereotype also applies to collaboration-to-collaboration references. (Collaborations are described in the next section.)

- *Call*—The call stereotype is one whose source and target objects are both operations. This stereotype infers that the source operation invokes the target operation.
- *Copy*—This stereotype infers that the source and target objects are not the same instance, but the values, states, and roles are the same.
- *Derived*—The derived stereotype has elements as source and target objects. This form of stereotype infers that the source object is derived from the target object.
- *Friend*—The source and target objects in a friend stereotype are both packages. This stereotype extends the visibility of the imported contents of one package instance to another.
- *Import*—As with the friend stereotype, the source and target objects are packages. The import stereotype causes the public contents of the target package to be referenceable in the source package.
- *Instance*—Instance implies that the source is an object instance, but the target is a type. For example, A is an instance of B.
- *Metaclass*—This stereotype has a type as a source object and a metaclass as the target object. This indicates that the target is the metaclass of the source.
- *Powertype*—The source object for a powertype is a generalization, and the target object is a type.
- *Refinement*—This stereotype is used when the source is a type, class, collaboration, or method, and the target object is a type.
- *Role*—This stereotype is used to show the source object as a type and the target as an association role.
- *Send*—The source for a send stereotype is an operation, and the target object is a signal. A send dependency indicates that the source sends the target signal.
- *Trace*—The trace stereotype has a model element as a source object while the target object will be a model element in the same or different model. This is the only kind of relationship that can span model boundaries. The trace stereotype infers that the source object traces back to the target object.

- *Uses*—This stereotype is a dependency where the source and target must both be *use cases* (use cases are defined in the section entitled, "The Modeling Diagrams Of The UML"). The source *use case* will include the behavior of the target use case.

The most direct influence on visibility comes from the friend stereotype. For example, in implementation visibility, element instances are not visible even to package instances that have the friend dependency. With private visibility, having the friend dependency allows visibility to element instances so long as the contents are imported first. The concept of visibility becomes clearer as familiarity with the UML is attained.

A direct correlation between the use of visibility and the treatment of packages, procedures, functions, and methods in Oracle8 can be made. All of the named program units afford the developer the opportunity to create public and private variables, and PL/SQL programs that emulate the concepts of visibility just described in the previous paragraph. At this point, the reader may wish to re-read the material on methods in Chapter 6 to cement the concepts just discussed.

Now that you have gained a better understanding of how relationships are handled in the UML, let's move next to a brief review of the supported model diagrams.

The Modeling Diagrams Of The UML

The modeling diagrams in the UML provide an open framework that facilitates the use of almost any development tool. Much of the syntax and notation found in the modeling diagrams accepts the standard notation and programmatic grammar from the native application tool being used. Programming languages in general use a variety of rules in the construction of type expressions, variables, and parameters. Programming languages also support the use of predefined and user-defined types.

The UML defines the use of the word *type* in a slightly more generic way than most languages, like C++ or Ada. The UML has defined *type* to more closely approximate *abstract data type*, while the definition of *class* is closer to the standard programming language definition of type. Because type expressions are language dependent, the UML avoids specific rules for constructing them. Even though language type expressions do not occur in UML diagrams, it is possible to generate them from UML types and classes. The attributes and parameters of elements in the UML can contain language type expressions that, in turn, can be used to generate code. For example, in the Oracle8 development environment, attribute specifications can be used to specify data column types, parameters to methods, and more. Such is the open and flexible nature of the UML modeling diagram environment.

Despite what might appear to be a comprehensive discussion of the UML modeling diagrams, there are many features and aspects not discussed here. For further information, you should review the most recent updates for the UML on the Web at **www.rational.com**.

There are seven general categories of modeling diagrams that exist in the UML. The seven model diagram types are listed here:

- Static structure diagram
- Use case diagrams
- Sequence diagrams
- Collaboration diagrams
- State diagrams
- Activity diagrams
- Implementation diagrams

At this point, we will review the basic structure and characteristics of each supported modeling diagram type, starting with the static structure diagram.

Static Structure Diagrams

The static structure diagram bears the most similarity to the entity relationship diagram familiar to most database designers. Static structure diagrams can be divided into two static types: class and object. The class diagram displays the static structure of a model (such as the types and classes), the internal structure of the types and classes, and the types' and classes' relationships to other elements of the model. Class diagrams can be organized into packages, as described in the previous section. Recall from Chapter 3 that classes are defined to be a descriptor for a set of objects with similar structure, behavior, and relationships. The class diagram serves to declare the classes in an application, and they are subsequently used in most of the other UML-supported diagrams. Class names must be unique within the package from which they are declared. There is adequate flexibility in the class diagramming structure to allow the suppression of the attribute and operation compartments. Also, additional

An Oracle8 Modeling and Design Methodology

compartments can be added to reflect predefined and user-defined properties. For example, business rules, events, and so on can be placed in the additional compartments. Figure 9.4 shows examples of class notation with varying degrees of detail.

An object diagram displays a model of object instances. Object diagrams can be considered a subset of class diagrams because an object diagram shows a snapshot of a specific detailed state for a part of a system at a given point in time. Object diagrams are useful in detailing the dynamics of the objects that it contains over a period of time. In other words, objects that transition from one state to another as a result of a connected event or process can be accurately described using an object diagram.

In the next section, I'll introduce an interesting diagram type useful in the analysis phase of development.

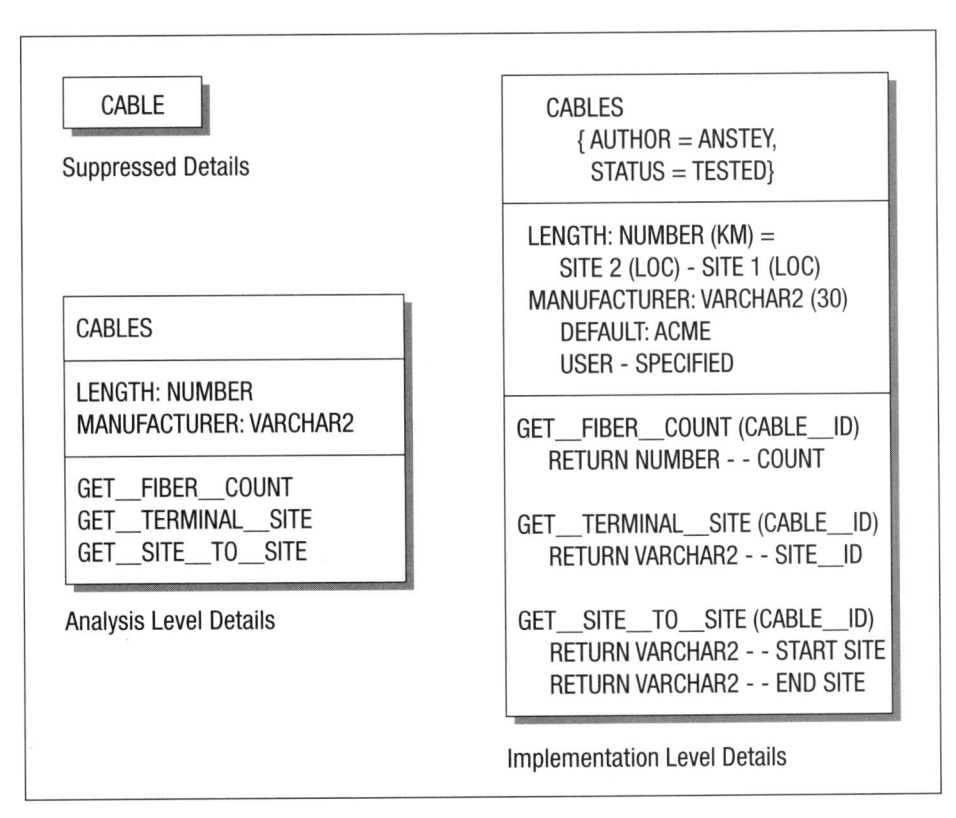

CABLE
Suppressed Details

CABLES
LENGTH: NUMBER
MANUFACTURER: VARCHAR2

GET__FIBER__COUNT
GET__TERMINAL__SITE
GET__SITE__TO__SITE

Analysis Level Details

CABLES
{ AUTHOR = ANSTEY,
  STATUS = TESTED}

LENGTH: NUMBER (KM) =
  SITE 2 (LOC) - SITE 1 (LOC)
MANUFACTURER: VARCHAR2 (30)
  DEFAULT: ACME
  USER - SPECIFIED

GET__FIBER__COUNT (CABLE__ID)
  RETURN NUMBER - - COUNT

GET__TERMINAL__SITE (CABLE__ID)
  RETURN VARCHAR2 - - SITE__ID

GET__SITE__TO__SITE (CABLE__ID)
  RETURN VARCHAR2 - - START SITE
  RETURN VARCHAR2 - - END SITE

Implementation Level Details

Figure 9.4
Varying degrees of class notation.

Use Case Diagrams

A use case diagram defines a system's functional requirements using *use cases*. A use case is essentially a sequence of actions that a system will perform to obtain a particular *actor* result (an actor is a stereotype of type, meaning an entity outside of the system). The stereotype symbol for actors is the easy-to-draw stick man (luckily for nonartistic persons like myself). Use case diagrams share a functional similarity to data flow diagrams and functional decomposition charts in the relational model in that entities and events (or processes) are documented. Use case diagrams are practical in the analysis phase of a project because requirements and functions can be clearly identified and labeled. Iterative levels of use case diagrams can be created, each showing a greater level of system granularity. Because of their ease-of-use and highly descriptive nature, use case diagrams are suitable for enterprise-level system planning down to the detailed business-unit level. Figure 9.5 shows a basic example of a use case diagram.

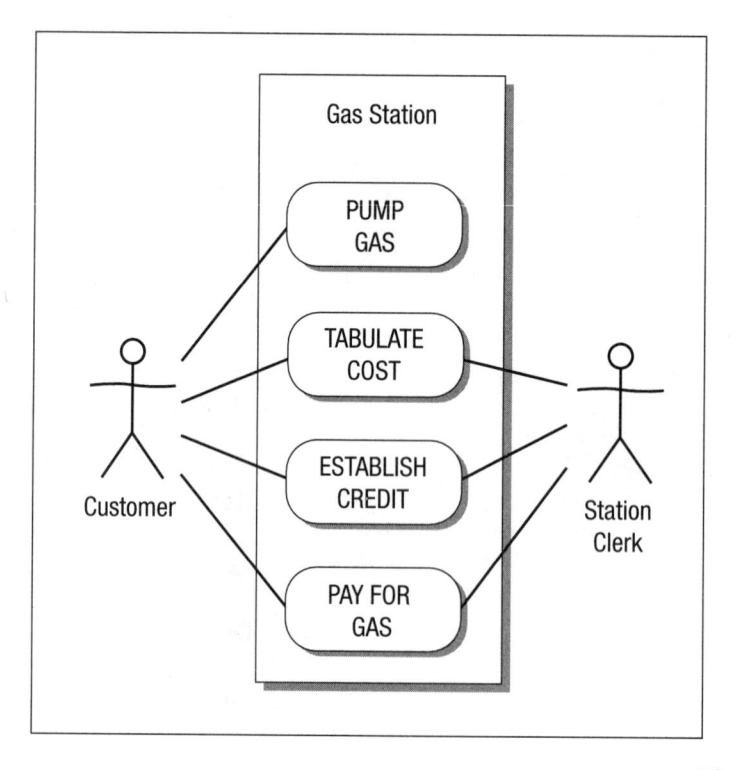

Figure 9.5
A simple use case diagram.

The use case diagram makes use of three types of relationships:

- *Communicates*—This relationship indicates that an actor "communicates" with the use case. The notation for this type of relationship is a solid line or path.

- *Extends*—The extends relationship is a form of generalization. The notation for an extends relationship is a solid path with an arrow pointing from the use case providing the extension to the base use case. For example, an extends relationship running from use case A to use case B signifies that an instance of B can include a specific behavior from A.

- *Uses*—The uses relationship signifies inclusion of a particular behavior from one use case to another. For example, a uses relationship running from use case A to use case B shows that an instance of A will include the behavior from B. Note that there is only a slight difference between the extends and uses relationships. The first indicates an optional condition, while the latter indicates mandatory compliance.

An illustrative example of the implementation of relationships in a use case diagram is found in Figure 9.6.

Now that the basics of the use case diagram have been explained, let's move on to sequence diagrams.

Sequence Diagrams

A sequence diagram shows the types of objects that participate in a use case scenario. Specifically, sequence diagrams show an interaction constructed in a time sequence. Participating objects are displayed along with the messages that are exchanged over a period of time. In a sequence diagram, the associations between objects are not displayed. Sequence diagrams can be shown in two different ways. The first is a generic format whereby all of the possible events or sequences for participating objects are displayed. The second is a diagram depicting only one specific sequence. The sequence must be consistent with the activity shown in the generic format. In other words, the specific sequence must be a subset of the generic diagram. Sequence diagrams are displayed against two axes. The first (vertical dimension) represents time, while the second (horizontal dimension) represents the objects in the diagram. There is no significance to the ordering of objects on the horizontal axis, and, therefore, objects can be organized into *swimlanes*. Developers and analysts familiar with the

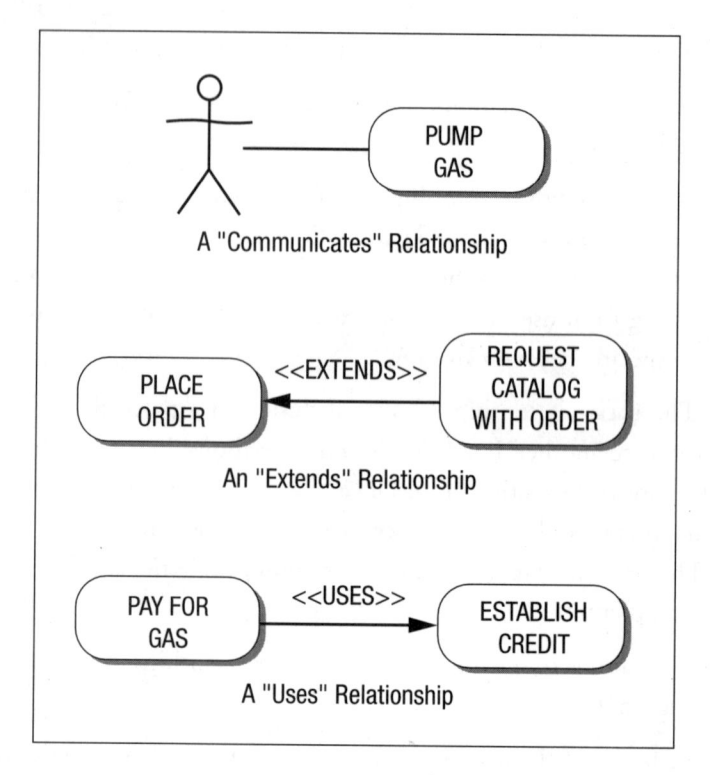

Figure 9.6
Relationships in a use case diagram.

Designer/2000 tool will find the sequence diagram somewhat similar to the Process modeler. Figure 9.7 illustrates a basic example of a sequence diagram.

One particular special notation found in the sequence diagram is the *object lifeline*. The object lifeline is a vertical dashed line that represents the existence of an object at a particular time. The lifeline denotes periods where an object can be created or destroyed. If a creation event is indicated, then the message creating the object is drawn with an arrow pointing at the object symbol. If a destruction event is exercised, then a large *X* is used to illustrate this activity. Lifelines can split into two or more concurrent lifelines. This signifies that there is a conditional branch in the message flow.

Messages have been mentioned in the previous paragraph, and, while you might be familiar with the meaning, the definition is repeated here in the context of the UML modeling diagrams. Messages are the communications between objects with the expectation that some action or event will result. Messages in the sequence diagram are

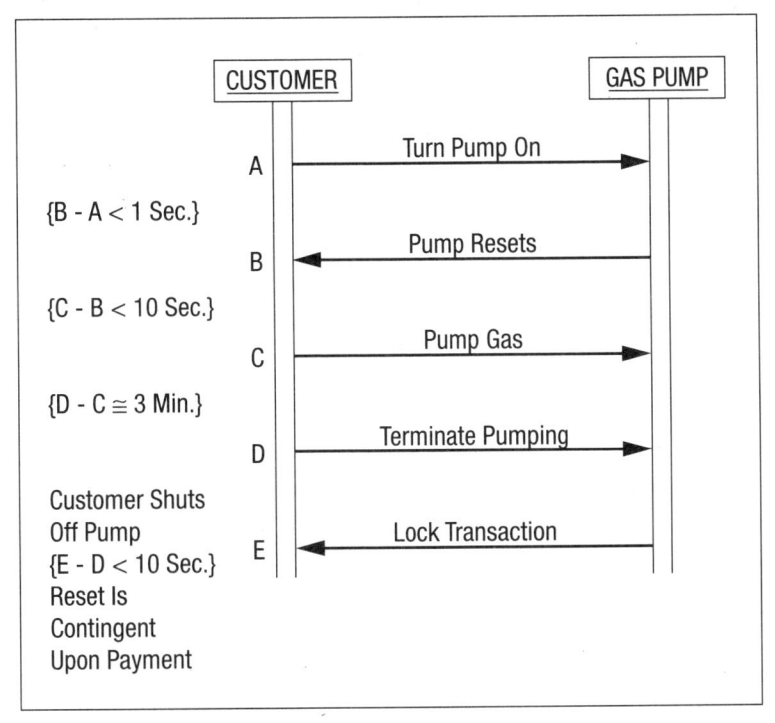

```
                CUSTOMER              GAS PUMP

                    │   Turn Pump On     │
                  A │───────────────────▶│
{B - A < 1 Sec.}    │                    │
                    │    Pump Resets     │
                  B │◀───────────────────│
{C - B < 10 Sec.}   │                    │
                    │     Pump Gas       │
                  C │───────────────────▶│
{D - C ≅ 3 Min.}    │                    │
                    │  Terminate Pumping │
                  D │───────────────────▶│
Customer Shuts      │                    │
Off Pump            │   Lock Transaction │
{E - D < 10 Sec.} E │◀───────────────────│
Reset Is            │                    │
Contingent          │                    │
Upon Payment        │                    │
```

Figure 9.7
A basic sequence diagram.

shown as a horizontal solid arrow from the lifeline of an object to the lifeline of another object. If messages occur in a particular sequence, then this can be annotated by numbering the messages.

From the time-sensitive nature of sequence diagrams, we next move to a diagram type that describes interactions—collaboration diagrams.

Collaboration Diagrams

A collaboration diagram displays interactions around objects and the links between those objects. Particular emphasis is placed on the messages involved in accomplishing a task, and less focus is given to relationships between objects. Collaboration diagrams are composed of *collaborations*, so it is appropriate that we define this term in the context of its use in the UML. A collaboration is a modeling unit describing a set of interactions among types. Collaborations can be attached to types, operations, or use cases to describe their external effects. They can also be attached to classes and methods to describe internal implementations. A collaboration used for internal implementation is described at a finer granularity than one used for external specification. Collaboration diagrams do not show time as one of the units of measure, so tracking the sequence of events is usually done with sequence numbers. Sequence diagrams and collaboration diagrams show similar information but present it in slightly different ways. Sequence diagrams are used to show an explicit sequence of messages and are well-suited for realtime specifications. Collaboration diagrams, on the other hand, are better for understanding the effects on a particular object and for the conduct of procedural design. Figure 9.8 shows a simple example of a collaboration diagram.

The context of a collaboration (the modeling unit) can be depicted as an object diagram. Recall that object diagrams are one of two static structure type diagrams. A collaboration can be depicted in an object diagram in one of two ways:

- *Methods*—This type of depiction shows an implemented operation with its associated target object and any objects that the target object calls on. The only objects displayed are those involved in the operation being modeled. The context of the diagram should include objects present before, during, and after the operation. Three stereotypes are used to label the participating objects: <<new>>, <<destroyed>>, and <<transient>>.

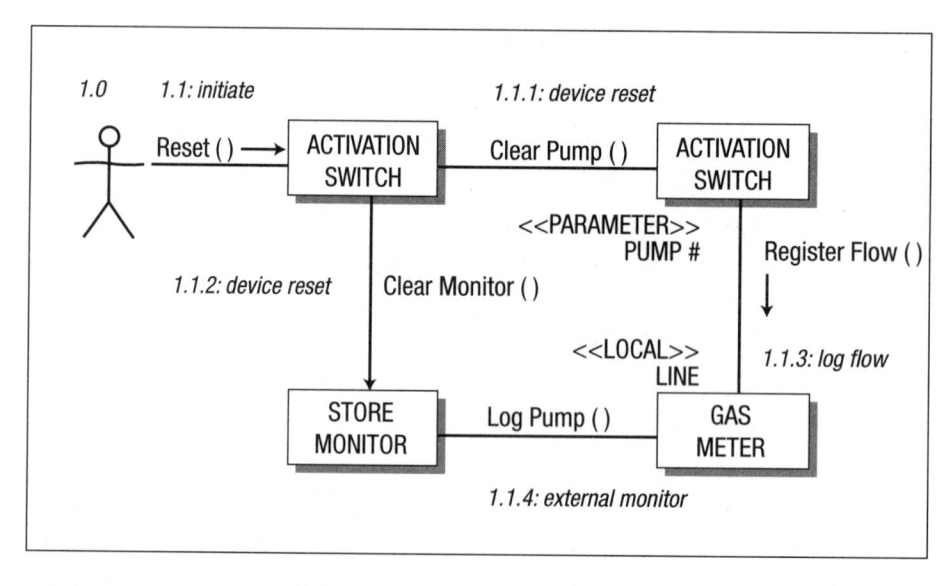

Figure 9.8
A collaboration diagram example.

An Oracle8 Modeling and Design Methodology

- *Types and operations*—A types and operations diagram is a variant of a collaboration diagram that meets several conditions. The necessary conditions are when a completed type definition is displayed, and the context of its object diagram includes the type's constituents and the related objects affected by operations on the type described by the collaboration. Message flows are not shown in the object diagram for this depiction of a collaboration. This way of showing collaborations is used to display behavior specifications for the type definition. To help illustrate this concept, Figure 9.9 shows an example of a collaboration depicted under the types and operations category.

The next modeling diagram to be discussed is the state diagram.

State Diagrams

State diagrams show the sequence of *states* that an object or process goes through during its life cycle. Full accounting is made for received inputs, along with the responses

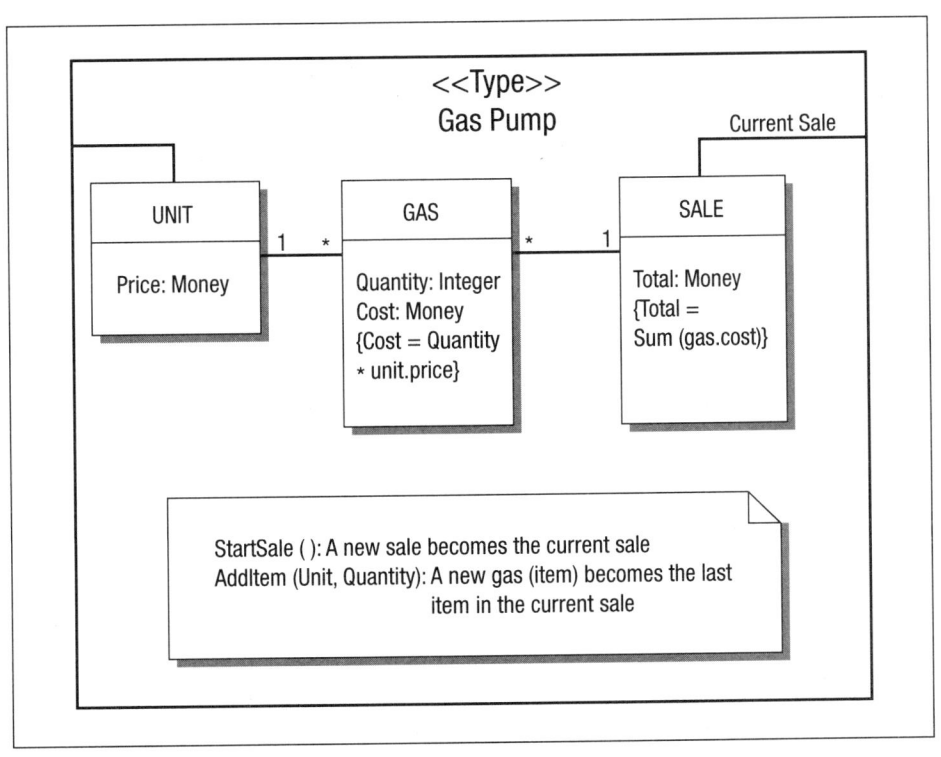

Figure 9.9
Types and operations object diagram view of a collaboration.

and subsequent actions. A state diagram includes all transitions and timelines associated with an object. A state is defined in the UML to be a condition during the life of an object or an event under which a specified condition is satisfied, performed, or anticipated. A state can include *do actions*, which are performed in an ongoing process. Do actions can be interrupted by outside processes or events, which indicates that they do not have to be atomic in nature. Do actions have a specified starting point when the state is entered. They can terminate independently, or they can require an external influence to do so. States can be further subdivided into subregions, each of which can have their own start and termination points. Transitioning to a final state indicates that an activity or process is complete. Figure 9.10 shows an example of a state diagram.

States can be further refined into substates using **and** and **or** relationships. These states are known as composite states, because one or more conditions can reside

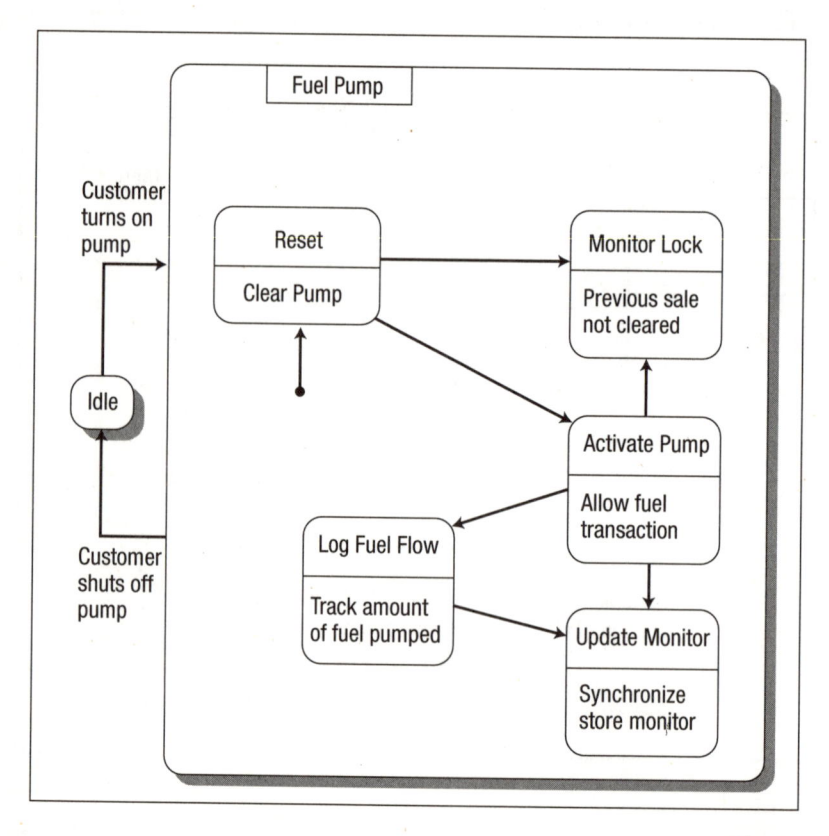

Figure 9.10
An example of a state diagram.

simultaneously within a state. An **and** relationship further defines a state into a concurrent substate, while the **or** relationship defines it into mutually exclusive disjoint substates. When states are refined in this manner, only one of the two (concurrent or mutually exclusive) can be exercised. The two substate conditions can be thought of in this way: Concurrent substates indicate that one or more substates can be held simultaneously with other concurrent substates under the same parent state. The mutually exclusive substate (also known as *disjoint substate*) cannot coexist with any other substate under the same parent state. Figure 9.11 illustrates the difference between concurrent and disjoint substates.

From this basic discussion on state diagrams, we'll move on to a model diagram type that has strong ties to the state diagram—the activity diagram.

Activity Diagrams

An activity diagram is a special case state diagram where most, if not all, of the states are action states. Additionally, most or all of the transitions from one state to another are executed via the completion of all actions in the source state. An activity diagram is connected to a class, process, or use case in the model. The purpose of an activity diagram is to provide insight into the flow of internal processing without the distraction of external influences. It is appropriate to use activity diagrams to illustrate modules where the events represent the completion of internally generated actions. For example, if we were to evaluate the activity "prepare lunch," a series of steps, including decisions, would be executed to arrive at the termination point where lunch is served. Figure 9.12 illustrates the use of the activity diagram.

Both state and activity diagrams use decisions to redirect the flow of processing to different transitions when a choice (boolean) must be made. The UML provides a stereotype to show a decision point. This stereotype is the diamond symbol with one input arrow and two or more outgoing arrows, each representing a separate outcome of the decision.

Activity diagrams also allow for the use of swimlanes, as described in the section explaining sequence diagrams. Swimlanes act as a form of package to help in organizing responsibility for activities within a class. Swimlanes often correspond to organizational units in the business model. An activity diagram can be divided into swimlanes, as illustrated in the example found in Figure 9.13.

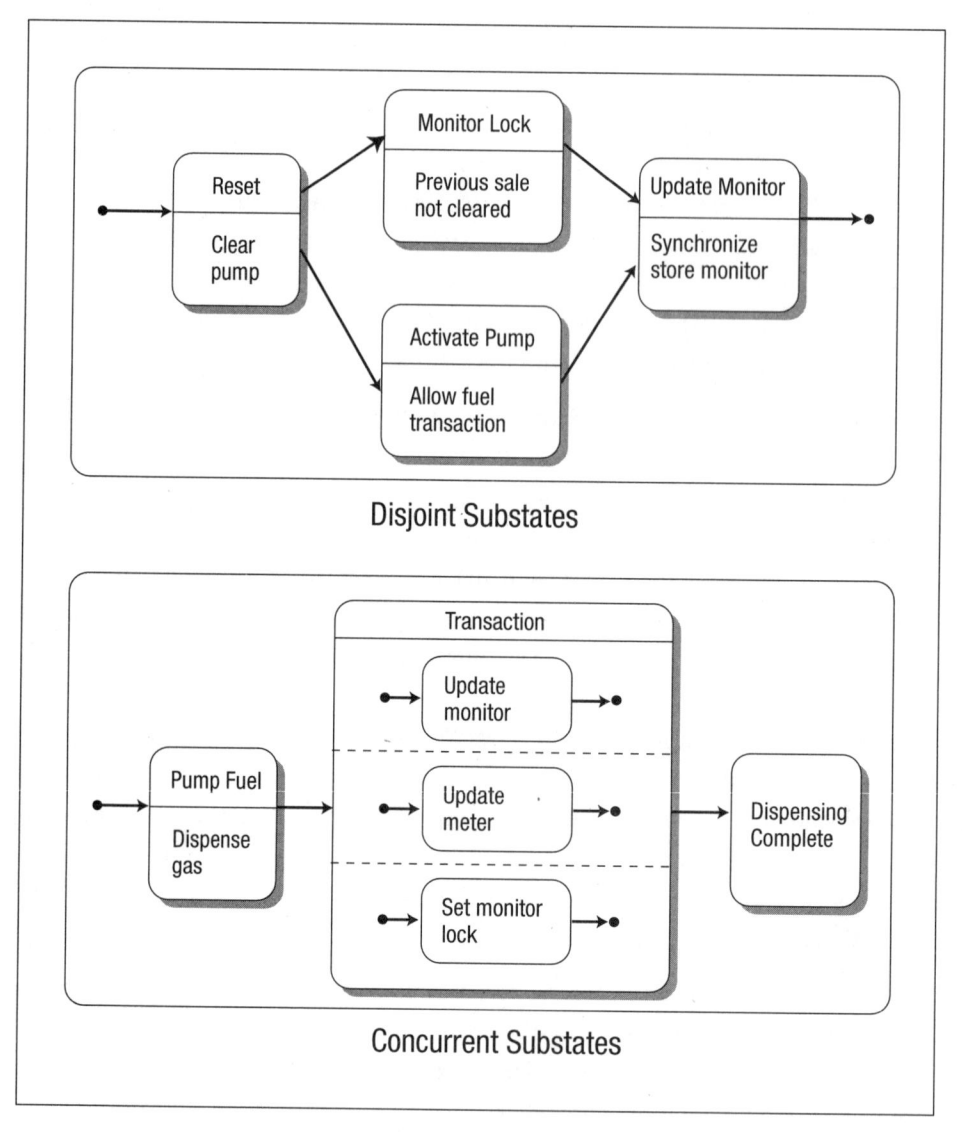

Figure 9.11
A comparison of concurrent and disjoint substates.

As you can see in Figure 9.13, each swimlane represents an area of responsibility. There is no significance to the order of the swimlanes. Also, transactions can traverse lanes, because there is no significance to the route or path that they take.

Now that our discussion of activity diagrams is complete, we can move on to the last of the model diagrams to be introduced—implementation diagrams.

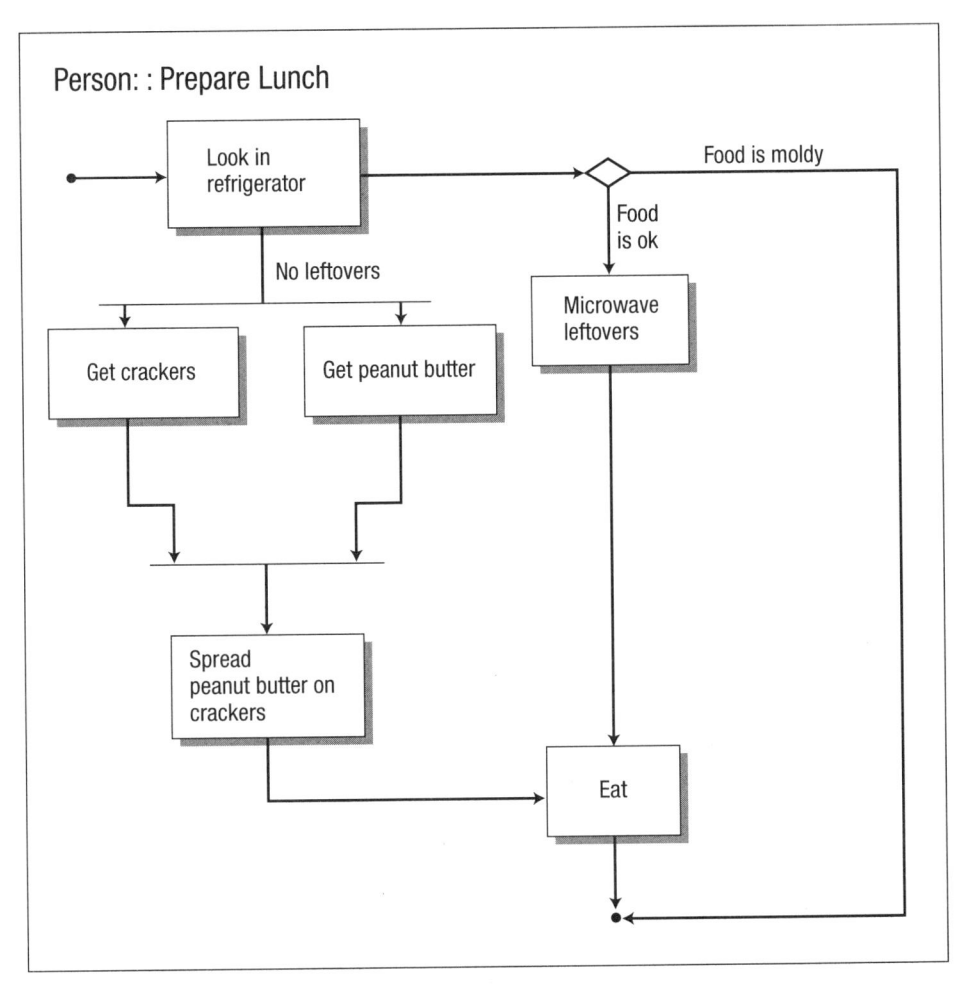

Figure 9.12
An example of an activity diagram.

Implementation Diagrams

Implementation diagrams are useful for showing source code structure and runtime implementation structure. There are two varieties of implementation diagrams: component diagrams and deployment diagrams. A component diagram serves to illustrate the dependencies among software components to include source code, binary code, and executables. The component diagram illustrates implementation structure by displaying software components as:

- Connected by dependency relationships, or
- Contained by other software components

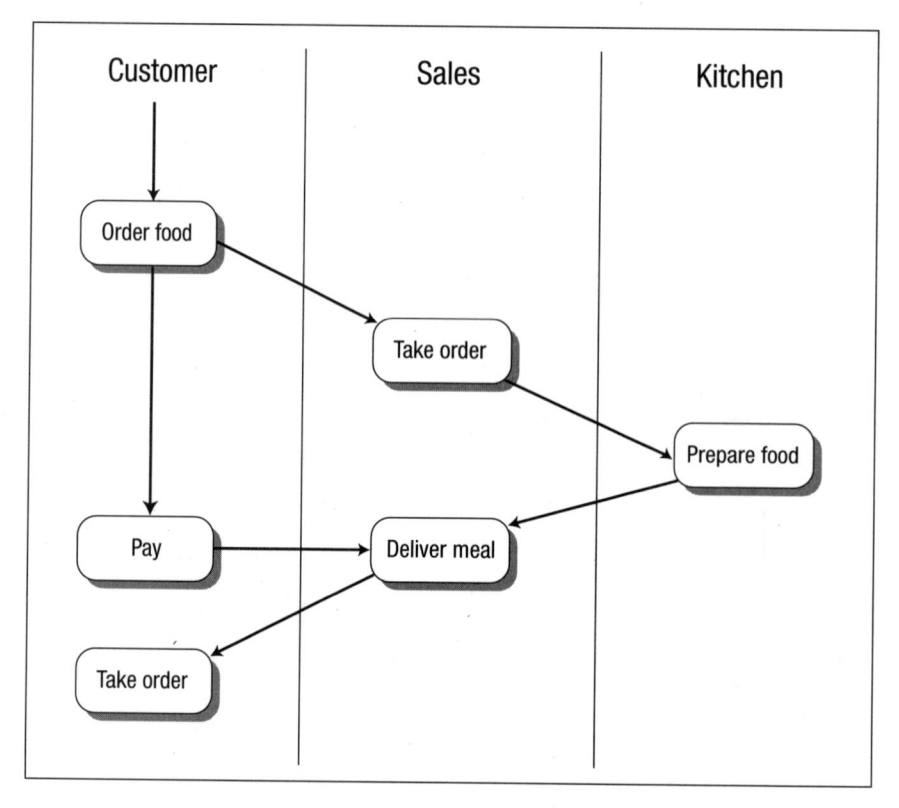

Figure 9.13
An activity diagram with swimlanes.

Software components can exist at different periods of the software transition phase. For example, some components can exist during compile time, others at link time, and still others at runtime. The component diagram will accurately illustrate software component types but not their instances. A component diagram can be used to show software component types, nodes, and compiler dependencies specific to the programming language being used. Figure 9.14 shows a basic example of a component diagram.

Deployment diagrams show how runtime elements (and runtime elements only) are configured, including their associated software components, processes, and objects. The visual depiction of a deployment diagram consists of *nodes* connected by communication associations. A node is a physical runtime object representing a particular computational resource having memory and processing capability. Nodes can be represented as types and instances. The nodes can contain instances of components

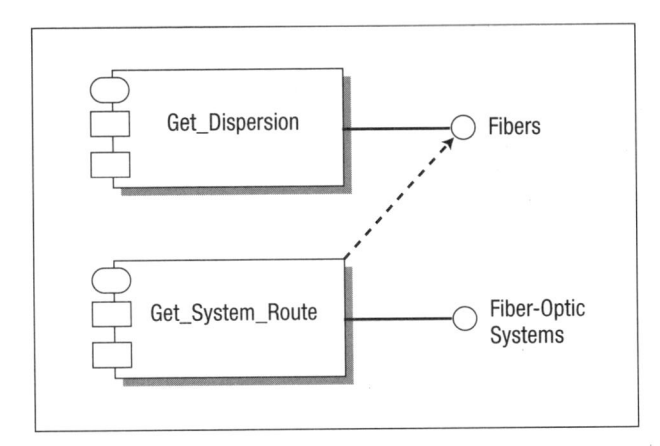

Figure 9.14
A sample component diagram from the implementation diagram family.

indicating that those components run from the specified node. Software components can, in turn, have objects showing that the object is a part of the component. A number of stereotypes are used in describing certain behaviors that nodes, components, and objects can participate in. For example, a component that migrates from node to node would be labeled with the <<becomes>> stereotype, while a component running on a particular node might be assigned the <<supports>> stereotype. Figure 9.15 illustrates the use of a deployment diagram.

Now that the basics of UML modeling diagrams have been presented, let's discuss how these tools support the object relational modeling effort.

The Object Relational Model And The UML

Because the object relational model is a marriage of two conceptual worlds, a modeling approach based purely in one discipline or another is inadequate to describe its entire character. Just as the UML is the logical choice as the modeling paradigm to formulate the database object model, so it is also appropriate to return to the UML to satisfy the diagramming needs for designing object relational database systems.

From the standpoint of the system development life cycle described in Chapter 3, any and all of the diagramming schemes just described in the previous section can be effectively incorporated into the various stages of the life cycle. The issue of greater importance is whether all of the diagrams have to be assimilated. The answer to this is, of course, no. Not all of the modeling diagrams will have relevance to every database

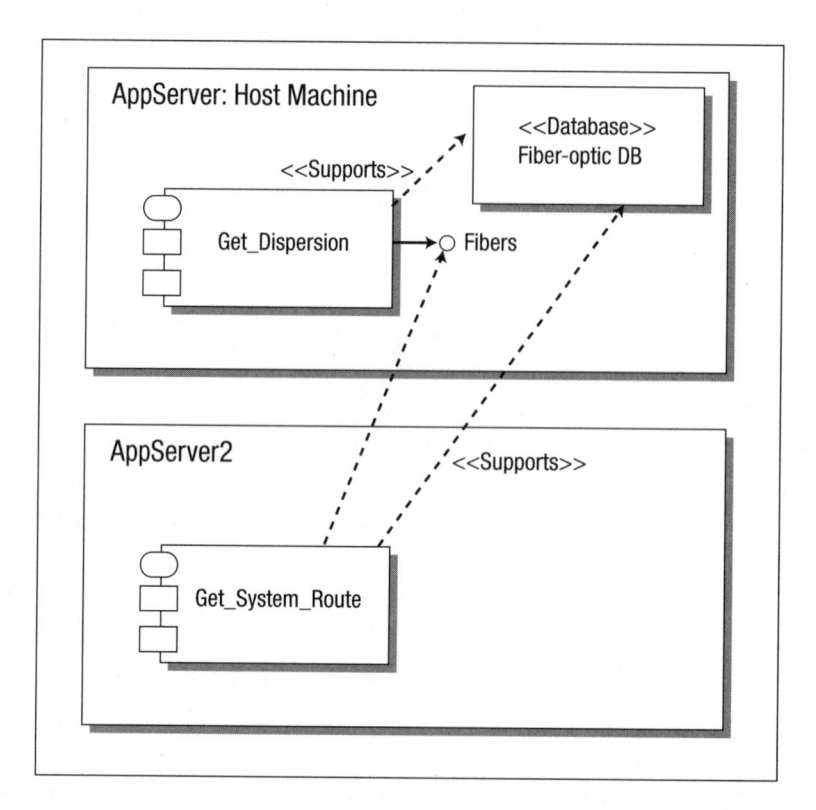

Figure 9.15
An example of a deployment diagram from the implementation diagram family.

application that is to be designed. There are, however, a few diagrams that should be a part of every system design effort. Figure 9.16 illustrates the correlation between the modeling diagrams discussed in this chapter with the systems development life cycle introduced in Chapter 3. To illustrate this point, let's discuss the purpose of each diagram in the context of the system development life cycle for Oracle8.

In the strategy phase when the system requirements are first ascertained, it is helpful to begin the organization of requirements with a use case diagram. The use case diagram will serve two important functions: It will group requirements and functions, and it will provide an overall view of the application that is being designed. Use case diagrams can depict varying levels of detail and are good surrogates to conventional data flow diagrams. A later section provides an illustrative example of their use.

An Oracle8 Modeling And Design Methodology

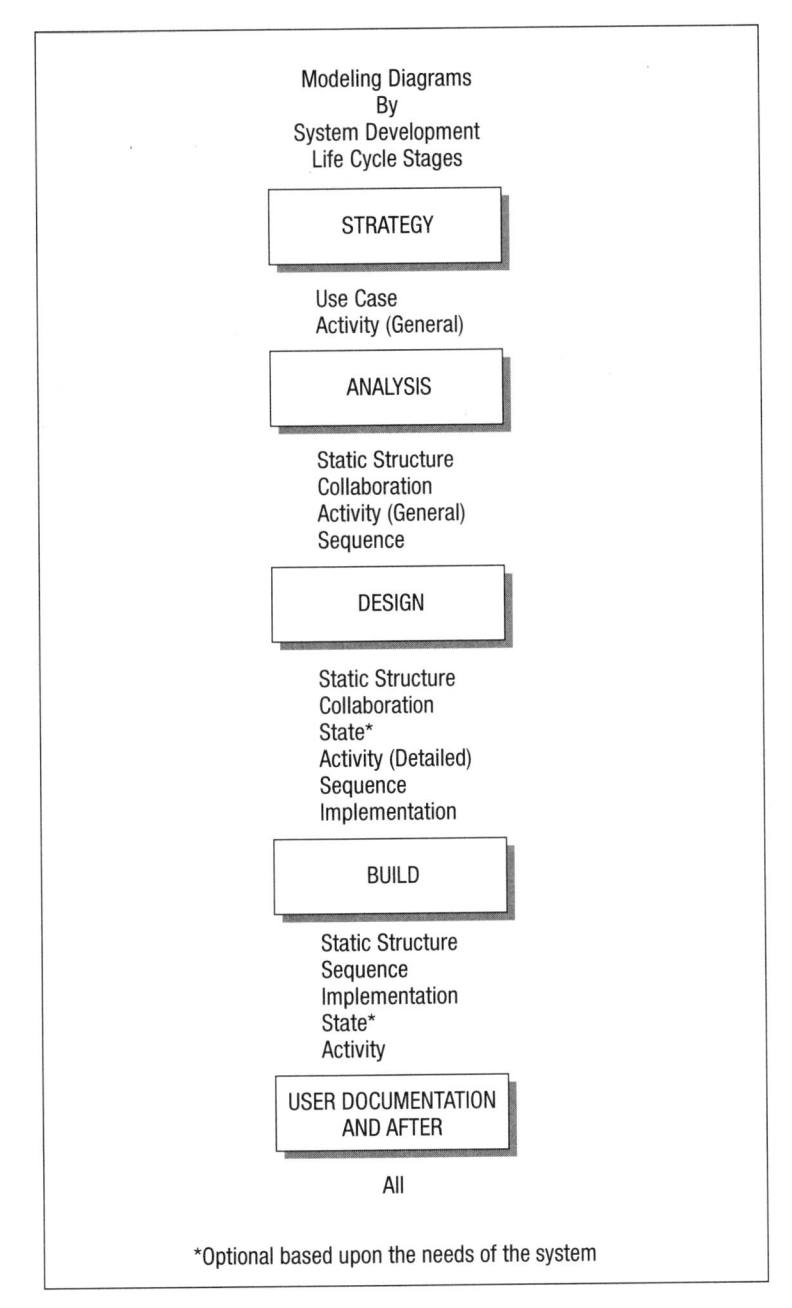

Modeling Diagrams
By
System Development
Life Cycle Stages

STRATEGY

Use Case
Activity (General)

ANALYSIS

Static Structure
Collaboration
Activity (General)
Sequence

DESIGN

Static Structure
Collaboration
State*
Activity (Detailed)
Sequence
Implementation

BUILD

Static Structure
Sequence
Implementation
State*
Activity

USER DOCUMENTATION AND AFTER

All

*Optional based upon the needs of the system

Figure 9.16
The correlation between the UML modeling diagrams and the systems development life cycle.

The analysis phase is the appropriate point to introduce static structure diagrams. As the integral objects in the application are identified, it is important to establish their purpose and relationships within the model. The static structure diagram will become one of the most important diagrams produced. It supplants the conventional entity relationship diagram used in the relational model. The complex nature of object relational designs can be captured through this venue.

Collaboration diagrams are useful in the decomposition of the functional flow within an application system. Because collaborations are useful in describing a set of interactions among types, they are an effective means of planning methods when combined with the use case diagrams. Collaboration diagrams will be one of the key sources of information when planning a method topology, as described in Chapter 6. Collaboration diagrams should come into favor during the analysis and design phases.

If the nature of an application system requires the use of state diagrams, they should be introduced during the design phase. In the context of designing for Oracle8 applications, the use of state diagrams is entirely optional and may only be useful in circumstances where the application under consideration requires detailed behavioral modeling. A good example of this might be an automated assembly line system where crucial iterative steps or events must take place at a certain time, in a certain order.

The activity diagram, as you might recall, is a special variation of the state diagram. Unlike the state diagram, the activity diagram will find a useful place in the design effort more frequently. Activity diagrams do not show relationships, but their treatment of actions, states, and decisions makes them a good complement to the use case diagram. These two diagrams will solidify the strategy and analysis of an application system and solidify the decomposition of processes that eventually will become methods. Activity diagrams can also represent action-object flows so that the aspect of elements can be tied in to show the correlation of database entities with their respective behaviors.

Sequence diagrams can be useful in establishing the iterative process flow at atomic levels of a system or, even more generically, at the business unit level. If the application being designed requires the documentation of events that build on each other, then the sequence diagram is essential. The automated assembly line example mentioned in the last paragraph is a good candidate for sequence diagrams. As a car chassis proceeds down the assembly line, different parts are added. First, the drive train is installed, followed by the passenger compartment frame, then various body panels. Each of these assembly steps could be further subdivided. For example, the passenger compartment frame must be installed with seats, dashboard, carpeting, and so on. All of these examples illustrate a sequential process, each step reliant on the success of the previous step. From the main assembly line to the detailed level of the passenger compartment, multiple levels of processes must be modeled.

During the design and build phases, the implementation diagram can assist developers in mapping source code structure and runtime implementation. The implementation diagram should be a culmination of the information gathered through the previous diagrams. The nature of the component diagram should encourage good modular code design by pointing out redundancies and inconsistencies (recall that the component diagram is the source code variant of the implementation diagram). The deployment diagram is the complement to the component diagram, and, together, they describe the nature of how the code will be organized and structured. The implementation diagram will be the framework from which the actual generated code is produced.

The chart in Figure 9.16 is intended to be a guideline for designers and developers to stage the use of the various modeling diagrams in their application development process. Successful systems do not require the creation of every one of the seven diagrams. Assess the nature of the application to be built, and select the graphical mechanisms that provide the necessary coverage.

Now that the appropriateness of each modeling diagram has been discussed, I'll present a discussion on implementing the new modeling diagrams, accompanied by illustrative examples.

Implementing New Diagrams In The Object Relational Design

Diagramming is a means of conveying complex or difficult-to-understand concepts in a way that makes them clear to the individuals who must implement the concepts. Modeling diagrams are the visual means of communicating the many aspects of a system design. The primary reason diagrams are used is that they carry a powerful ability to communicate ideas in ways that simple text cannot. Diagrams can cross cultural divides, because the supporting textual notation is secondary to the symbology that they contain. Most of us are visual learners. Facts and information are quickly assimilated through what we observe. To illustrate this, imagine yourself preparing for a lengthy road trip. As the principle driver, would you prefer a detailed set of written directions or a good roadmap? My guess is that you would choose the roadmap without hesitation. This is because the roadmap conveys significance beyond the written word. It provides a sense of placement and proportion that words cannot easily describe. The same holds true in developing database applications. Diagrams help validate that the development team has correctly interpreted what the client has asked for. Mutual agreement of their interpretation speeds the development process and improves the accuracy of what is eventually built.

Now that the importance of modeling diagrams has been emphasized, let's examine a couple of the most frequently used diagrams by presenting their use in an example.

Using Use Case And Activity Diagrams In Method Design

The importance of the use case diagram in organizing the requirements in the strategy phase has already been pointed out. Of particular interest is that using the use case diagram in conjunction with the activity diagram results in an effective means of formulating the methods that will be used in the application. To illustrate how these two diagram types might be used, we'll model the Ptomaine Palace Restaurant. The Ptomaine Palace is under new management and is eager to please its patrons. The essential high-level use cases represented in the first cut of the model diagram are illustrated in Figure 9.17.

Our diagram identifies four actors that take part in the model. These are the customer, waiter, cook, and manager. The use case, as you might recall, is essentially a sequence of actions that a system will perform to obtain a particular actor result. In the diagram displayed in Figure 9.17, the use cases are **PLACE ORDER, FILL ORDER, PREPARE MEAL, EAT, FILE COMPLAINT,** and **PAY BILL**. Note that there are two relationship types displayed on the model. The first is a communicates relationship and is used between actors and use cases. This relationship shows interaction between the actor and the use case. It is a solid line and has no labeling. The second is a generalization and is an extends relationship. This relationship is notated with a solid line tipped with an arrow and labeled with the extends stereotype. The use of this relationship infers that paying the bill can include a complaint regarding the

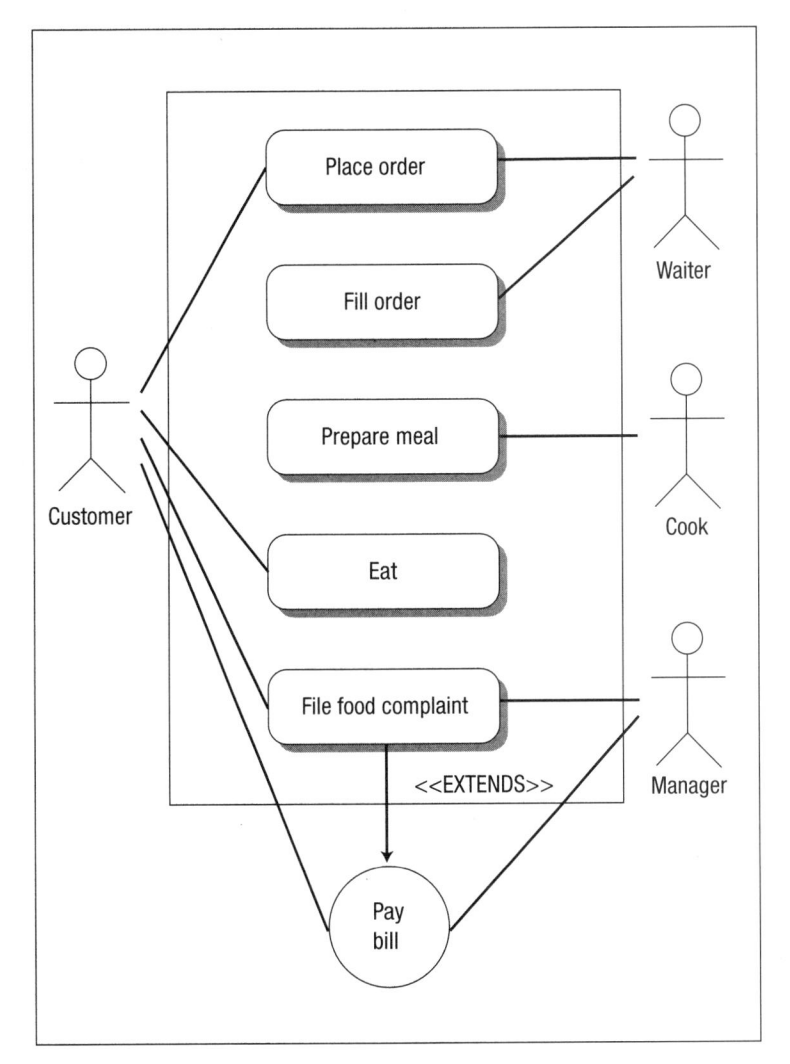

Figure 9.17
The use case diagram for the Ptomaine Palace Restaurant.

food. Each use case maintains a correspondence with one or more actors. Actors are connected to those use cases where they have a direct participation. For example, a customer will **PLACE ORDER**, but the waiter participates in this activity too. Therefore, a communicates relationship is drawn to the waiter as well.

Looking at the diagram, you can see that customers place orders, eat, occasionally complain about the food, and pay the bill. Waiters take orders and fill orders while the cook prepares them, the manager becomes involved when the customer complains and/or pays the bill, and so forth.

Now, let's examine the activity diagram for a specific use case that is produced from the events at the Ptomaine Palace Restaurant. Figure 9.18 shows the activities that take place during the prepare meal transaction.

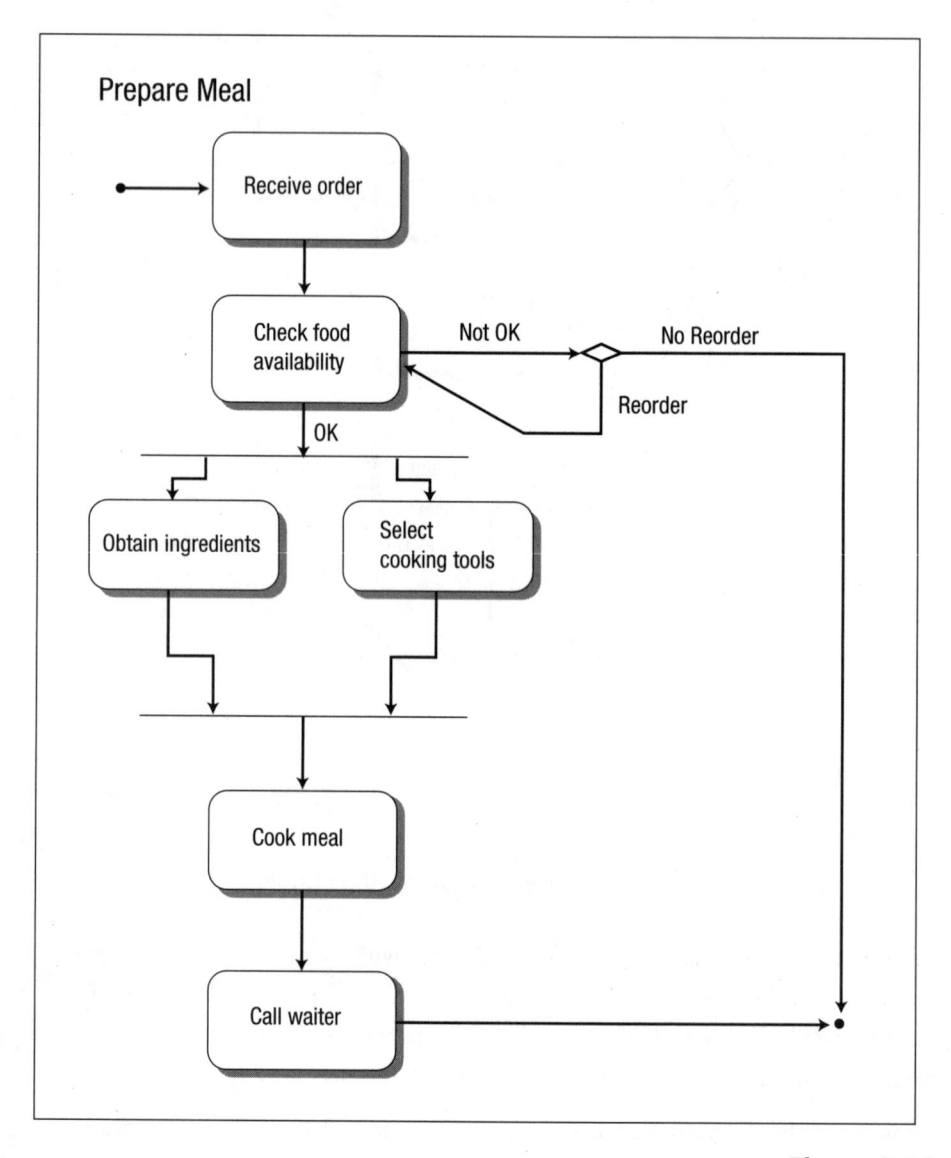

Figure 9.18
The activity diagram for the Ptomaine Palace Restaurant.

An Oracle8 Modeling And Design Methodology

We can see the iterative flow of activity that takes place when a cook prepares a meal. Note that all of the transitions are triggered by the completion of an action in the source states. Activity diagrams must be attached to classes, implementations of operations, or use cases. In this circumstance, the diagram is attached to the use case illustrated in Figure 9.17. A similar diagram is produced for each use case to document the flow of activity.

The next step is to compare and evaluate the two diagrams in order to formulate behaviors that we can assign to the database elements, in other words, identify the methods. Every activity is a candidate for method generation. What differentiates the activities that become methods from those that will not is how an activity is categorized. For example, in the use case diagram, there is a use case called **EAT**. This is a physically executed activity performed by an actor and does not assume a specific behavioral correlation to any possible database entities. On the other hand, the use case **PAY BILL** requires the execution of a number of steps in order to successfully complete it. If we take a closer look at the detailed activity and use case diagrams for **PAY BILL**, we will find that several processes or steps are good candidates. Figure 9.19 shows the detailed use case and activity diagrams for the use case **PAY BILL**.

The activity of paying for a meal involves updating the **PAYMENTS** element. Assuming that a credit card is used, a payment cannot be recorded until the following activities take place:

- Process credit card
- Detect invalid card
- Process payment

Note that the second item, detect invalid card, is a subprocess of process credit card. What has been established is the start of the method topology discussed in Chapter 6. For each atomic-level use case and activity diagram, the data-related processes are organized and grouped. A preliminary hierarchy of method instances is created. The preliminary method topology produced is again compared to the static structure diagram during the design phase, and the methods are finalized. Because the static structure diagram plays such an important role in the system design process, we will shift our focus to this pivotal model diagram type.

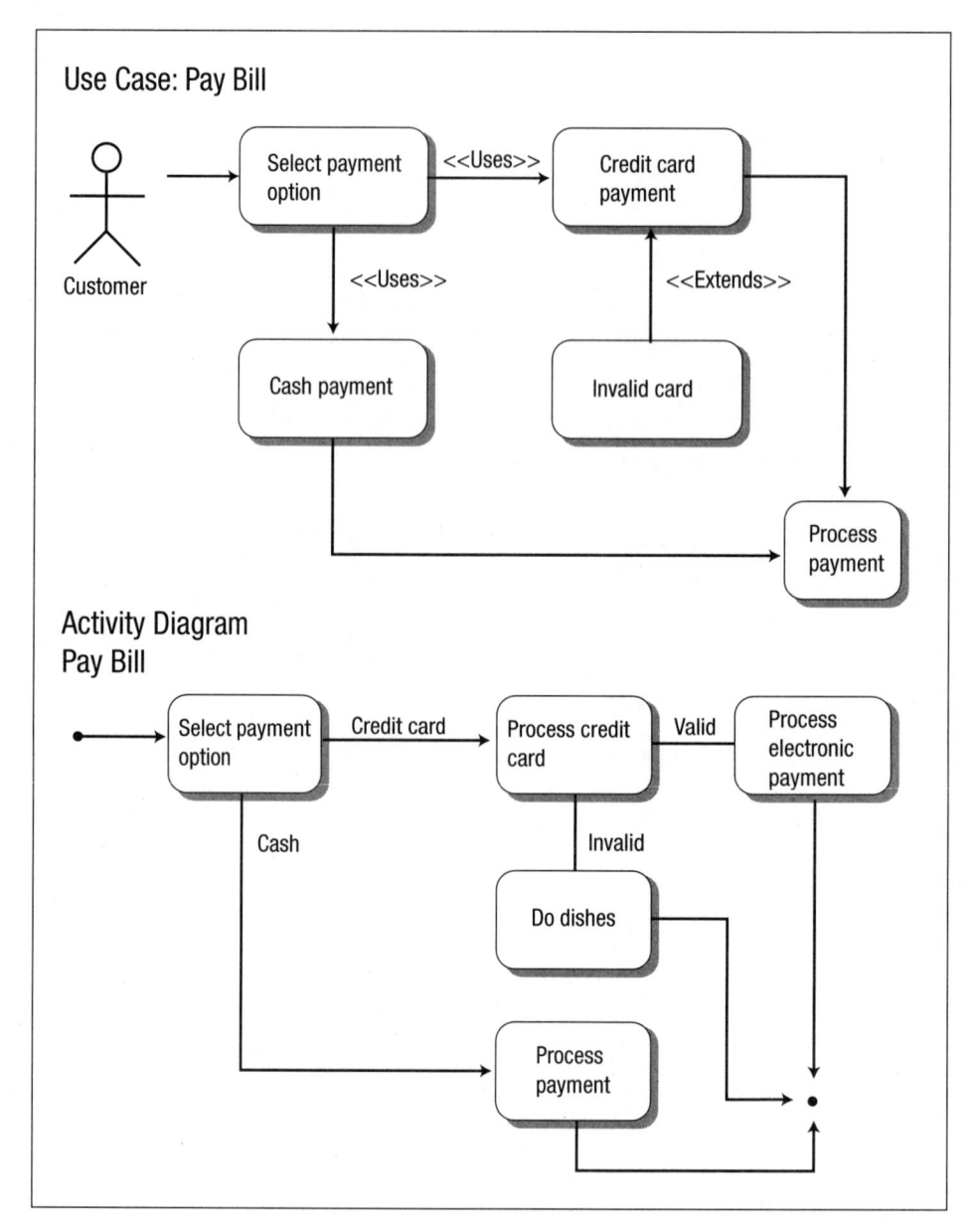

Figure 9.19
The detailed use case and activity diagrams for **PAY BILL**.

Implementing The Static Structure Diagram

The static structure diagram gets its start during the analysis phase, much like the entity relationship diagram does for relational modeling. The static structure diagram is of supreme importance, because it illustrates the combined aspects of the system to include elements and relationships. The subject of our modeling example will shift back to the fiber-optic network introduced in Chapter 8 because of the unusual nature of the entities and the relationships between them. Figure 9.20 shows the static structure diagram for the fiber-optic network.

Recall in Chapter 8 that Figure 8.14 shows a clumsy (and not completely resolved) entity relationship diagram for the network-like character of how the various entities in the fiber-optic system associate with one another. Looking at the diagram in Figure 9.20, it is quickly realized that the great power in this diagram type is the ability to represent detailed relationship types in conjunction with stereotypes. With this object relational tool, we have stepped beyond the limiting nature of entity relationship diagrams and can more effectively resolve intricate many-to-many relationships in a far more elegant way. For example, take the relationship between **DEVICES** and **SYSTEMS**. The relationship that exists between the two is of type association because there are shared aggregations of object instances to collections of type instances. This association would have an association role specifying multiplicity or the number of instances of a type that are participating in the association. The relationship between **CABLES** and **FIBERS** is more aptly defined to be a generalization, because there is an implied unidirectional inheritance relationship going from **CABLES** to **FIBERS**. Recall that many attributes are common to both of these object types, but **FIBERS** are dependent on **CABLES** for their existence. If stereotypes are used in the generalization, then <<subclass>> or <<subtype>> would be the most likely candidates to elaborate on the character of the relationship between **CABLES** and **FIBERS**.

DEVICES represents a class of objects. The notation available in the static structure diagram allows us to display implementation-level details about this class, unlike this diagram type's relational predecessors. For the sake of comparison, various levels of detail are represented in the different elements and classes to illustrate the graphical flexibility offered in the static structure diagram. Notation to indicate methods is also shown using the methods identified in the analysis of the fiber-optic network in Chapter 8.

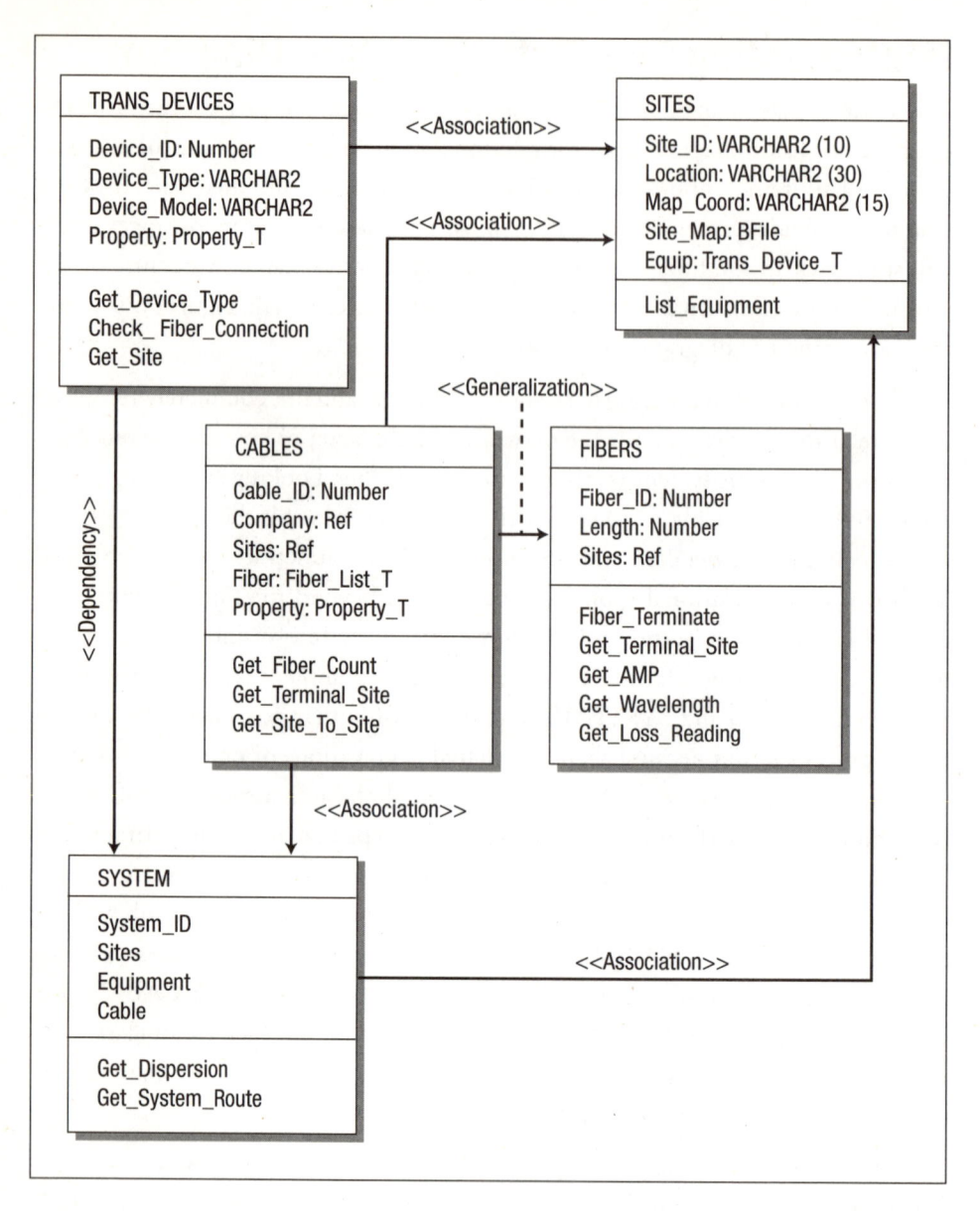

Figure 9.20
The static structure diagram for the fiber-optic network.

Summary

The power and flexibility of the new modeling diagrams found in the UML offer contemporary database designers and developers the ability to more accurately represent real-world systems. The most obvious advantages to the new diagrams are their extensive treatment of relationships and element diagramming. The disadvantage is that the notation and rules are not as intuitive as the relational methodology familiar to most developers. For any application being designed in the object relational paradigm, the modeling diagrams of the UML require our full consideration.

In the next chapter, we'll examine an introduction of Oracle8's object relational capabilities in a data warehousing environment.

HIGH PERFORMANCE

Oracle8 Design For The Data Warehouse

CHAPTER 10

To see a world in a grain of sand
And a heaven in a wild flower
Hold infinity in the palm of your hand
And eternity in an hour.
—William Blake

HIGH PERFORMANCE

Oracle8 Design For The Data Warehouse

Without question, the advent of the data warehouse ushered in a new level of analytical capability within the business world. Businesses needed a way to tap into their vast accumulations of corporate data, and the data warehouse provided an answer.

The nature of today's business world places a demand on companies to improve operations in order to stay competitive. Rapid assimilation of inventory status, product sales statistics, market forecasts, and so on cannot wait a month or more until summary reports are produced. Access to aggregated data, in finely focused categories, allows today's businesses to respond quickly to market trends. This, in turn, makes companies more profitable and efficient. Businesses now have the ability to focus their marketing and manufacturing efforts with an agility that was not possible only a few short years ago. All of this presumes that organizations have been able to effectively tap into their vast amounts of data to glean the information that facilitates market agility.

Achieving success in the data warehouse arena requires more than a set of spreadsheets and a keen eye for market trends. A successful data warehouse is the result of careful planning and intensive customer participation. Entire sets of books have been written on the subject of data warehousing, and Bill Inmon, the "father" of Data Warehousing, has published more than 25 books on the topic. Suffice it to say that the material in this chapter provides only the basics of working in the data warehousing arena under Oracle8. If you are planning on immersing yourself in an Oracle8 data warehouse project, I recommend that you obtain further guidance. A good reference text to consult is *High Performance Oracle Data Warehousing*, by Donald Burleson, published by The Coriolis Group. In light of all that Oracle8 has to offer, the primary focus of this chapter is to describe what database options can be used in a data warehousing environment and how they are implemented.

CHAPTER 10

An Overview Of Data Warehousing

Before springing headlong into the details of building an Oracle8 data warehouse, it is appropriate to conduct a basic overview of what data warehousing is and how data warehouses are built. Probably more than any other area of database design, data warehousing has been greeted with overly optimistic attitudes and naive notions by developers and businesses alike. Flippant attitudes and oversimplifications of what it takes to deploy successful data warehouses have led to many disappointing deployments. Indeed, a successful data warehouse implementation in some aspects is actually more difficult to produce than an OLTP system for the following reasons:

- The analysis of a data warehouse requires more background planning to ensure that timely information and system performance are achieved. A greater understanding of the corporate data stores, both historical and current, is necessary.

- Data warehouses require more in-house political support because they are generally secondary to the overall corporate information systems mission.

- Data warehouses are not as forgiving in the area of tuning and performance when compared to conventional online transaction processing systems (OLTP). Remember that the quantity of data used in a data warehouse is most likely orders of magnitude greater than that found in an OLTP system.

- The data in a data warehouse must be kept current with that found in the production system. Data currency introduces a problem that few analysts and designers have had to deal with directly on such a large scale. This, of course, relates back to how thoroughly the analysis was performed.

So, in essence, the data warehouse is really a consolidation of data from one or more OLTP sources where the data has been transformed, scrubbed, and aggregated to meet a specific business need. The start of any data warehousing effort should be the identification of a class or category of problem that the data warehouse should solve.

Generally, data warehouses address the needs of a *decision support system*. A decision support system is a combination of two components: a structured component consisting of decision rules, and an intuitive, or creative, component driven by human intervention. A decision support system consists of the following properties or characteristics:

- *Obtains the solution to a nonrecurring problem*—A real world problem is modeled by simulating its behavior or behaviors.

- *Requires human input*—Users contribute to the decision-making process by providing input. This, in turn, affects the overall outcome.

- *Presents a testable hypothesis for the decision support system*—A proper decision support system allows users to produce models in order to simulate various behaviors in the system.

- *Allows ad hoc queries for data retrieval*—Ad hoc queries are used to gather information in support of the decision making process. Often, the results of one query spawns additional queries that address aspects of the decision support system that have not been previously considered.

- *Involves users who are knowledgeable about the problem to be solved*—Decision support systems require that the users understand the problem that is being solved. This is because pertinent user input is needed in the formulation of the solution. If a user is unable to provide meaningful input, then the result will be meaningless.

- *Enables more than one "correct" answer to be derived*—Decision support systems usually have a range of acceptable results. When the decision support system is first formulated, a valid domain is defined, thus setting the target that the desired goal must attain.

- *Uses external data sources*—Data classification from outside sources might be needed to further categorize the data that is being analyzed.

Transforming these concepts of the decision support system into a working data warehouse requires the integration and synthesis of several key components. The starting point for this activity should be the corporate data model. The corporate data model provides analysts with an enterprise-level view of the customer's data schema, the participating relationships between entities, and the framework for how the data is organized. The second component used in the transformation is the data warehouse data model. The data warehouse data model provides insight into the detailed, subject-oriented, strategic information that was the focus of the decision support system. Finally, a departmental data warehouse design featuring the highly categorized data of individual operational entities is incorporated. Figure 10.1 illustrates the transformation process leading to the data warehouse implementation.

Taking into account what has been discussed so far about decision support systems and data warehouses, the general characteristics of the data warehouse can be described as follows:

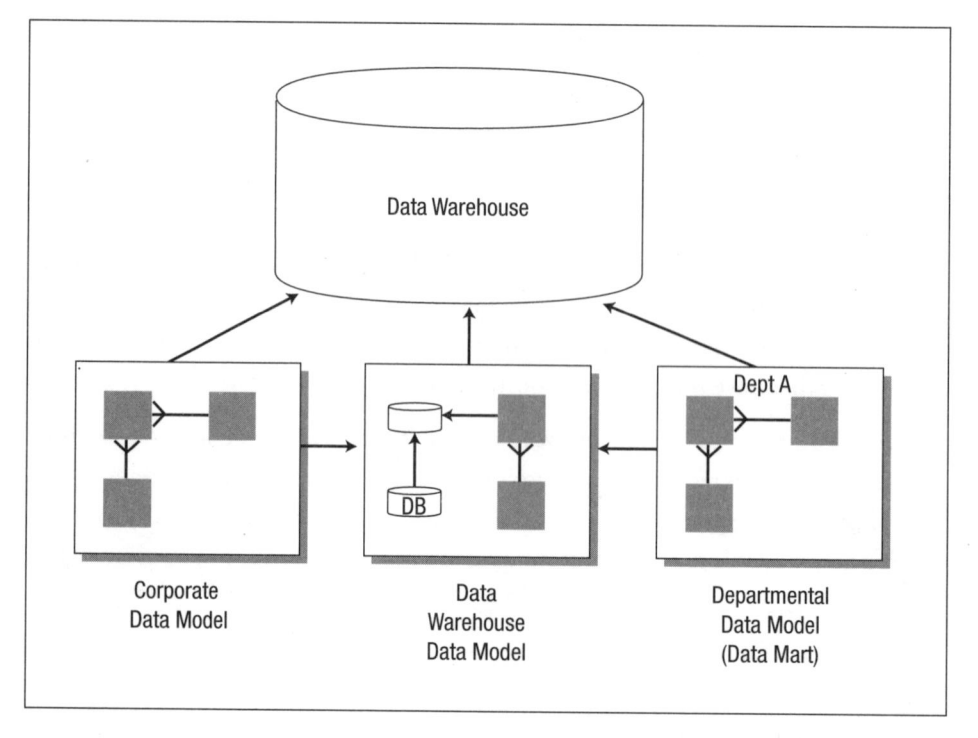

Figure 10.1
The process of formulating a data warehouse.

- *Data focused on a specific subject area*—The purpose of the data warehouse is to gather as much pertinent information as possible for a particular subject area from within an organization. For example, commodity trades, sales volume, and so forth.

- *Highly denormalized data structures*—Data warehouses customarily pre-join tables with many redundant columns.

- *Pre-aggregated data*—Data warehouses contain pre-calculated totals in order to improve runtime performance.

- *Read-only during queries*—Typically, data warehouses are loaded during off-hour time periods and used for read-only transactions during regular business hours.

- *Interactive ad hoc query capability*—Data warehouses must support the demand for data by users, at any time.

Data warehouses contrast significantly to OLTP systems in a number of ways. Table 10.1 highlights the differences between the two.

Table 10.1 Contrasting OLTP and data warehouse systems.

Characteristic	OLTP	Data Warehouse
Normalization	High	Low
Table sizes	Small	Large
Table row count	Small	Large
Transaction duration/size	Small	Large
Number of online users	High	Low
Typical operation	Update	Report
Analytical requirements	Low	Medium to high
Data level	Detail	Detail and summary
Data updates	Frequent	Off-peak hours
Full-table scans	Rare	Often
Historical data	Low (< 90 days)	1 or more years

Now that the basic features of data warehouses are understood, let's look at some of the concepts crucial to data warehouse analysis and design. Specifically, let's look at data marts and online analytical processing.

Data Marts

The picture that conjures up in your mind when you hear the phrase *data mart* may or may not be an accurate interpretation of what a data mart really is. In basic terms, a data mart is a smaller version of a data warehouse that places its focus on a smaller scale. Recall earlier, when we described the three key components of developing a data warehouse. The third component, a departmental data warehouse design, is indicative of a data mart.

A data mart focuses on featuring the highly categorized data of individual operational entities. For example, sales statistics for a single department or branch. As with a data warehouse, a data mart is a consolidation of data from one or more OLTP sources where the data has been transformed, scrubbed, and aggregated to meet a specific business need. Due to its smaller size, a data mart might not require the same structural and performance tuning techniques of a data warehouse. Also, a data mart typically supports the larger requirements of a data warehouse through the

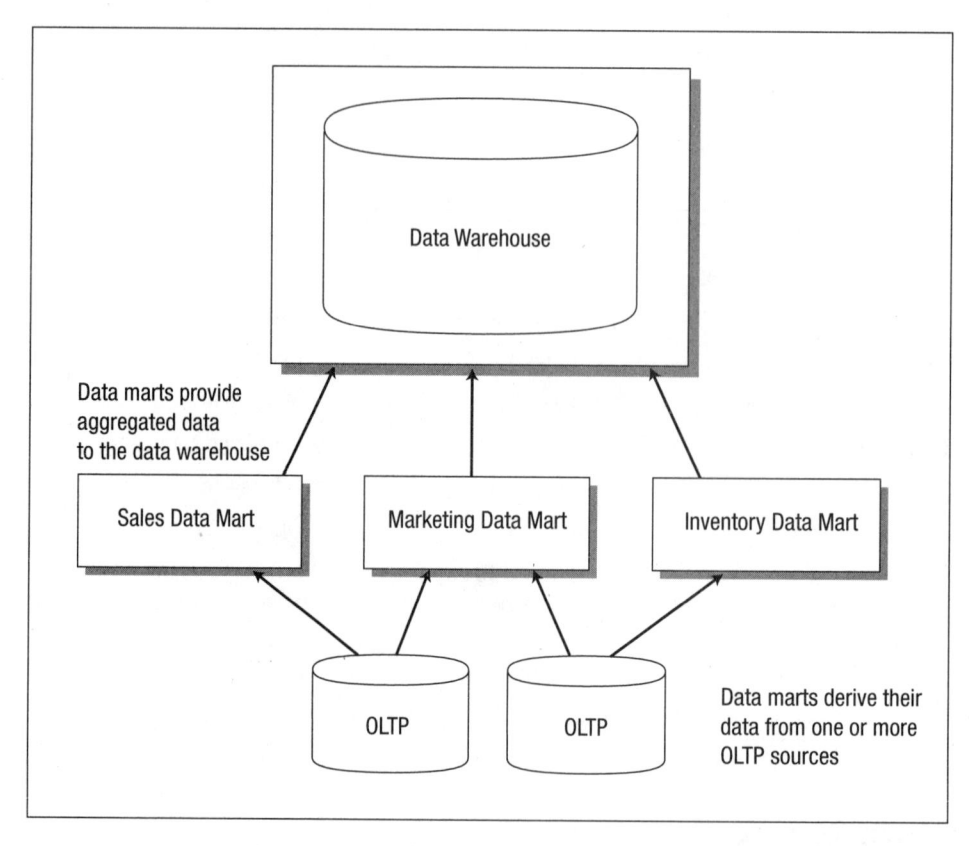

Figure 10.2
The relationship between a data mart and a data warehouse.

consolidation or aggregation of its data. Figure 10.2 illustrates the relationship between the data mart and data warehouse. Understanding the difference between the two will be imperative later, when we discuss Oracle8 data warehouse design.

A data mart is the highest level in which the object extensions in Oracle8 can be used. Depending on the sizing and performance characteristics of the data mart to be built, object extensions might not be used at all. The reasons for this become clear later in this chapter, in the section that describes the Oracle8 features that support data warehousing. Before proceeding to this discussion, let's address the important concepts relating to online analytical processing.

Online Analytical Processing And Multidimensional Databases

Online analytical processing, or OLAP, is the means of (or tool for) presenting facts or information in a cross-referenced style. This concept enables users to determine cross-referencing criteria, or *dimensions*. For example, a user can choose to store sales totals cross-referenced by time period, product, territory, and salesperson. Although Dr. E. F. Codd first coined the phrase in a white paper published in 1993, the concept was not new and had been incorporated into one or more data analysis engines for more than 20 years. Traditionally, OLAP has been implemented as an analytical front-end product to the relational database itself. The wide variety of products intended for this purpose has grown significantly in recent years, adding to the complexity of selecting the right tool for the right job.

A *multidimensional database* is a non-relational database architecture that stores summarized information in a way that the dimensions are cross-referenced with each other. Over time, there has been some confusion over the use of the terms *OLAP* and *multidimensional database* due to their close association. Keep in mind that OLAP is considered a tool, while the multidimensional database is, well, a database. The two are often used together with an OLAP product such as Oracle Express as the front end to the multidimensional database. OLAP products can draw from several types of data sources, including:

- Multidimensional databases
- Relational databases
- Spreadsheet data (for example, Excel, Lotus 123, and so on)

Utilizing OLAP as a front end to multidimensional databases has come to be known as *multidimensional OLAP*, or MOLAP. The concept of the multidimensional database was first introduced in 1972 by Management Decision Systems (MDS) in conjunction with the Wharton School of Business. The two organizations first teamed up to implement the Express multidimensional database in decision support systems for numerous clients.

The multidimensional database data model makes use of what is known as a *cube* strategy in the structure of the cross-referenced dimensions. Figure 10.3 illustrates the concept of the multidimensional database cube.

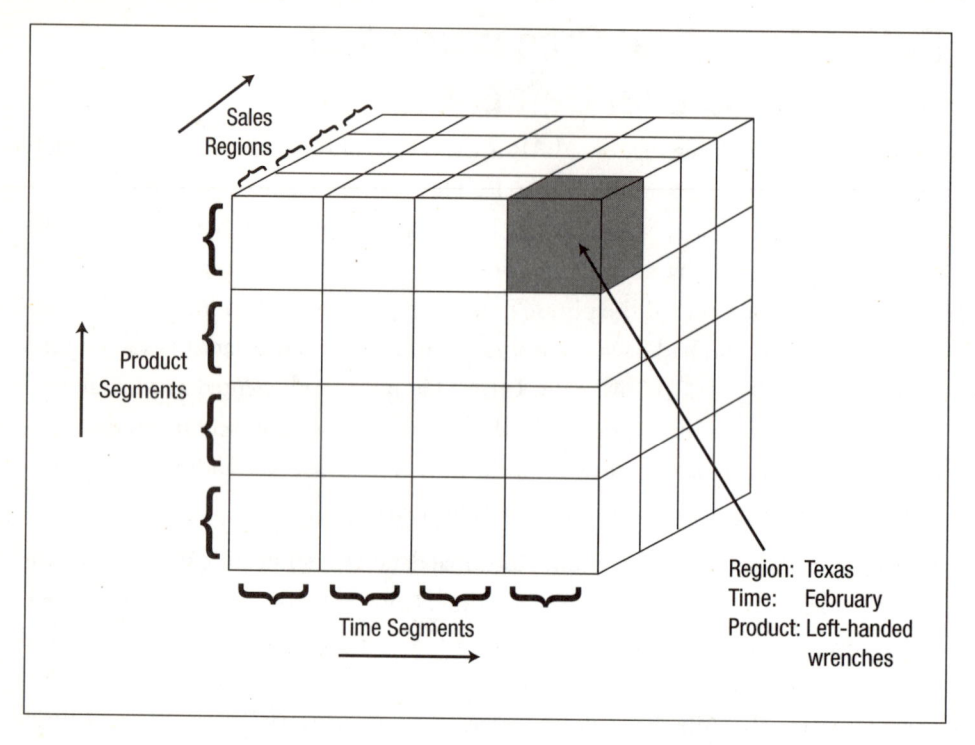

Figure 10.3
The multidimensional database cube concept.

Each smaller cube represents an association of variables with a dimension. Note in Figure 10.3 that dimensions run along the edges of the cube. In this way, each axis represents each dimension. By defining the three axes that give the cube depth, length, and width, individual cells are created that represent the contained value sets that lie within the cross-referenced boundaries of the three dimensions. For example, an individual cell might contain the data for the Texas sales team during the month of February for the product sales of left-handed wrenches. From this example, you can see product specificity cross-referenced with a subset of the entire sales force for a given segment of time.

Relational and multidimensional databases differ in their data model concept. The relational model uses the flat table as the basis of its structure. Compare this to the three-dimensional aspect of the multidimensional database. As you can see, the multidimensional database more closely approximates the characteristics of an array, where the cross-referencing of several dimensions gives depth to the character of the data being assembled.

Although there is little or no apparent difference between an OLAP implementation and a multidimensional database to the end user, there are significant operational differences between the two. An OLAP implementation against a relational database (ROLAP) offers tremendous flexibility through the use of ad hoc queries. Contrast this to the multidimensional database whose queries are predetermined. On the other hand, the multidimensional database engine pre-summarizes data and, therefore, achieves very fast response times. The ROLAP implementation must query the data and perform the necessary summarizations dynamically and, therefore, is not as fast. Finally, multidimensional databases pay the price for maintaining pre-summarized data by requiring a greater amount of storage space when compared to a ROLAP system. Table 10.2 contrasts the characteristics of ROLAP and multidimensional databases.

As mentioned earlier, ROLAP implementations are an OLAP tool used in conjunction with a relational database. ROLAPs are characterized by the following properties:

- Runtime data is extracted from a relational database.
- Summarized data appears in a cross-tabular format.
- A mechanism is incorporated for translating the relational data into a multidimensional format.

The driving force behind the ROLAP concept is to find a way to present relational data to users in a multidimensional structure. Several methods have been devised to accomplish this special form of aggregation, including specialized ROLAP middleware tools created by third-party vendors. Another method is to download pre-aggregated data into what is known as a *pivot table* (a table commonly found in spreadsheet

Table 10.2 Contrasting the characteristics of ROLAP and multidimensional databases.

Characteristic	ROLAP	Multidimensional
Speed	Slow to Moderate	Fast
Queries	Ad hoc	Fixed
Storage	Low	High

applications comprised of fact and dimension columns). Finally, a metadata server can be used as an intermediary between a relational database and a query tool. The metadata tool provides the definitions of the dimensions, supplies the mapping rules to the relational database, and tracks any hierarchies between dimensions. Hierarchies between dimensions can be subcategorical groupings, such as departments within a company's division. Because of the flexible nature of ROLAP systems, their use is characterized in situations where the data changes frequently, the volume of data is large and storage is at a premium, and the nature of queries is dynamic.

Now that you have a basic understanding of data warehousing concepts, let's examine the data warehouse features supported by Oracle8. In the next section, we'll pay particular attention to features that impact design and performance.

Oracle8's Data Warehousing Features

If you consider the features and improvements made in Oracle8 over its predecessor Oracle7, even without object extensions, you'll find that significant strides have been made in the areas of performance and maintainability. Some of the information presented here is not new to Oracle8. For example, bitmapped indexes are available in version 7.3 of the Oracle RDBMS. Other features, however, make their debut in Oracle8, and they will impact on how data warehouses, as well as OLTP implementations, are designed and tuned. Let's start off with a discussion of bitmapped indexing.

Bitmapped Indexes

Bitmapped indexes are a powerful tool in the use of query performance. The bitmapped index function was first introduced in Oracle7 but has undergone some improvements with the introduction of Oracle8. In Oracle8, there are now five indexing schemes:

- *B*-tree indexes (currently the most common)*—This is the standard index structure used by the Oracle database engine.

- *B*-tree cluster indexes*—This is the B*-tree index counterpart for clusters rather than individual tables. Clusters are data from multiple tables stored together.

- *Hash cluster indexes*—A hash cluster is a cluster stored by a hash key, which is a computed value based on the object's disk location. Therefore, the object is tracked by physical location rather than index key.

- *Reverse key indexes*—A reverse key index reverses the bytes of each column indexed (except the **ROWID**) while keeping the column order. These are used to reduce performance degradation in Oracle Parallel Server environments.

- *Bitmap indexes*—This is an index scheme used in low cardinality situations where bitmaps are created for each data row. The bits in a bitmap mark the rows that meet query criteria.

These indexing schemes provide complementary performance functionality. This means that the greatest performance benefit is derived when they are used in combination. In a bitmap index, a bitmap is used for each key value rather than a list comprised of **ROWID**s. Every possible **ROWID** has a corresponding bit in the bitmap, whereby setting the bit means that the row with the corresponding **ROWID** contains the key value. Oracle uses a mapping function to convert the bit position to an actual **ROWID**. Bitmap indexes are best when used on data with a small set of varying values. For example, a **GENDER** column can have, at most, three values: **MALE**, **FEMALE**, and **UNKNOWN**. To illustrate the concept of bitmap indexes, Figure 10.4 shows portions of a company's work force data and bitmapped entries for the **WORK_SHIFT** column.

From the graphics in Figure 10.4, you can see that work force data in the **EMPLOYEE** table is comprised of numerous columns, many of which are low cardinality columns. In this particular case, note that only three possible work shifts exist. The second graphic in Figure 10.4 shows how each bit corresponds to a single row in the table. Because there are three possible values for **WORK_SHIFT**, a separate bitmap is created for each occurrence, as shown. The value entered for each bit in a bitmap depends on the value of **WORK_SHIFT** for each row in the table. Bitmap indexing efficiently merges indexes that correspond to several conditions in a **WHERE** clause. Rows that do not satisfy the conditions in a **WHERE** clause of a query are removed from consideration before the table is accessed. This results in a dramatic improvement in response time.

Bitmap indexes are not suitable for OLTP applications with large numbers of concurrent transactions modifying the data. Bitmapped indexes should be used for decision support systems in data warehousing applications where DML activity is low and query rate is high.

Now that bitmapped indexing has been explained, let's move next to an introduction of index-organized tables, a new feature in Oracle8.

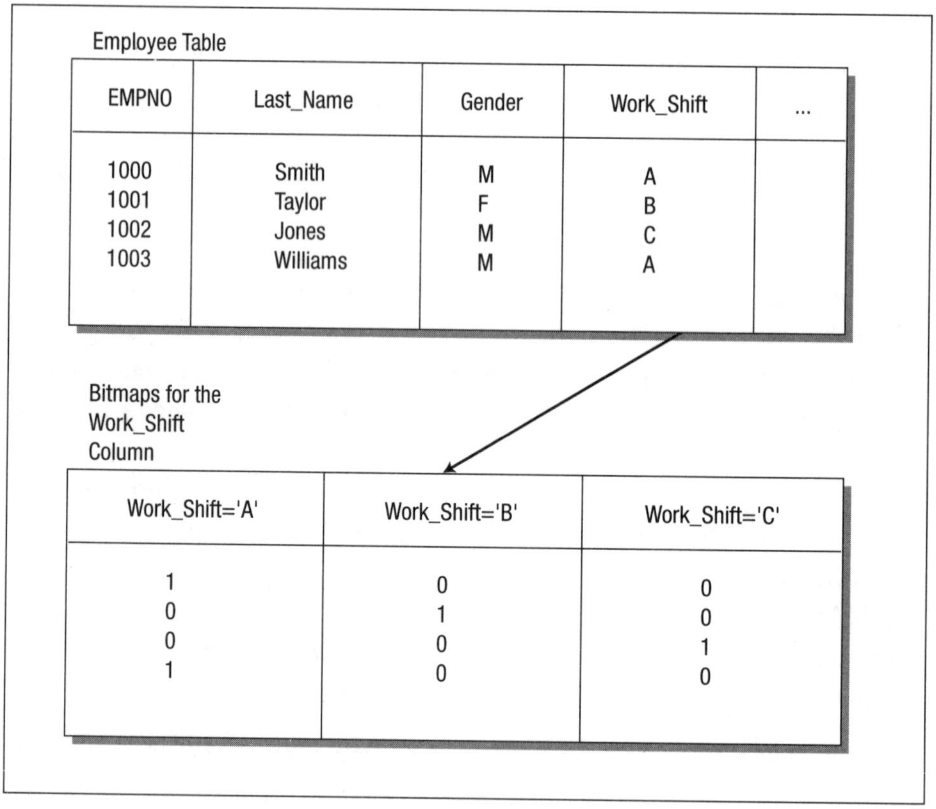

Employee Table

EMPNO	Last_Name	Gender	Work_Shift	...
1000	Smith	M	A	
1001	Taylor	F	B	
1002	Jones	M	C	
1003	Williams	M	A	

Bitmaps for the Work_Shift Column

Work_Shift='A'	Work_Shift='B'	Work_Shift='C'
1	0	0
0	1	0
0	0	1
1	0	0

Figure 10.4
Selected workforce data with a bitmapped **WORK_SHIFT** column.

Index-Organized Tables

Index-organized tables differ from their regular table counterparts in that the data for the index-organized table is placed in the corresponding index. When data is changed through the process of adding, updating, or deleting rows, only the index-organized table is changed. Index-organized tables are much like conventional tables with an index on one or more of the columns. Rather than maintain two separate storage objects for the table and the B*-tree index, the database system maintains only the B*-tree index, which contains both the encoded key value and the associated column values for each corresponding row. Index-organized tables do not maintain the **ROWID** as the second element. Instead, the actual data row is stored in the B*-tree index.

The data rows are built on the primary key for the table. Each B*-tree index entry is structured in the following manner:

```
<primary_key_value, table_column_values>
```

Index-organized tables are suitable for accessing data via primary key or, in the case of concatenated primary keys, via any portion of the concatenated key. Key values are not duplicated in the second element reserved for the row data.

Index-organized tables can be manipulated in the same way conventional tables are manipulated—by using SQL statements. In cases such as this, the database will use the B*-tree index to perform all data-access operations. Table 10.3 shows how index-organized tables compare to regular tables.

By storing the row data with the index, actual data access speeds are increased. In addition, storage is saved because index and table objects are combined into one, eliminating the use of the **ROWID**.

From this interesting database construct, let's move to one of the most exciting and highly anticipated features to be offered in Oracle8—the partitioning option.

Table 10.3 A comparison of index-organized tables and regular tables.

Regular Table	Index-Organized Table
ROWID will uniquely identify a row; primary key optionally specified	Primary key uniquely identifies a row; primary key must be specified
Implicit **ROWID** column; secondary physical indexes allowed	No implicit **ROWID** column; secondary physical indexes not allowed
Access by **ROWID**	Access by primary key
Sequential scan returns all rows	Full-index scan returns all rows in primary-key order
UNIQUE constraint and triggers allowed	Triggers allowed but not **UNIQUE** constraints (Oracle8 restriction)
Can be stored in a cluster containing other tables	Cannot be stored in a cluster
Distribution, replication, and partitioning supported	Distribution, replication, and partitioning not supported (Oracle8 restriction)

The Partitioning Option

The partitioning option is, as its name implies, an option and is not included with the baseline Oracle8 DBMS product. The features of partitioning present some interesting benefits for large database implementations that do not allow adequate downtime to perform full or incremental backups. The basic concept of partitioning is that large tables and views can be broken into several logical standalone substructures that can be manipulated independently.

Oracle considers the partitioning option as part of the object relational strategy for Oracle8, despite the fact that partitioning cannot be used with the object extensions in the current version of the database. This point is elaborated on further in the following section. As of this writing, nothing has been released about support for the object extensions by the partitioning option. In order to delve further into the concept of partitioning, let's explore the database constructs that use partitioning, starting with partitioned views.

Partitioned Views

Recall from your experience that a *join view* is defined as a view with more than one table or view in its **FROM** clause. Join views are also restricted from using the following clauses in the constructing **SELECT** statement: **DISTINCT, AGGREGATION, GROUP BY, START WITH, CONNECT BY, ROWNUM,** and set operations (**UNION ALL, INTERSECT,** and so on). Oracle8 introduces the updatable join view, which involves two or more base tables or views and permits **UPDATE, INSERT,** and **DELETE** operations. This feature represents an extension to the query-only nature that views once possessed. Updatable columns in an updatable join view can be identified by looking in the following data dictionary views:

- ALL_UPDATABLE_COLUMNS
- DBA_UPDATABLE_COLUMNS
- USER_UPDATABLE_COLUMNS

Partition views can be used to divide very large tables into multiple, smaller pieces (or partitions) in order to achieve significant improvements in availability, administration, and performance. The basic concept of the partition view is to divide a large table into multiple physical tables using a partitioning criteria. The partitions are then joined together as a contiguous object for query purposes. Each partition can have its own key ranges. Queries using a key range will access only the partitions that are addressed by the key range. For example, if a **CUSTOMER** table has been partitioned into key ranges of alphabetical groupings by last name, then only the partition containing the **A** names will be accessed if the query is searching for **Anstey**. Figure 10.5 illustrates query access to a partitioned view.

Partitioned views can also incorporate the use of check constraints and **WHERE** clauses. Listing 10.1 shows the preferred method for implementing check constraints.

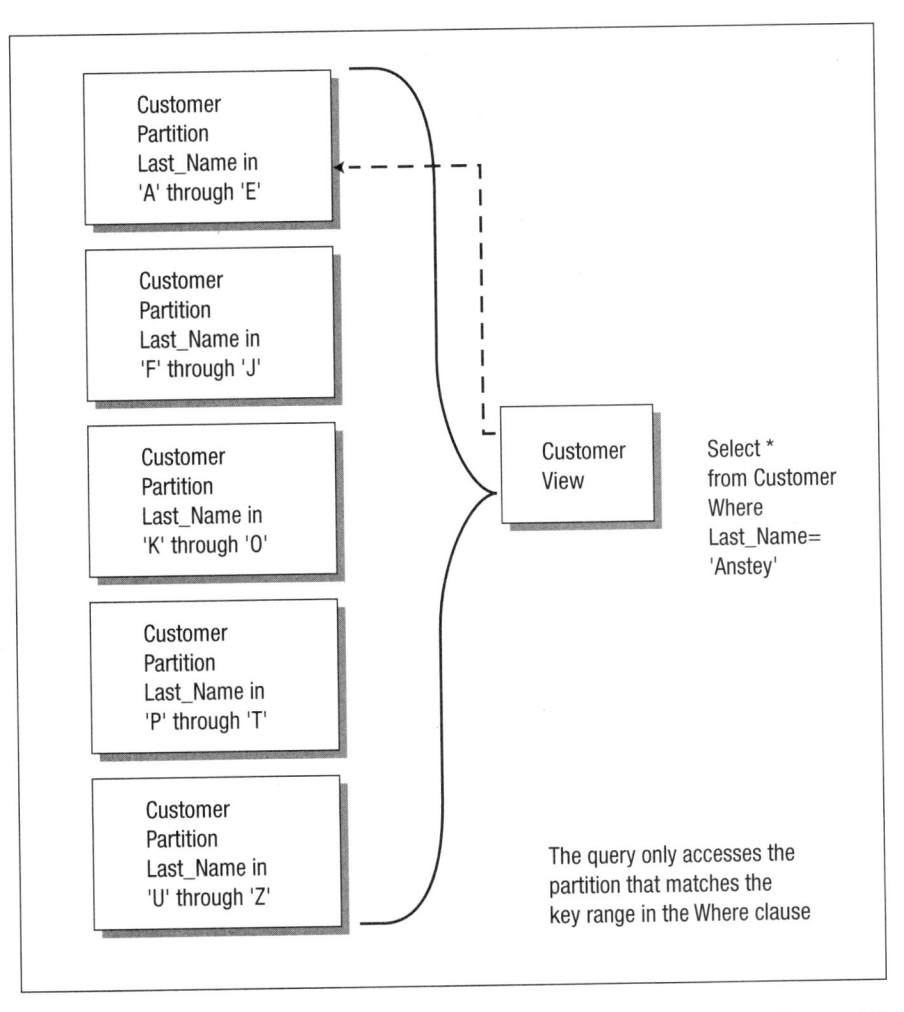

Figure 10.5
Query access to a partitioned view.

Listing 10.1 A partitioned view implementing check constraints.

```
ALTER TABLE WRENCH1_SALES ADD CONSTRAINT C_WRENCH1
    check (sale_date between '01-JAN-1998' and '31-MAR-1998');
ALTER TABLE WRENCH 2_SALES ADD CONSTRAINT C_ WRENCH 2
    check (sale_date between '01-APR-1998' and '30-JUN-1998');
ALTER TABLE WRENCH 3_SALES ADD CONSTRAINT C_ WRENCH 3
    check (sale_date between '01-JUL-1998' and '30-SEP-1998');
ALTER TABLE WRENCH 4_SALES ADD CONSTRAINT C_ WRENCH 4
    check (sale_date between '01-OCT-1998' and '31-DEC-1998');

CREATE VIEW wrench_sales AS
SELECT * FROM WRENCH 1_SALES UNION ALL
SELECT * FROM WRENCH 2_SALES UNION ALL
SELECT * FROM WRENCH 3_SALES UNION ALL
SELECT * FROM WRENCH 4_SALES;
```

The method described in Listing 10.1 offers two advantages. First, the check constraint predicates are not evaluated for every row during a query. Second, the predicates guard against the insertion of rows in the wrong partitions. For example, wrench sales for the month of May cannot be inserted into any other partition except for **WRENCH2_SALES**.

Alternatively, the criteria for the partitioned view can be addressed in the **WHERE** clause of the view's DML statement. Listing 10.2 illustrates the use of the **WHERE** clause to stipulate the selection criteria.

Listing 10.2 Using the WHERE clause to stipulate partitioned view criteria.

```
CREATE VIEW wrench_sales AS
SELECT * FROM WRENCH 1_SALES WHERE sale_date between
'01-JAN-1998' and '31-MAR-1998' UNION ALL
SELECT * FROM WRENCH 2_SALES WHERE sale_date between
'01-APR-1998' and '30-JUN-1998' UNION ALL
SELECT * FROM WRENCH 3_SALES WHERE sale_date between
'01-JUL-1998' and '30-SEP-1998' UNION ALL
SELECT * FROM WRENCH 4_SALES WHERE sale_date between
'01-OCT-1998' and '31-DEC-1998';
```

Using the method shown in Listing 10.2 has several disadvantages over the method demonstrated using check constraints. First, the partitioning predicate is applied at runtime for all rows in all partitions that are not skipped. Second, if a row with a sale date of '05-APR-1998' is mistakenly inserted into the **WRENCH1_SALES** partition, then the row will "disappear" from the partition view. Finally, partitioning criteria is stored in one, consolidated view definition, making the retrieval of specific partition criteria difficult. This forces the user to fish through code to find the partition criteria desired.

One significant benefit of partition views is that they enable data management operations like data loads, index creation, and data purges for individual partitions rather than on the entire table. This leads to a dramatic savings in time to perform these operations because a table can be manipulated a subset at a time. A tremendous advantage to the independence of each partition is that operations can still be exercised against one or more partitions, even when an unused partition is offline. For example, users can be executing queries against **WRENCH1_SALES** while **WRENCH2_SALES** is offline and being backed up. The Oracle Server incorporates the intelligence to explicitly recognize the status of partition views. The Oracle server engine uses this intelligence to enhance query optimization and query execution. Query optimization and execution are enhanced in the following ways:

- *Partition elimination*—For each query, the specific criteria is evaluated, and unneeded partitions are eliminated (this is known as *partition pruning*). For example, if a query only involves wrench sales in the first quarter, then there is no need to retrieve data from the remaining three partitions. Smart behavior on the part of the database engine results in substantial performance improvements because the entire table is not scanned.

- *Partition-level query optimization*—Oracle selects the most appropriate access path for query optimization at runtime. Optimization takes place at the level of the underlying physical tables. For example, Oracle would derive the proper optimization path to a partition view of **WRENCH_SALES** consisting of 12 partitions, one for each month: **WRENCH_JAN, WRENCH_FEB,… WRENCH_DEC**. If data involving only two partitions is being queried, then the remaining 10 partitions will not be considered because the query does not involve them.

It is apparent that partition views are useful in data warehouse environments due to the large volumes of data. In the next section, we'll discuss a related database object—the partition table. The benefits of a partition table closely match those of the partition view.

Partition Tables

As you saw in the previous section, the partitioning option offers a great deal in the way of maintenance and query performance. Much of what is described for partition views also applies to partition tables. Not only is partitioning possible for tables and views, but indexes can also benefit from this feature. Partitioning addresses the key problem of supporting very large tables and indexes by allowing users to decompose them into smaller and more manageable pieces.

> **Note:** *Oracle only supports partitioning for tables and indexes. It does not support partitioning of clustered tables and their indexes, nor of snapshots.*

Even though all partitions of a table or index have the same logical attributes (columns and their definitions, for example), their physical attributes can be set to different specifications. For example, the partitions in a table will contain the same columns, constraints, and so forth. At the same time, partitioned indexes will address the same columns, however, storage specifications and other physical attributes such as **PCTFREE**, **PCTUSED**, **INITRANS**, and **MAXTRANS** might be different for each partition of each table or index. In this way, the specific physical needs of each partition can be tailored to the particular nature of the partition. Although partitions are logically grouped, they will not always have the same number of rows. The flexibility to independently specify each partition's physical attributes means better utilization of resources.

Partitions are stored in separate segments. As an option, each individual partition can be assigned to a separate tablespace. Segregating partitions by tablespace offers the following advantages:

- Damaged data can be contained to prevent the total loss of a table.
- Each partition can be independently backed up.
- I/O load can be balanced by mapping partitions to disk drives.

Partitions offer a special benefit in a decision support system environment. Ad hoc queries can be executed using a partition scan, rather than a table scan, when rows from only selected partitions are needed. For example, a query that requests data generated in the fourth quarter of 1997 can scan just the rows stored in the fourth quarter 1997 partition, ignoring other rows generated over numerous years. Partition scans improve response times and often reduce the temporary disk space required for queries that require full-table sorts.

Partitioned tables have particular restrictions on logical attributes that all Oracle analysts and developers must be aware of. Partitioned tables cannot have any columns with **LONG** or **LONG RAW** data types, **LOB** data types (**BLOB**, **CLOB**, **NCLOB**, or **BFILE**), or object types. Bitmap indexes can be created on partitioned tables. The only restriction is that bitmap indexes must be local to the partitioned table and, therefore, cannot be global indexes.

The rules for partitioning tables are quite straightforward as long as the following conditions are met:

- The table cannot be a part of a cluster.
- The table cannot contain **LOBs**, **LONG** or **LONG RAW** data types, or object types.
- The table cannot be an index-organized table.

Based on these three criteria, it is obvious that the partitioning option cannot be exercised against object tables and views.

> *Note: As a result of the data type restrictions for partitioned tables, use of the objects option must be segregated from that of the partitioning option. In other words, the options cannot be used together against the same data table at the same time. This presents a significant obstacle to developers faced with the task of developing sophisticated data warehousing projects. In all likelihood, the objects option will be waived in order to take advantage of the partition option's benefits.*

Now that an overview of the features in Oracle8 that support the data warehouse have been properly introduced, I will proceed to a discussion of planning and implementing a data warehouse using Oracle8.

Oracle8 And Data Warehousing

If I could use only one word to describe the design strategy of a data warehouse, it would have to be *aggregation*. By the same token, much of what the object extensions offer the database designer is a means to effectively aggregate data objects in order to mimic real world systems and simplify what users, developers, and interfaces have to work with. Unfortunately, in data warehousing environments, developers are extremely limited in how they can combine performance and object extensions. Can an effective plan for integrating both be devised? If so, is it a sound approach? We will explore both questions in the next two sections.

Planning The Data Warehouse In Oracle8

The concepts presented earlier in this chapter describe the characteristics of data warehousing, OLAP, multidimensional databases, and so on in a way that conveys no particular preference for one vendor's product over another. Indeed, many third-party vendors provide tools, utilities, and specialized database engines to serve the data warehousing community. Depending on the methodology being pursued (OLAP, ROLAP, MOLAP, and so forth), the data model behind the database varies according to the desired role. The most striking example of this is the comparison between the relational and multidimensional databases. Oracle's philosophy is that a single database server (such as Oracle8) can fulfill all the needs of decision support systems given that the proper enhancements and specialized technologies are applied.

The success of any data warehousing project depends entirely on how well the analysis and design efforts are performed. As with the development life-cycle stages used for OLTP systems, the data warehousing effort must undergo a development effort focused heavily on extracting the specific requirements of the decision support system.

The first step in the process of planning a data warehouse is to ascertain the need. Earlier, we discussed how warehousing efforts are usually a secondary mission for IS staff. The project that does not secure the wholehearted support of management traverses the quick road to failure.

The second step is to accept the fact that a data warehousing system is more complex than the typical client/server project that most developers are accustomed to. Not only is there more data to deal with (lots more), but it must be aggregated to suit the decision support system. In addition, there is a plethora of tools and utilities designed for use in data warehousing efforts that makes the job of the analyst more complicated. If this is your first data warehousing project, admit your naiveté, and secure the help of experienced professionals to guide you and your staff on the development journey. The expense in consulting dollars will quickly pay for itself in the form of saved mistakes.

The third step is to carefully evaluate the technical competence of your user community. In most cases, there will be the opportunity for ad hoc queries. The responsibility for their execution must be determined at the onset of the project. If your users truly understand basic SQL, then it will be acceptable to pass this task to them. On the other hand, if your users are at the novice level and cannot find most of their applications when a shortcut icon has been created for them, then they shouldn't be granted the ability to run queries. This is an important point because most IS staffs are too busy on an average day to run queries whenever someone decides to call. Even experienced users can benefit from a refresher course in SQL, thereby alleviating the burden on the IS people after the data warehouse is deployed.

The fourth step is to determine the regularity and concept of data synchronization. Data in a data warehouse is useless if it trails the OLTP system by three weeks. Part of the design effort is to formulate a detailed plan for refreshing the data in the warehouse tables. It is not sufficient to "draw it out" on paper and declare success. A well-planned data warehouse design effort includes several prototype data synchronization schemes, each tested on the system to be deployed. Timing metrics, shortcomings in load scripts, and so on should be identified as soon as possible to avoid problems during deployment. In addition, sizing estimates (for storage requirements) should be calculated and triple checked. Just as it is prudent to fudge by 20 percent on how much paint you might need to cover the exterior of your home, it is wise to do the same for estimating the amount of storage that a system might require to meet the data needs of the decision support system.

I once consulted on a large hospital project to integrate the patient records for approximately two dozen hospitals. I arrived after the initial analysis had been performed. During a progress meeting, we decided to recalculate the storage requirements based on the customer's requirements. Much to everyone's astonishment, the initial figures had underestimated the needed disk storage by half! Unfortunately, hardware had already been purchased, and the task of contacting the client fell on our project lead. I'm not sure, but he might still be selling T-shirts on the beach.

The fifth step is to manage your customer's expectations. In order to avoid surprises or disappointments, users must be aware of what the data warehouse will and will not do for them. In this regard, I have used the analogy of the starship Enterprise from the popular television show *Star Trek*. Many nontechnical users have the impression that a request for data, services, or features will come as simply to them as ship repairs come when Spock jumps under the control console on the bridge and declares only moments later that damages to the computer are repaired. That is fiction—this is reality. Nothing is that easy. Maintaining a constant line of communication with users ensures your ability to fulfill user requests and alleviates the *Star Trek* syndrome.

Once you, as the analyst, have gone over the basics, it is time to get the project started in earnest. In analyzing the requirements for the data warehouse, you must start at the end to get to the beginning. What I mean by this is that a full assessment of the intended output must be plainly stated. A complete list of standard reports, anticipated queries, and item-for-item matching of the data requirements from the decision support system must be made.

Chances are that the data source for the data warehouse will be from one or more OLTP systems, one or more data marts, historical data, or a combination of all three. OLTP systems will support the use of the object extensions for Oracle8, but if you must use performance features like partitioning or bitmapped indexes in your database applications, then you will not be able to take advantage of the objects option.

One strategy for getting the best of both worlds is to shield the data warehouse from object types. Figure 10.6 illustrates the concept of layering object types at the lowest detail level away from the data warehouse.

The plan of action illustrated in Figure 10.6 is implemented in the following manner. Detail tables from the underlying OLTP system incorporate various object types. A preliminary aggregation of data is performed to "cleanse" out object types by rolling data from object types and collection types (nested tables and **VARRAY**s) into denormalized tables and/or views. This constitutes the protective layer between the OLTP and OLAP schemes. The resulting data tables and views can then be used to populate the larger aggregated entities that will drive the data warehouse.

Creation of the protective layer of conventional tables and views is not an effort to be trivialized. Complex conversion code in the form of PL/SQL scripts must be written if the strategy is to succeed. This adds to the complexity of maintaining synchronized data between the lower OLTP system and the data warehouse tables. Such an arduous task can be sufficient reason to abandon any attempt to use the object option in a data warehousing environment. But, before ruling out that possibility, it

Oracle8 Design For The Data Warehouse

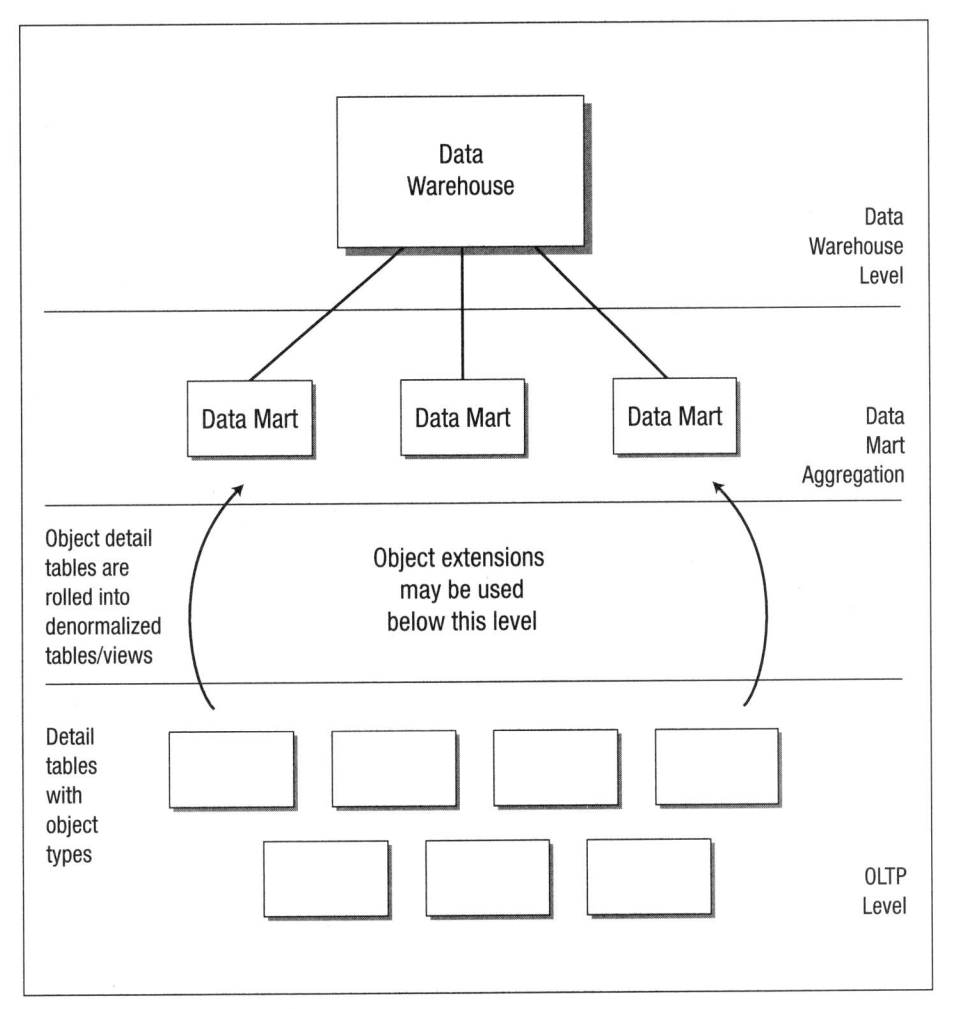

```
                    Data
                  Warehouse                        Data
                                                 Warehouse
                                                   Level

        Data Mart      Data Mart     Data Mart    Data
                                                   Mart
                                                Aggregation

Object detail        Object extensions
tables are            may be used
rolled into           below this level
denormalized
tables/views

Detail
tables
with
object
types                                              OLTP
                                                   Level
```

Figure 10.6
Layering object extensions below the data warehouse.

will be necessary to consider the source data. You might be required to create a data warehouse from an OLTP source that has already implemented the object option in Oracle8. If this is the case, then the strategy outlined earlier will most likely be your best course of action.

If you are planning a data warehouse effort in Oracle8, then it will most likely implement what is known as a *star query*. In the next section, we'll look at what star queries are and how they are used in Oracle8.

Using Star Queries

The star schema is the data representation of choice for many data warehousing implementations. Essentially, a star schema consists of one very large table, known as a *fact table*, and several smaller tables termed *dimension tables*. Fact tables consist of primary information. For example, in a human resources data warehouse, the **EMPLOYEE** table might list every company employee worldwide. Another example might be for a factory outlet chain where the **SALES** table contains all products sold by all stores. Dimension tables consist of reference, or *lookup*, information. Referring to the factory outlet example, a fact table might contain specific product information while another maintains time period data. Figure 10.7 illustrates the star schema using the factory outlet example.

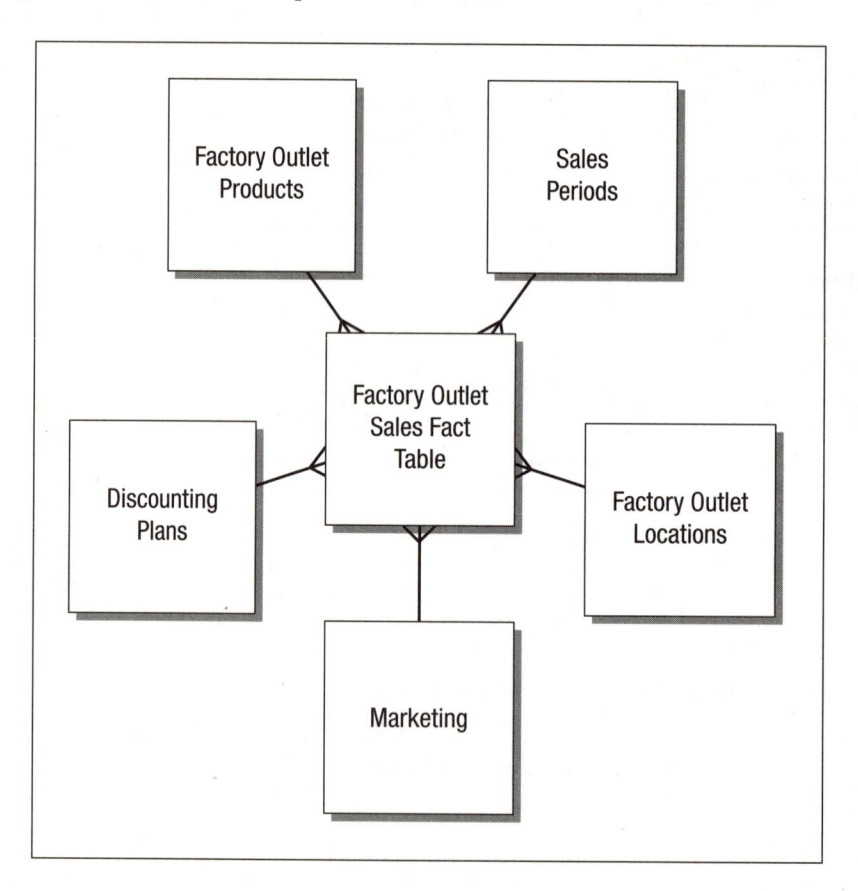

Figure 10.7
An example of a star schema.

A star query is a join between a fact table and a number of dimension tables. Each dimension table is joined to the fact table using a primary-key-to-foreign-key relationship. Note from the illustration in Figure 10.7 that the dimension tables are not joined to each other. The Oracle cost-based optimizer recognizes star queries and generates efficient execution plans for them. Oracle's rule-based optimizer is not capable of detecting star queries.

As of version 7.3, Oracle offers a new data access hint called the star query hint. In order to use this hint, the query must be performing a full-table scan, and the fact table must also have a concatenated index with every key from the dimension tables. In Oracle8, the star query optimization algorithm has been improved, eliminating the creation of Cartesian product joins. The Oracle8 star query join executes in two phases. First, it fetches only the necessary rows from the fact table via bit-mapped index. Second, the result set from the fact table fetch is joined to the relevant dimension tables. The new optimization algorithm is also completely parallelized, allowing parallel index scans on partitioned and non-partitioned tables.

Typical star schema fact tables contain keys and measures. For example, a simple fact table might contain the measure **Sales** (from our factory outlet example) and keys to **Time_period**, **Product**, and **Market**. In this case, there would be corresponding dimension tables for **Time_period**, **Product**, and **Market**. The **Product** dimension table would have information about each product number that appears in the fact table. A star join is a primary-key-to-foreign-key join of the dimension tables to a fact table. Fact tables typically have concatenated indexes on the key columns to facilitate the star join.

To illustrate the use of star queries, look at the code in Listing 10.3.

Listing 10.3 Sample code for a star query.

```
SELECT SUM(dollars)
FROM sales, time_period, product, market
WHERE market.region = 'East Coast'
AND product.brand = 'Acme'
AND time.year = 1998
AND time.month = 'January'
AND time_period.key = sales.time_period_key
AND product.pkey = sales.product_key
AND market.key = sales.market_key;
```

Note from the code in Listing 10.3 that the primary keys of the dimension tables are joined to the corresponding fact table's foreign keys. The cost-based optimizer must be used to maximize star query efficiency. A good start is to evaluate the star query using the **ANALYZE** command to gather statistics for each table accessed by the query.

In Listing 10.3, a concatenated index would be constructed on the columns **time_period_key**, **product_key**, and **market_key**. Column order in the index is critical to performance because the columns in the index will take advantage of any ordering of data. Adding rows to the large (fact) table in time order suggests that the **time_period_key** should be the first in the index. Performance gains can be realized during static extracts from another database by sorting the data on the key columns before loading it. If all queries specify predicates on each of the small tables, a single concatenated index suffices. Additional indexes will be useful when queries are executed that frequently omit leading columns in the concatenated index.

Analyzing tables will normally cause the optimizer to select an efficient star plan. Providing hints to the optimizer will improve the plan and, subsequently, performance. The most effective method for obtaining the best performance is to order the tables in the **FROM** clause in the order of the keys in the index, followed by the large fact table last. The following hint assists the optimizer in selecting the most efficient plan:

```
/*+ ORDERED USE_NL(sales) INDEX(sales sales_concat) */
```

Another method for enhancing performance via the optimizer is through the use of the more generic **STAR** hint, as follows:

```
/*+ STAR */.
```

Extended star schemas can be further extended by replacing the dimension tables with a join of several smaller dimension tables. For example, it is possible to further reduce the product table into model and manufacturer tables. Performance problems commonly arise if dimension tables are reduced to an extremely atomic level. The first problem that arises from normalizing the dimension tables too far is that the optimizer must consider substantially more permutations of table joins. A second problem results from the multiple executions of the multiple dimension table joins. This scenario is a perfect case where denormalization resolves the problem by reducing complexity and increases query performance. Views can be created to relieve the work performed by the optimizer while maintaining a more normalized structure. Listing 10.4 shows the use of a view to resolve a performance problem.

Listing 10.4 A sample denormalized view of multiple dimension tables.

```
CREATE VIEW product_view AS SELECT /*+ NO_MERGE */ *
FROM model, mfgrs WHERE model.mfkey = mfgrs.mfkey;
```

The hint shown in Listing 10.4 will reduce the optimizer's search space and cause the database engine to cache the result of the view.

Another means of improving efficiency of star queries is through the use of what is known as a *star transformation*. A star transformation is a cost-based query transformation. The star optimization is well-suited for schemas with a small number of dimensions and dense fact tables. The star transformation is ideal when any of the following conditions exist:

- There is a large number of dimension tables.
- The fact table is sparsely populated.
- There are queries where not all dimension tables have constraining predicates.

A significant benefit of the star transformation is that it does not perform a Cartesian product of the dimension tables. This fact makes it a better alternative in situations where the fact table is sparse and/or many of the dimension tables would produce a sizable Cartesian product yielding a small percentage of rows matching the fact table. In addition, the star transformation combines bitmap indexes on individual fact table columns for improved performance. The transformation requires few concatenated indexes because it combines indexes from the dimension tables in use. This alleviates the need to create numerous concatenated indexes to support the multiplicity of query patterns. The star transformation works by generating new subqueries that can be used to drive a bitmap index access path for the fact table. For example, assume you have three dimension tables named **A**, **B**, and **C**, and a fact table named **fact**. Listing 10.5 shows the code for the initial query, and Listing 10.6 shows the resulting subqueries.

Listing 10.5 The initial query.

```
EXPLAIN PLAN FOR
SELECT * FROM fact, A, B, C
```

```
WHERE fact.c1 = A.c1
AND fact.c2 = B.c1
AND fact.c3 = C.c1
AND A.c2 IN ('Acme', 'Widget')
AND B.c2 < sysdate
AND C.c2 = 100;
```

Listing 10.6 The resulting subqueries from a star transformation.
```
SELECT * FROM fact, A, B
WHERE fact.c1 = A.c1 AND fact.c2 = B.c1
AND A.c2 IN (1, 2, 3, 4)
AND B.c2 < 100
AND fact.c1 IN (SELECT A.c1 FROM A WHERE A.c2 IN ('Acme', 'Widget'))
AND fact.c2 IN (SELECT B.c1 FROM B WHERE B.c2 < sysdate)
AND fact.c3 IN (SELECT C.c1 FROM C WHERE C.c2 = 100);
```

Assuming that there are bitmap indexes on **fact.c1**, **fact.c2**, and **fact.c3**, as shown in Listing 10.5, the resulting subqueries, shown in Listing 10.6, can be used to drive a bitmap index access path. For each value of **A.c1** that is retrieved from the first subquery, the corresponding bitmap for that value is retrieved from the index on **fact.c1**, and these bitmaps are merged. The result is a bitmap for precisely those rows in the fact table that match the condition on **A** in the subquery **WHERE** clause.

The same operation is performed for the second and third subqueries, yielding corresponding bitmaps. The three merged bitmaps can then be linked with the **AND** clause, resulting in a bitmap corresponding to those rows in the fact table that meet the conditions in all three subqueries simultaneously. This bitmap can be used to access the fact table for retrieval of the selected rows. The resulting rows are then joined to tables **A**, **B**, and **C** to return the overall query product. As this example demonstrates, no Cartesian product is required.

Star transformations are enabled by setting the value of the initialization parameter **STAR_TRANSFORMATION_ENABLED** to **TRUE**. Use the **STAR_TRANSFORMATION** hint to make the optimizer use the best plan in which the transformation has been used. If you intend to use star transformations, keep in mind that tables with the following properties are not supported:

- Tables with table hints incompatible with a bitmap access path.
- Tables with too few bitmap indexes (there must be a bitmap index on a fact table column).

- Remote tables (remote dimension tables are allowed in the generated subqueries).
- Anti-joined tables.
- Tables already used as a dimension table in a subquery.
- Unmerged views (those that are not view partitions).
- Tables possessing a good single-table access path.
- Small tables that don't make the transformation worthwhile.

Summary

This chapter discusses Oracle8's tremendous support for data warehousing. In the early sections, we focused on a brief overview of data warehousing and how you must plan for a data warehouse. Of critical importance is the fact that the coexistence of object extensions and performance-oriented features in Oracle8 is not usually possible. This poses a dilemma to analysts and developers facing a mixed environment where incompatibilities must be reconciled. From the standpoint of data warehouse design, we discussed a series of crucial steps necessary to ensure a successful project, and wrapped up the discussion with a detailed description of the nature and use of the star schema in Oracle8. In the next chapter, our discussion moves on to an explanation of distributed systems and the Oracle8 features that impact the design effort in that complex environment.

HIGH PERFORMANCE

Oracle8 And Distributed Systems

CHAPTER 11

HIGH PERFORMANCE

The real question is not whether machines think but whether men do.
—B. F. Skinner

Oracle8 And Distributed Systems

In the 1990s, we're witnessing an expansion of information technology unlike any other era in human history. Islands of information are rapidly being linked to one another in an effort to increase data access speeds. Data management efforts are focusing on the technologies required to bridge dissimilar database systems into one cohesive system. The degree of challenge in successfully developing and maintaining a distributed database system (DDS) rises dramatically when compared to the independent, single-node/server implementation. Indeed, the set of problems that must be conquered in deploying a successful DDS are a level of magnitude greater than those of a basic OLTP system. The factors that impact a distributed database system include accessing remote nodes, replicating data, linking databases from multiple vendors, executing SQL across a network, implementing Net8 (the successor to SQL*Net), and more. In the sections that follow, we'll explore the nature of distributed systems, Oracle8's distributed environment features, and distributed systems design techniques.

An Overview Of Distributed Systems

An appropriate way to begin the discussion of distributed systems is by defining the essential terminology. Oracle Corporation differentiates between the terms *distributed databases* and *distributed processing*. While the terms are used together frequently, the following statement places them in the proper context: Oracle distributed databases utilize a distributed processing architecture in order to operate. In a more pragmatic sense, this could mean that an Oracle server can act as a client when requesting data from another Oracle server. This behavior also holds true if the Oracle server is requesting data from a non-Oracle server. Systems supporting multiple database vendors are *heterogeneous*. This concept is explained later in this chapter, in the section entitled, "Features And Properties Of Oracle8 Distributed Database Systems." The definitions for distributed database and distributed processing as used by Oracle are given here:

- *Distributed Database*—Distributed databases are comprised of two or more databases stored on multiple computers that appear to applications as a single database.

- *Distributed Processing*—Distributed processing takes place when an application system distributes its tasks among different computers in a network. In an Oracle environment, it is common for the GUI front-end processes to be executed from client PCs or network computers, while the actual SQL statements are carried out on a back-end database server. Distributed database application processing systems are commonly referred to as *client/server* database application systems.

There is some disagreement in the computing industry over the standard definition of a distributed database system. In most situations, a distributed database system is a multiplicity of database products, usually from the same vendor, geographically spread over multiple servers or nodes. The term is interpreted differently by front-end application vendors who see the distribution in an architectural sense rather than a physical sense. Even hardware vendors have produced their own interpretation of DDS, which to them means a system composed of different databases running on the same brand of hardware products.

Early on, a general definition for distributed database system was offered by Chris Date, computer systems author and co-inventor of the relational database model. In his definition, Chris Date stated that a distributed database system should have the following 12 characteristics:

- *Local autonomy*—This means that data in the distributed database is owned and managed by the local nodes or database servers. Each local node or database processes and owns data independently from the distributed system.

- *No reliance on a central site*—In a perfect world, each remote site is considered a participating equal, and no one site maintains governing authority over any of the other nodes on the distributed system. Each site should maintain its own data dictionary and provide database security for the tables and objects that it owns.

- *Continuous operation*—Continuous operation means that each node must be available 24 hours a day, 7 days per week. Although each node operates independently, it is also a member of the distributed database system. Each node on the distributed database system must have access to the data residing on the other nodes in order to maintain continuous operation. This means that Oracle hot backups are part of a routine maintenance schedule in order to meet constant data demand from other remote nodes.

- *Location independence*—The key to location independence is establishing data transparency. From a typical user standpoint, the physical location of a specific piece of data is inconsequential. This means that the mechanisms necessary to execute data transactions without referencing specific site locations (from the user's perspective) is essential.

- *Fragmentation independence*—This concept refers to the ability for logically related data to be stored at different physical nodes or sites. Fragmentation can occur in two forms: horizontal partitioning and vertical partitioning. *Horizontal partitioning* places different rows of data from the same table on different remote sites. *Vertical partitioning* allows a distributed system to store data columns from the same table at various locations on the network. Figure 11.1 illustrates the use of horizontal and vertical partitioning.

- *Replication independence*—Replication independence occurs when copies of the master database are created and stored on remote nodes or sites. Oracle calls these copies *snapshots*, and each snapshot can contain an entire database or a subset thereof. Due to the reduced cost of storage, it makes sense from a performance aspect to maintain replicated copies of various portions of the master database at some or all remote sites. An additional benefit of replication independence is that master data is available to all independent nodes, even when the network between sites goes down.

- *Distributed query processing*—There are two aspects to distributed query processing. The first aspect is the obvious benefit of accessing multiple databases with a single query. The second, and perhaps more important, aspect is that the resources used to execute the query can be distributed between nodes. For example, let's assume that a query is executed to retrieve the highest spending customers from each regional territory in the U.S. Even though the query is initiated in Dallas, the data retrieval for Los Angeles and New York will be executed on those respective nodes. The node initiating the query will perform the merge of the resulting data from each territory. Figure 11.2 illustrates the concept of distributing processing resources among several nodes or sites.

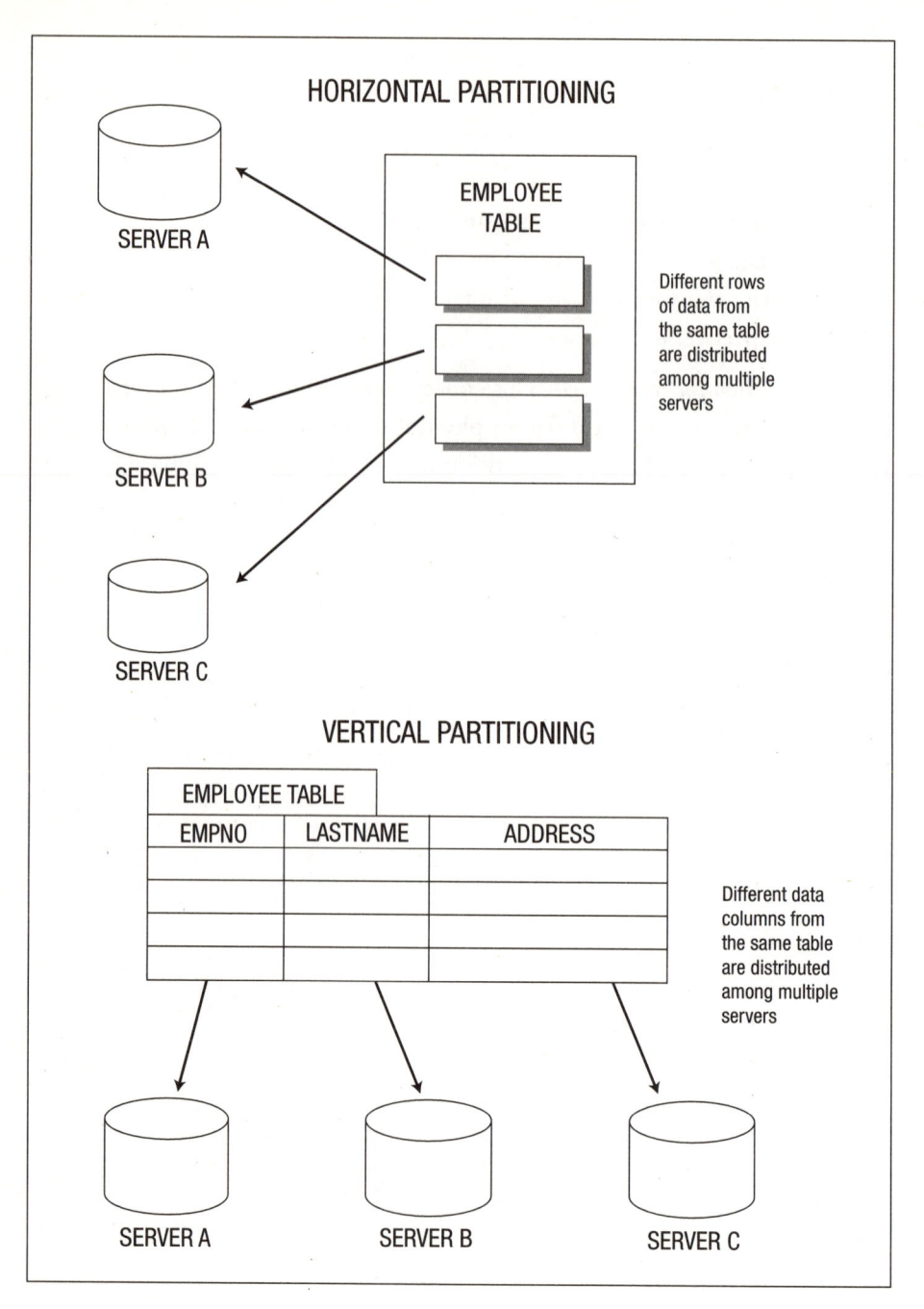

Figure 11.1
Horizontal and vertical partitioning.

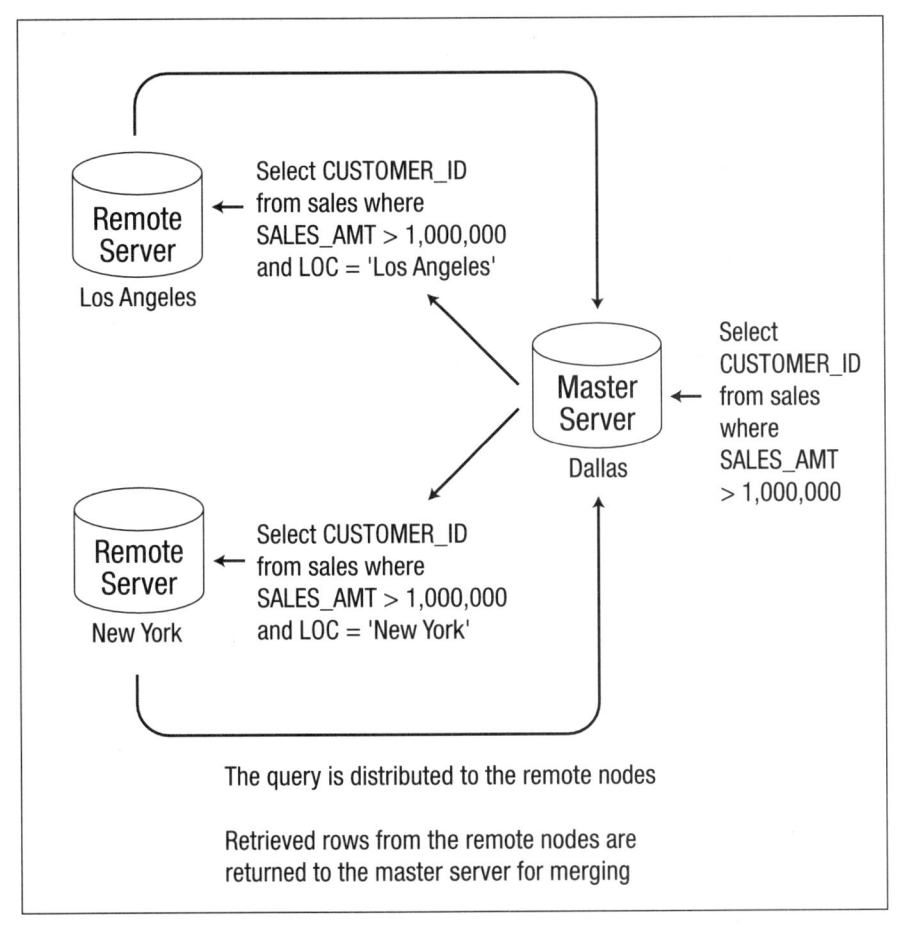

```
                                    Select CUSTOMER_ID
         Remote          ←─────     from sales where
         Server                     SALES_AMT > 1,000,000
         Los Angeles                and LOC = 'Los Angeles'
                                                                    Select
                                                                    CUSTOMER_ID
                                          Master           ←─────   from sales
                                          Server                    where
                                          Dallas                    SALES_AMT
                                                                    > 1,000,000
         Remote                     Select CUSTOMER_ID
         Server          ←─────     from sales where
         New York                   SALES_AMT > 1,000,000
                                    and LOC = 'New York'

         The query is distributed to the remote nodes

         Retrieved rows from the remote nodes are
         returned to the master server for merging
```

Figure 11.2
Resource utilization in a distributed query process.

- *Distributed transaction management*—Distributed transaction management, or *update processing*, involves Oracle's ability to perform DML operations (**INSERT**, **UPDATE**, and **DELETE**) against multiple databases from a single command. The Oracle database engine uses a technique known as a *two-phase commit*. The two-phase commit guarantees that data updates on remote nodes are completed before the entire transaction is committed. An error raised at any point during a two-phase commit will cause the database to roll back the entire transaction. Because of the importance of distributed transaction processing in Oracle distributed database configurations, this topic is discussed in further detail in an upcoming section.

- *Hardware independence*—This concept refers to the ability to execute SQL transactions against data on any node on a system without regard to the hardware platform on which it resides.

- *Operating system independence*—Distributed database systems should not be restricted by differences in operating systems between independent nodes. For example, queries executed from a node hosted by a Unix server should allow the access of data from a VMS server. Users should be isolated from any operating system peculiarities when retrieving data from the system as a whole.

- *Network independence*—As with operating system independence, network protocols should not act as a barrier or hindrance to accessing data on a distributed database system. To reduce network-access problems resulting from differences found in various protocols, Oracle includes a multiple-community feature as part of SQL*Net and its successor, Net8. Oracle8 requires the use of Net8 as the connectivity mechanism between Oracle8 and other databases and/or application tools.

- *Database independence*—This is the last characteristic required for distributed database systems. Database independence means that data can be retrieved and updated from different database architectures. Oracle establishes access to non-Oracle databases by means of the Oracle Open Gateway products.

Now that the basic terminology has been defined, let's examine the types of distributed database systems that you can expect to see implemented in a typical business environment.

Types Of Distributed Databases

Distributed database systems are not restricted to a single design pattern. As a matter of fact, distributed database systems can be categorized into three varieties: horizontal distribution, vertical distribution, and architectural distribution. Each of these implementations has particular characteristics that set it apart from the others. Let's examine each of the distributed database system types, starting with horizontal distribution.

Horizontal Distribution

Distributed databases configured under horizontal distribution run under the control of separate processors and are geographically distributed. Keep in mind that the geographical distribution of databases is only a physical configuration. This means that databases can be located miles apart or in the same room. Horizontal distribution also describes symmetric multiprocessing (SMP) configurations, where each database can be run on a dedicated processor on the same machine. Regardless of whether the horizontal distribution is configured with independent servers or a single SMP system, Net8 is required to negotiate the communication between the CPUs used to support each database. Figure 11.3 illustrates multiple databases configured in a horizontal distribution.

Vertical Distribution

A vertical distribution, also referred to as a *platform distribution*, describes a database configuration where the databases reside on a variety of hardware platforms. Under this configuration type, it is common to find databases from more than one vendor, because this is often used in client/server deployments. For example, a PC-based

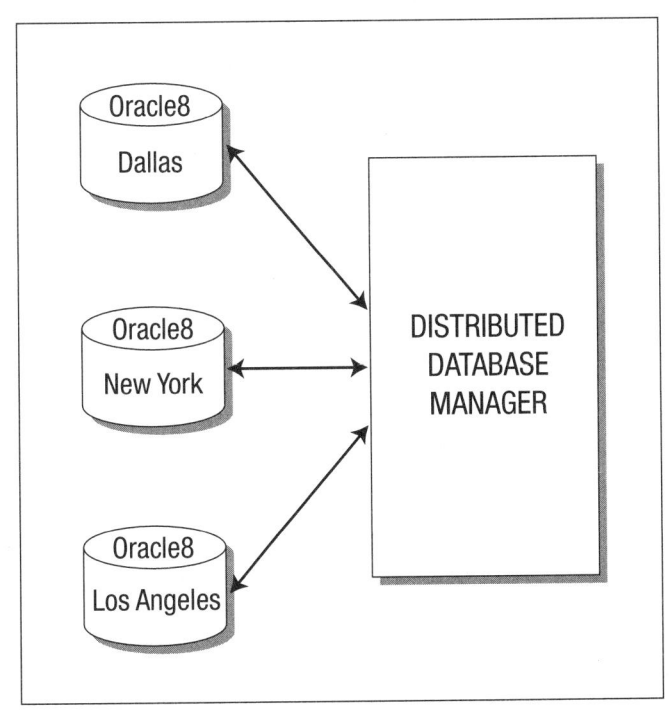

Figure 11.3
A horizontal distribution of a distributed database system.

database tool like Microsoft Access could be deployed on a PC network, while the connected mainframe database is Oracle8 running on a RISC-based Unix server. Vertical distribution deployments are very common and provide a great deal of versatility, but they are more difficult to maintain. Figure 11.4 illustrates the concept of vertical distribution using the client/server example just described.

Architectural Distribution

The architectural distribution describes a distributed database system that incorporates more than one database architecture. This means that non-relational databases can also be participating nodes in the DDS. A combination of state-of-the-art and legacy database systems can exist in an architectural distribution. This design approach to distributed database systems makes the most sense when large amounts of legacy data (residing, perhaps, on a hierarchical database) must be fused with current database applications built on Oracle8 or on an object-oriented database like Raima.

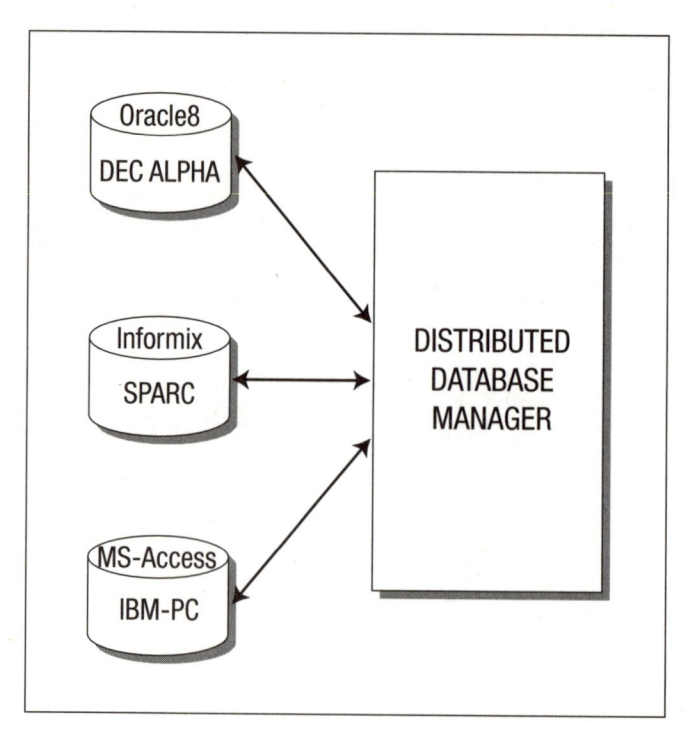

Figure 11.4
A vertical distribution example.

As with hierarchical and relational distributions, the combination of old and new systems will be common where the cost of migrating legacy data to a new system like Oracle8 is prohibitive.

So far, I have discussed what distributed database systems are and what characteristics they must possess. I have also described three configurations common to DDS design. Let us next explore Oracle8's features that support the distributed database system environment.

Features And Properties Of Oracle8 Distributed Database Systems

The Oracle8 database management system offers a number of functions and features that support distributed database system implementations. Database developers must be acutely aware of the options available to maximize database system designs.

As pointed out in Chapter 10, Oracle8's object extensions are not currently compatible with certain other Oracle8 options or features. Despite the limited object-extension support by Oracle8's other enhancements in the current release, it is worthwhile to entertain the notion of their combined use in version 8.1. The last section of this chapter includes object extensions when discussing design issues for Oracle8 distributed database systems. At the time of this writing, the restrictions, limitations, performance impact, and syntactical requirements of the fully integrated object extensions have not been determined.

> *Note:* Object extensions are not supported by the following in version 8.0.x of Oracle8: partitioning, bitmapping, distributed databases, and the parallel option. Support of object extensions is currently limited to relatively basic implementations. The first release of Oracle8 allowing the combined use of object extensions with the other named extensions and features is scheduled for version 8.1.

Before venturing into the area of design issues, let's explore Oracle8's features and functions designed to support distributed database systems.

Heterogeneity And Transparency

Earlier in this chapter, the term *heterogeneous* is used to present an overview of distributed database systems. As you may recall, a heterogeneous distributed database system contains at least one non-Oracle database system. Distributed database systems consisting of databases from multiple vendors are increasingly common as organizations seek to integrate corporate data. (Chapter 10 outlines the importance of bringing a company's informational resources together.) In an Oracle environment, the *Oracle Open Gateway* provides access to non-Oracle data.

An Oracle Open Gateway provides access to the non-Oracle system from an Oracle Server. The Oracle Server, when combined with the gateway product, provides full connectivity and transparency to data residing on a non-Oracle database server. In other words, an application accessing data does not need to be aware that it is accessing a non-Oracle system. Oracle gateways are product specific and must be ordered to match the non-Oracle system to be accessed. For example, if data from a DB2 database is part of a distributed database system, then the gateway for DB2 must be installed. Due to the numerous possibilities and combinations in a heterogeneous environment, you should consult Oracle's *Oracle Open Gateway Technology Guide* for detailed information on implementing gateways.

Transparency is the means of hiding users from the complex data transaction processes on an Oracle distributed database system. In other words, the semantic details of updating or retrieving data from an Oracle database to any non-Oracle databases on the distributed database system are hidden from users. The idea behind transparency is to make a distributed database system appear as though it is a single Oracle database. Transparency infuses the development and production environments with a level of simplicity that eliminates distracting complexities.

The Oracle8 Server allows *location transparency*, which hides the physical location of database objects from applications and users. Location transparency exists when a user can access a database object regardless of whether it belongs to an Oracle or non-Oracle database.

The common approach to establishing location transparency is to have a DBA create synonyms for the tables and supporting objects in an application schema. Listing 11.1 shows an example statement using synonyms.

Listing 11.1 A sample synonym statement.

```
CREATE PUBLIC SYNONYM widget
FOR texas.widget@sales.ansteyville.com
```

The creation of the synonym in Listing 11.1 means that accessing data in the remote database can be accomplished with shorter and more lucid SQL statements. Users are only aware that the data is in the object known as **widget** instead of **texas.widget@sales.ansteyville.com**. Views and stored procedures can also be used to aid in the establishment of location transparency by aggregating the necessary data elements into a consolidated database object.

As part of Oracle's effort to maintain seamless connectivity in a heterogeneous environment, Oracle8 now includes a utility called *Heterogeneous Services*. Heterogeneous Services is an integrated component within the Oracle8 Server. The intent is to provide an enabling technology for Oracle's next generation of Open Gateway products. Heterogeneous Services is designed to provide a common architecture and administration mechanisms for future Oracle gateway products. According to Oracle Corporation, future releases of Oracle Open Gateways taking advantage of Heterogeneous Services are slated to include the following features:

- *Distributed transactions*—A heterogeneous transaction linking Oracle and non-Oracle systems will guarantee that DML statements are either committed or rolled back utilizing Oracle's two-phase commit mechanism. The two-phase commit mechanism and distributed transactions are covered in more detail later in this chapter.

- *SQL transparency*—As described earlier, data transparency will be available from non-Oracle systems into the Oracle environment to gain the appearance that the data is stored in a single, local database. SQL statements issued by an application will be converted into SQL statements that can be interpreted by the non-Oracle systems.

- *Procedural access*—Procedural systems, such as messaging and queuing systems, will make use of PL/SQL remote procedure calls via the Oracle8 Server.

- *Data dictionary translations*—Conversion of non-Oracle database systems for the purpose of making them appear as Oracle servers will be performed through a series of SQL statements containing references to Oracle's data dictionary tables. In turn, these SQL statements will be translated into SQL statements containing references to a non-Oracle system's data dictionary tables.

- *Pass-through SQL*—Oracle will allow direct access to non-Oracle systems via the native SQL of the non-Oracle system.

- *Stored procedure access*—Stored procedures in SQL-based non-Oracle systems will be accessed in the same fashion as Oracle's PL/SQL remote procedures.

- *National language support*—Oracle Open Gateways will support multibyte character sets and character translation, as a part of the national language support feature.

- *Global query optimization*—The Oracle8 query optimizer will consider features like cardinality and table indexes from the non-Oracle system. Then, the non-Oracle performance features will be decomposed to produce efficient SQL statements on the non-Oracle system.

Not all features listed will apply to every version of the Open Gateway product. You should consult the gateway documentation to determine which features are supported.

The next topic to be discussed—data replication—is of particular importance when trying to establish replication independence. It is also of vital concern to DBAs responsible for the safety and reliable access to data by remote nodes.

Data Replication

Data replication is extremely useful for a number of reasons. In data warehousing environments, replication improves reliability and query response times. In distributed database systems, replication ensures that data is accessible if one or more of the remote databases becomes unavailable. In OLTP configurations, replication helps with data load balancing. Often, it is difficult to balance processing requirements among applications that require light data use, like OLTP, and heavy demand use, like data warehousing systems. Data replication is a good strategy to take when there are concurrent data demands from multiple applications, such as OLTP and data warehousing, and fast response times must be balanced with intensive I/O operations against the system. One of the biggest disadvantages of data replication is the fact that there is a period of time where the database replica is out of synchronization with the master database object. Every organization must determine what their acceptable threshold for a non-updated database replica is. This presents the classic trade-off of data currency for performance.

Oracle8 supports two general kinds of replication: basic and advanced. Let's examine these replication concepts more closely.

Basic Replication

Oracle's definition of *basic replication* can be paraphrased as the creation of data replica objects that provide read-only access to the table data originating from a primary or master site. Data replication objects, termed *snapshots*, can be queried by applications, thereby avoiding network traffic. If it becomes necessary to perform DML commands against the data, then the DML must be executed against the original data stored at the primary site. DML against a snapshot is not permitted. Figure 11.5 illustrates the concept of basic replication.

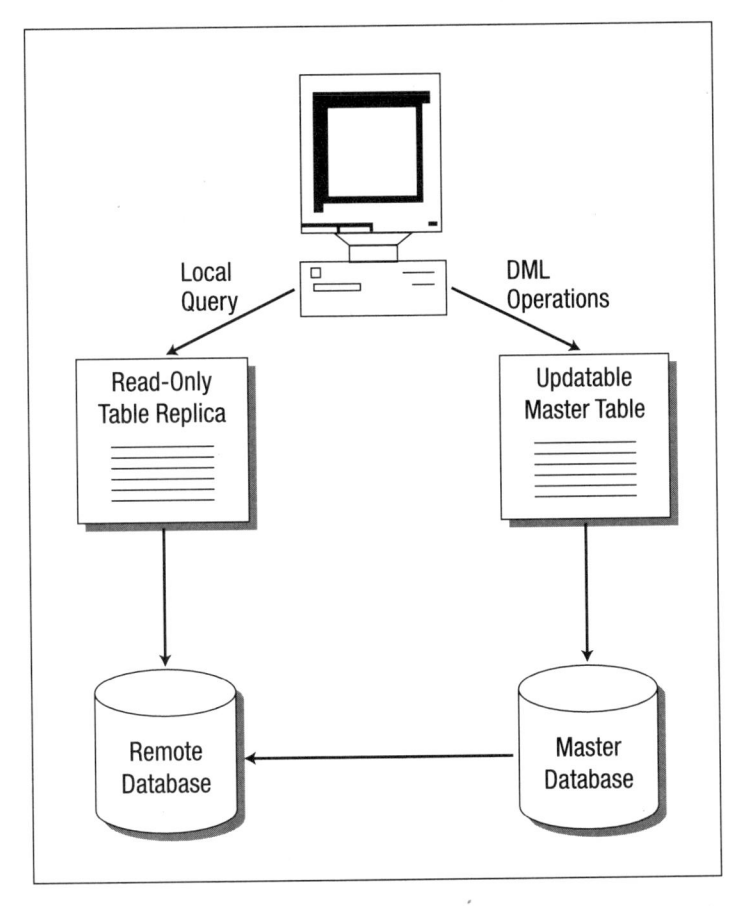

Figure 11.5
An example of basic replication.

Database replication is a preferred alternative to established database links when a number of conditions exist. First, if the replicated tables are predominantly read-only, then the database is a good candidate for replication. Second, if the objects to be replicated are accessed on a frequent basis, then they should be replicated. Replication can be considered as a strategy to help alleviate networks that are congested with SQL traffic. Response times will improve and so will database performance.

As mentioned earlier, basic snapshots are read-only copies of table data from one or more remote master tables. Oracle defines a snapshot by using a defining query that references the data in the remote master tables. Defining queries are constructed such that each row in the snapshot corresponds directly to a row or a part of a row in a single master table.

Oracle's use of basic snapshots does not include the use of the following functions or clauses in the defining query: distinct or aggregate functions, **GROUP BY**, **CONNECT BY**, multitable joins, restricted types of subqueries, and set operations. Listing 11.2 shows a sample snapshot definition.

Listing 11.2 A basic snapshot definition.

```
CREATE SNAPSHOT anstey.widgets AS
SELECT * FROM anstey.widgets@us.texas.com
```

Defining queries must always reference all the primary key columns in the master table. Snapshots from advanced replication can include restricted types of subqueries that reference multiple tables. The purpose of a subquery in a defining query for a snapshot is to filter rows from the snapshot's master table. Subquery snapshots can be used to roll up many-to-one references between parent and child tables.

By now, you have probably surmised that the data in a snapshot might not be absolutely current when compared to the data in the master table. Snapshots reflect data available at a specific point in time, namely, when the snapshot was created. In order to maintain currency between a snapshot and its master table, the snapshot must be refreshed on a regular basis. Refreshing snapshots can be conducted as batch operations, thus reducing interference with user access while providing a more current version of the data.

Complex snapshots are those that include distinct or aggregate functions, **GROUP BY** or **CONNECT BY** clauses, multitable joins, restricted types of subqueries, or set operations. Listing 11.3 shows an example of a complex snapshot definition.

Listing 11.3 A complex snapshot definition.

```
CREATE SNAPSHOT anstey.widget AS
SELECT widget_id, product_code
FROM anstey.widgets@us.texas.com a, anstey.products@us.texas.com b
WHERE a.product_id = b. product_id
SORT BY widget_id;
```

Oracle cannot perform fast refreshes of complex snapshots. The only alternative is to perform a complete refresh. This has the disadvantage that network performance is adversely affected during the complete refresh operation.

While there are definite operational advantages to using basic replication, some situations require DML activity. The second replication type to be examined—advanced, or *symmetric*, replication—allows DML activity.

Advanced (Symmetric) Replication

Advanced replication extends the capabilities found in basic replication. With advanced replication, it is possible for applications to update table snapshots. With advanced replication, snapshots throughout the distributed database system can be queried or updated. The participating Oracle Servers automatically handle the collation of DML activity against table snapshots, thereby ensuring transaction consistency and data integrity.

Updatable snapshots were first introduced in Oracle version 7.3. Snapshots are created by selecting a destination system with the **CREATE SNAPSHOT** command, whereby the snapshot is created from the master table. Oracle provides two techniques for refreshing the data: complete refresh and fast refresh. The complete refresh is generally performed by dropping and subsequently recreating the snapshot over again in order to obtain a newer picture of the data. A fast refresh refreshes only the changes that have taken place on the master table. Updatable snapshots are always simple, fast-refreshable table snapshots. Any changes made through an updatable snapshot to the snapshot's remote master table are propagated throughout the system by the Oracle engine. Advanced replication is useful in many circumstances where special requirements exist in the application system. The following examples highlight special-requirement scenarios found in real world distributed database system environments:

- *Application load distribution*—Certain applications place heavy demands on one or more nodes simultaneously. Advanced replication can be used to distribute the transaction processing. Common applications that place heavy demands on system resources are data warehousing operations.

- *Disconnected environments*—Advanced replication can be used with transaction processing applications in the field. For example, let's say a sales force equipped with laptop computers records sales transactions during the day and downloads the data from the day's activity to a centralized server via modem at night. The collected data from the sales representatives updates the primary server and allows timely updates of sales performance figures.

- *Movement of information*—Advanced replication can be used as an information transport mechanism. For example, an advanced replication system can be used to off-load data from an update-intensive operational database to a data warehouse or data mart.

- *Providing a failover site*—Advanced replication is useful to protect data in a mission-critical database. For example, an entire database can be duplicated using an advanced-replication system, and the replicated data can be stored at a secondary facility. The secondary facility or node can be used in the event of system crashes, network outages, or other unforeseen calamities. Use of a failover site reduces the risk of downtime and ensures continuous operation of a distributed database system.

Now that we've discussed the concept of data replication, let's explore some important issues to consider when deploying database applications in a distributed environment. In the next section, we'll particularly focus on using procedures.

Database Applications In A Distributed Environment

Deploying applications in a distributed database system environment requires more sophisticated techniques in deploying and executing SQL statements than in a single database configuration. As stated in previous chapters, the effective use of procedures in the form of methods will be extremely important to future implementations of object relational application systems. One practice that occurs with frequency in the distributed database system configuration is the use of remote procedure calls, or *RPCs*.

The distributed database system environment supports the use of PL/SQL packages and procedures to support applications acting on the distributed database. Developers can write applications that utilize local procedure calls against the local database while remote procedure calls (RPCs) perform work at remote databases. Remote procedures are executed by passing the necessary parameters from the local server to the remote server in the procedure call. An example of such a procedure call appears in Listing 11.4.

Listing 11.4 A sample remote procedure call.

```
BEGIN
texas_group.add_widget@sales.ansteyville.com(901);
END;
```

As with any PL/SQL program unit, errors can arise, causing handling exceptions to occur. This, of course, is a possibility whether the procedure is executed locally or remotely. Debugging procedures at remote nodes presents special challenges and are best completely tested at their native location before implementation in a distributed environment. The following exceptions can occur when a procedure is executed locally or at a remote location:

- *PL/SQL user-defined exceptions*—These are declared by using the keyword **EXCEPTION**.

- *PL/SQL predefined exceptions*—These exceptions are built using predefined keywords in the body of the exception statement, such as **NO_DATA_FOUND**.

- *SQL errors*—Common examples include ORA-00900 (invalid SQL statement) and ORA-02015 (cannot select **FOR UPDATE** from remote table).

- *Application exceptions*—Application exceptions are generated using the **RAISE_APPLICATION_ERROR()** procedure.

If you are working with local procedures, then the messages just listed can be trapped by writing an exception handler. Listing 11.5 shows an example exception handler.

Listing 11.5 An example of an exception handler.

```
DECLARE

BEGIN

EXCEPTION
   WHEN NO_DATA_FOUND THEN
/* ...specific steps to handle the exception */
END;
```

The **WHEN** clause must be given a specific exception to be handled. In Listing 11.5, the **NO_DATA_FOUND** exception is specified. Not all possible exceptions are declared. In cases where no exception is available, such as those generated with **RAISE_APPLICATION_ERROR**, you can use the **PRAGMA EXCEPTION_INIT**, as shown in Listing 11.6.

Listing 11.6   The use of **PRAGMA EXCEPTION_INIT**.

```
DECLARE
no_widgets EXCEPTION;
PRAGMA EXCEPTION_INIT(no_widgets, -20101);
BEGIN

RAISE_APPLICATION_ERROR(-20101, 'There are no widgets');

EXCEPTION
WHEN no_widgets THEN

END;
```

Exceptions in a remote procedure can be handled by an exception handler in a local procedure. The remote procedure returns an error number to the local procedure, which then handles the exception. User-defined exceptions in a remote PL/SQL procedure return an ORA-06510 to the local procedure. Because of this type of generic response from a remote procedure, distinguishing between user-defined exceptions is impossible. This points out the importance of debugging remote procedures at their local sites whenever possible. All other remote exceptions that do not involve user-defined exceptions can be handled directly by error number. Additional information on the proper use of exception handlers appears in Chapter 6.

Listing 11.4 brings up a very important point about the database application process. On numerous occasions throughout this book, it is pointed out that developers must be keenly aware of the database topography and the overall development plan. A complete understanding of the functional decomposition and the database schema is supremely important in a distributed environment. Because developers are responsible for integrating code from various nodes, there is an increased risk that some code might be needlessly duplicated, or worse, made incompatible with other modules. Developers must have a complete understanding of what each program unit does at each remote node as well as how to return the results to a calling application.

Aside from remote procedure calls, developers are also responsible for the creation of remote and distributed SQL transactions. *Remote queries* are queries that retrieve information from one or more remote tables located at the same remote node. The following line of code illustrates a remote query:

```
SELECT * FROM anstey.widgets@us.texas.com;
```

DML commands can also be executed against remote tables as illustrated in the sample update statement shown in Listing 11.7.

Listing 11.7   A sample remote update command.

```
UPDATE anstey.widgets@us.texas.com
SET color = 'green'
WHERE partno = 99;
```

While the remote query only addresses one remote node, the distributed query selects information from two or more nodes. Listing 11.8 illustrates a distributed query.

Listing 11.8   A sample distributed query.

```
SELECT widget_id, product_code
FROM widgets a, anstey.products@us.texas.com b
WHERE a.product_id = b.product_id
SORT BY widget_id;
```

Distributed updates modify data on two or more nodes. A distributed update can be executed using a procedure or trigger. Listing 11.9 shows an example of a distributed update. Each remote node is called on to execute the portion of the update that pertains to the data it is responsible for. Should any portion of the distributed update fail, then the entire distributed update program unit will fail. This tactic prevents the possibility of partial updates.

Listing 11.9   A sample distributed update.

```
BEGIN
UPDATE anstey.widgets@us.texas.com
SET color = 'green'
WHERE partno = 99;
UPDATE products
SET type = 'widget'
WHERE product_id = 99;
END;
```

As might be expected, remote and distributed transactions closely parallel the characteristics of remote and distributed queries and updates. The primary difference between the two groups is essentially quantifiable. A remote transaction contains one or more remote statements, all of which reference the same remote node. Listing 11.10 illustrates a typical remote transaction.

Listing 11.10 A remote transaction.

```
UPDATE anstey.widgets@us.texas.com
SET color = 'green'
WHERE partno = 99;
UPDATE anstey.products@us.texas.com
SET type = 'widget'
WHERE product_id = 99;
COMMIT;
```

A distributed transaction is similar to a distributed update, except that the distributed transaction includes statements that individually or as a group update data on two or more distinct nodes of a distributed database. Listing 11.11 shows a distributed transaction.

Listing 11.11 A distributed transaction.

```
UPDATE anstey.widgets@us.texas.com
SET color = 'green'
WHERE partno = 99;
UPDATE products
SET type = 'widget'
WHERE product_id = 99;
COMMIT;
```

The process of how distributed transactions are conducted is extremely important in a distributed database systems environment. Therefore, the following section presents a detailed discussion describing distributed transactions in Oracle8. Such a discussion is important to developers who must understand the implications of simultaneous data transactions.

Understanding Distributed Transactions

The mechanisms for maintaining data integrity in a distributed database environment are understandably more complex than in a single-node configuration. In a distributed database environment, many transactions from throughout the network can execute queries against the data simultaneously. In addition, many DML transactions can also be occurring against the data at the same time. To ensure that the data is properly maintained, Oracle practices a sophisticated distributed transaction management technique, called the *two-phase commit*.

Oracle8 automatically controls and monitors the commit or rollback of a distributed transaction and maintains the integrity of the databases participating in the transaction. A distributed transaction in Oracle8 is directed to the **TEMP** tablespace of the initiating node for processing. This is an important fact to make note of when considering the sizing requirements for the **TEMP** tablespace. The mechanism for performing a distributed transaction is the two-phase commit. The two-phase commit is completely transparent and requires no special actions on the part of the user or developer. The distributed transaction mechanism is broken into two phases: prepare and commit. Both phases are executed automatically whenever a **COMMIT** statement is passed to the server. The following sections describe the actions that take place during each phase.

The Prepare Phase

The prepare phase sets the initial conditions required for all nodes to accept the **COMMIT** command. All nodes to be addressed in the distributed transaction are instructed to prepare. The exception to this is the *commit point site*, which is responsible for initiating a commit or rollback, as instructed by the global coordinator. One node on a distributed database system is always designated as the commit point site by the system administrator. A commit point site is determined by assigning each node a commit point strength in the session tree. Usually, the node storing the most critical data, such as the master database, is selected as the commit point site. The global coordinator, or *initiating node*, asks the participating nodes to prepare. When all the participating nodes indicate that they are prepared, then the global coordinator gives the signal to commit the transaction. In the event that one or more nodes cannot prepare, then the transaction is rolled back.

When a node acknowledges the prepare command, it records the necessary information to conduct the transaction, even if a system failure should occur. Nodes that are prepared will not make a unilateral decision to commit or roll back the transaction. Locked data involved in a transaction involving a two-phase commit cannot be accessed until both phases have completed. Fortunately, all the required actions are performed in an extremely short period of time.

Nodes can give one of three responses when asked to prepare by the global coordinator:

- *Prepared*—A distributed transaction has modified data on the node, and the node is successfully prepared.
- *Read-only*—No data on the node has been, or can be, modified (only queried), so no prepare is necessary.
- *Abort*—The node cannot successfully prepare.

Once all nodes are successfully engaged in the prepare phase, the next phase of the distributed transaction mechanism takes place—the commit phase.

The Commit Phase

Once all nodes have successfully acknowledged the prepare phase, the next step is to commit the data in the distributed transaction. As mentioned earlier, all nodes have guaranteed to act in compliance with the instruction to either commit or roll back. The commit phase consists of two steps.

1. The global coordinator instructs all nodes to commit the transaction.
2. Oracle8 commits the local portion of the distributed transaction at each node and releases the locks. Redo logs are updated to reflect the fact that the transaction has been committed.

All of the data on the distributed system is consistent when the commit phase is complete. To reinforce the two-phase commit steps just described, I will now present an illustrative example.

A Two-Phase Commit Example

Crazy Dave's Electronic Emporium has witnessed explosive growth over the last year. The chain of stores now spans the continental United States with more than 400 outlets. The sales and inventory data for Crazy Dave's is maintained on a distributed database system located in various parts of the country. One server is dedicated to sales data while another is used for inventory data. The other servers maintain data for other areas of the company, such as human resources and payroll.

Whenever sales transactions are recorded, the associated records in inventory must be updated accordingly. The following sections describe what happens when a distributed transaction for a sales order is entered.

At one of the retail outlets, a salesperson enters, then commits a sales order via a database application, like Oracle Forms. The application sets into motion one or more SQL statements that enter the order into the **SALES** database and update the inventory in the **INVENTORY** database. The SQL statements are part of a single distributed transaction, all must succeed or fail as a unit. Data integrity is maintained in this way, preventing partial updates to closely linked data. If sales transactions were able to process without the inventory update, then there would be a product discrepancy when any form of reconciliation activity took place. Each of the SQL statements in the transaction causes the session tree to be defined. Figure 11.6 illustrates the construction of the session tree.

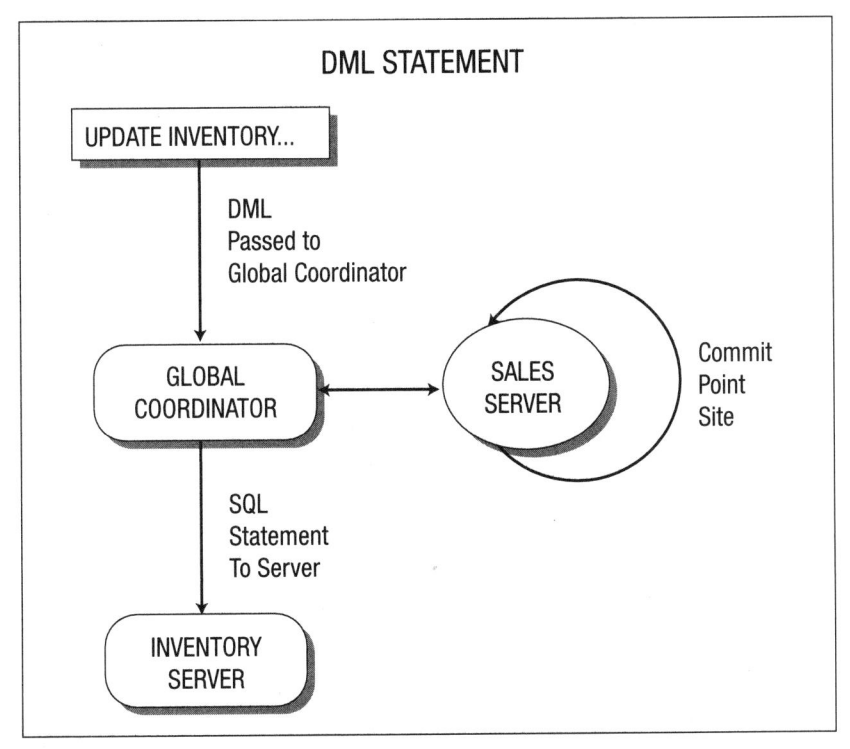

Figure 11.6
The construction of the session tree.

Because an order-entry application initiates the transaction, the **SALES** database becomes the global coordinator for the distributed transaction. The order-entry application inserts a new sales record into the **SALES** database and updates the product count in the **INVENTORY** database. Both the **SALES** and **INVENTORY** databases are servers for session-tree purposes. Additionally, the **SALES** database is considered to be a client of the **INVENTORY** database, because **SALES** performs an update against **INVENTORY**. The last two statements complete the definition of the session tree for this specific distributed transaction. In the process of constructing the session tree, each of the two nodes has acquired the necessary data locks to execute the SQL statements that reference local data. The locks will remain in place, even after the SQL statements have been executed, until the two-phase commit is complete.

Now that the transaction has been entered, the next step is to commit the data. The issuance of the **COMMIT** command initiates the two-phase commit process. The commit phase begins with the selection of a commit point site, which is determined immediately after the **COMMIT** statement is issued. Based on the information found in the session tree, the **SALES** database is determined by the global coordinator to be the commit point site.

After the commit point site has been determined, the prepare message is sent out by the global coordinator to the participating nodes. The only exception to this is the commit point site. In our Crazy Dave example, the **INVENTORY** database is the only node asked to prepare. When prompted, the **INVENTORY** node responds with one of the three possible choices named earlier in the section describing the prepare phase. If the **INVENTORY** node can guarantee that it can commit the locally dependent part of the transaction and can record the commit information in its local redo log, then the node can successfully prepare.

When the **INVENTORY** node prepares, it sends a message back to the **SALES** node. The following two actions can occur based on the response given by the **INVENTORY** node:

- If the **INVENTORY** node responds with an abort message, then the global coordinator instructs all nodes to roll back the transaction, completing the process.
- If the **INVENTORY** node responds with a prepared or a read-only message to the global coordinator, then the global coordinator asks the commit point site (the **SALES** node) to commit the transaction.

Once these steps have been completed and acknowledgement has been made back to the commit point site, the commit point site (**SALES** node) commits the transaction locally and records this fact in its local redo log. Despite the fact that the **INVENTORY** node might not have committed yet, the transaction will be committed at both nodes, even if the **INVENTORY** node is unable to commit at the present time.

The global coordinator is now informed by the commit point site that the transaction has committed. Since the commit point site and global coordinator are one in the same (in this example), no operation is required. The commit point site maintains the status of the committed transaction until the global coordinator receives confirmation from the other nodes that the transaction has been committed. Locally held resource locks for the transaction in question are released as each node commits.

Once all the participating nodes and the global coordinator have committed the transaction, the global coordinator informs the commit point site. The arrival of this message begins a series of status erasures regarding the distributed transaction. Because the transaction has been successfully committed, the nodes no longer have a requirement to maintain data on the transaction status. The final step occurs when the commit point site informs the global coordinator that it has cleared the transaction. The global coordinator finalizes the transaction by clearing the transaction status.

With an understanding of distributed transactions, you are now ready to move on to a discussion about the design issues involved with a distributed architecture.

Designing A Distributed Architecture With Oracle8

Preparing a design in Oracle8 for a distributed database system generally derives its nature from one of two approaches. The first type of approach occurs when your organization intends to integrate existing database systems (Oracle and non-Oracle) into a DDS. The second approach occurs when the implementation will be all new from the ground up and will require detailed design and analysis for each planned node. Keep in mind that, despite the greater size of implementation and variety of database configurations, the project must be driven by detailed business objectives.

Chapter 11

The primary goals of any distributed database system should be:

- Availability
- Accuracy
- Concurrency
- Recoverability

The data location is the most important factor to consider when designing a distributed database system. You must ensure that local clients have quick access to the data they use most frequently and that remote operations do not occur very often. Replication is one means of dealing with remote-node access.

When planning a distributed database system, there are several key issues that will drive the direction that the design takes, including:

- Network configuration
- Distributed database design
- Symmetric replication
- Table snapshots and snapshot logs
- Procedures, packages, and functions

Part of the database design effort involves consultation with the database administrator to ascertain the best location for the data. The analysis of a distributed database system to be built will reveal the factors that will be most important to your users. Some particular issues to consider during the analysis are:

- Number of transactions executed from each node
- Amount of data required by each node
- Performance characteristics of the network
- Reliability of the network
- Performance factors of the hardware at each node
- Impact to the DDS if a node is down (this helps determine data replication requirements)
- Referential integrity requirements between nodes

Unfortunately, declarative referential integrity across nodes is not permitted by Oracle in a distributed system. In other words, a declarative referential integrity constraint on one table cannot specify a foreign key that references a primary or unique key of a remote table. As a surrogate to referential integrity across nodes, triggers can be used to obtain a desired result. Keep in mind that using triggers to establish referential integrity across the nodes of a distributed database can limit the accessibility of not only the parent table but also the child table.

Part of the analysis and design effort must include an evaluation of the configuration options that best suit a client's needs. Selecting configuration options means determining how to organize the distributed database system. Possible configurations include business function and organization. For example, you might want to configure a DDS by region, or, perhaps, it could be organized by departments within the company (sales, marketing, and so on). Consider the structure of the company implementing the distributed database system. Are all of the data users located in one branch of the company? If so, then the DDS should be configured to address realtime demands for data while reducing remote-node access.

The integration of the object extensions in any distributed database system must wait until the release of Oracle8.1. At this time, it is unknown whether support for third-party object extensions will be supported. For example, the use of Datablades with Informix might be a plausible non-Oracle participant in a heterogeneous configuration. The use of the object extensions will adhere to the same rules of object accessibility that have been prescribed for conventional data objects in this chapter. The combination of methods with the functionality of remote procedure calls opens new possibilities in manipulating data behavior.

Collection types can be integrated into the overall DDS concept to play a role in replication. One of the great benefits of object views and tables will be their ability to create powerful aggregations that can be replicated on multiple nodes, thus increasing location independence and reducing network conflict.

Any distributed database system design incorporating the object extensions should be approached in a phased implementation. Distributed database systems require a great deal of customization from establishing connectivity between databases to synchronization of data. From a technical standpoint, two implementation plans should be used. The first should address the overall goals and requirements of the DDS. The second implementation should set forth the design for each individual node. Once the individual node plans are combined, a seamless integration with the global DDS design must be attained.

Snapshot Design Considerations

Snapshots are powerful tools at the disposal of the DBA. Despite the fact that table replication activities have become very stable and provide a means of improving performance across the distributed database, they are not maintenance-free. Numerous administrative problems are possible in the application of snapshots that increase the number of possible failure points. Errors can occur while trying to write to the **SNAPSHOT_LOG** table, or difficulties with Net8 can result in update failures leaving the DBA to resolve the discrepancies.

Creating snapshots is an iterative process that requires planning and coordination. Before implementing snapshots at any or all nodes on the distributed database system, two scripts must be run: CATSNAP.SQL and DBMSSNAP.SQL. The first script populates the Oracle data dictionary with the required system tables used to manage snapshots. The second script creates the stored procedures used in the manipulation and handling of the snapshots.

The DBA must also set several parameters in the init.ora file before snapshots can be used.

- SNAPSHOT_REFRESH_INTERVAL—This parameter sets the refresh interval in a number of minutes.

- SNAPSHOT_REFRESH_PROCESSES—This parameter defines the number of refresh processes on the instance. The minimum value is 1.

- SNAPSHOT_REFRESH_KEEP_CONNECTIONS—This parameter determines whether remote connections should be maintained after a refresh operation. The recommended setting is **FALSE**.

The next step in creating snapshots is to design each snapshot site. A snapshot site will be a selected node on the DDS. The intent of the snapshot site is to support simple read-only and updatable snapshots of table data at the master site. Snapshot site data should have a one-to-one correspondence to the replicated tables at the master site. A snapshot group can also contain other replication objects such as procedures, packages, functions, synonyms, and views.

For every snapshot site that is established, it is important to create a corresponding snapshot log at the master site. A snapshot log is necessary for every master table that supports at least one simple snapshot with fast refreshes. Refresh groups are created to support the snapshot groups and snapshots for each snapshot site. Oracle organizes and refreshes individual snapshots as part of a refresh group.

In a distributed system where there is a high degree of interaction between nodes, a single point of failure can have wide ranging affects on daily operations. To alleviate the potential problems associated with this interdependency, snapshot lookup tables can be created from the master database tables to all nodes that require frequent access. Create the snapshots of required tables on a nightly basis. The DBA should then create views on the snapshots to provide a seamless layer to the application. Under this configuration, databases can then work independently of each other. Real-time updates should be reserved for only the most critical data. Since most reference data changes on an infrequent basis, real-time updates are not justified.

Restoring a database to a previous point-in-time can become complicated. Updates performed on the master database result in changes cascading down to other remote nodes. In order to guarantee the integrity and consistency of the data, all databases should be restored to the same point in time, even if only one required the restoration. Distributed database systems whose remote nodes depend upon each other for information to include frequent data exchange, cannot be properly restored with a single instance point in time recovery without consequences.

Performance Enhancements With Oracle8

Oracle8 introduces a number of new features aimed at improving the distributed database system environment. Each new feature should be carefully evaluated by users in order to derive the maximum benefit possible. Performance improvements for use in a DDS environment include the following:

- Parallel Propagation of Deferred Transactions—This feature is intended to improve throughput performance by parallelizing a replication transaction stream while maintaining consistency and transaction dependencies.

- Internalized Replication Triggers—Oracle8's replication triggers will now improve response time performance, reduce processing overhead, and require less administration.

- Reduced Data Propagation—This feature means that Oracle8 reduces the amount of replicated data traveling over the network. One direct benefit of reduced data propagation is in the handling of large objects (LOBs). Propagation can be reduced to column updates, column conflict detection and resolution, and primary key values.

One feature of note that developers must be aware of is the upgrade of SQL*Net to the new Net8 service. Net8 is essentially a version upgrade to the familiar SQL*Net product, but Net8 is required when using Oracle8. Net8 is considered part of the program interface in network communications. Net8 uses the communication protocols or application programmatic interfaces (APIs) supported by a wide range of networks to provide a distributed database and distributed processing capability for Oracle database systems. Net8 supports communications on all major network protocols. As with SQL*Net, Net8 makes use of the tnsnames.ora file found on both the server and all client machines. The tnsnames.ora file specifies detailed protocol and domain information that Net8 must use in order to establish a connection between two machines. The tnsnames.ora file can maintain information on multiple server connections. As a DBA or developer, it is important to map the connectivity that each client and remote node will require to properly access data, snapshots, and other database objects on the distributed database system. Administration of Net8 requires many details that are specific to the protocols and operating systems in use. The reader is directed to the Net8 Administration Guide for more detailed information.

Summary

In this chapter, we covered the essential elements of distributed systems. Oracle8 offers many performance features in support of distributed database systems. We discussed specific details regarding heterogeneity, data replication, distributed transaction management, and remote SQL. Oracle8's support of the object extensions in the distributed environment lies in the future release of Oracle 8.1. In the meantime, the concepts presented in this book offer a solid foundation from which to build future object-relational distributed database systems. In Chapter 12, we'll discuss the object extensions to SQL and briefly touch on the emerging industry SQL standard.

Object Extensions To SQL And The Emerging SQL3 Standard

HIGH PERFORMANCE

CHAPTER 12

HIGH PERFORMANCE

Standards are always out-of-date. That is what makes them standards.
—Alan Bennett

Object Extensions To SQL And The Emerging SQL3 Standard

Since 1986, the American National Standards Institute (ANSI) has set and monitored the industry standard for SQL. In addition, as technological improvements have been introduced to the database community, the ANSI SQL standards have set the pace for the database community as a whole. The user community has grown accustomed to seeing new revisions to the SQL language about every three years.

The recent emergence of object-relational databases has been anxiously anticipated for a number of years as developers struggled to merge object-oriented and relational methodologies. The introduction of universal database servers, however, has brought about a curious integration of two divergent paradigms that place greater demands on the SQL language. The existing semantics and constructs found in the current SQL standard are quickly becoming inadequate to meet the needs of object types hosted by the new breed of object relational databases. The shift in database paradigms, coupled with the functional demands of working with new object types, has placed the ANSI and International Organization for Standardization (ISO) groups in a difficult position. Once accustomed to leading the industry, they now find themselves in the awkward position of trying to catch up before vendors adopt completely proprietary solutions to the SQL language.

Individual database vendors face an interesting predicament. On one hand, there is a demand for the functionality found in object relational databases like Oracle8. On the other hand, there is the standardization of language semantics so important to an open computing environment. In an effort to address functional shortcomings, database vendors are racing to create their own versions of the SQL language that will service the new object extensions. The ANSI committee has been working for at least five years on the successor to the SQL92 standard. How the various flavors of SQL will merge with the new SQL3 standard once it is released is of justifiable concern to developers who are neutral to proprietary extensions. In this chapter, we'll discuss the emerging SQL3 standard currently under development as well as the object extensions to PL/SQL found in Oracle8.

The Emerging SQL3 Standard

The SQL language is recognized as the most important data description and access standard in the relational database community. All database vendors utilize some form of SQL to access data from the database engine. At the international level, the ISO is responsible for defining the specifications and enhancements that characterize the SQL language. In the United States, ANSI controls the approval and standards mechanism. SQL is really only one of many program standards addressed by ANSI and ISO. The process used to bring a language into standardization is quite complex and time-consuming. A detailed explanation of the process is beyond the scope of this book; however, the basic steps go something like this:

1. Special committees are formed to review additions and changes to a language standard.

   Committees are comprised of members from around the world (in the case of the ISO), each representing the interests of his or her country in the adoption of the SQL standard.

   In the case of SQL, the ANSI and ISO groups decided to split the development of the SQL standard into multiple parts. Each part can be approved individually as an addendum to the existing SQL92 standard.

2. Details are compiled and voted on by committee members, and a draft document is eventually assembled.

3. Committee members comment and vote on the draft document, and the process proceeds until consensus is reached and the new standard is approved.

ANSI conducts the standardization effort for the United States. Once a standard is approved at the national level, it undergoes validation by the National Institute of Standards and Testing (NIST). NIST maintains validation tests for approved levels of standardization. The requirements and testing criteria are produced as Federal Information Processing Standards, or FIPS.

As early as 1993, ISO recognized the need to enhance the current standard (SQL92) in order to address object-oriented concepts like abstract data types and methods. The added complexity of adding object-oriented concepts into the existing relational framework has proven to be a daunting task for ISO and ANSI. The release of SQL3 has been delayed until possibly as late as 1999. Consensus has been difficult to achieve, and many skeptics doubt that a standard will be released at all. Maintaining an open standard is important for integration of heterogeneous environments, however. The lack of an accepted standard complicates system development. By 1999, most, if not all, vendors will have developed proprietary solutions to the existing SQL standard.

It is unknown at this time how closely vendors are adhering to the proposed direction of SQL3, but Oracle has made efforts to follow the direction proposed as closely as possible thus far. Until a draft standard is produced, it is impossible to anticipate all possible changes in function and semantics appearing in the final document. The importance of the SQL3 standard to the development community is addressed further in the section entitled, "Issues Affecting The New Standard." If you wish to pursue the continuing debate on the emerging SQL3 standard, you should follow Jim Melton's regular column, entitled "SQL Update," in *Database Programming And Design Magazine*.

In the next section, we'll review the different parts of the SQL3 development effort currently under way.

The SQL3 Development Effort

As mentioned in the previous section, the ISO and ANSI groups chose to split the development of the next SQL standard into several parts. Individual committees are responsible for the development of the standard under their area of influence. The SQL3 effort is broken down into the following seven parts:

- SQL/Framework
- SQL/Foundation
- SQL/CLI
- SQL/PSM

Chapter 12

- SQL/Bindings
- SQL/XA
- SQL/Temporal

A brief description of each part along with the anticipated delivery timelines is described in the following paragraphs. Figure 12.1 illustrates the decentralization of the SQL3 effort into multiple parts.

SQL/Framework

The framework portion of the SQL3 standard effort encompasses a nontechnical description of the overall emerging standard's structure. The overall document describes, in layman's terms, the complete body of SQL3, including supported functionalities and programmatic extensions that address the intent and requirements of object-model integration with the existing relational standard. One goal of the ISO is to produce a document that is upwardly compatible with the existing SQL92 standard.

A great degree of effort has been made to integrate the object-oriented data model, supported by the Object Database Management Group (ODMG) and their standard known as Object Query Language (OQL), with the relational concepts of the SQL standard. Many experts believe that a unification of the two models might eventually be possible. Jim Melton, in a paper entitled, "Accommodating SQL3 And

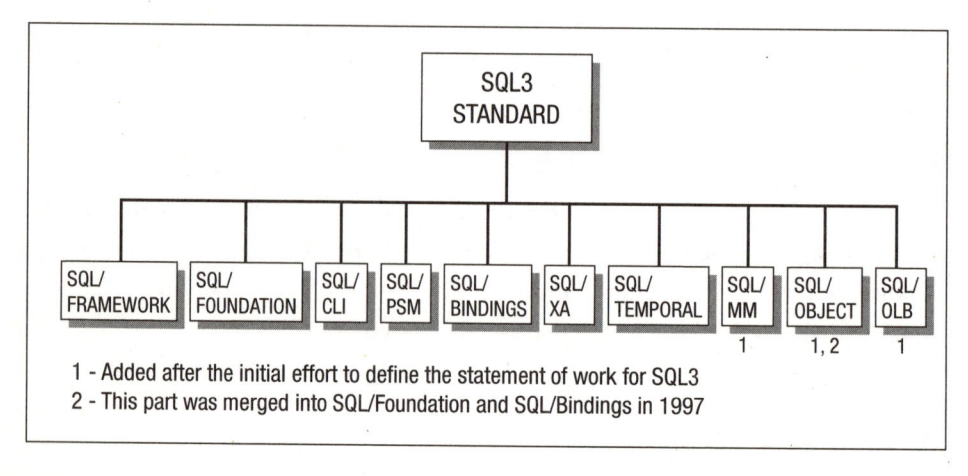

Figure 12.1
The constituent parts of the SQL3 standards development effort.

1 - Added after the initial effort to define the statement of work for SQL3
2 - This part was merged into SQL/Foundation and SQL/Bindings in 1997

ODMG," describes the principal differences between the two standards and suggests that a merger or unification might ultimately be possible.

SQL/Foundation

The foundation portion of the SQL3 standard comprises a significant part of what will emerge as the final approved document. SQL foundation describes the core components to be included in SQL3 and specifies the requirements for the following enhancements:

- The baseline capabilities defined under SQL/PSM.

- The introduction of new data types.

- Semantics and overall enhancements to triggers.

- Details supporting the use of subtables.

- The introduction of abstract data types (ADTs). Oracle refers to these constructs as user-defined data types.

- Various object-oriented capabilities.

The efforts to expand the object extensions to the SQL standard focus on type and table facilities in SQL. The current standard already defines the use of what is known as *built-in data types*. These include the familiar character and number constructs with which developers are quite familiar. SQL/Foundation also includes two new built-in data types: **BOOLEAN** and **ENUMERATED**. **BOOLEAN** data types allow three distinct values: **TRUE**, **FALSE**, and **UNKNOWN**. The UNKNOWN value will be addressed with **NULL**. The use of **NULL** to represent the UNKNOWN state is an important concept in SQL3 because applications will have the leverage to define the meaning that **NULL** assumes. For example, possible assignments to the meaning of **NULL** might be *unknown, missing, not applicable*, or *pending*. Different associations to the **NULL** value will be given different representations in the database, so the various uses can be distinguished from one another. The use of NULLs presents a point of contention with the existing ODMG data model for object-oriented databases, which do not support the use of **NULL**s. **ENUMERATED** data types permit the user to create or define a domain with values confined to a small set or range. For example, if a domain of **VEHICLES** were created consisting of **CAR**, **TRUCK**, and **MOTORCYCLE**, then a column can be defined with the **ENUMERATED** data type, which will restrict the acceptable entries to the column to those that are in the domain **VEHICLES**.

The concept of the abstract data type is also being introduced in SQL3. The SQL3 standard defines an abstract data type as one that encapsulates an attribute and its associated operations together. Operations and attributes are implemented by means of procedures termed *routines*. ADTs can also be defined as subtypes of other ADTs. A subtype inherits the structure and behavior of its supertypes. Within SQL3, the concept of multiple inheritance is supported. Multiple inheritance is an indispensable object-oriented concept expanded upon in Chapter 13. Instances of ADTs can be persistently stored in the database only by storing them in columns of tables. There is no facility in SQL3 to name individual instances of an ADT and store them persistently in the database using only that name.

SQL3 defines two kinds of ADTs: Object ADTs and Value ADTs. The main characteristic of the Object ADT is its use of an object identifier (**OID**). As you probably recall from our earlier discussions, Oracle8 introduces the use of **OIDs** for use with user-defined data types. The **OID** is an implicit part of the Object ADT, somewhat like the **ROWID** is implicitly attached to data rows in an Oracle table. Object ADTs also specify whether the ADT reference refers to an actual ADT instance (which includes its **OID**) or an **OID** of an ADT instance located elsewhere. Recall in Chapter 5 that Oracle's use of pointers or **REFs** utilize the **OID** in the same fashion. If an Object ADT is used in a type definition (for example, a column definition) or in a variable definition of a procedure or function, the ADT type reference consists of the ADT name, followed by an optional *elaboration mode*, represented by the keyword **INSTANCE**. If the definition does not specify **INSTANCE**, then the data item (column, variable value, and so forth) contains an **OID** that identifies an instance of the abstract data type. Otherwise, the item contains an actual instance of the ADT. This means that both reference and embedding semantics are supported with the Object ADT. An ADT instance that physically resides in one column of a table can be referenced from other columns of the same or different tables by storing its **OID** in those columns.

A Value ADT contains the actual instance of an object excluding the **OID**. Each instance of a Value ADT represents itself just like values of primitive data types. The use of **OIDs** described in SQL/Foundation is quite similar to the use of **OIDs** found in Oracle's implementation, described earlier in Chapter 5.

Object Extentions To SQL And The Emerging SQL3 Standard

An SQL routine for an ADT is basically a subprogram. A routine can be either a function or a procedure. A routine reads or updates components of an ADT instance or accesses any other parameter declared in its parameter list. A routine can be either an SQL routine or an external routine. An SQL routine has a body that is written completely in SQL. An external routine has an externally provided body written in some standard programming language.

Table facilities are enhanced in SQL/Foundation in a number of ways. Tables will include a new row identifier facility allowing databases to maintain a unique identifier for each row. The row identifier can be used by applications in situations requiring a unique key. Developers familiar with Oracle will recognize the similarity between this facility and Oracle's **ROWID**. A row identifier can also be used as a column value and/or foreign key. Base tables are assigned a row identifier by specifying the **WITH IDENTITY** clause in the table definition. For every table **A** for which a row identifier is defined, a new subtype—**A IDENTITY**—of the row identifier data type is also created.

Another enhancement to the table construct is the introduction of the subtable facility. A table can be declared as a subtable of one or more supertables by using the **UNDER** clause in the table definition. This new functionality implies the use of multiple inheritance. When a subtable is defined, the subtable inherits every column from its supertable(s) and can also define columns of its own. The concept of subtable is completely independent from the ADT subtype concept. Any base table which has a subtable or supertable has a row identifier implicitly defined. An example of the planned syntax for subtables appears in Listing 12.1.

Listing 12.1 The creation of subtables.

```
CREATE TABLE employee
   (name CHAR(20),
    sex  CHAR(1),
    age  INTEGER,
    spouse person IDENTITY);

CREATE TABLE manager UNDER employee
   (salary FLOAT);
```

The concept of subtables in the SQL3 standard closely resembles Oracle's implementation of nested tables. More importantly, it establishes a precedence for the use of inheritance in the object relational database. Oracle intends to support inheritance in version 8.1; however, the syntax for its use has not yet been released. Inheritance is discussed in greater detail in Chapter 13. As with Oracle8's use of nested tables and **VARRAY**s, SQL/Foundation supports collection types for sets, lists, and multisets.

A row type is a sequence of field name/data type pairs resembling a table definition. The row type provides a data type that can represent the types of rows in tables. So, complete rows can be stored in variables, passed as arguments to routines, and returned as return values from function invocations. This facility also allows columns in tables to contain row values. Listing 12.2 displays an example of row types in the **CREATE** statement for SQL3.

Listing 12.2 An example use of row types in SQL3.

```
CREATE TABLE personnel
    (name CHAR(40),
     address ROW(street CHAR(30),
                 city CHAR(20),
                 state CHAR(2),
                 zip ROW(original CHAR(5),
                         plus4 CHAR(4))));
INSERT INTO personnel
VALUES('David Anstey, ('123 Maple St.,
  'Dallas', 'TX', ('12345', '9876'))));
```

A *named row type* is one that has a name assigned to it. A named row type is effectively a user-defined data type with a nonencapsulated internal structure (consisting of its fields). They are used to specify the types of rows in table definitions.

A named row type can also be used to define a reference type. The value for a reference type, as defined for a specific row type, is a unique value that identifies a specific instance. A reference type value can be stored in one table and used as a direct reference (a *pointer*) to a specific row in another table, just as an object identifier in other object models allows one object to directly reference another object. The same reference type value can be stored in multiple rows, thus allowing the referenced row to be shared by those rows. SQL3 provides row types as literal structures. Instances of row types can be used as values in tables. A number of predefined parameterized collection types are also defined. A collection can be specified as **SET**(*<type>*), **MULTISET**(*<type>*), or **LIST**(*<type>*). In each case, the *<type>* parameter (called the *element type*) can be a predefined type, an ADT, a row type, or another collection type.

Object Extensions To SQL And The Emerging SQL3 Standard

SQL3 supports polymorphism for both ADTs and tables in subtable hierarchies. In addition, SQL3 also supports template types, allowing the specification of user-defined parameterized types.

Each component (attribute or routine) of an ADT has an encapsulation level of either **PUBLIC**, **PRIVATE**, or **PROTECTED**. **PUBLIC** components form the interface of the ADT and are visible to all authorized users of the ADT. **PRIVATE** components are totally encapsulated and are visible only within the definition of the ADT that contains them. **PROTECTED** components are partially encapsulated; they are visible within their own ADT and within the definition of all subtypes of the ADT.

SQL3 also supports encapsulation for tables to the extent that views are considered as providing encapsulation. In SQL3, a table can be defined as either a set table, a multiset table, or a list table. By default, a table is a multiset table (a table is a multiset of rows in SQL92). Set tables and list tables share all the properties of multiset tables, but they have additional properties. A set table can contain no duplicate rows, and a list table has an ordering defined for the rows. Each table has a data type, which consists of the specification of whether the table is **MULTISET**, **SET**, or **LIST**, and the row type of the table. The row type of a table is the sequence of pairs (column name, data type) specified in the table definition. These data types can include ADTs as well as built-in types.

An ADT can be defined as a subtype of one or more ADTs by defining it as **UNDER** those ADTs (multiple inheritance is supported). In this case, the ADT is referred to as a direct subtype of the ADTs specified in the **UNDER** clause, and these ADTs are direct supertypes. A type can have more than one subtype and more than one supertype. An instance of a subtype is considered an instance of all of its supertypes. An instance of a subtype can be used wherever an instance of any of its supertypes is expected. If an ADT is defined as a VALUE ADT, then its supertypes must be VALUE ADTs, and the same relationship is true for OBJECT ADTs.

SQL/Foundation includes many other features too numerous to mention here. The most significant topics have been presented, but a detailed examination of other minor functionalities is left for you to pursue independently.

SQL/CLI

The SQL/CLI part of the standards development effort deals with the specification of a programming call-level interface to SQL databases. SQL/CLI addresses the ability of third-party software to interface directly to the RDBMS. In 1992, the original document was published as the Microsoft Open Database Connectivity (ODBC) specification. The goal for SQL/CLI is to provide standards for implementation-independent call-level interface access. Additionally, the standard calls for the specification of database access via dynamic link libraries (DLLs) for client/server application tools.

SQL/PSM

The SQL/PSM part of the new SQL specifications defines the use of stored procedures to include the computational mechanisms used therein. Work on the SQL/PSM standard under SQL92 guidelines was considered complete in mid-1997, but changes to the SQL foundation portion for SQL3 make certain sections of SQL/PSM obsolete. It is anticipated that SQL/PSM will be reopened by the committee in order to update portions that made direct reference to the older SQL92 standard.

Much of what is to be specified in the SQL/PSM document will be familiar to current Oracle developers. SQL/PSM will describe procedural language extensions to the standard SQL functionality. Today, Oracle's PL/SQL provides the procedural extension to SQL*Plus. SQL/PSM specifies the use of flow-control statements and other programming that include the following functionality:

- IF statements
- Looping constructs
- Exception-handling capability
- Case statements
- Begin/end blocks
- Variable declarations
- Value assignment through the use of **SET** statements
- Program unit diagnostics via process and status information

Developers familiar with PL/SQL programming will find common ground with much of the material detailed in SQL/PSM.

SQL/Bindings

SQL/Bindings is the part of the standard that deals with dynamic SQL and embedded SQL. Dynamic SQL pertains to the syntax and use of dynamically created SQL during runtime. Embedded SQL refers to the integration of SQL constructs with other programming languages. The bindings from SQL92 were the starting point for this portion of the standard. The major points of discussion for SQL/Bindings were how mappings from object-oriented languages would be handled for SQL3. Resolution of outstanding issues for this part had to wait until the object model for SQL3 had stabilized. SQL/Object (discussed in the section entitled, "Additional SQL3 Enhancements") was presented for committee draft status in 1997. During committee discussions, it was decided to merge SQL/Object into the parts most affected by its endorsement, namely SQL/Foundation and SQL/Bindings. SQL/Bindings was also presented to the committee for draft in 1997 having resolved the object-oriented mapping issue to the satisfaction of the standards group. It is anticipated that SQL/Bindings along with SQL/Foundation will be among the first parts of the SQL3 standard to be ratified.

SQL/XA

SQL/XA is also known as the interface-specialization standard. The goal of SQL/XA is to standardize the application program interface (API) between the global transaction manager and the resource manager. The intended recipient for this standard is the distributed database system environment where heterogeneous configurations can be present. Under this SQL standard specification, the explicit input and output parameters as well as the semantics are laid out for the function calls described in the ISO document for SQL resource managers supporting the two-phase commit ("Distributed Transaction Processing").

SQL/Temporal

SQL/Temporal deals with specific time-related capabilities within SQL. Temporal SQL deals with the storage, retrieval, and manipulation of temporal data in an SQL database environment. At first blush, this might seem rather trivial, but it is not. At issue is the ability for SQL to retrieve specific data values at specific times without the use of cumbersome or complicated joins. Valid-time support is not available in the current version of SQL. Many common temporal queries found in real-world applications are either difficult to simulate in SQL or require embedding SQL in a procedural language. This is a result of SQL's lack of support for valid-time tables in its data model and query constructs. For example, if a user wishes to find the current salary of a particular employee, the fetch operation is quite simple. The task becomes far more complex if the user wishes to extract salary changes over time based on job title or advancement. The aim of the SQL/Temporal standard is to prescribe the proper semantics to add valid-time support mechanisms to the DBMS implementation. The result would be a dramatic simplification of queries, optimized storage structures, and significant performance improvements.

After the delineation of the SQL3 effort into the seven parts just described, it was determined that current technological advancements warranted the inclusion of additional sections to the overall SQL3 standard.

Additional SQL3 Enhancements

The first additional SQL3 enhancement, mentioned in the SQL/Bindings section, was SQL/Object. SQL/Object outlines the object-model features to be included in the new SQL3 standard. SQL/Object addresses support for the following object-oriented structures:

- User-defined types (ADTs, named row types, and distinct types).
- Type constructors for row types and reference types (pointer-based object navigation).
- Type constructors for collection types (sets, lists, and multisets—also referred to as aggregate objects).
- User-defined functions and procedures.
- Support for large objects (**BLOB**s and **CLOB**s).

Much of the discussion surrounding the object enhancements for SQL/Object has already been presented in the section describing SQL/Foundation. As mentioned earlier, the efforts being conducted under SQL/Object were merged into the SQL/Foundation and SQL/Bindings parts in 1997.

The second enhancement added to the SQL3 effort was SQL/MM, or SQL multimedia. Recognizing the importance of multimedia objects, such as images, sound files, video clips, and so on, the committee elected to extend the initial standards development effort in late 1993. In 1994, the SQL/MM part was added to the SQL3 effort. This new effort will specify packages of SQL abstract data type definitions using the facilities for ADT specification found under SQL/Foundation and other pertinent standard parts. SQL/MM intends to standardize class libraries for science and engineering, full-text and document processing, and methods for the management of multimedia objects, such as image, sound, animation, music, and video. The standard will also incorporate the necessary language bindings for multimedia objects. Under the ISO, there are other standardization bodies that dictate the standards for documents, images, video, and so on. The specifications produced by these other groups will be used in the SQL/MM standard. The recent popularity of the Java language encouraged the ISO to consider further standardization efforts in that direction. The next section examines the relationship of SQL3 and Java.

SQL3 And Java

The overwhelming popularity of Java as a programming language has pointed out the importance of addressing its incorporation into the SQL standard. At the time that the first SQL3 committees were formed, Java was not an active factor. In fact, in 1993, the explosive growth of the Web as a development venue had not even occurred. No one today would question the importance that the World Wide Web has on business activity and commerce. The dominance of Java as a programming language has not been lost to the ISO or ANSI. Discussion has been raised to propose that a project for the embedding of SQL into one or more object-oriented languages take place. While languages like C++ and Smalltalk might be included in this effort, the obvious focus will be on the Java language. The ISO and ANSI have approved the commencement of such an effort, but the delivery of an approved document could be a long way off. Early in 1997, the ISO approved the formation of the new project, which now constitutes another developmental part of the SQL3 standard effort. The project for developing the specifications of Java and SQL has been named SQL/OLB, or SQL/Object Language Bindings. Integration of Java programming with object relational databases is still a fairly new technology. This committee may find it possible to deliver a working standard before widespread proprietary solutions are deployed by database vendors. Despite the enormous efforts being put forth by the various committees, there are a number of issues that impact upon the chances for its success. These issues are explored next.

Issues Affecting The New Standard

In July 1997, the National Institute of Standards and Technology (NIST), an agency within the United States Department of Commerce, elected to drop independent conformance testing of the SQL standard. There has been a tremendous amount of fallout as a result of this decision. Reasons cited for discontinuing support for SQL conformance testing were budgetary in nature. It is widely recognized that NIST's contributions to the SQL standard were invaluable to the database industry. NIST's efforts provided a level of consistency by which vendors could achieve product consistency and universal compliance. The decision to withdraw came at a particularly sensitive juncture, as critical data management-related standards were (and still are) poised to start standardizing objects, multimedia data, complex data structures, and data definition standards.

The potential for fragmentation of the SQL standard is great if you consider the recent decision made by NIST. Additionally, the delay of the overall SQL3 document from ISO leaves database vendors no alternative but to pursue their own proprietary solutions to the mapping of object functionality into the SQL language. As database developers, this should raise a certain level of concern, because the environment in which we do business will most likely become far more complex.

Organizations that continue to adopt one vendor's solutions to their data management efforts will not be as dramatically impacted as organizations that seek to create heterogeneous systems utilizing products from multiple vendors. In the absence of accepted SQL standards, devising applications that can execute transactions between different database systems will become very difficult. Different vendors might not choose to adopt the same functional extensions in their proprietary versions of SQL. If like functionalities are present, they might not be semantically compatible.

In all likelihood, SQL3 will not receive the level of acceptance that SQL92 enjoys today, even after it is adopted. The SQL3 standard was originally scheduled for completion around 1996. By the time SQL3 is completed (circa 1999), many vendors will have charted their own course for object functionality in SQL. IBM, Oracle, and others are strong advocates of the SQL3 specifications, but it remains to be seen if industry giants such as these are enough to help the database community keep a unified course.

As the importance of integrating object-oriented concepts has taken hold in the relational database community, some experts have expressed their concern for extending a relational standard that has difficulty managing data more complex than an alphanumeric string. Chris Date, one of the original proponents of the relational database model, has spoken in favor of devising a new query language that deals with abstract concepts like user-defined data types and methods. The object-oriented model goes well beyond set theory and predicate logic, so it follows that the query mechanism for any database supporting the object paradigm would benefit from a language that better supports classes, aggregation, collection types, and more. Much of the argument in favor of uniting the SQL3 and OQL efforts can be derived from these concerns.

That concludes our discussion of the SQL3 standards process. Now, it is appropriate for us to examine the features and extensions included in Oracle's new version of PL/SQL in support of the object-relational character of Oracle8.

An Overview Of The New Features In PL/SQL

Oracle Corporation uses particular extensions to the ANSI SQL language. The PL/SQL product, while adopting the elements of ANSI SQL, is Oracle's procedural derivation designed to augment the use of SQL by supporting basic programming logic, like loops and branches. PL/SQL allows developers to write powerful functions and procedures in an SQL format for the purpose of accessing or modifying data. Unlike basic SQL, PL/SQL allows for the logical grouping of many SQL statements into a single program block. PL/SQL is an indigenous tool to Oracle, and very little can be accomplished, whether building or using database, without writing PL/SQL code at some point. PL/SQL also supports the use of Data Definition Language (DDL) and Data Manipulation Language (DML) commands, just as SQL*Plus does.

PL/SQL continues its long-standing reputation for tight integration with the database while providing a robust procedural-style language, based entirely on SQL. Oracle's basic philosophy behind PL/SQL is that it improves developer productivity in four ways. With the introduction of object support, the following reasons become all the more valid:

- *Ease of use*—PL/SQL reduces the need for implementing 3GL languages in order to obtain procedural capabilities.

- *Code reuse*—The ability to implement server-side stored procedures and packages encourages the concept of code reuse by allowing many applications to access the same program unit.

- *Execution safety*—This refers to the concept that errors are detected at compile time rather than runtime. This allows developers to diagnose and fix problems before deployment.

- *Encapsulation*—Oracle implements the concept of encapsulation through the use of the specification and body paradigm in PL/SQL packages. Program units and variables can be created as public or private using the package mechanism.

In order to support the object extensions now included in Oracle8, SQL and PL/SQL require a number of extensions to support user-defined data types, collection types, methods, and more. This section outlines the features and extensions added to PL/SQL in support of Oracle8. Detailed discussions on the design and use of these extensions are found in various chapters throughout this book. In this chapter, you'll find a consolidated overview, enabling you to review the new features categorically.

Categorically, the improvements to PL/SQL (and SQL*Plus, for that matter) for Oracle8 can be classified into three areas: object type support, database extensibility, and performance improvements. Our focus in this chapter will be with the first two areas of improvement. The details regarding the enhancements to performance are predominantly internal mechanics and will, therefore, be omitted from the discussion. The first of these is the focus of the next section and is of greatest interest to developers with an intent to create applications using the object extensions in Oracle8.

Object Type Support

The most exciting and pertinent enhancements to PL/SQL are those relating to object type support. The first, and perhaps most significant, improvement is in the area of user-defined object types.

Object Types

Object types created in Oracle8 represent abstractions of real-world entities. Recall that object types were discussed in greater detail in Chapter 4. Object types are considered templates for objects that internalize their structure. An object type can be defined and created once and utilized by many objects. All object types are composed of three distinct components:

- *Name*—Uniquely identifies an object.

- *Attributes*—Define the nature of the entity being modeled. Attributes are comprised of Oracle built-in data types and/or user-defined data types.

- *Methods*—Dictate the behavior of the object. Methods can be composed of PL/SQL program units stored in the database or C programs stored externally in the file system.

PL/SQL constructs support the use of objects as bind variables for use in program units and methods. Object types can be composed of several attributes to include scalar types, other objects, references to other objects (as in the use of **REFs**), or sets of objects. In order to utilize object types, Oracle has created a set of DML and DDL commands that include **CREATE TYPE, DROP TYPE, ALTER TYPE,** and **GRANT/REVOKE TYPE.** Server-side implementation of object type methods is performed via PL/SQL procedures (discussed in greater detail later in this chapter).

The **CREATE TYPE** command closely follows the syntax found in PL/SQL packages. In fact, developers who have done a fair amount of PL/SQL programming will recognize that the use of **TYPE** is used in the creation of PL/SQL tables.

Creation of object data types can be fully specified or start out as an incomplete type. Incomplete types allow developers to address other object definitions that rely on an object type that requires further analysis. Typical incomplete type statements appear like this:

```
CREATE TYPE Chemical_t;
CREATE TYPE Buyer_address_t;
```

At this point, no further definition is provided. In the next code example, the data type definition is completed:

```
CREATE TYPE Buyer_address_t AS OBJECT (
    Address_id      NUMBER,
    Buyer_name      VARCHAR2(30),
    Address_ship    Address_t
    );
```

Note from the preceding example that the attribute **Address_ship** is declared as a user-defined data type. The data type **Address_t** could be declared as follows:

```
CREATE TYPE Address_t AS OBJECT (
    Address1        VARCHAR2(30),
    Address2        VARCHAR2(30),
    Address3        VARCHAR2(30),
    City            VARCHAR2(20),
    State           VARCHAR2(2),
```

```
    Zip              NUMBER(5)
);
```

The complex structure of user-defined data types is hidden from the user by Oracle's internal mechanisms. Data from user-defined data types is stored in tables, and the database system automatically maps these constructs into the simpler relational table constructs familiar to users.

User-defined data types support the development of complex data models, because the business functions can be constructed intact while retaining the declarative behavior of the relational database. For example, assume for a moment that a company has adopted a complex pricing structure for its products. Because of the way sales are negotiated, it is possible for a single sale to have more than one discounting structure applied to it. By incorporating the pricing structure in an object table, the data and its behavior (in this case, the business rules governing the application of discounts) is stored in one convenient database object. Furthermore, by exercising this kind of abstraction in the data object, the server is able to support the client request in a single retrieval, thereby reducing transmission traffic and improving performance.

An integral part of object type support is the incorporation of methods. Let's take a look at PL/SQL's support for handling methods.

Methods

Oracle8 functionality is extended through its support of methods. A complete discussion on methods can be found in Chapter 6. Methods constitute the mating of behavior with data, and this object-oriented concept is accomplished in Oracle via PL/SQL. Objects can be defined to have three types of methods: constructor, user-defined, and comparison. Each method is described as follows:

- *Constructor method*—A function that creates a new object based on the definition stated in the object type's specification. Oracle names the new constructor method the same name as the new object type. The parameters are the same as the attributes named in the object type definition. Constructor methods are implicitly created and are, therefore, unobtrusive.

- *User-defined method*—This method is completely scripted and defined by a developer. User-defined methods allow developers the greatest flexibility in programmatic control. While a method defined in an object declaration must be a

PL/SQL program unit, the program unit can call other external procedures written in other languages, such as C. Much of the power derived from user-defined methods is in the coding. Chapter 6 covers user-defined methods in greater detail. External procedures are covered in greater detail later in this chapter, in the section entitled, "Database Extensibility."

- *Comparison method*—This method is subdivided into two groups: **MAP** and **ORDER**. **MAP** methods provide a way to compare two objects to determine a quantitative outcome. **ORDER** methods utilize internal logic to compare two objects. Order methods are well-suited to making comparisons of small groups of instances against a single value. The returned value is not quantitative but, rather, qualitative. The following code example shows the proper use and syntax for **MAP** and **ORDER** methods:

```
CREATE OR REPLACE TYPE bird (
    bird_id         NUMBER,
    speed           NUMBER
MAP MEMBER FUNCTION  find_max_speed
    RETURN INTEGER IS
      BEGIN
        RETURN  speed;
      END;
);

CREATE OR REPLACE TYPE bird (
    bird_id         NUMBER,
    speed           NUMBER
ORDER MEMBER FUNCTION  find_max_speed (speed   INTEGER)
    RETURN INTEGER IS
      BEGIN
        IF speed < SELF.speed THEN
           RETURN  -1;
        ELSIF site > SELF.site THEN
           RETURN 1;
        ELSE
           RETURN 0;
        END IF;
      END;
);
```

Now that the essential extensions to PL/SQL covering methods has been discussed, let's move on to collection types.

415

Collection Types

In PL/SQL, collection types are composed of nested tables and **VARRAY**s. A *nested table* is essentially a table within another table and linked to a specific column. Nested tables are suitable in situations involving a table in which one or more columns are to be used as parameters, variables, or ADTs. They are also ideal when the number of items is indeterminate and the storage must be directly managed. Nested tables are stored out-of-line and have a more robust access than **VARRAY**s. A nested table is stored in a store table, which must be specified in the **CREATE TABLE** command for each nested table used. In order to implement a nested table, a pointer is defined in the column that references it. If a column is so designated to reference the nested table, then all column entries for that column must contain a pointer to a nested table of the exact same definition. The clause necessary for the implementation of a nested table is as follows:

```
nested table Employee_t store as
       Employee_List_tbl;
```

The implementation of nested tables lends itself well to the modeling of hierarchical structures. Nested tables offer a simpler database design by reducing the number of actual tables created or traversed during data manipulation. Much like conventional arrays, nested tables are an ordered collection of elements of the same type. Each element has a unique index number assigned to it that determines its order in the collection. Nested tables vary from arrays in that they are unbounded. This means that the size of a nested table can change dynamically. Nested tables do not require consecutive index numbers and can, therefore, implement an indexing scheme of any integer series.

Variable arrays, or **VARRAY**s, bear a certain resemblance to PL/SQL version 1 tables. **VARRAY**s are suitable when the subset of information is static and the subset is small. **VARRAY**s function much like arrays found in most third-generation languages in that a single identifier can be associated with an entire collection. **VARRAY** constructs are stored inline. This means that the **VARRAY** structure and data are stored in the same data block as the rest of the row as a **RAW** data type. The appropriate syntax for the creation of **VARRAY**s is shown here:

```
CREATE OR REPLACE TYPE
   Markets AS varray(4) of VARCHAR2(20);
```

This **CREATE** statement demonstrates the creation of a **VARRAY** with four cells. Elements of a **VARRAY** can consist of scalars, object types, and references to object types, but they cannot include nested tables or other **VARRAY**s.

Oracle permits the use of collection types as variables in PL/SQL procedures, functions, and packages. This should be of considerable interest to developers as they now have the capability to pass nested tables and **VARRAY**s as parameters between client-side applications and server-side PL/SQL stored procedures. Nested tables and **VARRAY**s can also be used to define nonpersistent object types within PL/SQL packages for programmatic use. From the aggregated nature of collection types, let's move on to a discussion of object tables and views.

Object Tables And Views

Object tables are special tables that hold objects while providing a relational view of those objects' attributes. For details on object tables, refer to Chapter 4. Attributes in an object table are composed of top-level attributes of a particular type. Object tables use a specific syntax in their DDL statements for their creation and alteration. The following code segment illustrates a typical **CREATE** statement:

```
CREATE  TABLE address OF Address_t;
```

Note the use of the key word **OF**. This implies that the an object table of **Address_t** object is to be created. The object type **Address_t** can be comprised of numerous attributes, as described in the object types section earlier. When an object table is created, a corresponding **OID** is added for every row that can be used in **REF**, **DEREF** and **VALUE** commands.

Object views are a virtual representation of one or more object tables. As an extension of the view functionality, object views become a virtual object table of built-in and user-defined data types from relational and object tables in the database. For example, an object view can contain attributes of type **NUMBER**, **VARCHAR2**, and an assortment of user-defined data types gathered from one or more relational and object tables. Object views can even be created from other object views. The syntax for the creation of an object view is similar to that of the object table, as the following code segment indicates:

```
CREATE VIEW Employee_view OF Employee _t
   WITH OBJECT OID (Employee _id) AS
```

```
SELECT    c.Employee_id,
   c.Title,
   c.Pay_grade,
   c.Specialty_code
FROM      Employee_history c
WHERE     c.title = 'Manager';
```

The use of the **WITH OBJECT OID** specification indicates to Oracle that the object identifier corresponds to the primary key of the **Employee_history** table. Note that the specification of an object identifier in an object view must reference a unique data item, such as a unique or primary key. In addition, any column addressed in the **WITH OBJECT OID** clause must also be an attribute of the referenced object type—in this example, data type **Employee_t**. If the object view involves a join of two or more tables, then it is incumbent on the user to specify the key to be used as the unique identifier for the view.

Object views provide the ability to restrict access to data that is not appropriate to all users of the system by screening out particular columns. Because deletions are not possible from the view without the creation of an **INSTEAD OF** trigger, data is protected from accidental or intentional misuse.

Join views are not updateable, nor are single table views updateable if they have set operators or group functions. Oracle8 introduces a PL/SQL extension to produce the same result as a DML statement against a view known as the **INSTEAD OF** trigger. The **INSTEAD OF** trigger replaces the standard functionality of a DML statement. When an **INSERT**, **UPDATE**, or **DELETE** is executed against the object view, the trigger replaces the DML statement behind the scenes. The following code example illustrates the use and syntax of an **INSTEAD OF** trigger construct:

```
CREATE OR REPLACE TRIGGER
   Employee_view_insert_tr INSTEAD OF INSERT ON Employee _view

BEGIN
   INSERT INTO Employee _history VALUES (
      :NEW.Employee_id,
      :NEW.Title,
      :NEW.Pay_grade,
      :NEW.Specialty_code);
END;
```

OBJECT EXTENTIONS TO SQL AND THE EMERGING SQL3 STANDARD

With the introduction of the **INSTEAD OF** trigger construct, Oracle gives views a parallel functionality with tables. In the next section, a further discussion on the use of **REF**s is presented.

REFs

Oracle has introduced several new extensions for the manipulation of **OID**s. The **REF** command returns the **OID** of an object instance. The **OID** contains no actual data but merely "points" to the object table in question. The **REF** construct allows objects or tables to refer or point to a row object. **REF**s encapsulate the reference activity between the host and target objects.

A table can consist of top-level **REF** columns or **REF** attributes that have been embedded inside of an object type column. Tables can have a combination of **REF** columns and **REF** attributes, each referencing a different object table. The following code segment demonstrates the proper use of a **CREATE** command with embedded **REF** columns in the definition:

```
CREATE OR REPLACE TABLE Employee (
   Employee_id      NUMBER,
   Emp_bio          REF emp_info_t ,
   Photo_id         NUMBER,
   Resume_id        NUMBER,
   Emp_name         cand_name_t,
   Emp_address      address_list_t
);
```

While the **REF** command provides a means to retrieve an **OID**, the raw value is meaningless in and of itself. In order to support the extraction of the referenced value, Oracle has included the **DEREF** statement. The **DEREF** routine is used to retrieve the value or values pointed to by the **REF** statement. SQL **SELECT** statements do not support the implicit dereferencing of **REF**s within PL/SQL programs but do so in SQL*Plus. The use of **DEREF** is required to obtain the value(s) contained in the target table within a PL/SQL block. The proper syntax for the use of the **REF** and **DEREF** constructs together to retrieve a meaningful value is shown in the next code example:

```
DECLARE
   info              emp_info;
```

```
    emp_info_t    REF     emp_info;
    name                  VARCHAR2(20);
BEGIN
    SELECT DEREF (emp_info_t)
    INTO   info
    FROM   DUAL;

    name := info.emp_name;
END;
```

One final extension that has been added to support the use of **OIDs** is the **DANGLING** clause. If a **REF**ed value is deleted without removing the **REF** value in the dependent table and a subsequent operation attempts to access the missing **REF**, an error condition will occur. To avoid this problem, the **DANGLING** clause is used to check for missing or deleted **REFs**. The **DANGLING** clause can be used with the **IS** and **IS NOT** modifiers. An illustrative example of the **DANGLING** clause is shown in the next code segment:

```
UPDATE emp_info_t
   SET emp_info = NULL
 WHERE emp_info
    IS DANGLING;
```

The next topic of object support to be discussed is the extended functionality provided for large objects.

Large Objects (LOBs)

Oracle extends its support of unstructured data by introducing the large object, or **LOB**. The **LOB** construct is intended as a replacement to the previous data types—**LONG**, **RAW**, and **LONG RAW**. **LOBs** are ideally suited for the storage of unstructured multimedia data, such as images, video, and sound files. **LOB** data types store identifier values known as locators that specify where the actual **LOB** data is stored. **LOB** data is either stored out-of-line inside the database (in the case of **BLOBs**, **CLOBs**, and **NCLOBs**) or as an operating system file (in the case of **BFILEs**).

LOBs can be categorized into two types: internal and external. Internal **LOBs** are objects that are physically stored in a database. **LOBs** stored in a database are subject to the same conditions as other object types. For example, a **LOB** data type can be updated, selected, and so forth, much as a **VARCHAR2** or **NUMBER** data type. Internal **LOB**s come in the following three varieties:

- **BLOB**—This is a **LOB** whose value is composed of raw or unstructured binary data.

- **CLOB**—This **LOB** subtype contains values composed of single-byte fixed-width character data corresponding to the character set used in the database.

- **NCLOB**—This subtype contains values having fixed-width multibyte character data that corresponds to the NLS character set defined in the Oracle8 database.

Oracle has provided a new PL/SQL package intended for the manipulation of **LOB**s called **DBMS_LOB**. **DBMS_LOB** contains a set of built-in procedures and functions that can read, update, and otherwise manipulate **LOB** data. Additionally, a new Oracle Call Interface (OCI) has been added for additional programmatic texture.

Oracle8 extends the capability of including **LOB**s in a data table. In previous releases of Oracle, users were limited to a single **RAW** or **LONG RAW** column per table. In Oracle8, each table can support multiple **LOB**s and each can be of a different type. The sample code segment shown here illustrates the incorporation of multiple **LOB** types in a single table:

```
CREATE TABLE Employee_bio (
   Employee_id          NUMBER,
   Resume               BLOB,
   Photo                BFILE);
```

Because **BFILE**s reside on the operating system, it is necessary to retain storage information in order for Oracle to access it. This has led to the creation of another extension known as **DIRECTORY**. In order to link an operating system file with the attribute of type **BFILE**, it is necessary to first create a **DIRECTORY** object. The **DIRECTORY** object administers the access of **BFILE** data types in Oracle8. **DIRECTORY** serves as an alias for the physical directory on the host server where the binary file(s) are located and names the file to be used.

Now that object support in PL/SQL has been covered, the next pertinent topic to discuss is database extensibility.

Database Extensibility

Oracle achieves database extensibility through the use of external procedures. In Oracle8, the PL/SQL functionality is extended to allow the invocation of programs external to the database system. PL/SQL stored procedures can "call out" to a C program registered with the server. Keep in mind that other programs written in other languages can be subsequently invoked as long as they are callable from the C language. Figure 12.2 illustrates the architecture behind the execution of an external procedure.

In order to execute external procedures, the procedures must be registered in a library. Oracle requires a schema object, called an *alias library*, representing the DLLs to be used. This is performed with the use of the **CREATE LIBRARY** command. Users authorized to implement the DLLs must be granted **EXECUTE** privileges on the alias library. The following code segment illustrates these last two concepts:

```
CREATE LIBRARY  bird_progs AS '/home/dlls/bird.dll';

GRANT EXECUTE ON bird_progs TO anstey;
```

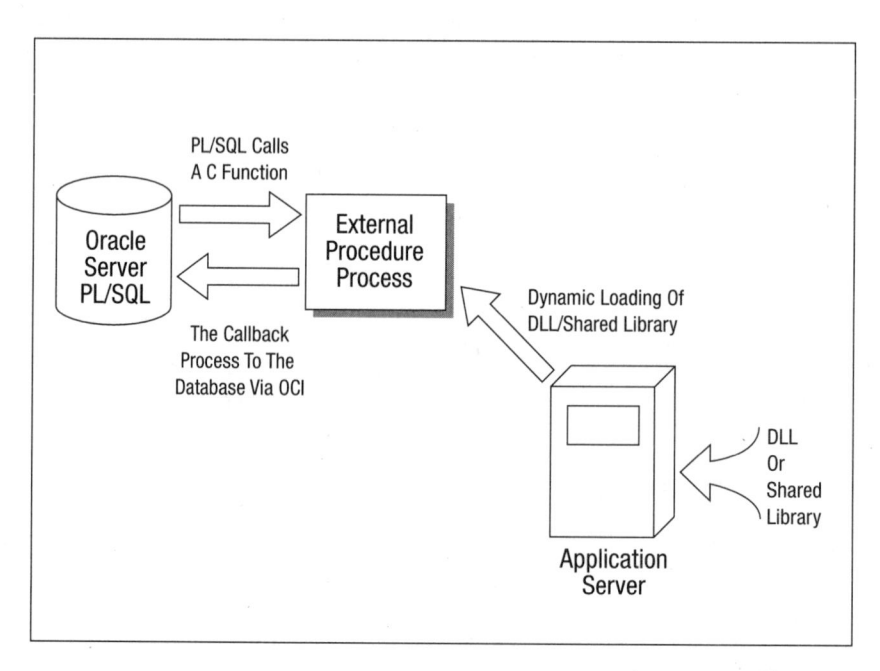

Figure 12.2
The process of implementing an external procedure.

The PL/SQL program unit used to call the external procedure must have knowledge of the whereabouts of the library. To accomplish this, the library must be *registered*. Registering is performed by creating a standalone PL/SQL package to act as a proxy for the external procedure. The syntax for registering an external procedure is as follows:

```
CREATE   FUNCTION bird (
    sc1              BINARY_INTEGER;
    sc2              BINARY_INTEGER;

RETURN   BINARY_INTEGER AS EXTERNAL
    LIBRARY          bird_progs
    NAME             "bird_speed"
    LANGUAGE         C
    CALLING STANDARD C;
```

Once the C programs are written and compiled into a shared library, they can be called dynamically from a server-side PL/SQL program. The shared library is dynamically loaded at runtime, and the program will execute in the same transaction as the calling PL/SQL program. The C program also has the capability to call back to the database via one of Oracle's server interfaces, like OCI.

Summary

The relevance of the emerging SQL3 standard to developers and the applications that they will write in the future cannot be discounted. This chapter describes the iterative process that the international standards committees must take in bringing the next incarnation of SQL to the development community. We have looked at the different parts of the emerging standard and compared and contrasted some of the features of Oracle8 against the proposed extensions for SQL3. Finally, we categorically took an overview look at the new functionalities in PL/SQL. In Chapter 13, we'll move on to a discussion of class hierarchies and inheritance. The discussion in Chapter 13 focuses on strategies for utilizing object classes in anticipation of the functionality currently slated for Oracle version 8.1.

HIGH PERFORMANCE

Planning For Class Hierarchies And Inheritance In Oracle8

CHAPTER 13

HIGH PERFORMANCE

The more things change, the more they are the same.
—Alphonse Karr

Planning For Class Hierarchies And Inheritance In Oracle8

Two of the most fundamental concepts of the object-oriented paradigm are type classes and inheritance. C++ programmers have long recognized the power and versatility of creating type classes as the mechanism to create objects. The concept of classes is absolutely indispensable in the art of object-oriented programming. From a real-world perspective, the concept of classes is a natural extension of how we view the world. From the moment we awaken each morning until the time we doze off to sleep at night, our minds constantly compare the things around us. Making comparisons is the process of considering the similarities among objects as well as contrasting the differences. Methodically organizing object properties and attributes and categorizing different variations of the same elemental object is what defining classes is all about. Up until the advent of Oracle8, relational database developers were restricted in terms of how class structure could be represented. From a logical sense, supertype and subtype constructs could be modeled, but the physical implementation always required a design compromise. For example, we could model a vehicle with all of its properties and attributes, but we would have trouble modeling those attributes that were unique to a specific type of vehicle, such as the **sail_size** attribute, which applies to sailing vehicles, but would not apply to automobile vehicles.

Of equal importance is the ability for objects to share, or inherit, similar properties. Inheritance is the essential ingredient that allows object-oriented programmers to create class hierarchies. The integration of true inheritance has never been possible before in the relational environment, because the physical representations of class objects in the relational structure lacked persistence. In addition, true type classes combine data with their associated functions and procedures (behaviors). Until the release of Oracle8, this was not possible in the relational paradigm. With the introduction of Oracle version 8.1, developers will benefit from their efforts to model real-world systems in the same fashion as object-oriented programming systems.

The focus of this chapter is the presentation of classes and inheritance in anticipation of Oracle's release of version 8.1. In the sections that follow, we'll discuss the concepts and ideas necessary to prepare analysts and developers for what lies ahead.

An Object-Oriented View Of Classes And Inheritance

The value of understanding object-oriented programming increases on a daily basis. More and more applications developed today are being built with languages like C++. The most noteworthy example, of course, is Java. Java is considered by many to be one of the only true object-oriented languages, and its impact on today's applications cannot be disputed. The Web has taken everyone by storm and many software vendors are directing their developmental attentions to it as the user interface of choice. You don't need to look any further than Oracle to see the dramatic impact that Web application development is having on our industry. For example, version 11 of Oracle Applications (Financials, Manufacturing, and so on) will be delivered for Web access first and may not be released as the client/server product that we have come to know.

At the same time that this exciting revolution is taking place in system applications, the need to access data has grown proportionately (if not more so). Before the introduction of the object relational database, programmers were required to handcraft front-end applications in a way that accommodated the non-persistent, declarative structure of relational tables. The object extensions in Oracle8, including classes and inheritance for version 8.1, will alleviate the developmental imbalance. Data structures can now be designed and created to more closely match the capabilities and characteristics of the object-oriented programming languages so much in vogue in today's applications.

As you might recall, classes and inheritance are introduced in Chapter 1. Our discussion for this chapter begins by revisiting these important concepts. It is important that our discussion of classes and inheritance focuses on a purely object-oriented perspective. This will give you a greater appreciation for the theory behind both classes and inheritance. In addition, a lively discussion from the perspective of the C++ language will aid in presenting the material in the sections that follow.

Classes Revisited

Recall that a class is a data type that consists of data members and their functions. If you are familiar with the C language, you might recognize the similarity of *structures* and classes. In a sense, classes are structures, except that classes also incorporate methods and they possess the ability to hide one or more members from programs outside of the class. In other words, classes include the ability to encapsulate various data members.

The data elements, constructor and destructor functions, and member functions (all participating elements as methods) are known as *class members*. When we say that a class has the ability to hide various members (this includes the method members), then we are referring to class member visibility. Recall from Chapter 3 that the concept of visibility is one of the basic core elements that defined the UML's meta-model. Here again, visibility for object-oriented languages dictates what sort of access the mechanisms outside of the class will have to that class's constituent elements. Figure 13.1 illustrates a class with public and private members.

In C++, visibility is determined by one of two access specifiers, named *public* and *private*. Private members in a class can only be accessed by member functions (methods) in that class. Public members can be accessed by the class's member functions as

```
CLASS WIDGET {
   // PRIVATE FUNCTIONS
   INT GET_PART

   // PUBLIC FUNCTIONS
   VOID FIND_PART(INT NUM)
   INT ADD_PART
```

Private Functions And Variables Are Declared Immediately After The Class Declaration

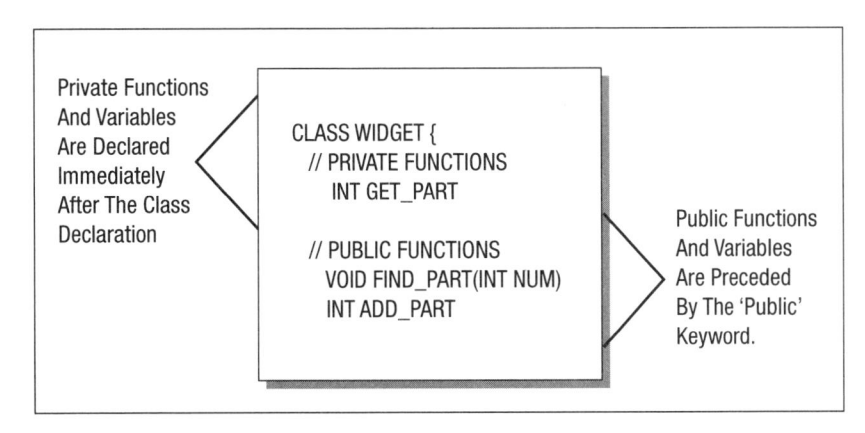

Public Functions And Variables Are Preceded By The 'Public' Keyword.

Figure 13.1
An object-oriented class with public and private members.

well as other functions outside of the class. As with any programming language, there are exceptions. For example, *friend functions* are those that exist outside of the defined class but are given special permission to access private members within the class in question.

In object-oriented methodology, the starting point for the class structure is the base class. A base class equates to what is often termed a *generalization*. The base class contains the high-level properties and supporting functions that are common to all object classes. In object-oriented terms, the class is a logical abstraction that describes the characteristics that an object type will assume. Classes do not contain or represent actual instances of objects. Instead, objects take on the properties of classes under which they have been defined. As a basis of discussion, let's return to the fiber-optic network example used in Chapter 8. Recall that a host of various lightwave devices were used to construct a working fiber-optic system. We could create a base class for the devices with the attributes and functions illustrated in Figure 13.2.

Note from the illustration in Figure 13.2 that the class members are very general. This is because the class members must characterize all fiber-optic system elements. If the devices in our fiber-optic system were all the same and performed identical functions, we might be content to create only one class. Obviously, this is not the case. While each individual device falls under the generic description of the base class, each has its own distinctive properties and functions. In order to address the distinctive nature of specific devices under the base class, it is necessary to define

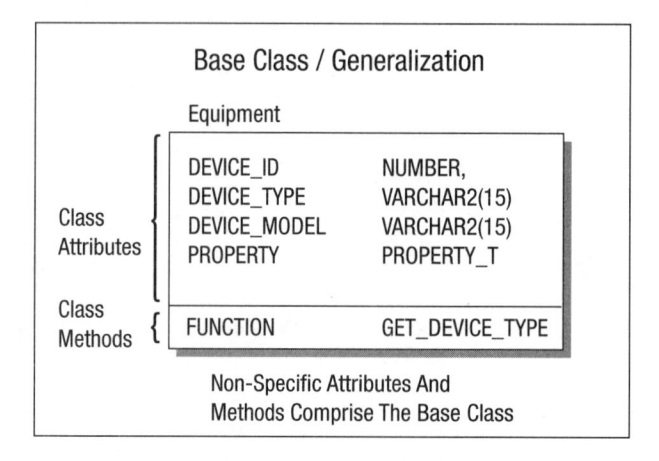

Figure 13.2
An example base class using the fiber-optic network model.

specializations or derived classes. Notice how the process of creating derived classes closely resembles the activity that takes place in a functional decomposition. The creation of this class tree, or hierarchy, is the first step in establishing a pattern of inheritance.

Inheritance

In order to practice the concept of inheritance, we must establish one or more *derived* classes to our base class. The principle behind the derived class is that a specific implementation of the base class is being defined. For example, in the previous section, we created a base class for the fiber-optic system equipment. If we were to specify a subclass called LRE to describe all varieties of light retransmission devices, then this would constitute a derived class. The derived class maintains all attributes and functions of the base class, but it can also specify additional properties and functions of its own. The relationship between the base class and the newly created derived class represents a *generalization-specialization structure* (*gen-spec structure*, for short). A generalization-specialization structure must pass a reasonableness test in order to be valid. If the generic statement holds true that *specialization* is a kind of *generalization*, then the gen-spec structure is valid.

There are several good reasons for creating class hierarchies in object-oriented programming:

- It might be possible that the source code for the base class is not accessible for other developers to modify. Often in a C++ development environment, the source code from supporting member functions to the base class or third-party class libraries is not available and cannot be changed.

- The base class is most likely used by numerous modules in the program code. Changes to the base class would require developers to change existing routines and programs. If the scope of the programming effort is large, all the affected modules might not be found, causing errors to arise.

- Building a class hierarchy allows the programmer to reap the full benefits of the object-oriented paradigm. Creating class hierarchies establishes a set of general purpose classes with self-modifying behavior driven by the derived classes that will use them. Class hierarchies support a technique known as a *virtual function mechanism*. This technique is described later in the section entitled, "Multiple Inheritance."

- In object-oriented programming, it's possible that the base class is an abstract class, meaning its sole purpose is to provide a generic shell or framework from which derived classes add their own specific implementation details.

The process of creating derived classes requires special consideration as to why the class is being created and what the class is for. Class hierarchies can become insidiously complex if good analysis and design are not performed. This is because there is an inherent desire to specialize every deviation from the base class, even when there are other means to address the design problem. For example, a properly analyzed derived class can often address more than one specialized object. If a derived class cannot be constructed to meet the needs of two or more object types, it is sometimes possible to create a derived class through multiple inheritance. Multiple inheritance is described in detail in the next section.

Oftentimes, the problem within a class hierarchy is not with the proliferation of derived classes so much as it is with the fact that the derived classes are badly defined. The scope of the application system must be taken into consideration, assuming the entire time that there might be "sibling" classes or functions that need to be addressed. Carefully review related business functions to find similar data types that can be combined. To illustrate this point, recall from the fiber-optic network model that both the **SITE** and **SYSTEM** entities possessed a user-defined data type that described the equipment used. Through singular evaluation of each entity in the functional decomposition process, we might arrive at the properties describing **EQUIPMENT** from two different perspectives. We know from our previous analysis of this modeling problem that the classification of **EQUIPMENT** is quite straightforward. A single equipment class addresses the attribute requirements for **SITE** and **SYSTEM**. In a team development environment where hundreds of entities, attributes, and methods are being designed, the functional overlap will not be so obvious.

When a derived class inherits the properties of the base class, it does so in the same visibility scheme that was defined for the base class. For example, if the base class includes both public and private members, then those members will retain their same visibility status in the derived class. Figure 13.3 illustrates this basic principle of inheritance.

There is an additional aspect of member visibility that plays a role in inheritance. C++ includes a visibility property called *protected*. Recall earlier that private members are not accessible to any other class outside of the one that declares them to

Planning For Class Hierarchies And Inheritance In Oracle8

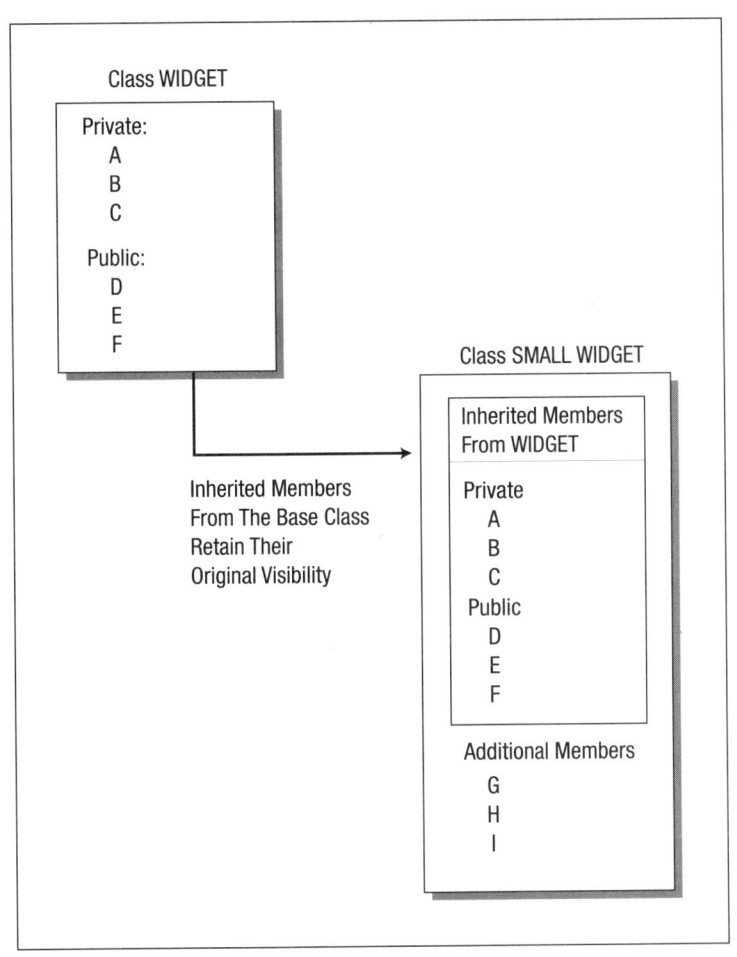

Figure 13.3
The visibility of inherited class members.

include derived classes. With protected visibility, derived classes have public access to base class members defined under protected mode. Any class that is not one of the derived classes of the base class does not have access to protected members. This is one way that C++ exercises the concept of encapsulation.

Because derived classes inherit all class members from the base class, including methods, the question of overriding inherited values certainly pops up. A derived class can override the standard characteristics and/or functionality of a base class member function as long as that member is public. In order to do so, the derived class function must share the same name and parameter list types. To illustrate this point, Figure 13.4 shows the concept of overriding inherited functions.

Class member overriding is an important tool in adding specificity to a derived class when the base class function is too broad in scope. For example, assume that there is a base class function called **maximize**. In the base class, **maximize** might be used to

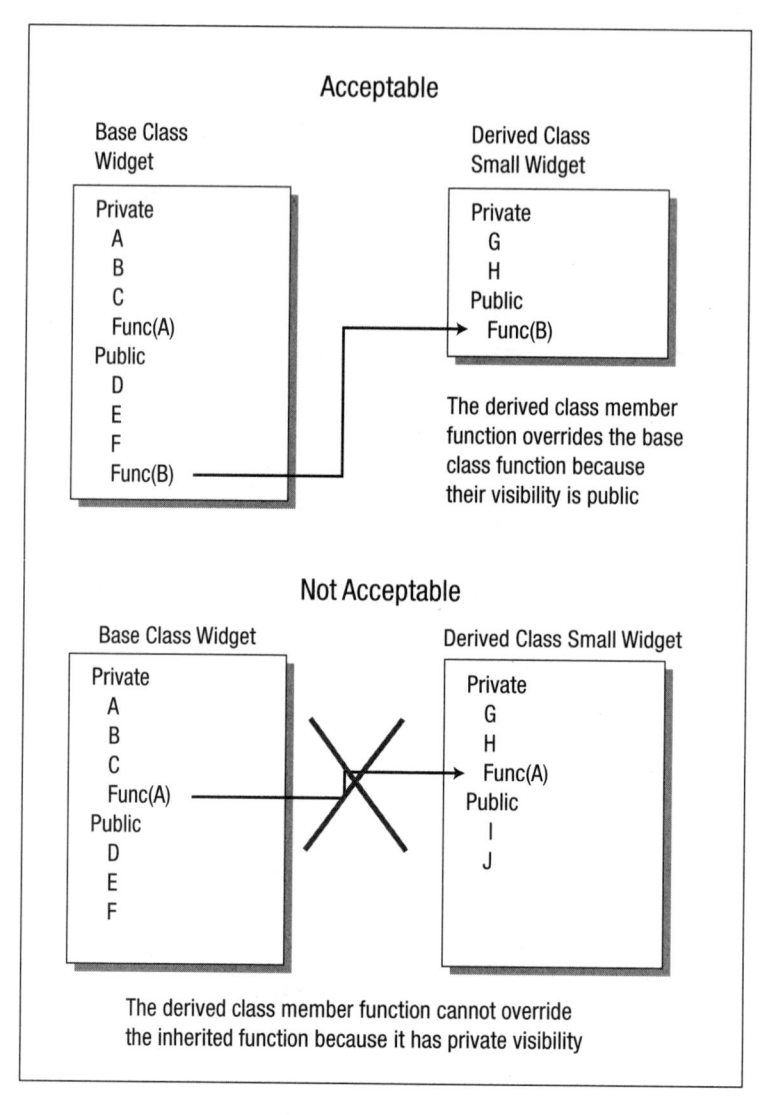

Figure 13.4
A derived class function overriding an inherited base class member function.

find the greatest score on a math exam. The derived class version of **maximize** could be used to find the most frequently missed question on the same math exam.

Designing a class hierarchy for object-oriented languages undergoes an analysis process similar to the process relational database developers are already accustomed to. During the design phase of a relational database project, functional decomposition is performed on business objectives to formulate lower-level processes and data interactions. Analysis of potential class hierarchies in object-oriented programming undergoes a rigorous process of decomposition, as well. The following steps iterate the proper actions in performing class analysis:

1. *Assess the business requirements carefully to avoid derived class overkill.* It is easy for project requirements added after the design has begun to perpetuate an endless generation of additional derived classes. Once this happens, confusion and duplicity set in, not to mention the difficulty in mapping the logical design to a physical implementation.

2. *Utilize a "compare and contrast" technique in creating derived classes.* In many respects, this technique resembles the actions described when creating a method topology, as depicted in Chapter 6. Recall that building a method topology requires the decomposition of each method into atomic functions. Processes that perform the same functionality are tagged, and later, during the build phase, redundancies are eliminated. The basic idea behind the compare and contrast technique is that derived classes are examined for similar structure (class members, including member functions). Similar derived classes are also scrutinized for differences. Oftentimes, minor differences can be reconciled, and a single class can be generated where there might have otherwise been two or more.

3. *Establish standards or conventions that derived classes must follow.* This rule addresses more of the "how" than the "what" aspect of class design. In simple terms, a base class should be used to describe or define one or more conventions that will be used by all derived classes. For example, assume that your application will perform a reasonable amount of date/time manipulation. One likely convention that might be established is that date-comparison processes will calculate and compare to the nearest hour. Another convention might be that all data returns of type date will be in a specific format, such as DD-MON-YYYY.

So far, the discussion on inheritance has focused on the basic concepts and mechanisms. In the next section, I will introduce multiple inheritance—the aspect of inheritance that adds real depth to the design of class hierarchies.

Multiple Inheritance

Multiple inheritance is a natural extension of the class hierarchy concept. In multiple inheritance, a derived class can have multiple base classes. Additionally, the derived class can itself become a base class for further derivations. The latter case is sometimes termed a *multifaceted class hierarchy*. The execution of multiple inheritance can appear deceptively simple, yet there are a number of pitfalls that adversely impact on physical implementation and on component reuse. Figure 13.5 illustrates the two types of multiple inheritance.

At this point, you might recognize that the multifaceted class hierarchy resembles the pattern established when we created a method topology in Chapter 6. The multifaceted class hierarchy is the more common variation used in establishing multiple inheritance. Because class member functions are inherited down the hierarchy, you might wonder how C++ performs member function resolution when derived classes have implemented overriding methods. Depending on the function type, execution might proceed from the base class to the derived class. In other cases, the direction is the opposite. Earlier in this chapter, constructor and destructor functions are listed as integral components of a class. Constructor functions essentially perform initialization for the object using the class in question. Destructor functions basically destroy or reset an object, based on the class in question. In a configuration where at least two or more classes (to include multifaceted class hierarchies) are linked via inheritance, the constructor is executed from the base class first then to the lower derived class or classes. The behavior for a destructor operates in the opposite direction, starting first at the lowest derived class and working upward to the base class.

As stated earlier, multiple inheritance can present certain problems in its implementation, particularly in a configuration where a derived class has multiple base classes. Look closely at the class hierarchy found in Figure 13.6. This illustration points out one of the more common problems that can arise in a multiple inheritance scheme.

In the class hierarchy shown in Figure 13.6, a base class is inherited by two derived classes. In turn, a new derived class is created that inherits the characteristics of the first two derived classes. The ambiguity arises at compile time when the C++ language

Multiple Inheritance

Type I

Type II (Multifaceted Class Hierarchy)

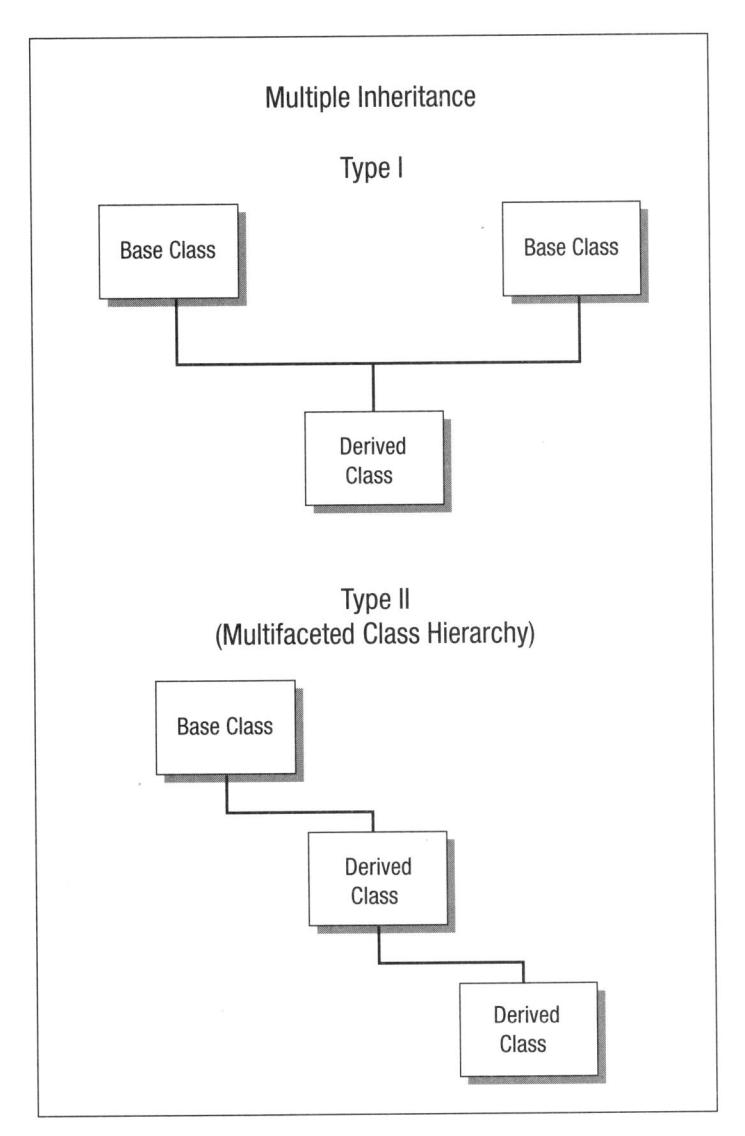

Figure 13.5
The two types of multiple inheritance.

tries to resolve the inheritance of the base class by the third derived class twice. In the C++ language, such ambiguities are resolved through the use of what is known as a *virtual class*. In order to prevent a doubling of inheritance demonstrated in this example, the base class is addressed with the keyword *virtual* in the specifier line for the declaration of the derived class. By declaring a base class as virtual, you are telling

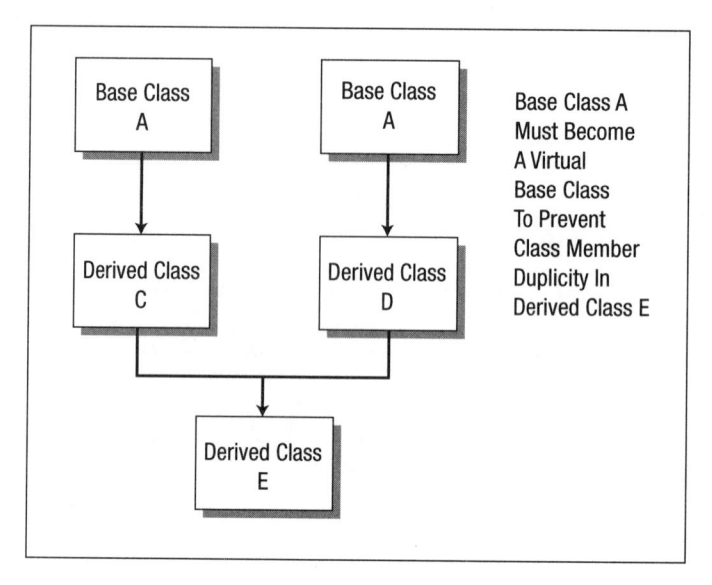

Figure 13.6
Multiple inheritance with virtual base classes.

the compiler that only one instance of the base class is required, regardless of its source. From a logical sense, there is no difference between a base class and a virtual class. It would certainly be tempting to use the virtual keyword whenever possible in a multiple inheritance configuration simply to avoid any possibility of inheritance ambiguity. The virtual keyword, however, cannot be used indiscriminately, because there are rules that govern its use. If you are interested in pursuing this topic further, refer to a good C++ language reference text. Keep in mind that the behavior of base class duplicity affects all class members, whether they are data types or functions (methods).

The introduction to classes and inheritance that we have just covered provides a good foundation on which to build on in the area that is of main concern—the design and creation of classes and the use of inheritance in the next version of Oracle8. This is the focus in the next section.

Oracle8 And Type Classes

The implementation of class hierarchies and inheritance in Oracle8 will bear a significant resemblance to the object-oriented approach. Even with the enhancements slated for version 8.1 of Oracle8, there remain certain fundamental gaps in how the object relational database can exercise these valuable concepts. Keep in mind that Oracle Corporation will incrementally extend the coverage for object-oriented functionality with each subsequent release. While version 8.1 introduces support for inheritance, only a subset of the full capabilities will be available in the first release. For example, multiple inheritance will not be supported initially. There are many in the database modeling community that do not feel that multiple inheritance is needed. It should be noted, however, that it is viewed with enough importance by the international community to have been included in the new SQL3 specification. In the sections that follow, I address the implementation of classes in the object relational scheme. There are two aspects of class structure and inheritance that apply to the design of Oracle8 systems. The first is the application of classes and inheritance to data types. The second involves the design of tables. In Chapter 6, we discussed how a topology of methods could be analyzed, designed, and built. The topic of dealing with methods in a class hierarchy is the subject of discussion later in this chapter. Before dealing with the ways in which classes can be mapped to an Oracle8 application, let's first discuss how classes impact the design.

Oracle Implementation Of Classes

In our earlier discussion of classes, I described the base class or generalization to be the simplistic property set for an object type. In object-relational terms, the base class is synonymous with the supertype. At this point, it is useful to emphasize that the concepts of classes and inheritance are applicable to both user-defined data types and table constructs. Each is addressed separately in this chapter, because there are particular nuances that are singular to the application and/or implementation of class structure and inheritance to each level of database object. Recall from Chapter 12 that the new SQL3 standard will support inheritance at the data type and table levels. Interestingly enough, the new SQL3 standard provides support for multiple inheritance at both the data type and table level.

At the time of this writing, the specific syntactical arguments needed to construct classes in Oracle8 were not available. There are two interesting approaches as to how class construction might be accomplished. In all likelihood, the grammar used in creating user-defined data types and object tables will form the basis for creating generalization-specialization classes in Oracle8. For example, the current syntax for creating a typical user-defined data type appears in Listing 13.1.

Listing 13.1 The syntax for creating a user-defined data type.

```
CREATE TYPE Address_t AS OBJECT (
    Address1        VARCHAR2(30),
    Address2        VARCHAR2(30),
    Address3        VARCHAR2(30),
    City            VARCHAR2(20),
    State           VARCHAR2(2),
    Zip             NUMBER(5)
);
```

The SQL3 standard is quite specific in its treatment of user-defined data types and the implementation of inheritance. Subtyping of data types is handled through the use of the **UNDER** clause. The **UNDER** clause indicates in the create script that the subtype is subordinate, or *under*, the supertype. Listing 13.2 illustrates the use of the **UNDER** clause from SQL3 modified to match existing Oracle8 syntax.

Listing 13.2 Anticipated syntax for the creation of a data subtype.

```
CREATE TYPE employee_t AS OBJECT
    (employee_id        NUMBER,
    last_name           VARCHAR2(30,
    first_name          VARCHAR2(20),
    pay_grade           VARCHAR2(10),
    dept_id             NUMBER);

CREATE TYPE manager_t AS OBJECT
    UNDER employee_t
    (dept_level         VARCHAR2(20),
```

In the example shown in Listing 13.2, a subtype **manager_t** is created from the user-defined data type **employee_t**. Note from the example that the **manager_t** subtype includes an additional attribute. If we were to examine the final attribute list for **manager_t**, we would find that it consists of the following data members:

```
employee_id
last_name
first_name
pay_grade
dept_id
dept_level
```

Any methods associated with the **employee_t** data type would be inherited by **manager_t**.

Another possible approach to the syntax of creating classes in Oracle8 might involve the use of Java. The Java language is recognized to be at the forefront of current application technology. Oracle corporation has committed to the full integration of the Java language in their entire range of database products. The JSQL initiative will provide the Java language with compile-time access to Oracle's database schema. JSQL is intended to be a seamless integration of Java and SQL. Oracle is producing JSQL as a continuing initiative of language integration with SQL. Similar efforts have included Pro*C, Pro*COBOL, and Pro*FORTRAN to name a few. JSQL is an extension of the capabilities first put forward in the JDBC initiative. JDBC set out to provide a simple call-level library interface for use with Oracle's database.

Java bears some similarity to C++ in terms of how classes are implemented. Java differs from the C++ class structure convention in that a single-object file serves as the interface definition for a type. Java also utilizes similar syntactical conventions as Oracle in that Java objects and internal methods are accessed via dot notation. Java does not require the manipulation of pointers in order to execute object referencing as does C and C++. One major difference between Java and Oracle8 is that objects are not persistent in Java while Oracle8 allows the flexibility to enable persistence. Java and Oracle8 support forward referencing thus eliminating the need for header constructs like those used in C and C++.

The use of Java or JSQL for the construction of classes will probably not address all the functional requirements for an indigenous language in Oracle8. PL/SQL will continue to be a product mainstay, and, therefore, developers should expect to see SQL3-compliant syntax to appear in Oracle's SQL tools. Chapter 14 presents additional discussion on Oracle's JSQL initiative.

Now that some syntactical speculation has been laid out for the support of classes in version 8.1, let's proceed to the topic of building data type classes in Oracle8. For demonstrative purposes, SQL3 conventions are integrated into the code examples describing the creation of class constructs. Let's first consider the execution of classes and inheritance for user-defined data types.

Building User-Defined Data Type Classes

Developers will find that the implementation of class structure and inheritance is quite similar to the creation of types, as discussed in Chapter 4. The idea behind developing a data type hierarchy is that basic core components are developed with the intent that they will form simple, easy-to-use representations of objects that would normally be complex or tedious to use. When we first discussed the data type hierarchy concept in Chapter 4, we did so without making presumptions about extended functionality, such as with inheritance. In Chapter 4, the hierarchy concept built from the atomic data level and gradually moved up the chain to larger data constructs, such as tables and views. The intent was to reduce as much of the leaf-level attribute referencing as possible and incorporate attributes into self-contained data types suitable for reuse in many parts of an application. It's understood that well-documented libraries of user-defined data types reduce the complexity of business objects. Simple, easy-to-access data objects, tables, and views replace circuitous SQL statements needed to ferret out the appropriate aggregations.

With the ability to exercise inheritance, the process of building data type hierarchies reaches maturity. The start of the class development effort takes place during the design phase. The reason for this is that attributes are generally not addressed until that phase of the life cycle. Contrast this practice with that of building classes of object tables, which begins during the analysis phase and carries on into the design.

In certain respects, designing and building data type classes proceeds in the reverse direction as the process proposed in Chapter 4. The opportunity to initially target data hierarchy prospects is during the detailed phase of creating the data flow diagram. Recall in Chapter 9 that we noted that new modeling diagrams can be used to embellish or supplant the conventional data flow diagram. The most effective modeling diagrams for this purpose are the use case and collaboration. These diagram types are well-suited to mapping natural data aggregations, complex data constructs, and unusual business criteria that manifest themselves on the data stores and intended entities.

For illustrative purposes, let's return to Chapter 8's fiber-optic system model. Because all fiber-optic equipment has certain functional properties like transmitted wavelength, bitrate, and so on, we might want to create a data type base class that describes the general properties of any piece of equipment. Listing 13.3 shows the atomic-level attributes that comprise the new user-defined data type base class.

Listing 13.3 The user-defined data type base class for equipment properties.

```
CREATE TYPE property_t AS OBJECT
    (property_id          NUMBER,
```

```
      property_type         VARCHAR2(15),
      value                 VARCHAR2(10)
MEMBER FUNCTION
   f_add_property
   RETURN INTEGER IS
      BEGIN
         RETURN  added_yn;
      END;
);
```

The example in Listing 13.3 shows the **property_t** type with its constituent attributes. Note that a method has also been defined intended for use when properties are added to various devices. This base class is adequate for most general applications of properties to equipment, because it addresses all the basic facts about device properties.

Let's now assume that a derived data type is needed to address the specific characteristics of equipment properties that pertain to light transmission. Recall from the discussion in Chapter 8 that light signals traveling along an optic fiber will diminish with distance and must therefore be amplified. The derived class for equipment properties must address the aspect of range. The resulting derived data type class would be created using the code shown in Listing 13.4.

Listing 13.4 The derived data type class for equipment properties.

```
CREATE TYPE wave_property_t AS OBJECT
   UNDER property_t
   (range                NUMBER,
    dispersion_level     NUMBER
MEMBER FUNCTION
   f_calc_disp_rate
   RETURN INTEGER IS
      BEGIN
         RETURN   rate;
      END;
);
```

Under this definition, **wave_property_t** inherits all the class members from **property_t** to include the method **f_add_property**. Assume for a moment that the declaration for the new derived data type class included a method by the same name and parameter list as that occurring in the base class. If this had been the case, the derived class method would override the base class method in execution. Had the methods contained different parameter lists, they would have constituted overloaded procedures.

In an application manipulating a data type defined under the derived class, the method under the derived class would be attempted first, followed by the method under the base class if the functions were overloaded. This practice once again demonstrates the use of polymorphism in Oracle8 methods.

As you can see, class structure will offer many design and implementation benefits in developing object relational application systems in Oracle8. Creating data type classes is only the first step. The use of classes and inheritance is also pertinent to the design and construction of object tables.

Building Table Classes

The emerging SQL3 standard clearly defines the support for classes in the form of supertype and subtype constructs. What was applicable to data types is also pertinent to object tables. The design of entities and tables commences in the analysis phase. Recall that the logical entity definition precedes the physical construction of tables. In the object-relational database paradigm, the supertype (base class) is the abstraction of a general set of properties or attributes and normally has no instances of data associated with it. However, it is possible for a base class to be a table containing instances or rows of data. The difference lies in the way object types and table declarations are carried out. It is possible to create an object type for the purposes of establishing a subsequent table definition, as the following lines of code demonstrate:

```
CREATE TYPE Address_t AS OBJECT (
    Address_id      NUMBER;
    Address1        VARCHAR2(30),
    Address2        VARCHAR2(30),
    Address3        VARCHAR2(30),
    City            VARCHAR2(20),
    State           VARCHAR2(2),
    Zip             NUMBER(5)
);

CREATE TABLE address OF Address_t;
```

In this scenario, the type **Address_t** has no instances of data, but the associated object table **address** does. Alternatively, a declared table (with data) can be used as a base class for subsequent creation of subtables or derived classes.

In the previous section, we covered how user-defined data type classes can be constructed. The product of that effort will be integrated into the formulation of object table classes. In the initial stages of design, table-level base classes may be incomplete because further analysis of the business requirements is necessary before the attributes associated with the table can be fully developed. In the first stages of the functional decomposition, detailed attributes are not identified. It is only as the functional decomposition progresses and further collaboration diagrams are produced that a complete picture of a table's characteristics can be fully realized.

Returning to the fiber-optic system model once again, we have created a base class for the object table level to represent the general aspects of fiber-optic equipment. Listing 13.5 shows the code used to create the base class.

Listing 13.5 The equipment object table base class.

```
CREATE TYPE equipment_t AS OBJECT (
    Device_id       NUMBER,
    Device_type     VARCHAR2(15),
    Device_model    VARCHAR2(15),
    Property        property_t
    MAP MEMBER FUNCTION get_device_type
);

CREATE TABLE equipment OF equipment_t;
```

The type **equipment_t** carries no data instances. Note that **equipment_t** implements the user-defined data type **property_t** described earlier. At this point, we are at liberty to create derived object table classes or additional object type classes. For example, if we wish to extend the functionality of **equipment_t** to address a specific type of equipment, say, a cable, we can define a derived object type from **equipment_t**, as shown in Listing 13.6.

Listing 13.6 A derived class of **equipment_t**.

```
CREATE TYPE cable_t AS OBJECT
  UNDER equipment_t (
    length          NUMBER
    MEMBER FUNCTION get_dark_fiber
);
```

This example merely reiterates what we are able to do with objects. If we wish to create a sub-table based on equipment from the earlier example, the code would look something like that shown in Listing 13.7.

Listing 13.7 A derived sub-table from equipment.

```
CREATE TABLE cable
   UNDER equipment (
   length           NUMBER
   MEMBER FUNCTION get_dark_fiber
);
```

Note the slight variation in syntax. The major difference is that Listing 13.6 created another derived object type and Listing 13.7 created a derived object table. In both cases, the constituent attributes and methods include those from **equipment_t** and any added in the declaration of the subsequent derived object type and object table, respectively.

The implementation of class structures and inheritance is rather straightforward. In the next section, we'll examine the treatment of multiple inheritance issues in anticipation of its support in Oracle8.

Dealing With Multiple Inheritance Issues

Despite the fact that the SQL3 standard is scheduled to support multiple inheritance for data types and tables, there has been no indication that Oracle8 version 8.1 will do so. Oracle intends to implement object-oriented features in a phased approach. The first release of Oracle8 includes the functionalities outlined in this book. With subsequent versions, Oracle will include inheritance (discussed in this chapter), improved treatment of polymorphism, encapsulation, and so on.

While the implementation of basic inheritance for a single base/derived class proves to be somewhat elementary, a closer examination of multiple inheritance issues shows that careful planning will be needed to maintain a clean and uncomplicated design. As mentioned in an earlier section, multiple inheritance comes in two forms. The first to be addressed here (and certainly the simplest) is the multifaceted class hierarchy. This form of multiple inheritance passes class members along a single line, so its implementation should be quite similar to that described in the previous section for basic inheritance.

Drawing once again from the fiber-optic system model, a multifaceted class hierarchy of equipment-to-LRE-to-multisystem LRE would be constructed, as shown in Listing 13.8.

Listing 13.8 A multifaceted class hierarchy of equipment classes.

```
CREATE TYPE equipment_t AS OBJECT (
   Device_id         NUMBER,
   Device_type       VARCHAR2(15),
   Device_model      VARCHAR2(15),
   Property          property_t
   MAP MEMBER FUNCTION get_device_type
);

CREATE TYPE lre_t AS OBJECT
   UNDER equipment_t (
   system_type       VARCHAR2(15),
   system_config     VARCHAR2(15)
   MEMBER FUNCTION assign_system
);

CREATE TYPE ms_lre_t AS OBJECT
   UNDER lre_t (
   bidirectional_yn VARCHAR2(1),
   concurrent_sys    NUMBER
   MEMBER FUNCTION config_sys
);
```

Describing the hierarchy, we find that **equipment_t** is the object type base class. The first level derived class is **lre_t**. **lre_t** also functions as the base class for **ms_lre_t**. Note that **equipment_t** is considered the direct superclass of **lre_t**, just as **lre_t** is the direct superclass for **ms_lre_t**. **lre_t** possesses all the class members (attributes and methods) from **equipment_t** plus the additional members that it has defined. **ms_lre_t** includes all the class members from any and all superclasses above it plus any that it has added.

When multiple derived classes are spawned from a single base class, the resulting derived classes are known as *sibling classes*. Although sibling classes inherit the same characteristics from the base class, they do not share any additional members or properties between the two of them. Figure 13.7 illustrates the relationship that exists between sibling classes.

There are some interesting points to be made about multiple inheritance where two base classes are used to define one or more derived classes. Consider the syntax for creating a derived class from two base classes, as shown in Listing 13.9.

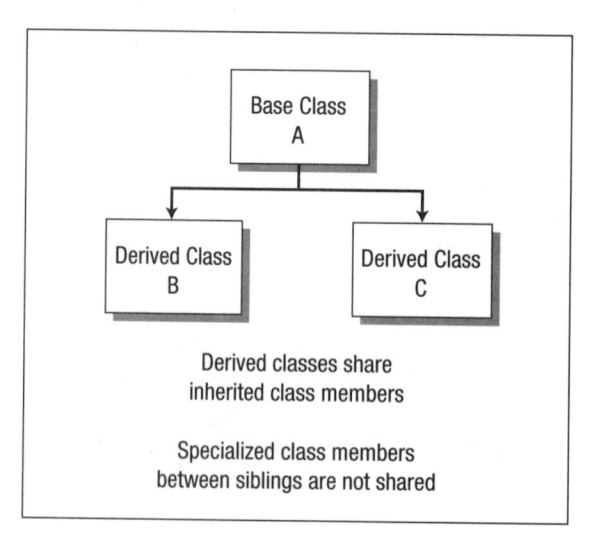

Figure 13.7
The relationship between sibling classes.

Listing 13.9 Multiple inheritance with two base classes.

```
CREATE TYPE equipment_t AS OBJECT (
   Device_id        NUMBER,
   Device_type      VARCHAR2(15),
   Device_model     VARCHAR2(15),
   Property         property_t
   MAP MEMBER FUNCTION get_device_type
);

CREATE TYPE system_t AS OBJECT
   system_id        NUMBER,
   Sites            REF site_t SCOPE IS Sites
   MEMBER FUNCTION get_dispersion
);

CREATE TYPE fiber_t AS OBJECT
   UNDER equipment_t
   UNDER system_t          (
   fiber_id         NUMBER,
   bidirectional_yn NUMBER,
   dark             VARCHAR2(1)
   MAP MEMBER FUNCTION fiber_terminate,
   MAP MEMBER FUNCTION get_terminal_site
   MEMBER FUNCTION get_wavelength
);
```

The derived class object **fiber_t** inherits the members from both **equipment_t** and **system_t**. Drawing from our discussion earlier in the chapter, you might be wondering how duplicated class members are handled. Although the example in Listing 13.9 does not create this situation, the consequences of such an occurrence deserve some thought. At the time of this writing, the mechanism in Oracle8 for dealing with duplicity arising in multiple inheritance had not been published. Duplicate attributes are not allowed in a single table construct, so any attempt at such an action would result in an error condition. At a later date, a keyword or clause might be incorporated to handle duplicity as it is done in C++ through the use of the virtual keyword. In the case of methods, so long as the parameter lists are different, duplicated methods will be incorporated as overloaded functions. In all likelihood, the order in which supertypes are defined in the derived class declaration will probably dictate some sense of precedence with regard to duplicated attributes. For example, the first base class appearing in the derived class declaration might be considered the primary source, and, therefore, it would override subsequent attributes of the same name that appear in the next base class.

Now that some of the issues surrounding the use of inheritance in Oracle8 have been discussed, let's turn our attention to the ways that class hierarchies can be planned for.

Designing Class Hierarchies

The process of designing for class hierarchies in Oracle8 applications is really the effort of emphasizing reuse while implementing a logically structured schema of base classes and their associated derived classes. Most texts on object-oriented design agree that formulating classes requires a thorough functional decomposition of the application system to be built. In traditional approaches to functional decomposition, the application at large was broken into smaller problem domains or business objectives. This section describes the steps required to develop a data type hierarchy.

The primary goal of constructing class hierarchies is to develop the correct balance of detail and data type aggregation in order to achieve simplicity in code development and information retrieval. Evaluating the system requirements and business rules does accomplish this task. Once this effort has begun, you should:

- Define appropriate data aggregations in order to resolve complex business rules.
- Strive for object reuse in application development.

- Seek out class constructs that improve system performance via simplified retrieval.
- Look for commonalities in the schema in order to consolidate type and table classes.

An effective opportunity to initially target data hierarchy prospects occurs during the detailed phase of creating the data flow and/or collaboration diagrams. It is at this point when natural data aggregations, complex data constructs, and unusual business criteria manifest themselves on the data stores and intended entities. You should select candidates for class definitions carefully so that they are flexible. Adding too many "special interest" derived classes reduces the probability that the composed data type will have utility in other parts of the application. In addition, select attributes and group them logically, much as you would relational tables, in order to achieve the highest level of normalization possible. Data redundancy is acceptable, but why introduce it if it isn't necessary?

At the beginning of this chapter, a validity test is described for use in inheritance situations. Classes must lend themselves to the generalization-specialization test. The "is-a-kind-of" relationship spawns hierarchies of object classes because each constituent member or object is a part of the next object class. For example, an automobile engine is comprised of parts, the engine is a part of the automobile. Is-a-kind-of relationships imply a successive level of attributes or properties that gradually define a class hierarchy. In short, they devise a plan for the logical consolidation of leaf-level attributes for the purpose of simplifying data access and program design through the use of object type and table classes.

Next, we will briefly discuss the steps for applying the framework of methods to a class hierarchy. As class members, methods form an integral part of any class definition. In the next section, I will address some of the aspects of mapping methods to classes.

Mapping Methods To Oracle8 Classes

In the object-oriented paradigm, methods are constituent members of a defined class. Because of the tight integration of data with behavior, designing class hierarchies in languages like C++ is a singular task. Oracle's treatment of methods with data is a more loosely defined association.

When attempting to map methods to classes, try to keep three key points of method design and development in mind:

- Work to encapsulate object behaviors.
- Plan ahead, and design for situations where polymorphism is called for.
- Analyze the design carefully to identify method dependencies.

When methods are defined for a supertype, they are inherited by all subtypes under the supertype. This points out two important aspects of object type and method design:

- Created behaviors are shared under an object type class.
- Each subtype receives the exact same behavior (method).

The first of these aspects represents an economy of effort, because behaviors and processes will cascade down a class hierarchy. If a variant behavior is required from the method in the derived class, remember that methods can be overloaded to achieve a sense of polymorphism. In this type of situation, the method in the derived class will be tagged for execution first unless the parameter list does not match. If the parameter list doesn't match, then the Oracle engine will walk up the class hierarchy until it finds the overloaded method with the appropriate parameters.

The treatment of methods continues as described in Chapter 6. While the design of a method topology does not change, its integration with object classes varies in certain aspects to the way that methods were mapped to groups of tables and types. The following highlights some of the points to keep in mind when integrating a method topology with classes:

- Remember that the class hierarchy provides for inheritance. This has two points of special significance to developers. First, a method can be assigned once at a specific point in the hierarchy and all subclasses will inherit that method. Second, variations in behavior for derived classes require an overloaded function or other mechanism in order to achieve the desired behavior.

- Avoid unwanted conflicts with methods of the same name. User-generated methods from derived classes override the base class method if an overloaded configuration is not in affect.

- Beware of conflicts arising in multiple inheritance schemes. Creation of derived classes that draw from multiple base classes presents the possibility of class member duplicity. Closely examine the class hierarchy structure for possible conflicts.

Summary

In this chapter, we covered the exciting features of classes and inheritance. Although the first release of Oracle8 to support them is limited in scope, each successive iteration will introduce expanded coverage of true object-oriented behavior. The ability to incorporate inheritance expands the dynamic abilities of the object relational database. In the final chapter of this book, I discuss the current trends at work in the Oracle8 development environment. The future direction of Oracle8 and the tools that support it are also the focus of Chapter 14.

HIGH PERFORMANCE

Current Trends And Future Directions

CHAPTER 14

HIGH PERFORMANCE

I never think of the future. It comes soon enough.
—Albert Einstein

Current Trends And Future Directions

The wheels of progress have begun to turn, and the advent of the object relational paradigm is ushering in new opportunities for technological growth. The immense popularity of the Java language (thanks to the World Wide Web) is driving the demand for object-oriented support like never before. The course that we now see before us was inevitable. Dramatic progressions in user interfaces, applications, complex data types, and multimedia have spurred the advancement of databases and programming tools to meet the challenge.

Oracle has undertaken an ambitious effort to change the direction of computing from client/server to network computing architecture (NCA). The goal of NCA is for any Java-enabled Web browser to be able to run Oracle database applications without any software running on the client browser. The introduction of object extensions in Oracle8 is one part in the larger picture of transforming the database system into an environment where integration of multiple programming languages and tools is as seamless as possible. In addition to this, Oracle recognizes the inherent difficulties of deploying and maintaining the traditional two-tier client/server architecture. Object support in Oracle8, the incorporation of Java-enabled tools, the introduction of software components called *cartridges*, and more are escorting clients and developers into the next generation of application development. Improvements and extensions are not limited to the database server. Oracle's family of development tools will also follow suit in incorporating the newest technologies that provide a seamless link between application and data.

Many initiatives have already begun. In some cases, the extensibility and functionality will be introduced incrementally. In others, functionality will be introduced in the near future. In the sections that follow, I'll guide you through the current status of features underway, as well as touch on the features planned for the future.

The Current Technological Trends In Oracle8

Without a doubt, the most significant factor driving the adoption of object-oriented functionality in Oracle8 is Java. This is not to say that other demands have not played a part in the eventual genesis of the object relational database. Complex application systems, like telecommunications, have contributed to the demand for a more robust database paradigm, as well. Difficult modeling problems have long been recognized in the relational database community. In large part, the success of purely object-oriented databases has been fueled by the failures of the relational methodology. Object-oriented databases have not enjoyed the universal popularity that relational databases have, however. To some degree, this can be attributed to reticence on the part of analysts and developers who are well-versed in relational methodology. Many developers find the nature of objects quite alien and unintuitive. The introduction of Oracle8 will aid in transitioning hesitant clients from management on down, because the core functionality (SQL, table constructs, and so on) remains relatively intact.

Because of Java's significance, the first part of this discussion focuses on Java and how Oracle is integrating this incredibly popular language into the database.

Oracle8 And Java

Presently, Oracle is aggressively adopting a number of initiatives for the advancement of integration and compatibility between its flagship product, Oracle8, and the Java language. Oracle recognizes that Java provides the means to bring about a platform-independent application environment. Not only that, but Java will enable organizations to create distributed object computing systems and networks in the future.

Oracle has purchased the Borland JBuilder product and is currently working on a project code-named Valhalla. Valhalla will be the extension of the JBuilder product to add Oracle interfaces and create a Java-based application development environment.

While Java bears some similarity to C and C++, it also possesses many advantages over them. Java and C++ both support inheritance, encapsulation, polymorphism, class structures, and so on. Unlike C++, which derives its object orientation by extending the C language, Java is a pure object-oriented language. Java is considered easier to learn and use because much of the high-level programming aspects have been omitted. For example, Java does not use header files, operator overloading, or pointer arithmetic. Java will advance the cause of user acceptance because of its indispensable role in creating applications for the Web.

One of the enabling factors for use of Java is the JavaBeans initiative. JavaBeans is a component architecture for Java created by Sun Microsystems, and it is fully compliant with the CORBA Internet Inter-ORB Protocol (IIOP) standard. JavaBeans enables developers to create and reuse universal software components capable of being run on any platform that will support a browser. JavaBeans will also integrate with third-party products and toolkits, like Microsoft's ActiveX controls.

Because of the importance of the Java language to the overall application strategy that Oracle has put forth, the company started two product initiatives to complement the use of Java with Oracle8—JDBC and JSQL.

JDBC And JSQL

Oracle fully intends to build Java support into the database at the language and system levels. Currently, two product initiatives extend the database developer's ability to establish dynamic and static SQL access to the database with Java.

The first of these initiatives is a collaborative effort by Oracle, JavaSoft, and others called *JDBC*. JDBC is the standard dynamic call-level interface used by Java to access the SQL language. JDBC is vendor independent and supports the following functionalities:

- Multiple database connection management.
- Transaction management.
- Query access to the database.
- SQL statement manipulation via the use of bind variables.
- Execution of stored procedures on the database.
- Database dictionary access.

Oracle has introduced two implementations of the JDBC drivers, each targeted for a specific operating situation. The first driver accommodates traditional client/server configurations. The second driver addresses the thin client, or NCA environment. Both drivers are complete implementations of the JDBC 1.22 standard and incorporate specific extensions for Oracle8. The extensions include performance optimization utilities to reduce roundtrip traffic and data type support for Oracle data types. Because of the platform-independent nature of JDBC, certain Oracle8 data types are not supported. For example, **LOB**s, user-defined data types, and collection types (nested tables and **VARRAY**s) cannot be accessed. Future extensions of the product might provide support for these and other data types particular to other vendor database engines.

Additional driver types have also been developed for specific programming needs. The OCI driver uses low-level JDBC calls as native methods. These native methods are written in C and are supported through Oracle's OCI interface. The thin driver is written in Java and is ideally suited for Java-enabled browsers.

Oracle, IBM, and Tandem have joined forces to create JSQL. JSQL is intended for static SQL utilization predefined at compile time. JSQL represents the standard for embedding SQL statements within Java programs. JSQL implementations are shorter, more type safe, and efficient than JDBC-centric programs. JSQL's implementation is based on a precompiler generating Java code with JDBC calls. JSQL offers several benefits to the database developer:

- JSQL creates binary and source code that can be ported to a multitude of platforms, thus enforcing the code reuse concept.

- JSQL closely integrates the use of Java and SQL for a more seamless application of program code.

- JSQL provides the mechanisms to map SQL types to Java types, thereby simplifying the process of information transfer.

- JSQL is checked at compile time. Checking data types at this stage significantly reduces the possibility of runtime errors.

JSQL has been submitted to the ISO for consideration as an industry standard contingent on the standardization and approval of Java. Production-level versions of JDBC and JSQL began shipping with Oracle8 version 8.04 in December 1997.

Another particular initiative at Oracle that started in conjunction with the enthusiastic rush to Java was for support of plug-in *cartridges* that would extend the programmatic functionality of the code that accesses and manipulates data.

Oracle Cartridges

A *cartridge* is a software component that can reside on a client, application server, or database. The use of cartridges supports the concept of an open, network-based architecture for distributed computing environments. Cartridges are written primarily in Java and are designed to provide extensibility to the application environment that they support. For example, Oracle provides a product called the *ConText cartridge* that provides for the manipulation of unstructured text sources, such as documents. Cartridges use what is known as an interface definition language (IDL) that allows the cartridge to identify itself with other objects in a distributed object system environment. Numerous cartridges have already been developed for use with Oracle's Web Server. In 1997, Developer/2000 was released with a Web cartridge allowing for the lion's share of processing to be placed on the application server, while only the GUI portion of the application is processed by the client. In this case, the client is a Web browser. The concept of how cartridges are implemented can be found in Figure 14.1, which also illustrates the overall concept of network computing architecture.

	Client	Application Server	Database
Development Tools	Designer/2000 Developer/2000 Object Database Designer	Java Access To PL/SQL Designer/2000 Developer/2000 Object Database Designer	Designer/2000 Developer/2000 Object Database Designer
Applications	Oracle Applications Oracle Interoffice Internet Commerce Server	Oracle Applications Oracle Interoffice Internet Commerce Server Java Cartridges	Java Cartridges
Interfaces	JDBC - OCI JDBC - THIN SQL	JDBC JSQL Web Tool Kit	JDBC JSQL
Java Virtual Machine Support		Java In Web Application Server	Java In Database 1. Triggers 2. Stored Procedures 3. Methods 4. Data Cartridges

Figure 14.1
The overall concept of network computing architecture.

Cartridges address the application layer of the NCA concept but are capable of implementation on any of the three tiers described in the NCA strategy: client, application server, and database. Cartridges are designed to work together or individually, extending the programmatic capability of the Web and the database. Cartridges can also be written to ease the integration of legacy systems into the distributed environment of Oracle8. Such cartridges would address the transactional aspects of moving data back and forth between a legacy system and Oracle. To integrate cartridges into the NCA concept, *Universal Cartridge Services* are provided to help make a more manageable environment. Universal cartridge services include mechanisms for installation, registration, activation, execution, administration, monitoring, and security. Many of these services are CORBA compliant. Cartridges are given access to other services through the use of the Inter-Cartridge Exchange (ICX). The ICX is an object bus that facilitates the cross-network communication of cartridges. ICX natively utilizes both IIOP and HTTP protocols, thus improving the environmental transparency during communication between cartridges and other services.

Future Initiatives With Oracle8

The object relational database is still in its infancy. While a tremendous amount of functionality has been introduced in the object extensions for Oracle8 thus far, there are still a number of advancements that await incorporation before Oracle8 can truly be considered fully compliant with the basic principles of object-oriented programming and design. Oracle's strategic direction is to emphasize the NCA concept. In keeping with that strategy, the object relational enhancements to the database and the *n*-tier approach to applications development will favor server-side development, integrated code and data repositories, and CORBA compliance. While it is particularly difficult to predict the future of computing technology, the following sections outline the current plans for Oracle8 and the tools that support it.

Server-Side Advancements With Oracle8

There are a number of improvements and enhancements that developers should expect to see in the near future with regard to the database engine. Release 8.04 of the database engine includes production versions of JSQL and JDBC. It also includes support for the new Java Development Kit (JDK), time-stamped data support, enhanced support for image data stored as **BLOB**s, and multithreaded callouts.

Oracle has adopted an incremental approach to releasing object-oriented extensions. Developers can expect to see improvements in the following areas in upcoming versions:

- Extended support for inheritance.
- Enhanced functionality of collection types, specifically, **VARRAY**s.
- Advanced indexing features (slated for version 8.1).
- Support for true polymorphism and encapsulation.

Recognizing the importance of the data warehousing market, Oracle has begun development of a metadata repository architecture based on the object relational model. The purpose of the new repository will be to consolidate sources of data in the Oracle8 data warehouse to include data extraction mechanisms, transformation processes, schemas, and overall database design. The repository will also support an object relational model describing the warehouse dimensions and hierarchies.

One of the strengths of Oracle's plan is that the object repository will allow DBAs and developers to maintain data about a data warehouse and application development tools in one repository. Central storage of all pertinent data from a database system will aid in maintainability and encourage code reuse.

The current schedule places the new object repository in beta sometime around the middle of 1998. The production version should be ready for commercial distribution by the end of 1998.

Application Development Tools And PL/SQL

The Designer and Developer application development tools used to support Oracle8 database systems have the most ground to cover in order to become fully compliant with the features and functionalities in the Oracle8 database engine. New product initiatives predominantly centered around the Java language will eventually converge with the existing tools to provide a seamless development environment. The sections that follow address the various development tool groups and what the plans are for the near future.

The Designer/2000 Family

In Chapter 7, I introduced the newest member of Oracle's database design family, Object Database Designer. Object Database Designer fills a gap in the current arsenal of tools. If you are familiar with Designer/2000, you'll recognize that the current release is unable to support the object extensions in Oracle8. The latest version of Designer/2000 (version 2) will be released almost concurrently with the publication of this book. Although most of the object extensions will not be supported in version 2, it is anticipated that the following will be supported in this new release:

- Large Objects (including **BLOBs** and **CLOBs**)
- Index-organized tables
- Partitioned tables
- Deferred constraint checks

Analysts and developers anticipating full support for Oracle8's object extensions will most likely have to wait for Designer/2000 version 3. Object Database Designer offers full support for the design of objects in Oracle8, so developers can expect an eventual combination of this tool with Designer/2000.

You might recall that Object Database Designer strongly supports the use of UML in its representation of types and models. Because the UML does not prescribe the specific mechanisms under which application tools and languages implement the physical model, expect Oracle to provide a full set of options that seamlessly navigate the transition of logical model to physical implementation.

Developer/2000

Many database developers who are not conversant with Oracle's design and development tools might not realize the close functional relationship between Designer/2000 and Developer/2000. Because the Designer product offers the ability to generate Developer components (Forms and Reports), it is essential that the two product lines maintain functional parity. The most recent version of Developer/2000 (release 2) has garnered much praise from the development community. Much like its sibling product, Designer/2000, it does not yet offer support for the object extensions in Oracle8. The new version of the tool does, however, support the use of several new features in Oracle8. Developer/2000's support of Oracle8 features includes the following:

- Implementation of Oracle8's Advanced Queuing and Deferred Transaction Support.
- DML against partitioned tables.

- Ability to exercise the parallel processing option via SQL hints. This ability includes queries and transactional operations.

- Support of NCA by including Developer tool components as cartridges.

- Sharing of multiple client connections through a single transport connection via a technique known as *connection pooling*. This must be enabled by using Net8.

- Access to unstructured text, video, and spatial data in support of the ConText, Oracle Video Server, and Spatial options on the Oracle8 database engine.

Previous versions of Developer/2000 did not support the same version of PL/SQL as did the database. Having dissimilar versions of PL/SQL in the database and the application tools presented certain problems in writing code that could be deployed. PL/SQL in Forms and Reports applications lacked the robustness of server-side PL/SQL program units. This shortcoming has been corrected in Developer/2000 version 2, meaning that the full functionality of PL/SQL can be exercised across all levels of application development.

Although the current release of Developer/2000 supports the generation of Web-enabled forms, expect to see expansions for this functionality. Current versions of Developer/2000 now support the full integration of the Java language and allow the definition of Java applets to implement Oracle applications. This builds on Oracle's current initiative to extend Java support throughout the product line.

Another significant change to the Developer/2000 (and Designer/2000) product is that it has moved from the client, or desktop, back to the application server. This is being done to consolidate applications and to support the NCA concept. There is a strong possibility that the development tools will no longer be available in desktop versions starting sometime in 1998.

Other Tool Initiatives

As mentioned earlier, Oracle is planning a new tool strategy that includes a product comprised primarily of class libraries and collected objects called *Java Business Objects*. Java Business Objects is intended for capturing definitions, methods, rules, and validations of objects targeted for reuse. The tool is slated to operate with a number of products, including Designer/2000, third-party Java products, and, another proposed Oracle tool, Java Integrated Development Environment (Java IDE). Oracle's Java IDE is intended to allow developers to produce Java code that can be run on client machines and on the server. Java IDE is based on Borland's product Jbuilder. Java IDE has the capability to create Java-based business objects packaged as CORBA objects or JavaBeans components. Java IDE will integrate with the other development tools and support Oracle8's JSQL. To support the use of Java Business Objects, Oracle will also release an object repository for use in providing object definitions, impact analysis mechanisms, and multiple object version merger capabilities. Java Business Objects and its accompanying object repository should be commercially available by the second half of 1998.

Oracle is also pursuing a new project called *Aurora*, currently targeted for Oracle8 version 8.1. Aurora will be a major initiative allowing the construction of Java stored procedures in the database.

PL/SQL

The many enhancements and extensions added to PL/SQL in support of Oracle8 are addressed in several chapters of this book. As the functionality of the database continues to grow, further extensions will be added. PL/SQL is the common thread that runs through the database, as well as the development tools, like Developer/2000 and Designer/2000. PL/SQL's versatility has been expanded in the current version through the incorporation of external procedures and consistent integration throughout the development products. In the future, Oracle intends to pursue several key factors in an effort to improve and extend the versatility of PL/SQL:

- Oracle intends to develop a tighter integration between PL/SQL and SQL. The aim is to simplify the use of PL/SQL in the SQL*Plus environment. Array support for bulk processing of DML statements is slated for a future release. An additional aspect of this closer integration of the two tools is an ongoing effort to improve performance and reduce the memory usage associated with accessing SQL from PL/SQL.

- Oracle intends to improve product usability by introducing improved error messages and exception handling capabilities. In addition, APIs for improved debugging and tracing will be a welcome functionality for developers. Other APIs will be written to allow third-party tools to integrate fully functional GUI-based development environments for PL/SQL.

- Support for external procedures will be expanded to allow construction of database cartridges for user-defined data types, user-defined operations (methods against individual data types), user-defined storage and access structures, and functional querying on data type instances.

- Extended support and tighter integration with data cartridge functionality in the database server will allow full incorporation of third-party tools with the database server.

- PL/SQL will be integrated within the NCA. PL/SQL's role in the NCA will be important because it is Oracle's intent to map PL/SQL to CORBA. PL/SQL will be given the ability to call out to CORBA objects transparently. Conversely, CORBA objects will have the ability to call in to PL/SQL programs.

- PL/SQL initially had the ability to execute in the database server as early as version 7. In the future, PL/SQL will be enabled across multiple tiers of the NCA. This means that not only will PL/SQL operate in the server- and client-side environments, but it will also exist in the middle tier in the Oracle Web Server as a Web cartridge.

- Subsequent releases of Oracle8 will see the seamless interoperability of PL/SQL and Java. The current plan is to provide strong support for Java in all three tiers of the NCA, just as PL/SQL will. Oracle anticipates a balanced coexistence between PL/SQL and Java as major languages in the database environment. While the popular favorite of SQL programmers will continue to be PL/SQL, Java will be targeted as the language of choice for application cartridges in the server.

- Oracle is promoting language transparency through the interoperability of PL/SQL and Java. The current plan is to allow PL/SQL applications to call JSQL methods. The reverse will also hold true. Ultimately, as developers expand the nature of their object relational constructs, they will have the freedom to write methods in either language.

The continued expansion of support for the NCA will usher in further improvements to PL/SQL. It is clear that Oracle intends to establish a close-knit functional relationship between PL/SQL and Java.

Summary

We covered a great deal of information in this book. We have looked at the new object extensions of Oracle8 in great detail. We examined the paradigm shift required to design and build future applications, and we considered the appropriateness of using objects in a variety of developmental environments. The changing environment of computing today is ushering in exciting new technologies at a rate that boggles the mind. Oracle's entry into the object relational realm brings a heightened level of design and developmental functionality. At the same time, this new strategy for application and database implementation introduces new challenges to everyone who develops present-day database systems. We must embrace a sense of forward thinking and expose ourselves to the challenges that await. The new capabilities found in Oracle8 give us the opportunity to create applications like never before. As comforting as it might be to resist the transition to a new methodology, the pioneers in our profession will blaze the trail that others will follow. I hope that the information in this book helps to guide you on your way as one of the pioneers.

HIGH PERFORMANCE

Naming Convention Standards

Appendix A

Naming Convention Standards

This appendix outlines a recommended convention for naming database objects in Oracle8. One of the most frequent topics of discussion at user group meetings and consulting jobs is a plan of action for naming schema objects for a database application. The material covered in this appendix addresses two aspects of standard naming convention practice. The first aspect is the naming restrictions and requirements imposed by Oracle. The second aspect encompasses the optional recommendations that make the database environment easier for DBAs and developers. The optional recommendations are intended as a starting point for organizations wishing to develop and define a standard naming practice. One important point to keep in mind is that other development and design tools used in the database development process can have an impact on how objects are named. For example, developers who have used Designer/2000 know that the tool's generators subscribe to a specific set of object naming techniques. Developers intent on using this product might want to bring their organizational naming standards in line with how Designer/2000 names objects.

Oracle Schema Object Naming Requirements

The Oracle corporation prescribes a set of rules that developers must follow in naming the various schema objects. The rules are quite simple and straightforward, but they will get you in trouble if you disregard them. Oracle differentiates between two distinct groups of database objects for the purposes of naming requirements: schema objects and other objects that span the entire database.

Oracle defines a *schema* as a collection of logical structures of data, or *schema objects*. Schema objects are owned by a database user and include objects like tables, views, indexes, packages, procedures, sequences, synonyms, and so on. The *Oracle SQL*

Appendix A

Language Reference Manual contains a complete listing of schema objects. You should consult the Oracle documentation for a complete listing of schema objects, as well as an exhaustive list of reserved words that cannot be used in database object names.

The other distinct group of objects (not considered schema objects) are those that are stored in the database but do not belong or reside in a specific schema. These objects are considered universal to all schemas and reside in a database-owned namespace.

The concept of namespace is important because it dictates valid boundaries for object names. Object names cannot be duplicated within a namespace. Figure A.1 illustrates namespace boundaries for both database object types described.

Object names within a namespace boundary must be unique. For example, snapshots and tables are resident in the same namespace. It is not allowed to name a table **EMPLOYEE** and subsequently name a snapshot **EMPLOYEE** in the same namespace. Keep in mind that namespaces are owned by a specific schema, so the name **EMPLOYEE** could be used in another schema under the same namespace boundary. One exception to keep in mind is the use of procedures and functions. Program units with the same name are allowed in the same namespace under the same schema as long as the arguments are different. This is required to support the concept of overloading described in Chapter 6 of this book.

Within each namespace, there are several other rules that must be adhered to. The following list addresses these:

- Oracle object names are not case sensitive; therefore, they can be addressed as **employee** or **EMPLOYEE**, for example.

- Object names must be from 1 through 30 bytes in length. Database names cannot exceed 8 bytes and database links cannot exceed 128 bytes.

- Object names cannot contain quotation marks within the body. Note the rule below that does allow the use of quotation marks for creating object names with blanks and case sensitivity.

- Oracle object names must begin with an alphanumeric character and can only contain characters from the database character set used to include _, $, and #, but Oracle does not recommend the use of the $ and # characters.

- Database object names cannot use Oracle reserved words, DUAL, or SQL language keywords. The *Oracle SQL Language Reference Manual* contains a complete listing of all reserved words and keywords.

SCHEMA OBJECT NAMESPACES

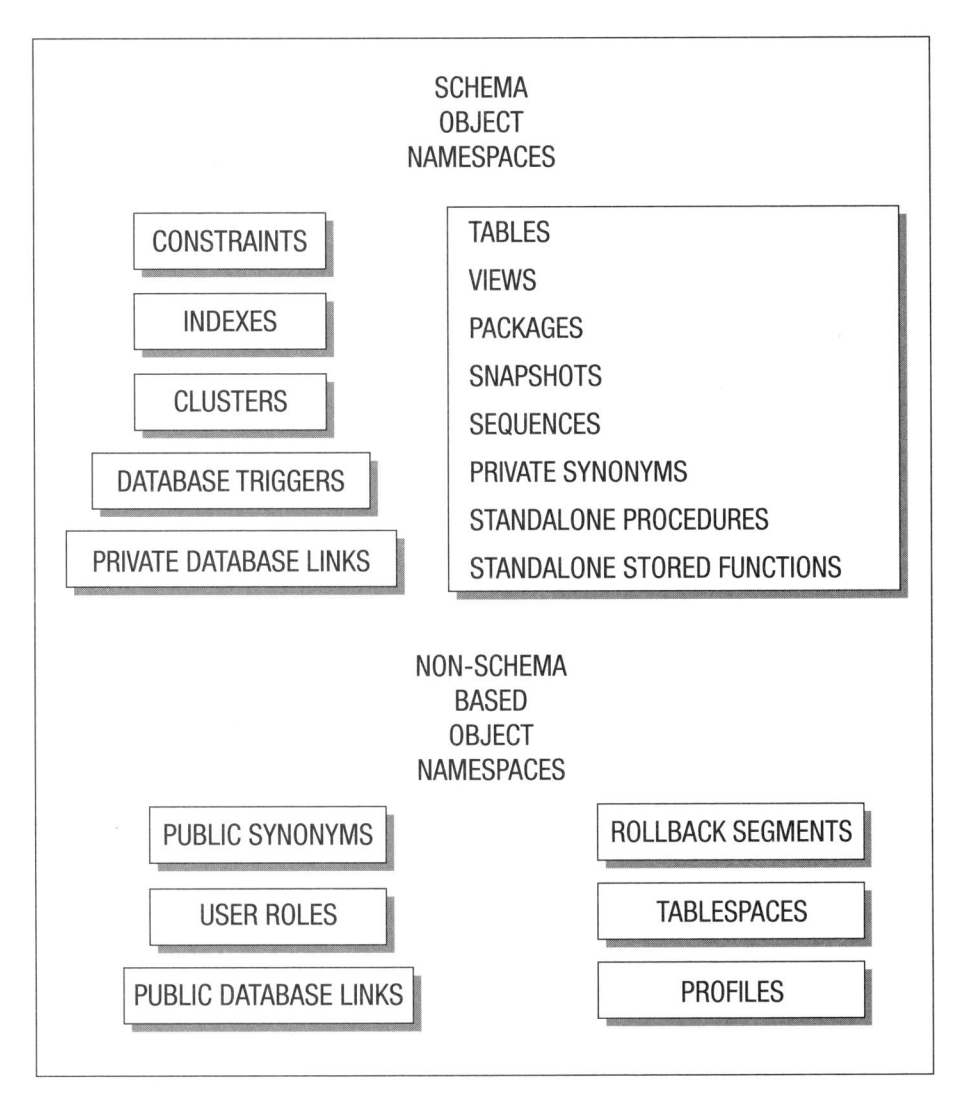

- CONSTRAINTS
- INDEXES
- CLUSTERS
- DATABASE TRIGGERS
- PRIVATE DATABASE LINKS

- TABLES
- VIEWS
- PACKAGES
- SNAPSHOTS
- SEQUENCES
- PRIVATE SYNONYMS
- STANDALONE PROCEDURES
- STANDALONE STORED FUNCTIONS

NON-SCHEMA BASED OBJECT NAMESPACES

- PUBLIC SYNONYMS
- USER ROLES
- PUBLIC DATABASE LINKS
- ROLLBACK SEGMENTS
- TABLESPACES
- PROFILES

Figure A.1
Oracle namespace boundaries.

- Oracle allows object names to be enclosed in double quotes. This allows developers the freedom to use names with spaces and case sensitivity. Keep in mind that once a name has been defined with double quotes, it must be addressed in double quotes from that point on.

This summarizes Oracle's required conventions for object naming. In the next section, we'll cover the other recommended naming practices.

Recommended Naming Conventions

Nothing will cause a developer revolt quicker than the implementation of obtuse, nonsensical naming patterns in a database. Despite the fact that Oracle grants the liberty to use short object names, this freedom should never be taken to extremes. I once went to a client site where the previous group of consultants had named the tables **tbl1**, **tbl2**, **tbl3**, and so forth and the columns **col1**, **col2**, **col3**, and so on. The first thing we set out to do (after figuring out what each table and column was for) was to rename everything in the database.

The following recommendations are just that, *recommendations*. You should extend or modify the suggestions presented here to suit the needs of your organization.

Tables And Views

All database objects should be given a descriptive name without an application-specific prefix. With respect to tables and views, the names should reflect the general purpose or content of the object. For example, the following code line shows a good example of a table/view name:

EMPLOYEES

This is a good descriptive name that follows all the prescribed guidelines. Note that the name is indicated in the plural sense. As a general convention, entities are named using the singular while tables, views, and other physical manifestations use the plural tense. Now, let's look at another table/view name:

HUMAN_RESOURCES_EMPLOYEES

This name meets the length and alphanumeric character requirements set forth by Oracle, but the application name is unnecessary. Here is a good example of what you should *not* do:

TBL1

This type of naming usually indicates that the development team needs to be replaced. And, here's one final example of a naming practice you should avoid:

XYBTOOL1

This name meets the basic naming requirements, but no one will remember what the name represents six months from now.

Columns

Column names must follow the same basic naming requirements as tables, views, and so forth. Column names must be unique within a table but should remain consistently the same across tables and views. For example, if a column **EMPLOYEE_ID** is used in the **EMPLOYEE** table, then any other table using a column for that purpose (like a foreign key) should retain the same name. Columns of the same meaning should retain the same name, data type, and domain across the schema and usually the database. Figure A.2 illustrates the right and wrong methods for name usage between tables.

Sequences

For clarity, sequence names should be based on the column that they support followed by _S. For example, the column **EMPLOYEE_ID** might have a sequence named **EMPLOYEE_ID_S**.

Indexes

There are several useful guidelines for naming indexes. Index names should consist of the name of the table being indexed followed by the suffix **_UIDX**n for unique indexes and **_NIDX**n for nonunique indexes where the *n* represents a sequential number. The following examples demonstrate proper index naming procedures:

```
EMPLOYEES_UIDX1
EMPLOYEES_NIDX3
```

Alternatively, unique and nonunique indexes can also employ the column name along with the table name for further clarification. Even though this information can be obtained from the data dictionary, it is often useful when the name is sufficiently descriptive to identify its use and meaning. Formulating a meaningful name, however, can be difficult under the 30-byte limitation. Following is one example of an index name employing the column and table names:

```
EMPLOYEES_EMPNO_UIDX1
```

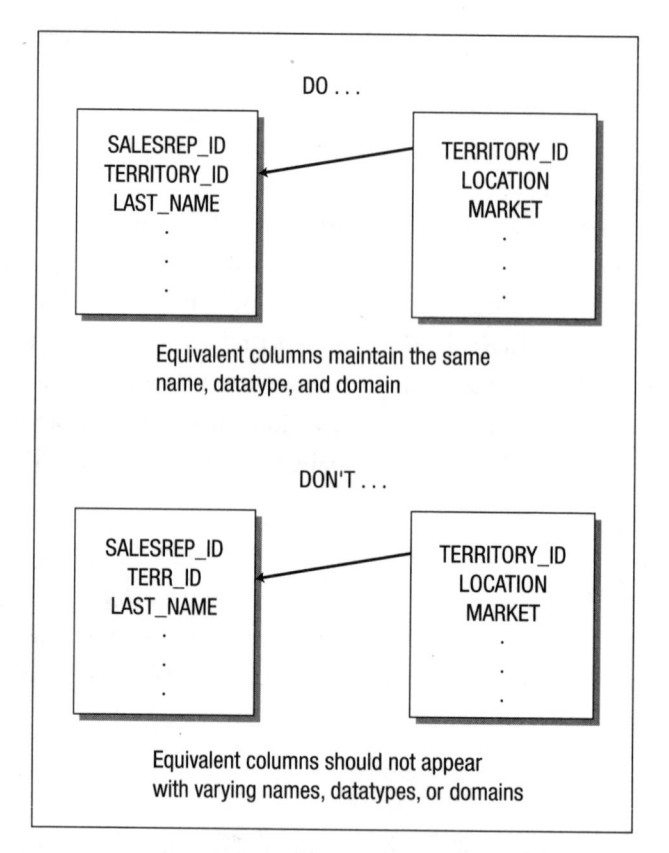

Figure A.2
Column name usage between tables.

Constraints

Primary key constraints should be named using the table name followed by the suffix **_PK**. Likewise, foreign key constraint names should consist as much as possible of the name of the foreign key followed by the suffix **_FK**. The next lines of code show primary and foreign key constraints:

```
EMPLOYEES_PK
DEPT_EMP_ID_FK
```

Note in the latter example that the entities creating the foreign key relationship are used in the constraint name. This is because constraints belong to the same namespace and must, therefore, be unique within the schema. In order to avoid clashes with similar foreign keys, the participating tables are identified in the name. Violation of this rule (unique constraint name within a namespace) generally yields a cryptic system error such as SYS_0001716.

Database Triggers

Database trigger names should consist of the table name with a prefix containing the trigger type and intended actions. PRE-action triggers should be identified by *aX_* where *a* indicates *ante* (before) and X denotes the action (I for insert, U for update, and D for delete). The following lines are examples of this form of database trigger:

```
aI_EMPLOYEES
aU_EMPLOYEES
aD_EMPLOYEES
```

POST and ON action triggers should likewise follow the same database trigger naming conventions set forth for PRE-action triggers. POST-action triggers should use the prefix **pX_** where X denotes the same lettering style for INSERT, UPDATE, and DELETE. The ON-action triggers should use the prefix **oX_**. Examples of these triggers are shown in the following code lines:

```
pI_EMPLOYEES
pU_EMPLOYEES
oU_EMPLOYEES
oD_EMPLOYEES
```

Program Units

Procedures, packages, and functions should bear names that are as descriptive as possible. To differentiate between the three program unit types, **PKG_**, **P_**, and **F_** prefixes should be used. The **PKG_** prefix indicates that the database object is a package:

```
PKG_CREDIT_CHECK
```

The **P_** prefix is used to indicate a procedure:

```
P_CREDIT_CHECK
```

The **F_** prefix is used to indicate a function name:

```
F_CREDIT_CHECK
```

Object Types

The introduction of object extensions added new responsibilities to adequate naming standards. Now that there are additional constructs to administer, it becomes more important to maintain a consistent pattern of object naming. A simplified approach to naming all object types is to merely add the suffix **_t** to the object name as the next code line illustrates:

```
address_t
```

The disadvantage to this approach is that it becomes impossible to differentiate between the various object types. The following naming conventions resolve the ambiguity of deciphering the various object types used. The **_t** suffix should be used to denote object types such as user-defined data types and object tables:

```
person_t
```

The **_ov** suffix can be used to label object views. Alternatively, some variation of **_ovw**, **_oview**, and so on can be used depending upon the preference of the development team:

```
employees_ov
```

The **_v** suffix should be used to name **VARRAY**s:

```
grades_v
```

Nested tables are identified by using the **_list** suffix:

```
courses_list
```

REF columns can be identified by using the **_r** suffix:

```
empno_r
```

All **OID** indexes should bear the **OID** prefix followed by the table name:

```
oid_employees
```

Development teams may wish to consider writing DDL statements with native data types in capital letters while user-defined types appear in lowercase.

Glossary

abstraction—The concept of creating a data class containing only the essential elements of that class. An abstraction represents a generalization of a type.

ADT—Abstract data type. Also known as a user-defined data type.

ANSI—American National Standards Institute.

association (UML)—A bidirectional connection between two objects. One of the relationship types defined in the UML.

attribute—An attribute specifies the detailed properties of an entity.

base class—A class of high-level properties and supporting functions; a generalization.

BDAM—Basic Direct Access Method. A database access technique that uses what is known as a hashing algorithm, taking the symbolic key and converting it into a location address on the physical medium.

BFILE—External Large Objects composed of binary or raw data stored in a server-side operating system file.

BLOB—Binary Large Object. A **LOB** subtype containing values composed of raw or unstructured binary data.

cardinality—Cardinality defines the expected number of occurrences of an object type on each side of a relationship.

CASE—Computer-aided software engineering.

class—A data type that consists of data members and their functions.

CLOB—Character Large Object. This **LOB** subtype contains values composed of single-byte fixed-width character data corresponding to the character set used in the database.

CODASYL—Committee On Development Of Applied Symbolic Languages. This group formulated the first network model for databases.

Glossary

collection type—A data unit made up of an indefinite number of elements, each of the same data type. Collection types are similar to arrays except that collections can have only one dimension.

constructor method—A function that creates a new user-defined data type based on the definition stated in the object type's specification.

CORBA—Common Object Request Broker Architecture. A distributed object standard.

dangling REF—A REFed value that is deleted without removing the **REF** value in the dependent table.

data mart—A smaller version of a data warehouse that places its focus on a smaller scale.

DDL—Data Definition Language. SQL statements used in database object creation.

DDS—Distributed database system.

decision support system (DSS)—The basis for data warehousing comprised of two parts: a structured component consisting of decision rules and an intuitive, or creative, component driven by human intervention.

dependency (UML)—One of the five relation types in the UML. A unidirectional relationship where a source object has a dependency on a target object.

DEREF—A routine used to retrieve the value or values pointed to by a **REF** statement.

derived class—a specific implementation of a base class; a specialization.

Designer/2000—Oracle's software engineering tool used for the design and generation of database schemas. Designer/2000 utilizes the CASE method.

Developer/2000—Oracle's application development suite comprised of Forms, Reports, Graphics, and Procedure Builder.

distributed database—A database system comprised of two or more databases stored on multiple computers that appear to applications as a single database.

distributed processing—Distributed processing takes place when an application system distributes its tasks among different computers in a network.

distributed transaction—DML statements that individually or as a group update data on two or more distinct nodes of a distributed database.

DLL—Dynamic link libraries.

DML—Data Manipulation Language. SQL statements used to alter data.

element (UML)—The most basic object in the set of core parts in the UML. Elements comprise the base class for most objects in the UML.

encapsulation—The process of defining a class with data members and functions into a definition. In other words, the mechanism that binds code and data together while protecting or hiding it from outside of the class.

entity—A representation of an object for which specific information is maintained, such as vehicle, person, and so forth.

generalization (UML)—A unidirectional inheritance relationship used in supertype/subtype hierarchies where an instance of the subtype is substitutable for an instance of the supertype.

hierarchical database—A database structure where pointers are used to establish relationships between data elements.

ICX (Inter-Cartridge Exchange)—An object bus that facilitates the cross-network communication of cartridges.

IDL (Interface Definition Language)—A mechanism that allows the cartridge to identify itself with other objects in a distributed object system environment.

IIOP—Internet Inter-ORB Protocol.

IMS—Information Management System. The first commercial database fielded by IBM.

inheritance—The ability for one class to inherit the properties of its ancestor.

ISAM—Indexed Sequential Access Method. A sequential storage method using flat files.

ISO—International Organization For Standardization.

Java—A purely object-oriented language used for development of Web applications.

JavaBeans—A component architecture for Java created by Sun Microsystems.

Glossary

JDBC—The standard dynamic call-level interface used by Java to access the SQL language.

JSQL—The standard for embedding SQL statements within Java programs.

leaf-level attribute—The most atomic-level object type where no further decomposition takes place. Leaf-level attributes are generally part of a collection.

leaf-level scalar attribute—A leaf-level attribute that exists outside of a collection.

link (UML)—A relationship type that specifies the instances of processes and elements that describe an interaction. One of the relationship types defined in the UML.

linked list—The technique of linking multiple objects or data elements in a sequential fashion in order to establish an order or hierarchy.

LOB—Large Object. The new data type in Oracle8 that replaces **LONG** and **LONG RAW**.

map method—A comparison method used to provide a way to compare two objects to determine a quantitative outcome.

message—An executed function belonging to a class member. The message will include the function call and its associated arguments.

meta-model—A model of how a model is defined or expressed, or in simpler terms, a model of a model.

method—A method in object-oriented programming is a function of a particular class. In Oracle8, it represents any program unit designed to manage behavior of a data type to which it is assigned.

model (UML)—A subtype of element defining an abstraction of a system or a subsystem being modeled.

ModelElement (UML)—This component is one of only two immediate subtypes to element. A ModelElement describes an abstraction drawn from the modeled system.

MOLAP—*See* multidimensional database.

multidimensional database—A nonrelational database architecture that stores summarized information in a way that the dimensions are cross-referenced with each other.

multifaceted class hierarchy—A version of multiple inheritance where a hierarchy of classes is established.

multiple inheritance—A derived class having multiple base classes or a derived class that itself becomes a base class to further derivations.

name (UML)—A label given to an element.

NCA—Network Computing Architecture.

NCLOB—A **LOB** subtype containing values having fixed-width multibyte character data that corresponds to the NLS character set defined in the Oracle8 database.

nested table—A table embedded within another table and linked to a specific column. One of the two collection types supported in Oracle8.

NIST—National Institute Of Standards And Testing.

Object Database Designer—Oracle's database design tool configured to the design of object relational databases, specifically Oracle8.

object tables—Special tables that hold objects while providing a relational view of those objects' attributes. Attributes in an object table are composed of top-level attributes of a particular type.

object view—A virtual representation of one or more object tables. Object views become a virtual object table of built-in and user-defined data types from relational and object tables in the database.

ODBC—Open Database Connectivity.

ODMG—Object Data Management Group.

OID—Object Identifier. An **OID** is a 128-byte base-64 number generated internally by the Oracle engine. When an object table is created, a corresponding **OID** is added for every row that can be used in **REF**, **DEREF**, and **VALUE** commands. **OID**s are used only by object tables, and they do not change or repeat.

OIDINDEX—Indexes created on **OID**s.

OLAP—Online Analytical Processing. The means of (or tool for) presenting facts or information in a cross-referenced style.

OLTP—Online Transaction Processing.

Glossary

OMG—Object Management Group.

OMT—Object Modeling Technique. This is an object-oriented modeling methodology and a precursor to the UML.

OOSE—Object-Oriented Software Technique. This is an object-oriented modeling methodology and a precursor to the UML.

OQL—Object Query Language.

order method—A comparison method that uses internal logic to compare two objects. Order methods are used for making comparisons of small groups of instances against a single value.

overloaded program units—The creation of more than one program unit with the same name where each program unit differs in function and parameters.

owns (UML)—Defines what elements are aggregated or owned by a specific package. One of the five relationship types in the UML.

package (UML)—A generalized grouping mechanism for elements.

pivot table—A table commonly found in spreadsheet applications comprised of fact and dimension columns.

pointer—An address to a data object. Pointers come in two varieties: address and symbolic. Address pointers make use of the physical address of a targeted data element. Symbolic pointers are composed of a unique name or identifier, instead of a physical location address.

polymorphism—The ability for different objects in a class hierarchy to have different behaviors in response to the same message.

REF—An Oracle-supplied routine that returns the **OID** of an object instance.

references (UML)—A means by which a referenced element can be addressed or seen by other elements not within the same package.

Referential Integrity (RI)—The means by which the database guarantees that the value or values from one column maintain their dependency on another column through the use of integrity constraints.

relationship—Relationships describe the significance or association that one object has with another.

replication—The creation of data replica objects that provide access to the table data originating from a primary or master site.

ROLAP—An OLAP implementation against a relational database.

ROWID—Data types used for the unique identification of each row of data in a non-clustered table.

RPC—Remote procedure call.

sequential allocation—A technique of storing equivalently sized data elements in sequential order on a physical device or in memory.

SMP—Symmetric Multiprocessing.

SQL—Structured Query Language.

SQL3—The new SQL standard currently under development by the ISO and ANSI.

stereotype (UML)—Stereotypes are the classification instrument for elements.

subclassing—*See* inheritance.

system—A name for a grouping of business functions, entities, programs, and so on.

system (UML)—This is a subtype of element and represents a collection of objects gathered to perform a specific purpose.

transition (UML)—A behavioral relationship that specifies the state change of an object. One of the relationship types of the UML.

type-instance dichotomy—The preparation of generic descriptions that define multiple specific items.

UML—Unified Modeling Language. An open standard modeling language containing notation and semantics for object modeling.

VARRAY—Variable Array. This is one of two collection types in the object extensions found in Oracle8. This is a single-dimensional array structure stored inline.

Glossary

ViewElement (UML)—A textual and graphical depiction of a collection of model elements.

virtual class—A class definition used in C++ to prevent the inheritance of the same base class more than once in multiple inheritance configurations.

visibility (UML)—Visibility establishes the degrees to which an element can be seen from outside of its enclosure, whether the enclosure is a package or a model.

Index

A

Abstract data types. *See* ADTs.
Abstraction, 20-21
Access methods
   basic direct, 4
   indexed sequential, 4
Access speed
   data warehouses, 78
   scoped referencing, 152
Activity diagrams, 313-315
   in method design, 324
Address pointers, 145. *See also* Pointers.
ADTs, 14, 19, 24-26, 120-133
   collection types, 120, 124-125
   elaboration mode, 402
   encapsulation level, 405
   nesting, 25
   object ADTs, 402
   object types, 120, 122-124
   persistent, 25
   routines for, 403
   value ADTs, 402
Aggregate data types, 24, 28, 96-102
   pointers, 149
Alias library, 191, 422
Aliasing, 85
ALTER TABLE command, 149
ALTER TYPE command, 413
American National Standards Institute. *See* ANSI.
ANALYZE command, 41, 358
Anonymous blocks, 178. *See also* PL/SQL.
ANSI, 12, 397
Application cache, 29
Architectural distribution databases, 372
Association, 87, 299
   roles, 299-300
Attributes, 56, 81

B

B*-tree indexes, 342
Base class, 430
Basic direct access method. *See* BDAM.
BDAM, 4
Becomes stereotype, 301
BFILE type, 118-119, 281
Bill-of-materials relationship, 63, 273
Bind stereotype, 301
Bitmapped indexes, 342
BLOB subtype, 114, 421
Booch, Grady, 13, 73
BOOLEAN data type, 401
Burleson, Donald, 333
Business objects, 14

C

C++, 16
   access specifiers, 429
   compared to Java, 456-457
   function overloading, 19

INDEX

generator for persistent classes, 74
generator in Object Database Designer, 233
methods, 175
protected visibility, 432
Call stereotype, 302
CALLING STANDARD, 192
Cardinality, 57
   determining in relationships, 92
   one-to-many relationships, 60
Cartridges, 28, 455
CASE
   life cycle development process, 35
   method, 36
   in Oracle, 35. See also Designer/2000.
Case study—fiber-optics model
   analysis, 261-266
   components, 257-261
   data model, 280-
   defining relationships, 266-276
   methods design, 276-279
CAST operator, 170
Center of the universe rule, 264, 276
CHAR data type, 110
Character data types, 110-111
CHECK constraints, 347-348
Chen, Peter, 56
Circular referencing, 159
Classes
   abstract, 20
   base, 430
   defined, 17-18, 429
   derived, 431
   encapsulation, 21-23, 429
   hierarchies, 69, 263, 431, 449
   implementation in Oracle, 439
   inheritance, 19
   mapping methods to, 450
   members, 429
   notation, 305

overriding inherited values, 433
static structure diagrams, 304
steps for analyzing, 435
type, 263, 438
virtual, 437
virtual function mechanism, 431
visibility, 429
Client/server database applications systems, 366. See also Distributed systems.
Client-side objects, 29
CLOB subtype, 115, 421
CODASYL, 4, 143
Collaboration diagrams, 309
Collection types
   nested tables, 98, 416
   in PL/SQL, 416
   in SQL3, 404
   variable arrays, 97, 416
Committee on Development of Applied Symbolic Languages. See CODASYL.
Comparison methods, 187-190
   differences between map and order, 189
   map methods, 188, 415
   order methods, 188-189, 415
Complex object view example, 167-170
Computer-Aided Software Engineering. See CASE.
Constraints
   check, 347
   with DML statements, 8
   with nested table creation, 100
   in UML modeling diagrams, 295-296
Constructor methods, 186, 203, 436
Constructs
   deciding which to use, 77-78
   DEREF, 153-154
   linked list, 146

INDEX

OIDs, 150
REFs, 151
VALUE, 156
ConText cartridge, 459
Conventional referencing, 151. *See also* REF command.
Copy stereotype, 302
CORBA, 460
CREATE DIRECTORY command, 281
CREATE LIBRARY command, 192
CREATE TABLE command, 98, 282
   and complete types, 101
   generation of OIDs, 150
   with embedded **REF**s, 151
CREATE TYPE command, 413

D

DANGLING clause, 155, 416
Data flow diagrams
   initial, 37
   fiber-optic network, 262
   modeling for objects, 73-77
Data manipulation statements. *See* DML.
Data replication
   basic, 377
   symmetric, 379
Data structures, 144
Data types
   aggregate, 24, 28, 96-102
   built-in, 108-119
   complex, 97
   hierarchy concept, 137-139
   large object (LOB), 28
   unstructured data typing, 97
   user-defined, 24
Data warehousing
   bitmapped indexes, 342
   characteristics, 336
   contrasting with OLTP systems, 337
   data marts, 337-338
   decision support systems, 334-335
   index-organized tables, 344
   online analytical processing, 339-342
   overview of data warehousing, 334-337
   partitioning option, 346
   planning, 352-355
   star queries, 355-361
Database object model, 94
Database systems
   aggregate objects, 96
   client/server systems, 5
   design problems, 68
   evolution of, 3–11
   illustration of evolution, 10
   hierarchical architecture, 3, 4
   legacy systems, 4-6
   object-relational, 11
   relational model, 6-8
   triggers, 179-180
Datastore objects
   with nested data objects, 76
Date, Chris, 366
Date data type, 111
DBMS_LOB, 421
Decision support systems, 334
   characteristics of, 334-335
Dependency, 84, 87, 299
DEREF, 153, 419
Derived stereotype, 302
Design, 34-70. *See also* System development.
Designer/2000, 9, 41
   future trends, 461-462
   history of, 46
   strengths, 47
Destructor methods, 436

487

INDEX

Development life cycle, 33-70
    analysis phase, 38-39,
    build phase, 41
    design phase, 39-41
    impact of Oracle8, 48-50
    production phase, 46
    requirements identification, 258-259
    strategy phase, 36-37
    transition phase, 44-46
    user documentation phase, 43-44
Developer/2000, 19, 47
    future trends, 462-463
Diagram window (in OR-Compass), 238
Digital Equipment, 74
DIRECTORY object, 421
Disjoint substate, 313
Distributed systems, 365-394
    architectural distribution, 372
    characteristics of, 366-370
    designing, 389-391
    distributed databases vs. distributed processing, 366
    exception handling, 381
    features in Oracle8, 373-388
    horizontal distribution, 370
    performance enhancement, 393
    remote procedure calls, 380-381
    snapshot design considerations, 392
    transaction management, 369
    vertical distribution, 371
Domain
    data integrity, 82
    defined, 56
DML, 8
    assignment statements, 81
    relational operators, 81
DROP TYPE command, 413

E

Elements, 83
Element type, 404
Encapsulation, 12, 21-23
Entity relationship
    diagram, 39, 293
    modeling, 56-65
Entity type, 56
ENUMERATED data type, 401
ER modeling
    attributes, 56
    cardinality, 57
    domains, 56
    history, 56
    object extensions impact, 58
Events
    external, 50
    realtime, 51
    system, 51
Exception handlers, 179.
    See also PL/SQL.
    identifying when needed, 200
    remote procedures, 381
    user-defined, 201
Exclusive relationships, 64
Explain Plan utility, 101
Extensibility, 30
Extensions
    object-oriented, 23-29
    pointers, 27, 143-172
External procedures, 190
    registering, 192
    support on PL/SQL, 422-423

F

Federal Information Processing Standards. *See* FIPS.

INDEX

Fiber-optic system case study
   analysis, 261-266
   components, 257-261
   data model, 280-284
   defining relationships, 266-276
   methods design, 276-279
FIPS, 399
First normal form, 6
   when to violate the rule, 102
Flat-file systems, 4-6
FOREIGN KEY constraint, 82
Friend
   functions, 430
   stereotype, 302
Functional decomposition, 38, 50-54
Functions, 180. *See also* PL/SQL.
   return clauses, 182

G

GeneralizableElement, 300
Generalization, 87, 300, 430
Generalization-specialization
   structure, 431
Global coordinator, 386
GRANT TYPE command, 413
GROUP BY, 188
Groups
   objects, 286
   repeating, 60, 103

H

Hash cluster indexes, 342
Hashing algorithm, 4
Heterogeneous Services, 375
Hewlett-Packard, 74
Hierarchical database architecture, 3-4

Hierarchies
   method hierarchy planning, 204-212, 278
   multiple inheritance, 436
   multifaceted class hierarchy, 436, 446-447
   reasons for using hierarchies, 431
   use of pointers, 5
Hints, 357
Horizontal
   distribution databases, 370-371
   partitioning, 368

I

ICON Computing, 74
Icons, 294
IDMS, 5
i-Logix, 74
Impedance mismatch, 89
Implementation
   diagrams, 316
   visibility, 301
Import stereotype, 302
IMS, 4
IN, 182
Index-organized tables, 344-345
Indexed sequential access method. *See* ISAM.
Indexes
   bitmapped, 342-343
   of OIDs, 156-157
Information hiding, 216
Information Management System. *See* IMS.
Inheritance, 12
   definition, 19-20
   multiple, 436-437
   overriding derived values, 434

INDEX

Inmon, Bill, 333
IN OUT, 182
INSTEAD OF trigger, 180, 418
ISAM, 4
Instance stereotype, 302
Inter-Cartridge Exchange (ICX), 460
Intersection, 61

J

Jacobson, Ivar, 73
Java, 26, 428, 455
    compared to C++, 456
    JavaBeans, 457
    JDBC, 457
    JSQL, 441, 457-458
Julian date calendar, 111

L

Large object data type. *See* **LOBs**.
Leaf-level attributes, 122
Legacy systems, 4-6
Linked lists, 144, 148
Links, 88, 300
LIST collection type, 404
LOBs, 28
    accessing with pointers, 149
    internal, 114-118
    external, 118
    support in PL/SQL, 420
Locators, 28
Logic Works
    OR-Compass, 74, 236-251
LONG data type, 110
    converting to LOB, 116
LONG RAW data type, 112

M

MAKE_REF command, 170
Mandatory to mandatory relation, 60
Mandatory-to-optional relation, 60
Many-to-one relationships, 60
Many-to-many relationships, 60, 266-271
MAP methods, 188
MCI Systemhouse, 75
MDBS2, 5
Messages
    definition, 18, 175
    in UML modeling diagrams, 308
Metaclass stereotype, 302
Metamodels, 78
    comparison, 95
    object, 83-87
    relational, 79-82
Methods, 26-27, 120, 175-217
    activity diagraming for, 324
    building in PL/SQL, 194-204
    calling, 203-204
    chaining, 204
    comparison methods, 187-190, 415
    constructor, 187, 203, 414
    creating prototypes, 213-216
    definition, 18
    dependency considerations, 197
    external procedures, 190-193
    hierarchy planning, 204-212, 278
    identifying duplicate behaviors, 211
    map methods, 188
    object views, 29
    order methods, 188
    prototype mapping, 206, 277
    reasons to use, 185-186
    supertype/subtype configuration, 195

use case diagrams, 322
user-defined, 414
vs. database triggers, 26
Microsoft Corporation, 75
MLSLABEL data type, 114
Model explorer (in OR-Compass), 237
ModelElement subtype, 84
Modeling conventions, 35-46
Modeling diagrams (UML)
   activity diagrams, 313
   collaboration diagrams, 309
   conventions, 294-298
   implementation diagrams, 315
   relationships, 298-303
   sequence diagrams, 307
   state diagrams, 311
   static structure diagrams, 304
   use case diagrams, 306
Modsects, 285
MOLAP, 339
Multidimensional
   databases, 339-340
   OLAP, 339
   VARRAYs, 27
Multiple inheritance, 436
   multifaceted class hierarchy, 436, 446-447
   with two base classes, 448
MULTISET
   collection type, 404
   operator, 170

N

National Institute of Standards and Testing. *See* NIST.
Navigator, 223, 232-233
NCA, 9, 460
NCHAR data type, 110
NCLOB subtype, 115, 421

Nesting
   dereferencing, 161-165
   methods, 205
   rules for nested tables, 101-102
   sample nested table, 99
   tables, 26, 27, 97
   using pointers, 146-147
Net8, 394
Network Computing Architecture. *See* NCA.
Network databases, 4-5
NIST, 398
Non-first normal form data structures
   modeling, 102
Non-persistent ADTs, 25
Normalization
   data integrity, 81
   impact of pointers 143
   rules of, 6-7
NOT NULL constraint, 82
Number data types, 110

O

Object Data Management Group. *See* ODMG.
Object Database Designer, 13, 74, 221-237
   C++ generator, 233
   component descriptions, 223-225
   Design Recovery, 235
   Navigator, 223, 232-233
   prerequisites for using, 222
   Quality Check Utility, 235-236
   Server generator, 234
   toolbar, 226
   Type Modeler, 223, 227-232
   working environment, 225-231
Object identifier. *See* OID.
Object Management Group. *See* OMG.

INDEX

Object Modeling Technique. *See* OMT.
Object models
   creating, 75-79
   database object model benefits, 94
   metamodel, 83-88
   metamodel comparison, 95
   sample model, 256-290
   using tools to help create, 221-251
Object-oriented extensions, 12, 13
   classes, 17-18
   features of Oracle8, 23-29
   deciding when to implement, 16
Object-Oriented Software Technique. *See* OOSE.
Object-relational databases, 11-13, 143
   case studies, 256-290
   enhancing existing schemas, 235
   incorporating methods, 178
   using diagrams, 321
   when to implement, 14
Objects
   client-side, 29
   diagramming, 305
   groups, 286
   lifeline, 308
   relations, 287
   tables, 26, 417
   tracking by order, 284
   types, 24
   views, 29, 128-130, 417
ODMG, 12, 400
OF keyword, 417
OID, 14, 25, 150
OIDINDEX, 156-157
OLAP, 339
OLTP, 4
   contrasting data warehouse systems, 337
OMG, 12
OMT, 13

Online analytical processing. *See* OLAP.
Online transaction processing. *See* OLTP.
One-to-many relationships, 60, 271-273
One-to-one relationships, 59
OOSE, 13
Optional-to-optional relation, 60
OQL, 12, 400
Oracle Corporation
   Designer/2000, 9, 41, 47
   Developer/2000, 47
   Object Database Designer, 13, 48, 222-237
   Open Gateway, 374
Oracle8
   data warehousing features, 342-351
   distributed database systems features, 373-388
   future directions, 455-466
   history, 9
   modeling for, 13-16
   object option, 120
   object-oriented features, 23-29
   partitioning option, 346
   reasons to migrate from version 7, 11
OR-Compass, 74, 236-251
   building model elements, 240-243
   components, 237-239
   data types, 242
   design environment, 239-240
   features, 236
   forward engineering, 248-249
   internal routines, 246
   relation types, 243-246
   reverse engineering, 249-250
   row types, 241
   table types, 241
   toolbars, 238
ORDER BY, 188
Order methods, 188-189
OUT, 182

Overloading
    packages sample, 19, 279
    program units, 195-196
Owns, 85

P

Package Explorer (in OR-Compass), 237
Packages
    advantages to using, 196
    body, 182
    contents, 5
    overloaded, 279
    program units, 182
    purity level, 201-202
    sample package script, 183
    specifications, 182
    in UML modeling diagrams, 295
PARAMETER clauses, 193
Partitioning
    horizontal, 367
    tables, 350
    vertical, 367
    views, 346
Paths (in UML modeling diagrams), 295
Persistent
    ADTs, 25
    storage, 88
Pig tails, 62
PL/SQL
    anonymous blocks, 177-179
    creating methods, 176, 194-204
    database extensibility, 422
    exception handlers, 179
    external procedures, 190, 422
    functions, 180-181
    future enhancements, 464-465
    large objects, 420
    methods support, 414
    object tables, 417

object types, 412
packages, 182
registering libraries, 192
specifying indicators for
    parameters, 193
stored procedures, 182
Platform distribution database, 371
Pointers, 27-28, 143-172
    address, 146
    circular referencing, 159
    dangling REFs, 155
    dereferencing, 153-154
    nested dereferencing, 161
    object identifiers, 150. *See also* OIDs.
    recursion, 157
    re-sequencing, 164-167
    returning the value of an object, 156
    symbolic, 146
    vs. linked lists, 148
Polymorphism, 12, 17
    definition, 18
    illustration, 20
    support in SQL3, 405
    using nested procedures, 199
    using overloading, 196
Poplists, 97
Powertype stereotype, 302
PRAGMA EXCEPTION_INIT, 382
Primary key, 7, 82
Private
    class members, 17
    visibility, 301
Pro*C, 176
Procedures, 182
Process flow analysis, 54
Protected visibility, 301
Public
    class members, 17
    visibility, 301

INDEX

Purity level, 202. *See also* RESTRICT_REFERENCES PRAGMA command.

Q

Queries
  distributed, 369
  star, 356-361

R

Rational Software Corporation, 12, 75
RAW data type, 112
Realtime events, 51
Recursive relationships, 62
  modeling, 159
Redundancy
  benefit of, 7
  relational, 65
REF command, 14, 26. *See also* Pointers.
  circular referencing, 159
  conventional vs. scoped, 151
  dangling, 155
  limitations, 153
  nested dereferencing, 161
  purpose, 151
  support in PL/SQL, 419
Reference type, 404
Referencing, 85,
  conventional vs. scoped, 151
Referential Integrity
  constraints, 82
  history, 8
  maintaining with triggers, 180
  sample table creation script, 8
Refinement stereotype, 302

Relational databases
  assignment statements, 81
  differences from multidimensional databases, 340
  drawbacks for networked systems, 256
  entity relationship diagrams, 293
  normalization rules, 6-7
  key to success, 3
  model, 6-8
  object-oriented extensions, 13, 73-82
  operators, 81
  referential integrity, 8-9
Relational metamodels, 79-82
  basic characteristics, 81
Relationships
  bill-of-materials, 63
  direction of, 93
  embedded, 93
  exclusive, 64
  many-to-many, 60
  in object metamodels, 87
  one-to-many, 60
  one-to-one, 59
  recursive, 62
  scope, 288
  types in the UML, 299-300
Remote procedure calls, 380-
Repeating groups, 60
  advantages and disadvantages, 103
RESTRICT_REFERENCES PRAGMA command, 201
RETURN clause, 182
REVOKE TYPE command, 413
Reverse key indexes, 343
ROLAP, 341-342
Role stereotype, 302
Round-trip engineering, 235
Routine Explorer (in OR-Compass), 238
Row types, 404
  named, 404

ROWID data type, 112-114
  bitmap indexes, 343
  differences from OIDs, 150
Rumbaugh, Jim, 73

S

Samples
  Acme Telephone Company, 256-290
  Bob's Fertilizer, 134-138
  Complex object view example, 167-170
  Consult Rite, 131-134
Scalar, 122
SCOPE clause, 151-153
  restricting a column's REF value to a specific table, 152
  restricting a column's REF values to a column, 153
Scoped referencing, 151. *See also* REF command *and* **SCOPE** clause.
Second Normal Form, 6
Self-association, 157. *See also* Recursive relationships.
Send stereotype, 302
Sequence diagrams, 307
Sequential allocation, 144
SET collection type, 404
Snapshots, 377-379
  design considerations, 392
SQL. *See also* PL/SQL.
  declarative structure, 89
  introduction, 6
SQL3, 12, 398-411
  additional enhancements, 408
  issues, 409-411
  SQL/Bindings, 406
  SQL, CLI, 405
  SQL/Foundation, 401
  SQL/Framework, 400

SQL/PSM, 406
SQL/Temporal
SQL/XA, 407
support for Java, 409
State diagrams, 311-313
Static structure diagrams, 304
  class diagrams, 304
  implementing, 327-328
  object diagrams, 305
Stereotypes, 85, 297
  dependency metamodel class, 301
Stored procedures, 180
Structured query language. *See* SQL.
STAR hint, 358
Star
  queries, 356-361
  transformation, 359
Store tables, 101
Strings (in UML modeling diagrams), 295
Subclassing. *See* Inheritance.
Subtables, 403
Supertype, to subtype relationship, 20
Symbolic pointers, 145. *See also* Pointers.
System development
  analysis phase, 38-39, 261-266
  build phase, 41-42
  common design issues, 68
  design phase, 39-41
  determining the central focus, 264-265
  diagrams to use in each phase, 318-321
  entity relationship modeling, 56-65
  impact of Oracle8 extensions, 48-50
  process flow analysis, 54-56
  production phase, 46
  strategy phase, 36-37
  transition phase, 44-46
  user documentation phase, 43-44

Index

T

Table classes, 444
Tables
   index-organized, 344-345
   nested, 26, 27, 98
   subtables in SQL3, 403
   partition, 350
Texas Instruments, 75
Thin client, 9
Third Normal Form, 7
Trace
   stereotype, 302
   utility, 101
Transition, 87, 300
Transitive dependencies, 7
Triggers
   database, 179-180
   INSTEAD OF, 29, 418
Twizzling, 164
Two-dimensional symbols, 295
Two-phase commit, 369, 385-389
   commit phase, 386
   prepare phase, 385
Type classes, 263
   derived data, 443
   user-defined data, 442
Type-instance dichotomy, 296
Type Modeler, 223, 227-232
   associations, 230
   creating objects, 228
   generalizations, 229
   interfaces, 228
   operations, 231
   relation types, 228
   roles, 230

U

UML, 12-13, 73-75
   See also Modeling diagrams (UML).
   diagrams, 303-320
   modeling diagram conventions, 294-298
   modeling relationships, 298-303
UNDER clause, 440
Unified Modeling Language. *See* UML.
UNIQUE constraint, 82
Unisys, 75
Universal Cartridge Services, 460
UPDATE command
   preventing dangling REFs, 155
Use case diagrams, 306-307
User-defined data types. *See* ADTs.
User documentation development, 43
Uses stereotype, 303

V

VALUE construct, 156
VARCHAR data type, 110
VARCHAR2 data type, 110
VARRAYs, 26, 27
   description of, 124
   differences from nested tables, 125
   multidimensional, 27
   repeating groups, 60
   re-sequencing pointers, 164
   rules for using, 101
   when to use, 97
Vertical
   distribution databases, 371
   partitioning, 368
ViewElement, 87

Views, partitioned, 346
Virtual
   class, 437
   function mechanism, 430
Visibility, 87
   degrees of, 301
   protected, 432

W

WITH CONTEXT clauses, 193

Y

Year 2000, 111-112

Notes...

Notes...

Notes...

Notes…

Notes…

Notes…

Notes...

HIGH PERFORMANCE

Meet Advanced Demands with High Performance

The High Performance series explains the advanced tool features that introductory books just can't cover. The heavy-duty projects in each book force readers to think through the development process at an expert's level. These books strive for technical depth, presenting the underlying theory of the technology being discussed and backing it up with example code or demonstration projects.

Books in the High Performance series are edited by recognized industry experts Jeff Duntemann and Don Burleson. Co-founder and Editorial Director of The Coriolis Group, Jeff Duntemann is the author of seven books and innumerable articles on computer technology. Don Burleson has 15 years' experience as an Oracle developer and is the author of numerous books and articles on database management.

High Performance Oracle8 Tuning
Donald Burleson
1-57610-217-3 • $49.99/$69.99 (US/CAN)
Available Now

High Performance Oracle Database Automation
Jonathan Ingram
1-57610-152-5 • $39.99/$55.99 (US/CAN)
Available Now

High Performance Oracle Data Warehousing
Donald Burleson
1-57610-154-1 • $39.99/$55.99 (US/CAN)
Available Now

High Performance Oracle8 SQL Programming & Tuning
Pete Cassidy
1-57610-213-0 • $39.99/$55.99 (US/CAN)
February 1998

High Performance Oracle8 Object-Oriented Design
David A. Anstey
1-57610-186-X • $39.99/$55.99 (US/CAN)
February 1998

High Performance Windows Graphics Programming
Stan Trujillo
1-57610-148-7 • $39.99/$55.99 (US/CAN)
Available Now

High Performance Windows NT 4 Optimization & Tuning
Arthur Knowles
1-57610-164-9 • $49.99/$69.99 (US/CAN)
Available Now

High Performance Visual Basic 5 Web Development
Scott Jarol
1-57610-063-4 • $39.99/$55.99 (US/CAN)
Available Now

High Performance Delphi 3 Programming
Don Taylor, Jim Mischel, John Penman and Terence Goggin
1-57610-179-7 • $49.99/$69.99 (US/CAN)
Available Now

High Performance ISAPI/NSAPI Web Programming
Tony Beveridge and Paul McGlashan
1-57610-151-7 • $39.99/$55.99 (US/CAN)
Available Now

High Performance Borland C++ Builder
Matt Telles
1-57610-197-5 8 $39.99/$55.99 (US/CAN)
Available Now

CORIOLIS GROUP BOOKS
An International Thomson Publishing Company ITP

(800) 410-0192 • International Callers (602) 483-0192 • Fax (602) 483-0193 • www.coriolis.com

Prices and availability dates are subject to change without notice.
©1998 by Coriolis Group Books. All Rights Reserved. AT/GS 10/97